"The events of the last month had satisfied me that the [...] me was without enterprise and possessed [...] amounted to timidity."

  — Jubal Early, sizing up Phil Sheridan before the Battle of Third Winchester

"I tell you it did look really frightful to watch them. They started toward us a full half mile distant from the extreme left of their line. First at a trot, but gathering momentum as they came, by the time they were half way toward us they were on a full gallop, nearer, nearer, they came . . ."

  — A cavalryman serving with the 2nd Ohio describing a Confederate
      charge at Third Winchester

"The broad blue wave surged forward with a yell which lasted for minutes. In response there arose from the northern front of the woods a continuous, deafening wail of musketry without break or tremor. For a time I despaired of the success of the attack, for it did not seem possible that any troops could endure such a fire."

  — Capt. John W. DeForest's description of the charge by the Army of
      West Virginia at Third Winchester

"The veterans of Stonewall Jackson fired amazingly low, so that the grass and earth in front of the Regiment was cut and torn up by a perfect sheet of lead. Their bullets sought the hiding places of the men with fatal accuracy, and by ones and twos and threes, they went crawling to the rear, with their blue clothes defaced with streaks and lots of crimson gore. Blood was on everything—was everywhere . . . was spattered upon bushes—was gathered in ghastly puddles upon the ground."

  — Surgeon Harris H. Beacher, 114th New York, Nineteenth Corps

"For once in their lives they know they are whipped—yes skinned alive."

  — Surgeon Daniel M. Holt, 121st New York, Sixth Corps

The Last Battle
of
WINCHESTER

Scott Charles Patchan

Above left: Maj. Gen. Phil Sheridan; Above right: Lt. Gen. Jubal Early.
Library of Congress

Phil Sheridan, Jubal Early, and the
Shenandoah Valley Campaign,

August 7 - September 19, 1864

Savas Beatie

California

First paperback edition, first printing
ISBN-13: 9781611215762

Patchan, Scott C., 1966-
The last Battle of Winchester : Phil Sheridan, Jubal Early, and the Shenandoah Valley campaign, August 7-September 19, 1864 / Scott Charles Patchan. — First edition.
pages cm
Includes bibliographical references and index.
ISBN 978-1-932714-98-2
1. Winchester, 3rd Battle of, Winchester, Va., 1864. 2. Sheridan, Philip Henry, 1831-1888–Military leadership. 3. Early, Jubal Anderson, 1816-1894–Military leadership. 4. Shenandoah Valley Campaign, 1864 (August-November) 5. Virginia–History–Civil War, 1861-1865–Campaigns. I. Title.
E477.33.P38 2013
973.7'32–dc23
2013003604

SB
Savas Beatie LLC
989 Governor Drive, Suite 102
El Dorado Hills, California 95762
www.savasbeatie.com (web)
sales@savasbeatie.com (email)

Savas Beatie titles are available at special discounts for bulk purchases in the United States by corporations, institutions, and other organizations. For details, please contact us at sales@savasbeatie.com.

Printed in the United States of America.

In memory of my Father-in-Law

Lt. Thomas J. Richardson, 1940-2011
Fairfax County Police Department

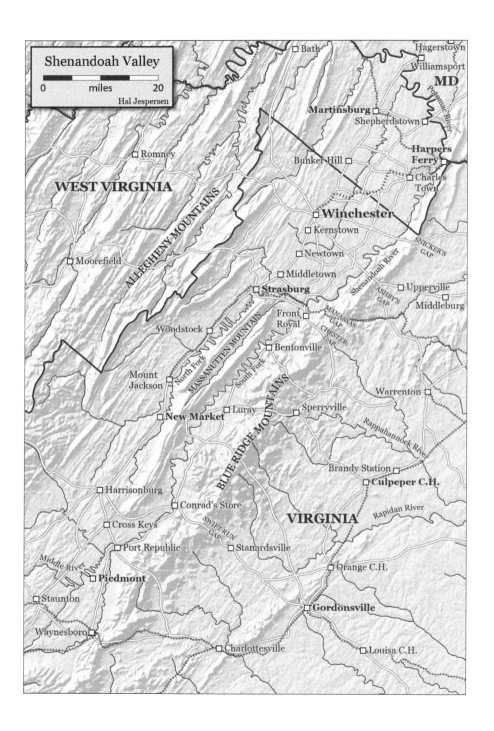

Shenandoah Valley

0   miles   20

Hal Jespersen

Bath
Hagerstown
Williamsport
MD
Martinsburg
Shepherdstown
Potomac River
Romney
Bunker Hill
Harpers Ferry
WEST VIRGINIA
Charles Town
Winchester
Kernstown
SNICKER'S GAP
Newtown
Shenandoah River
Moorefield
Middletown
Upperville
ALLEGHENY MOUNTAINS
Strasburg
ASHBY'S GAP
Middleburg
Front Royal
MANASSAS GAP
Woodstock
North Fork
CHESTER GAP
Bentonville
MASSANUTTEN MOUNTAIN
South Fork
Mount Jackson
Warrenton
Luray
Sperryville
New Market
BLUE RIDGE MOUNTAINS
Rappahannock River
Brandy Station
Culpeper C.H.
Harrisonburg
Conrad's Store
VIRGINIA
Rapidan River
Cross Keys
SWIFT RUN GAP
Port Republic
Stanardsville
Orange C.H.
Middle River
Piedmont
Staunton
Gordonsville
Waynesboro
Charlottesville
Louisa C.H.

Contents

Contents (continued)

Contents (continued)

———————————

Maps and illustrations appear throughout the book for
the convenience of the reader.

Introduction

The Shenandoah Valley has long been recognized as one of the great scenic wonders of the United States. Throughout human history, the Valley has served as a vital transportation corridor. For centuries, American Indians such as the Delaware, Shawnee, Catawba, and Seneca lived in and traveled the Valley, hunting buffalo, farming, and warring before Virginia Governor Alexander Spotswood and his Knights of the Golden Horseshoe visited in 1716, opening the door for European settlement. The English from eastern Virginia were hesitant to cross the Blue Ridge Mountains and settle the Valley, but by the middle of the 18th century, industrious Germans from Pennsylvania and hardy Scotch-Irish pioneers quickly turned the Shenandoah into a bountiful granary during colonial and antebellum times. When the secession crisis erupted in 1861, the Valley's residents remained strong Unionists. When President Abraham Lincoln issued a call for Virginia to provide troops for an invasion of the Deep South, however, a large majority of those who lived in the Valley cast their lot with the Confederacy, as did most Virginians.

During the Civil War, the Shenandoah served as a granary and a workshop for the primary Confederate army operating east of the Blue Ridge. Its most lasting legacy during the war was how the Confederates utilized the Valley to continually disrupt the strategic balance in Virginia. In 1861, Confederate Gen.

Joseph E. Johnston moved his army from the Valley to Manassas Junction, where his additional numbers played a decisive role in winning First Manassas. In 1862, Maj. Gen. Thomas J. "Stonewall" Jackson baffled and defeated the Federals in the Valley in a series of sharp engagements that prompted President Lincoln to withhold critical reinforcements from Maj. Gen. George B. McClellan's campaign against Richmond. This, in turn, allowed Gen. Robert E. Lee the time to bring Jackson east and launch the Seven Days' Battles, which saved the Confederate capital from capture. In 1863, the Shenandoah served as an avenue for invading the North. Lieutenant General Richard S. Ewell crushed the foolhardy abolitionist Maj. Gen. Robert Milroy at the Second Battle of Winchester before moving on to join the balance of the army at Gettysburg. For Lincoln and the Union cause, the Shenandoah Valley had, indeed, become the "Valley of Humiliation." The year 1864 would prove no different.

As much as anything, the Valley's geographic location and topography vexed Lincoln and his commanders since the onset of hostilities in 1861. It stretches 160 miles from the James River south of Lexington to the Potomac River at Harpers Ferry, with an average width of 25 to 30 miles. The rugged Allegheny Mountains form the Valley's western wall while the scenic Blue Ridge separates the Shenandoah from the central Virginia Piedmont region farther east. Numerous gaps and passes through the Blue Ridge (such as Snickers, Ashby, Manassas, and Swift Run) allowed the Confederates to slip in and out of the Shenandoah at will, befuddling opponents as Jackson did in 1862. In the center of the Valley, Massanutten Mountain hovers over the countryside for 50 miles from Front Royal to Harrisonburg. This shadowy blue outgrowth divides the Shenandoah into two sections, the Shenandoah proper to the west, and the Luray or Page Valley to the east. Only one readily accessible gap cuts through Massanutten. Running from New Market east to Luray, it, too, was used by Jackson with much effect in 1862.

The Shenandoah Valley's namesake river begins its journey to the Potomac in the form of two forks fed by several smaller streams and rivers in the southern and western reaches of the basin. The North Fork rises in Rockingham County near the eastern edge of the Allegheny Mountains, meanders northward through the main Valley, and passes around the northern tip of Massanutten between Strasburg and Front Royal. The headwaters of the South Fork, the North, Middle, and South rivers, flow primarily through Augusta County until they come to a confluence at Port Republic in Rockingham County. From there, the South Fork courses northward through the narrow Luray Valley until joining the North Fork near Front Royal.

Forming the Shenandoah River proper, the scenic waterway continues the journey north toward the Potomac River at Harpers Ferry.[1]

The general northward water flow in the Shenandoah Valley has given rise to a unique geographic nomenclature in the region. When one heads northward, he is moving downstream or "down the Valley" toward Winchester, the primary town in the "Lower Valley." Conversely, a wagon rolling southward on the Valley Pike is said to be moving "up the Valley" toward Staunton or Lexington in the "Upper Valley."

Between the ranges of the Allegheny and the Blue Ridge and upon the bottomland along the rivers was some of the most verdant land in the entire South. Its fertile farms and granaries earned the region the sobriquet "Breadbasket of the Confederacy," though in truth the term was overstated. Even before the war began in 1860, the Valley had supplied Virginia with less than 20% of the Commonwealth's entire wheat, corn, oats, and hay production. The region also accounted in 1860 for no more than 11% of Virginia's livestock. During the first year of the war, agricultural productivity in the Valley declined by more than 50%. The Valley was not the Confederacy's primary source of provender by 1864.

This fact was not lost upon the Confederates who used the Valley's reputation and geography to their every advantage. On October 1, 1862, General Lee informed the Confederate secretary of war that he feared a Federal movement against the Virginia Central Railroad in the Shenandoah Valley because "they [the Federals] think we depend upon it for our supplies." Although the Valley's significance to the Confederacy as a whole was inflated, it was still an important locale that produced many essential resources for Confederate forces operating in Virginia and served as a tactical corridor that the Confederates continually utilized to their advantage.[2]

Because the Shenandoah Valley runs southwest to northeast, Union forces entering from the northern end would march southwest or "up" the Valley. In doing so, they moved away from Washington, exposing the capital to a

1   John Wayland, *The German Element of the Shenandoah Valley of Virginia* (Charlottesville, 1907), 1-5.

2   For an excellent study on the true role of the Shenandoah Valley during the Civil War, see Michael G. Mahon, *The Shenandoah Valley, 1861-1865: The Destruction of the Granary of the Confederacy.* (Mechanicsburg, PA, 1996), 74-75, 133-134; United States War Department, *The War of the Rebellion: A Compilation of the Official Records of the Union and Confederate Armies* (Washington, 1880-1901), Series 1, vol. 19, Part 2, 640-642, hereafter cited as *OR.* All references are to Series 1 unless otherwise noted.

Lt. Gen. U. S. Grant
LC

potential counterstroke from the Virginia Piedmont east of the Blue Ridge. At the same time, those advancing Union troops were actually moving away from Richmond, the primary Federal objective in Virginia. These distinct disadvantages did not hold true for the Confederacy. Instead, the Valley provided an excellent corridor for the Southerners to invade and threaten the North. The Shenandoah Valley provided the Confederates with a direct route toward Washington. They could move quickly from the Virginia Piedmont through the gaps of the Blue Ridge and into the Shenandoah, baffling Union forces operating along the Potomac River. The end result was that any Confederate force emerging from the northern end of the Valley was in an ideal position to threaten the important northern cities of Washington, Baltimore, Philadelphia, and Harrisburg. General Robert E. Lee did precisely that in 1863 to set up his invasion of Pennsylvania during the early stages of the Gettysburg campaign.[3]

The way the United States Army waged war against the rebellious Southern states changed during the early months of 1864 when President Abraham Lincoln selected Lt. Gen. Ulysses Simpson Grant to lead the Union's armies. Grant owned a steady string of victorious campaigns, including Fort Donelson, Shiloh, Vicksburg, and Chattanooga. His victories went well beyond the hollow tactical sort of successes that did not alter the general course of the war. Carefully planned, Grant's campaigns achieved maximum impact toward the overall goal of saving the Union. Now that he was in command of all U.S. forces across the continent, he planned a simultaneous offensive from Virginia to the Mississippi River and beyond to maintain pressure on the Confederacy in every theater of war.

Previous uncoordinated Federal efforts permitted the South to reinforce threatened areas from inactive theaters of war. For example, in the late summer of 1863, the Army of the Potomac's inaction allowed Lt. Gen. James Longstreet to take two divisions from the Army of Northern Virginia and reinforce the Braxton Bragg's Army of Tennessee in North Georgia, where that luckless command won its only clear-cut victory of the war at Chickamauga. Grant was determined not to allow that to happen again. To prevent any such recurrence, the new Federal commander-in-chief included every able-bodied soldier in the grand strategic plan, significantly limiting the usage of large forces to defend strategic points such as Washington. He reasoned that the garrison forces "guarded their special trusts when advancing from them as well as when remaining at them."[4]

In the Deep South, Grant's strategy called for Maj. Gen. William T. Sherman's group of three armies to press Gen. Joseph E. Johnston's

---

3 In Shenandoah Valley parlance, to move south was to move "up" the Valley, and to move north was to march "down" the Valley.

4 U. S. Grant, *Personal Memoirs of U. S. Grant, Selected Letters 1839-1865*. (New York: Literary Classics of the United States, 1990), 478.

Confederate Army of Tennessee in Georgia. Grant tasked Sherman with defeating Johnston and capturing Atlanta, a vital railroad and manufacturing center. At the very least, a persistent advance by Sherman would prevent Johnston from reinforcing General Lee in Virginia. The Union's military chieftain also instructed Maj. Gen. Nathaniel Banks to assemble his forces at New Orleans and advance on Mobile, Alabama, a key Confederate port situated on the Gulf coast. The final and perhaps most important part of Grant's strategy would unfold in Virginia.[5]

Grant planned four simultaneous advances in the Old Dominion. Major General George G. Meade would lead the Army of the Potomac across the Rapidan River against Lee's army while Maj. Gen. Benjamin Butler's Army of the James operated against Gen. Pierre Gustave Toutant Beauregard's Confederate force along the James River line. From the mountains of western Virginia, meanwhile, Brig. Gen. George Crook's army would descend upon southwest Virginia to sever the vital Virginia and Tennessee Railroad, which connected Petersburg to the important resources in southwest Virginia and east Tennessee. After severing the railroad, Crook had orders to march north to Staunton in the Shenandoah Valley and join forces with Maj. Gen. Franz Sigel, whose Army of the Shenandoah was advancing up the Valley from Martinsburg, western Virginia. A cavalry division under Maj. Gen. William W. Averell would be detached from Crook to lay waste to the Confederate salt and lead mines in southwest Virginia. If Grant's designs succeeded, they would prevent the Confederates in Virginia from reinforcing each other through constant pressure in all departments. Grant's plan was the most comprehensive the Union high command unveiled during the entire war. Yet, as in most military campaigns, unforeseen difficulties and battlefield failures made significant alterations in strategy necessary when the campaign opened in early May.[6]

Lee's Army of Northern Virginia remained one step ahead of Meade, frustrating his designs to crush the Confederates and seize Richmond. Butler's appearance made things tense in Richmond for a while, but a reinforced Beauregard bottled the despised Butler at Bermuda Hundred along the James River several miles southeast of the capital. Cavalry under John Hunt Morgan and William E. "Grumble" Jones stopped Averell near Wytheville. George

5 Ibid., 478.

6 Ibid., 478-479.

Crook achieved the only clear Union victory that May when he routed Maj. Gen. Albert Gallatin Jenkins's force at Cloyd's Mountain and severed the Virginia and Tennessee Railroad at New River Bridge. However, a captured telegram that falsely reported a Confederate victory over Grant in the Wilderness convinced Crook to return to his base in western Virginia instead of moving into the Shenandoah Valley. With Grant supposedly driven back across the Rapidan River, Crook feared that Lee would detach an overwhelming force to western Virginia to deal with Union forces operating in that region. Crook's premature withdrawal removed his forces from active operations for nearly one month.

From the outset of active campaigning in the spring of 1864, military operations in the Shenandoah Valley sullied Grant's plans for subduing Virginia. Less than two weeks after Grant ordered the Army of the Potomac across the Rapidan River and into the Wilderness, a Southern army under Maj. Gen. John C. Breckinridge defeated the inept Sigel at New Market on May 15. This defeat prompted the German to retreat nearly 40 miles to the north side of Cedar Creek. In the aftermath of New Market, General Lee urged Breckinridge to either pursue Sigel across the Potomac to disrupt Grant's operations, or join the embattled Army of Northern Virginia army above Richmond. Breckinridge decided against pursuit and joined Lee in the defense of the Southern capital. He marched his men south to Staunton, where they boarded cars on the Virginia Central Railroad and headed for Hanover Junction. Lee certainly could use the manpower against the tenacious Grant, but pulling Breckinridge out of the Shenandoah denuded the region of valuable veteran troops. The *Richmond Examiner* sarcastically called the movement "that wise order, which brought Breckinridge to Hanover Junction, where he was never needed."[7]

Grant replaced the defeated Sigel on May 21 with Maj. Gen. David Hunter. Hunter rejuvenated U.S. forces in the Shenandoah and moved quickly, taking advantage of Breckinridge's absence. Lee belatedly learned of the renewed Union offensive in the Valley and hastily scrambled forces from southwest Virginia and east Tennessee under Grumble Jones to save Staunton from capture. On June 5 near the tiny village of Piedmont, Hunter routed Jones on the lush farmland of Augusta County in shadow of the Blue Ridge. Hunter's victory effectively eliminated all credible Confederate opposition to his continued advance. It also resulted in Jones's death, which further confused an

7 *Richmond Examiner,* June 13, 1864.

already disjointed Confederate command situation in the Valley. Hunter occupied Staunton the next day, destroying mills, workshops, warehouses, and significant portions of the Virginia Central Railroad.

Reinforced by two divisions under Brig. Gen. George Crook, Hunter's enlarged force moved on Lexington at the southern end of the Valley. There, they destroyed the Virginia Military Institute, segments of the James River and Kanawha Canal, and burned the home of former Virginia governor John Letcher. Hunter's ultimate objective was Lynchburg, a vital logistics center where the Virginia and Tennessee Railroad joined the Orange and Alexandria to form the Southside Railroad. The Southside ran east to Petersburg, and was critical to the success and survival of the Confederacy.

Hunter's success prompted an immediate reaction by Lee. When he learned of Hunter's victory at Piedmont, Lee returned Breckinridge's division to the Shenandoah. The Kentuckian's force, however, was too small to do anything beyond blocking Hunter's access to the gaps in the Blue Ridge east of Staunton. Most notably, Breckinridge's presence prevented Hunter from seizing and destroying the Blue Ridge Tunnel, which bore the Virginia Central Railroad through the mountains. When it became clear to Lee that Hunter was moving on Lynchburg, the Confederate commander rushed the Army of Northern Virginia's famed Second Corps under Lt. Gen. Jubal A. Early to save that vital town from falling to Hunter. Early arrived not a moment too soon and defeated Hunter on June 18 and forced a Federal retreat into the mountains of western Virginia, where they would be of no use for nearly a month.

Hunter's withdrawal immediately freed western Virginia from Federal control and opened the door for Early to seize the initiative. As Lee had preordained, Early consolidated his force with Breckinridge, advanced down the Shenandoah Valley, crossed the Potomac River into Maryland, and defeated a hastily assembled Federal force at Monocacy Junction on July 9. Early's force appeared in front of the Washington defenses two days later. With his troops suffering under a deadly heat wave, Early postponed any attack until the following morning. During the night, Confederate cavalry passed on reports to Early that two U.S. army corps were on the way to the national capital from Grant's army. Morning light confirmed the accuracy of the report, and Early withdrew back into Virginia, narrowly avoiding being trapped between Hunter's returning force in western Maryland and the troops Grant sent to Washington.

Once back in Virginia, Early rested his troops for a day at Leesburg before continuing his withdrawal into the Shenandoah Valley on July 16. A small

Union cavalry force from the vanguard of Hunter's force struck the center of Early's retreating column, creating consternation among the wagon train before being driven off. Hunter's field force, now under the command of George Crook, joined forces with the troops pursuing Early from Washington. The pursuers attacked Early near Snicker's Gap on July 18, but the Virginian parried their thrust in a rearguard action at the battle of Cool Spring. On the following day, Early's cavalry repulsed Union flanking efforts on his right at Berry's Ferry near Ashby's Gap and on his left near Charlestown. Another Union column under Averell was moving south from Martinsburg toward Winchester, so Early promptly withdrew his army deeper into the Shenandoah Valley. His only setback came when Maj. Gen. Stephen D. Ramseur disobeyed orders and went out looking for a fight with Averell on July 20. Ramseur's disobedience resulted in substantial loss of troops and artillery, and proved to be the only blot on Early's splendid campaign from Lynchburg to Washington and back to the Valley.

In the Western theaters, the situation looked slightly better for the Union cause. By May 15, Sherman and Johnston had battled to a standstill at Resaca, but Johnston's Army of Tennessee retreated intact. Johnston fell back inexorably toward Atlanta as Sherman flanked him out of one position after another throughout May and June. With the Army of Tennessee pressed against the fortifications ringing Atlanta, President Jefferson Davis sacked Johnston in the middle of July and replaced him with Lt. Gen. John B. Hood, who immediately assumed aggressive offensive operations. The result was three defensive Union victories in just eight days (July 20-28), but Atlanta remained in Confederate hands.

The situation in Nathaniel Banks's department verged on disastrous. The Massachusetts politician barely escaped from his ill-fated Red River campaign, which had begun before Grant assumed command. Banks's debacle and bedlam created by Confederate cavalryman Nathan Bedford Forrest in Tennessee eliminated the possibility of any immediate operations against Mobile, Alabama. The gulf coast port ultimately remained in Confederate hands until April of 1865. The South was indeed pressed on all fronts, but victory continued to elude the Lincoln administration.

In the closely monitored eastern Virginia theater of operations, Grant's spring offensive produced heavy casualties but fell far short of final victory. By late June, Grant had settled into a siege in front of Petersburg and Richmond that would be plagued by embarrassing failures throughout the summer. Many politicians in the North reacted by calling for an end to the war, and more importantly, the number of citizens sharing that sentiment was growing as the Federal casualty lists lengthened. Many people in the North wondered aloud if the cost of preserving the Union was simply becoming too high. Republicans openly debated dumping Lincoln from their ticket in the 1864 presidential election. Although Lee successfully fended off Grant's heavy attacks, he lost tens of thousands of irreplaceable veterans and forfeited the initiative to the tenacious Midwesterner. Lee knew the Confederacy could not in the end prevail against a siege, but waning Northern will to continue the war remained the South's last hope. Even Lincoln began to doubt his own reelection chances.

Operations in the Shenandoah Valley that late summer and early fall would play a critical role in determining the outcome of the epic Grant-Lee struggle in Virginia. While the two giants maintained the status quo along the Petersburg and Richmond fronts, the more fluid and wide ranging operations in western Virginia and Maryland ultimately changed the strategic balance in the Virginia.

* * *

The genesis of *The Last Battle of Winchester* occurred in the summer of 1993 in Manassas, Virginia. I was preparing a talk on Third Winchester that I delivered on September 9, 1993. It was my first foray into public speaking, and my friend William J. (Bill) Miller was listening to my rehearsal speech. As we went through the talk, Bill asked probing questions and shared his experience in speaking. When we were done, Bill said something to the effect of, "You really know a lot about that. You should write a book on it." In doing so, Bill opened the door to a whole new world for me, and I am forever grateful for his encouragement. I have written several books and dozens of articles between then and now, but without the suggestion and encouragement of a professional historian, author, and editor like Bill, I doubt that any of them would have been written. Thanks, Bill.

Another person I want to extend profound thanks to is Chief Nicholas Picerno of Bridgewater College, a.k.a. "The Chief of Third Winchester Battlefield." In addition to contributing numerous photographs for this book and opening his immense collection for my research, Nick was the key player in the preservation of the Huntsberry Tract at the Third Winchester Battlefield. His perseverance resulted in saving that bloodstained ground where so many Union and Confederate soldiers gave "their last full measure" on September 19, 1864. His friendship and comradery in exploring the Valley battlefields are greatly appreciated and enjoyed.

There are many other individuals who come to mind after two decades of research and writing. This list is by no means all-inclusive and I sincerely apologize to anyone I may have overlooked. My fading memory by no means negates your contributions. To avoid showing any favoritism, I have listed these names alphabetically. Keith Bohannon forwarded many rare sources and leads, especially from Georgia; Paul Chronic shared rare 16th Georgia Cavalry Battalion sources. My good friend Gary Ecelbarger reviewed several early drafts and accompanied me on many research trips and battlefield visits. Between both of us we have managed to raise six kids who will forever associate the Shenandoah Valley Campaigns with "Dinosaur Land," located at Double Tollgate. Hal Jespersen produced the wonderful maps that appear throughout this book. Hal is a rising star in the world of Civil War topographical engineers, following as he does in the footsteps of Jed Hotchkiss.

Robert E. L. Krick shared many sources and provided me with the lead on the SMU Photographic collection of the Third Winchester Battlefield. Esteemed historian Robert K. Krick assisted in research in the Fredericksburg Spotsylvania National Military Park collections in his former office at Chatham Manor, and shared sources on the Valley campaign over the years. Thanks to Rodger Lemly, retired miner from Maple Creek Coal Mine in western Pennsylvania, for sharing his ancestor's diary from the 15th West Virginia; Terry Lowry shared 22nd Virginia Infantry and West Virginia Confederate sources. Over the years, Dana MacBean of Beaufort, South Carolina, shared many maps and discussed many aspects of the campaign that greatly aided my understanding of the location of various obscure events. Ted Mahr, the author of *Showdown in the Shenandoah*, which remains the definitive work on the battle, enthusiastically shared ideas and research material over the years and has served as an inspiration to persevere in the face of obstacles. Manuel and George Semples of Winchester guided me on several trips over the battlefield, sharing their extensive archeological knowledge of that ground.

Fred Ray offered assistance over the years and shared his extensive knowledge of the Army of Northern Virginia sharpshooters. Ben Ritter shared his extensive knowledge of Winchester and many sources as well. Larry Strayer of Dayton shared photographs from his Cumberland Gallery Collection and steered me to many Ohio sources. Bryce Suderow provided important research throughout the course of this project, as did Allan Tischler, who kindly shared his research on many aspects of the battle, including his in-depth knowledge of Sheridan's Scouts and Medal of Honor recipients. He also guided me to the Alfred R. Waud drawings. The dean of cavalry historians, Eric Wittenberg, shared cavalry sources and read and reviewed an entire draft of the manuscript, improving the overall quality of this book. Alfred Young generously shared his extensive research on casualties in the Army of Northern Virginia in 1864, which greatly enhanced my understanding of Third Winchester.

Many others have assisted in small but important ways throughout this long process, helping with research needs or listening to ideas, offering opinions, sharing general knowledge, or performing a special favor. They include: Gary Arnold, Ohio Historical Society; Brandon Beck, formerly of Shenandoah University; Nan Card, Rutherford B. Hayes Presidential Center; James Creed (23rd Illinois); Walter DeGroot (5th New York Heavy Artillery); Rod Gainer; United States Army historian; Pat Goodman, previous owner of Hackwood Farm; Lee Hadden (4th North Carolina); John McAnaw, U.S. Army, retired; Linda Meenegahn (5th New York Heavy Artillery); Steve Meserve, Loudoun County historian; J. Michael Miller, U.S.M.C. University Historian at Quantico; Jonathan Noyalas, Professor at Lord Fairfax Community College; Don Phanz, Fredericksburg-Spotsylvania National Military Park; Jerry Reed and Gordon Rhea; Craig Swain, artillery specialist; and Joe Whitehorne, U.S. Army retired.

I also want to extend my sincere appreciation to Theodore P. Savas, Marketing Director Sarah Keeney, editors Lucas Cade and Alexandra Savas, and the rest of the Savas Beatie staff for their patience and dedication to this project. The final stages took significantly longer than expected, but their commitment remained firm. My family and I are most appreciative of that and Ted's unwavering encouragement.

*   *   *

Finally I must thank my family, especially my beautiful, patient, and encouraging wife Nancy for putting up with my pursuit of history. She and all three of my children have spent good chunks of their childhood visiting battlefields and other historical sights and we have all shared many good times along the way. Andrew, Elena, and Sophia, thanks for sharing those days with me. My now 24-year-old son Andrew in particular has experienced the Third Battle of Winchester at several stages of his life, but always remembers our visits to Hackwood in the mid-nineties, when it was owned by a family who used it to care for homeless animals and endowed cats. The large, scraggly, but friendly dog became his fast friend and followed us around whenever we visited and is an everlasting memory of those times. My youngest daughter Sophia created a promotional trailer for this project on her iPad for use on YouTube, showcasing her technical knowledge and creativity.

Union infantry skirmishing along the Halltown line. *A. R. Waud, LC*

WORTH HIS WEIGHT IN GOLD

Sheridan, Grant, Lincoln, and Union Strategy in the Shenandoah Valley

Shrill blasts from a train whistle pierced the air around Monocacy Junction to announce the arrival of the new commander of the Army of the Shenandoah. When Maj. Gen. Philip Henry Sheridan stepped onto the station platform, his future was as unclear as the smoke wafting along the tracks. His prospect for achieving victory in Virginia's Shenandoah Valley seemed unlikely. The history of the Union's fortunes in that "Valley of Humiliation," coupled with Sheridan's inexperience as an army commander, provided little reason to believe otherwise. To most, it seemed more probable that he would soon join the long list of Union generals whose careers derailed in the Shenandoah Valley. Sheridan, however, had the confidence of his commander, Lt. Gen. Ulysses Simpson Grant, and every promotion received bore the date of a hard fought battle.

In an age when martial pomp, flamboyant uniforms, and dramatic proclamations were commonplace among men of high military rank, this unspectacular little Irish-American from Ohio hardly fit anyone's image of an ideal general. But then again, neither did Grant. President Abraham Lincoln initially saw only "a brown, chunky little chap, with a long body, short legs, not enough neck to hang him, and such long arms that if his ankles itch he can scratch them without stooping." Indeed, Sheridan stood only five-feet-five-inches tall and weighed a slight 115 pounds. Crowned with a black, flat-topped, pork-pie hat, he donned the simple blue coat of the common soldier only slightly embellished by regulation shoulder straps bearing the two stars of a major general. "There was nothing about him to attract attention," observed a reporter, "except his eye . . . that seemed a black ball of fire." Grant had seen that fire blazing on the battlefield at Chattanooga, and it was exactly what he wanted in the Shenandoah Valley.[1]

In an age of fierce anti-Catholic and anti-Irish prejudice in America, Sheridan's family heritage contrasted sharply from the lineage of the typical U.S. Army officer. Men of rank were chiefly composed of Anglo-Saxon Protestants from the aristocratic South or gentry from the Mid-Atlantic and New England states. While he claimed birth in America, some evidence indicates that Sheridan may have been born during his family's trans-Atlantic voyage or even back in Killinkere Parish, County Cavan, Ireland. Generations before his birth, the English had brutally repressed the native Irish Catholics and attempted to repopulate the area with lowland Scots and English settlers. Nevertheless, the Sheridan family and its forebears steadfastly adhered to their religious beliefs as they struggled to eke out a living on a small leased tract, land that centuries before had been taken from the Irish by the English. Oppression and limited economic opportunities finally induced the family's immigration to the United States in 1831, the year of Philip's birth. After spending time in Boston and Albany, the family moved west, settling in the then frontier town of Somerset, Ohio. Nestled in the rolling green hills of southeastern Ohio, this small town had become a haven for Irish Catholics who had flocked there to work construction jobs along the ever expanding National Road.[2]

Life in Ohio was not easy for the Sheridans. Like most people of that era, the daily routine revolved around providing for necessities of life. Philip's

---

1 *National Magazine,* August 1904, 596.

2 Sheridan's birthplace is a matter of much debate. While Sheridan claimed birth in Albany, New York, evidence indicates that he may have been born in Ireland. William F. Drake, *Little Phil: The Story of General Philip Henry Sheridan* (Prospect, CT, 2005), 7-11; Eric Wittenberg, *Little Phil: A Reassessment of the Civil War Leadership of Gen. Philip H. Sheridan* (Washington, DC, 2002), 1-2; Philip H. Sheridan, *Personal Memoirs of Philip Henry Sheridan,* 2 vols. (New York, NY, 1904), vol. 1, 3-4; Richard O'Connor, *Sheridan the Inevitable* (New York, NY, 1953), 34.

father, John, worked as a laborer on the National Road but still struggled to support his wife Mary Meenagh and their children. There were no servants at the Sheridan home so "Little Phil," as he became known, performed daily chores around the family's modest three-room log cabin. With his father away from home working on the construction crews, Sheridan's mother provided his "sole guidance." He later acknowledged that her "excellent common sense and clear discernment in every way fitted her for such maternal duties." He received only the bare basics of an education in a one-room schoolhouse. The Irish schoolmaster, a Mr. McManly, "one of those itinerant dominies of the early frontier," as Sheridan recalled him, fully implemented the old adage that "to spare the rod was to spoil the child." When in doubt, the schoolmaster "would consistently apply the switch to the whole school," thus never failing to catch the miscreant. Even worse for young Phil, McManly was an old acquaintance of his mother from the days in Ireland, so he paid particular attention to the development of her son.[3]

Young Sheridan longed for a military career. Like so many boys, he was captivated by martial pomp and circumstance. Somerset's annual Fourth of July celebrations provided him with the perfect opportunity to experience American military history in the flesh. When Sheridan was six or seven years old, the event's organizers rolled out an aged Revolutionary War veteran "in a farmer's wagon, seated on a split-bottom chair." When Phil saw the crowd eagerly gathering around the veteran and leading him to a place of honor on the platform, Sheridan asked a friend, Henry Greiner, why everyone was making such a fuss over the man. Upon hearing that he "had been a soldier under Washington" and had fought in five battles, Sheridan transfixed his eyes upon that living piece of history. "I never saw Phil's brown eyes open so wide or gaze with such interest as they did on this old revolutionary relic," recalled Greiner. Seeing this "comrade of Washington . . . was probably the first glow of military emotion that he experienced." Thereafter, Sheridan spent long hours watching the local militia drill in the town square, dreaming of the day that he would lead men into battle. "Little Phil" evidently impressed the people of Somerset in that regard. An elderly friend actually crafted a tin sword for the boy that was used to lead companions in mock military drills and battles.[4]

---

3 Sheridan, *Memoirs*, 3-4.

4 Henry C. Greiner, *General Phil Sheridan As I Knew Him, Playmate-Comrade-Friend* (Chicago, IL., 1908), 15-17; O'Connor, *Sheridan the Inevitable*, 25.

Living along the National Road allowed Philip to meet a host of characters, few of whom were as colorful as the tough-talking teamsters seeking a brief respite in Somerset after a long haul. Their rough language and combative tenacity impressed the young Sheridan, who later emulated their style on many a Civil War battlefield. Although he was very small in stature, the boys of Somerset quickly learned that his fierce Irish temper compensated for his diminutive proportions in a brawl. Many of these fights were the outgrowth of a generations-old cross-town rivalry. Sheridan and his comrades of the vaunted "Pig Feet" gang battled their adversaries, the "Turkey Feet" in Somerset's adolescent turf wars, even though the cause of the rivalry had been long forgotten.[5]

Although stories of his boyhood high jinks were widely told after Sheridan became a national hero, he successfully completed his formal schooling at just 14. The time had come to find his station in life. Many years of firsthand observation had convinced a local businessman and neighbor that Sheridan was an intelligent and dependable youth with the potential to do much more with his life than the average boy from Somerset. Sheridan jumped at the opportunity to work with the merchant, but was also encouraged to "improve himself" through further study in "mathematics [and] select works of history." While Philip excelled as a storekeeper, he longed for what he believed was a more exciting career in the U.S. Army. After three years of clerking, Sheridan applied for an opening to the U.S. Military Academy at West Point from Somerset's congressional district. "There came a letter, accompanied by no testimonials, no influential recommendations, or appeals from wealthy parents," recalled Sheridan's Congressman Thomas Ritchey. "It simply asked that the place might be given to the writer, and was signed 'Phil Sheridan.' The boy needed no recommendations, for I knew him and his father before him, and I appointed him at once." The opportunity to live his dream had arrived.[6]

At West Point, Sheridan discovered that his Irish-Catholic heritage and working-class roots set him apart from an academy dominated by cadets from the South and the eastern seaboard cities. Further, a large segment of the cadet

5   Ibid., 21; Whitlaw Reid, *Ohio in the War: Her Statesmen, Generals and Soldiers* (Cincinnati, OH, 1868), 1:499.

6   The slot at West Point was available because the original appointee failed his entrance exam. Reid, *Ohio in the War*, 1,499. Ezra J. Warner, *Generals in Blue: Lives of the Union Commanders* (Baton Rouge, LA,1986), 437.

corps was pro-slavery, a doctrine Sheridan was unwilling to tolerate. These differences, combined with his inborn sharp temper, resulted in "various collisions" with fellow his cadets. The hot-headed Ohioan resented "even the appearance of an insult"—even if he knew the resulting altercation would end with his classmates carrying him back to his quarters. On one occasion he assaulted a Virginian in front of the entire company of cadets. This action resulted in a one-year suspension and delayed his graduation. Ironically, the Virginian, James Terrill, would remain loyal to the Union in 1861, fight with Sheridan in the Army of the Ohio, and die in battle at Perryville, Kentucky, in October 1862. In spite of the culture clash in upstate New York and his intemperate actions, Sheridan graduated in 1853 ranked 35th of 53. Following graduation, Sheridan entered the infantry, where he served for eight years in Texas and Oregon, gaining some combat and leadership experience fighting Indians.[7]

Sheridan was serving in Oregon with the 4th U.S. Infantry when Southern forces opened fire on Fort Sumter in April 1861. Just as it did for thousands of other men, the war presented Sheridan with an opportunity for career advancement, and he intended to take full advantage of the chance. The fiery Ohioan, recalled a subordinate, "believed intensely that rebellion was a crime, and that it ought to be put down, no matter what the cost."[8] To Sheridan's dismay, he remained in Oregon until the fall of 1861 when orders finally arrived assigning him to the 13th U.S. Infantry. The journey to Jefferson Barracks in Missouri was a long one. Sheridan left Fort Yamhill in Oregon by ship and sailed to San Francisco. From there he sailed to the Isthmus of Panama, which he crossed to catch another ship north to New York City. After a brief sojourn back home in Somerset, Sheridan made his way to St. Louis. Upon his arrival, Maj. Gen. Henry Halleck, then commander of the Department of the Missouri, selected Sheridan for staff work.[9]

One of the first tasks Halleck assigned Sheridan was auditing the fiscal mess and cleaning up rampant corruption in Maj. Gen. John C. Fremont's Department of Missouri. Sheridan called upon his years of experience as a store

---

7 Gen. R. A. Alger, *Eulogy on the Late General Philip H. Sheridan* (Detroit, 1888), 3; O'Connor, *Sheridan the Inevitable*, 34; Harriet Beecher Stowe, *Men of Our Times or Leading Patriots of the Day* (Hartford, CT, 1868), 407.

8 Alger, *Eulogy*, 11.

9 Ibid., 10.

Warehouse in Harpers Ferry containing Quartermaster stores
for Sheridan's Army. *A. R. Waud, LC*

clerk back in Ohio and approached the assignment with methodical
steadfastness, displaying the same diligence and dedication he would later bring
to planning military campaigns. After successfully completing the audit, Halleck
rewarded Sheridan with an appointment as the chief quartermaster and
commissary of the Army of Southwest Missouri under Maj. Gen. Samuel
Curtis. At the time, Curtis's army was conducting the Pea Ridge campaign, and
Sheridan's efforts proved critical. The position provided Sheridan with a firm
understanding of the importance of logistics and supply to an army in the field.
This knowledge would profoundly influence his decisions during the 1864
Shenandoah Valley campaign.

It did not take long for Sheridan to run afoul of the irascible Curtis. The
confrontation was set in motion when officers in the quartermaster's
department requested payment from Sheridan for horses they had stolen from
civilians. The Ohioan refused their demand and, instead, confiscated the
animals for army use. The rebuffed officers were allied with Curtis and
unwilling to go away empty-handed. When they complained about Sheridan's
actions, the army commander ordered payment of the claims. Sheridan stood
by his decision and refused. "No authority can compel me to jay hawk or steal,"
he argued. "If those under my supervision are allowed to do so, I respectfully
ask the General to relieve me from duty in his district as I am of no use to the

service here, unless, I can enforce my authority."[10] General Curtis was outraged and leveled charges against Sheridan; however, the proceedings stopped short of a full court-martial when General Halleck interceded on the Ohioan's behalf and returned him to staff duty.

After the Confederate defeat at the battle of Shiloh in April 1862, Sheridan served as an assistant to General Halleck's topographical engineer during the army's snail-like advance toward the important logistical center of Corinth, Mississippi. In reality, Sheridan carried out any number of functions around headquarters and on the march. No matter the task, he approached it with his trademark "intense earnestness that made his success." Sheridan still longed for a combat command, but an appointment did not appear imminent. Even the influential Maj. Gen. William T. Sherman was unable to secure a commission for "Little Phil." Several fellow officers, including Brig. Gen. Gordon Granger and Capt. Russell Alger, lobbied the governor of Michigan to appoint Sheridan as colonel of the 2nd Michigan Cavalry. Despite his lack of mounted experience, the officers helped secure the appointment on May 27, 1862. General Halleck reluctantly approved the promotion, although he regretted losing such an efficient staff officer. Halleck later joked that no one could pitch headquarters tents as well as Sheridan.[11]

Sheridan's first combat opportunity arrived several weeks later on July 1, 1862, during one of the few pitched conflicts of the Corinth operation. He led a small brigade of 900 troopers to victory over several thousand Confederate horsemen at Booneville, Mississippi. His cleverness, innovative tactics, and outstanding intelligence work impressed Maj. Gen. William Rosecrans, commander of the Army of the Mississippi. He promptly urged the Ohioan's promotion to general. "Brigadiers scarce. Good ones scarcer," declared Rosecrans, "and the undersigned respectfully beg that you will obtain the promotion of Sheridan. He is worth his weight in gold." Sheridan was promoted to brigadier general on September 13, 1862, to rank from the date of his success at Booneville.[12]

10 Charges and Specifications against Capt P. H. Sheridan, Actg. Asst. Quartermaster, Sheridan Papers, Library of Congress.

11 Alger, *Eulogy*, 11.

12 Warner, *Generals in Blue*, 438; Philip Henry Sheridan Commission Branch File, National Archives.

Although Sheridan emerged from the war with the exalted reputation as the Union's leading cavalryman, his true legacy was as the Union's premier front line combat commander. More than a dozen years after the war, sculptor James E. Kelly complimented Sheridan's countenance as having "the character of the cavalryman." In an unguarded, spontaneous response, Sheridan retorted, "Yes, yes, but I commanded infantry." His promotion landed him command of an infantry division in Maj. Gen. Don Carlos Buell's Army of the Ohio. At Perryville, Kentucky, on October 8, 1862, Sheridan displayed prudent aggressiveness and a willingness to act independently as the situation demanded. His real baptism of fire occurred on December 31, 1862, during the first day's fighting at the battle of Stones River outside Murfreesboro, Tennessee. Suspecting that a Confederate attack was imminent, Sheridan placed his division under arms at an early hour and readied it for action. When the attack came, the Southerners drove the unprepared divisions on his right from the field. Sheridan, however, fought his division with a fierce determination, maneuvering and counterattacking as the situation demanded. "I knew it was infernal in there before I got in," recalled fellow division commander Lovell Rousseau, "but I was convinced of it when I saw Phil Sheridan, with hat in one hand and sword in the other, fighting as if he were the devil incarnate." The Ohioan's stellar efforts helped save General Rosecrans's Army of the Cumberland from defeat. The grateful Rosecrans rewarded Sheridan with a promotion to major general. "If he lives and has a chance," Rosecrans told a reporter, "Sheridan will rise to the highest rank in the army for he is not only a born fighter but a great general."[13]

At the battle of Chickamauga in September 1863, Sheridan's Division became caught up in the Federal rout. Given the stream of Union fugitives fleeing the Confederate onslaught, Sheridan fought his division as well as he could. He recognized the hopelessness of the situation as officers tried to force men back into the ranks only to watch them be mowed down by the Confederate musketry. Sheridan shouted above the din of battle, "Let them go! Let them go for their lives!" Sheridan withdrew the shattered remnants of his division from the battlefield, but was unable to join Maj. Gen. George H. Thomas on Snodgrass Hill. The defeat at Chickamauga weighed heavily on

13 William B. Styple, ed., *Generals in Bronze: Interviewing the Commanders of the Civil War* (Kearny, NJ, 2004), 10-11; Reid, *Ohio in the War*, 1:505-506; James Roberts Gilmore, *Personal Recollections of Abraham Lincoln and the Civil War* (Boston, MA, 1898), 123-124.

Maj. Gen. Philip H. Sheridan
LC

Sheridan. One Union colonel remembered seeing the Ohioan in tears, so great did defeat weigh upon him.[14]

14 Donald Allendorf, *The Long Road to Liberty: The Odyssey of a German Regiment in the Yankee Army, The 15th Missouri Volunteer Infantry* (Kent, OH., 2006),125; "Sheridan in Battle," *St. Louis Post-Dispatch*, in the *Morning Oregonian*, August 17, 1888.

Any lingering questions about Sheridan's performance at Chickamauga were erased two months later at Chattanooga. Here he led his division as it charged its way up Missionary Ridge and helped sweep a large part of the Confederate Army off the high ground surrounding the city. Although his men were not the first to reach the crest, Sheridan distinguished himself as the only officer able and willing to keep his troops in hot pursuit of the beaten enemy once the Confederate line broke and ran. His instinct to go for the kill caught the attention of Maj. Gen. Ulysses S. Grant, who had taken charge of the operations at Chattanooga. The future president had witnessed the assault from his command post at Orchard Knob and had a grand view of the entire operation. "To Sheridan's prompt movement, the Army of the Cumberland and the nation are indebted for the bulk of the capture of prisoners, artillery, and small arms that day," explained Grant. "Except for his prompt pursuit, so much in this way would not have been accomplished."[15]

In March 1864, Grant appointed Sheridan commander of the Army of the Potomac's Cavalry Corps. Sheridan was the only combat officer brought from the west by Grant. Sheridan experienced a disappointing start to his Cavalry Corps career in the Wilderness and on the road to Spotsylvania that boiled over into a heated feud with Maj. Gen. George G. Meade, commander of the Army of the Potomac. After promising Meade in the midst of a heated argument that he (Sheridan) would "whip Stuart if you will only let me," Sheridan went out and led the Federal cavalry to victory over Maj. Gen. J. E. B. Stuart's Confederate cavaliers at Yellow Tavern near Richmond on May 11. On Sheridan's next raid, Stuart's replacement, Maj. Gen. Wade Hampton, repulsed efforts to raid Gordonsville at the battle of Trevilian Station on June 11 and 12. At risk of running out of ammunition, Sheridan cut his losses and returned to the Army of the Potomac, failing to achieve any of the objectives for his raid. Afterward, he and his cavalry served around Richmond and Petersburg in an unspectacular manner. His tenure as Cavalry Corps commander was clearly marked by a more aggressive use of the Union mounted arm and improved confidence among the rank and file. Nevertheless, Sheridan's record as a battlefield commander did not live up to the expectations that his performances in the west had established as his benchmark. Consequently, Sheridan's assignment to the Valley command in August of 1864 came as a surprise to many. The appointment was made at Grant's discretion, largely due to his belief

---

15 Peter Cozzens, *The Shipwreck of their Hopes: The Battles for Chattanooga* (Chicago, IL, 1994), 392.

that the little Irishman from Somerset, Ohio, could infuse some of Grant's own resolve to the situation and lead the Union to victory in the Shenandoah Valley.[16]

Although Sheridan brought an aggressive approach to warfare in the Valley, he was not the reckless and impulsive commander often portrayed in historical literature. When he made up his mind to strike, he hit hard, but only after careful deliberation and planning. Before committing to action, Sheridan almost always factored in political, military, and logistical considerations. His hunger for information about enemy strength and dispositions served him well in that regard. Dating back to his days as colonel of the 2nd Michigan Cavalry in 1862, Sheridan had regularly used scouts, spies, and guides to obtain intelligence. "No matter how great the extent of the country over which he was to operate, he had the rare faculty of possessing a full knowledge of it," recalled Col. Russell A. Alger, who served with Sheridan in Mississippi in 1862 as well as in the Army of the Potomac's Cavalry Corps two years later.[17]

Sheridan's words and deeds confirmed Alger's claim. When he arrived in Harpers Ferry in early August 1864, Sheridan recorded that he "did what [he] never failed to do during the whole course of the war—make a map, or rather an information map, of the surrounding country." Indeed, Sheridan obsessed over such things. "My mind ran to the accumulation of knowledge of this kind," he recalled. As an independent commander, Sheridan understood the importance of logistics and how they impacted the outcome of any campaign. Much of this understanding was the result of his earlier staff service under Halleck and Curtis. Time and again that experience would influence Sheridan's Shenandoah Valley campaign in ways that contrasted sharply with his impetuous, roughrider image.[18]

*   *   *

---

16 Sheridan, *Memoirs*, 368-369; Wittenberg, *Little Phil*, 28-30, 39.

17 C. L. Martzolff, "General Philip H. Sheridan," *Ohio History Sketches* (Columbus, OH, 1903), 271; Hiram C. Whitley, *In It* (Cambridge, MA, 1894), 77; Charles Haven Ladd Johnston, *Famous Cavalry Leaders* (New York, NY, 1918), 313-358.

18 R. A. Alger, *Eulogy on the Late General Philip H. Sheridan*. 9, 11; *New York Times*, March 4, 1886 (original appeared in *Detroit Free Press*).

Phil Sheridan's arrival in the Shenandoah Valley was the culmination of a series of events dating back to May 1864. From the outset of active campaigning in the spring of 1864, military operations in the Shenandoah Valley had sullied General Grant's plans for subduing Virginia. Less than two weeks after Lt. Gen. Ulysses S. Grant ordered the Army of the Potomac across the Rapidan River and into the Wilderness, a Southern army under Maj. Gen. John C. Breckinridge defeated Maj. Gen. Franz Sigel's Federals at New Market on May 15. Confederate commander Robert E. Lee urged Breckinridge to either pursue Sigel across the Potomac to disrupt Grant's operations, or join the embattled Army of Northern Virginia above Richmond. Breckinridge decided against pursuit, but joined Lee in the defense of the Southern capital. He marched his men south to Staunton where they boarded cars on the Virginia Central Railroad and headed for Hanover Junction. Lee certainly needed the manpower to stop Grant, but pulling Breckinridge out of the Shenandoah denuded the region of valuable veteran troops.

After Sigel's defeat, Grant replaced him with Maj. Gen. David Hunter on May 21. Hunter moved quickly and took advantage of Breckinridge's absence. On June 5, he routed a force under Brig. Gen. William E. "Grumble" Jones at Piedmont, effectively eliminating all credible Confederate opposition to his continued advance. Hunter occupied Staunton the next day, destroying mills, workshops, warehouses, and portions of the Virginia Central Railroad. Reinforced by two divisions under Brig. Gen. George Crook, Hunter's enlarged force moved on Lexington at the southern end of the Valley. There they destroyed the Virginia Military Institute, segments of the James River and Kanawha Canal, and burned the home of former Virginia governor John Letcher. Hunter's ultimate objective was Lynchburg, a vital logistics center where the Virginia and Tennessee Railroad joined the Orange and Alexandria to form the Southside Railroad. The Southside ran eastward to Petersburg and was critical to the success and survival of the Confederacy.

Only days after the Confederate victory at Cold Harbor on June 3, Lee learned of Hunter's victory at Piedmont and occupation of Staunton. Breckinridge's Division was immediately dispatched back to the Valley. When Crook joined Hunter at Staunton and they moved on Lexington, Lee realized that the Federals intended to capture Lynchburg. The loss of that logistical center would make it nearly impossible to maintain a viable defense of Richmond. Although his army was already sorely depleted, Lee had little choice but to send additional reinforcements to prevent the fall of Lynchburg. On June 13, Lt. Gen. Jubal Anderson Early's 8,000 Second Corps veterans departed the

Confederate trenches around Richmond, boarded trains at Hanover Junction, and headed toward Lynchburg.

When Early's troops arrived there on the afternoon of June 17, advance elements from Hunter's army were driving several cavalry brigades under Brig. Gen. John D. Imboden toward the city of Lynchburg. The combative and profane "Old Jube" galloped to the front through flocks of retreating cavalrymen, shook his fist at the approaching Federals, and shouted, "No buttermilk rangers after you now, damn you!" With a bugler from the old Stonewall Brigade sounding the charge, Early interposed Maj. Gen. Stephen D. Ramseur's Division between Lynchburg and Hunter's advancing army. Running low on ammunition and intimidated by the arrival of veteran infantry reinforcements from Lee's Army of Northern Virginia, Hunter retreated into the mountains of West Virginia. His precipitate withdrawal uncovered the Shenandoah Valley, the traditional Confederate invasion route to the North. At Lee's behest, Early marched his men down the Valley, crossed the Potomac River into Maryland, and routed Maj. Gen. Lew Wallace's makeshift army at Monocacy Junction just east of Frederick on July 9, 1864.[19]

Two days later, Early's exhausted veterans arrived on the outskirts of Washington, but he quickly realized that the searing summer heat and stifling humidity had wreaked havoc upon his command. "Natural obstacles alone prevented our taking Washington," asserted General Ramseur. "The heat & dust was so great that our men could not possibly march farther." Early deferred his assault until morning to rest his army and to allow stragglers to rejoin the ranks. That same night, Early learned that Grant had dispatched two Union corps from Petersburg to reinforce Washington and that these veterans now manned the defenses. Early refused to risk his 16,000-man army against the reinforced fortifications surrounding Washington. On July 12, Early prudently headed back toward the Potomac under cover of darkness and reached the safety of Virginia on the morning of July 14.[20]

The belated Union pursuit by elements of two Federal corps did not get underway until July 13. Their overall commander, Maj. Gen. Horatio G. Wright, was loathe to cross the Potomac into Virginia, but did so when he learned that the advance of Hunter's returning army might be endangered by

---

19 John W. Daniel, "Memorial of Gen. Jubal A. Early," *Southern Historical Society Papers*, vol. XXI, 296.

20 Ramseur to My Darling Wife, July 15, 1864, SHC-UNC.

Early. Hunter's vanguard struck Early's wagon train at Purcellville on July 16, but Early escaped into the Valley after suffering a small loss of wagons and men. Two days later, Early repelled his pursuers in a sharp engagement at Cool Spring near Snickers Gap. Wright concluded that Early was in full retreat toward Richmond—despite the clash that had taken place between Brig. Gen. William W. Averell and Confederate Maj. Gen. Dodson Ramseur four miles north of Winchester at Rutherford's farm. Wright promptly returned the VI Corps to Washington, leaving only Hunter's small force under General Crook's immediate command to confront Early near Winchester. Lincoln and his administration were deeply disappointed in Wright. Assistant Secretary of War Charles A. Dana lamented that "Wright started back as soon as he got where he might have done something worth while." Lincoln was even less charitable, quipping that Wright feared "he might come across the rebels and catch some of them."[21]

After Wright's departure, Crook's cavalry patrols skirmished with Early's men between Strasburg and Kernstown for several days. Although the horsemen reported that Early was present in full force, Crook clung to Wright's incorrect assessment of the strategic situation and instead chastised the reports as exaggerated. When Early's vanguard appeared south of Kernstown on the morning of July 24, Crook threw caution to the wind and advanced a small force to confront the Confederates. Acting under General Lee's directive to do all he could to prevent additional reinforcements from being returned to General Grant at Richmond and Petersburg, Early struck Crook at the Second Battle of Kernstown. Crook soon realized his mistake and rushed reinforcements to Kernstown, but he was too late. Early launched dual flanking attacks which made short work of Crook and sent the Federals streaming into Winchester. In what one Virginian termed "the most easily won battle of the war," the Confederate Army of the Valley inflicted 1,200 Federal casualties while losing only 200 men. "I have never witnessed a more perfect stampede," recalled one of Early's veteran officers. "Helter skelter they fled, abandoning every species of property."[22]

---

21 Tyler Dennet, *Lincoln and the Civil War Diaries and Letters of John Hay* (New York, NY, 1939), 209; OR 37, pt. 2, 427.

22 For detailed study on Early's campaign following his retreat from Washington, see Scott C. Patchan, *Shenandoah Summer: The 1864 Valley Campaign* (Lincoln, NE, 2007); Journal of Captain

The magnitude of the Kernstown defeat assumed larger proportions when Early dispatched 3,000 cavalrymen on a raid into Pennsylvania under Brig. Gen. John C. McCausland. In retaliation for Hunter's destruction of the homes of prominent Virginia secessionists in the Shenandoah Valley, Early ordered McCausland to collect a ransom from Chambersburg, Pennsylvania, or burn the town to the ground. When no ransom was forthcoming, McCausland carried out Early's order and destroyed hundreds of homes and businesses. On a less spectacular but logistically important note, Early's advance also continued the disruption of the Baltimore and Ohio Railroad, the vital link between Washington and the western states. Railroad crews were repairing the damage Early had inflicted during his Washington Raid when the Confederates appeared a second time. Soldiers who had served under Stonewall Jackson in his actions against that rail line in 1862 quipped that "Early [was] finishing 'Stonewall' Jackson's contract on the B. & O. R. R."[23]

Viewed from the War Department in Washington, the tactical situation in the northern Shenandoah Valley and along the Potomac was in complete chaos. Neither Hunter nor Crook seemed up to the challenge of sorting out the confusing intelligence reports and reacting appropriately to the deteriorating situation.[24] President Lincoln and General Grant recognized that the status quo could not continue and that a change in the region's military leadership was essential for political as well as military reasons. Hunter's actions demonstrated that he was incapable of managing the Department of West Virginia and Crook, the administration's handpicked leader of Hunter's field army, had failed at Kernstown.

The root of the military problem was largely the organizational structure that existed in the affected regions. The large and unwieldy command structure in and around the Shenandoah Valley hampered the Union's ability to address emerging Confederate threats in the region. When Early advanced into Maryland in July, he confronted troops belonging to the Department of West Virginia. As he moved east, Federals from the Middle Department challenged his advance at Monocacy. Soldiers from the Department of Washington manned the defenses of the capital city. McCausland's torch-bearing

---

Seaton Gales contained in *Our Living and Our Dead*, March 4, 1874; John Worsham, *One of Jackson's Foot Cavalry* (Wilmington, NC, 1987), 160.

23 G. Q. Peyton Memoir, Manassas Library.

24 Augustus Forsberg Memoir, Washington and Lee University, 31.

cavalrymen at Chambersburg were operating in territory under the jurisdiction of the Department of the Susquehanna. The Shenandoah Valley belonged to the Department of West Virginia. As a result, no single Union commander possessed the overall authority to address the threat posed by Confederate forces operating out of the Shenandoah Valley. Departmental commanders acted on their own accord with little, if any, effective coordination of action between departments. Jubal Early had been exploiting this weakness in the Union's command structure since the first days of July. As Assistant Secretary of War Dana previously told Grant, "There is no head to the whole and it seems indispensable that you should appoint one."[25]

The organizational structure left Maj. Gen. Henry Halleck, now President Lincoln's military chief of staff, as the region's de facto leader. Halleck's distaste for taking decisive action and his obsession with bureaucratic wrangling rendered him unsuitable for such a role. "It seemed to be the policy of General Halleck and Secretary [of War] Stanton to keep any force sent here, in pursuit of the invading army, moving right and left, so as to keep between the enemy and our capital," observed Grant, "and generally speaking, they pursued this policy until all knowledge of the whereabouts of the enemy was lost. To remedy this evil," Grant concluded, "it was evident in my mind that some person should have the supreme command of all the forces [in those departments]." Unlike Halleck, Grant was a man of decision, and he moved to consolidate the departments under the newly created Middle Military Division.[26]

Grant's first choice to command the new enlarged department was Maj. Gen. George G. Meade, commander of the Army of the Potomac. Meade wrote his wife that Grant "had thought proper to communicate to me that he had nominated me for a command in Washington." The news buoyed Meade's sagging spirit, for he longed to serve where he could make command decisions without Grant and his ever-present staff scrutinizing his every move. Meade was not the only candidate being considered for the job. Grant also had his eyes on the Army of the Potomac's aggressive cavalry commander, Maj. Gen. Philip Henry Sheridan, whose primary experiences had been leading infantry in the Army of the Cumberland and as a proficient logistics officer during the first year of the war.

---

25 *OR* 37, pt. 2, 223.

26 U. S. Grant, *Personal Memoirs of U.S. Grant and Selected Letters 1839-1865.* (New York, NY, 1990), 614; *OR* 36, pt. 1, 29.

On July 31, 1864, President Lincoln journeyed to Fort Monroe at the tip of the Virginia peninsula near Norfolk to discuss the overall military situation with Grant. One of the items on the agenda was finding a commander for the Middle Military Division. Several names surfaced during this discussion: Meade, Sheridan, William B. Franklin, Winfield S. Hancock, and even George B. McClellan. Political considerations in a presidential election year quickly dashed Meade's hopes. Lincoln had stood by Meade when Lee escaped after Gettysburg when many Republicans were calling for Meade's removal from command of the Army of the Potomac. The president worried that voters would construe Meade's transfer away from the prominent Army of the Potomac as a sign that the war was not going well. Grant understood and did not press the issue. Franklin and Hancock likely were never considered seriously for the position. McClellan's name surfaced merely as a tactic to eliminate the popular general as a political rival to Lincoln. When the meeting ended, General Hunter retained administrative command of the new Middle Military Division; however, Lincoln acquiesced to Grant's choice of Sheridan to lead "all the troops in the field."[27]

Back at Petersburg, news of the 32-year-old Sheridan's appointment ruffled some feathers in the Army of the Potomac. Some officers, Hancock among them, thought Sheridan's recent performance as cavalry corps commander had been sluggish and inconsistent. "[S]ome political chicanery [was] at the bottom of it, and that they are afraid in Washington to give us a chance to do anything that others cannot swallow up," complained Hancock. General Meade adopted a more charitable view of the situation. "I intend to look on the affair in the most favorable light," he informed his wife, "particularly as I have my hands full with the Burnside imbroglio [the failed battle of the Crater], and must remain here to see to it." Viewed through the clarifying lens of historical hindsight, Grant's selection of Sheridan to lead the Army of the Shenandoah seems nearly inevitable, but in August of 1864, it was clearly an unconventional choice.[28]

Grant's choice of Sheridan propelled him ahead of several older and more experienced senior officers. It also represented a significant leap in responsibility. Sheridan had never led more than 12,000 men in any capacity,

---

27 George Gordon Meade, ed., *Life and Letters of George Gordon Meade, Major General United States Army* (New York: Charles Scribner's Sons, 1913, 2: 218; Bruce Catton, *Grant Takes Command*, (New York, NY, 1968, 1969), 2 vols. 336; Grant, *Memoirs*, p. 615.

28 Meade, *Life and Letters of General Meade*, 2:219.

but Grant expected him to guide the reorganized Army of the Shenandoah against a successful veteran enemy in a region synonymous with Confederate victory. Adding to the weight of the responsibility, Grant expected Sheridan to do so in the same determined and aggressive style Grant himself espoused. Few men made the successful leap to army commander during the course of the war. Many generals with stellar combat records as subordinates failed as independent commanders. Only victory would remove any lingering doubts Lincoln, Stanton, and others harbored about Sheridan.

"I am sending General Sheridan for temporary duty whilst the enemy is being expelled from the border," Grant informed Halleck on August 1. "Unless General Hunter is in the field in person, I want Sheridan put in command of all the troops in the field, with instructions to put himself south of the enemy and follow him to the death. Wherever the enemy goes let our troops go also. Once started up the Valley they ought to be followed until we get possession of the Virginia Central Railroad. If General Hunter is in the field," concluded Grant, "give Sheridan direct command of the 6th Corps and cavalry division."[29]

Grant's aggressive tone lifted Lincoln's sagging spirits, but the president understood the realities of Washington politics and military bureaucracy. The message would not get through the War Department to the field commanders without alteration by Stanton or Halleck. "I have seen your dispatch. . . . This, I think, is exactly right as to how our forces should move," Lincoln wired back to Grant. "But please look over the dispatches you may have received from here, even since you made that order, and discover, if you can, that there is any idea in the head of any one here, of 'putting our army south of the enemy' or of 'following him to the death' in any direction. I repeat to you it will neither be done nor attempted unless you watch it every day, and hour, and force it."[30]

Grant read Lincoln's dispatch on August 3 and knew immediately what needed to be done. Still, he hesitated to initiate any action from City Point that might expose Washington to Early's Southern Army. That same day Grant was aboard a steamboat plying through the choppy waters of Chesapeake Bay bound for Washington. He passed through the capital city without stopping

29 Grant, *Memoirs*, 615.

30 To get orders to Union commanders in the Shenandoah Valley, Grant had to send them through the War Department in Washington. Once there, the orders were interpreted by Maj. Gen. Henry Halleck and Secretary of War Edwin Stanton, and were often diluted in their intent because of Halleck's natural cautiousness. Ibid., 615-616.

and caught a northbound train. When the train arrived at Relay House, Maryland, Grant stepped onto the wooden platform wearing a simple coat adorned with three stars. Puffing on one of his trademark cigars, he found a seat and "smoked and talked with the four staff officers who accompanied him for an hour or more." The commanding general left Relay House, Maryland, at 5:00 p.m. on a westbound train headed to Monocacy Junction. He arrived two hours later, hopped into a carriage, and headed directly to Hunter's headquarters at the Thomas house on the Monocacy battlefield. As he passed through the army's camp along the way, veteran soldiers from the VI Corps saw Grant approaching and "cheered him grandly."[31]

Grant wasted no time on niceties or small talk with Hunter, and instead asked for the latest intelligence on Early's forces. Hunter admitted "he was so embarrassed with orders from Washington moving him first to the right and then to the left that he had lost all trace of the enemy." Unfazed, Grant confidently replied, "I will find out where the enemy is." The resolute leader ordered Hunter's forces to push four miles above Harpers Ferry into the Shenandoah Valley. Grant clearly understood the logistical realities of Early's situation. The irascible Virginian would quickly rear his head when Union forces threatened to sever Confederate communications with Winchester and the upper Valley, regardless of his current whereabouts along the upper Potomac.[32] That evening Grant set forth in detail his orders for Hunter:

> In pushing up the Shenandoah Valley, as it is expected you will have to go, first or last, it is desirable that nothing should be left to invite the enemy to return. Take all provisions, forage, and stock wanted for use of your command; such as cannot be consumed, destroy. It is not desirable that the buildings should be destroyed; they should rather be protected; but the people should be informed that so long as an army can subsist among them recurrences of these raids must be expected, and we are determined to stop them at all hazards. Bear in mind the object is to drive the enemy south, and to do this you want to keep him always in sight. Be guided by the course he takes.[33]

31 Correspondence of the *Philadelphia Enquirer* contained in the *Belmont Chronicle*, August 18, 1864; Letter from the 151st New York, September 17, 1864, contained in the *Orleans American*, October 14, 1864.

32 Grant, *Memoirs*, 616.

33 *OR* 43, pt. 1, 698.

Grant's directive would guide the coming campaign and ultimately serve as the impetus for the infamous "burning" of the Shenandoah Valley.

Once the army had its marching orders, Grant suggested that Hunter establish his departmental headquarters "at any point that would suit him best, Cumberland, Baltimore, or elsewhere. Sheridan would command the troops in the field." At 11:30 p.m. on August 5, he telegraphed Halleck, "Send Sheridan by morning train to Harpers Ferry. . . . Give him general command of all the troops in the field within the [Middle Military] division." Hunter perceived his own irrelevance in Grant's design long before Sheridan arrived and tendered his resignation, his second in three weeks. Grant accepted it without hesitation and later praised Hunter for "a patriotism that was none too common in the army." Phil Sheridan would command the newly created Middle Military Division in its entirety. Not only would he have to lead the Army of the Shenandoah in the field, Sheridan was also responsible for all operations and logistical considerations of a vast military division that extended from the Eastern Shore of Maryland west to the Ohio River. The duties included the defense of Washington and guarding the critical Baltimore and Ohio Railroad through the guerrilla-infested mountains of West Virginia and Maryland. Both Halleck and Stanton openly questioned Sheridan's ability to handle the enormous responsibility.[34]

While Grant conferred with Hunter, Sheridan remained in Washington. On August 4, he met with President Lincoln and Secretary of War Stanton at the White House. "Mr. Lincoln candidly told me that Mr. Stanton had objected to my assignment to General Hunter's command," recalled Sheridan. Lincoln added that he agreed with Stanton's assessment, but reassured a humbled Sheridan. "Since General Grant had 'ploughed round' the difficulties of the situation by picking me out to command the 'boys in the field,' he felt satisfied with what had been done and 'hoped for the best.'" Stanton sat in stolid silence while Lincoln spoke. When the meeting adjourned the secretary accompanied Sheridan back to the War Department and indelibly impressed upon the new commander the "necessity for success from the political as well as from the military point of view." Stanton's lecture to the young general and the reminder

---

34 For all of Hunter's patriotism, this was the second resignation he had submitted in less than one month. He tendered his resignation when the Lincoln administration assigned George Crook to command Hunter's troops during the pursuit of Early from Washington. He had previously threatened to resign when things were not to his liking while serving as commander of Union forces operating along coasts of the Carolinas and Georgia. Grant, *Memoirs*, 616-617.

of Lincoln's uncertain future in the upcoming election had a lasting impact on the course of the developing campaign.[35]

On August 6, Sheridan's army marched into Harpers Ferry and on to Halltown with rousing strains of patriotic music filling the air. Its new commander, however, waited impatiently at Monocacy Junction for "an hour or two" before boarding a train to join his men. When he arrived, Sheridan established his headquarters in a dilapidated hotel and summoned Lt. John R. Meigs, the chief engineer for the Middle Military Division, for a meeting. Meigs was "familiar with every important road and stream and with all points worthy of note west of the Blue Ridge," Sheridan wrote, "and was particularly well equipped with knowledge regarding the Shenandoah Valley, even down to the farm-houses." Meigs's detailed understanding of the Valley's terrain and cartography came from service under Generals Hunter and Sigel in 1864 and Brig. Gen. William W. Averell in 1863. Sheridan also had a good eye for terrain, and together the two men poured over the maps of the region. The new commander grasped the military implications of the geography and knew it would play a pivotal role in the forthcoming campaign.[36]

Accurate information on Jubal Early's whereabouts and intentions was sorely lacking. Numerous reports of Early crossing into Maryland poured into Sheridan's headquarters. One outpost reported that 2,000 Confederates had splashed across Cherry Run twenty miles west of Harpers Ferry. Another report claimed 6,000 Southern cavalry crossed the Potomac River in Loudoun County, ten miles east of Sheridan's position. Exaggerated reports of Confederate activities around Sharpsburg and Hagerstown abounded. Given the dizzying array of information, Sheridan was unsure if the Confederates were mounting a full-scale invasion, a raid, or only a brief diversion. Further, his options for discovering Early's true intentions were limited because of an immediate lack of competent cavalry. Two mounted divisions en route to the Shenandoah via Washington had not yet arrived, and Averell's division was chasing down Brig. Gen. John McCausland's raiders in West Virginia. "Affairs here," Sheridan informed Grant, are "somewhat confused," but he assured his chief that he would "soon straighten them out."[37]

---

35 Sheridan, *Memoirs*, vol. 1, 463-464.

36 Ibid., 467-468.

37 OR 43, pt. 1, 710.

These constraints did not shackle Sheridan. Immediately, he dispatched Col. Charles R. Lowell's 1,000-man makeshift brigade to conduct a reconnaissance mission toward Martinsburg. The Ohioan remained at Harpers Ferry, waiting "anxiously" for information. Brigadier General Alfred T. A. Torbert's elite cavalry division soon arrived from Washington after being transported there from Petersburg. "[H]urry up your Second Brigade and send word to General Merritt to push on and report to [me] here," he urged the division commander. Within 24 hours, Sheridan concluded that Early's brief presence north of the Potomac was a ruse based on the reports of his cavalry. "Early crossed the river and took dinner at Sharpsburg," Sheridan informed Grant, "but returned immediately."[38]

---

38 OR 43, pt. 1, 690, 699, 710-712, 720.

Chapter 2

PERPETUAL FERMENT

Jubal Early and Confederate Strategy

The Confederates did not remain obligingly idle while the Union army worked through its thorny command issues. On August 5, 1864, Southern soldiers belonging to Lt. Gen. Jubal A. Early's Army of the Valley District took a well-deserved opportunity to rest along the banks of the Virginia side of the Potomac River. The momentarily carefree Confederates shaded themselves beneath the trees from the hot summer sun. As the churning water slipped past them, they removed their shoes and rolled up their pant legs in preparation for yet another river crossing into Maryland. Low rations and excessive marching during the taxing spring and summer campaigns in Virginia and Maryland had reduced the men to "skin and bones." The sight of their emaciated legs—or "spindle shanks," as the soldiers called them—elicited exchanges of good-natured hooting and laughter.

When the order came down, the barefoot veterans of so many campaigns and skirmishes splashed into the water, waded across the rocky river bottom, and climbed their way up the opposite bank. This was the third time in the past month that Early's army had sojourned upon Northern soil. Like the crossings that had preceded this one, the Southern thrust above the Potomac River alarmed President Abraham Lincoln and his administration. No one in the

United States Army or government could grasp Early's intent, estimate the composition of his command, or accurately discern his precise whereabouts at any particular time.[1]

"We are keeping the Yankee nation in a perpetual ferment," declared Maj. Jedediah Hotchkiss, the Second Corps' topographical engineer who served as the map maker for Stonewall Jackson in 1862. Another Confederate officer accurately deemed the Federals "completely mystified and kept in perpetual apprehension of a renewal of invasion." Although Jackson died 15 months earlier, Southern forces had continued his proud legacy of dominance in the Shenandoah Valley. In Jackson's place now stood Lt. Gen. Jubal Early, a aging, combative, and cunning Virginian. When Early's troops crossed the Potomac River entered Maryland on August 5, "Old Jube," as his soldiers called him, stood at the pinnacle of his military career and was the present military master of the Shenandoah Valley.[2]

In August 1864, Jubal Anderson Early was 47 years old, stood nearly six feet in height, and weighed about 170 pounds,—a good-sized man for that era. However, a severe illness contracted during the Mexican War left his body wracked with arthritis and other joint and skeletal ailments commonly summarized in the mid-1800s as simply "rheumatism." As a result, his hunched body robbed him of the dominating stature normally associated with a man of his dimensions. The Virginian's graying hair and unkempt beard only added to the image of Early as an old man. One observant soldier described the army commander as "a very malignant and very hairy old spider." Even more damning than his gruff exterior was a cantankerous personality that meshed perfectly with his aged appearance. Early's physical attributes and acerbic disposition earned him several descriptive monikers among his soldiers, including "Old Jube," "Old Granny," or "Old Lop Ear." Staff officer Lt. Peter Hairston described his superior as "decidedly a character—a fine officer, very active and energetic in the discharge of his duties with some peculiarities which render him very amusing." Jubal Early also excelled at the usage of profane language, and it was widely rumored that no other soldier in the entire Army of

---

1   George Quintus Peyton, "A Civil War Record for 1864-1865," University of Virginia (UVA hereafter).

2   J. Hotchkiss to wife, August 4, 1864, Hotchkiss Papers, Library of Congress (LC hereafter); "Journal of Captain Seaton Gales," contained in *Our Living and Our Dead*, March 4, 1874; Edward A. Pollard, *The Early Life, Campaigns, and Public Services of R. E. Lee: With a Record of the Campaigns and Heroic Deeds of his Companions in Arms* (New York: E. B. Treat and Co., 1871), 478.

Lt. Gen. Jubal A. Early
LC

Northern Virginia could get away with uttering such words in front of Gen. Robert E. Lee. Although General Lee was 10 years senior to Early, the beloved army leader affectionately dubbed his subordinate his "Bad Old Man." Like Stonewall Jackson, Early made no show in his dress. Instead, he appeared to be "a plain farmer looking man . . . but with all, every inch a soldier," noted one man in the ranks. This opinion was echoed by a foreign observer who, upon meeting Early, described him as "a gruff-looking man, but with a high reputation as a soldier."[3]

Early was also an outspoken character and gave free voice to his opinions without any consideration whatsoever. On one of the few occasions when the irreverent Virginian attended church in early 1865, the minister postulated upon the dead buried in the surrounding churchyard rising up and speaking to those in the congregation. The preacher rhetorically asked the congregation how they would react to such an event. Silence overcame the congregation as its members pondered that miraculous thought. In the midst of the attentive silence, "Old Jube" leaned over toward a staff officer seated beside him and with the "voice of a stentor" whispered, "I'd conscript every damned one of them."[4] On another occasion, Early's second-in-command, Maj. Gen. John C. Breckinridge of Kentucky, questioned a group of Virginians about their constant references to the "FFV's" or "First Families of Virginia." He inquired of the Virginians about the disposition of the state's second families. Although not participating in the immediate conversation, Early overheard the question and proved unable to resist his sarcastic urge. Jubal chimed in, "They moved to Kentucky," to the laughter of those around him.[5]

Jubal Early was born in 1816 among the rolling hills of Franklin County, Virginia, as the third of Joab and Ruth Early's 10 children. Joab prospered as one of the area's largest slave owners and possessor of more than 1,300 acres of productive land. Biographer Charles C. Osborne described Early's upbringing as "lapped in wealth and unassailable position—albeit in a remote part of the world." He received the best education available, attending boarding schools in nearby Lynchburg and Danville.[6] Tragedy struck the Early family in 1832 when his mother died. "Old Jube" recalled her passing as a source of "the deepest

3   Gary Gallagher, "Two Generals and a Valley: Philip H. Sheridan and Jubal A. Early in the Shenandoah," *The Shenandoah Valley Campaign of 1864* (Chapel Hill, NC, 2006), 7; Charles C. Osborne, *Jubal: The Life and Times of General Jubal A. Early, CSA* (Chapel Hill, NC: Algonkin Books of Chapel Hill, 1992), 30-31, 210; Jubal Early, *Autobiographical Sketch and Narrative of the War Between the States* (Philadephia: J.B. Lippincott Co.), xviv-xxv; Peter Hairston to wife, Nov. 3, 1863, Hairston Papers, SHC-UNC.

4   Samuel J. C. Moore Papers, Southern Historical Collection (SHC hereafter), University of North Carolina (UNC hereafter).

5   Samuel J. C. Moore Papers, SHC-UNC; Miscellaneous Notation, John Warwick Daniel Papers, University of Virginia (UVA hereafter).

6   Early, *Autobiographical Sketch*, xvii; Osborne, *Jubal*, 6-7.

grief" for his entire family. Life went on, and Early's well-rounded preparatory education helped him obtain an appointment to the United States Military Academy at West Point, New York. By his own admission, he "was never a good student and was sometimes quite remiss." Early later remembered that he "was not a very exemplary soldier . . . [and] had very little taste for scrubbing brass," a menial task excelled at by more ambitious cadets. He did not relish a career in the U.S. Army. The promise of a low-paying position as a military officer and the hardships of army life did not appeal to Jubal. Instead, he sought a more lucrative career and luxurious lifestyle. At one point, he seriously considered resigning from the academy; however, when his brother informed Jubal how proud their father was to have his son at West Point, Early dutifully remained at the academy and attained a "respectable" standing in his academics. His stormy nature occasionally led to fights with other cadets, including noted future generals Joseph Hooker and Lewis A. Armistead. Nevertheless, Jubal Early persevered and graduated in the Class of 1837, ranked 18th out of 50 cadets.[7]

After graduation, Early served his mandatory year of service on active duty in Florida's Seminole Indian War. "Though I heard some bullets whistling among the trees," recalled Early, "none came near me and I never saw an Indian." He resigned in July 1838 and returned to Rocky Mount, the seat of Franklin County, where he plunged into the study of law to ensure a successful future as a lawyer. Early soon became a successful practitioner of law and eventually won election to several local political offices. Although a successful attorney in the court room, he failed to properly manage the details of his business affairs and never truly attained the wealth he sought. Unlike most nineteenth-century men in the prime of life, Early never married. He once fell deeply in love with a beautiful girl from Philadelphia named Lavinia, whom he met at White Sulphur Springs, Virginia. They planned to reunite the following year at the springs. Instead, Early received an envelope from Philadelphia that contained a newspaper clipping announcing Lavinia's marriage to another man. The news crushed Early's spirit. Many have speculated that this failed romance prompted Early to remain a lifelong bachelor. While he never married, he did have a significant relationship with Julia McNealey of Rocky Mount. Between 1850 and 1864, the long-lasting affair produced four children who bore the

---

7 Early, *Autobiographical Sketch*, xvii-xviii.

Early family name. Although Jubal supported the children, Julia eventually married another man in 1871.[8]

It has been said that it was because of his own failed relationships that "Old Jube" resented officers whose wives accompanied them in the field. He directed most of his criticisms in that regard at Maj. Gen. John B. Gordon, the rising star in the Army of Northern Virginia and a man whom Early seemed to resent. Early once exclaimed, "I wish the Yankees would capture Mrs. Gordon and hold her till the war is over!" While passing through Winchester, Early noted a civilian carriage among the army wagons and asked what it was doing there. Upon learning that it was Mrs. Gordon's conveyance, Early quipped, "Well I'll be damned! If my men would keep up as she does, I'd never issue another order against straggling." Although Gordon attracted Early's attention, the wives of generals John C. Breckrinridge and Robert E. Rodes had also spent time visiting their husbands during the campaign. However, their presence did not seem to attract the same enmity from Early that Gordon's wife did. Perhaps Gordon in later writings exaggerated Early's feelings regarding the presence of Fanny Gordon, or maybe Early simply focused on Gordon because of the two men's already rocky military relationship.[9]

Professionally, Early prospered as a lawyer in Franklin County and won election to Virginia's House of Delegates for one term. During the war with Mexico, he served as a major in the Virginia Militia and military governor of Monterrey, but saw little combat. While in Mexico, he contracted the severe cold and fever that afflicted him with chronic rheumatism that plagued him for the rest of his life. The illness wreaked havoc on his body, and he was "bent with arthritis like a man more than twice his age [and] bore little resemblance to the tall, upright youth the citizens of Franklin County had last seen." Although only 31 years old, Early "was already grizzled."[10]

When he returned home, he persevered as a successful lawyer in Rocky Mount and won election as the Commonwealth's Attorney for Franklin County in 1851. When the Civil War broke out, Jubal Early was still serving as a simple country prosecutor. The citizens of Franklin County elected him to represent

---

8   Millard K. Bushong, *Old Jube: A Biography of General Jubal A. Early*, 18-19; Osborne, *Jubal*, 13-14, 20-21, 30, 31, 34-35, 485; Early, *Autobiographical Sketch*, xix.

9   John B. Gordon, *Reminiscences of the Civil War* (New York: Charles Scribner's Sons, 1904), 319.

10   Ibid., 30-31.

their Unionist viewpoint at the Virginia Secession Convention. There, Early fervently opposed secession and argued vehemently on behalf of the Union. In the second round of voting, Early supported secession, motivated largely by the course of actions pursued by the Lincoln administration. Although Virginia's Ordinance of Secession brought "bitter tears of grief" to Early's eyes, he nonetheless stayed dutifully loyal to his home state. "I fought through the entire war without once regretting the course I pursued with an abiding faith in the justice of our cause," explained Early. As a lawyer with a West Point education and barely two years of army experience, he became colonel of the 24th Virginia Infantry. At that rank, he led a brigade at the First Battle of Manassas in July 1861, counterattacking on Chinn Ridge and sweeping the Federals from his sector of the battlefield. In recognition of his services on the battlefield, General Beauregard promoted Early to brigadier general to rank from July 21, 1861. In May 1862, he was seriously wounded while leading an ill-fated frontal attack at Williamsburg during the Peninsula campaign. He returned home to convalesce at Rocky Mount, and rejoined the army later that summer to begin his rapid ascent to prominence in the Army of Northern Virginia.[11]

General Early matured rapidly as a combat leader during the second half of 1862, acting decisively while serving under Maj. Gen. Stonewall Jackson. At Cedar Mountain, Early's Brigade arrived on the field and helped to stem the initial Union success. At Second Manassas, his brigade helped throw back the attacking legions of Maj. Gen. John Pope's army. On September 17, 1862, amidst the vicious fighting at Antietam, Jubal Early ascended to divisional command when his commander went down in the combat. Early assisted Stonewall Jackson in defending the West Woods and helped wreck Maj. Gen. John Sedgwick's division. By Fredericksburg, Early had ascended to permanent division command, and his division played a critical role in restoring the Southern line after a Federal breakthrough on the Confederate right at Prospect Hill. In 1863, Early earned Lee's praise for carrying out his role at Chancellorsville, but the former Franklin County prosecutor starred in the Second Battle of Winchester on June 14. Early's Division stormed an important fortified U.S. position, capturing a six-gun battery in a well-planned and executed assault that marked the beginning of the end for the Federals at Winchester. At Gettysburg, he broke the stalemate on the first day, smashing into the Union right flank and driving it into the town in chaos. In spite of this

11 Early, *Autobiographical Sketch*, viii.

tactical success, his critics focused on the inability of the Confederates to secure Cemetery Hill, with some blaming Early for that failure. Nevertheless, in the first year after his wounding at Williamsburg, Early had fought in six pitched battles where he and his command had played critical roles that favorably affected the Confederate outcome. Early had been a difference-maker in the Army of Northern Virginia, and had accumulated more combat experience in barely a year than his soon-to-be opponent in the Shenandoah, Phil Sheridan, had obtained during his entire Civil War career to date.[12]

On November 7, 1863, Early and his command witnessed its "first serious disaster." Lee had posted parts of Early's Division on the north bank of the Rappahannock River at Rappahannock Station. Early's troops occupied a salient with the deep river at their backs. Early "objected to the engineering" and told Lee he thought the position "was bad." When troops from the Army of the Potomac's Sixth Corps launched an unprecedented night attack, Early's worst fears were manifested. The Federals quickly overran the Confederate defenses, and Early lost 1,600 of the 2,000 men that had been deployed to the north bank. When Lt. Gen. Richard S. "Dick" Ewell took leave of his command a few days later, Lee placed Early in temporary command of the Second Corps during the Mine Run campaign. The ensuing actions proved relatively uneventful and provided Early with little combat opportunity at his brief elevated level of command.[13]

By the middle of December, General Ewell resumed command of the Second Corps sending Early back to his division. A severe cold snap blanketed central Virginia at about the same time U.S. Brig. Gen. William W. Averell led his cavalry division on a raid against the Virginia and Tennessee Railroad at Salem. Lee wasted no time in assigning Jubal Early to an independent command that was assembled to meet Averell's incursion. Early buffeted himself against the biting cold with a woolen skull cap pulled firmly over his ears and a long overcoat that brushed the ground as he moved along. He rode the rails of the Virginia Central from Orange to Staunton in the heart of the Shenandoah Valley, followed by two brigades of infantry and two cavalry brigades from

---

12 For an objective discussion on Jubal Early and the combat on the first day at Gettysburg, see Harry W. Phanz's *Gettysburg: The First Day* (Chapel Hill: North Carolina: The University of North Carolina Press, 2000), 343-349. Douglas Southall Freeman, *Lee's Lieutenants: A Study in Command*, 3 vols. (New York, Charles Scribners and Sons, 1942), vol. 2, 253; Osborne, *Jubal*. 168-171.

13 Ibid., 205-212.

Lee's army. Lee expected Early to trap Averell's command before it could return to its base in West Virginia, but he narrowly escaped. The campaign succeeded only in fomenting Early's bias against the Western Virginia cavalry commands of Brig. Gen. John D. Imboden and Col. William L. Jackson. Early roundly criticized them and their troops in communications with Lee creating bad feeling among them. As fate would have it, Imboden and Jackson's commands became part of Early's Army of the Valley District later in 1864.[14]

Early began the 1864 Overland campaign still serving as a division commander under Lt. Gen. Richard S. Ewell. Early's Division put in a solid defensive performance in the Wilderness, but his supposed unwillingness to promptly act upon the suggestion of Brigadier General Gordon may have cost Lee an opportunity to seriously damage Meade's army. While the impact of Early's delay at implementing Gordon's proposed flanking attack against the Federal right can be debated, the events of the day clearly strained the relationship between Early and his leading brigadier general. When Lt. Gen. A. P. Hill grew ill in May 1864, Lee elevated Early to temporary command of the Third Corps. During the bloody operations at Spotsylvania Courthouse, Early demonstrated marked ability as a corps commander and gained Lee's increased confidence. Hill soon recovered and returned to his command, sending Early to his division in Ewell's Second Corps. When Ewell became incapacitated later that May, Lee again appointed Early to command the Second Corps and made him a temporary lieutenant general. Early performed so well that when Ewell attempted to reclaim his position in early June, Lee balked and retained "Old Jube" as the leader of the Second Corps.[15]

Early's operations in the Shenandoah Valley and adjoining regions in late June and July 1864 only enhanced his reputation. He had saved Lynchburg from the fiery clutches of U.S. Maj. Gen. David Hunter, threatened Washington, and kept the Baltimore and Ohio Railroad inoperable for more

14 For a complete account of Averell's Salem raid, see Darrell Collins, *General William Averell's Salem Raid: Breaking the Knoxville Supply Line* (Shippensburg, PA: Burd Street Press, 1999); Osborne, *Jubal*, 215-217.

15 For a detailed and objective assessment of the Gordon-Early-Ewell controversy in the Wilderness, see Gordon Rhea, *Battle of the Wilderness* (Baton Rouge, LA: Louisiana State University Press, 2004). As usual, Gordon overplayed his own importance in the matter and heightened the culpability of Ewell and Early. Rhea, *Battle of the Wilderness*, 407-409, 412-416; Rhea, *The Battles for Spotsylvania Courthouse* (Baton Rouge, LA: Louisiana State University Press, 2005), 322-323.

than a month. Most importantly, Early's actions in the Valley had pulled five infantry and two cavalry divisions (30,000 men) from Grant's operations at Petersburg. For Robert E. Lee, that result alone justified Early's continued presence in the Shenandoah. The "Bad Old Man" was not finished, either. He was about to tap dance on the B & O at Martinsburg and initiate another round of deception along the Potomac River.[16]

On August 4, Early initiated another chapter of Lee's bold strategy in the Shenandoah Valley by moving north to Martinsburg and disrupting the vital Baltimore and Ohio Railroad. Brigadier General John C. Vaughn's brigade, with Col. James W. Gillespie filling in for the wounded Vaughn, led the advance and drove a Federal detachment out of Martinsburg. The Confederate forces had rendered much destruction in Martinsburg during their previous visits, and their presence was not welcome. "Martinsburg was a strong Union town and its populace very bitter against the South," recalled a Tennessean. The town's female population taunted Early's Southerners, with one group claiming, "Our folks will soon be back and drive these rebels out, and we can have a nice time with our boys eating ice cream."[17]

When Early crossed the Potomac River and entered Maryland with 11,000 men of all arms on August 5, his primary goal was to cover McCausland's return from the Chambersburg raid through the appearance of making a much larger raid into Maryland. Gillespie's mounted Tennesseans led the way, fording the Potomac at Williamsport. Next came Maj. Gen. Robert E. Rodes's wing of the small army consisting of his own and Stephen Ramseur's infantry divisions. John Breckinridge's Corps, composed of the divisions of Maj. Gen. John B. Gordon and Brig. Gen. Gabriel C. Wharton, crossed near Shepherdstown with Col. William L. "Mudwall" Jackson's Virginia cavalry screening the movement. Early posted General Imboden's 700-man cavalry brigade near Shepherdstown, where he feigned an advance toward Harpers Ferry and screened the army's right flank.

In the end, General Early's movement to cover McCausland's withdrawal was not entirely successful. In spite of Early's efforts, a Union cavalry force under Brig. Gen. William W. Averell tracked McCausland down and routed him at Moorefield on August 7, capturing more than 400 prisoners and a battery of

16 Patchan, *Shenandoah Summer*, 316.

17 Reuben Clark Memoirs, Georgia Department of Archives and History (GDAH hereafter), 14.

horse artillery. Nevertheless, Early's push above the river launched another round of wild speculation on the part of the Federal authorities. Many believed that Early's second raid of the North in less than a month was now underway. The jittery Northern reaction to Early's brief appearance in Maryland underscored the political sensitivity of operations in the northern Shenandoah Valley.[18]

Early's brief foray into Maryland entered familiar territory that stirred memories of Sharpsburg and the horrendous retreat from Gettysburg. The Confederate vanguard skirmished with some Union cavalry from Maryland and shoved them across Antietam Creek with little trouble. Rodes's wing camped on the grounds of Saint James College a couple of miles east of Williamsport and about halfway between the river town and the old Sharpsburg battlefield. Around them were the weathered but forbidding breastworks they had constructed during the retreat from Gettysburg. While Gordon's division marched through Sharpsburg and across the battlefield, Early and Jed Hotchkiss took time out to roam the war-scarred field. As Early recalled his role on that bloody September day, Hotchkiss sketched the position of Early's brigade during that battle.[19]

During the Confederate sojourn in Maryland, Early's forces gathered up whatever supplies they could find. The results were a far cry from the immense bounty gathered earlier that summer during Early's first raid into Maryland. The commissary department rounded up only 150 horses, 2,000 bushels of corn, and a large cache of leather. Troops were permitted to purchase personal goods from the Marylanders at the standard U.S. dollar prices using worthless Confederate currency. This arrangement permitted staunch moralists in the Southern ranks to fleece Marylanders with a clean conscience. Even Hotchkiss procured gifts for his family back in Virginia, buying a bonnet for his wife and scarves for his daughters. He also purchased spools of black and white thread with sewing needles, precious commodities in the resource-strapped Confederacy.

Some of Gillespie's Tennesseans ventured into Hagerstown, which had been occupied multiple times since the Confederates' first invasion of Maryland in 1862. They were well received by the town's residents, who offered dinner

---

18 Patchan, *Shenandoah Summer*, 315-316.

19 Jed Hotchkiss Journal, contained in *OR* 43, pt. 1, 567.

and good company. "It was almost like an ovation. Hagerstown, unlike Martinsburg, was a rebel town," declared one Tennessee officer. Jonathan Hager Lawrence, "a very elegant old gentleman," as well as an avowed Unionist and descendant of the town's fathers, treated Capt. Reuben Clark of the 59th Tennessee "royally," sharing "his fine wine and cigars" while the two men debated the politics of secession.[20]

Early's entry into Maryland ended as quickly as it began. Although Federal authorities feared he would end up in Pennsylvania, he returned to Virginia on August 6. Since Grant had sent the Federal forces at Frederick, Maryland, back to Harpers Ferry, Early was compelled to withdraw all the way to Bunker Hill located 10 miles south of Martinsburg. Here, his army obtained several days of much needed rest.

*   *   *

In Richmond, General Lee learned that Grant had raised the ante in the Valley by dispatching Sheridan with two cavalry divisions. Lee promptly matched Grant as far as the Confederacy's limited resources permitted. On August 6, General Lee called South Carolinian Lt. Gen. Richard H. "Dick" Anderson to his headquarters for a conference with Confederate President Jefferson Davis. Anderson was acting commander of the Confederate First Corps while Lt. Gen. James Longstreet recovered from wounds received in May at the Wilderness. Davis approved Lee's plan to send Anderson with three divisions—one infantry and two cavalry—to Culpeper. His command was to operate east of the Blue Ridge Mountains while Early remained in the Shenandoah Valley. Lee hoped to lure Sheridan into detaching troops from the Valley to confront Anderson. If Sheridan obliged, Early would presumably be well-positioned to strike the weakened Union force remaining in the Shenandoah. The plan was sound, and Lee had full confidence in his army's ability to successfully carry out his designs.[21]

Lee instructed Maj. Gen. Fitzhugh Lee, the commander of one of the cavalry divisions under Anderson, to join the South Carolinian's force at Culpeper and "march towards Alexandria." The elder Lee was pulling no punches in his effort to win the war. He realized the Confederacy's slim hopes

20 Reuben Clark Memoirs, GDAH, 14.

21 *OR* 43, pt. 1, 991.

for independence might well lay in Lincoln's defeat in the coming November presidential elections. Anything that Lee did to cause confusion or panic in the North would chip away at Lincoln's re-election chances. By sending a cavalry division into Northern Virginia, Lee hoped to draw Federal troops away from both Petersburg and the Shenandoah Valley to defend Washington. Wherever the Federals weakened their forces, Lee would strike.[22]

The dispatch of Anderson and his divisions was a rather remarkable gamble. Trapped in the trenches around Petersburg and Richmond, the Army of Northern Virginia was under constant and heavy pressure from Grant. The Federal commander relentlessly extended his flanks and aggressively thrust at Lee's communications, all while keeping a tight grip on the static trench lines. Already heavily outnumbered, the detachment of so many men underscored how important Lee believed another major victory in the Shenandoah Valley might be for the Southern cause. Major General Joseph Brevard Kershaw's 4,000 foot soldiers constituted the nucleus of Anderson's command. Major Generals Wade Hampton and Fitz Lee each commanded a cavalry division, along with the usual allotment of horse artillery, while Maj. Wilfred W. Cutshaw's Battalion of three artillery batteries rounded out Anderson's force. Given the Northern propensity for exaggerating the strength of Confederate armies, it was not unreasonable to assume that Anderson's command at Culpeper might be perceived as comprising at least 20,000 troops. Lee knew from experience that Anderson would pose a larger threat in the minds of Federal commanders than his 9,000 veterans actually were.[23]

Anderson departed Richmond on August 7 with elements of Kershaw's Division and arrived at Mitchell's Station on the Orange and Alexandria Railroad. The balance of the division joined Anderson the following day, and the entire command moved several miles north to Culpeper. Fitzhugh Lee's cavalry and Cutshaw's artillery arrived three days later. Suspicions of a Federal move against Richmond prompted Lee to hold Hampton's cavalry division until August 11.

On August 11, Lee telegraphed General Anderson in Culpeper and outlined the goals of the South Carolinian's independent campaign:

22 Maj. Gen. Fitzhugh Lee's Report of Operations for 1864, Museum of the Confederacy.

23 OR 43, pt. 1, 243, Richmond operations, ANV returns.

You had better take position north of Culpeper Court-House and let the cavalry operate north of the Rappahannock River. Should the enemy's forces move west of the Blue Ridge range, leaving Washington uncovered, the cavalry might cross the Potomac east of the mountains and demonstrate against that city. Should he concentrate all of his cavalry in the Valley, unless it can be withdrawn by other operations ours must meet it, and General Hampton must take command of all the cavalry when united. Any enterprise that can be undertaken to injure the enemy, distract or separate his forces, embarrass his communications on the Potomac or on land, is desirable.[24]

The Shenandoah Valley had proven to be the Confederacy's trump card in Virginia time and time again. Its effective use played an important role in Confederate victories at Manassas in 1861, and helped save Richmond when General McClellan threatened to capture it during the Peninsula campaign in the spring of 1862. From 1863 onward, Lee had used the Shenandoah to launch operations north of the Potomac River. Now, as the summer of 1864 wound down, the commander of the Army of Northern Virginia rolled the dice once more and sent Anderson and his foot soldiers westward toward the old Valley of Virginia.

24 Ibid., 995.

Officers and Armies

Sheridan, Early, and their Subordinate Commanders

Phil Sheridan faced a daunting task. Not only did he have to protect Washington D.C., Maryland, and Pennsylvania from further Southern incursions, but he also had orders to clear the expansive Shenandoah Valley of all remaining Confederate forces. Although he would soon have an overwhelming advantage in manpower and materiel, he faced a skillful and battle-hardened opponent. Prior Union commanders in the Valley and elsewhere had proven that having more men and supplies did not guarantee victory. Indeed, no Union general had achieved anything more than temporary success in the Valley. Jubal Early's Second Corps from Robert E. Lee's Army of Northern Virginia continued to use the Valley to instill fear in the halls of Washington. Qualitatively speaking, Early's Southerners outmatched Sheridan's disparate army in both experience and *espirit de corps*. Simply put, Sheridan's new command was an army in name only, and he had yet to mold his varying commands of infantry, cavalry, artillery, and support services into an efficient and effective fighting force.

Sheridan's most formidable challenge was to reconstruct the Army of the Shenandoah into a cohesive fighting force from several disparate commands that had little shared history. His most experienced unit, the Army of the

Maj. Gen. Horatio G. Wright
LC

Potomac's Sixth Corps under Maj. Gen. Horatio Wright, was not the same command that had crossed the Rapidan River and marched into the Wilderness three months earlier. Enormous combat losses, including the death of its beloved commander, Maj. Gen. John Sedgwick, and the expiration of thousands of enlistments had devastated the corps' potency. The Sixth Corps began the Overland campaign in early May 1864 with nearly 23,000 officers and enlisted men. By July 12, some 14,000 of them (60 percent) had been killed, wounded, captured, or were missing. Large numbers of veteran troops walked away from the army when their three-year enlistments expired throughout the summer. The majority of the replacements were conscripts and bounty men who lacked the reliability and experience of the veterans. An officer from another corps that had not been with the Army of the Potomac observed, "They seem to be badly demoralized by the severe service." In spite of the losses, the Sixth Corps still possessed a solid cadre of combat-seasoned officers and soldiers who had learned their trade battling the vaunted Army of Northern Virginia for more than two years. Sheridan expected much from them in the Shenandoah.[1]

The commander of the Sixth Corps, Horatio Wright, was a 44-year-old West Point-trained engineer from Connecticut who had graduated second in the class of 1841. He had taught engineering at the academy and worked on several notable public works projects, including the harbor at St. Augustine, Florida. When the Civil War broke out, he helped construct the ring of forts that protected Washington, D.C. Although a respected engineer, his combat experience prior to 1864 was limited. He served in minor operations along the Atlantic coast from South Carolina to Florida and commanded the Department of the Ohio, where he served in a largely administrative capacity during the 1862 Confederate invasion of Kentucky. His performance there did not impress many in Washington, and the U.S. Senate declined his promotion to major general. Wright joined the Army of the Potomac in 1863 as a division commander in the Sixth Corps, but played only a minor role at Gettysburg. The zenith of his combat career prior to 1864 came during the Mine Run campaign in November 1863. General Wright orchestrated a rare night attack that overran a Confederate division dangerously isolated on the north bank of the Rappahannock River. He survived the culling of generals that occurred when Meade downsized the number of corps in the Army of the Potomac and served dutifully in the battle of the Wilderness. When Sedgwick was killed by a sniper's bullet at Spotsylvania on May 9, 1864, Wright assumed command of the Sixth Corps as the senior division commander.[2]

---

1 The Sixth Corps casualties and strength were compiled from several volumes from the *Official Records* that relate to the Overland Campaign and the battle of Monocacy. John William DeForest, *A Volunteer's Adventures: A Union Captain's Record of the Civil War* (Baton Rouge: Louisiana State University Press, 1996), 165.

2 Jubal Early was in command of the division that was overrun at Rappahannock Station.

As an inexperienced combat officer and corps commander, Wright struggled at Spotsylvania and Petersburg. In July 1864, he led the half-hearted pursuit of Early from Washington. After one week of uninspired effort, Wright proclaimed Early safely driven back to Virginia and on his way to Richmond. A few days later, Early devastated General Crook's small army at Kernstown, and Wright's Sixth Corps about-faced for the Valley once more. Noted Overland campaign historian Gordon Rhea wrote of Wright, "His actions betokened a general promoted beyond his ability." With no viable alternative, Wright remained commander of the Sixth Corps, but would have to grow into the job under Sheridan's leadership in the Valley.[3]

Morale in Maj. Gen. William H. Emory's Nineteenth Corps was higher than in Wright's Sixth Corps and its ranks contained regiments of veteran soldiers. However, Emory's men lacked the extensive combat experience that the Sixth Corps men had gained at such a terrible price. The Nineteenth Corps was also a cold command—it had not seen any noteworthy combat since Maj. Gen. Nathaniel Banks's disastrous Red River campaign in Louisiana earlier that spring. Although the Louisiana campaign proved a fiasco, the Nineteenth Corps produced solid performances and tactical successes at Port Hudson and along the Red River. After Banks's front had collapsed at Mansfield (Sabine Cross Roads) on April 8, a division from Emory's corps stood tall and stopped Lt. Gen. Richard Taylor's victorious Confederates, saving much of the army from destruction. The next day, the Nineteenth Corps played a determined role in throwing back Taylor's attacks at Pleasant Hill. After enduring a trying sea voyage from Louisiana that left many of its men ill, the Nineteenth Corps slowly filtered into Washington and then to the Valley. When Sheridan first took command, however, the largest division of the Nineteenth Corps had yet to join the army. Overall, Emory's command was the true unknown of Sheridan's army. No one could predict how it would react against Early's veterans.[4]

General Emory was affectionately known as "Old Bricktop" to his old army comrades for the bright red hair he had in his younger days; however, many of the men who served under him during the Civil War simply called him "The Old Man." His entire adult and family life had been dedicated to the U.S.

---

3   Gordon C. Rhea, *The Battles for Spotsylvania Courthouse and the Road to Yellow Tavern, May 7-12, 1864* (Baton Rouge: LSU Press, 1997), 317.

4   For a detailed history of the corps see William Irwin, *History of the Nineteenth Army Corps* (New York, 1892).

Bvt. Maj. Gen. William H. Emory
LC

Army. He wed a great-granddaughter of Benjamin Franklin, and the marriage produced four boys and two girls. One of his sons graduated from West Point in 1861 and served as an officer in the 9th U.S. Infantry during the Civil War. Another son went to Annapolis in 1862 to attend the United States Naval Academy and would go on to become a prominent naval officer.[5]

5 "Major General Emory, Death of the Famous Commander of the Nineteenth Corps," *National Tribune*, December 8, 1887.

As for the soon to be 53-year-old Emory, he was born on Maryland's Eastern Shore in 1811 and graduated from West Point in 1831, the same year that Sheridan was born. Emory served four years in the 4th U.S. Artillery, stationed at the notable posts of Fort McHenry and Charleston Harbor. He resigned from the army in 1836 and became an Assistant United States Civil Engineer. After only two years in the civilian sector, he rejoined the army and was assigned to the Topographical Engineers, where he quickly earned a reputation as an outstanding mapmaker. His maps were used extensively in the exploration of the trans-Mississippi west, and he accompanied several exploration and survey parties, including that of Gen. Stephen Kearney to California. When the Mexican War broke out, Emory initially served as the chief engineer in the Army of the West, but was soon promoted to lieutenant colonel in a regiment of Maryland and Washington, D.C. volunteers. He led them in Gen. Winfield Scott's campaign from Vera Cruz to Mexico City.

When the Civil War erupted, Emory was promoted to colonel of the 5th U.S. Cavalry. In 1862, he became a brigadier general and commanded the Army of the Potomac's Regular Army cavalry brigade. Emory led it capably during McClellan's Peninsula campaign, particularly distinguishing himself at Hanover Courthouse where he cut off and captured an entire Confederate regiment. Later in 1862, he organized a division of infantry in Baltimore which eventually sailed to New Orleans.[6]

He led this division as part of the Nineteenth Corps during the campaign for Port Hudson, Louisiana. During those operations, some officers on the staff of Maj. Gen. Nathaniel P. Banks feared that Emory's "timid counsels" limited the army's chance of success. In actuality, Emory won Banks's praise for his "skillful movements" during rear guard actions in the Red River campaign that allowed the defeated Federal army to escape destruction. It was Emory's finest hour thus far in the war, and enhanced his already well-established reputation as a reliable officer. In Emory's new assignment to the Army of the Shenandoah, Sheridan could expect dutiful performance and old army obedience to orders from Emory. Initiative, dash, and flexibility, however, would be provided by others.[7]

6 Ibid.

7 David Hunter Strother, *A Virginia Yankee in the Civil War* (Chapel Hill, NC: University of North Carolina Press, 1961), 177; Nathaniel Banks's Report on the Red River Campaign. *OR* 34, pt. 1, 201.

Brigadier General George Crook's little Army of West Virginia experienced significant action in western Virginia during the spring and early summer campaigns of 1864. The results were mixed, but most of Crook's men proved themselves to be solid fighters in varying engagements, including Cloyd's Mountain, New Market, Piedmont, Lynchburg, and Snickers Gap. The extensive marching through the Valley and Appalachian Mountains of western Virginia earned them nicknames such as the "Buzzards" and "Mountain Creepers." The polished and well-drilled Easterners of Wright's Sixth Corps and Emory's Nineteenth Corps looked down on the rugged Westerners. However, an officer from the 34th Massachusetts, the only New England outfit in Crook's command, observed that the Buzzards "could fight like wildcats and yell like coyotes, [and] both at the same time." Sheridan recognized their tenacity and appreciated their experience and proficiency at marching and maneuver. Consequently, he used Crook in the traditional role of a light infantry command. Under Sheridan, Crook's soldiers would lead reconnaissance missions and initiate difficult flank marches that often turned the tide of battle in favor of the Union. But that was all to come in the near future. In their engagement on July 24 at Kernstown, Early outfoxed Crook and routed his men in confusion. The "Mountain Creepers" had experienced victory and defeat in varying degrees, but had never had cause to be ashamed of their conduct prior to Kernstown. Since that ignominious rout, the "Buzzards" eagerly sought an opportunity to even the score.[8]

Born on September 8, 1828, near Dayton, Ohio, George Crook grew up on his father's farm along the banks of the Miami and Erie Canal. He possessed "wonderful self-poise" and "was as cool in adversity as in success." One schoolmate recalled Crook as "A farmer's boy, slow to learn, but what he did learn was surely his. He was older, somewhat, than his comrades," he continued, "and was good-natured, stolid and was like a big Newfoundland dog among a lot of puppies. He would never permit injustice, or bullying of the smaller boys."[9]

8   The Army of West Virginia was not the Eighth Corps, as it is often erroneously referred to both now and at the time of the campaign. The Eighth Corps was based out of Baltimore and was under the command of Lew Wallace. Elements of that organization fought Jubal Early at the battle of Monocacy. A. C. Soley, "Sheridan at Winchester: How the 34th Massachusetts Had a Hand in the Whirling," *Springfield Republican*, February 14, 1887.

9   *The American Tribune*, May 2, 1890; Martin F. Schmidt, ed., *General George Crook: His Autobiography* (Norman, OK: University of Oklahoma Press, 1946), xxii.

In 1852, Crook graduated 38th out of 43 cadets in his West Point class. He would eventually become the lowest ranking West Point graduate to reach the rank of major general. Crook gained considerable prewar combat experience against warring American Indians in the Pacific Northwest, giving him a familiarity with battle that few officers possessed in 1861. One of these frontier clashes left an arrowhead imbedded in his hip for the rest of his life and served as a constant reminder of the deadly reality of war. Crook became the colonel of the 36th Ohio in the summer of 1861 when the Civil War erupted.

While the Civil War produced its share of unique personas, George Crook provided an unusual departure from the norm of the day. In an army where officers regularly drank and smoked, Crook shunned not only alcohol and tobacco, but also eschewed coffee and tea as they "spoiled the nerve." In an era of bombastic and vainglorious military men, Crook remained an affable, unpretentious individual as he rose through the ranks. Like Sheridan, Crook possessed the ability to inspire and lead men in battle, albeit in his own moderated manner. An Ohio colonel noted that Crook said little, but "his presence somehow charged the men with electricity." By August 1864, Crook had amassed a record as a competent military leader. The one serious blight on his record occurred at Kernstown on July 24. Crook's faulty battlefield decisions led to the disastrous Union defeat which culminated in the burning of Chambersburg, Pennsylvania, by Confederate raiders. Now, both he and his men longed to wipe that stain from their record.[10]

Interestingly, the commander of the Army of West Virginia was Phil Sheridan's closest confidante during the Valley campaign even though he was not the next ranking officer in the army. The two men eventually experienced a falling out during the Indian Wars that broke wide open when they disagreed over terms that Crook had offered the Apaches. When Geronimo escaped and went on the warpath, Sheridan criticized Crook's methods, prompting him to submit his resignation to his old friend. To Crook's dismay, Sheridan readily accepted it and appointed Gen. Nelson Miles in Crook's place. It was only the latest in a series of disagreements over Indian policy between the two old friends from West Point. In the midst of these events of the 1880s, Crook drafted his autobiography. Not surprisingly, the Geronimo affair was fresh in Crook's mind. He never forgave Sheridan for questioning his methods, and

10 James Comly Diary, Rutherford B. Hayes Presidential Center Library, Fremont, OH (RBHPC hereafter).

Crook looked upon all of his relations with Sheridan in the most negative light, shading the truth at times. In fairness to Crook, his memoirs, unlike Sheridan's, were never finished during his lifetime and what survived were drafts that ended up in print during the 1930s. However much their relationship deteriorated in the future, it is important to understand that George Crook was Sheridan's primary confidant in 1864. Their discomfiture was years away, and had no impact upon the 1864 Valley campaign.[11]

Sheridan's thorniest internal issue was the appointment of a cavalry chief for the assembling Army of the Shenandoah. Brigadier General William Averell was the senior cavalry general in Sheridan's army and had displayed a certain talent for handling the mounted arm as an independent commander. Most recently, he achieved the only Union successes against Early during the summer campaign. At Rutherford's farm on July 20, an outnumbered Averell attacked Maj. Gen. Stephen D. Ramseur, capturing 250 prisoners and four cannon. On August 7, Averell once again found his force badly outgunned but nevertheless attacked and routed Brig. Gen. John C. McCausland at Moorefield, seizing another battery and hundreds of prisoners. Clearly, Averell had shown promise as an autonomous leader of a small command, but he chafed at serving as a subordinate in a larger army. In 1863, Averell's sulking and inaction during the Chancellorsville campaign had cost him command of a division in the Army of the Potomac's Cavalry Corps. Many of those same men with whom he had clashed were now on their way to the Valley. Although Averell was deserving of the command of Sheridan's cavalry, that privilege went to another.[12]

As commander of the Army of the Potomac's Cavalry Corps, General Sheridan had come to know and trust Brig. Gen. Alfred Torbert during the trying spring and summer campaigns of 1864. Torbert clearly did not have Averell's experience, but he also did not have his prickly reputation. Recently promoted to the largest and most important command of his career, Sheridan needed someone he could trust as commander of the Army of the Shenandoah's cavalry. Sheridan preferred Torbert, but because Averell out-ranked Torbert, Sheridan forwarded the issue to General Grant. He

---

11 It is important for readers to note that Sheridan and Crook were on very cordial terms during the 1864 Valley Campaign and formed a solid leadership team. Both men believed they could rely on the other in a tight situation. Schmidt, *General George Crook*, 264-265; Paul Andrew Hutton, *Phil Sheridan & His Army* (Norman, OK, 1985), 125, 366-367.

12 Patchan, *Shenandoah Summer*, 320; Stephen W. Sears, *Chancellorsville* (Boston, 1996), 218-219, 399, 391, 392.

advised Sheridan on August 7, the same day that Averell won his victory at Moorefield, "Do not hesitate to give commands to officers in whom you repose confidence, without regard to claims of others on account of rank. If you deem Torbert the best man to command the cavalry, place him in command and give Averell some other command or relieve him from the expedition." Sheridan did precisely that and appointed Torbert as the army's chief of cavalry, leaving a much chagrined Averell to serve under him as a division commander.[13]

Alfred Thomas Archimedes Torbert was born in Georgetown, Delaware, and graduated from West Point in 1855. He was commissioned a lieutenant in the 5th U.S. Infantry. In 1861, he was tendered a commission in the Confederate Army but turned it down. He spent the first three years of the Civil War as a commander of New Jersey infantry and earned commendations for his actions as a brigade commander at Second Bull Run, South Mountain, and Antietam. He received a promotion to brigadier general in November 1862 and continued his command of the Sixth Corps' New Jersey brigade at Chancellorsville and Gettysburg. In the spring of 1864, he was a surprise choice to command a division in Sheridan's Cavalry Corps. Although he battled illness during the Overland campaign that often kept him away from his division, Torbert had gained Sheridan's trust and would lead the Union cavalry in the Valley.[14]

Sheridan's experienced, well-equipped, and splendidly mounted cavalry corps was his supreme advantage. Torbert's elevation to Cavalry Corps commander placed 28-year-old Brig. Gen. Wesley Merritt in command of the First Cavalry division. Merritt was born in New York City where he spent the first four years of his life. His father, John Willis Merritt, moved his family to a farm near Belleville, Illinois, where Wesley spent most of his youth. As a boy, he did not harbor dreams of a military career. Instead, "his train of thought had always been toward a career in the law." Although Merritt and his brothers

---

13 George Crook had viewed Averell as a rival during their tenure as division commanders in the Department of West Virginia through spring and early summer campaigns. Crook later accused Averell of being drunk on the battlefield at Kernstown, although no other evidence supporting that claim has ever surfaced. It may be that Crook's negative opinion influenced Sheridan in his choice of cavalry commanders as well. Major General David Hunter also had a very low opinion of Averell from the Lynchburg Raid and voiced as much to Grant. This information likely influenced Grant who probably passed that information on to Sheridan when he arrived at Monocacy Junction. Hunter blamed Averell's incompetency for Hunter's failure to capture Lynchburg. OR 43, pt. 1, 719.

14 Warner, *Generals in Blue*, 508-509.

Maj. Gen. Philip Sheridan, Brig. Gen. Wesley Merritt,
Maj. Gen. Alfred Torbert, and Brig. Gen. James H. Wilson.
LC

spent much time working the family farm, his father saw to it that his boys took full advantage of the educational opportunities that were available to them. His father started a daily newspaper and Wesley became very involved in its operations, managing the business office and gaining "considerable skill" as a printer. At 16, Merritt began to study law in the office of a judge in nearby Salem. Shortly thereafter, his father raised the possibility of attending West Point. Although it was not what the younger Merritt had in mind, he complied with his father's wishes, graduated in the class of 1860, and received assignment to the 2nd U.S. Dragoons. For the first two years of the Civil War, he served in cavalry staff positions for officers that included Generals Phillip St. George Cooke and George Stoneman. Shortly before Gettysburg, Merritt received a promotion to brigadier general and command of the famed Reserve Brigade of the Army of the Potomac. Thereafter, he continually proved his skill and worth on many fields of battle, such as Gettysburg, Todd's Tavern, Yellow Tavern, and more. Merritt's horse soldiers composed what was arguably the best mounted division in the entire Union army in 1864, and they would play a leading, if not decisive, role in the Valley campaign. For the initial campaign, however, Merritt's division was joined only by a small, hastily assembled cavalry brigade under the command of Col. Charles R. Lowell. It was composed of the odds and ends of several cavalry regiments from the Washington defenses and the Shenandoah Valley. Torbert's other divisions had not yet joined the army in the field.[15]

Although Phil Sheridan possessed many excellent organizations in his command, there was little shared history among the units. The Sixth Corps and Cavalry Corps, for example, had a limited familiarity from the Army of the Potomac and that army's "personality." Much of the infantry had served briefly together during the pursuit of Jubal Early from around Washington, D.C., in July. By no means, however, was this assortment of troops a cohesive army in early August of 1864. To Sheridan belonged the task of molding them into a successful fighting force.

In contrast, Jubal Early had rebuilt the successful Army of the Valley District throughout the summer. The Second Corps of the Army of Northern Virginia, numbering about 8,000 troops, formed the backbone of the organization. It had begun the Wilderness campaign with nearly 16,000 troops and now counted only half that number in its ranks. The casualties were heavier than simple math would indicate as additional units and replacements had joined in the interim. The corps' organizational structure was essentially reconstructed after the devastating losses at Spotsylvania's Mule Shoe on May 12. Officers of all grades were needed to fill the numerous vacancies stemming from the high casualty lists. Regiments and brigades were consolidated and transferred, and additional units were added during the course of the campaign to reinforce the battered outfit. Although some of the changes did not sit well with the men, the shared history as Stonewall Jackson's foot cavalry kept the overall cohesiveness intact. From Lynchburg to Monocacy and back to the Shenandoah Valley, officers and men gained experience and grew comfortable

15 "General Wesley Merritt," *New York Times*, May 29, 1898. Brigadier General James H. Wilson's Third Division, Army of the Potomac had not yet reached the Valley and would not for several days. Averell's division was en route from Moorefield, West Virginia. Brigadier General Alfred Duffie's small division was still north of the Potomac.

with their new roles and organizations. Although supply, discipline, and morale problems surfaced away from the battlefield, Early had rejuvenated the Second Corps' fighting spirit and once again transformed it into a force to be reckoned with.

Breckinridge's division from the Department of Southwest Virginia added roughly 2,000 foot soldiers to Early's force. The veterans of the Second Corps had derisively designated this command "Breckinridge's Wagon Guard" due to the role it played during the Washington Raid. While these troops lacked the Second Corps's extensive combat experience, two of its three brigades retained excellent officers, a solid organizational structure, and some of the largest regiments in Early's army. As the campaign progressed, the division's role intensified, culminating with the critical flank attack that devastated the remaining Union troops at Kernstown on July 24.

The Confederacy's mounted arm in the Shenandoah Valley was the weak link of Early's army. Five poorly equipped brigades composed the outfit, and they were only nominally led by Maj. Gen. Robert Ransom who spent more time sick in an ambulance than actually leading his division in the field. Early in the campaign, the Confederate cavalry's performance was adequate. Brigadier General John McCausland was praised for his delaying tactics during Hunter's march on Lynchburg and his aggressive role in locating and attacking the Union left flank at Monocacy. Brigadier General John Imboden's brigade received praise for its herculean efforts during the New Market campaign against Franz Sigel. Brigadier General Bradley Johnson's brigade had ridden into the suburbs of Baltimore during Early's Washington raid, creating much consternation at the U.S. War Department. Yet Ransom had been unable to take these five brigades of mountaineers who excelled in "the silly practice of whooping and hallooing" and turn them into a cohesive cavalry division. Johnson called them his "wild western Virginians." Ransom's ill health had precluded him from taking an active role in operations much of the time. The inefficient Brig. Gen. John C. Vaughn substituted for Ransom until a battlefield injury sent him to the rear and necessitated a change in command. Jubal Early did not help matters as he took little or no action to rectify the situation, although he was well aware of his horsemen's shortcomings both from the summer campaign and his time in western Virginia the previous winter.[16]

---

16 Bradley Johnson to Wife, July 15, 1864, Bradley T. Johnson Papers, Duke University.

Although the Valley Cavalry (as Early's troopers came to be known) performed adequately during the spring and summer of 1864, their fortunes dramatically reversed on August 7 at Moorefield, West Virginia. There, General Averell surprised and routed Early's two largest mounted brigades under McCausland and Johnson. These brigades had numbered at least 3,000 troopers at the outset of the Chambersburg Raid, but lost nearly a third of their men and all of their artillery in the contest at Moorefield. Discipline during the raid evaporated. Security measures were so lax that Averell completely surprised the Southerners in their camps; resistance was token at best. Aside from the physical losses of Moorefield, these commands became completely demoralized, a contagion that soon spread to the other brigades. It was the worst possible time for disaster to befall Early's cavalry. The arrival of Sheridan's mounted arm from the Army of the Potomac would only worsen the situation.

In his infantry, Jubal Early commanded subordinates who had extensively worked together. They knew and understood each other's intricacies and had placed the Confederate cause above their personal differences thus far in the ongoing campaign. This familiarity and ability to work as a team allowed Early's small army to accomplish so much that summer of 1864. The rejuvenated leadership of Stonewall Jackson's former Second Corps had emerged as a tight-knit, hard fighting outfit throughout the 1864 Virginia campaign in spite of the enormous combat losses suffered during the Overland Campaign. Officially, Early's army consisted of four infantry divisions, a single five-brigade cavalry division, and three battalions of artillery. Throughout most of the summer, Early had given his two senior officers (John Breckinridge and Robert Rodes) command of unofficial infantry "corps." In practice, this helpful arrangement was often set aside as circumstances dictated.

Jubal Early's army possessed a number of solid combat commanders. Two of them, Maj. Gens. Robert E. Rodes and John B. Gordon, stood head and shoulders above all the rest. Rodes had commanded the largest division in Stonewall Jackson's old corps since Chancellorsville. The respected Jed Hotchkiss pronounced Rodes "the best division commander in the Army of Northern Virginia." Jackson's former cartographer considered Rodes "worthy of and capable for any position in" the army. A native of Lynchburg, Virginia, the 33-year-old Rodes graduated from the Virginia Military Institute in 1848. He later worked as an assistant engineer on the Southside Railroad until 1854, and then transferred to Tuscaloosa, Alabama, to work for the Alabama and

Chattanooga Railroad. Rodes fell in love with and married a local girl and adopted Alabama as his home. He remained there until the war began.[17]

When that conflict began, Rodes organized the 5th Alabama Infantry, and its soldiers elected him as their colonel that May. Six months later, Rodes received a promotion to brigadier general and command of the first Alabama brigade in what became the Army of Northern Virginia. While leading his Alabamians at Seven Pines on May 31, 1862, Rodes was disabled by a serious wound for several months. Returning to active duty later that summer, Rodes fought tenaciously at South Mountain holding off George Meade's Pennsylvania Reserves and guided his brigade's valiant defense of the Sunken Lane at Sharpsburg. In perhaps his finest moment of the war, Rodes commanded the division that spearheaded Stonewall Jackson's stunning flank attack at Chancellorsville that crushed Joe Hooker's right flank. Rodes's judgment at Gettysburg was suspect like that of many of his comrades; however, he repeatedly demonstrated his worth to Lee's army during General Grant's Overland Campaign. Most notably, he helped block the Union breakthrough at Spotsylvania on May 12. On July 18, Rodes's division gained a hard fought victory in the bitter contest at Cool Spring. By the summer of 1864, Rodes had emerged as Early's most trusted subordinate, at times commanding two divisions of infantry. Furthermore, Rodes's rapport with the Valley army's commander had a mitigating effect on Early's caustic personality.[18]

Early also had the services of former U.S. Vice President John C. Breckinridge of Kentucky. As commander of the Department of Southwest Virginia, Breckinridge served as Early's unofficial second in command. Like Rodes, Breckinridge commanded two divisions, his own and General Gordon's. Early and Breckinridge hit it off and became friends, or as close as anyone ever got to being friends with Jubal Early. Although his role as a corps commander figured more on paper than in reality, he buffered Gordon from Early, keeping a lid on that simmering feud. An Alabamian in Early's army thought the Kentuckian "a magnificent looking man, weighing over two-hundred pounds. He wears a heavy moustache, but no beard, and his large piercing blue eyes are really superb."[19]

17 Jed Hotchkiss to Wife, September 23, 1864, Hotchkiss Papers, Library of Congress.

18 Clement A. Evans, ed. *Confederate Military History*, Alabama-Mississippi, 441-443.

19 *SHSP*, Diary of Robert E. Park, Late Capt. Twelfth Alabama Regiment, 385.

Breckinridge was a political general, but he had attained some reputation during the Civil War. He earned his first combat laurels at Shiloh in April 1862. As a member of the Confederacy's much maligned Army of Tennessee, Breckinridge served capably on many hard-fought fields in the Western Theater, including Stones River. He was also a politically connected detractor of his controversial commander, Gen. Braxton Bragg. The Kentuckian served capably, earning the praise of the Confederate Congress for his leadership at Baton Rouge and ultimately rising to corps command on the heels of the Southern victory at Chickamauga. However, allegations of drunkenness hounded the Kentuckian, and he was reportedly intoxicated on the battlefield during the Confederate disaster at Chattanooga. In 1864, he departed the Army of the Tennessee and assumed command in southwest Virginia. General Lee heaped additional responsibility upon the Kentuckian's broad shoulders by informing him that he must also be ready to assist in the defense of the Shenandoah Valley. That spring, Breckinridge soon found his vast new charge besieged by two Union offensives pouring out of West Virginia. He rushed his forces to the Shenandoah Valley and defeated Franz Sigel at New Market in May 1864. He then took his division to Richmond and served briefly with Robert E. Lee at Cold Harbor before returning to the Valley. He played a critical role in Early's victory at Kernstown.[20]

Major General John Brown Gordon, a protégé of Rodes, saw his star rise faster since the summer of 1863 than any other officer in the Army of Northern Virginia. What few things he couldn't do on the battlefield were later accomplished in his postwar writings. His memoirs, published in 1904 after most of his contemporaries had passed away, embellished an already admirable record. James Longstreet declared, "He has made a grand newspaper record since the war," but such criticisms were 40 years away in the summer of 1864. Without a doubt, Gordon possessed a knack for the tactical offensive and the ability to inspire troops in a way that few men could. One Georgian crowed, "He's the prettiest thing you ever did see on a field of fight. It'd put fight into a whipped chicken just to look at him."[21]

Born in Georgia in 1832, Gordon had no military experience prior to the Civil War. At the outset, he organized a company called the "Raccoon Roughs" and was assigned to the 6th Alabama Regiment. He soon became that

---

20 William C. Davis, *Breckinridge: Soldier, Statesman, Symbol*, 394-395.

21 Nichols, *A Soldier's Story of his Regiment*, 141-142.

regiment's colonel and learned the art of war serving in Rodes's brigade. Gordon wasted no time in establishing a reputation as an aggressive combat leader. In his first engagement at Seven Pines, he lost 373 men killed and wounded. When a Union bullet severely wounded Rodes at that battle, Gordon assumed command of the brigade. He was severely wounded while leading his regiment's defense of the Sunken Lane at Antietam. When he recovered from his wound, Gordon received command of Brig. Gen. Alexander R. Lawton's Georgia brigade prior to Chancellorsville.

This promotion placed Gordon under Early's command and started a sometimes stormy relationship. Tall, handsome, and straight as a ramrod, Gordon charmed the ladies and drew the admiration of the men serving under him. The Georgian came to the forefront in the Wilderness, launching a crippling counterstrike that threw the attacking Federals into chaos on May 5. On the following evening, Gordon rolled up the right flank of Grant's army and captured hundreds of prisoners, including two general officers. With Early leading Hill's Corps at Spotsylvania, Gordon commanded the Virginian's division and played a crucial role in staving off disaster. At Monocacy, Gordon's division delivered the blow that routed the Federals from the field. Unlike Lee who cultivated his subordinates, Early grew suspicious and distrusting. "Old Jube" apparently lacked complete confidence in his own abilities as an independent commander. Conversely, Gordon had questioned Early's tactical judgment on several occasions beginning with the first day at Gettysburg and later at the Wilderness. Gordon later wrote:

> Like the brilliant George B. McClellan (whom I knew personally and greatly admired), and like many other noted soldiers who might be named in all armies, he lacked what I shall term official courage, or what is known as the courage of one's convictions—that courage which I think both Lee and Grant possessed in an eminent degree, and which in Stonewall Jackson was one of the prime sources of his marvelous achievements. This peculiar courage must not be confounded with rashness, although there is a certain similarity between them. They both strike boldly, fiercely, and with all possible energy. They are, however, as widely separated as the poles in other and essential qualities.[22]

---

22 John B. Gordon, *Reminiscences of the Civil War* (New York, 1904), 317.

Under this cloud of distrust and suspicion, Early and Gordon labored throughout the Shenandoah Valley campaign. However, Breckinridge's intermediary role and summertime success kept any controversy in check for the time being.

In early August, Sheridan possessed a numerical advantage over Early that would soon grow to an overwhelming difference. Sheridan's army numbered 26,000 while Early barely mustered a force of 13,000 at that time. At least 6,000 horse soldiers of Wilson's, Averell's, and Duffie's divisions and 8,000 infantrymen of the Nineteenth Corps had not yet joined Sheridan in the Valley. The 2,000 disorganized and dispirited survivors from McCausland's defeat at Moorefield would bolster Early's force on August 9. Upon taking command, Sheridan knew Early had enough men to oppose his force in the Valley. Confederates had confronted two-to-one odds throughout the war, and in Virginia it proved to be no barrier to victory.

Put Yourself South of the Enemy

Sheridan Moves Against Early

The day of August 9, 1864, was eventful and frenetic around Harpers Ferry. Men of the quartermaster and ordnance departments bustled about ensuring that the Army of the Shenandoah was well supplied as it prepared to make its next trek up the Valley under its new commander. General Torbert's splendid division of cavalry finally rode into town providing Sheridan with the mobile strike force he desperately needed. Simultaneously, Sheridan and his staff remained inside his headquarters pouring over maps of the region and filtering through the latest scouting reports on Early's strength and location. They conceived a plan they hoped would position their army south of Early's force, which was then centered about 11 miles north of Winchester at Bunker Hill.

Scrutinizing the maps, Sheridan selected Winchester as his objective. Would Early remain stationary at Bunker Hill while Sheridan's army stole a march to Winchester? Moving undetected was critical because Sheridan had to cover more than double the distance that Early had between his army and Winchester. Sheridan hoped, "to bring [his] troops, if it were at all possible to do so, into such as position near that town as to oblige Early to fight." If Sheridan could win the race to Winchester, the Confederate Army of the Valley would be in dire straits.[1] To that end, Sheridan issued marching orders for the following day:

1. At 4:00 a.m., Torbert's horsemen were to march from Charlestown to the intersection of "the pike from Millwood to Winchester with the pike from Millwood to White Post." From there, Torbert was to send "strong parties" to the crossings of Opequon Creek and leave Lowell's brigade at Summit Point to cover the army's right flank.

2. At 5:00 a.m., Wright's Sixth Corps was to move along a dirt road to reach Clifton.

3. At 5:00 a.m., Crook's Army of Western Virginia was to march to Berryville.

4. Also at 5:00 a.m., Emory's Nineteenth Corps was to march, take position between Berryville and Clifton, and open communications with Wright and Crook. Sheridan would establish his headquarters with Emory.

U.S. Cavalry riding out of Harpers Ferry to join the Shenandoah Valley Campaign.
A. R. Waud, LC

---

1   Sheridan, *Memoirs*, 1:476.

5. Wagon transportation would be limited and the subsistence trains would remain at Bolivar Heights until otherwise ordered.[2]

Although Sheridan was assembling an ever-increasing Union force around Harpers Ferry, Jubal Early was in no mind to cede the initiative. Indeed, the aggressive Early was devising his own plan to strike northward once again toward Martinsburg with two divisions of infantry. These plans changed when alarming news began to filter into his headquarters at Bunker Hill throughout August 9. First, he received confirmation of McCausland's disaster at Moorefield, requiring him to rush Ramseur's division to Winchester in case Averell pursued the beaten Confederates eastward on the Romney Road. At 10:00 p.m., a courier from Imboden's brigade at Shepherdstown dashed into Early's headquarters to report the advance of Union cavalry "up the Shenandoah." Imboden also informed Early that "the 6th, 8th & 19th [Corps] are at Harpers Ferry & Halltown under [Major General Joseph] Hooker." Imboden was wrong about Hooker, but correctly stated that strong enemy forces were on the move. The larger part of the Nineteenth Corps had not yet reached the Valley, but Sheridan still had twice the infantry that Early did. As Halltown was just 17 miles east of Bunker Hill, the news startled Early. He realized that his command was now dangerously exposed, and that his right flank could be turned. If Early carried out his planned advance toward Martinsburg, he would be exactly where Sheridan wanted him—trapped in the northern reaches of the Shenandoah Valley.[3]

Sheridan's plan was sound, but Jubal Early—as he had been all summer—remained one step ahead of Union efforts to trap him. Early issued orders at 11:00 p.m. on August 9 instructing his army to fall back to Winchester at sunrise. Thus, while Sheridan's troops were stirring in their camps early on the morning of August 10, the Confederate Army of the Valley District began

2 OR 43, pt. 1, 739-740.

3 In correspondence with General Lee, Early downplayed McCausland's defeat as exaggerations of the Northern newspapers. Readers should note that errant references to the "Eighth Corps" equate to Crook's Army of West Virginia. The actual Eighth Corps served under Lew Wallace in the defenses of Baltimore and was not present in the Shenandoah Valley under Sheridan. That corps had previously served in the Valley and some of its troops were under Crook, resulting in a constant though incorrect reference to Crook's command as the Eighth Corps by both Federals and Confederates. Historians have continued this error into the 21st Century. William W. Old Diary, Library of Congress; OR 43, pt. 1, 991-993; George Q. Peyton Diary, UVA.

shifting its center of operations 11 miles south from Bunker Hill to Winchester. Ramseur shifted his men from the west side of town to the junction of the Millwood Pike and Front Royal Road southeast of Winchester, covering the southeastern approaches from Front Royal and Millwood. Breckinridge posted Brig. Gen. Gabriel Wharton's division on the Berryville Pike, four miles east of Winchester where that road crossed Opequon Creek. Gordon's division occupied the ground north of the Berryville Pike to cover several Opequon crossings on Wharton's left flank. Rodes's division moved to Stephenson's Depot, four miles north of town. Part of his division advanced to Jordan Springs where it guarded potential avenues of advance from Harpers Ferry via Charlestown and Summit Point. Deftly performed, Early's moves quickly and thoroughly covered the fords along Opequon Creek between Winchester and Harpers Ferry. His army was now positioned within a day's march of the commanding heights of Fisher's Hill 19 miles farther south. This important position provided the Southern army with a natural fortress where they could make a stand against a larger force. The men had been there before when Early withdrew up the Valley from his Washington raid the previous month. It was a routine move for the Southerners, and there was no panic in the Confederate withdrawal. When the army reached Winchester, Early halted and waited for Sheridan's next move.[4]

Torbert's cavalry rode out of its camps at 5:00 a.m. on August 10, one hour behind schedule. Merritt's division headed south out of Halltown, West Virginia, for 17 miles to Berryville, Virginia, located nine miles east of Winchester. When the Union cavalry rode through Charlestown, where the abolitionist John Brown was tried and executed, the troopers sang "the John Brown Song." It was a stirring scene, recalled one Union trooper, with "[e]ach regiment in turn taking it up until several thousand voices composed a grand chorus singing under the inspiration of the circumstances as we had never heard it before, nor have we since." As the horse soldiers moved through the lush Shenandoah countryside, a trooper of the 6th New York couldn't help but observe that "[t]he country was rich and healthful, with plenty of good water." It was indeed a vast change from the dank, disease-ridden environment of their prior environs around Petersburg and Richmond. When the horsemen reached the picturesque village of Berryville, Torbert dispatched Brig. Gen. George Armstrong Custer's Michigan brigade to reconnoiter the Berryville Turnpike

---

4 William W. Old Diary, LC; OR 43, pt. 1, 992-993.

west toward Opequon Creek. Custer met and dispersed the covering Confederate cavalry pickets, but promptly encountered the 30th Virginia Sharpshooter Battalion from Wharton's division. Just east of the Opequon, the battalion was deployed on a prominent rise known as Limestone Ridge. The Virginians were backed up by artillery and Wharton's full division of infantry on the creek's west bank.

Custer skirmished with the 30th Virginia Battalion briefly, but prudently retired before suffering a serious loss. This encounter informed the Federals that Early was aware of their movement and had won the race to Winchester. While Custer engaged the Virginians, Torbert moved the balance of Merritt's division eight miles southward on the road running from Berryville toward White Post. The Federals scattered a small Confederate cavalry force encountered near the Millwood Pike and then went into camp for the evening. Colonel Luigi di Cesnola's 6th New York Cavalry picketed the army's extreme left flank at the village of Millwood. He also sent a strong detachment toward Ashby's Gap to keep an eye out for the stealthy Col. John Singleton Mosby and his hard-hitting Rangers of the 43rd Virginia Battalion.[5]

On Sheridan's right flank, Col. Charles R. Lowell's brigade of cavalry had likewise moved out of Halltown at 5:00 a.m. Lowell covered the army's right flank, passing through Charlestown at 7:30 a.m. He covered roughly 10 miles to Summit Point and continued riding west toward the Opequon, where he found the Confederates waiting for him. While skirmishing along that stream, Lowell captured 15 men from Imboden's brigade and 13 infantrymen from Rodes's infantry division. Realizing that a substantial Confederate force lay in his front, Lowell fell back a short distance toward Summit Point and camped for the night.[6]

The Union infantry had followed Lowell's cavalry out of Halltown and experienced an uneventful march. Lieutenant John M. Gould of the 29th Maine and a veteran of the 1862 Valley Campaign was amused as the army passed through Charlestown. He found "the same old secesh style of sour looks and down-right ugliness" that was exhibited when he marched through in 1862. A

5 The John Brown song was the foundation for the Battle Hymn of the Republic. J. R. Bowen, *Regimental History of the First New York Dragoons During Three Years of Active Service in the Great Civil War* (New York, 1900), 209; Hillman A. Hall, *History of the Sixth New York Cavalry (Second Ira Harris Guard)* (Worcester, MA, 1908), 210-211; OR 43, pt. 1, 438, 471.

6 Ibid., pt. 1, 486; Diary of Valorus Dearborn, 2nd Massachusetts Cavalry.

Vermont officer in the Sixth Corps reported that the infantry moved mainly through "woods and fields, which, as the woods in that region are free from underbrush, and the fields are quite level, made very comfortable travelling indeed." By the end of the day, the foot soldiers occupied a line running nearly four miles from Clifton on the north to Berryville in the south, with Wright's Sixth Corps on the right, Emory's Nineteenth Corps in the center, and Crook's small West Virginia army holding the left. Brigadier General David Russell's Sixth Corps division pushed out a strong advance guard to screen the Opequon Creek crossings between Merritt's and Lowell's commands on the flanks.[7]

The Confederate halt at Winchester convinced Sheridan that "Early could be brought to stand at that point." Sheridan issued orders to his commanders to secure the fords along the Opequon southeast of Winchester so that his army could approach the town from that direction. Most importantly, he ordered Torbert "to push Merritt's division up the Millwood pike toward Winchester, attack any force he might run against, and ascertain the movements of the Confederate army." This maneuver would determine whether or not the Union had an opportunity to trap Early at Winchester. The infantry commands were likewise ordered to advance toward the Opequon and secure the fords where the various roads led to Winchester from Berryville and White Post. Lowell's brigade continued to cover the army's right flank.[8]

At 5:00 a.m. on August 11, Sheridan's army continued its drive to seize the Valley Turnpike around Newtown while Early positioned his army to guard the eastern and southeastern approaches to Winchester. On this day, Torbert sent Custer's Michigan cavalry up the Millwood Pike to reconnoiter toward Winchester. Custer's Wolverines crossed the Opequon, shunted aside a covering force of Confederate cavalry, and advanced to within two miles of Winchester before encountering two brigades from Ramseur's division. This clash triggered a two-hour "right sharp scrimmage" along the Millwood Pike. Custer deployed Maj. Angelo Paldi's 1st Michigan Cavalry as skirmishers, while Maj. Thomas M. Howrigan advanced his battalion of the same regiment toward Winchester. Custer ordered a section of Capt. Dunbar Ransom's 3rd U.S. Artillery forward to support the cavalrymen who had edged close enough to Winchester to see Early's wagon trains retreating up the Shenandoah Valley

---

7 Tom Ledoux, ed. *Quite Ready to be Sent Somewhere: The Civil War Letters of Aldace Freeman Walker* (Victoria, Canada, 2002), 287.

8 Sheridan, *Memoirs*, 479.

toward Newtown. As Custer's men drew closer, the aggressive Ramseur attacked with Brig. Gen. John Pegram's Virginia brigade.[9]

Here, the ground presented a series of ridges, depressions, and dense undergrowth that allowed Pegram to deploy his brigade undetected by Custer. The Virginians formed into a single rank battle line and charged, surprising Howrigan's troopers on both flanks. "Thus flanked," noted an observer, "Major H.'s party retreated under a galling fire, and very naturally in some disorder." Custer quickly dispatched the 7th Michigan to reinforce his sagging left flank. At the same time, Capt. James Mathers led a dismounted detachment from the 6th Michigan Cavalry to save the advanced section of Ransom's battery. Mathers got his men quickly into position, and had grabbed a carbine from one of his horse holders to join the fight when a bullet struck him in the forehead, killing him instantly.[10]

Pegram's Virginians kept coming, but Custer held firm. His band "struck up a lively air," and his men kept up a heavy fire with their Spencer repeating rifles. The Confederates shot the horse out from under Major Paldi, but the line held. When the Virginians reached the top of one ridge, Capt. Dunbar Ransom's 3rd U.S. Artillery opened up and "fired point blank into us with grape and canister," halting the advance. "We were pretty close," recalled Pvt. George Q. Peyton of the 13th Virginia, "and the balls made the bushes hum for a while." Pegram's men wisely withdrew to their original position, content to have driven back Custer's advance. Custer lost five men killed and eighteen wounded in the engagement along the Millwood Pike, but he held his final position until ordered away to rejoin Merritt's division later that day. Custer's encounter with Ramseur's infantry proved to Sheridan that he was "mistaken" about bringing Early to bay at Winchester. "Old Jube" had already begun to retreat. The Ohioan promptly altered his plans and ordered Merritt's division to strike for Newtown.[11]

While Custer and Ramseur battled along the Millwood Pike, Torbert dispatched Merritt with the balance of his division to seize the Front Royal and Winchester Pike five miles to the south. Previously, Merritt had ordered Col.

9   OR 43, pt. 1, 422, 438, 466; William W. Old Diary, LC; A Bugler, "From the Fifth Michigan Cavalry," *Detroit Advertiser and Tribune*, August 26, 1864.

10   E. A. Paul, "The Middle Department," *New York Times*, August 20, 1864.

11   J. H. Kidd, *A Cavalryman with Custer* (New York: Bantam Books, 1991), 270; George Q. Peyton, Journal, Manassas Library; Early, *Last Year*, 71.

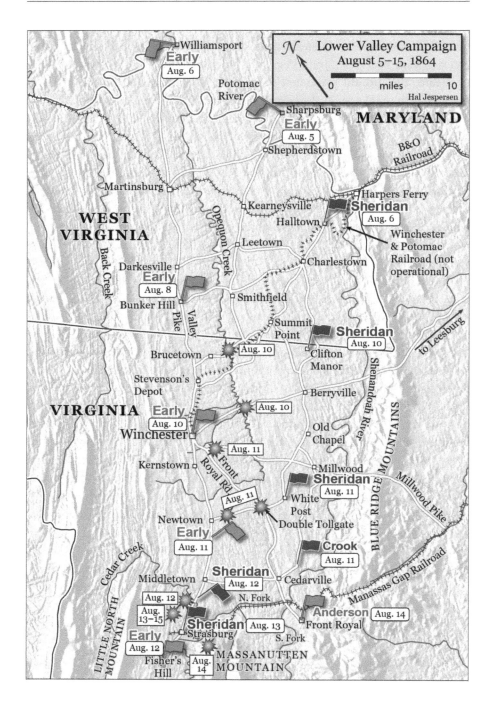

Williamsport
Early
Aug. 6

Potomac
River

Sharpsburg
Early
Aug. 5
Shepherdstown

MARYLAND

B&O
Railroad

Martinsburg

Kearneysville
Halltown

Harpers Ferry
Sheridan
Aug. 6

**WEST
VIRGINIA**

Opequon Creek

Leetown

Winchester
& Potomac
Railroad (not
operational)

Back Creek

Darkesville
Early
Aug. 8
Bunker Hill

Charlestown

Smithfield

Summit
Point

Sheridan
Aug. 10

to Leesburg

Valley Pike

Brucetown
Aug. 10

Clifton
Manor

Stevenson's
Depot

Berryville

VIRGINIA   **Early**
Aug. 10
Winchester
Aug. 10

Old
Chapel

Shenandoah River

Kernstown

Front Royal Rd.

Aug. 11

Millwood
Sheridan
Aug. 11

White
Post
Double Tollgate

BLUE RIDGE MOUNTAINS

Millwood Pike

Aug. 11

Newtown
Early
Aug. 11

Crook
Aug. 11

Cedar Creek

Middletown
Sheridan
Aug. 12

Cedarville

N. Fork

Manassas Gap Railroad

Aug.
13–15

Aug. 12

Sheridan   Aug. 13
Strasburg

Anderson   Aug. 14
Front Royal

S. Fork

Early
Aug. 12
Fisher's
Hill

Aug.
14

**MASSANUTTEN
MOUNTAIN**

LITTLE NORTH MOUNTAIN

N   **Lower Valley Campaign**
August 5–15, 1864

0   miles   10
Hal Jespersen

Luigi di Cesnola of Col. Thomas C. Devin's brigade to Newtown. Fearing that Early's retreating infantry might run into Cesnola's small regiment, Torbert changed the Italian's destination to White Post six miles east of Newtown. Cesnola was born into Italian nobility in 1833 and was educated at the Royal Military Academy in Turin. He fought in Italy's War for Independence and the Crimean War before immigrating to the United States in 1860 and settling in New York City. He began his Civil War career as major in the 11th New York Cavalry, but was quickly promoted to command of the 4th New York Cavalry. While under arrest for trumped up charges, he was wounded and captured after leading his men into a fight at Aldie without weapons on June 17, 1863. All in all, Cesnola was a natural leader of men "with the power to charm others into a love of their duty."[12]

Within a short time Cesnola's eclectic command of Germans, Irish, Poles, and Italians reached the village of White Post. At 8:30 a.m., he encountered advance pickets from Brig. Gen. John C. Vaughn's brigade of roughly 600 mounted Tennesseans and Georgians. Under the command of Col. James W. Gillespie of the 43rd Tennessee Mounted Infantry, the Confederate troopers were charged with covering Early's southern or right flank. Cesnola's troopers pushed them back through some woods toward the intersection of the Front Royal and Newtown Pikes, dubbed the "Double Tollgate" by locals because tolls were collected in both directions. As the Southerners fell back, Cesnola captured 29 wagon loads of harvest that had been gathered up by the Confederate forces as they withdrew toward Newtown.[13]

By 11:00 a.m., Colonel Gillespie, a veteran of the Vicksburg campaign, had dismounted his 600 men behind fences and stone walls astride the road to Newtown between White Post and the Double Tollgate. His position also covered the Front Royal-Winchester Pike. Gillespie's sole objective was to delay the Union cavalry while Early shifted other troops into position near Newtown in sufficient force to hold open the Valley Pike. If the Tennessean

12 OR 43, pt. 1, 769-770. For a full biography on Cesnola, see Frank W. Alduino and David J. Coles, *Sons of Garibaldi in Blue and Gray: Italians in the American Civil War* (Youngstown, NY, 2007), 133-169.

13 The brigade was composed mainly of Tennesseans with the small 16th Georgia Cavalry Battalion attached. I refer to this brigade as Tennesseans for the sake of brevity—with all due respect to the Georgians. OR 43, pt. 1, 770.

failed, Merritt's cavalry would be poised to disrupt Early's line of retreat at Newtown, just four miles to the west.[14]

When Cesnola reported Gillespie's presence to his commander, Devin rushed the balance of his brigade toward White Post. Colonel Thomas C. Devin was an Irish-Catholic businessman and prewar militia officer from New York City. He rose to brigade command under the tutelage of Maj. Gen. John Buford, and gained a reputation as "Buford's Hard Hitter" or "Old War Horse" for his tenacity in combat. Devin earned the respect of his men who simply called him "Uncle Tommy." Though he had more experience than the younger West Pointers such as Custer and Merritt, he had not yet received a brigadier general's star. Indeed, the 42-year-old New Yorker had commanded a brigade since the Fredericksburg campaign. Nevertheless, Buford had declared, "I can't teach Col. Devin anything about cavalry; he knows about the tactics [better] than I do!"[15]

The 6th New York Cavalry arrived near the Double Tollgate accompanied by Merritt with Devin arriving shortly thereafter, and found Cesnola's 4th New York skirmishing with Gillespie's Tennesseans. Devin quickly deployed his brigade for action, posting the 17th Pennsylvania and the 6th New York to the right of Cesnola's regiment. The 9th New York held a position a mile down the Front Royal Pike toward Winchester, keeping a wary eye northward in case any Confederate infantry filtered up from Custer's front. Merritt decided that Gillespie's left flank could be broken with a mounted charge by the 6th New York Cavalry. The New Yorkers charged splendidly, jumping over a half dozen stone walls. Gillespie's Tennesseans leveled their Enfield rifles and fired incessantly, driving the New Yorkers back.

Unable to drive the Tennesseans with a mounted attack, Devin deployed a section of Capt. Edward Heaton's Battery B and L, 2nd U.S. Artillery and quickly opened fire on the dismounted Confederates. Gillespie did not have any artillery to call upon, so his men were forced to endure the pounding. The stone walls that had protected them against bullets proved a deadly liability when subjected to severe and accurate Federal artillery fire: rocks and stone fragments turned into lethal projectiles every time a shell struck the wall. The situation on

14 Vaughn was wounded at Martinsburg on July 25, and was no longer actively commanding his brigade. *New York Times*, August 20, 1864.

15 Edward G. Longacre, *The Cavalry at Gettysburg* (Rutherford, NJ, 1986), 51.

Gillespie's left was especially dire, and the troops in that position fell back to avoid the intense shelling.[16]

Realizing the Confederate left was "partially uncovered," Devin dismounted the 6th New York and 17th Pennsylvania Cavalry regiments and sent them against the weakened Confederate flank. Their small arms fire killed Maj. R. S. Vandyke of the 1st Tennessee Cavalry along with several other men of the brigade. When Gillespie went down with a serious wound, Lt. Col. Onslow Bean of the 16th Tennessee Cavalry Battalion assumed command. Flanked out of their position and taking losses, the Tennesseans beat a hasty retreat toward Newtown. The route to the Valley Pike now appeared open.[17]

As luck would have it, Early had shifted Brig. Gen. John D. Imboden's Virginia cavalry brigade from his left flank to his right near Newtown. When reports of Merritt's appearance at Double Tollgate reached Early, he rushed Imboden to Gillespie's assistance. When the Tennesseans saw the approaching Virginians, they halted and reformed their broken ranks. The united commands then fell back in good order to a stand of woods about one mile west of the original Confederate position at Double Tollgate. Imboden, a veteran artillerist himself, deployed Capt. John McClanahan's battery of horse artillery. Devin immediately responded by feeding another section of Captain Heaton's horse artillery into the fight. The Regulars quickly silenced McClanahan's guns and continued to shell the Confederate troopers, hurrying them along toward Newtown.[18]

It was 3:30 p.m. and there were still several hours of daylight remaining. Merritt ordered Col. Alfred Gibbs's reserve brigade to take the lead in the pursuit, with Devin's brigade close behind him. Gibbs deployed his former regiment, the 1st New York Dragoons under the command of Maj. Rufus Scott, and headed for Newtown. "The country between White Post and Newtown," observed the *New York Times* war correspondent, "though not particularly uneven or rugged is nevertheless favorable for defensive operations, being intersected by numerous fences and oak groves so particular to Western Maryland and the Shenandoah Valley."[19]

16 OR 43, pt. 1, 471-472; *History of the Sixth New York Cavalry*, 211.

17 OR 43, pt. 1, 471-472.

18 Ibid., 472; William W. Old Diary, LC.

19 OR 43, pt. 1, 487; E. A. Paul, "The Middle Department," *New York Times*, August 20, 1864.

While Gillespie delayed the Federal advance, Early promptly positioned Maj. Gen. John B. Gordon's division of 2,500 men one-and-a-half miles east of Newtown to cover the road from Double Tollgate. Brigadier General William Terry's Virginia brigade deployed on the left of that road. This unit included the last vestiges of the old Stonewall Brigade which numbered little more than 300 officers and men. Brigadier General Zebulon York's Louisiana brigade, the skeletal remnants of 14 proud Pelican State regiments, shook out a battle line on the right side of the road. The Virginians and Louisianans formed their lines along the edge of some woods. Colonel Edmund N. Atkinson's Georgia brigade anchored the division's right flank, deploying in an open field. All across Gordon's developing line, soldiers quickly threw up crude breastworks of fence rails, rocks, and tree limbs. Gordon sent his division's sharpshooters across the fields in front of his battle line and deployed them in a thick skirmish line in some open woods.[20]

By 4:00 p.m., the New York Dragoons had driven the last of the Confederate horsemen out of the way and run into Gordon's skirmishers posted in the woods. Scott dismounted his Dragoons and drove the butternuts back to their previously constructed fortifications. A brisk skirmish ensued, but the New Yorkers made no headway against the Confederate infantry. About 6:00 p.m., Gordon launched several sorties against the Dragoons using thick lines of skirmishers. The loosely arrayed Southerners advanced, forming a semicircle that overlapped both of Scott's flanks. Although the Southerners poured a "murderous" fire into the New Yorkers, the embattled Dragoons held off the worst of the onslaught with their seven-shot Spencer repeating carbines. "Our boys fired with such rapidity and so incessantly that Sergeant Jackson and several of his band were called to our aid," recounted a New Yorker, "and all were kept busy distributing cartridges." The situation was especially dire on the left, where elements of Col. Edward Atkinson's Georgia brigade overlapped the Dragoons's flank.[21]

Colonel Gibbs witnessed Scott's plight and poured reinforcements into the fight. Captain David S. Gordon's 2nd U.S. Cavalry extended the right flank, and Capt. Nelson Sweitzer's 1st U.S. Cavalry rushed into line on the left where the Georgians were making things hot. The Regulars charged across a wide, plowed

---

20 Jed Hotchkiss, 1864 Sketchbook, August 11, 1864, Map 51; Inspection Report of Gordon's division, August 20, 1864, National Archives.

21 *OR* 43, pt. 1, 487; Bowen, *Regimental History of the First New York Dragoons*, 211.

field. "We went across with a cheer, in double time, drove the enemy for the moment from the timber," recalled one Regular. Nevertheless, the Confederates continued to pour an enfilading fire into the left flank of Gibbs's line. Atkinson fed more men into the fight, pressed steadily ahead, and again forced Gibbs's line to fall back. Major Scott went down wounded, and his Dragoons fell back for 110 yards, halted, and reformed their line of battle. Captain Moses Harris of the 1st U.S. Cavalry recalled pulling back "at least as expeditiously as when we advanced." The retreat did not stop until "we found that inanimate friend of the soldier, a good substantial rail fence, and soon had rail barricades in our front which we held in spite of every effort of the enemy to dislodge us."[22]

Gordon continued to harass the Union troopers with swarming attacks by his sharpshooters. Merritt reacted by unlimbering Captain Heaton's horse artillery and adding its firepower to fray. Despite the added fire, Georgians from Atkinson's brigade continued pressing heavily against Gibbs's left. A squadron of the 6th Pennsylvania and the entire 17th Pennsylvania from Devin's brigade were sent to bolster the threatened left. With darkness now engulfing the Valley and having accomplished his mission of securing Early's line of retreat at Newtown, Gordon withdrew his men back to their breastworks. Torbert and Merritt remained content to hold the ground they had gained that day. With Early's entire army lurking about the vicinity of Newtown, the Federals dared not push any farther. Once Gordon was assured that the Federals had ceased their efforts to advance, he fell back to a position closer to Newtown.[23]

Once it became known that Early was abandoning Winchester, the Union infantry adjusted its march to shift farther south. The foot soldiers pressed forward toward Opequon Creek and bivouacked on the east bank. The Sixth Corps was on the right at the Millwood Pike, Crook was at Senseney Road, and the Nineteenth Corps anchored the left near Parkin's Mill. Lowell's cavalry brigade joined Merritt that evening on the road between White Post and Newtown. The Confederate withdrawal from Winchester on August 11 left the town's residents anxious. Early's recent burning of Chambersburg, Pennsylvania, left them fearful of Federal retaliation. "The Yankees are roused up to anything by the burning lights at Chambersburgh," noted Mrs. Hugh Lee.

22 OR 43, pt. 1, 17, 487; Moses Harris, "With the Reserve brigade," *Journal of the United States Cavalry Association*, March 1890, 13.

23 OR 43, pt. 1, 17, 487.

Pvt. John J. Rhodes of the 5th Virginia Infantry, part of the Stonewall Brigade, was captured on August 12 during the retreat to Fisher's Hill. *LC*

Her sister-in-law concluded that Jubal Early's fateful order had doomed Winchester to the same fate when the Union army returned to town.[24]

Sheridan had no intention of burning Winchester, but that did not stop Union soldiers from taunting the town's secessionists. When the first Federal troops entered the town, some residents inquired if the Union Army would burn Winchester. The Yankee soldiers replied that "they were not the burning party, but that they [the burners] would be in tomorrow." The townspeople spent several nervous days, but the town was spared the torch.[25]

Early's Army of the Valley District camped for the night just south of Newtown. With Sheridan's army closing in, the Confederates broke camp at 3:00 a.m. and marched south toward Strasburg and Fisher's Hill. This commanding defensive position was Early's ultimate objective; however, as the Southerners passed through Middletown and crossed Cedar Creek, he halted and formed his army into line of battle on Hupp's Hill, another commanding eminence between Strasburg and Cedar Creek. There he awaited Sheridan's next move.[26]

---

24 Mrs. Hugh Lee had hosted Mrs. John B. Gordon and her son in her home during the Valley Army's stay in Winchester. The general's family departed on August 10. Their departure provided the Lee family with advance warning of Early's pending departure. Diary of Mrs. Hugh Lee, Winchester-Frederick County Historical Society Collection, Handley Library; Michael G. Mahon, *Winchester Divided: The Civil War Diaries of Julia Chase and Laura Lee* (Mechanicsburg, PA: Stackpole Books, 2002), 161-162.

25 Ibid., 163.

26 Early, *Last Year of the War*, 60.

On the evening of August 11, Sheridan reformulated his plans. The time had passed for moving the Army of the Shenandoah south of Early. Instead, Sheridan issued orders for a straightforward pursuit of Early's forces. On August 12, Sheridan cautiously followed Early's force up the Valley Pike with Merritt's cavalry division in the van. Merritt headed south on the pike with Lowell's, Custer's, and Gibbs's brigades. Devin's brigade moved farther west until it reached the Back Road, a country track that ran parallel to the Valley Pike near the eastern base of Little North Mountain. The New Yorker turned southward and continued the advance while covering Sheridan's right flank. Lowell's brigade soon encountered Early's skirmishers along the north bank of Cedar Creek. The Federals immediately dismounted and skirmished with their Southern counterparts. George Crook's Army of West Virginia arrived on the scene, and his infantry helped Lowell shove the Confederates across Cedar Creek. The encounter, however, did not develop into a serious engagement. By nightfall, Sheridan's entire army was in position: Crook on the east side of the pike, Emory's Nineteenth Corps detachment immediately west of that road, Wright's Sixth Corps on Emory's right flank, and the cavalry covering both flanks.[27]

As Early observed the Federal build-up in his front, he found "that the enemy was advancing in much heavier force than I had yet encountered." Outnumbered at least two-to-one, Early pulled his army back to Fisher's Hill. The eminence was really a series of hills sandwiched between the Shenandoah River and Little North Mountain to the west, where it was more susceptible to flanking. At Fisher's Hill, the 2,000 survivors from Gen. John McCausland's ill-fated raid on Chambersburg rejoined the army. Although occupying an intimidating position against a frontal assault, Early feared that Sheridan would send his cavalry up the Luray Valley east of Massanutten Mountain and flank the Confederate position at Fisher's Hill. To guard against such an occurrence, he sent Imboden's brigade to Front Royal to cover the approaches to the Luray Valley.[28]

Early had been duly reporting developments in the Valley to Robert E. Lee at Richmond. Lee informed Early about Lt. Gen. Richard H. Anderson's presence at Culpeper on August 8, so "Old Jube" understood that support was

27 Sheridan, *Memoirs*, 480.

28 Early, *Last Year of the War*, 60.

nearby. With Sheridan concentrating such a large force and suddenly bearing down on Early in the Valley, Lee changed the game plan for Anderson. There would be no diversionary action east of the Blue Ridge. On August 12, Lee directed Anderson to march Kershaw, Fitz Lee, and Cutshaw to Sperryville, located 20 miles west of Culpeper at the eastern foot of the Blue Ridge. From Sperryville, Anderson was only 24 miles from Front Royal via Chester Gap. Lee directed Anderson to "be governed by circumstances," and "keep in communication with Early." That very day, Early notified Anderson of the developments in the Valley and requested him to march his command to Front Royal and protect the Luray Valley.

Anderson's movement toward the Valley would have a profound impact upon the course of Sheridan's developing campaign. Any hopes for a quick change of fortune in the Shenandoah would soon be dashed.[29]

---

29 Early also added that Wade Hampton's cavalry division should join Anderson by August 15, but this never materialized because General Lee recalled Hampton to meet a new threat from General Grant opposite Richmond and Petersburg. OR 43, pt. 1, 996-997; Early, *Last Year of the War*, 60.

THE NICEST FIGHT OF THE SEASON

The Battle of Guard Hill (Crooked Run)

Phil Sheridan's opportunity to position the Army of the Shenandoah south of Jubal Early's Army of the Valley District and cut him off from the rest of the Confederacy had slipped away. The prospect of failure rankled the Union commander, but it did not temper his resolve.

On the morning of August 13, Sheridan telegraphed Grant, "I was unable to get south of Early but will push him up the Valley." Immediately that same day, he issued orders he hoped would put significant pressure on the Confederates and force a battle. Sheridan advanced Horatio Wright's Sixth Corps to the heights immediately west of Strasburg at 7:00 a.m. Merritt's cavalry moved later along the Middle Road to the west. That track was "a most horrible mountain road," recalled an officer of the 1st New York Dragoons. The Union forces found "the enemy in force in entrenchments about a mile beyond the town" upon Fisher's Hill. It was, noted one trooper, "one of the strongest positions in the valley." While Sheridan considered how to attack Early's fortified position, he received intelligence reports of Lt. Gen. Richard H. Anderson's approaching Confederate force of 500 officers, 5,500 enlisted soldiers, and 20 pieces of artillery. These reinforcements were not new recruits or backwater garrison soldiers, but experienced veterans from the Army of Northern Virginia.[1]

This news alarmed Sheridan. His army was now south of Front Royal facing southwest to confront Early at Fisher's Hill. With Anderson on his way to Front Royal, the Southerners could easily threaten the Federal left flank and rear. Anderson's arrival would increase the total effective Confederate forces in the Valley to nearly 21,000. Meanwhile, Sheridan's army still lacked Grover's division of the Nineteenth Corps and Wilson's cavalry division from the Army of the Potomac. Sheridan reported his "effective line of battle strength was about 18,000 infantry and 3,500 cavalry," but on paper his force was closer to 30,000. The elimination of Sheridan's decisive numerical advantage and his now vulnerable position near Strasburg combined to cause him "much anxiety."[2]

When Sheridan's operations ground to a standstill at Strasburg, inquisitive reporters prodded staff officers for information on the army's forthcoming movements. Under previous commanders, staff officers freely shared inside information with the press, but the reporters quickly learned that things would be different with Sheridan at the helm. "It is almost impossible to learn anything positive regarding the future movements of the Army of Western Virginia,"

---

1   OR 43, pt. 1, 783; Howard M. Smith Journal, Library of Congress; Sheridan, *Memoirs*, 481.

2   On August 31, Kershaw's division numbered 377 officers and 3,445 enlisted men present for duty. During August, Kershaw experienced significant losses on the 16th at Cedarville of 300 and on the 26th at Halltown of 125. Assuming the normal flow of men into the regiment from convalescence and extra duty, Kershaw likely had at least 3,800 men when he arrived in the Valley. Fitz Lee's division numbered 115 officers and 1,591 men on June 30. Captured reports from Lee's division for September show 1,370 present for duty, but does not break out officers and men. It will be assumed that this figure is an aggregate total. Given the heavy duty experienced by Lee's division from the time it arrived in the Valley, it is safe to assume that he had at least 1,500 men when he reached the Shenandoah, not including the horse artillery. Cutshaw's Battalion counted 17 officers and 364 men armed with 12 guns on September 29, 1864. Sheridan had earlier reported his total force at 26,000. The 21,500 "line of battle strength" does not include his artillery and must exclude all officers and extra duty men. As stated, the mounted divisions of William W. Averell, Alfred A. Duffie, and James H. Wilson had not yet joined Sheridan, nor had most of Cuvier Grover's four Nineteenth Corps brigades. For a brief time and a brief time only, Sheridan's effective force was nearly on par with the Confederates in the Valley. In similar fashion, Jubal Early refers to "muskets" in his accounts of the campaign which represent a decrease of 15 to 20 percent from the reported present for duty for his army that appears in the *Official Records*. See OR 42, pt. 2, 1,213, and Ibid., 43, pt. 1, 42; Luman Harris Tenney, War Diary of Luman Harris Tenney, 1861-1865 (Cleveland: Evangelical Publishing House, 1914), 132; Confederate Inspection Reports, National Archives, *New York Times*, August 18, 1864.

complained a *New York Times* correspondent. "Staff officers are very taciturn on the subject."[3]

Sheridan reacted quickly to Anderson's reported approach, dispatching a cavalry brigade from Merritt's division to Front Royal "to ascertain definitely, if possible, the truth of such reports." Merritt sent the reliable Col. Thomas Devin to Cedarville on the Front Royal and Winchester Turnpike, a few miles north of the former town. Devin's troopers rode out of their camps near Middletown at 7:00 p.m. and covered five miles before halting for the night. His advance pickets occupied the crossroads hamlet of Cedarville. The next morning, August 14, Devin's New Yorkers and Pennsylvanians struck the turnpike and continued south toward Front Royal. The Federals encountered Imboden's Cavalry brigade guarding Early's right flank at Guard Hill, a commanding eminence on the north bank of the Shenandoah River's north fork. The hill was a key position, because it overlooked the fords and roads leading to Front Royal from the north; the turnpike actually passed over Guard Hill before it descended toward the river. Devin quickly shoved Imboden across both forks of the Shenandoah River, and promptly posted two squadrons of the 9th New York Cavalry as pickets. Imboden's horsemen lingered in the distance on the opposite side of the rivers, but more serious trouble was on the way as Anderson's command headed across the Blue Ridge.[4]

Meanwhile, on August 13 near Berryville, a more immediate and potentially serious nuisance lashed out at Sheridan's supply lines. Colonel John Singleton Mosby, the famed Confederate partisan known as the "Gray Ghost," was carefully monitoring Sheridan's supply line. Mosby planned to hit the Union wagon trains as they rolled out of Harpers Ferry. On August 12, his scouts spotted 600 wagons under the protection of Brig. Gen. John Kenly's brigade[5] slowly making their way toward Berryville. When the report reached Mosby, his Rangers of the 43rd Virginia Battalion were hiding out at the eastern base of the Blue Ridge 11 miles east in Loudoun County. Late that afternoon, Mosby

---

3   The Army of Western Virginia is a reference to Sheridan's force. It was unofficially known as the Army of the Shenandoah, and that title would not be made official until November 1864 after the active campaigns in the Valley had ended. George F. Williams, "The Middle Division," *New York Times*, August 21, 1864.

4   *OR* 43, pt. 1, 42-43.

5   Kenly's brigade was attached to the post at Harpers Ferry and was not assigned to Sheridan's combat force. It consisted of Maryland Home Guards and Ohio National Guardsmen serving for 100 days. Sheridan's brother, John, served in one of these regiments.

marched his command of "something over 300 men with two mountain howitzers" through Snickers Gap along the road to Berryville. They crossed the Shenandoah River near sunset and went into hiding for the night. Mosby sent a scout to reconnoiter the area, and rested in an old barn while awaiting the scout's return.[6]

The scout located the vulnerable wagon train parked just north of Berryville and promptly notified Mosby. The partisan leader took a few men and rode ahead to plan the attack, leaving Capt. William Chapman to bring up the rest of the command. When Mosby arrived on the scene, he found a most inviting target: the supply train belonging to the Reserve brigade of Merritt's cavalry division. The potential for trouble started when Capt. E. P. McKinney, the Reserve brigade's commissary of subsistence, "without orders permitted the train to go into park, the drivers to unhitch and unharness their animals and lie down and go to sleep." Making matters worse, the wagon guards, National Guardsmen from Ohio serving a 100-day stint, failed to adequately picket the area. In the darkness of night, the fatigued soldiers gave little thought to proper security measures. Such laxity often proved a fatal error in Mosby's Confederacy, as his rangers seldom missed an opportunity to hit vulnerable Union detachments.[7]

Mosby assessed the situation quickly and called up Captain Chapman and the full battalion. Under cover of a thick predawn fog, Mosby's men unlimbered one of the howitzers on a knoll no more than 100 yards from the Federals. Unfortunately, the crew planted the gun on a hornet's nest. When the angry insects swarmed out, the men panicked and one accidentally jerked the lanyard, setting off the gun. At the roar of the cannon, Mosby's men burst into the midst of the Federals, firing their Colt revolvers to the left and right. With most of the rangers wearing blue coats, confusion reigned among the Federals who could not readily tell friend from foe. One column of the partisans bolted toward the parked wagons and scattered the infantry guards. One Ohioan recalled, "The raiders were shooting our men down in every direction," so he leapt into a pile of hay and survived the attack. A second column struck Devin's train as it entered Berryville. Most of the startled Ohio soldiers fled after firing a token round into the early morning mist, but one small detachment took refuge behind the brick walls of Buck Marsh Baptist Church on the outskirts of town.

6 OR 43, pt. 1, 630, 634.

7 Ibid., 632.

They fiercely resisted the Rangers until Mosby's howitzer shelled the church and drove them out. With the Federals driven off, Mosby's men picked through the abandoned wagons, took what they could carry, including a cache of musical instruments, and then burned the rest. The raid proved to be quite a success. Mosby's Rangers burned or captured 100 wagons, and snared 100 prisoners, 200 beef cattle, and numerous draft animals. When the Rangers returned to their camp in Loudoun County, one of them recalled that the command presented "quite a sight, displaying their ornate, new blue uniforms, laughing and singing, and playing the untuned musical instruments, accompanied by the noisy cattle." The physical damage that Mosby inflicted upon the train impacted Sheridan's campaign negligibly. It did not, as Mosby claimed, force Sheridan to withdraw from Early's front at Strasburg due to a resultant lack of supplies. Nevertheless, the threat of Mosby's guerrillas forced Sheridan to increase vigilance to the rear and divert troops from the pursuit of Early's army to strengthen the wagon guards.[8]

In addition to developments on the ground in the Shenandoah, Sheridan continued to learn about the political realities of campaigning so close to Washington. J. W. Garrett, the president of the vital Baltimore and Ohio Railroad, expressed considerable concern over the government's failure to protect his rail line. Small bands of partisans constantly damaged the rails and harassed repair crews, especially between Harpers Ferry and Back Creek, a few miles west of Martinsburg. "I hope General Sheridan will have it in his power to detail at once an effective force for this purpose," Garrett told Stanton. The railroader suggested that Sheridan utilize Averell's division, which was just then reaching the Valley, to protect the vital railroad town of Martinsburg and its surrounding environs. Within 24 hours, Sheridan issued that very order to Averell. When Garrett talked, people in Washington listened, and Sheridan seemingly understood that reality.[9]

---

8   Ibid., 619-632; John S. Mosby, *Gray Ghost: The Memoirs of Colonel John S. Mosby* (New York: Bantam Books, 1992), 227-228; James Joseph Williamson, *Mosby's Rangers: A Record of the Operations of the 43rd Battalion Virginia Cavalry from its Organization to the Surrender* (New York: Ralph B. Kenyon, Publisher, 1896), 207-211; Hugh C. Keen and Horace Mewborn, *43rd Battalion Virginia Cavalry Mosby's Command* (Lynchburg, VA, 1993), 159; George Perkins, *A Summer in Maryland and Virginia or Campaigning with the 149th Ohio Volunteer Infantry* (Chillicothe, OH, nd), 34-36.

9   *OR* 43, pt. 1, 780.

At U.S. Army headquarters in City Point, General Grant worried about the strong forces under Anderson that Gen. Robert E. Lee was sending to the Shenandoah Valley. A man of action, Grant initiated an offensive against Richmond to prevent Lee from further reinforcing his forces in the Valley. The movement on Richmond also covered an effort by Meade's Army of the Potomac to break the Weldon Railroad south of Petersburg. Grant's effort north of the James River resulted in the Second Battle of Deep Bottom. While Grant failed to achieve his tactical objectives at Richmond, he did cause Lee to reconsider his plans for sending reinforcements to the Shenandoah. He telegraphed Maj. Gen. Wade Hampton, already en route to Culpeper, "Halt your command and return to Richmond." Without Hampton and his 3,000 troopers, Anderson's force lost much of its potential, and Jubal Early lost a cavalry commander who understood the realities of late-war mounted and dismounted operations better than anyone else in the Army of Northern Virginia. Grant's continued probing of Lee's defenses north of the James River clearly aided Sheridan's cause in the Valley.[10]

Back at Cedar Creek, nagging problems continued to plague Sheridan and his army. A Confederate signal station operating atop Signal Knob on the northern end of Massanutten Mountain was particularly troublesome. "Every daylight movement of our troops could be seen by the enemy better than if they were in our camp." Sheridan determined to shut it down and establish one of his own. He turned to George Crook and his "Mountain Creepers" to carry out the assignment. On August 14, a 60-man detachment from the 12th West Virginia Infantry ascended Signal Knob, drove off the Confederates, and established a Union signal station. However, after only a few hours, the sharpshooters of Gordon's division climbed the mountain and counterattacked. They drove off the West Virginians and reestablished the Confederate station on Signal Knob. The next morning Crook tried again, this time sending Lt. Col. George W. Taggart's 14th West Virginia supported by the 116th Ohio. This force crossed the Shenandoah River in the early morning hours of August 15, the men stopping to fill their canteens with the cool, clear water. They gained the cover of timber at the northern base of Signal Knob and began the hazardous ascent. "The underbrush was so dense," recalled one West Virginian, "that it was with great difficulty a man could get through." Taggart sent one company ahead as an advance guard, but it lost its way and moved

10 Ibid., 999; Wittenberg, *Glory Enough for All*, 313-314.

directly up "the mountain at its north end, where from the summit some distance down there was no timber." Confederates posted behind rocks opened fire, compelling the company to retire. The brief clash distracted the defenders from discovering the rest of the Union force winding its way up the mountain through timber and brush.[11]

By 10:00 a.m., Taggart's band had reached the summit, but the exhausting climb in the hot August morning took its toll upon his men. Taggart deployed his regiment in a defensive position, while the Signal Corps troops attempted to establish their station. From the peak, the West Virginians looked down upon the Valley and saw "a grand sight-two armies in repose," as Sheridan and Early stared each other down around Strasburg. The Confederate infantry discovered Taggart's presence and attacked. The West Virginians charged and drove them back to their stone breastworks on the top of the mountain. With news of a larger enemy force concealed on the Strasburg side of the mountain, Taggart buried his dead under rocks and prudently withdrew his parched West Virginians from the mountaintop. With great difficulty, they carried their wounded down the slope in blankets, lowering them down from one squad to another at steep points in the descent. Unable to obtain water throughout the day, Taggart's troops were so thirsty when they finally reached the Shenandoah River that "the men drank water and vomited and drank more and did the same thing over." When they finally reached their camp around midnight, one soldier remembered being "more dead than alive." Another mountaineer summed up the day's effort as "a hard march that brought poor returns." Sheridan did not get his signal station on Massanutten and Jubal Early retained his commanding view of Union operations in the vicinity.[12]

In the meantime, uneventful skirmishing had continued throughout August 14, around Strasburg while Sheridan sifted through intelligence reports. The situation became clear when Col. Norton P. Chipman of the War Department arrived at Sheridan's headquarters with a message from General Grant. Chipman and his escort hastily rode from Washington through Snickers Gap to personally deliver it to Sheridan. Chipman, a confidant of both Lincoln and Stanton, was more than a simple messenger. He remained on the scene and

---

11 William Hewitt, *History of the Twelfth West Virginia Volunteer Infantry* (n.p., n.d.), 171; Theodore Lang, *Loyal West Virginia* (Baltimore, 1895), 295; Jesse Tyler Sturm, *From a "Whirlpool of Death . . . to Victory": Civil War Remembrances of Jesse Tyler Sturm* (Charlestown, WV, 2002), 74-75.

12 Lang, *Loyal West Virginia*, 295; Sturm, *Remembrances*, 76-77.

observed firsthand Grant's new commander in the Shenandoah Valley for the rest of August. The note Chipman delivered read, "It is now certain two divisions of infantry have gone to Early and some cavalry and twenty pieces of artillery." Grant warned that Sheridan "must be cautious and act on the defensive until movements here [Richmond/Petersburg] force them to detach [troops] to [Richmond/Petersburg]. Grant added, "Early's force, with this increase cannot exceed forty thousand men, but this is too much for General Sheridan to attack." On a positive note for Sheridan, Grant's overestimation of the Confederate strength did facilitate the release of Grover's division of the Nineteenth Corps from the defenses of Washington. Furthermore, Grant's assessment completely altered Sheridan's approach to the campaign. No longer would he attempt to follow Early "to the death." Instead, the little Irishman from Somerset, Ohio, would patiently wait for Early to send some of those troops back to Lee before striking out again.[13]

In preparation for a withdrawal from Strasburg, Sheridan sought "a defensive line—a position where a smaller number of troops could hold a larger number, for this information led me to suppose that Early's force would greatly exceed mine when Anderson's two divisions of infantry and Fitzhugh Lee's cavalry had joined him." Sheridan saw only one suitable position on his map—Halltown, about four miles west of Harpers Ferry. It was indeed a strong position, with the Potomac River protecting the right flank and the Shenandoah River the left. In anticipation of the withdrawal, Sheridan directed General Emory to march the Nineteenth Corps to Winchester at 11:00 p.m. on August 15. Sheridan also instructed Merritt to join Devin opposite Front Royal with Custer's and Gibbs's brigades at 8:00 a.m. that same day.[14]

In removing his army to Halltown, Sheridan would be closer to his arriving reinforcements. Brigadier General James H. Wilson's cavalry division was expected to reach the Valley via Snickers Gap, and Brig. Gen. Alfred Duffie's 900-man mounted division would join Sheridan at Berryville. Averell's division was nearing the Valley region from West Virginia. Typical of Averell, he complained that, "One-third of my horses are totally unfit for further service at present." He also lamented shortages of forage and the heavy toll that the hard campaign against McCausland had inflicted upon his command. In truth, Averell's losses were minimal. With all of the hard combat and campaigning

13 *OR* 43, pt. 1, 43.

14 Sheridan, *Memoirs*, 483-484.

that Sheridan's cavalry experienced throughout the spring and summer of 1864, the army commander had little sympathy for Averell's situation. "I shall use every endeavor to be ready for the field in five or six days," assured Averell. This uninspiring response did little to bolster Averell's reputation in eyes of his new commander. It only confirmed the worst that Sheridan had heard from Crook and officers of the Cavalry Corps.[15]

Sheridan reacted to Anderson's advance not a moment too soon. The South Carolinian's command had passed through Chester Gap and reached Front Royal on the previous afternoon, August 14. Major General Fitzhugh Lee's cavalry arrived first that morning, and Kershaw's First Corps infantry division marched into town that afternoon. Detachments from Kershaw's command picketed the south bank of the South Fork of the Shenandoah River and watched the road leading north to Winchester. Anderson rested his tired command for the remaining hours of the day. Kershaw's men used the respite, their first since the campaign opened back in May, to partake in "the delight of a bath, and in the pure, clear waters of the Shenandoah, [it] was a luxury indeed." "We had a fine time there," recalled a Georgian, "and went in swimming every day." Although the troops were still at war, the Shenandoah Valley provided them a more pleasant and healthful environment than the vile trenches around Petersburg and Richmond.[16]

While Early had been notified of the approaching reinforcements, he had not yet communicated with Anderson. On August 16, the First Corps commander sent Fitz Lee "to seek an interview" with Old Jube and arrange, on Anderson's behalf, for an immediate attack. Lee departed Front Royal at daylight, accompanied by a lone staff officer. With the direct road to Strasburg in Sheridan's hands, Lee was forced to cross the rugged Massanutten Mountain. "The ascents and descents were so precipitous and rough," recalled Lee, "that we were obliged to ride mules." Lee reached Early's headquarters that afternoon, and the two men finalized a joint attack plan against Sheridan for the following day, August 17.[17]

---

15 OR 43, pt. 1, 801-804.

16 D. Augustus Dickert, *History of Kershaw's Brigade: With Complete Roll of Companies, Biographical Sketches, Incidents, Anecdotes, Etc.* (Dayton, OH, 1976), 418; Jim Parrish, "50th Georgia: The Shenandoah Valley," 2.

17 Fitzhugh Lee, Report, MOC.

While Fitz Lee was conferring with Early at Fisher's Hill, Anderson grew concerned about the Union force occupying Guard Hill on the north bank of the North Fork of the Shenandoah River. It was an important position as the Front Royal and Winchester Turnpike crossed both forks of the Shenandoah River there and then ascended Guard Hill. Controlling that dominating high ground would be vital to any advance Anderson would make, but would also facilitate easier communications with Early. On the morning of August 16, Brig. Gen. Thomas Devin's Union cavalry controlled that vital high ground. To pry Guard Hill from Devin's grasp, Anderson sent Brig. Gen. Williams C. Wickham's cavalry brigade of Lee's division. In Lee's absence, Wickham commanded the division while Col. Thomas H. Owen led the brigade in the pending action. Anderson closely supported the cavalry with the veteran Georgia infantry of Brig. Gen. William T. Wofford's brigade from Kershaw's division.[18]

Captain Daniel W. Lapham's squadron of the 9th New York Cavalry of Devin's brigade picketed Guard Hill and the nearby fords. Devin's encampment was located at Cedarville on the west side of the Front Royal and Winchester Pike, one mile north of Guard Hill. Crooked Run, a deep stream with steep banks, separated the bivouac from Lapham's squadron. Devin had deployed Capt. Timothy Hanley's dismounted squadron from the 9th New York to guard the bridge over Crooked Run and form a skirmish line behind the stream. By 2:00 p.m., Maj. Gen. Wesley Merritt had joined Devin at Cedarville with both Custer and Gibbs. Custer posted his Michigan brigade on the east side of the pike and deployed 150 troopers from Maj. Charles W. Deane's 6th Michigan to picket his front, relieving Devin's men of responsibility for that sector. Deane posted his pickets along the northern bank of the Shenandoah River and atop Guard Hill. He established a reserve line along Crooked Run immediately north of Guard Hill. Gibbs's reserve brigade rode two miles northward on the pike to Nineveh, where they halted and established camp. The Union horsemen anticipated nothing more than routine screening duty while they protected the army's left flank. "Horses were unsaddled and brigade and regimental headquarters had their tents pitched," observed a correspondent on the scene. "Officers and men were for once, they thought,

18 Report of Lt. General Richard A. Anderson, 1864, FSNMP; Civil War Reminiscences of Robert Thruston Hubard, Robert T. Hubard Papers, UVA.

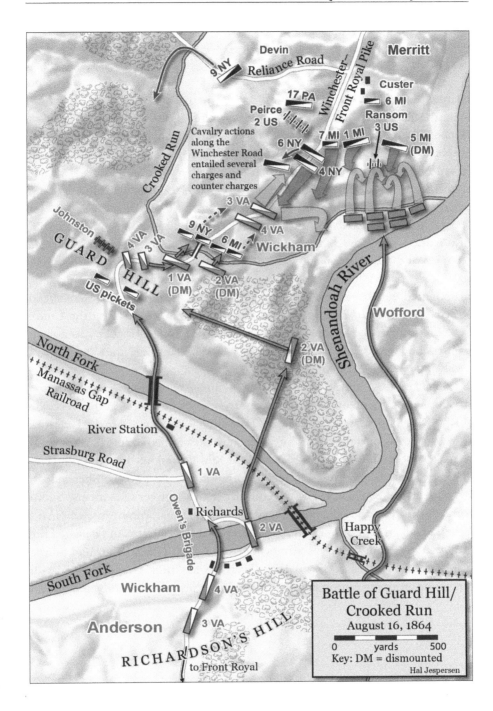

Cavalry actions along the Winchester Road entailed several charges and counter charges

Battle of Guard Hill/
Crooked Run
August 16, 1864

0   yards   500
Key: DM = dismounted

Hal Jespersen

partaking of a quiet meal." Contrary to expectations, their Shenandoah respite did last long.[19]

At 3:00 p.m., Wickham's Virginia Cavalry splashed into the river and charged the New Yorkers picketing the northern bank. Colonel Owen rode with the advance squadron of the 1st Virginia Cavalry, the spearhead of Wickham's assault. The 4th and 3rd Virginia followed in column while the 2nd Virginia crossed the Shenandoah River's North Fork on the right a short distance downstream from the ford at the pike. Lapham's New York pickets scurried up Guard Hill and halted on the crest. Here, they rallied upon their reserves and fired at the 1st Virginia, slowing the Confederate advance for several minutes. Concurrently, the 2nd Virginia came up on the right, dismounted, and moved through some woods on the top of the hill. When the troopers of the 2nd Virginia saw the exposed left flank of the Federals atop the hill, they opened fire, throwing the cavalrymen into confusion. Wickham dismounted the 1st Virginia and united it with the 2nd Virginia, advancing and shoving the Federals down the northern face of the ridge toward the Union picket reserves posted behind Crooked Run. Anderson's objective was now in Confederate hands, but the Union cavalry lurked below and the skirmish was escalating quickly.[20]

Crooked Run quickly became the defining geographic feature of the developing engagement. The creek wound its way southward on the west side of the Winchester and Front Royal Pike until Guard Hill blocked it from flowing directly into the Shenandoah River. Instead, the hill forced the stream to make a horseshoe bend so that Crooked Run flowed northward on the east side of the pike. The run continued on until it merged into the Shenandoah River, nearly one mile north of the confluence of that river's North and South forks. A bridge carried the pike over the stream at the northern foot of Guard Hill. A small growth of trees on the southern bank of the stream facilitated the stealthy movement of troops advancing from Guard Hill. The ground on the inside of the horseshoe formed by the run was "broken and rolling, with limestone cropping out on every hand, and the view only obstructed here and

---

19 OR 43, pt. 1, 423, 439, 472; *New York Times*, August 25, 1864.

20 Hubard, Reminiscences, UVA.

there by a locust-tree." While it offered little cover for the Union forces operating in that sector of the battlefield, it was ideal for mounted operations.[21]

Before continuing his attack, Wickham quickly consolidated his foothold on Guard Hill by deploying his entire brigade. The dismounted troopers of the 1st and 2nd Virginia battled the Federals of the 9th New York and 6th Michigan across Crooked Run. Atop Guard Hill, Capt. Philip P. Johnston's Virginians muscled the Stuart Horse Artillery into position upon the summit and unlimbered his guns astride the Winchester-Front Royal Turnpike. The gunners sited their cannon upon Merritt's main position located roughly 1,000 yards north on the pike and began shelling his encampment.[22]

The dismounted Virginians battled Hanley's New Yorker's for possession of the bridge that carried the pike over the run. Hanley deployed his troopers on the high ground on the west side of the road, while Major Deane deployed his Michigan men to the east. Captain Lapham rallied his squadron at the bridge, where they joined the reserves and checked the advance of the dismounted Virginians. A Confederate trooper noted that the New Yorkers "poured a hot fire into our men, and so effective that of about ten men brought to the rear, seven or eight were shot through the breast."[23]

Custer had watched the developing action with keen interest from atop a hill within the Federal lines, and he reacted without hesitation. The young general rushed Maj. Harvey H. Vinton with a squadron of the 6th Michigan to reinforce his skirmish line on the east side of the pike. Reacting to the presence of the Stuart Horse Artillery on Guard Hill, Custer deployed Capt. Dunbar R. Ransom's four-gun battery of the 3rd U.S. Artillery on a ridge in the center of his line. As soon as the guns were loaded, they opened fire at the Confederate pieces on the opposite hilltop. The Regulars' first three shots scattered a large group of Confederates who had assembled around the artillery to watch the action unfolding in the valley below. Johnston then redirected the fire of three

---

21 E. A. Paul, "The Cavalry Engagement at Crooked Run," Berryville, August 17, 1864, in the *New York Times*, August 25, 1864.

22 Johnston initially deployed two guns, but Federal accounts indicate that perhaps as many as nine guns were deployed on Guard Hill. That number appears high. It is more likely that the Confederates deployed six guns.

23 OR 43, pt. 1, 472; Hillman A. Hall, *History of the Sixth New York Cavalry (Second Ira Harris Guard)* (Worcester, MA: The Blanchard Press, 1908), 213.

of his six guns from Devin's cavalry to provide counter-battery fire against Ransom.[24]

Wickham watched as the 1st and 2nd Virginia slowly drove back the Federal skirmish line from its position behind Crooked Run. When he spotted Vinton's dismounted squadron of the 6th Michigan coming forward to reinforce the sagging Federal skirmish line, Wickham ordered Col. Thomas H. Owen of the 3rd Virginia to "charge as far as possible and if overpowered to fall back." Lieutenant Robert T. Hubard overheard the order and quickly concluded that it reflected "more courage than prudence." It was a needless effort as Guard Hill had been taken. Owen rode over to Hubard and said, "You all will have a difficult job, but whip them follows and see that the Regt. does its duty and I'll try to be near you." Owen ordered the charge and the 3rd Virginia pounded down the pike "through a storm of shell and small arms." The mounted Confederates shattered the Federal skirmish line and poured over Crooked Run, firing at the retreating Federals from horseback in a most chaotic scene. Moments later, Wickham quickly followed with the 4th Virginia.[25]

Devin reacted immediately and charged the approaching Virginians on their flank with Col. Luigi de Cesnola's 4th New York Cavalry. The Italian colonel drew his saber and dashed out in front of the 4th New York and personally led the way. The regiment surged ahead with drawn sabers "under a perfect sheet of leaden fire" from the Virginians. Cesnola struck the flank of the advancing Confederates and shoved them back across Crooked Run. The New Yorkers slashed in among the retreating Confederates and nabbed a number of prisoners. The 3rd Virginia fell back several hundred yards and reformed. Private Frank Leslie captured the colors of the 3rd Virginia and received the Medal of Honor for his effort.

With the immediate threat on the pike neutralized by Cesnola's charge, Devin quickly deployed the rest of his command for action. In the camp of the 6th New York, troopers had been standing in line and waiting to be paid when the attack came. The bugler sounded "To Horse" and the New Yorkers rushed to their mounts. Leaving the regiment partially unpaid, the paymaster closed up his safe box and declared, "I want to see a cavalry fight," and followed the men into action. At Devin's direction, Maj. William E. Beardsley's 6th New York

---

24 Paul, "The Cavalry Engagement at Crooked Run," *New York Times*, August 25, 1864; A. Bugler, "Our Army Correspondence," *Detroit Advertiser and Tribune*, September 27, 1864.

25 Hubard, Reminiscences, UVA.

Cavalry followed Cesnola into the fray and took position in a ravine, shielded from Confederate fire. Nearby, Capt. Charles H. Peirce unlimbered his battery of the 2nd U.S. Artillery, supported by the 17th Pennsylvania Cavalry. The Regular Army gunners opened fire and made "sad havoc" in the Confederate ranks. Devin sent the remaining squadrons of the 9th New York to a range of hills well off to the right, west of Crooked Run. He ordered its commander, Col. George S. Nicholls, to advance and threaten the left flank of Wickham's position, but little came of this movement.[26]

The action intensified on the east side of the pike in front of Custer's brigade. The first shots by Devin's picket line had caused no alarm among the Michigan troopers. A lieutenant from Devin's staff soon dashed into Custer's camp and informed the general that Wickham was advancing in force and driving Devin's pickets across Crooked Run. Again, Custer reacted quickly. In fewer than 10 minutes, his entire brigade stood ready for action. Custer did not even wait for his own horse to be saddled, but instead mounted an orderly's steed and galloped to the nearest eminence to reconnoiter the situation. He immediately spotted the advancing Confederates and deployed his brigade for battle. Custer positioned Maj. Angelo Paldi's 1st Michigan behind Ransom's guns. Colonel Russell A. Alger's 5th Michigan anchored the brigade's left flank, while Col. Melvin Brewer's 7th Michigan guarded the right next to Devin. The remaining portion of Col. James H. Kidd's 6th Michigan remained in reserve.[27]

While Custer monitored the progress of Devin's fight, a new threat emerged on the extreme left of the Union battle line. Captain Levant W. Barnhart, Custer's asssistant adjutant general, had galloped up a hill on the left of the line and saw Brig. Gen. William T. Wofford's Georgia brigade crossing the Shenandoah River at a ford downstream. To meet this emerging threat, Custer advanced a section of Ransom's battery to Barnhart's Hill. He also shifted Colonel Alger's 5th Michigan and Major Paldi's 1st Michigan into position behind the hill. The blond general instructed Alger to dismount the 5th

---

26 OR 43, pt. 1, 472-473; *New York Times*, August 25, 1864.

27 Major Angelo Paldi was born in Sardinia, Italy, in 1816, educated at the military academy at Turin, and was noted as an "experienced officer" when the Civil War broke out. In Detroit, he was an architect and draftsman, and a prewar militia officer who also painted the frescoes on the ceiling of Saints Peter and Paul Catholic Church in 1848. *Johnston's Detroit City Directory and Advertising Gazetteer of Michigan* (1861); *New York Times*, August 25, 1864; "The 5th Michigan Cavalry," *Detroit Advertiser and Tribune*, September 2, 1864, "Our Army Correspondence," *Detroit Advertiser and Tribune*, September 27, 1864.

Michigan and form his line of battle behind the crest of the hill to the left and rear of Ransom's guns. To Alger's right, Paldi held his regiment in readiness to launch a mounted charge. Atop the eminence, the Regulars sited their guns on Wofford's 1,200 Georgians as they moved under cover of brush and trees along the river and opened fire. Wofford saw the seemingly unsupported artillery and moved to capture it. He formed the 16th Georgia, 24th Georgia, and Cobb's Legion into line of battle and directed them to charge and "easily capture the guns."[28]

Wofford's Georgians charged out of the woods "with a yell like so many demons." Ransom's two guns belched canister into the Confederate ranks but failed to halt their jubilant advance up the hill. Behind the guns, Custer's Wolverines waited anxiously for the pending collision out of sight on the reverse slope of the hill. "The moment we awaited the attack," reported one trooper, "was one of the most intense suspense." As the Georgians neared the crest, Alger rode out in front of the 5th Michigan and ordered the advance. The troopers "arose from the grass as one man," trudged up the slope, and opened fire with their repeating carbines into the faces of the stunned Georgians. "For a few minutes," reported a correspondent, "there was one incessant roll of musketry." Wofford's front line staggered but soon recovered and struggled to move forward again.[29]

In preparation for the coming theatrics, Custer pressed his hat firmly to his head as he rode rapidly along the ridge under heavy rifle fire. As he dashed toward the 5th Michigan, a Confederate bullet clipped one of his golden locks, which fell to his shoulder. When he reached Alger's position, Custer "waved his hat and shouted to them to advance; the bugler sounded the advance." With an enthusiastic cheer, the dismounted troopers of the 5th Michigan charged into the ranks of Wofford's brigade, firing their Spencers with reckless abandon. One bullet plunged into Lt. Col. Edward B. Stiles of the 16th Georgia and killed him instantly. Corporal Frederick A. Pond of the 5th Michigan grabbed the staff of the 16th Georgia, but color-bearer Wave Ballard ripped the flag free and

28 Wofford's brigade contained 843 men on September 29, 1864, and lost nearly 350 men killed, wounded, and captured at Guard Hill. His ranks contained at least 1,200 men on August 16. Inspection Report for Wofford's brigade, September 29, 1864; *New York Times*, August 25, 1864; *Detroit Advertiser and Tribune*, September 2 and 27, 1864.

29 *New York Times*, August 25, 1864; *Detroit Advertiser and Tribune*, September 2 and 27, 1864; Gerald J. Smith, *One of the Most Daring of Men: The Life of Confederate General William Tatum Wofford* (Murfreesboro, TN, 1997), 129.

Lt. Horatio David of the 16th Georgia, Wofford's brigade. The young officer was wounded in the fighting at Crooked Run. *LC*

sprinted away, leaving Pond holding only the staff. As the Southerners fell back in confusion, Major Paldi's 1st Michigan stormed out from behind the hill and struck Wofford's left flank "with drawn sabers like a whirlwind." Custer and Alger "with hats off and sabers drawn, rushed up and down the ranks, exposed to a most murderous fire, cheering the men." Paldi's men "used their sabers with telling effect." One Michigan officer wrote home, "No men alive could withstand the impetuosity of such a charge. The enemy gave way, hurrying back like a great wave in the wildest confusion."[30]

The devastating onslaught of Custer's Wolverines shattered Wofford's advance. The Georgians retreated toward Crooked Run in disorder, where they attempted to make a stand on the unbloodied second line of the brigade. The 5th Michigan pursued the Southerners and "slaughtered them by the score." Major Paldi's battalion of the 1st Michigan swung around and cut the Georgians off from reaching Crooked Run. The Michiganders shot Wofford's horse out from under him, violently slamming the general to the ground. He recovered enough to flee on foot and swim across the run; however, his injuries ended his career with the Army of Northern Virginia and deprived Kershaw of a competent and experienced brigadier.[31]

30 *New York Times*, August 25, 1864; *Detroit Advertiser and Tribune*, September 2 and 27, 1864; Gerald Smith, *One of the Most Daring of Men*, 129-130.

31 Ibid.

On Custer's right flank, "Uncle Tommy" Devin's keen eye spotted Wofford's rear column maneuvering into line of battle to support their comrades who were being driven by Custer. Devin rushed Cesnola's 4th New York and three squadrons of the 6th New York into the fray. The Empire State troopers pitched into the Georgians before they could form and drove them into Crooked Run, capturing dozens of prisoners. Private Thomas Kelly snared the battle flag of the Cobb Legion infantry. In Custer's front, "[t]he enemy tried to turn our left," reported Merritt, "but they found us 'laying for them,' and we corralled them, shooting them down until they cried for mercy." Many Georgians threw down their loaded muskets and followed General Wofford to safety across the creek. Several drowned in the effort, and nearly 250 became prisoners of war. Eighty dead and wounded rebels lay in front of Merritt's position.[32]

While Merritt's horsemen finished off Wofford's infantry, Wickham renewed the cavalry action on the Federal right. He personally led the 4th Virginia Cavalry up the pike and into a gap in the Union line that was created when Devin diverted much of his strength against Wofford. Only two squadrons of the 6th New York remained concealed in a ravine west of the pike. They held their fire until the Virginians were upon them and then emptied their Spencer rifles into the Confederate horsemen at close range. The cheering New Yorkers then drew sabers and charged, driving the 4th Virginia toward Crooked Run. Wickham finally halted the retreat and rallied his routed cavaliers. "The rebel charge was led by General Wickham with great gallantry and coolness," admired one of Devin's troopers. "He was at one time within fifty feet of us."[33]

The rallied 3rd Virginia Cavalry charged shortly after Wickham attacked and encountered the 4th Virginia as it retreated. The 3rd Regiment veered off to the right and threatened the right flank and rear of the Federals still rounding up prisoners from Wofford's brigade. Custer saw the developing threat posed by Wickham's Virginians and ordered Lt. Col. Melvin Brewer's 7th Michigan Cavalry forward. Although Brewer's troopers endured a storm of iron from Johnston's horse artillery, the Wolverines drew sabers and charged the 3rd Virginia. As the Federals approached, the Virginians plainly saw Custer's flag

---

32 *New York Times*, August 25, 1864; *Detroit Advertiser and Tribune*, September 2 and 27, 1864; Gerald Smith, *One of the Most Daring of Men*, 129-130; *The Daily National Intelligencer*, August 25, 1864.

33 Hall, *History of the Sixth New York Cavalry*, 214; Hubard, UVA.

moving among the Michigan men as the yellow-haired general inspired his Wolverines.

To the left of the 3rd Virginia, Wickham rallied the 4th Virginia on the pike and charged the 6th New York, only to be repulsed again. The 7th Michigan honed in on the right flank of the 3rd Virginia, threatening to cut it off from the crossing over Crooked Run. The Virginians turned and retreated, with an unhappy Wickham galloping among them. He called out, "Halt men, halt. Where the hell are you going to? Rally 'round your general." The words had barely left Wickham's mouth when one of his troopers pointed out that the 7th Michigan was already between them and the bridge over Crooked Run. "In a twinkling," Wickham dashed off for safety with the rest of his men. The Federals pursued them briefly, but reigned in their mounts at Crooked Run when they came under the guns of the Stuart Horse Artillery. Covered by the severe and accurate artillery fire, Wickham and his men reached the safety of Guard Hill. Anderson reacted to the rout of Wofford's Georgians and the defeat of Wickham's cavalry by sending Col. James P. Simms's Georgia infantry brigade to stabilize the Confederate hold on Guard Hill and the fords. These fresh Georgians skirmished briefly with Merritt's horsemen, but did not attempt to renew the attack against the victorious U.S. horse soldiers.[34]

Tactically, Merritt had dealt Anderson a bloody repulse at Crooked Run, losing only 70 troopers in the process. However, the South Carolinian had achieved his objective when Wickham's cavalry secured the fords over the Shenandoah River and Guard Hill. Wickham's and Wofford's misguided venture beyond Guard Hill cost the Confederacy more than 300 irreplaceable veterans. "Lt. Genl. Anderson, Major Genl. Kershaw and (acting) Major Genl. Wickham all witnessed and were together responsible for the stupid, bungling way in which this fight was conducted," complained a Virginia cavalryman. At Anderson's headquarters, however, a lighter mood prevailed. Staff officers joked, "Wofford swung his right and made a water haul." Anderson explained that the repulse was due to "our troops, pushing forward with too much boldness into the open ground north of Crooked Run, were rather roughly

---

34 Simms's brigade apparently arrived sooner than Anderson indicated in his report. The 51st and 53rd Georgia lost eight wounded and eight captured in the action. Federal reports speak of a second column of infantry moving forward to support Wofford after his repulse; this was apparently Simms's brigade. Hubard, UVA; Report of Lt. General Richard A. Anderson, 1864, Fredericksburg and Spotsylvania National Military Park.

handled."[35] When Gen. Robert E. Lee read Anderson's after action report, he found little to laugh about, telling Anderson:

> I fear that at Front Royal, the enemy was too strong for the force you sent against him. I think in all cases it is the best to employ all our available force without reference to the weakness of the enemy. If we have the advantage of numbers, it renders success more certain, the loss less. I hope that you will always endeavor to bring your whole force to bear upon the enemy when possible as in that way alone can superiority of numbers be made valuable.[36]

On the Union side of the run, Col. Russell Alger, Sheridan's old comrade from his 2nd Michigan days, perched himself upon a stone wall to watch the troopers of his 5th Michigan regroup and mount their horses. Wesley Merritt trotted up to Alger and congratulated him on "the nicest fight of the season." Merritt, Custer, Devin, and their troopers received universal accolades in the wake of the battle. "Colonel Devin, who acquitted himself with conspicuous skill and gallantry," praised Merritt, "was painfully wounded in the foot, though he kept the field to the end of the battle." An officer of Custer's brigade declared, "I do not see how the Government can any longer withhold a star from Col. Devin." Colonel Kidd of the 6th Michigan praised his comrades of the 5th Michigan, "I do not believe that a single regiment, on either side, at any time during the war, performed a more brilliant deed."[37]

The engagement at Crooked Run, or Cedarville as it was alternately known, proved to be a watershed event in the Shenandoah Valley. Sheridan's cavalry proved that it could stand and fight toe-to-toe with the battle-hardened infantry of the Army of Northern Virginia. From that moment forward, Sheridan's cavalry tangled with the Confederate foot soldiers on an almost daily basis. The U.S. horse soldiers became more adept at fighting infantry with each encounter. Ultimately, this experience proved to be a decisive factor in the campaign.

With Anderson lurking menacingly at Front Royal, Sheridan promptly withdrew his headquarters from Cedar Creek to Newtown on August 16. No

---

35 Hubard, Reminiscences, UVA; Francis W. Dawson, *Reminiscences of Confederate Service, 1861-1865* (Baton Rouge: LSU Press), 121.

36 Hubard, Reminiscences, UVA; Francis W. Dawson, *Reminiscences of Confederate Service* 121; Robert E. Lee to Lt. Gen. R. H. Anderson, August 29, 1864, Gilder Lehrman Collection.

37 *New York Times*, August 25, 1864, *Detroit Advertiser and Tribune*, September 2 and 27, 1864; J. H. Kidd, *A Cavalryman with Custer*, 272.

Col. Thomas C. Devin earned his brigadier general's star on August 16, 1864, for the way he fought his cavalry at Crooked Run, one of the campaign's many engagements. *LC*

sooner had he done so than he heard the reverberations of artillery rumbling down the Valley. These thunderclaps notified the Union commander that his forces were already engaged with Anderson's troops. With most of Sheridan's army still positioned near Cedar Creek, the sounds of battle near Front Royal worried the Federal commander that Anderson might cut off his retreat to Winchester.

The engagement provided Sheridan with "absolute confirmation" of Grant's warning of Anderson's arrival in the Valley, satisfying Sheridan "with the wisdom of my withdrawal." Over on the Valley Pike, Sheridan's retreat from Cedar Creek proceeded without incident. Emory's 19th Corps arrived at Winchester at five o'clock on the morning of August 16. Emory surveyed the area's terrain and told Sheridan, "This place is entirely indefensible." The corps commander suggested "that the crossing of the Opequon is a better position." Sheridan agreed and ordered Emory to send the army's subsistence trains to Harpers Ferry with a brigade escort. The balance of Emory's force would hold itself in readiness to march at 4:00 a.m. the following morning. The 6th Corps and the Army of West Virginia would withdraw from their positions at Cedar Creek at 8:00 p.m. that same evening, leaving Lowell's cavalry to bring up the rear. Early's and Anderson's forces remained in their respective positions at Fisher's Hill and Front Royal until the next morning, August 17.

Had Merritt not slammed the door shut on Anderson at Crooked Run, the following day might have turned out quite different for Sheridan.[38]

---

38 Sheridan, *Memoirs*, 488-489; *OR* 43, pt. 1, 815.

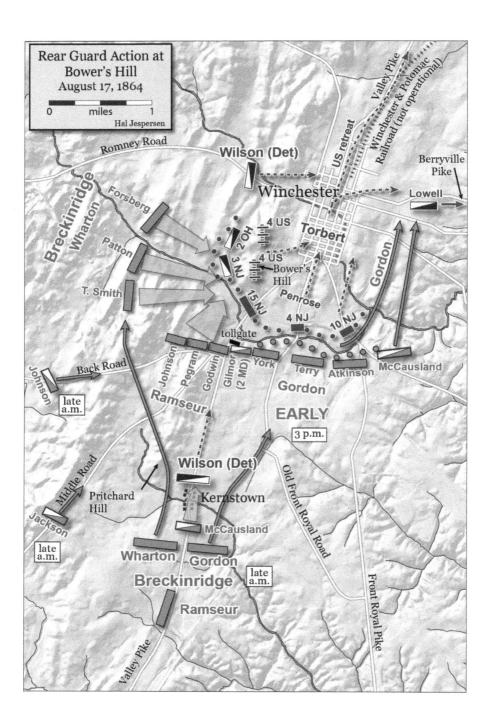

Rear Guard Action at
Bower's Hill
August 17, 1864

0   miles   1

Hal Jespersen

Romney Road

Wilson (Det)

Winchester

Valley Pike

Winchester & Potomac
Railroad (not operational)

US retreat

Berryville
Pike

Lowell

Breckinridge

Wharton

Forsberg

Patton

T. Smith

2 OH

3 NJ

4 US

4 US

Bower's
Hill

Torbert

Gordon

15 NJ

Penrose

4 NJ

10 NJ

tollgate

Johnson

Pegram

Godwin

Gilmor
(2 MD)

York

Terry

Atkinson

McCausland

Johnson

Back Road

Ramseur

Gordon

EARLY

3 p.m.

late
a.m.

Middle Road

Pritchard
Hill

Wilson (Det)

Kernstown

Old Front Royal Road

Jackson

McCausland

late
a.m.

Wharton

Gordon

late
a.m.

Breckinridge

Front Royal Pike

Ramseur

Valley Pike

Chapter 6

A BACKWARD MOVE

Confederate Resurgence, August 17 - 19

the sun rose on August 17, the Confederates discovered that Sheridan's army had vanished. Before long, they saw smoke rising from all parts of the lower Valley from the barns, hay, and wheat stacks set afire by Union cavalry. This sight inspired a stronger purpose within the Southerners, and Early promptly put his army in pursuit mode. "On both sides of the road," noted a correspondent from Early's headquarters, "flaming stores of wheat and fodder mapped out their march, and the smoke that overhung the Valley from Strasburg to Winchester was as heaven's 'black flag.'" The billowing, black pillars ushered in a new component to the Valley conflict and raised the stakes considerably. The destruction of private property signaled that the local citizenry were now directly involved in the fight.[1]

Although Anderson's arrival at Front Royal forced Sheridan to abandon his position at Strasburg, he implemented another phase of Grant's strategy for the Valley. Back in July, Grant had directed Hunter to "eat out Virginia clear and

---

1 In Civil War parlance, the term "Black Flag" represents a "take no prisoners" approach to combat, wherein prisoners would be summarily executed. Special Correspondent, "From the Valley," August 18, 1864, contained in the *Richmond Enquirer*, August 26, 1864.

clean as far as they go, so that crows flying over it for the balance of this season will have to carry their provender with them." When Sheridan took over in August, Grant passed on similar, albeit more reserved, orders regarding the Valley: "It is desirable that nothing should be left to invite the enemy to return." To that end, Sheridan now directed Torbert, "You will seize all horses, mules, and cattle that may be useful to our army. . . . No houses will be burned, and officers in charge of this delicate, but necessary duty must inform the people that the object is to make this Valley untenable for raiding parties of the rebel army." When the cavalry began the retrograde movement at 5:00 a.m. on the morning of August 17, they fanned out across the lower Valley and began the work of confiscation and desolation. "This duty, not among the most agreeable assigned to soldiers," reported General Merritt, "was thoroughly and delicately done."[2]

Newly minted Maj. Gen. Lunsford Lindsay Lomax led Early's cavalry into action for the first time on August 17. He had just replaced the ailing Maj. Gen. Robert Ransom who had been forced from active service by chronic illness. The Virginia native and 1856 West Point graduate faced a Herculean task: whip Early's Valley cavalry into shape so that it could stand up to Sheridan's well-equipped mounted legions. Lomax had served as a staff officer in the western theater for the first two years of the war and then secretly organized partisan units in the Shenandoah Valley, including Mosby's Rangers. In 1863, he became colonel of the 11th Virginia Cavalry and was promoted to brigadier general following the Gettysburg campaign. He had displayed sound judgment and solid leadership during the many cavalry encounters of the spring and summer of 1864. He quickly became popular with the men of his new command in the Valley. Major Harry Gilmor of the 2nd Maryland Battalion, C.S.A., opined, "Lomax was one of the most generous, honest-hearted men in the service, brave to a fault and he deeply felt the loss of every man; since the days of Ashby there was none I loved better."[3]

Lomax's division led the pursuit of Sheridan's army down the Valley. McCausland's 1,000-man brigade advanced down the Valley Pike. Colonel William L. Jackson's Brigade of 700 moved on the Middle Road to the west, while Brig. Gen. Bradley T. Johnson's 1,100-man command took the Back Road even farther west. The brigades of Imboden and Vaughn remained with

2   OR 43, pt. 1, 57, 440, 816; John Y. Simon, *The Papers of Ulysses S. Grant*, vol. 11, 243.

3   Warner, *Generals in Gray*, 190-191; Gilmor, *Four Years in the Saddle*, 239.

Anderson near Front Royal under the operational control of Fitz Lee. Early's infantry and artillery followed Lomax down the Valley Pike. The clash of arms began at noon when Early caught up with the Yankee rearguard at Kernstown four miles south of Winchester.[4]

Brigadier General James H. Wilson's 3,000-man cavalry division from the Army of the Potomac stood in the path of the approaching Confederates. Wilson's force joined Sheridan's army that very day. Upon Wilson's arrival at Winchester, Torbert deployed Wilson's force as the primary component of the Federal rear guard. "Harry" Wilson was an Illinois native who graduated from West Point in 1860. Several of his classmates were already participating in the Valley Campaign: Merritt and Col. James Warner as comrades and Maj. Gen. Stephen D. Ramseur in the opposing ranks. Wilson served as a topographical engineer during his brief prewar Regular Army career. When the war began, Wilson served in a variety of roles across several theaters. He was chief topographical engineer on the Port Royal expedition in 1861 and 1862, served on McClellan's staff during the Antietam campaign, and joined Grant's staff as an engineer and inspector general during the Vicksburg campaign. In the fall of 1863, Wilson was promoted to brigadier general and served on Sherman's staff at Chattanooga and then Knoxville. He served briefly as the chief of the cavalry bureau in Washington in early 1864. Grant then picked him to command the Army of the Potomac's Third Cavalry Division. Considering Wilson's complete lack of experience as a combat commander, he did reasonably well in his new role. However, he did struggle at times such as the first day of the Wilderness fighting and during the failed Wilson-Kautz Raid near Petersburg.[5]

When Wilson arrived at Winchester, he joined the rearguard assembling south of town under Torbert's direction. Sheridan bolstered the cavalry with Col. William H. Penrose's 850-man New Jersey Brigade of the Sixth Corps.[6] Torbert, the respected former commander of the Jersey men, deployed the infantry in an arc around Bower's Hill, covering all of the roads leading into Winchester from the south and west. One of Wilson's regiments went out on

4   OR 43, pt. 1, 569.

5   Warner, *Generals in Blue*, 566-567.

6   OR 43, pt. 1, 166, 172, 424; James H. Wilson, *Under the Old Flag: Recollections of Military Operations in the War for the Union, the Spanish American War, the Boxer Rebellion, etc.* (New York: D. Appleton and Company, 1912), 539; Charles R. Paul Diary, Murray J. Smith Collection, United States Army Military History Institute (hereafter USAMHI).

Col. William Penrose was the infantry commander of the New Jersey Brigade. LC

the Romney Road and from there covered the western approach. To the south, Penrose posted the 15th New Jersey in front of Bower's Hill, astride the Valley Pike on his right flank. The 10th New Jersey guarded the Front Royal Road on the brigade's left. The 4th New Jersey went into position between its sister regiments and held the center. The line extended for nearly two miles, a very long distance for such a small brigade to cover. The New Jersey men compensated by deploying in skirmish order and effectively utilizing the available cover. "Our line was well protected by the nature of the country, stone walls, & c," reported Capt. Baldwin Hufty of the 4th New Jersey. Behind the infantry, horse Battery C, 4th U.S. Artillery, unlimbered on Bower's Hill supported by two companies of the 2nd Ohio Cavalry.[7]

While the infantry deployed in the southern outskirts of Winchester, Wilson advanced a sizeable portion of his division south to Kernstown, "that village of ill omen for marauding and incendiary Yankees" in reference to Early's July 24 victory at that locale. Wilson established an advanced line and skirmished with McCausland's troopers. At the same time, Lowell's brigade was moving down the Valley toward Kernstown from Cedar Creek, burning crops and barns and driving confiscated livestock ahead of them as they went. "The infernal invaders," wrote a Confederate, "had illuminated their progress down our lovely valley with burning barns, hay ricks, and pasture fields." Spurred on

---

7 OR 43, pt. 1, 166, 172; Camille Baquet, *History of the First Brigade, New Jersey Volunteers* (Trenton: Published by the State of New Jersey, 1910), 152-153.

by the devastation they had witnessed, Lomax's Confederate cavalry caught up with a portion of Lowell's brigade between the Middle and Back roads as it wreaked havoc upon the Glass family farm. Lowell initially held off Jackson, but Johnson's Brigade flanked the Federals and drove them off, saving the Glass farm from further damage. Before the Confederates could follow up their gains, elements of Wilson's division arrived and assisted Lowell in checking their advance.[8]

Any Federal success was short lived. Breckinridge's corps arrived at Kernstown, and he deployed John Gordon's division to the right of the pike and Gabriel Wharton's to the left. Both units quickly deployed their sharpshooters who advanced rapidly, firing on the run, and forcing the Union cavalry to retreat toward Winchester. With the Union horsemen in retreat, Lomax's cavalry resumed its position in the vanguard. On the Middle and Back roads, Johnson and Jackson renewed their advance, shoving Lowell's brigade back toward Winchester. On the right, McCausland's Brigade cautiously followed Wilson's detachment down the Valley Pike.[9]

The retreating cavalrymen reached Torbert's rear guard south of Winchester at 2:00 p.m. and took position with the infantry. Wilson's men joined the waiting battle line, but Torbert sent Lowell to guard the Berryville Pike east of Winchester. By 3:00 p.m., dismounted troopers from the brigades of Jackson and Johnson were attacking the 15th New Jersey on the right of the Union line. Troopers from Johnson's Brigade seized a hill on Penrose's right flank, but the reserve line of the 15th New Jersey "advanced with a yell" and easily drove the Virginians from the eminence. The Jersey troops exchanged fire with the Southern horsemen, who made no further effort to directly assault the position for the next two hours. Fulfilling their directive, Torbert's rearguard held the Southerners at bay, which allowed Sheridan's infantry to file out of Winchester and head toward Berryville and safety.[10]

From the Union position at Bower's Hill, "large columns of the enemy could be seen moving both to our right and left, evidently forming for an attack." The situation looked ominous for the Union defenders as Jubal Early

---

8   OR 43, pt. 1, 569; Augustus Forsberg Memoir, Washington and Lee University; *The Official Military Atlas of the Civil War*, LXXXIV, 31; Bradley Johnson to wife, August 30, 1864, Bradley Johnson Papers, SHC-UNC; *Richmond Examiner*, August 26, 1864.

9   OR *Atlas*, "Attack on the Federal Outpost near Kernstown," LXXXIV, 31.

10 Charles R. Paul Diary, Murray J. Smith Collection, USAMHI.

had arrived on the scene with his infantry and was readying his troops for action. "Old Jube" acted with deliberation and made sure that his attack was delivered with overwhelming force. Jed Hotchkiss, Early's topographical engineer and the man who had mapped the Shenandoah Valley for Stonewall Jackson back in 1862, led the brigade of another engineer, Swedish-born Col. Augustus Forsberg, westward across several farm lots to the Middle Road. Forsberg's Virginians drove back Federal skirmishers on the Middle Road before sliding into position west of that stretch of track. General Breckinridge quickly reinforced Forsberg with the balance of Wharton's division, deploying his three brigades to the left of the Back Road in an arcing line that resembled a scythe poised to slice down on Torbert's right flank. In the waning daylight, the Kentuckian advanced a thick line of sharpshooters against the stiff resistance that had earlier checked Lomax.

While Breckinridge was posting Wharton on the left, Gordon was deploying his division of infantry into line of battle extending eastward from the Valley Pike to cover both the old Front Royal "Plank" Road and the Front Royal Pike, both of which fed into Winchester from the southeast. Ramseur's division arrived and slid into position between Wharton and Gordon. Lomax, in turn, shifted McCausland's brigade farther around to the right, hoping that he could gain the Berryville Pike and cut off Torbert's retreat route to the east. The battle plan seemed familiar to many Confederates, though the roles had changed among the units. Jubal Early had, in fact, used the same basic plan at Second Kernstown a few weeks earlier with devastating results.[11]

The attack began in earnest around 5:00 p.m. In the center, Ramseur advanced his division sharpshooters, but kept his main battle line concealed. On the left, Breckinridge dashed out in front of Wharton's Division and scanned the Federal position at Bower's Hill. Wearing a long pale linen duster over his uniform, Breckinridge rode back to Wharton and Forsberg. With bullets whizzing about their heads and artillery rounds bursting in the air, he calmly instructed Wharton to launch an attack en echelon. Forsberg initiated the assault on the far left, and then Col. George S. Patton's Brigade picked up the movement in the center followed by Col. Thomas Smith's Brigade on the right. On the opposite end of Early's battle line, Gordon's Division attacked about the same time as Forsberg. Once again, Early had executed a well-timed

11 *OR* 43, pt. 1, 569.

Brig. Gen. Gabriel C. Wharton graduated from the Virginia Military Institute (VMI). He fought up and down the Shenandoah throughout much of 1864, including the battle at New Market that May. LC

attack against both flanks of Torbert's rear guard while Ramseur's division remained stationary directly in front of the heavily outgunned Federals.[12]

The heaviest combat developed along Wharton's front farther west. Forsberg's sharpshooters advanced into heavy resistance from the 3rd New Jersey Cavalry and 15th New Jersey Infantry. The gunners from the 4th U.S. Artillery at Bower's Hill enfiladed the 45th and 51st Virginia of Forsberg's brigade, "which made some havoc in our ranks." Breckinridge deployed some Confederate artillery to support his advance. Nevertheless, the 4th U.S. Artillery continued to pound the Southerners, with one of them admiring how the Union battery was "beautifully served." As the attack en echelon developed, Patton and then Smith moved forward on Forsberg's right, forcing the 15th New Jersey to abandon its advanced position and take cover behind a stone wall at the base of Bower's hill. There they redeployed with the 2nd Ohio Cavalry and the 3rd New Jersey Cavalry on the right. On the left of the Federal line, Gordon's sharpshooters attacked the 10th New Jersey's left flank. Gordon's men advanced rapidly and forced the Federal regiment into a confused retreat. On the opposite end of the Confederate line, Forsberg's Brigade eventually flanked the 15th New Jersey on its right, and the entire Union battle line unraveled. A Federal cavalryman observed, "The rebels

12 Forsberg Memoir, WLU; OR 43, pt. 1, 569; Evans, *Confederate Military History*, vol. 3, 491.

gained possession of the stone wall and one-half of its brave defenders fell into their hands." Lieutenant Colonel Charles H. Tay and 150 men of the 10th New Jersey quickly became prisoners of war. The soldiers of the 4th U.S. Artillery fired "grape and canister until the guns were almost surrounded." They limbered up and started to the rear on the double quick, narrowly avoiding capture as the Southerners did not see the battery withdrawing in the "bewildering darkness."[13]

The break quickly spread to Wilson's entire division. As the stampede progressed, "thousands of excited men were rushing past and gaining shelter within the town." As the 1st Vermont Cavalry withdrew through Winchester, several residents fired from their dwellings at the New Englanders, "showing how bitter was their hate." The commander of Wilson's first brigade, Brig. Gen. John B. McIntosh, found himself without a command or staff but still remained calm amidst the chaotic night scene. He soon located Maj. A. Bayard Nettleton's battalion of the 2nd Ohio Cavalry, which had maintained good order amidst the pandemonium. McIntosh ordered the Ohioans to "protect the rear and check the enemy as long as possible, [so] that the stampeded column might have time to reform." McIntosh and Nettleton stood on the firing line with the Buckeyes "where the bullets were thickest," shouting encouragement to the men over the din of battle. By then, "Night deep and dark had settled upon the scene and both friend and foe were invisible," reported a Buckeye, "save when the deep flash of the rifle lit up the line and exposed the opposing forces for a moment to view."[14]

On the Southern left, Wharton's division entered Winchester and pursued the Northerners through the town. The Confederates felt their way through the dimly lit streets guided by the sounds of footsteps and horseshoes pounding on cobblestone. Friendly fire incidents were common, and shouts of inquiry and confusion echoed through the night. As Capt. R. C. Hoffman led men of the 30th Battalion Virginia Sharpshooters of Forsberg's brigade through town, his request for identification was answered by "the full fire of a superior force." Some Virginians of Col. Thomas Smith's Brigade pursued the retreating

---

13 "Old Po' Keepsie," Camp of Co. G, 2d Ohio Cavalry, August 23, 1864, in the *Painesville Telegraph*, September 1, 1864; Charles R. Paul Diary, Murray J. Smith Collection, USAMHI; *Richmond Enquirer*, August 16, 1864.

14 *Vermont Chronicle*, September 3, 1864; *Painesville Telegraph*, September 1, 1864; Baquet, *History of the First New Jersey Brigade*, 152; *Richmond Enquirer*, August 26, 1864.

Federals beyond Winchester and captured a battle flag from one of the New Jersey regiments. One Southerner noted that the well worn banner was "a glorious but dilapidated remnant of drygoods."[15]

On the Confederate right, Gordon's division closed in on the town from the southeast via the Front Royal Road. At the same time, Ramseur's division advanced due north down the Valley Pike. As the Confederate line neared Winchester on these converging roads, the adjoining flanks of the two Southern divisions overlapped in a dense cornfield. In the darkness, they mistook each other for the enemy and opened fire, creating chaos and confusion. Ramseur sent the cavalryman Maj. Harry Gilmor to straighten out the situation. Gordon's division subsequently shifted to the right and continued the pursuit around the east side of Winchester where it engaged McIntosh's 2nd Ohio posted upon a hill along the Berryville Pike. "Here," reported a Confederate observer, "the flashing of musketry around the slope of the night-curtained hill afforded a pyrotechnic display of no ordinary beauty." As the Federals quietly drew off into the darkness, the firing gradually subsided.[16]

Major Gilmor and Holmes Conrad, an officer from the Laurel brigade who was unaccountably in the Valley at the time, rode out into the darkness after the retreating Federals. They suddenly found themselves in the presence of 50 Union cavalrymen sitting on their mounts in the darkness. Gilmor promptly turned to a darkened stone wall that lined the road and commanded, "lay low, and [do] not fire till I give the word." There were no Confederates behind the wall, but the bold Marylander turned to the Federals and yelled, "Throw down your arms and surrender or I'll blow you to the devil." The surprised Federals complied and, fortunately for Gilmor and Holmes, a Confederate skirmish line arrived on the scene and rounded up the prisoners. Major Gilmor used the captured horses to help remount the 2nd Maryland Cavalry Battalion, C.S.A, which had been severely weakened at the Moorefield fight 10 days earlier.[17]

The soldiers of the New Jersey Brigade experienced a harrowing retreat. Confederates broke through the brigade line as it attempted to rally, splitting the

---

15 The identity of the captured battle flag was not mentioned. *Richmond Enquirer*, August 26, 1864; J. H. P., "Vermont Cavalry," August 19, 1864, to the *Vermont Chronicle*, September 3, 1864.

16 Harry Gilmor, *Four Years in the Saddle* (New York: Harper and Brothers, Publishers, 1866), 227-230.

17 *Richmond Enquirer*, August 26, 1864; Gilmor, *Four Years in the Saddle*, 229-230.

command in two. Confusion and uncertainty among the troops on both sides intensified. "It was so close and so dark," wrote Capt. Charles R. Paul of the New Jersey brigade, "that the two lines were often mixed together, at one time Col. [Edward L.] Campbell [of the 15th New Jersey] took command of a Rebel regiment for his own, and commenced reforming it." In the darkness, the opposing sides became so mixed up that some retreating New Jersey troops captured an officer from Gordon's staff. The officer warned the Federals that they were surrounded and urged them to surrender. The Jersey men "did not see it in that light," and Captain Paul led 200 men to safety eastward via the Berryville Pike. Colonel Penrose escaped through the north end of Winchester with the rest of the survivors by following the Martinsburg Pike. "It has been a bad day for our brigade," complained Paul to his diary, "but I suppose we have accomplished all that was expected of us, namely delaying the enemy." Initial reports placed casualties at 450, but many of the missing men eventually showed up. The Confederates only claimed the capture of 250 men. Losses in the Confederate ranks numbered approximately 100 killed and wounded, along with a few prisoners lost in the darkness.[18]

The stiff resistance of the New Jersey Brigade on August 17 prompted Early to inform Robert E. Lee that the Valley Army had engaged two divisions from the Sixth Corps instead of a single small brigade. This report validated the opinion of Captain Paul, who mused, "I think the rebs will feel cheap when they find they employed all of one of their corps (Breckinridge's) to dislodge a skirmish line of 800 men."[19]

Over at Front Royal, Anderson had likewise roused his men out of camp at an early hour that morning and moved northward. Those not already at Guard Hill crossed the Shenandoah and marched down the Front Royal and Winchester Turnpike toward Winchester. Anderson's hopes for an attack on Sheridan's flank or rear had been dashed by Merritt's victory at Crooked Run on the previous day. Instead, Anderson conducted a relatively routine pursuit of Merritt's division. The mounted brigades of Imboden and Col. Onslow Bean led the columns down the Front Royal and Winchester Pike, skirmishing sporadically with a detachment that Merritt had left behind to slow the Confederate advance while his main force burned out the Valley's resources

18 Charles R. Paul Diary, Murray J. Smith Collection, USAMHI; *OR* 43, pt. 1, 168, 176, 569; *Richmond Enquirer*, August 26, 1864.

19 *OR* 43, pt. 1, 552; Charles R. Paul Diary, Murray J. Smith Collection, USAMHI.

during the retreat. Consequently, Anderson's force played no role in the day's events.[20]

Kershaw's division halted for the night around Parkin's Mill on Opequon Creek a few miles southeast of Winchester on the Front Royal Pike. Fitz Lee's cavalry command, which temporarily included Imboden and Bean's brigades, followed Merritt eastward to White Post 10 miles south of Berryville before turning toward Winchester and riding six miles to rejoin Anderson at Parkin's Mill. Although the Confederate forces had shoved Sheridan back toward the Potomac River, they lamented that "the opportunity for striking a blow was lost."[21]

Like so many times before, the residents of Winchester experienced a day of fear and hopeful expectation. Once again, Union troops taunted them with the prospect of burning the town as they passed through in retreat. "Three companies of Chambersburgh men are coming," chided some stragglers. An Ohio soldier asked one woman if she remembered his regiment from 1863. She did not but asked him why he had returned. "To burn the town," he retorted. Relief finally came to Winchester's secessionists when Early's army drove the Federal rear guard through the town in confusion. "Thank God we are safe once more," exalted Mrs. Hugh Lee. Major Henry Kyd Douglas of Ramseur's staff galloped up the street and stopped at her house where he received a hearty welcome. Mrs. Lee placed bright lanterns in her front windows and stood on her porch and waved to Lomax's passing Confederate cavalry. The horsemen cheered her as she handed out food and supplies to the passing troopers.[22]

August 18 brought even more pleasure to most of Winchester's residents as the Southern army occupied the town in daylight. Confederate officers of all ranks congregated at Mrs. Lee's house. The dedicated Southern patriot served home-cooked meals to soldiers and officers throughout the day. Fitz Lee, Lunsford Lomax, and their staff officers enjoyed a scrumptious breakfast. That evening, Generals Breckinridge and Gordon and their families joined a number of local officers and filled the parlor of the Lee house. The band of the Louisiana Tiger Brigade serenaded the crowd. "We dined very late, and I did

20 "Official Diary First Corps," J. William Jones, ed., *SHSP*, vol. 7, 503-512; James D. Ferguson Diary, Duke University; Maj. Gen. Fitzhugh Lee, Report of Operations 1864, MOC.

21 "Official Diary First Corps," J. William Jones, ed., *SHSP*, vol. 7, 503-12; James D. Ferguson Diary, Duke University; Maj. Gen. Fitzhugh Lee, Report of Operations 1864, MOC.

22 Mrs. Hugh Lee Diary, WFCHS, Handley Library.

not have a moment's time to rest the whole day," recorded Mrs. Lee. It was a welcome but all too brief respite from the anguish of war. Her spirits rose higher when the officers assured her that "the army moves tomorrow, burning with vengeance on the Yankees for the terrible devastation which has marked their progress."[23]

Not everyone in Winchester was happy to see Early's Confederate army arrive. It was business as usual for the town's tiny Unionist minority. "The same thing has taken place today that we always see. Our army never advances in the Shenandoah Valley but to take a backward move," complained Julia Chase. This was the fourth time in 1864 alone that the Union forces had gone up the Shenandoah Valley only to return well short of victory. Unlike the previous three attempts, Phil Sheridan managed his retrograde movement without any serious side effects to the overall Union cause there. For Unionists in Winchester, that provided little consolation once the Confederate forces moved into town and oppression began anew for Winchester's remaining loyalist families.[24]

In the midst of a steady rain that fell on August 18, Early deployed his divisions to cover the northern and eastern approaches to Winchester. Anderson marched a few easy miles north from his bivouac at Parkin's Mill to the Millwood Pike and encamped on the southeastern outskirts of Winchester. For the most part, however, Early allowed his troops to rest. On August 19, "a fine day, slight showers," as recorded by one atmospheric observer, Early shifted his forces 10 miles northward on the Valley Pike and deployed his infantry around the familiar hamlet of Bunker Hill, West Virginia. Lomax advanced his troopers to Martinsburg and Shepherdstown without incident. Aside from some minor cavalry scrapes along the Opequon, the situation remained relatively quiet for two days. Anderson and Fitz Lee's force remained in position at Winchester, maintaining its status as an independent command. Interestingly, Early's departure from Winchester marked the first of several occasions when Early relocated his forces immediately after Anderson joined him in the same general area. Both Early and Anderson seemed satisfied to cooperate with each other at a distance.[25]

23 Ibid.

24 Mahon, *Winchester Divided*, 164.

25 OR 43, pt. 1, 1,024.

After the rearguard action at Winchester on August 17, Sheridan had deployed his cavalry along the same line east of Opequon Creek that he had used during the previous week's advance. Wilson's division held Summit Point at its northern extreme while Merritt guarded Berryville to the south, with both commands picketing the roads crossing the creek. The infantry occupied a position farther to the rear and about two and a half miles west of Charlestown. While Jubal Early did not closely follow Sheridan, Mosby struck again outside of Berryville.[26]

Mosby's troopers had been prowling around the edge of Sheridan's army since it arrived in the vicinity of Berryville and Charlestown. One of Mosby's rangers came across a lone Union soldier skinning a stolen sheep he had just slaughtered. The ranger shot the Federal, severed a hoof from the dead animal, and crammed it in the soldier's mouth. Before leaving the scene, the ranger scrawled a hasty note and left it on the Federal's lifeless body. It read, "I reckon you got enough sheep now." This was only the first incident in an escalating rear area war between Mosby and the Union cavalry. On the night of August 18, Mosby roused his men from the camps along the Blue Ridge near Snickers Gap and rode west, crossing the Shenandoah River at Castleman's Ferry. He divided his command into several detachments. Captain A. E. "Dolly" Richards led Company B toward Charlestown while Mosby struck out with Company A for the road between Charlestown and Harpers Ferry. It was on the turnpike to Berryville, however, that Capt. William H. "Sam" Chapman with Companies C, D, and E initiated an action that came to typify the level of vehemence and animosity exhibited in the Valley in 1864.[27]

Four troopers from Col. Russell Alger's 5th Michigan Cavalry of Custer's brigade stood a lonely sentinel on the Berryville and Snickers Gap Pike on that moonlit night. Chapman and his men emerged from the darkness to the east dressed in civilian garb and Union blue and struck up a conversation with Corp. Alpheus Day. What happened next became a point of contention. According to the consistent Michigan accounts, Chapman gunned Day down in cold blood, although Mosby's man later denied it. The details mattered little as young Day lay lifeless on the ground in a pool of blood, another casualty of the heartless

26 Ibid., 44.

27 Wert, *Mosby's Rangers*, 195; James Joseph Williamson, *Mosby's Rangers: A Record of the Operations of the Forty-Third Battalion Virginia Cavalry* (New York, 1896), 211-213; William J. Miller, "Demons That Day," *Civil War: The Magazine of the Civil War Society*, December 1996, 47.

business of war. One hour later, a group of Mosby's men clad in blue uniforms fired at Pvt. John Connell of the 5th Michigan, wounding him in the hand. The remaining two pickets were taken prisoner, but escaped later that night into a ravine along the side of the Blue Ridge. Connell made it back to 5th Michigan's camp and sounded the alarm. Colonel Russell Alger deployed a skirmish line to reinforce his picket posts. The attacks on the Union sentinels persisted throughout the night. "Bushwhackers," as the Michigan men termed Mosby's partisans, were "continually creeping up and 'blazing away.'" The Michigan men promptly scattered into the darkness and took up hiding places of their own behind trees and among buildings, and, as one trooper noted, the Rangers' "fun is played out."[28]

Alger reported the incident to Custer the next morning. The commander immediately ordered retaliatory actions. He believed that local "citizen bushwhackers under Mosby" had carried out the attack, and he directed his vengeance against them. Custer ordered Alger to burn four houses "nearest to the post on which the men of your command were killed or lost." Alger's only constraint was "being careful that the occupant is not a loyal man." To send a firm message to the populace of Berryville and Clarke County, Custer added that Alger should "choose residences of considerable value" to make an impression upon the people. "Inform the inhabitants of this vicinity that this is done in retaliation for the men lost from my command," expounded Custer, "and that in the future for every man killed, wounded, or missing, I will burn a house of some prominent secessionist living in the vicinity of the outrage."[29]

Alger assigned the task to Capt. George Drake who led 50 men to carry out Custer's orders. Drake immediately burned three of the four homes selected and then led a small detachment to set the final house ablaze. The balance of his command waited on the narrow Sheppard's Mill Road near the already burning home of Benjamin Morgan. A few miles away, Captain Chapman and his pack of rangers were lurking near Castleman's Ferry on the Shenandoah River. When he saw the black smoke billowing in the western sky, he galloped toward its source and found one of the homes ablaze. The unfortunate inhabitants told

28 Ibid., 47-48; A. Bugler, "The 5th Michigan Cavalry," *Detroit Advertiser and Tribune*, September 2, 1864, and September 27, 1864; G. F. Williams, "More About the Massacre by Mosby: Rebel Treachery-Cowardly Cruelty," *New York Times*, August 25, 1864.

29 George C. Custer to Russell Alger, August 19, 1864, William L. Clements Library, University of Michigan.

Chapman of Custer's warning to the local population, sending the partisan officer into frenzy. He immediately brought up his command and headed toward Alger's unsuspecting Michigan troopers. Along the way, the Rangers passed another burning house and outbuildings where a heartbroken mother and her children stood crying in the rain. The sight moved Irish-born Ranger John F. Lynn to solemnly declare, "Jasus [sic], if that wouldn't make a man fight, I don't know what would."[30]

Chapman's 200 Rangers rode down the country road toward Benjamin Morgan's burning house where Lt. James Allen and the larger portion of the burning detail waited for Drake to return from firing the last house. Clothed in blue uniforms and rubber ponchos that concealed their identity, the Rangers closely approached Allen's detachment without raising any suspicion. Chapman achieved the element of surprise by moving at a walk and imitating one of the many Union detachments patrolling the area. He suddenly ordered a charge, bellowing, "Wipe them from the face of the earth! No quarter! No Quarter! Take no prisoners!" Allen saw the charge coming and attempted to wheel into line to meet it, but it was too late. The Rangers were upon them, one officer shouting, "Shoot the damn Yankee son-of-a bitch!"[31]

The Michigan troops turned and raced up the road toward Berryville but found their route blocked by a barricade that their pickets had erected. The barrier was so effective that horsemen could only pass by one at a time. Hemmed in by the barricade and numerous stone fences that were too high to jump, the trapped Michigan men were struck by the pursuing Confederates who mercilessly began cutting them down. True to Chapman's word, the Rangers took no prisoners and showed no mercy. Fourteen were killed outright and two were left for dead. Many were shot after they had surrendered, some with the very pistols they had just turned over to the Rangers. When the clash ended, the Rangers went back over the field and finished off any Federals who were still breathing. Nevertheless, two severely wounded troopers survived, one only long enough to tell his tale. The other eventually recovered but he bore a lifelong scar on his face, a constant reminder of that terrible day in Virginia.[32]

---

30 Miller, "Demons That Day," 49-50; Williamson, *Mosby's Rangers*, 215.

31 Wert, *Mosby's Rangers*, 196; Miller, "Demons that Day," 50-51.

32 Ibid., 52, 54; *Detroit Advertiser and Tribune*, September 2, 1864; *New York Times*, August 25, 1864.

Within 15 minutes of the attack, Alger had the entire 5th Michigan scouring the countryside for the perpetrators. The Rangers had vanished and were nowhere to be found. When Custer learned of the barbarity against his command, he ordered Alger to take the 5th and 6th Michigan cavalry regiments and burn the homes and barns of "the most prominent secessionist in that county." This time Custer cautioned Alger to "use every precaution against surprise, allowing no small parties to become detached from the main body." Alger willingly carried out the assignment and declared that "he will never bring another of Mosby's men alive into camp."[33]

As for Mosby himself, he saw little, if anything, wrong with what had occurred. He proudly reported to General Lee that his men had "shot to death" about twenty-five Federals and that "no quarter was shown." The tragic incident deeply impacted the men of the Michigan Brigade, and "cast a gloom over the whole command," observed one trooper. "In every heart burns an undying hatred, a desire for revenge," he wrote, "which only the blood of Mosby and his gang alone can satisfy." Sheridan reacted by ordering the arrest of "all able-bodied male citizens under the age of fifty who may be suspected of aiding, assisting, or belonging to guerrilla bands now infesting the country." For the most part, however, he remained focused on the larger campaign and did not allow Mosby's side show to become a distraction.

As tragic as this event was, it had little impact on the overall campaign in the Shenandoah Valley. Sheridan's army would continue withdrawing toward Harpers Ferry, and Jubal Early's army would soon stir from its camps and look for an opening to attack.[34]

---

33 George Custer to Russell Alger, August 19, 1864, William L. Clements Library, University of Michigan; *Detroit Advertiser and Tribune*, September 27, 1864.

34 *OR* 43, pt. 1, 634, 843; *Detroit Advertiser and Tribune*, September 27, 1864.

EARLY IS DOWN UPON US LIKE MAD

Confederate Charlestown Offensive, August 21

Robert E. Lee expected Richard H. Anderson and Jubal Early to cooperate for the good of the Confederate cause. However, Lee never intended for Early and Anderson to operate together in the Shenandoah Valley. Rather, Lee anticipated Anderson campaigning independently east of the Blue Ridge to complement Early's efforts in the Valley. Despite the Army of Northern Virginia's objective, subsequent events carried Anderson into the Shenandoah and created a potentially unwieldy command situation. Anderson was the senior officer of the pair, and so entitled to overall command. On the other hand, Early was in the midst of a very successful campaign that dated back to the middle of June at Lynchburg. When Early raised the topic of Anderson's seniority, Lee replied that he anticipated "no difficulty on that score." The personal history between the two generals indicated otherwise.[1]

Anderson and Early had feuded openly during the battle of Cold Harbor after Early requested Anderson's support for an unauthorized assault on the

1   OR 42, pt. 1, 1,006.

Federal lines. "This attack I cannot make without running over your troops," Early informed Anderson. The irascible Early went on to insinuate that Anderson had failed to obey a direct order from Lee to attack. Anderson retorted, "I have not, however, a high appreciation of your judgment and decline to be guided by it." He added, "I am sorry to see that a consciousness of the folly which you repeated on yesterday of sacrificing some eighty or a hundred of your men to obtain a little information, which added nothing to what was already known has put you in bad humor." To his credit Early reached out to Anderson to smooth over the contentious situation. The South Carolinian acknowledged Early's contrition and closed his response by stating, "Be assured that my private feelings will not be permitted ever to interfere with my public duty." The true nature of their subsequent relationship was about to be put to the test in the Shenandoah Valley.[2]

Jubal Early envisioned a grand offensive against Sheridan's army at Charlestown commencing on August 21. Like an angry thunderstorm blowing in from the west, the Confederate forces would roll eastward on a front nearly 17 miles wide along Opequon Creek. He informed Anderson of his intentions and suggested that the senior general act in concert, taking care not to offend the South Carolinian's sensibilities. Under this plan, Confederate forces would advance across the wide front upon several roads that converged on Charlestown. On the southern end, Maj. Gen. Fitzhugh Lee's cavalry division would ride out of Winchester along the Berryville Road toward its namesake town. Anderson's column would follow the Old Charlestown Road which ran east from the Valley Pike at a point three miles north of Winchester. Early's main force would march from Bunker Hill at sunrise headed for the Opequon crossing near the village of Smithfield. Lomax's cavalry division, having advanced toward Martinsburg two days previously, would head east toward Charlestown via Leetown, covering Early's left flank. With 20,000 men in the combined ranks of Early and Anderson, these movements were to be made "with the design of bringing on a general engagement."[3]

Sheridan's army, now increased to a "battle strength" of 23,000 infantry and 8,000 cavalry, occupied a defensive position to the west and south of

---

2 Correspondence between Gens. R. H. Anderson and J. A. Early, June 8, 1864, in the *Cincinnati Daily Commercial*, March 31, 1865.

3 OR 43, pt. 1, 569-570; Maj. General Fitzhugh Lee, Report of Operations 1864, MOC; E. R. Goggin to L. L. Lomax, September 27, 1867, Chicago Historical Society.

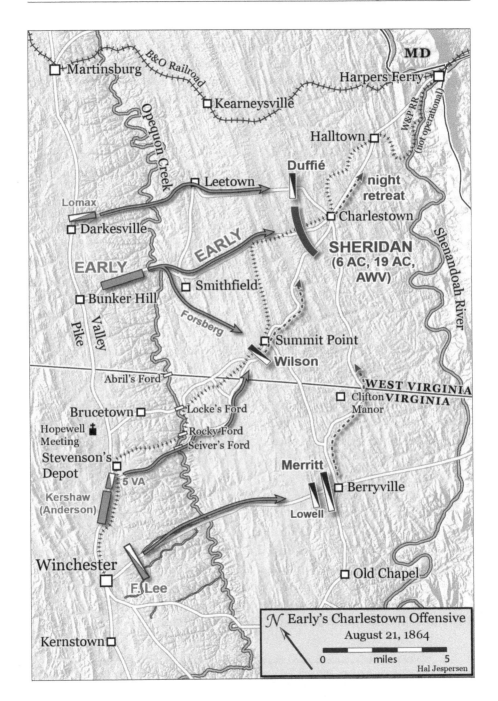

Martinsburg

B&O Railroad

Kearneysville

MD

Harpers Ferry

Halltown

W&P RR (not operational)

Leetown

Duffié

night retreat

Lomax

Opequon Creek

Charlestown

Darkesville

EARLY

SHERIDAN
(6 AC, 19 AC, AWV)

Shenandoah River

EARLY

Smithfield

Bunker Hill

Valley Pike

Forsberg

Summit Point

Wilson

Abril's Ford

WEST VIRGINIA
Clifton VIRGINIA
Manor

Brucetown

Locke's Ford

Hopewell
Meeting

Rocky Ford
Seiver's Ford

Stevenson's
Depot

Merritt

5 VA

Berryville

Kershaw
(Anderson)

Lowell

Winchester

F. Lee

Old Chapel

Kernstown

N Early's Charlestown Offensive
August 21, 1864

0   miles   5
Hal Jespersen

Charlestown. The Sixth Corps occupied a position near Flowing Spring two miles west of the town, covering the Smithfield Road. Emory's Nineteenth Corps held the pike that ran between Berryville and Charlestown about two miles southwest of the latter locale. Crook's Army of West Virginia deployed on Emory's left completing the infantry line. Torbert's cavalry held advanced positions to screen enemy approaches. Merritt's division remained at Berryville on the army's left, and Wilson was at Summit Point on the right. Both cavalry commands sent pickets out to Opequon Creek to watch all the crossings from Smithfield to the Berryville Pike.[4]

By 5:00 a.m., Jubal Early had the Second Corps and Wharton's division marching out of their camps at Bunker Hill and following the Smithfield Road toward Opequon Creek. The march continued without interruption until the column reached the covered wooden bridge that spanned the Opequon, which takes the dimensions of a small river by this point in its journey toward the Potomac River. At the bridge, the Confederates met 30 troopers of the 22nd New York Cavalry commanded by Lt. George Sperry; the lieutenant was tasked with picket duty that quiet Sunday morning as his first independent assignment. His commander had recently asked the New Yorker to serve as the regimental adjutant. The lieutenant refused on the grounds that he had promised his company that he would "fight the thing out with them." The commander looked at Sperry with a wry smile "having so much hell in it" and said, "Well Lieutenant, by God, you shall have your belly full." As a result, Sperry soon found his small command stationed at the Smithfield bridge with Jubal Early's Army of the Valley District bearing down on them. The New Yorkers put up a good fight, but the Confederates soon flanked their position in both directions.

Making matters worse, Brig. Gen. John McCausland's cavalry was moving northward from its position at Locke's Ford east of Brucetown and now threatened to cut the New Yorkers off from their reserves. Sperry's company was nearly surrounded as they sprinted back to the village of Smithfield under a cross fire. Sergeant H. C. Hammond later remembered that "we all got our 'bellies full,' some of us with chunks of cold lead thrown in." The New Yorkers joined their picket reserves in the village only to race down the Summit Point Road to rejoin Wilson's division, followed by a portion of McCausland's

---

4 "Battle strength" excludes detailed men and officers. It would be fewer than the regularly reported "present for duty" strength. Early typically used the term "muskets" when referring to his combat strength. When his present for duty was in the 10,000-man range, he typically reported it at approximately 8,500 muskets. Sheridan, *Memoirs*, 490-491.

brigade. The New Yorker's retreat along the Summit Point Road left the direct road to Charlestown wide open. McCausland's primary command rode out in front of Early's column and screened the Confederate advance toward Charlestown. Unsure of Anderson's whereabouts, Early sent Col. Augustus Forsberg's brigade to support McCausland's detachment in pursuit of the New Yorkers. Early also directed Forsberg to protect the army's rear and its wagon trains from Wilson's cavalry, which was operating only a few miles south of the Smithfield Pike.[5]

Anderson's column had more distance to cover than Early. The South Carolinian marched his force down the Valley Pike from Winchester until they reached the Old Charlestown Road, which they followed to Opequon Creek. At 8:00 a.m., Lt. Col. James H. Allen's 5th Virginia Cavalry led the way, driving pickets from the 3rd New Jersey Cavalry away from Seiver's Ford on the Opequon. The pickets scurried back toward Summit Point. "The Point," as the soldiers called it, was located about three miles west of Sheridan's main lines outside of Charlestown. The hamlet was centered around a depot on the Winchester and Potomac Railroad, a spur line of track that splintered off from the B & O at Harpers Ferry.[6]

Although the day was overcast, the sun "shone warmly" through the clouds, creating a "damp and very sultry day." At first, it did not appear as if there would be much action that day. Trooper Roger Hannaford of the 2nd Ohio Cavalry recalled, "Everything early in the morning betokened the Sabbath, quite still." Although his regiment had been ordered to relieve the 3rd New Jersey on the picket line at sunset, no one—from their commander Lt. Col. George Purington on down to the company cooks—"seemed to be in a hurry." Instead, the Ohioans "were generally shaving and cleaning up." Many had "been out foraging and luxuriated on mutton, chickens, green corn, potatoes, coffee and bread with a goodly supply of fresh milk."[7]

The relaxed scene abruptly ended when couriers brought word that the Confederates were advancing from Winchester. The Buckeyes sprang into their saddles as Brig. Gen. John B. McIntosh ordered Purington to advance the 2nd Ohio to the assistance of the retreating 3rd New Jersey. Soon after, Wilson

5 OR 43, pt. 1, 570; Joseph G. Snider Diary, WVU; H. C. Hammond, Historical Address of Serg't Maj. H. C. Hammond (Bainbridge, NY, 1995), 19.

6 Taylor, *Sketchbook*, 230-236.

7 Old Po'Keepsie, "2nd Ohio Cavalry," *Painesville Telegraph*, September 1, 1864.

ordered McIntosh to advance the balance of his brigade to a slight ridge about one-half mile west of its present position near Summit Point. Arriving at the designated place, McIntosh's troopers dismounted, hastily constructed some rail fortifications, and waited for whatever was coming their way.[8]

Purington's 2nd Ohio had not gone far when it encountered the retreating 3rd New Jersey Cavalry. The "Butterflies," as the Jersey men were known because of their golden-laced Hussar uniforms, were deployed on the road and to its left. Falling back slowly, they were "making a good fight" with their recently issued Spencer carbines. Seeing their hard-pressed comrades, the Ohioans trotted into the field on the right side of the road, dismounted, and rushed forward to take cover behind a rail fence. Major General Joseph B. Kershaw's skirmish line was only 25 yards away, and his main line of battle only 50 yards beyond that. These lines extended as far as the dismounted troopers could see in either direction. The Ohioans fired into the approaching Southerners and held the fence only long enough to cover the withdrawal of the 3rd New Jersey on their left. Then they dashed back to their horses and fell back toward Summit Point to join McIntosh's main line.[9]

By 10:00 a.m., Kershaw's infantry had arrived in front of McIntosh's brigade. The Southerners moved out of some woods and into the open field in front of the Union horsemen and "flaunted their miserable flag into our faces," recalled a New York soldier. The Confederates opened fire and attempted to force McIntosh's position, but the U.S. horse soldiers held firm. The Southerners charged, and the dozen guns belonging to Capt. La Rhett L. Livingston's U.S. horse artillery raked them with iron and "sent them 'kiting' to the woods again." Anderson did not deploy the artillery of Cutshaw's battalion to counter the Union gunners at this time, so Livingston's men fired without challenge. Undaunted, Kershaw redeployed his infantry and struck McIntosh simultaneously on both flanks. The Southerners let loose with the shrill Rebel Yell and defiantly waved their "blood red" battle flags as they trudged ahead. A few hearty Union troopers remained behind their rail breastworks until the Confederate infantry reached them, but most headed to the rear in great haste. The mounted portion of the 3rd New Jersey, which was supposed to have covered the retreat, broke first. Overwhelmed by Kershaw's foot soldiers,

---

8   OR 43, pt. 1, 516; Taylor, 230-236; G. F. Williams, "Battle at Summit Point," *New York Times*, August 24, 1864; Old Po'Keepsie, "2nd Ohio Cavalry," *Painesville Telegraph*.

9   Roger Hannaford, Reminiscences, Cincinnati Historical Society.

McIntosh's brigade fell back rapidly and in confusion to Summit Point. There Livingston's batteries held their position and fired canister into the approaching Confederates, compelling Kershaw's infantry to halt and consolidate its position. At Wilson's order, Brig. Gen. George Chapman dismounted his brigade and supported the artillery. Kershaw's Confederate sharpshooters attempted to force the position but were unable to make headway against Chapman and Livingston.[10]

Anderson soon received help from an unexpected direction. Forsberg's brigade, sent by Early to support McCausland's detachment, now arrived in the vicinity of Summit Point. The Swede had followed a country road leading from Smithfield to Summit Point until he encountered McCausland's detachment "making feeble resistance" to elements of Wilson's division. The Federals had taken position in some woods, requiring Forsberg to halt his brigade on the left side of the road behind a crest. He advanced his sharpshooters to clear the way, and Forsberg's Virginians promptly "scoured the woods and drove out in the open field a considerable number of mounted and dismounted Feds." Without hesitation, Forsberg followed them toward Summit Point, where he arrived about the same time that Livingston's batteries and Chapman's brigade checked Anderson's progress. The Swedish colonel's sharp eye quickly spied one of Livingston's six-gun batteries unlimbering and going into action against Anderson. Forsberg's sharpshooters advanced toward the battery's right flank, prompting its speedy withdrawal followed by Chapman's cavalry "in considerable confusion." Forsberg remained at Summit Point for two hours until he was certain that Wilson's cavalry would not return. With Wilson falling back to Charlestown and the pathway cleared for Anderson to renew his advance, Forsberg returned to Smithfield to guard the trains and camp for the night. The time was only 3:30 p.m., and several hours of daylight remained for Anderson to cover the five miles between Summit Point and Early's position west of Charlestown.[11]

Simultaneously with the infantry's advance, the Confederate cavalry moved forward on both flanks of the Confederate advance. Fitzhugh Lee's Virginians rode east on the Berryville Pike and reached the Opequon at 10:30 a.m. Lee's

10 Beadry, *History of the 5th New York Cavalry*, 165; *Painesville Telegraph*, September 1, 1864; Taylor, *Sketchbook*, 230-232; Early, *Memoir of the Last Year*, 74; Official Diary First Corps, August 21, 1864.

11 Augustus Forsberg Memoir, Washington and Lee University.

troopers advanced slowly against determined resistance from Col. Charles R. Lowell's brigade of Merritt's division throughout the morning. In the early afternoon, Sheridan began pulling the cavalry closer to Berryville, leaving Lowell to cover the rear. Lee's Virginians saw the withdrawal and charged, throwing a large portion of Lowell's command into confusion. He attempted to regroup his command on a ridge west of the town. There, Lt. Col. Andrew Greenfield's 22nd Pennsylvania Cavalry stood waiting in line of battle, and Lowell ordered them into the fray. "[We] charged into woods . . . let the 1st Maryland [U.S.A] go through us, and then went up on a gallop with raised sabers," recalled one Pennsylvania trooper. "When we came within thirty yards of the enemy, every man stopped and opened fire with carbine and revolver." For a few minutes, men fell rapidly on both sides, but the Pennsylvanians soon forced the Confederates to withdraw.[12]

The Southerners were not defeated, however, and had only fallen back to regroup. Fitz Lee deployed Maj. James Breathed's Stuart Horse Artillery beyond the sight of the Federals. When their mounted comrades were driven from the woods by the 22nd Pennsylvania, the Southern horse gunners opened fire and quickly knocked Greenfield's troopers out of the woods. Once again, the Virginia cavalry charged forward and occupied the vacated position among the trees. Lowell dismounted the 2nd Massachusetts Cavalry and 22nd Pennsylvania Cavalry on the left and right sides of the Berryville Pike respectively, and the two regiments charged ahead dismounted. The Bay Staters seized an old redoubt in their front, and the Pennsylvanians drove the Virginians from the woods a second time. "The fight at this point," recalled a member of the 22nd Pennsylvania Cavalry after the war, "was very severe, much of it at unpleasantly close quarters." By this time, Lowell had accomplished his mission as General Merritt had safely moved off with the balance of the division. Soon thereafter, Lowell quietly abandoned his position and headed north to Charlestown. Once there, the brigade took up another defensive position southeast of town behind Bullskin Run near Rippon. The Confederates were content to let the Union horsemen slip away unmolested. By

---

12 James D. Ferguson Diary, Duke; The Second Mass and Its Fighting Californians: The Diary of Valorus Dearborn, a copy of which is in the possession of the author; OR 43, pt. 1, 874; Samuel Clarke Farrar, *The Twenty-Second Pennsylvania Cavalry and the Ringgold Battalion* (Pittsburgh, 1911), 340-341.

the time Lee entered Berryville, it was sunset and active operations ceased for the day.[13]

On the northern flank of the Confederate front, Lomax headed east from Martinsburg, passing through the hamlet of Leetown, which was named for the disgraced Revolutionary War General Charles Lee.[14] At Leetown, Lomax turned eastward and moved toward Charlestown. He came in on the extreme left flank of the Confederate front and encountered opposition from the 900-man Federal cavalry division of Brig. Gen. Alfred N. Duffie. This command had attempted to rejoin the army on August 14 at Middletown, but a close inspection by Torbert and his medical staff sent the division back to Berryville as "unfit for active service, the Surgeon's report being adverse." Having been returned quickly to active duty more out of necessity than any significant improvement in the command's condition, Duffie's division now held the right (northern) flank of Sheridan's battle line. Perhaps it was thought this position would place Duffie's worn troopers out of harm's way; however, Lomax's horsemen were bearing down the Leetown-Charlestown Road with more than double the Frenchman's strength.[15]

Major Harry Gilmor and his two small Maryland battalions of Brig. Gen. Bradley Johnson's brigade spearheaded Lomax's drive up the Leetown-Charlestown Road. The combat commenced when Gilmor's troopers ran into stiff resistance from Duffie's division. The Marylander promptly requested reinforcements, which Lomax provided in the form of two Virginia regiments from Col. William L. "Mudwall" Jackson's brigade. Gilmor dismounted the Virginians, armed primarily with Enfield rifles, in some woods on the northern side of the road while keeping his own Marylanders as a mounted reserve. Elements of Duffie's division charged the Confederates posted among the trees, but the Virginians opened fire and threw their attackers into confusion.

13 OR 43, pt. 1, 486; The Second Mass and Its Fighting Californians: The Diary of Valorus Dearborn; Farrar, *The Twenty-Second Pennsylvania*, 340-341; James D. Ferguson Diary, Duke.

14 Charles Lee lived out his life on a nearby farm after George Washington relieved him of command during the battle of Monmouth in 1778.

15 This area of Virginia might be described as a sort of haven of sorts for discomfited Continental Army generals. In addition to Lee, Horatio Gates, disgraced on the battlefield at Camden, South Carolina, in 1780, and Adam Stephen, relieved of command after the battle in Germantown, Pennsylvania, in 1777 for supposed drunkenness, all resided within a few miles of one another. OR 43, pt. 1, 570; Gilmor, *Four Years in the Saddle*, 231; William B. Tibbits, Report of Service, National Archives.

The two mounted Maryland battalions saw the opportunity at hand and promptly attacked, driving Duffie's troopers back upon their reserves near Charlestown. Stirred by Gilmor's success, Lomax dashed over to the major and shouted, "Well done, Gilmor, well done." Gilmor continued to spar with Duffie's troopers on the north side of the road as the combat diminished to a routine skirmish, with neither side gaining any appreciable advantage. On Gilmor's right flank, Lomax deployed the rest of his division on the south side of the road, where his troopers skirmished with infantry pickets on the right flank of the Union Sixth Corps.[16]

Shortly before Lomax confronted Duffie, Jubal Early's troops appeared in front of the Sixth Corps on the Charlestown Pike. His command had rapidly covered the five miles between Smithfield and Sheridan's lines west of Charlestown. By 9:30 a.m., McCausland attacked the Sixth Corps's picket line at Cameron Depot, rousing its veterans to action. When McCausland's horsemen detected Sheridan's infantry, Early turned the advance over to Maj. Gen. Robert E. Rodes's division. McCausland sidled his command to the left, screened that area, and linked with Lomax to the north. At Cameron Depot, Rodes's division sharpshooters, commanded by Col. Hamilton A. Brown of the 1st North Carolina Infantry, quickly pounced upon the Sixth Corps's picket line. Brown's sharpshooters quietly slipped into position and relieved McCausland's horsemen. They took careful aim, picked a specific target, and then coolly delivered a steady and accurate rifle fire into the Union skirmishers. Under this sudden and lethal fire, the Federal pickets sprinted back to their camps.[17]

The fusillade from the Confederate sharpshooters surprised the Sixth Corps veterans that quiet Sunday morning. "Early is down upon us like mad," declared the surgeon of the 77th New York. The Federals had just readied for the usual Sunday inspection when the gunfire erupted on the picket line. Drummers beat the long roll and the troops struck their tents and fell into line of battle to await orders. Wright had previously posted Brig. Gen. David A. Russell's division on the right (north) side of the Smithfield Pike and Brig. Gen. George W. Getty's division to the left (south). Getty, a native of Washington, D.C., was an experienced division commander and Mexican War veteran who graduated from West Point in 1840. He began the Civil War as an artillery

16 Gilmor, *Four Years*, 232.

17 OR 43, pt. 1, 570; *New York Times*, August 24, 1864; Fred L. Ray, *Shock Troops of the Confederacy: The Sharpshooter Battalions of the Army of Northern Virginia* (Asheville, NC, 2006), 176.

Maj. Gen. Robert E. Rodes
LC

commander during the Peninsula and Antietam campaigns until he was
promoted to brigadier general and commanded a Ninth Corps division at
Fredericksburg. Serving in obscure actions such as Longstreet's siege of
Suffolk, Virginia, and a diversionary movement to the South Anna River during
the Gettysburg campaign, Getty did not make his mark until Grant's Overland
campaign. He proved his competence in the Wilderness and at Spotsylvania,
displaying a tenacity as a combat commander that was often lacking in the Army

Brig. Gen. George Washington Getty
LC

of the Potomac. His performance on August 21, 1864 at Charlestown proved no different.[18]

18 James M. Greiner, Janet L. Coryell, and James R. Smither, editors, *A Surgeon's Civil War: The Letters and Diary of Daniel M. Holt, M.D.* (Kent, OH: 1994), 239; Warner, *Generals in Blue*, 170-171.

Convinced by the suddenness of the attack that a full-scale assault was in the offing, Getty galloped into the woods overlooking the original picket line and into the camp of the Vermont brigade. Getty instructed its commander, Brig. Gen. Lewis A. Grant, to "move out at once and reestablish the picket line." At once, Grant deployed three regiments as skirmishers in the field immediately west of the woods "and dashed rapidly forward while the other regiments followed in line of battle." Grant's skirmishers advanced up a gently sloping hill covered by a cornfield that concealed Rodes's sharpshooters. The two sides exchanged volleys before the Vermonters plunged into the corn driving back the Confederates who "clambered over the fence at the further side of the field and vanished beyond the hill."[19]

Over on the north side of the Smithfield Pike, Russell quickly went to work restoring his picket lines where Lomax's dismounted troopers had broken through. He summoned the 2nd Rhode Island and 37th Massachusetts from Col. Oliver Edwards's brigade for the job. The Bay State soldiers had recently been armed with the Spencer repeating rifle, which carried eight rounds and could be loaded without having to leave cover. Edwards's men were eager to try their new armaments in action, and Early's appearance at Charlestown provided them that opportunity. Edwards "judiciously posted" his two regiments in a sunken road that dominated an open meadow in its front. "Almost immediately," recalled a Massachusetts soldier, "the spiteful crack of the Spencer rifle began to be heard." In its first field test with the Bay State soldiers, the rifle "grandly" achieved "the expectations which had been raised." The Confederates brought up two batteries to drive off the Union skirmishers, but the long range firing of the Spencers prompted the Southern artillery to withdraw to a safer position. In what would soon become a fairly common occurrence on several battlefields before the war ended, Sheridan galloped along the firing line of the Sixth Corps at Charlestown, scanning enemy positions and encouraging his soldiers. The general soon rode off as quickly as he appeared, but skirmishing continued. The troops dug in and prepared for the expected battle.[20]

---

19 Walker, *The Vermont Brigade*, 60-61.

20 Oliver Edwards, "Memorandum," Illinois Historical Society, 189; J. B. S., "From Sheridan's Army," *Daily True Delta*, September 10, 1864; James L. Bowen, *History of the Thirty-Seventh Regiment Mass. Volunteers in the Civil War of 1861-1865* (Holyoke, MA, 1884), 372-373.

Meanwhile, the action had continued unabated back on Getty's front. After the Vermonters passed through the cornfield, the brigade's right wing halted on the slight rise beyond. On the left, however, several regiments pressed on recklessly toward the main Confederate line "with more enthusiasm than discretion." Getty saw the overzealous Vermont men and rode after them. He was successful in stopping their advance before they blundered into the main Confederate line; however, the general almost paid the ultimate price. A Confederate sharpshooter barely missed his mark, killing the general's horse and forcing him to continue the battle on foot. The Vermonters withdrew and dug in on the ridge where their wiser comrades had halted. There they hastily gathered fence rails to fashion "feeble breastworks and scraped out hiding places in the sandy soil." Rodes did not allow the Federals to get too comfortable in their new position. He promptly reinforced his sharpshooters with the entire 43rd North Carolina, and advanced toward the waiting Federals in a formation that betokened modern combat. "The enemy attacked us from behind trees, ridges, fences, and walls with a force that could not be clearly made out," recalled Maj. Aldace F. Walker of the 11th Vermont.[21]

As the Confederate divisions arrived at Cameron Depot, Jubal Early promptly positioned them along his developing line. Ramseur's division arrived and went into position on Rodes's right flank. His sharpshooters suddenly found themselves engaged in a substantial encounter after they advanced and extended the line nearly to the Summit Point Road to the south. When Breckinridge reached the battlefield, Early massed his divisions along the Smithfield Pike behind Rodes. Gordon's division deployed to the right and Wharton to the left of that road. At some point, Gordon apparently deployed sharpshooters to the firing line as a few of his men were captured during the back and forth skirmish battles that flared along the lines that day.

Wright responded quickly to Ramseur's deployment by moving Brig. Gen. James B. Ricketts's Sixth Corps division from the reserve into position on Getty's left. As the skirmishing intensified, Getty reinforced Grant's Vermont troops with several regiments. The 61st Pennsylvania and 7th Maine from Brig. Gen. Daniel Bidwell's brigade went in on Grant's left. Four companies from the 93rd Pennsylvania of Brig. Gen. Frank Wheaton's brigade reinforced the line

---

21 Walker, *The Vermont Brigade*, 62-63.

near the Smithfield Pike. Two of these companies deployed in and around a house just south of that road, taking cover and battling the Confederates.[22]

As the skirmishing escalated, Getty stood near the Packett house, lamenting to another officer that his favorite horse had been shot out from under him. As the two men spoke, a Confederate bullet whistled between them. Although it was his second brush with death that day, Getty calmly said, "That came pretty near you, Major," in a "quiet and deliberate" tone. He then directed Maj. Aldace Walker to deploy some of his Vermonters in the Packett house, a stout brick structure atop a knoll on the left of Grant's line. However, several young ladies still occupied the house. Although they were warned to leave, the women "were overcome by the perversity of fear and . . . insisted upon taking refuge in the cellar." They remained there until the Confederates brought up artillery and began battering the house, which sent them scampering toward Charlestown in a panic.[23]

The firing of the Confederate sharpshooters was incredibly accurate. In addition to two near-misses on Getty, they also shot the horse out from under Grant, the commander of the Vermont brigade. Anything in blue that moved on the battlefield was fair game. Dr. Melvin John Hyde, surgeon for the 2nd Vermont, was moving along the front line, tending to the wounded and supervising their removal from the battlefield on stretchers. As Hyde made his rounds, he spotted the 11th Vermont "laying flat on their faces, the corn being literally cut off about three feet from the ground by the minié balls," whizzing barely over their prostrate forms. As the doctor assisted some medical orderlies, a bullet shot off the top of his hat. Moments later, a stretcher bearer seemingly stumbled forward and "fell headlong over the stretcher" dropping the wounded man to the ground. Hyde initially thought that the clumsy orderly had stumbled but quickly realized "that he was shot through the head, his brains being spattered all over the stretcher." Although the combat at Charlestown was primarily a high intensity skirmish, the casualty rates among the Federals highlighted the lethal effectiveness of the Confederate sharpshooter battalions.[24]

22 Fred R. Laubach Diary, Civil War Misc. Collection, USAMHI.

23 Walker, *The Vermont Brigade*, 64.

24 Geraldine F. Chittick, ed., *In the Field: Doctor Melvin John Hyde, Surgeon, 2nd Vermont Volunteers* (Newport, VT: n.d.), 105-106.

The intensity of the engagement across such a wide front prompted Sheridan to prepare for a full scale battle. He instructed Torbert to draw in Merritt's division from Berryville to shore up his southern flank. At noon, the little general from Ohio transferred a division of the Nineteenth Corps to shore up the right flank where elements of the Sixth Corps and Duffie's cavalry were confronting Lomax. Early desperately wanted to attack, but delayed initiating the engagement at Charlestown pending Anderson's anticipated arrival with Kershaw's infantry and Cutshaw's artillery. Anderson, however, never came, and Early did not attack. After driving Wilson from Summit Point, Anderson's force simply went into camp for the night at 3:30 p.m. although several hours of daylight remained. As a result, any opportunity that Early might have had to strike Sheridan at an advantage was lost. However, success was by no means assured as Sheridan had concentrated his army at Charlestown.[25]

Late that afternoon, the tempo of fighting increased on the northern sector of the battlefield where Lomax and Duffie confronted each other. The Frenchman attempted to maneuver one of his small brigades around Maj. Harry Gilmor's command that was holding the Confederate left flank on the Leetown Road. When Lomax learned of this, he cried, "For God's sake, Gilmor, don't let them turn your left flank; I am hard pressed myself by a heavy line of infantry skirmishers." Major Gilmor quickly shifted the 19th and 20th Virginia farther to the left in "a splendid position in a belt of woods." His Marylanders deployed in a cornfield beyond the trees, where they were hidden from Federal view behind a small hill. Before long, Col. William Bell's 12th Pennsylvania Cavalry charged and slashed through Gilmor's dismounted Virginians. Although the Southerners shot Bell, his adjutant, and 30 or so Pennsylvanians from their saddles, about 50 Union troopers broke through the dismounted Virginians. The Pennsylvanians' success was short-lived, however, as the Marylanders counter-charged and captured the 12th Pennsylvania's battle flag. Gilmor and his troopers attempted to pursue the beaten Federals back to their main line, but "as soon as he showed himself, every gun opened on him at short range." Gilmor withdrew the regiment as "it would have been useless slaughter," and the action slackened as the sun began to set.[26]

25 Early, *Last Year of the War*, 74.

26 Gilmor, *Four Years in the Saddle*, 234-235; Larry B. Maier, *Leather & Steel: The 12th Pennsylvania Cavalry in the Civil War* (Shippensburg, PA, 2001), 205-206; *National Tribune*, January 17, 1901.

August 21 had begun as a day with the potential for Jubal Early and Dick Anderson to combine forces and achieve a stunning victory over Sheridan as his army withdrew through the open ground of the northern Shenandoah Valley. However, reluctance on the part of both men to properly coordinate their movements and communicate effectively doomed any potential breakthrough from the beginning. Early simply advised Anderson of the Second Corps's intended operations and left Anderson to act in concert as the Carolinian saw fit. For his part, Anderson moved slowly in the combat at Summit Point and finally drove Wilson from his last position with the help of Forsberg's brigade from Early's column. Then Anderson failed to pursue Wilson to Charlestown and join Early in front of Sheridan's army. It was simply a harbinger of things to come as the Early-Anderson joint operations were concerned, and the situation did not improve.

Although no formal battle was fought on August 21 at Charlestown, the severe skirmishing and artillery fire exacted significant losses. Rodes lost 160 men killed or wounded, and the Sixth Corps endured the loss of 275 soldiers.[27] Sheridan assessed his situation at Charlestown and deemed his position "a very bad one" in the broader context of the campaign. He decided that, "As there is much depending on this army, I fell back and took up a new position in front of Halltown." Halltown sat four miles west of Harpers Ferry in the center of a peninsula formed by the Potomac and Shenandoah Rivers. The Halltown line offered Sheridan the ability to anchor each flank upon a river and placed his army in an excellent position to threaten Early's rear should he attempt to invade the North again. Starting at 10:00 p.m. on August 21, Sheridan withdrew his infantry from Charlestown. His soldiers marched through the town with only a "struggling moonlight" guiding their way through the partly overcast night. Once the infantry had withdrawn to Halltown, Sheridan withdrew Merritt and Wilson, posting them on his right where they could quickly respond to any Confederate attempt to cross the Potomac into western Maryland.[28]

Sheridan's withdrawal to Halltown was well received by the Confederates and impacted their assessment of the Ohioan's military ability. One confident Southern staff officer mused, "We will soon be in condition to resume the

27 OR 43, pt. 1, 19, 155-6, 570-1; *New York Times*, August 24, 1861.

28 OR 43, pt. 1, 19, 44, 156, 440, 516.

offensive again and start Sheridan on the track so well beaten by Banks, Fremont, Shields, Milroy, and Crooks and Co."[29]

The residents of Charlestown endured much suffering during the Civil War since their strongly secessionist town spent most of the conflict behind Union lines. Most recently, Maj. Gen. David Hunter had burned the home of his cousin, Andrew Hunter, who prosecuted John Brown for his fateful Harpers Ferry raid. After Sheridan withdrew, the town's residents came out in droves to welcome the Confederate forces. A Georgian from Rodes's division called the town "one of the greatest little places in the South." "Everything that the people could do to cheer, encourage or comfort the soldiers they did with no hesitancy whatever," related Joseph J. Felder. "It seemed to be a pleasure rather than a task to wait on or help a rebble Soldier in any way."[30]

At that time, Sheridan's withdrawal to Harpers Ferry appeared to be part of a deterioration of overall Union military fortunes in the late summer of 1864. While Sheridan and Early maneuvered in the Valley, Grant had continued his operations against the Weldon Railroad near Petersburg, attempting to sever Robert E. Lee's supply lines and preventing Lee from further reinforcing Early. These costly operations (Grant lost more than 4,200 men) secured a lodgment on the railroad and resulted in the recall of Wade Hampton's division, which had been en route to the Shenandoah at the time. An examination of Confederates captured by Grant around Richmond and Petersburg revealed that only Kershaw and Fitz Lee had gone to the Valley with Anderson. At the same time, Grant also wanted to assure Maj. Gen. William T. Sherman that no reinforcements from Lee would head south to assist Lt. Gen. John B. Hood in the defense of Atlanta. After winning several major victories in late July, Sherman's campaign slowed down. Atlanta was still in Southern hands and Hood's Army of Tennessee was still in the field and dangerous. As such, Grant continued his operations against Petersburg, but his situation continued to deteriorate. Within a week, he lost another 2,600 men when Maj. Gen. Winfield S. Hancock's battle-scarred remnant of the Second Corps collapsed at the battle of Reams Station. In the wake of recent disasters such as Burnside's failure in the battle of the Crater and the Confederate burning of Chambersburg, Halleck

---

29 J. Hotchkiss to Wife, August 18, 1864, JDH Papers, LC.

30 Joseph Jackson Felder to Dear Pa, August 19, 1864, GDAH.

Col. Norton P. Chipman served as the Federal War Department's observer in the Shenandoah Valley in 1864. LC

grew concerned about the course of Grant's overall operations and advised "taking in sail and not going too fast."[31]

Politics also loomed large in the Valley operations. Secretary of War Edwin Stanton's admonition about the political importance of Sheridan's operations echoed in the Irishman's ears. His withdrawal to Halltown raised the possibility of a renewed Rebel incursion across the Potomac River. Stanton worried whether the river crossings were adequately covered and had Col. Norton Chipman working aggressively to see that they were. Sheridan recalled, "It was generally expected that the reinforced Confederate army would again cross the Potomac, ravage Maryland and Pennsylvania, and possibly capture Washington." Such a crossing would not have bothered Sheridan in the least. He saw Early's striking northward across the Potomac as an opportunity for the Army of the Shenandoah to finally trap and destroy the Southerners. Although Sheridan "left everything [open] in that direction for them," Early did not cross, nor did the U.S. commander believe that he would.[32]

While Sheridan maneuvered the Army of the Shenandoah, Colonel Chipman had remained in theater, monitoring the situation for Stanton. Chipman gleaned information from Sheridan's subordinates, including Brig. Gens. John D. Stevenson at Harpers Ferry and William Averell. The latter had inaccurately informed Chipman that one of Fitz Lee's brigades had entered Martinsburg on August 19, accompanied by Harry Gilmor. Averell added that

---

31 Grant, *Memoirs*, 617-618; Noah Andre Trudeau, *The Last Citadel, Petersburg, Virginia, June 1864-April 1865* (New York: Little, Brown, 1991), 146, 152.

32 OR 43, pt. 1, 20, 880-881.

"Fitz Lee's cavalry was to cross at Shepherdstown and look after Averell." In truth, Fitz Lee was engaged in reconnaissance duties along the Winchester and Berryville Pike at that time. The information alarmed Stanton, creating concern that another Confederate incursion loomed north of the Potomac. Two days later, Averell added, again inaccurately, that Breckinridge's command had been in Martinsburg with Lee. Chipman would remain in the Valley until the end of August, his presence a visible reminder of the political importance of Sheridan's operations and the continued high-level skepticism of his appointment to such an important command. It was, as Wilson noted, a "season of doubt."[33]

33 Ibid., 858; James H. Wilson, *Under the Old Flag*, 1:540.

GIVE THE ENEMY NO REST

Halltown to Kearneysville, August 22 - 25

Military campaigns in the United States of America are fought at the direction of the duly elected political leadership. As such, politics played a major role in every campaign of the Civil War. Major General Philip H. Sheridan's campaign in the Shenandoah Valley was no exception. In fact, his army's proximity to Washington and the recent Union failures in that region only heightened the political impact upon Sheridan's operations. With direct responsibility for the defense of the national capital and the Potomac River crossings, the political consequences of Sheridan's actions in the Shenandoah assumed an importance that went well beyond their actual military significance.

In August 1864, President Lincoln's political prospects looked gloomy, and Sheridan's initial operations in the Shenandoah Valley had done nothing to improve them. The national chairman of the Republican Party informed Lincoln that if the election were held then, he would lose the crucial electoral votes from New York, Pennsylvania, and even his home state of Illinois. The news only confirmed what the president had long suspected. Some Republicans had actively sought a candidate to replace Lincoln or run against him on an alternative Unionist ticket. At the time, the radical Republicans had already nominated John C. Fremont to run against Lincoln in November under the banner of the Radical Democracy Party.[1] The latter move would all but ensure victory for the Democratic Party. As a result, Lincoln penned the following note to his cabinet:

Executive Mansion, August 23, 1864

This morning, as for some days past, it seems exceedingly probable that this Administration will not be reelected. Then it will be my duty to cooperate with the President-elect, as to save the Union between the election and the inauguration; as he will have secured his election on such ground that he cannot possibly save it afterwards.[2]

When the cabinet convened later that day, Lincoln folded the paper just enough to conceal the message and asked each member to endorse it without reading the hidden note. All signed without any objection. As dire as the situation seemed to Lincoln at that moment, timely Union victories in the right places could quickly rejuvenate Lincoln's electoral chances. Sheridan and his army happened to be in one of those key areas and, accordingly, held a large degree of influence in Lincoln's political fate.

From a purely military perspective, Sheridan handled his army deftly during his first two weeks at its helm. From a public relations standpoint, however, all that mattered was that Union forces in the Shenandoah Valley had once again failed as they had done throughout the war. When Sheridan's army reached the Halltown line on the outskirts of Harpers Ferry, pundits christened his force the "Harper's Weekly" because of its numerous retreats to that locale upon the heels of failed campaigns that summer. From a broader political perspective, Sheridan's test run down the Valley did nothing to improve President Lincoln's electoral prospects. Still, unlike the most recent excursions up the Valley,

1 The radical Republicans nominated Fremont in May at the Cleveland Convention. He would remain a candidate until September, when Lincoln placated them by removing the troublesome Montgomery Blair from his position as postmaster general. H. C. Phillips to Abraham Lincoln, August 20, 1864, Lincoln Papers, LC.

2 Abraham Lincoln, "Memorandum Concerning his Probable Failure of Re-election, August 23, 1864," in Lincoln, *The Collected Works of Abraham Lincoln* (Rutgers University Press, 1990), vol. 7, 514.

Sheridan avoided the defeats and acute embarrassments incurred by his predecessors.[3]

On the bright side, Sheridan's operations gained several advantages for the Union from a military perspective. His strong position at Halltown was virtually unassailable and strategically located. If Jubal Early wanted to cross the Potomac River, he could not do so without exposing his lines of retreat to Sheridan's army, which now numbered 40,000 men with the arrival of divisions under William Averell, Alfred Duffie, Cuvier Grover, and James Wilson. In contrast, Anderson's and Early's combined Confederate forces numbered only about half that figure. Still, Lt. Gen. Ulysses S. Grant believed the Confederates in the Valley were too strong for Sheridan to attack. With that mindset, Sheridan adopted a cautious "wait and see" strategy: he would remain vigilant until Early or Anderson sent troops back to Gen. Robert E. Lee at Petersburg before initiating any offensive operations. Ultimately, the cornerstone of Sheridan's entire operation hinged upon the departure of Confederates from the Valley. This course of action, initially proposed by Grant, was heartily approved by Secretary of War Edwin Stanton. With Maj. Gen. William T. Sherman inching closer to victory at Atlanta, the Lincoln administration feared another embarrassing setback in the Shenandoah region. Overarching political considerations shackled Sheridan's operational flexibility.

Sheridan cautiously deployed his army in its strong position around Halltown. George Crook's Army of West Virginia anchored the left, William Emory's Nineteenth Corps manned the center, and Horatio Wright's Sixth Corps held the right. Fatigue details immediately went to work, strengthening the lines. "We have been fortifying all day," observed one soldier, "and now have a line of works extending from the Shenandoah to the Potomac. . . . They are still building new works and improving the old." Colonel Charles R. Lowell's cavalry brigade patrolled the army's left flank, located on the Shenandoah River near Key's Ferry. Wilson's troopers formed on the right of the infantry above Halltown. Wesley Merritt's division took an advanced position near Shepherdstown and guarded Boteler's Ford. Duffie's small worn-out division crossed into Maryland at Point of Rocks and covered the lower Potomac crossings in Sheridan's rear. Averell's division guarded the fords of the upper Potomac near Williamsport, Maryland. With the army's

3 Aldace F. Walker, *The Vermont Brigade in the Shenandoah Valley 1864* (Burlington, VT: The Free Press Association, 1869), 28; *OR* 43, pt. 1, 19-21, 893.

Lt. Col. James Comly of the 23rd Ohio Infantry, 1st Brigade, Second Division, Gen. George Crook's Army of West Virginia.
R. B. Hayes Presidential Center

unprecedented strength and vigilance, a repeat of prior embarrassments in the Valley seemed unlikely.[4]

Sheridan now focused his efforts to learn the precise size and composition of the reinforcements that recently joined Jubal Early in the Valley. The Union army leader commenced a series of small-scale probing attacks against the Confederate lines in front of Halltown to determine which Rebel units confronted him. Sheridan assigned most of these efforts to Maj. Gen. George Crook's quick-hitting Army of West Virginia. Colonel Rutherford B. Hayes launched the first sortie early on the evening of August 22. About 6:00 p.m., the 23rd and 36th Ohio infantry regiments, together with the 5th West Virginia, sallied out of the woods and surprised a portion of Maj. Gen. Stephen D. Ramseur's skirmish line. Hayes's Westerners captured 20 Tar Heels and killed or wounded as many more. The Federals returned to their lines as swiftly as they had departed with only three men wounded. These brisk limited actions were not only tactically successful, but they also raised the morale of Sheridan's soldiers. Lieutenant Colonel James Comly of the 23rd Ohio confirmed as much when he later explained, "The men have not only not lost confidence, but have gained steadily, and are now ready

---

4   OR *Atlas*, 69:1-2; OR 43, pt. 1, 45; Ezra Walker Diary, USAMHI.

to do anything Sheridan and Crook may order. . . . Troops know when they are properly handled."[5]

The prisoners from Ramseur's division reaffirmed the presence of Lt. Gen. James Longstreet's (Anderson's) entire corps in the Shenandoah Valley. Sheridan doubted the story, as he suspected that only one division from Longstreet had come to Early's aid. Unfortunately, Federal scouts dressed as Confederates returned from Winchester and clouded the Union intelligence by likewise reporting the presence of Longstreet's entire corps. Brigadier General William W. Averell added to the confusion when he estimated Early's entire force at 30,800. He further reported that Maj. Gen. Charles W. Field's Confederate division was moving along the eastern base of the Blue Ridge Mountains. Moreover, rumors circulated that Maj. Gen. George Pickett's division entered the Valley as well. Grant, however, reassured Sheridan that the divisions of both Field and Pickett remained at Petersburg, but faulty information continued to filter back to the Irish general. "These various reports are embarrassing," complained Sheridan, "I have pursued a cautious policy and [act] on the defensive."[6]

On August 24, Sheridan tested Early's lines again. This time, seven regiments from Crook's infantry, four squadrons of Lowell's cavalry, and a detachment from the Nineteenth Corps carried out the mission. The objective was the capture of Ramseur's skirmish line posted 800 yards from the opposing Federals. The Southern skirmish line consisted of rail pens situated "in an open field, with a belt of woods on the right and left, and a large corn field in [the] rear." At noon, three West Virginia regiments from Col. Joseph Thoburn's division feigned an attack in front of the Confederates to grab their attention. At the same time, division commander Col. Isaac Duval advanced Col. Daniel D. Johnson's brigade on the left of Crook's line. The advance drove the Virginia sharpshooters of Brig. Gen. John Pegram's brigade back into the cornfield upon their reserves. Johnson's Ohioans and West Virginians fired furiously and shoved the Virginians back another 200 yards. The Union brigade turned to the right and rolled up Ramseur's entire skirmish line, driving them in confusion

5 OR 43, pt. 1, 399; James Comly Diary, RBHPC; "From The Valley," *Richmond Sentinel*, September 5, 1864.

6 Lieutenant General James Longstreet's First Corps was under the temporary command of Richard H. Anderson because Longstreet was severely wounded in the battle of the Wilderness on May 6, 1864, and was still routinely referred to as "Longstreet's Corps" by both Union and Confederate reports. OR 43, pt. 1, 19-20, 905.

toward Charlestown. As the Rebel skirmish line crumbled, troopers from Lowell's 2nd Massachusetts and Maj. Henry Myer's 22nd Pennsylvania Cavalry charged, captured a handful of prisoners, and created additional confusion among the Southerners.[7]

Major General Robert E. Rodes saw the developing break in the lines and rushed the 14th North Carolina from Brig. Gen. William R. Cox's brigade and a battery to Ramseur's assistance. The 14th North Carolina arrived on the scene and fired into the flank of Johnson's brigade, while the battery opened an enfilading fire from a commanding woodlot. Crook's artillery commander, Capt. Henry A. DuPont, retaliated with a dozen guns from Battery B, 5th U.S., and Battery D, 1st Pennsylvania, forcing the Confederate guns to withdraw after a 20-minute duel. With nothing more to be gained but further bloodshed, Crook withdrew his forces as his orders were to avoid a general engagement. The Union forces lost 50 soldiers killed and wounded in this small action, but captured 30 Confederates and a small herd of beef cattle. Ezra L. Walker of the 116th Ohio had observed the engagement from the protection of the Union works. "I do not know when I have seen so exciting a scene," recorded Walker. "The fight lasted about half-an-hour and resulted in our advancing our skirmish line 300 yards."[8]

Major General William H. Emory conducted a similar but smaller effort in front of the Nineteenth Corps and found the Southerners posted in strength. After Duval pulled Johnson back to the main Union line, Crook, DuPont, and Sheridan scanned the ground through their field glasses and discussed the situation. Suddenly, Lt. Col. James Comly of the 23rd Ohio excitedly galloped into their midst. The agitated officer dismounted, saluted Crook, and warned, "General, there is a brigade of the enemy in that ravine, right under the guns of Capt. DuPont's Battery. They are waiting to make an attack on our picket line!" In Comly's haste, he failed to recognize that the "little man" talking to Crook was General Sheridan. The commanding general promptly whirled around, stared sharply at Comly, and burst out, "What's that you say, Sir? Who are you?" Comly's first encounter with the fiery Ohioan proved awkward; however, some

7 "From the Upper Potomac," *Washington Daily National Intelligencer*, OR 43, pt. 1, 360, 399-400, 408-409.

8 Ibid., 399-400, 408-409; W. T. Patterson, "From the 116th Regiment, August 27, 1864," *Athens Messenger*, September 8, 1864; John V. Young to Dear Wife, August 26, 1864, WVU; Ezra L. Walker Diary, USAMHI.

kind words and a compliment from Crook smoothed things over. Sheridan verified the report and ordered DuPont to open fire. The artillery pinned the Southerners in the ravine for several hours before they could safely escape.[9]

Later that evening, Sheridan sifted through reports garnered from the day's actions. He learned that Rodes's and Ramseur's divisions were performing picket duty in front of the Union line at Halltown while Early kept the rest of his forces at Charlestown. The captured Southerners universally declared that two First Corps divisions had reached the Shenandoah Valley but disagreed as to whether Longstreet commanded them in person. Sheridan concluded that Early could not maintain his current advanced position nor could he cross into Maryland without exposing his line of retreat. Sheridan determined that Early "does not know what to do." Sheridan wired Grant, "I will commence operations seriously with the cavalry to-morrow." He instructed Torbert to launch a cavalry reconnaissance in force toward Leetown with Merritt's and Wilson's divisions that would hopefully draw Fitz Lee's cavalry into a fight.[10]

On August 25, Sheridan's operations and command decisions received the blessing of the War Department's man on the scene, Col. Norton Chipman. He told Stanton that Sheridan "showed no trepidation" when Anderson appeared at Front Royal "and at his leisure took up the retrograde down the Valley." Chipman noted that Sheridan guarded both flanks zealously and "at no time has it been possible for the enemy to have passed through the Blue Ridge for Washington, or to the right and into Pennsylvania without General Sheridan being almost immediately apprised of it." He continued, "Sheridan's army is in splendid condition, well in hand and manifesting the greatest anxiety for a fight. There is a feeling of entire confidence in their leader, and regiments talk about being able to whip brigades. Sheridan really has a very fine army here, and the universal good spirits that prevail and anxiety to fight manifested would make it a hard army to compete with." Chipman added, "Sheridan will begin from this time to harass them, and cannot fail to inflict severe punishment before they leave the Valley."[11]

Torbert's horse soldiers delivered the first dosage of harassment that very day. Coincidentally, Early had planned a movement of the Second Corps

9   James Comly Diary, RBHPC.

10 *OR* 43, pt. 1, 43, 440, 889, 898, 902, 908.

11 Ibid., 906-907.

toward the Potomac River that brought on a meeting engagement between the Union cavalry and Rebel infantry. Jubal ordered his commanders to have their troops ready to march for Shepherdstown on the Potomac River at sunrise. Anderson agreed to hold the line in front of Charlestown with Kershaw's infantry, Cutshaw's artillery, and two cavalry brigades. The operation entailed a great deal of risk for Anderson who confronted Sheridan's entire force of infantry with less than 6,000 men. As planned, Kershaw's division relieved Rodes and Ramseur at sunrise. The latter commands then followed Maj. Gen. John C. Breckinridge's corps, which had marched west toward Leetown. There, the column turned northward and followed the road to Shepherdstown. Fitz Lee simultaneously led several mounted brigades from both his own and Lomax's divisions toward Williamsport, Maryland, on the Potomac River "in order to keep up the fear of an invasion of Maryland and Pennsylvania."[12]

Torbert's divisions rode along parallel roads that joined at Walper's Crossroads, four miles southwest of Shepherdstown. There, Wilson's division joined Merritt and followed him southward to the hamlet of Kearneysville where the Baltimore and Ohio Railroad crossed the road leading from Leetown to Shepherdstown. Merritt's advance had scarcely passed the tracks when they encountered Col. William L. "Mudwall" Jackson's Confederate cavalry brigade riding through some thick woods in advance of Early's army. A cousin of the immortal Stonewall Jackson, "Mudwall" had received his name in "contradistinction" to his famous kinsman. Upon making contact with the Virginians, Merritt immediately dismounted Custer's and Cesnola's (Devin's) brigades and deployed the horse soldiers in a field to the right of the road. One observer wrote, "Custer's brigade opened the ball with great spirit (the way Custer always fights)," driving Jackson's Virginians from the woods. Beyond the trees, Early's infantry marched toward the unsuspecting Federal horse soldiers, who expected to fight the Southern cavalry. Neither side had anticipated a direct confrontation that day, but with such large forces moving through the limited countryside, a meeting engagement was inevitable.[13]

12 Ibid., 1,006; Report of Gen. R. H. Anderson, 1864 Valley Campaign, FSNMP, "Maj. Gen. Fitzhugh Lee, Report of the Operations," 1864, MOC; E. R. Goggin to L. L. Lomax, Sept. 27, 1867, Chicago Historical Society (hereafter ChHS).

13 Colonel Luigi de Cesnola was filling in for Devin, who was recuperating from wounds received at Crooked Run on August 16. Official Diary First Corps, *SHSP*, vol. 7, 509; *OR* 43, pt. 1, 425, 517; *Vermont Chronicle*, September 10, 1864; "Army Correspondence," *Detroit Advertiser & Tribune*, September 27, 1864.

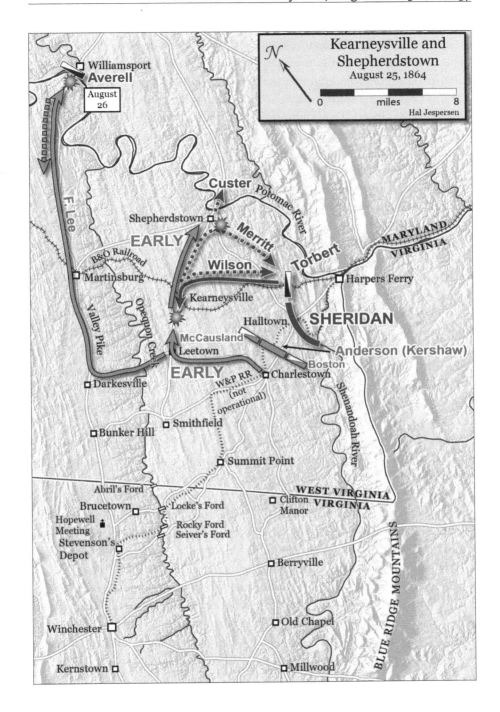

Kearneysville and
Shepherdstown
August 25, 1864

0   miles   8

Hal Jespersen

Williamsport
Averell

August
26

Potomac River

Custer

Shepherdstown

Merritt

EARLY

B&O Railroad

Torbert

MARYLAND
VIRGINIA

Wilson

Martinsburg

Harpers Ferry

Kearneysville

Valley Pike

Opequon Creek

Halltown

SHERIDAN

McCausland
Leetown

EARLY

Boston

Anderson (Kershaw)

W&P RR
(not
operational)

Charlestown

Darkesville

Shenandoah River

Smithfield

Bunker Hill

Summit Point

Abril's Ford

Brucetown

Locke's Ford

Clifton
Manor

WEST VIRGINIA
VIRGINIA

Hopewell
Meeting
Stevenson's
Depot

Rocky Ford
Seiver's Ford

Berryville

BLUE RIDGE MOUNTAINS

Winchester

Old Chapel

Kernstown

Millwood

F. Lee

Generals Early, Breckinridge, and Wharton rode near the front of the advancing Confederate column. Sharpshooters from Wharton's division led the butternut and gray column down the road toward Kearneysville. At 1:00 p.m., Jackson's cavalry tumbled back before the dismounted troopers from Custer's 1st and 7th Michigan. The Southern horsemen incorrectly informed Early that the Federal force consisted of a lone cavalry brigade. Early reinforced the sharpshooters with his largest infantry regiment, Lt. Col. John P. Wolfe's 51st Virginia, and assumed they would easily drive the Federal horsemen away. Wolfe's Virginians marched forward in skirmish order and boldly attacked, but Custer's battle line stood firm. The firing of the rifles and muskets created a "terrible uproar" that jolted both sides from their normal routine. Three color-bearers of the 51st Virginia were struck in quick succession, but the third man remained on the field despite his wound. The Virginians fought bravely, but they soon found themselves outgunned as Custer's troopers deftly plied their seven-shot Spencer rifles. Merritt posted three of Cesnola's regiments on Custer's right, dramatically increasing the pressure on the Virginians' left flank. Colonel Augustus Forsberg requested permission to reinforce the 51st Virginia, but "Old Jube" refused, believing they could handle the Union cavalry. On the opposite end of the Federal line, Torbert deployed several sections of horse artillery near the road. The gunners quickly spied the congregating group of Confederate generals and fired their cannon, sending the senior leadership of the Valley Army fleeing for cover.[14]

Torbert ratcheted up the pressure on Early by feeding Wilson's division into the fight. Wilson's men were armed entirely with Spencer carbines, a historic first. They dismounted rapidly and dashed into position with every fourth man leading the horses to the rear. Wilson's horse artillery wheeled into position well to the front, went into battery, and added its weight to the melee. Brigadier General John B. McIntosh's troopers scurried into position on Custer's left flank, extending the battle line across the road. Mounted and dismounted elements of Chapman's brigade marched "well off to the left" of the Federal battle line, placing the opposing Virginians at a great disadvantage. Before Torbert could capitalize upon the opportunity that Wilson's deployment offered, Jubal Early spotted the growing Union line and finally permitted Forsberg to reinforce the 51st Virginia. The Swede rushed the 45th Virginia

---

14 R. E. Wolfe to J. W. Daniel, October 5, 1905, John Warwick Daniel Papers, UVA; Forsberg, Memoir, 33-34, WLU.

into position to the right of the road and took shelter upon a wooded knoll. No sooner had they gotten into position than McIntosh's troopers charged. One of his troopers recalled that they went "with a forward rush and a fire of surprising volume" and "lusty cheers bursting from our throats at every step." The Union troopers halted their advance 250 yards short of the concealed 45th Virginia and took shelter in an old road cut lined with a sturdy post and rail fence. Although the Federals could not see any "Johnnies" on the wooded knoll, the steady shower of bullets and distant puffs of smoke affirmed their presence.[15]

The 45th Virginia had secured the Confederate right flank, but trouble was brewing on the left. Lieutenant Colonel Wolfe hastened to that end of his line where he discovered Cesnola's dismounted troopers attacking the left flank of the 51st Virginia. Wolfe asked Forsberg for reinforcements, but the Union attack struck before they arrived. Early's delay now proved costly. Cesnola charged with the 17th Pennsylvania on his left, 9th New York in the middle, and the 4th New York on the right. These regiments dashed across fields, leaped over walls, and smashed the left flank of the 51st Virginia, already occupied with the Michigan troopers in front. The Southerners collapsed rearward in a veritable panic. The Yankees shot down Wolfe in a cornfield as he vainly tried to rally his men, striking him in the neck and killing him almost instantly. On the Confederate right, the 45th Virginia now found itself in a precarious position with its left flank exposed to enfilading fire from Custer's Wolverines. Fortunately, Forsberg dispatched the 30th Virginia Battalion to aid the 45th Virginia.[16]

As the Virginians collapsed in confusion, Breckinridge burst into their midst with his long gray overcoat flowing in the breeze. With panic seizing men all around him, the Kentuckian kept his composure and never lost "his equipoise of manner or bearing." He calmed the startled soldiers, advanced the two remaining brigades of Wharton's division, and then galloped back to bring Maj. Gen. John B. Gordon's division into the fight. With these timely reinforcements, the Southern infantry quickly brought its strength to bear on

---

15 Wilson, *Under the Old Flag*, 541; *OR* 43, pt. 1, 517; Forsberg, 33-34, WLU; Hannaford, Memoir, Cincinnati Historical Society (hereafter CiHS).

16 R. E. Wolfe to J. W. Daniel, October 5, 1905, John Warwick Daniel Papers, UVA; Newel Cheney, *History of the Ninth New York Cavalry, War of 1861 to 1865* (Poland Center, NY: Jamestown, Martin Merz & Son, 1901), 213; Wilson, *Under the Old Flag*, 541; *OR* 43, pt. 1, 517; Forsberg, Memoir, 33-34, WLU; Hillman, *History of the Sixth New York Cavalry*, 217; E. A. Paul, "The Middle Military Division," *New York Times*, August 28 and 29, 1864.

the isolated Federal cavalry. To the left of the 45th Virginia, Wharton advanced the brigades of Col. Thomas Smith and Col. George S. Patton. Captain William M. Lowry's Wise Legion Artillery unlimbered in front of Cesnola's brigade and sent "some shrieking shells and ricocheting solid shot" into the Federal ranks. The combination of Wharton's fresh Virginia infantry and Lowry's artillery soundly checked Merritt's advance. Simultaneously, Breckinridge hastened the brigades of Brig. Gens. Zebulon York and William Terry from Gordon's division into position on Forsberg's right flank. With two infantry divisions now on the firing line, Early quickly gained the upper hand. Rodes's division eventually moved into position on Wharton's left flank, putting almost 8,000 Confederate infantrymen into line of battle with aggressive sharpshooter battalions leading the way.[17]

Although the situation turned decisively in favor of the Confederate forces, Union resistance did not evaporate. As Gordon deployed his division, a Spencer bullet from a Yankee rifle grazed his forehead. In spite of profuse bleeding, the rugged Georgian remained astride his horse and calmly directed his troops. For the rest of the day, he stayed on the front line and led his foot soldiers after the Union horsemen "all sprinkled with blood—the very personification of a hero." Not everyone shared Gordon's good fortune. Another shot killed Col. William Monaghan of the 6th Louisiana, commander of one of the regimental groups that composed York's brigade.[18]

Torbert reassessed his situation as the pressure began to overwhelm the outgunned Union horsemen. Confederate prisoners informed him that Early's entire army was on the scene, greatly dampening the Federal commander's enthusiasm for continuing the fight. "Having accomplished the object of the reconnaissance," reported Torbert, he ordered Merritt and Wilson to withdraw and return to their camps. As one Vermont horseman put it, "Our mission was accomplished; we did not wait for the whipping which they would gladly have given us, but went back by the way we came." Word passed so quickly along the firing line that an Ohio trooper in Wilson's division was "astonished and still more mystified" at the rapidity of the retreat for no apparent reason that he

17 R. E. Wolfe to J. W. Daniel, October 5, 1905, John Warwick Daniel Papers, UVA; Forsberg, 33, WL; Wilson, *Under the Old Flag*, 541; W. W. Stringfield, "Sixty-Ninth Regiment," *Histories of the Several Regiments and Battalions from North Carolina in the Great War, 1861-1865* (Goldsboro, NC: Nash Brothers Printers, 1901), 752, hereafter *North Carolina Regiments*; Roger Hannaford Memoir, CiHS.

18 Forsberg, Memoir, WLU, 34.

could see. Although the retreat began in an orderly fashion at 1:00 p.m., "a sort of panic struck most of the boys," recalled the same man. No doubt the rapid deployment of the Confederate infantry hastened the dismounted troopers along as they rushed to regain their horses. Once mounted, Wilson's men and the horse artillery covered the retreat of Merritt's division under heavy pressure from Gordon's division on the left. Still, Torbert's horsemen found a way to add some flair to the situation even in rapid retreat. As the 1st Rhode Island Cavalry withdrew behind the battery, its band struck up the "Star Spangled Banner" in the excitement and confusion of the moment.[19]

As Wilson withdrew his division, he staggered his artillery sections upon two ridges at intervals along the retreat route. The rear-most section fired for awhile to slow the Confederate pursuit and cover the withdrawal of the rear guard. That section then limbered up and retreated beyond another pre-positioned section that opened fire. The retreating section withdrew to the next ridge to the rear, unlimbered, and began the whole process again. By deploying their guns this way, the Union horse artillery forced the Confederates to maintain a respectful distance. Despite the artillery, the retreat from Kearneysville was still a close call for Wilson's cavalrymen, as the Confederates pressed the Federals closely until they arrived near Halltown.[20]

Early's infantry chased the retreating Federals from the battlefield at Kearneysville toward their camps near Shepherdstown and Halltown. Whenever the Union resistance stiffened, he halted his line of battle while the sharpshooters cleared the way. Although hotly pressed, Wilson's division arrived safely at Halltown, while Merritt's command rode leisurely farther northward to its camp located closer to Shepherdstown. After Wilson headed eastward to Halltown, Merritt deployed the 1st New York Dragoons from Col. Alfred Gibbs's reserve brigade to serve as his rear guard. As Early closed in, his scouts informed him of an opportunity to strike Merritt's division as it turned toward its camp, now that Wilson was no longer covering the rear. Early rode to the top of a high hill and looked down upon Merritt's isolated column as it moved along, completely oblivious to the Confederate presence just behind the

19 Wilson, *Under the Old Flag*, 753-753; *OR* 43, pt. 1, 517; Roger Hannaford, Memoir, CiHS; J.H.F., "Vermont Cavalry," Vermont Chronicle, September 10, 1864; Frederick Dennison, *Sabres and Spurs: The First Regiment Rhode Island Cavalry in the Civil War, 1861-1865* (Central Falls, RI: 1st Rhode Island Cavalry Regiment Veteran Association, 1876), 385.

20 Roger Hannaford, Memoir, CiHS; "Army Correspondence," *Detroit Advertiser & Tribune*, September 27, 1864.

hill. Wasting no time, Early rushed Gordon's division to attack this inviting target. Merritt attempted to meet the Southern infantry's attack, but the sudden fusillade of rifle fire from Gordon's men sent the Union troopers scurrying "in every direction." The Dragoons stood their ground but were cut off from the rest of the division. Fortunately, Merritt rushed Custer's brigade back to assist the beleaguered Dragoons.

As the New Yorkers were pondering whether to surrender or launch a desperate attack against infantry, they spied Custer leading his staff and headquarters guard over a hill to the east and galloping to their rescue. "His wide brimmed hat was flapping," recounted one of the stranded New Yorkers, "while his long golden curls were streaming in the air." Custer's advance "swept down like the wind" on the rear of the Confederate line between him and the rearguard. As he cut through to the Dragoons, he shouted to the New Yorkers, "Wheel about boys, and charge them! Forward! Charge!" The beleaguered Federals surged back through the Confederates and joined the balance of Custer's brigade. Even as Custer performed his daring rescue, Gordon quickly reinforced his own advance and sealed off the Michigan brigade's line of retreat toward Halltown. Merritt counterattacked with the 17th Pennsylvania to reopen an escape route for Custer and his crew, but the Confederates repulsed the effort. Custer now found himself in a situation akin to his experiences at Trevillian Station back in June when his command was cut off and besieged by Confederate cavalry. Only this time, Confederate infantry swarmed around his command. Making matters worse, the Potomac River was at his back.[21]

Initially, Custer did not realize the precariousness of his situation. With no enemy in sight, he halted his brigade in a wooded lot south of Shepherdstown, where his men dismounted around 3:00 p.m. One recalled that they "were all sitting or lying down with bridle reins in hand, taking our ease with more or less dignity, when a small body of Confederate horse [Jackson's brigade] made its appearance in the direction of Shepherdstown." The Michigan men jumped on their horses, charged, and repelled the Southern horsemen. Jackson, however, was only screening the advance of Breckinridge's corps. Before long, Custer's Federals saw Wharton's infantry entering the woods and quickly reined in their

---

21 Historian Eric Wittenberg referred to Trevillian as Custer's "First Last Stand." One might consider Shepherdstown Custer's "Second Last Stand." Worsham, *One of Jackson's Foot Cavalry*, 164-165; J. H. Kidd, *A Cavalryman With Custer*, 274; Henry P. Moyer, *History of the Seventeenth Regiment Pennsylvania Volunteer Cavalry*, 96; M. W. Lindsley, "Worthy of Custer," *National Tribune*, February 22, 1894; Maj. Howard M. Smith, Diary and Letter of August 26, 1864, LC.

Brig. Gen. George A. Custer
LC

mounts. With Gordon's division moving up on Wharton's right, Custer gamely formed his brigade into line of battle with its back to the Potomac River. The golden-locked general ordered his troopers to cheer and dared the Confederates to attack. Battery C, 3rd U.S. Artillery unlimbered in the center of the front line and "gave them a charge or two, right in their teeth." The battery then limbered up, headed to the rear, and deployed on a hill behind Custer's battle line. Once the guns had taken up their new position, Custer's command withdrew to the same hill, and the whole force repeated the process several times as they moved in retreat toward the Potomac River.[22]

Although Custer kept the Confederates at bay in his front, their overwhelming force quickly gained ground on his flanks. The Michigan brigade and the 1st New York Dragoons now found themselves surrounded "inside a horseshoe of infantry" with the river against the open heel. The Confederates on both flanks pushed for the river, threatening to sever Custer's line of retreat to the ford. Nevertheless, the indomitable Custer maintained his composure and continued the withdrawal "as if on parade, with Breckinridge and his corps for the spectators." Although the situation was tense, the Federals carefully plied their way to the river, safely crossed its murky waters into Maryland under cover of darkness, and camped at Antietam Furnace.[23]

The situation for the Union cavalry on the night of August 25 was anything but flattering. Back at Halltown, Sheridan, Torbert, and Merritt remained uncertain of Custer's fate throughout the night, and rumors of his demise flew rampantly through the Federal cavalry camps. As Wilson recalled, "Torbert and Merritt, with several mixed and miscellaneous detachments, drifted into my camp between nine and ten o'clock that night in a state of disorder and confusion." Further complicating matters, Sheridan was worried that Early might cross the Potomac and enter Maryland. To guard against that possibility, the Union commander immediately dispatched Wilson's division to the north side of that river opposite Shepherdstown via Harpers Ferry. Wilson's tired troopers marched through the dark of night and finally joined Custer near Antietam Furnace at daylight, ending concerns about Custer's fate.[24]

Overall, the engagements at Kearneysville and Shepherdstown did not change the military situation in the lower Shenandoah Valley. Ironically, both sides credited themselves with foiling a major movement by their opponents. The Union cavalrymen concluded that they certainly had thwarted another Confederate incursion across the Potomac. The Confederates believed that they had halted a major cavalry raid up the Shenandoah Valley. Simply put, these were quick-hitting meeting engagements between forces engaged in reconnaissance missions that had no real impact on the overall direction of the

22 Kidd, *A Cavalryman With Custer*, 274-275.

23 Ibid., 275-277; OR 43, pt. 1, 92, 517; Wilson, *Under the Old Flag*, 544.

24 OR 43, pt. 1, 101-102, 517; Wilson, *Under the Old Flag*, 543-544.

campaign. However, the action at Kearneysville did mark another step in the evolution of Sheridan's cavalry's ability to directly confront Jubal Early's vaunted "Foot Cavalry." The 51st Virginia alone lost 12 killed, 63 wounded, and 27 captured. One Confederate source reported the day's total losses at 215 men. Early also lost the services of cavalry commander Col. William L. "Mudwall" Jackson, who accidently shot himself in the leg while dismounting his horse in Shepherdstown after the fighting had stopped. Union losses numbered approximately 250.[25]

The events of August 25 convinced Sheridan that "there is not much doubt of the presence here of two divisions of Longstreet's corps." Sheridan concluded that Anderson must have had at least two divisions at Halltown to enable Early to march off with the entire Second Corps. Actually, Early and Anderson had completely bluffed Sheridan. Fewer than 6,000 Confederates faced Sheridan's 30,000 or more soldiers at Halltown. In fact, Sheridan missed a rare opportunity to devastate Anderson's isolated force. At the same time, Grant overstated the results of his Weldon Railroad operations at Petersburg. "I think it likely," he told Sheridan, "that all troops will be ordered back from the Valley except what they believe to be the minimum number to detain you." In this Grant was mistaken. The composition of the Confederates operating in the Valley would remain unchanged for several weeks, but active operations continued apace on a daily basis.[26]

25 *Staunton Vindicator*, September 23, 1864; John Mastin Diary, WVU.

26 It should be noted that Grant telegraphed Halleck on August 25, "Pickett's and Field's divisions are here (Petersburg). You can say this to General Sheridan and there is no doubt about it." The War Department did not forward Grant's direct message to Sheridan. This could be indicative of the administration's politically induced cautiousness, and a preference for Sheridan to remain on the defensive rather than risk another defeat in the Shenandoah. OR, 43, pt. 1, 905-906; 916-917.

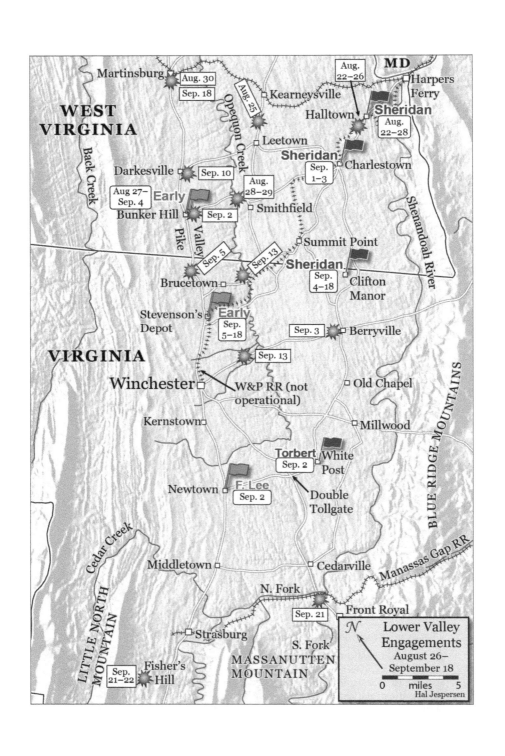

Lower Valley
Engagements
August 26–
September 18

0   miles   5

Hal Jespersen

I Think I Can Manage This Affair

Halltown to Smithfield, August 26 - 29

On August 26, Jubal Early fell back to Leetown, about midway between Halltown and the Confederates' favorite haunt at Bunker Hill on the Valley Turnpike farther west. Fitz Lee's cavalry had reached the Potomac River and skirmished with William Averell's division in front of Williamsport, Maryland. Lee drove Averell's vedettes from the Virginia side of the river, but found the Union position on the Maryland side too strong to attack. Averell reported Fitz Lee's attempt to cross at Williamsport for what it was: "no serious effort." The days of a mere Confederate appearance along the banks of the Potomac River creating uproar in the Union command structure vanished under Phil Sheridan's leadership. He had the resources needed to meet any threat and the wherewithal to use them effectively.[1]

---

1 After being relieved of command in late September, Averell reported "the enemy attempted to force a crossing of the river with his entire cavalry force supported by an infantry division with artillery. He was prevented and suffered loss without any casualties worth mentioning in my command." This greatly exaggerated report resulted from Averell attempting to justify the transfer of his command from Shepherdstown to the north side of the Potomac. Lee's movement was exceedingly tentative. OR 43, pt. 1, 21, 497.

Maj. Gen. George Crook, commander, Army of West Virginia.
R. B. Hayes Presidential Center

Meanwhile, the chess match along the Halltown-Charlestown line continued with Anderson remaining dangerously exposed to Sheridan's overwhelming force. After Sheridan's cavalry faced off with Early's Second Corps, the Union commander grew curious about the composition of the Confederates at Charlestown, so he instructed General Crook to "make a strong reconnaissance in your front at 4 p.m. today with one division of your army." One hour before the designated time, Sheridan rode over to Crook's headquarters to personally oversee the operation. Once more, Crook selected Col. Isaac H. Duval's trusted division for the work at hand, reinforcing him with a brigade from Col. Joseph Thoburn's division.

Crook instructed Thoburn to drive Kershaw's skirmish line from a small triangular wood lot on the south side of the Charlestown Road. He was to then hold the farther edge of the woods until Duval's division completed its operations on the right. Thoburn instructed Colonel Wells to burn some haystacks and shocks of wheat in the field beyond the woods that the Confederates were using to conceal sharpshooters. Thoburn personally supervised the deployment of Col. George D. Wells's brigade. At 4:00 p.m., Wells's skirmishers charged ahead and drove Kershaw's men back as ordered. Thoburn followed the skirmishers through the woods with the 5th New York Heavy Artillery and 116th Ohio in line of battle. As these regiments entered the woods, some of Kershaw's men fired into the Ohioans' right flank from the shelter of breastworks along the edge of some woods situated north of the Charlestown Road. The Confederate enfilading fire rendered the Federal position untenable, so Wells quickly maneuvered the 116th Ohio to meet the new threat. Lieutenant Colonel Thomas F. Wildes's Ohioans wheeled to their right and charged across the road, driving the Confederates from their works and deeper into the woods. The gray-clad infantry halted behind trees and showered the Buckeyes with a heavy fire, so Wells withdrew them to his "own woods" south of the road. There, the Ohioans traded shots with the Southerners across the road and kept them occupied while Wells carried out his assignment. Back at the western edge of the woods, the 34th Massachusetts rushed into the field, fired the hay and wheat, and then quickly returned to the trees. For now, Wells's entire force remained in the woods sparring with Kershaw's Confederates while Duval carried out his part of the assignment.[2]

After Thoburn gained Kershaw's attention, Duval moved out to attack north of the road. He formed six regiments into a line of battle in a wooded lot. Colonel Daniel Johnson's brigade deployed on the right and Col. Rutherford B. Hayes's brigade formed on the left. It was familiar ground for the Federals; Duval struck the same sector of the Rebel line as he had three days earlier. He

2 Ibid., 374-355; W. T. Patterson, "From the 116th Regiment," August 27, 1864, contained in *Athens Messenger*, September 8, 1864.

found the going much more difficult this day, as Kershaw's men had constructed substantial rail breastworks. As the line left the cover provided by a sheltering rise in the ground, one West Virginian on the skirmish line examined the situation and concluded that he would be shot when he reached the crest. To his surprise, Kershaw's South Carolinians "were entirely ignorant of our presence, sitting around unconcerned, not fifty yards from me." The Union skirmishers deliberately aimed and fired, prompting the South Carolinians to rush to their rail pens and loose a destructive volley into Duval's approaching line. Undaunted, Crook's Buzzards drove the Carolinians from their rail bull pens, clambered over the wood fences, and chased them toward the main Confederate breastworks. Seeing the break, Kershaw's reserves rushed into the works and met Duval's attack, but the swiftness of the assault caught the Southerners off guard and forced them back even farther to an inner line of works. There, Cutshaw's artillery roared into action and finally halted the Federal advance.[3]

As Duval carried the main breastworks, Col. Charles Lowell's 2nd Massachusetts Cavalry charged out of a ravine on the left of the infantry and bolted into the breach. A squad of Carolinians leveled their rifles at some horsemen who were tearing down a rail fence, but Lowell himself burst into their midst and whacked their rifles with his saber before they could fire. The Union cavalrymen swarmed around the Carolinians, but the Southerners did not give up easily. Fighting back with clubbed muskets, they killed an officer and wounded several others. The Union troopers quickly secured their prisoners and returned to their own lines. Crook's reconnaissance secured 95 South Carolinians, including a lieutenant colonel, three captains, and three lieutenants. The cost of this effort greatly surpassed Crook's probes on August 22 and 24. He lost 17 killed, 124 wounded, and one missing. Nevertheless, the boldness and vigor of Crook's sortie impressed Kershaw's veterans who also lost nearly 100 men killed and wounded. Accustomed to fighting against the hard luck Army of the Potomac, the South Carolinians quizzically asked Hayes's western troops, "Who the h-ll are you'uns?" The Southerners complimented Hayes's men on their brave actions and informed them that they

---

3   Jesse Tyler Sturm, From a "Whirlpool of Death . . . To Victory," *Civil War Remembrances of Jesse Tyler Sturm 14th West Virginia Infantry* (Charleston, WV: West Virginia Division of Culture and History, 2002) 84-85; "Battle Near Halltown," *Ironton Register*, September 8, 1864.

were not used to seeing such vigor on the part of their usual Yankee opponents from the Army of the Potomac.[4]

The results of the last few days buoyed Sheridan's confidence in his own ability to lead the Army of the Shenandoah. After reporting on the successful foray against Kershaw, Sheridan declared to Grant, "I think I can manage this affair. I have thought it best to be very prudent, everything considered."[5] On August 27, Grant responded:

> I now think it likely that all troops will be ordered back from the Valley except what they believe to be the minimum number to detain you. . . . Watch closely, and if you find this theory correct push with all vigor. Give the enemy no rest, and if it is possible to follow the enemy to the Virginia Central Railroad, follow that far. Do all the damage to the railroads and crops you can. Carry off livestock of all descriptions, and Negroes as to prevent further planting. If the war is to last another year, we want the Shenandoah Valley to remain a barren waste.[6]

Thereafter, Sheridan would closely monitor Confederate troop movements in the Shenandoah Valley and harass his Confederate opponents on a daily basis, waiting patiently for Early to send troops to Petersburg as Grant suggested.

At Confederate headquarters, Early likewise received guidance from his chief, Gen. Robert E. Lee. A few days earlier, Early had expressed concern over the greatly increased size of Sheridan's force and sought his commander's guidance on a course of action. Lee advised Early against any operations north of the Potomac River and suggested cavalry operations east of the Blue Ridge might force Sheridan to detach troops for the protection of Washington. Early also fretted about Sheridan's large cavalry force that had boldly attacked Confederate infantry on several occasions. To Early's disappointment, Lee replied that no additional Confederate cavalry would be sent to the Valley because Grant's cavalry force at Petersburg was "too strong." Lee also made it

---

4 James Comly Papers, Journal, RBHPC; Caspar Crowinshield to Henry Schrow, March 15, 1880, Schrow Pension File, National Archives; Charles A. Humphreys, *Field Camp, Hospital and Prison in the Civil War, 1863-1865* (Boston: Press of Geo. H. Ellis, 1918), 150; D. Augustus Dickert, *History of Kershaw's Brigade* (Morningside, 1973), 418-419; W. C. Hall Diary, Atlanta Historical Society.

5 OR 43, pt. 1, 21.

6 Ibid., 916-917.

clear that if Early could not effectively integrate Anderson's command into the operations in the Valley or east of the Blue Ridge, "I will order them back to Richmond."[7]

On August 27, Jubal Early withdrew his forces from the area between Shepherdstown and Leetown, marching the Second Corps to Bunker Hill which was located about midway between Winchester and Martinsburg on the Valley Pike. Anderson, "not liking the situation of my command near Charlestown," notified Early that he would withdraw behind the Opequon. The South Carolinian's command moved to Brucetown, a hamlet located six miles northeast of Winchester between the Valley Pike and Opequon Creek. The Confederate cavalry took position near Shepherdstown. Realizing that no Confederates remained in Sheridan's front, Early sent McCausland's brigade back toward Charlestown with orders to maintain a thin cavalry screen and provide advance warning of any Federal movements. With the Confederates pulling back from Sheridan's immediate front, August 27 marked the end of the Confederate offensive that had successfully forced the Army of the Shenandoah to fall back nearly 40 miles from Strasburg to Harpers Ferry. Unlike previous Confederate incursions down the Valley, Early found his pathway well-guarded, and could not maintain the initiative. Unfortunately for Sheridan, he misread Early's retreat as the withdrawal of Confederate forces from the Valley that Grant had predicted as the pending result of his operations at Petersburg. "The indications are that the rebel army is about leaving the valley," Sheridan telegraphed Grant that evening.[8]

On August 28, Sheridan responded to the Confederate pullback by advancing two miles west of Charlestown. Believing that Early would "fall back perhaps out of the Valley," Sheridan ordered his cavalry to follow Early closely in the event that he withdrew up the Valley. To do so, Sheridan recalled Wilson's division from Maryland and posted it at Shepherdstown. The Union commander ordered Averell to "join me via Martinsburg." Sheridan directed Merritt to advance his division through the countryside around Leetown and Smithfield, and then promptly inform army headquarters of his findings on Jubal Early's latest dispositions.[9]

---

7   Ibid., 1,007.

8   Ibid., 935, 937.

9   Ibid., 944-945.

Merritt's division rode promptly westward out of its Charlestown camp at 5:00 a.m. on another reconnaissance mission with Col. Alfred Gibbs's reserve brigade leading the way. When Gibbs reached the junction of the Leetown Road, his force turned south with Capt. William Henry Harrison's 2nd U.S. Cavalry leading the way. These Regulars forced pickets from "Mudwall" Jackson's brigade back upon their reserves north of Leetown. There, "several hundred" Virginians formed up to resist an attack, but Harrison halted his small regiment and requested support. Gibbs dispatched Maj. James Starr's 6th Pennsylvania Cavalry, and together the two regiments drove the Virginians through Leetown. After a short halt to reorganize, Merritt put Capt. Nelson B. Sweitzer's 1st U.S. Cavalry in the lead and followed Jackson's men.[10]

Reports of Merritt's approach had already filtered back to Maj. Gen. Lunsford L. Lomax. He turned to Maj. Harry Gilmor and told him that "two hundred of the enemy had been running" Jackson all morning. Lomax directed the Marylander to reinforce Jackson's brigade and reestablish the picket line at Leetown. Gilmor's men galloped through Smithfield and ran into Jackson's retreating force. Upon seeing Gilmor, Lt. Col. Dudley Evans of the 20th Virginia Cavalry told Gilmor that "there was not more than a regiment in our front." Gilmor suggested an ambush, so Evans dismounted his troopers and deployed them in a wooded lot on the west side of the Leetown Road. At the same time, Lt. Meredith Gilmor, Harry's brother, led 45 men armed with Enfield rifles into the woods east of the road and waited. Major Gilmor held the two Maryland battalions in the road and waited for an opportunity to strike. When Sweitzer's Regulars pounded up the road, the concealed Confederates in the woods let loose a rippling volley that stunned the approaching Union horsemen. Before they could regroup, Gilmor's mounted Marylanders crashed into the confused mass of Federal troopers and drove them back toward Leetown.[11]

Lieutenant Joseph S. Hoyer led the reserve squadron of the 1st U.S. Cavalry in the rear of the regiment. He quickly grasped the situation at the front and deployed his squadron four men abreast in the road. All that Hoyer and his men could see was "a dense cloud of dust" moving rapidly toward them. Sabers rattled as the men drew their blades from their scabbards, and Hoyer's bugler

10 Ibid., 488; Rodenbough, *Second Dragoons*, 346.

11 Gilmor, *Four Years in the Saddle*, 239-40.

sounded the charge. The approaching Marylanders slowed their pace but blazed into the Regulars with their revolvers. A rebel bullet mortally wounded Hoyer, but 26-year-old Lt. Moses Harris from New Hampshire grabbed the reins of command and pressed the counter attack. The Marylanders shot down Harris's horse, but the gritty Granite State Regular commandeered his bugler's horse and pushed his squadron forward. With stone walls lining the road, space was at a premium during the wild, close-quarter fight that ensued. Harris galloped out in front of the Regulars and led the attack down the narrow roadway under a heavy fire from the Confederates. The enlisted men followed close behind cheering, looking for room to join the melee at the front of the column. "We went through them with a crash – a fusillade of pistol shots – a few quick saber strokes – men and horses rolling in the dust of the pike," recalled Harris, "with the defiant yell dying on their lips, were in wild confusion and flight." The young lieutenant's front line leadership inspired the troops, turned the tide of the battle, and earned him the Medal of Honor.[12]

Meanwhile, the mortally wounded Hoyer struggled to the rear and requested assistance for his hard-pressed comrades in his dying moments. Captain Harrison of the 2nd U.S. Cavalry answered the call, turning to his troopers and shouting, "Draw Sabre! And Charge!" His horse soldiers galloped up the road and joined the wild, running fight with Jackson's Virginians and Gilmor's Marylanders. With the addition of Harrison's troopers, the weight of numbers favored Union arms and forced the Confederates back toward Smithfield, although the stone walls lining the narrow road constrained their movements. A squadron of the 2nd U.S. charged through the fields alongside the road and attempted to cut off and capture a number of Confederates from the 1st Maryland. Captain Gus Dorsey saved the Confederate horsemen from disaster. Dressed in blue pants, an officer's kepi, and wearing no coat, the Union troopers mistook Dorsey for one of their own. He ordered them to move to the right, and they obeyed long enough for the Confederates to evade the trap.[13]

The confused mass of Confederates raced into Smithfield. Snipers deployed in the houses and harassed the approaching Yankees, buying time for the majority of the Southerners to retreat to a ridge between the village and Opequon Creek. There, Fitz Lee and Lomax waited with most of Early's cavalry and at least one battery of artillery. With the Regulars exhausted from

12 Moses Harris, "With the Reserve brigade," 15-16; Moses Harris Medal of Honor File, NA.

13 Rodenbough, *Second Dragoons*, 346; Gilmor, *Four Years in the Saddle*, 239-240.

their charge, Starr's 6th Pennsylvania took over the lead, dashed into the village, and flushed out the Confederate snipers. As the Pennsylvanians exited the west side of the hamlet, the Confederate gunners swept the road with their artillery, checking the Pennsylvanians and setting several homes in Smithfield ablaze. Merritt countered quickly by unlimbering one of his horse batteries in a nearby field. The Union gunners opened counter-battery fire, forcing the Confederate artillery to switch its focus from the Pennsylvanians in the road to the Federal cannon. With the reserve brigade pressing the Confederates in front, Merritt sent Custer's brigade around the right to cut the Confederates off from the bridge over Opequon Creek. Unfortunately, Custer's skirmishers opened fire too soon, revealing their intentions. Fitz Lee recognized the danger and promptly ordered a retreat. The Southerners quickly limbered up their guns and pulled back. Lomax withdrew westward across the Smithfield bridge toward Early's force at Bunker Hill, and Fitz Lee pulled off to the south. He eventually crossed the Opequon about five miles upstream at Locke's Ford and encamped in front of Kershaw's infantry at Brucetown.

Merritt seized the bridge and posted his vedettes on the west bank of the Opequon, content to hold his position. Lomax's troopers found refuge behind their infantry near Bunker Hill. "Although somewhat bruised and battered," recalled Capt. French Harding of the 20th Virginia, "we were still in the ring." In the swirling action, the U.S. horse soldiers captured 30 or 40 prisoners, "many of them with sore heads from the strokes of our dull sabers," added a Federal.[14]

Merritt's victory over the Rebel cavalry prompted Early to place his infantry on alert in case of a full-scale Federal advance. Merritt, however, did not pursue beyond the creek, so the day proved to be one of rest and reprieve from duty for the Southern foot soldiers. "We have remained quietly in camp and there has been some preaching for the first time in a good while," wrote Maj. Jed Hotchkiss. "This is the first Sunday spent in camp since my return to the army [in January]," noted Lt. Henry H. Smith of the 5th North Carolina Infantry.[15]

14 OR 43, pt. 1, 47, 440, 448; Gilmor, *Four Years in the Saddle*, 239-240; Moses Harris, "With the Reserve Brigade," March, 1890, 15-16; French Harding, *Civil War Memoirs* (Parsons, WV: McClain Printing Co., 2000), 164-166; Moses Harris, Medal of Honor File, National Archives, Washington, D.C.

15 "Diary of Capt. H. W. Wingfield," Bulletin of the Virginia State Library, July 1927, 46; Caroline L. Shaffner, ed., Diary of Dr. J. F. Shaffner, Sr. (Winston-Salem, NC: n.p., 1936), 49;

Sheridan's general advance on August 28 continued his policy of harassing the Confederates with his cavalry and presaged a message from Grant of the same afternoon. After Sheridan's operations were well under way, Grant advised Sheridan to "feel the enemy strongly without compromising the safety of your position." Grant had no firm intelligence about Early returning any troops to Lee, but believed that Sheridan would "find the enemy in your immediate front weaker than you are." For his part, Sheridan received reports from Averell's scouts that "the rebels were moving up the Valley [southward]." He ordered Merritt to "send out at early dawn parties in the direction of Bunker Hill, if it is possible for them to get through, and ascertain whether or not the enemy's infantry are moving or have gone toward Winchester."[16]

Early the next day, Sheridan rode out to the front and personally surveyed the situation along the Opequon. Merritt dispatched Custer's brigade toward Bunker Hill and easily swept Lomax's troopers out of the way. Contrary to reports, Early had not detached any troops, as the Union cavalry on the road to Bunker Hill found out soon enough. As Merritt's cavalry approached Bunker Hill, Jubal Early unleashed Gordon's and Ramseur's divisions to drive away the Federals. These combative generals once again advanced their aggressive sharpshooter battalions, whose accurate fire forced Custer back to the east bank of the Opequon where he dug in. Ramseur followed the Federals on the direct road to Smithfield while Gordon led his division on a flank march south of that road, both arriving in front of the village at 10:00 a.m.

While Custer ventured up the road toward Bunker Hill, all was quiet at Smithfield. Several regimental bands soon gathered on a hill overlooking the Opequon and performed for the enjoyment of the gathering Union generals and officers. Officers on the knoll watched the progress of Custer's seemingly uneventful advance, until the booming crashes from a Confederate battery and the explosion of the shells near the hill quickly ended the merriment. "The hill was deserted in a twinkle," recalled Moses Harris. Soon after, Custer's retreating brigade appeared and rapidly withdrew across the wooden covered bridge to the east bank of the Opequon.[17]

Hotchkiss to wife, August 28, 1864, LC; H. H. Smith Diary, North Carolina Department Archives and History.

16 *OR* 45, pt. 1, 939, 945.

17 Moses Harris, "With the Reserve Brigade," 17.

When the Confederates appeared on the west bank of the Opequon in force, Merritt quickly prepared for action by dismounting most of his division. A section from Battery D, 2nd U.S. Artillery unlimbered on each side of the road upon the ridge between Smithfield and the bridge. In front, a dismounted squadron of the 6th Pennsylvania Cavalry occupied a rail breastwork. Gibbs dismounted the 1st New York Dragoons and the 1st and 2nd U.S. Cavalry and deployed them in some woods situated on a ridge overlooking the Opequon. Both sides traded shots across the Opequon between Merritt's dismounted troopers and the Confederate sharpshooters.

About 11:30 a.m., two Confederate batteries opened fire from the west bank and "made excellent practice, many case-shot and shells exploding in and about the battery and among the horses." Under cover of the artillery fire, Ramseur and Gordon forced their way across the bridge and deployed in front of Merritt's position. Heavy volleys went back and forth between the opposing sides as pressure mounted against the Federal cavalry. Merritt rushed reinforcements to the front line while the Confederates remained content to trade shots with the Union horsemen. While the standoff continued, Gordon sent Brig. Gen. Zebulon York to take position on the division's right to attack Merritt's left flank. Simultaneously, Ramseur moved against Merritt's right. Outflanked and outgunned by two divisions of Confederate infantry, Merritt withdrew his troopers from the fight. "So determined was their advance," admitted one of Gibbs's Regulars, "that the division was driven back a mile before we recovered our equilibrium." Then the Union cavalry fell back in a relatively orderly fashion, stopping to make frequent stands. Still, Gordon and Ramseur shunted Merritt back for nearly three miles. The retreat only ended when Sheridan brought up Brig. Gen. James B. Ricketts's division of the Sixth Corps. Gordon and Ramseur saw the approaching Union infantry, halted their march, and returned to their camps around Bunker Hill. The day's combat cost the Confederates 85 men killed and wounded while Merritt lost approximately 100 troopers.[18]

In the aftermath of the operations around Smithfield, Sheridan reversed course and concluded that no Confederate troops had left the Valley. He also put a stop to developing rumors that Breckinridge's corps was plunging deep into the heart of West Virginia and threatening to reach the Ohio River. Nevertheless, Sheridan continued to believe that he was outnumbered by Early,

---

18 OR 45, pt. 1, 489, 571, 952; OR *Atlas*, Plate LXXXII:7; Rodenbaugh, *Second Dragoons*, 345.

and as such, he maintained his cautious approach to the campaign. He was quite comfortable with his approach, as it conformed to both Secretary of War Edwin Stanton's and General Grant's assessment of the situation. Sheridan had at least hemmed in Jubal Early and prevented further mischief north of the Potomac River, something no one else had been able to do. Still, the Ohioan was not comfortable enough with the situation to undertake another offensive. "If Early has detached troops for Richmond," Sheridan told Halleck on August 30, "I will attack him vigorously; as yet I have not been able to learn that he has done so."

True to his word, Sheridan would not bring on a general engagement until he was absolutely sure that Early had been weakened.[19]

19 OR 43, pt. 1, 952, 961-962.

STRANGE BUSINESS

The Battle of Berryville, September 3

𝒜s August 1864 faded into the pages of history, Sheridan advanced his general position from Halltown, pressing closer to Opequon Creek and the Southerners waiting on the other side. The move represented a tentative first step in assuming the offensive, but it was by no means a full-fledged advance. That would have to wait until Jubal Early weakened his force by returning troops to Gen. Robert E. Lee. Fortunately for Sheridan, events in Georgia soon loosened the political bonds that had shackled his campaign.

On September 1, Maj. Gen. William T. Sherman's forces defeated Gen. John B. Hood's Army of Tennessee at the Battle of Jonesboro and occupied Atlanta the next day. While this was a major victory of military and strategic importance, Sherman's success had much larger implications as it instantly changed Lincoln's political fortunes for the better. His reelection was by no means guaranteed, and Jubal Early and his Confederate Army of the Valley District were still poised to be the most likely weapons of consequence to Lincoln. A military setback along the Potomac would be a stinging embarrassment and likely lead to negative political consequences for the Lincoln administration. Given the intense scrutiny and overemphasis that operations in Virginia received in the eastern newspapers, a defeat in the Shenandoah might be magnified beyond its actual significance. Moreover,

Lincoln needed to maintain Unionist majorities in Congress in the upcoming Congressional elections. In several important states, these elections occurred in September and early October, and any mishap in the Valley could unsettle the outcome.

In Chicago, the delegates to the Democratic Convention selected former Army of the Potomac commander George B. McClellan as their presidential nominee and George Pendleton, a reputed "peace-man" and southern sympathizer, for vice president. The defeatist Democratic platform called for ending the war and essentially granting the Southern Confederacy its independence. More than three years of bloody sacrifices made on behalf of the Union and emancipation would have gone for naught under that policy. In the South, the nomination of a presidential slate upon the peace platform heartened sagging expectations of Confederate victory. Confederates sensed that a Democratic electoral victory was their last hope for an independent Southern Confederacy. Major Jed Hotchkiss of Early's staff concluded that the Democrats "will all be for peace if the signs of the times are as much in our favor as they are now." The signs at that time included the stalemate of Maj. Gen. George G. Meade's Army of the Potomac in front of Richmond and Petersburg after four months of unprecedented bloodshed while Sherman rested his armies around Atlanta. As September wore on, Lincoln looked increasingly to Sheridan to ensure that those "signs" favored the Union Party.[1]

The fall of Atlanta adversely affected the mood in Jubal Early's army. The news particularly depressed Maj. Gen. John B. Gordon of Georgia. The developments in the Peach State raised concerns about loved ones at home among Early's Georgia soldiers. "I am getting very uneasy about home affairs," wrote Sgt. Joseph J. Felder to his sister. "Yesterday we received the very discouraging news [of] the fall of Atlanta and I don't think I ever was as blue for a short while." A Georgian from Kershaw's division declared, "I would like it very much if our Corps could again go to Georgia." Civilians in the Valley were not immune to the news and understood the consequences. In Winchester, one secessionist woman confided to her diary that the fall of Atlanta was "Bad News," that increased Lincoln's chances of reelection to the detriment of the Confederacy.[2]

1   J. Hotchkiss to wife, September 3, 1864, LC.

2   Joe Kershaw's division had gone to Georgia in 1863 with James Longstreet and participated in the Confederate victory at Chickamauga the previous September. Mrs. Hugh Lee Diary,

Even before the logistical and industrial center of Atlanta fell, Sheridan took a tentative first step on August 30 toward seizing the initiative in the Shenandoah Valley. He did so by dispatching Torbert to Berryville with two mounted divisions. The horsemen established their base camp there and reconnoitered the area south and west of town until September 2, when they returned to Charlestown. Torbert's presence at Berryville threatened the Confederate lines of retreat and communication south of Winchester. On August 31, Richard Anderson quickly moved Joseph Kershaw's infantry division together with Cutshaw's artillery battalion from its position at Brucetown three miles south to Winchester to deter the Union cavalry and protect those critical routes.

Although Sheridan had again encroached upon Early's vital southern flank, the cagey Virginian remained unfazed. Old Jube responded to the move by stretching his thin lines even farther. When Anderson moved Kershaw south to Winchester, Rodes's division, Early's largest infantry formation, marched north to Martinsburg that same day, further stretching the outnumbered Confederate forces. Rodes encountered Averell's pickets four miles south of Martinsburg and drove them back. Outgunned by the Confederate infantry, Averell retreated to Falling Waters, leaving a detachment of the 8th Ohio Cavalry to delay Rodes's advance. The Buckeyes offered stiff resistance, but Rodes deployed his old Alabama brigade and quickly routed them. "We had a pretty close race for about two miles," wrote one Ohio veteran, "the 'Johnnies' keeping our rear rather uncomfortable for stragglers." After driving Averell off, Rodes's division returned to Bunker Hill. In camp that night, an Alabama officer complained in his diary, "These reconnaissances may be very important and very interesting to general and field officers who ride [horses], but those of the line, and the fighting privates, wish they were less frequent or less tiresome." Rodes's brief movement to Martinsburg slowed repairs to the Baltimore and Ohio Railroad but did not affect the Union strategy. Sheridan even assured Averell that "your affair of yesterday is all right." From the Confederate perspective, moving Rodes to Martinsburg revealed Early's willingness to disperse his small force over a 23 mile front stretching from Winchester to Martinsburg with little concern for Federal interference. Sheridan's continued

WFCHS, 680; Joseph J. Felder to Dear Sister, September 8, 1864, GDAH; "A Georgian's View of War in Virginia," *Atlanta Historical Society Journal*, 23, 2, 121-12.

failure to react aggressively only reaffirmed the Confederate commander's assumptions.[3]

With Sheridan's cavalry remaining unusually passive, Early launched a reconnaissance in force east toward Summit Point on the morning of September 2. Rodes's division withdrew from Bunker Hill to Stephenson's Depot, four miles north of Winchester, to protect Early's northern flank. Brigadier General Bradley Johnson's Virginians and Col. Onslow Bean's Tennesseans of Lomax's division remained near Bunker Hill to keep an eye on Averell. Early's plans quickly went awry when the plucky Averell reoccupied Martinsburg. Finding no Confederates in the area, his division rode up the pike to Bunker Hill where Bean and Johnson attempted to stop the Union horse soldiers. Averell's horsemen attacked and routed the Southern cavaliers, capturing two battle flags, 55 prisoners, 20 wagons, and a small cattle herd. Averell chased them toward Winchester, but Rodes's infantry intervened and checked the Union cavalry near Stephenson's Depot. Averell withdrew back to Bunker Hill where his division spent a rainy night waiting in line of battle. Couriers notified Early of Averell's movement shortly after the Confederate infantry had crossed Opequon Creek on the way to Summit Point. Instead of risking disaster with Averell's cavalry lurking in his rear and Sheridan's large army in his front, Early reluctantly returned to the west side of the Opequon. On the Confederate southern flank, Sheridan rushed Torbert back to Berryville and soon after to White Post where he again threatened Confederate communications south of Winchester.[4]

The constant maneuvering about the lower (northern) reaches of the Shenandoah Valley ultimately flared into an unintended battle on September 3. Anderson had grown increasingly frustrated serving alongside Early with the Confederacy deriving little benefit from the presence of his First Corps detachment in the Valley. The cantankerous Virginian continually failed to effectively integrate Anderson's command into any meaningful operations in the Valley District. Instead, the South Carolinian operated as an independent commander, cooperating with Early at a distance. A member of Anderson's staff described the relationship between the two lieutenant generals as "strange

3 Cavalry, "From the Eighth Ohio Cavalry," *The Fayette County Herald*, September 22, 1864; Robert Park Diary, *SHSP*, 1:433; OR 43, pt. 2, 10; Early, *A Memoir of the Last Year of the War for Independence in the Confederate States of America* (Lynchburg, VA: Charles W. Button, 1867), 75.

4 OR 43, pt. 1, 497; Beach, *History of the 1st New York Lincoln Cavalry*, 416.

business." Anderson ranked Early but did not wish to take command of his troops, so the two commands "swung corners and chased in every direction to no good purpose that any of us could see."[5]

Anderson considered his position at Winchester "useless when the enemy declined an engagement and we could not compel one." He decided to march east, pass through the Blue Ridge at Snicker's Gap, and operate in the Loudoun Valley. His original orders from Robert E. Lee had outlined a similar plan with the hope that such operations would force Sheridan to split his force on both sides of that mountain range. Once in Loudoun, Anderson could create confusion in Sheridan's rear and threaten his lines of communication with Washington and Harpers Ferry. At the same time, Loudoun's comparatively unscathed farms could help feed Anderson's troops as that county had experienced considerably less military activity than their western neighbors in the Shenandoah Valley.[6]

On September 3, Sheridan advanced his army with no thought of bringing on a battle. Although the fall of Atlanta removed some of the political constraints that had been imposed upon Sheridan, he remained cautious. He later wrote that "the condition of affairs throughout the country required great prudence on my part, that a defeat of the forces of my command could be ill afforded." To that end, Sheridan remained true to his policy of bringing on a general engagement with Early only after he either detached troops to Petersburg, or could bring Early to battle on advantageous ground of the Irishman's choice.[7]

The Army of the Shenandoah, 40,000 strong, marched out of its position near Charlestown and headed toward its figurative Rubicon, Opequon Creek. Crook and Emory followed the Berryville-Charlestown Pike south to Battletown (as Berryville was often called.) Horatio Wright's Sixth Corps headed west on the Charlestown Road until it reached Clifton farm, where it halted and entrenched. Crook camped at Berryville, while Lowell's cavalry brigade covered the army's right flank at Summit Point. On the army's southern flank, Torbert sent Wilson and Merritt from White Post to patrol the area southward to Ninevah on the Front Royal Pike and west toward Newtown on

---

5   Dawson, *Reminiscences of Confederate Service, 1861-1865*, 123.

6   Lt. Gen. Richard Anderson, Report of Operations, 1864, FSNMP.

7   OR 43, pt. 1, 46.

the Valley Pike. Torbert discovered that Fitz Lee's division was protecting the vital Valley Pike just east of Newtown but did not attack the Virginian, despite outnumbering the Confederates. Aside from locating Lee, Torbert's patrols found no evidence that Early had returned any troops from the Shenandoah Valley to Robert E. Lee.[8]

Unlike his initial advance up the Valley in August to seize the Valley Pike, Sheridan's tentative movement on September 3 lacked any definitive objective. It simply advanced the Union position to within five miles of Opequon Creek and stretched his force from Clifton to Berryville. Once the movement was underway, Sheridan incessantly sought information concerning the size and composition of Early's army. The Ohio general realized that his force exceeded Early's but still errantly believed the Confederate force in the Valley was much larger than its actual size. Sheridan later explained, "Notwithstanding my superior strength, I determined to take all the time necessary to equip myself with the fullest information, and then seize an opportunity under such conditions that I could not well fail of success."[9]

At Winchester, Anderson learned that Torbert had withdrawn from Berryville (he did not know that Sheridan subsequently ordered him to White Post). The South Carolinian decided to take advantage of what he perceived to be an open road to Snickers Gap in the Blue Ridge beyond Berryville. Anderson had only 3,700 men under his direct command. Nevertheless, he marched Kershaw's infantry and Cutshaw's artillery eastward on the Berryville Pike with a small detachment of Fitz Lee's cavalry leading the way. Unbeknownst to Anderson, Crook's Army of West Virginia was moving toward Berryville from the opposite direction. A clash of arms was inevitable.

By late afternoon, Crook's 7,000-man force had bivouacked at Berryville. West of the town, Maryland Col. Robert S. Rodgers commanded Crook's picket line which consisted of men from Thoburn's division. Rodgers deployed the 1st West Virginia and 2nd Maryland Eastern Shore as pickets one and a half miles west of Berryville. At 4:00 p.m., Mississippians in the van of Anderson's force attacked Rodgers's post and drove them back upon their reserves, prompting the Marylander to request assistance from Thoburn.

Kershaw and Brig. Gen. Benjamin G. Humphreys scanned the situation and determined to attack Crook's left flank. Humphreys marched his brigade of

8   Ibid., pt. 2, 16.

9   Sheridan, *Memoirs*, vol. 2, 500.

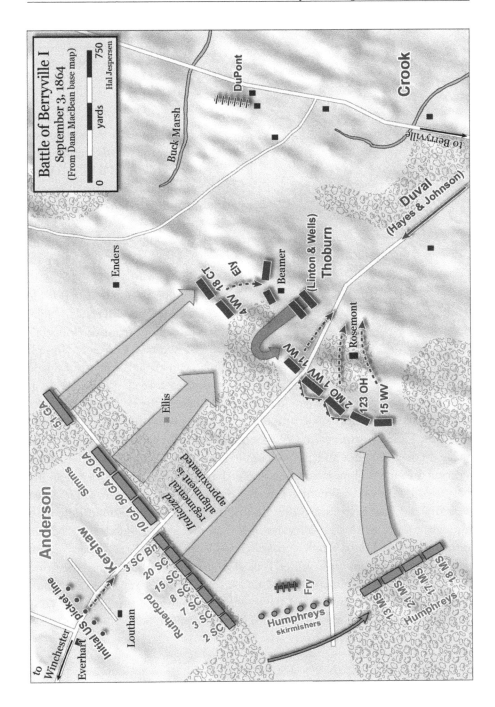

Battle of Berryville I
September 3, 1864
(From Dana MacBean base map)

Hal Jespersen

0   yards   750

Brig. Gen. Benjamin Humphreys, the commander of a Mississippi brigade. LC

Mississippi troops undetected into some woods south of the Berryville Pike, taking position opposite General Thoburn's left. At the same time, Joe Kershaw deployed his old South Carolina brigade under Col. William D. Rutherford and Col. James P. Simms's Georgia brigade astride the Berryville Pike directly in front of Rodgers's position. Colonel Joseph Armstrong's infantry brigade (Wofford's) remained in reserve. Kershaw's advance would follow the course of the Berryville Turnpike with Simms on the north side of the road and the other brigades to the south. From the Federal position, Lt. Col. Jacob Weddle of the 1st West Virginia heard firing on the picket line and galloped out to learn what he could of the situation. Peering through his binoculars, he saw Kershaw's division bearing down on the two small Federal regiments. Greatly outnumbered, Rodgers's 1st West Virginia and 2nd Maryland Eastern Shore regiments hung around only long enough to fire a single volley into the approaching Confederates before retreating toward Berryville.[10]

Back in the main camp at Berryville, Col. Joseph Thoburn heard the firing and led three more regiments from Lt. Col. John Linton's brigade to the front. Three-quarters of a mile west of the town, he encountered the confused West Virginians and Marylanders. He rushed into their midst, halted the retreat, and

10 OR *Atlas*, Plate LXXXII: 10; "Colonel Weddle's Experience," *Ironton Register*, December 16, 1886; Benjamin G. Humphreys, "The Sunflower Guards," Claiborne Papers, SHC-UNC; Dickert, *History of Kershaw's Brigade*, 420-421; W. C. Hall Diary, Atlanta Historical Society.

directed Rodgers to reform his troops on the south side of the road in some washed-out earthworks. Lieutenant Colonel Weddle remembered "the earthworks were hardly to be dignified by that name, not being over two or three feet high and affording very little protection." Thoburn deployed the reinforcements, bolstering Rodgers's dispirited troops. The 11th West Virginia took position in some woods on the north side of the road to cover Rodgers's right. On his left, the 123rd Ohio and 15th West Virginia moved into a clump of trees to guard that flank.[11]

Back in the main camp at Berryville, George Crook also heard the firing and rushed the balance of Thoburn's division to the front. Crook mounted his horse and galloped toward the firing line. Upon reaching the front, he found Thoburn and ordered him to post the balance of his division north of the road when those units reached the field. Colonel William G. Ely's brigade deployed to the right of the 11th West Virginia. Colonel George D. Wells's brigade was also moving forward to join the line. As they approached, Thoburn grew concerned as he plainly saw Kershaw's troops occupying woodlots in front opposite both of his flanks.[12]

In spite of that concern, George Crook was determined to turn the table on Anderson by launching a counterattack with Col. Isaac Duval's division. Crook accurately reasoned that Thoburn's division matched the strength of the attacking Confederates and should be able to hold until Duval deployed on the left. If the plan worked, Crook's flanking movement would roll up Kershaw's division and possibly destroy or capture much of it. This scenario might very well have succeeded if time had been on Crook's side.

Before Duval could complete his maneuver, Anderson and Kershaw seized the initiative from the deploying U.S. forces. Captain Charles W. Fry's Orange Battery unlimbered on an elevation near Kershaw's right flank and enfiladed Thoburn's left with heavy artillery fire. Another of Cutshaw's batteries shelled the Federal line from the front. Kershaw's brigades finished their deployment, their battle line advancing in a semi-circle that wrapped around both Federal flanks. Humphreys's Mississippians let out a yell to signal Kershaw that the attack had begun and then rushed from the woods. The 15th West Virginia greeted the Mississippi Rebels with "a furious volley," but it failed

11 OR 43, pt. 1, 360-361, 367; *Ironton Register*, December 16, 1886.

12 OR 43, pt. 1, 367.

to slow the Southerners who quickly routed the Mountaineers. The 123rd Ohio also "failed to make a stand" and retreated in haste and confusion, exposing the left flank of Rodgers's troops in the breastworks.[13]

Colonel Rutherford's South Carolinians heard the yells and charged through a cornfield on Humphreys's left, easily scattering the 2nd Maryland Eastern Shore. Only the 1st West Virginia offered any resistance to the Confederate attack south of the road. When the line crumbled to their left and right, the West Virginians abandoned their position and joined the retreat. Their commander, Lt. Col. Weddle, lingered too long at the breastworks. He recalled that a "tall reb made a jump at me and sought to reach me with the lunge of his bayonet." The blade drew blood, but a fellow Mountaineer saw his commander's dilemma and "jumped up and placing his musket near the fellow's head pretty nearly blew it off." On the north side of the pike, Col. Simms's Georgians attacked before Ely and Linton had completed their deployment. On Simms' left, the 51st Georgia struck Ely's right flank and forced the Federal brigade to withdraw. The retreating Federals quickly engulfed Wells's arriving brigade, throwing it into confusion before it could deploy. In fairly short order, Kershaw had routed Thoburn's entire division, sending the panicked Federals fleeing in confusion toward Berryville.[14]

The confusion quickly spread to troops who had not even been deployed on the firing line. Retreating fugitives raced through Wells's brigade as it attempted to deploy. Wells's normally reliable troops panicked and joined the masses in hasty retreat. "What magic power the enemy could employ to make enfeminate our daring soldiers, to paralyze their courage, particularly the 116th which had never failed before," lamented Captain Patterson of the 116th Ohio. The Southern magic was the sound generalship displayed by Anderson and Kershaw, who advanced aggressively before the Federal lines could be completely formed. Nevertheless, Thoburn despaired at the failure of his troops to make a stand, having led them throughout the spring and summer in many tight situations. "It is with mortification that I report the giving way of the command on the left," complained Thoburn, "the men and officers feel their disgrace and also believe themselves capable of doing better things."[15]

13 Ibid.; Benjamin G. Humphreys, "The Sunflower Guards," Claiborne Papers, SHC-UNC.

14 OR 43, pt. 1, 367, 1,026; *Ironton Register*, December 16, 1886.

15 OR 43, pt. 1, 367; William T. Patterson Diary, OHS.

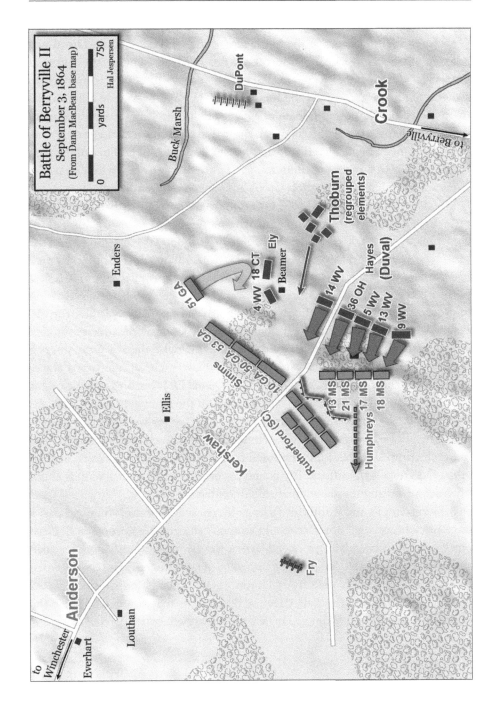

Battle of Berryville II
September 3, 1864
(From Dana MacBean base map)

0   yards   750

Hal Jespersen

When the first shots of the battle rang out, Col. Isaac Hardin Duval was relaxing on a campstool outside of his headquarters tent in the camp at Berryville. His troops were raising their tents while the commissaries slaughtered livestock to feed the hungry soldiers. "We had made a light day's march," recalled a West Virginian of Duval's division, "and we were happy as larks." Suddenly, a courier dashed into camp and delivered a message to Duval. Moments later, a bugle blared, and a drummer beat the long roll to call the men to formation. In a matter of minutes, the entire division was marching to the front and carrying out its part in Crook's planned counterattack.[16]

As Duval deployed his troops on Thoburn's left, fugitives from the latter's division retreated through the line, shattering Crook's plans. Instead of launching an attack, he was suddenly forced to use Duval's division to seal the breach and prevent disaster. Given the rough handling and rout that his men had experienced at Kernstown in July, Crook surely worried about a repeat performance. Amidst the confusion, Duval kept his veteran Kanawha division in good order and quickly shook out a line of battle. Colonel Rutherford B. Hayes deployed his three regiments behind a stone fence on the reverse slope of a small plateau. Hayes placed the 36th Ohio on his right, the 5th West Virginia in the center, and the 13th West Virginia on the left. Duval reinforced Hayes with the 9th and 14th West Virginia of Col. Daniel D. Johnson's brigade on his left and right flanks respectively. The ground on the front side of the wall was level with the top of the fence, forming a terrace. As they waited for Kershaw's men, Duval's Federals stooped down behind the wall, fired off some caps to dry out their damp rifles, and then rammed fresh rounds down the barrels of their guns. On Duval's right flank, Ely halted his brigade in Beamer's Woods south of the road, setting the scene for further combat.[17]

Humphreys's and Rutherford's brigades chased Thoburn's fugitives past a large brick house like "some cruel old women" shaking her apron at a flock of chickens. The Federals leapt over Hayes's troops, who were lying concealed behind the terrace wall. In spite of the torrent of retreating troops, Duval's men weathered the storm. In their front, Humphreys's jubilant Mississippians closed to within 200 yards of the wall, cheering defiantly as they charged between the house and several outbuildings. Duval's men saw them coming, fixed bayonets,

16 Sturm, *A Whirlpool of Death*, 87.

17 OR 43, pt. 1, 400-1, 405, 409-10; "The Fifth Virginia Infantry," *Ironton Register*, September 29, 1864.

Col. James P. Simms led a brigade of Georgia infantry in Joe Kershaw's First Corps division. *LC*

and steeled themselves to confront the Rebel onset. Hayes jumped upon the wall and called out, "Go for them boys!" The Ohioans and West Virginians fired a short-range volley into the rushing Rebels, clambered over the wall, and charged into the midst of the stunned Southern troops. One Mountaineer related, "The boys fired, yelled and scrambled up the wall, the sergeants pushing, boosting some of the less active, and the boys pulling each other, and then such a yelling and firing of those two lines you can't conceive." Duval's hard charging Federals ran over the 17th and 18th Mississippi and drove them back to the washed-out breastworks they had taken from Thoburn. There, the 13th and 21st Mississippi opened fire and saved the hard-hit regiments from further loss. Duval's counterattack killed at least 24 Rebels and captured 59 prisoners. Humphreys was seriously wounded in the chest and never returned to duty. Kershaw's old South Carolina brigade saw their comrades' plight and attempted to come to the aid of the Mississippians, but Duval's veterans stopped them cold. "Prisoners say it is the first time their division was ever flogged in a fair fight," bragged Colonel Hayes.[18]

While the Mississippians and South Carolinians were being driven back to the breastworks, Col. Simms's Georgians continued their advance north of the

18 Ibid.; R. B. Hayes to Dear Uncle, September 6, 1864, RBHPC; Benjamin G. Humphreys, "The Sunflower Guards," Claiborne Papers, SHC-UNC.

Berryville Road, pressing after Ely's brigade. The Georgians had advanced with "great spirit and gallantry," but the withdrawal of Rutherford and Humphreys on Simms's right prevented further progress. Although the Georgians had advanced with "great spirit and gallantry," Simms halted his advance to avoid the firestorm that struck his fellow brigadiers on the right.[19]

The fight now developed into a twilight standoff with neither side attempting to break the opposing battle line. Both Crook and Anderson fed more men into battle, but the tactical situation had stabilized. For more than two hours, the combatants located their targets by firing at the opposing muzzle flashes in the darkness. Many soldiers on both sides emptied their cartridge boxes in this manner. The entire 14th West Virginia ran out of ammunition, so Crook called in the 23rd Ohio from picket duty on the army's far left flank to relieve the Mountaineers. Captain William McKinley of Crook's staff later recalled, "The night battle of Berryville . . . was a brilliant scene; the heavens were fairly illuminated by the flashes of our own and the enemies' guns."[20]

As the battle lines stabilized, Anderson deployed another battery of Cutshaw's battalion, which "behaved gallantly and rendered good service." His foot soldiers kept up a heavy small arms fire, and it appeared as if a general engagement was shaping up. Finally, dwindling ammunition, fatigue, and rain ended the fighting. The engagement at Berryville cost Crook 23 men killed, 141 wounded, and 19 missing for a total of 183 Union casualties. Anderson lost at least 166 men in Humphreys's brigade while Simms lost another 30 killed and wounded. Total Confederate losses for the fighting at Berryville were at least 220 men.[21]

After the combat subsided, Crook's men interacted with the prisoners from Kershaw's division. The surgeon of the 12th West Virginia handed a Rebel captain a newspaper whose headlines heralded the fall of the city of Atlanta. The Southerner's spirit sagged at the news, and he announced that "their people might as well give up now as anytime, no use of being so stubborn about it."[22]

19 OR 43, pt. 1, 590.

20 *Ironton Register*, September 29, 1864; William McKinley, 23rd Ohio Reunion Speech, LC.

21 Confederate casualties are from Alfred Young's unpublished research on the 1864 losses of the Army of Northern Virginia. Author copy courtesy of Mr. Young. U.S. losses are contained in OR 43, pt. 1, 367, 401.

22 Richard R. Duncan, *Alexander Neil and the Last Shenandoah Valley Campaign* (Shippensburg, PA: White Mane, 1996), 62-63.

When Sheridan learned of the fighting, he hastened to Berryville and established a temporary headquarters. He errantly concluded that Anderson's advance had been an attempt to cut Torbert off from the balance of the Army of the Shenandoah. At 9:00 p.m., Sheridan withdrew Crook's Army of West Virginia to the east side of Berryville where it would be closer to Emory's Nineteenth Corps. "In this position," wrote Sheridan, "the line will be short, compact, easily reinforced, and on very good ground." Thirty minutes later, he informed Torbert of the results of the day's combat and reeled the cavalryman's command in from White Post back to Berryville. The cavalry was to close up on Crook's left flank and guard the roads running into Berryville from the west, south, and east. Sheridan's forces completed these dispositions early the next morning. If a general engagement ensued, Sheridan planned to fight it on the defensive; a plan that once again let Anderson's small force escape a potential disaster. Although the South Carolinian had failed in his objective of reaching the Loudoun Valley, his unexpected movement forced Sheridan to abandon the initiative and assume a defensive posture. In doing so, the Union commander forfeited another golden opportunity to overwhelm Anderson's isolated force for the second time in little more than a week.[23]

On the opposite side of the battlefield, Dick Anderson dispatched a messenger to Early "to inform him of the state of affairs and to urge him to join me by daylight the following morning." Late that night, Anderson belatedly learned that Torbert had moved through White Post and threatened the Valley Turnpike. He did not know that Torbert had already returned to Berryville by then but feared that the Union horsemen "would be able to do a great deal of harm to us if not cut-off entirely all our sources of supply." Jubal Early roused his troops very early on September 4 and marched to Anderson's support. Slowed by the muddy roads, he did not arrive until 9:30 a.m., and found Kershaw's division skirmishing with its Union adversaries. Early saluted Anderson and remarked, "Those Yankees came might near getting you yesterday." A miffed Anderson shot back, "Yes, General, and it is not your fault that they did not." The contentious relationship between Anderson and Early continued.[24]

23 OR 43, pt. 1, 23, 45-46; 43; pt. 2, 18-19; Early, *A Memoir of the Last Year of the War*, 76-77.

24 Lt. Gen. Richard Anderson, Report of Operations, 1864, FSNMP; Dawson, *Reminiscences of Confederate Service, 1861-1865*, 123.

Setting their differences aside for the moment, the two generals studied Sheridan's position and decided to take the offensive. Leaving Ramseur's division with Anderson on Kershaw's left, Early led Rodes and Wharton toward Sheridan's right flank to initiate the battle. The South Carolinian would follow with Kershaw and Ramseur when Anderson heard the sound of Early's guns. After marching two miles, Early reached an elevated position three and one-half miles north of Berryville, where he thought he may have a vantage point. He scanned the Federal position with his field glasses and, to his alarm, discovered that Sheridan's position extended well beyond the Confederate left "and was too strong to attack." It was the first time the Confederates had seen Sheridan's entire army deployed since it had been substantially reinforced. Old Jube promptly abandoned offensive operations and assumed a defensive position of his own. Anderson concurred with the decision, and the Confederates withdrew under the cover of darkness, returning to their previous positions west of the Opequon.

On the opposite side of the battlefield, Sheridan had hoped that Early and Anderson would attack the strong Federal position. He went so far as to inform Halleck that, "The indications look to an engagement to-morrow."

It never came.[25]

25 OR *Atlas*, Plate LXXXI: 10; OR 43, pt. 1, 572, 1,026; Early, *A Memoir of the Last Year of the War*, 77; Official Diary of the First Corps, *SHSP*, 7:509-510.

WHENEVER YOU HAVE AN OPPORTUNITY

Advance and Retreat, September 3 - 15

the next two weeks, infantry of both armies remained in their same relative positions, in a figurative stare down across Opequon Creek. During this period, the Union cavalry continued its dynamic pace and set the tone for the rest of the campaign. General Sheridan had directed Brig. Gen. William Averell "to push up the Valley so far as is prudent. Whenever you have an opportunity, attack the enemy." Averell enthusiastically complied with these instructions, attacking Jubal Early's northern flank on an almost daily basis, exhausting the outnumbered Confederate cavalry. Averell's quick-hitting excursions continually forced the Southern infantry to march out of camp and drive the Federal cavalry away, fatiguing the men and adding to the general wear and tear on Early's foot soldiers.[1]

Averell's aggressive performance of his duty in these actions probably saved his job—at least for the time being. On September 1, U.S. Grant complained to Sheridan that "the frequent reports of Averell's falling back without much fighting . . . and being able to take his old position without opposition, presents a very bad appearance at this distance. You can judge

1 OR 43, pt. 1, 504.

better of his merits than I can, but it looks to me as if it was time to try some other officer in his place." Grant was concerned about Averell's suitablility for the important role he filled. "If you think as I do in this matter," Grant told Sheridan, "Relieve him at once and name his successor." Sheridan retained Averell for the time being, as the New Yorker's heroic victories against long odds at Rutherford's farm on July 20 and Moorefield on August 7 did not justify his removal from command. In fact, communications between the two generals appeared pleasant, and Sheridan seemed satisfied with Averell's performance, especially with the detailed and relatively accurate intelligence garnered by the New Yorker's scouts.[2]

At 10:00 a.m. on September 3, the same day as the fight at Berryville, Maj. Gen. Lunsford Lomax led three of his cavalry brigades to Bunker Hill and attacked Averell's picket line. The Confederates drove the pickets two miles back to Darkesville, a village situated seven miles south of Martinsburg. There, Averell's main force waited in line of battle. When the Confederates appeared, the Union horse artillery opened a telling fire, halting Lomax's advance. Averell's cavalry counterattacked, driving the Confederates back in confusion. Lomax rallied his troopers back at Bunker Hill under cover of his own artillery. The Confederates checked Averell as he initially attempted to cross Mill Creek; however, the Federal commander fed more troops into the fight and broke the Confederate line. The U.S. troopers nearly captured the Southern artillery, but the creek slowed their advance. With the collapse of Lomax's division on his left flank, Early called out his old "Foot Cavalry" to seal the breach. In what had become a routine occurrence, Rodes's division marched out and checked Averell's pursuit, saving Lomax from any further embarrassment.[3]

Averell's attacks against Lomax between Bunker Hill and Stephenson's Depot on the Martinsburg Turnpike became a habitual event. "There was a fight every day," recalled a West Virginian of Averell's division, "the rebel cavalry . . . attempted to stop [Col. William H.] Powell's brigade; they would

<hr />

2 General Grant's assessment is puzzling, and brought about by Averell withdrawing from Martinsburg on September 1. Sheridan routinely reported the matter to Halleck. Sheridan described the whole matter as "not of much consequence and he is going back to Martinsburg." Grant apparently read more into the report and wanted Averell replaced. Although Sheridan did not act upon Grant's suggestion, Grant surely planted a seed in Sheridan's mind. He had previously encouraged Sheridan to overlook Averell's seniority when the former appointed Torbert to command the cavalry corps. OR 43, pt. 2, 3-4.

3 *Baltimore American*, September 6, 1864.

Brig. Gen. William Woods Averell
LC

soon be scattered and chased, until infantry and artillery, in large numbers would be encountered." These actions weakened the already disadvantaged Confederate cavalry and wore down the infantrymen who marched to their rescue. "Usually the men were in the saddle almost constantly from sunrise until dark," recalled a New Yorker, "and each day had its casualties."[4]

4 For more on this fascinating series of actions, see Joseph J. Sutton, *History of the Second Regiment West Virginia Cavalry Volunteers During the War of the Rebellion* (Portsmouth, OH: 1892),

On September 5, Averell's division headed south on the Martinsburg Pike. He soon encountered two of Lomax's brigades under the overall command of Col. George H. Smith from the 62nd Virginia Mounted Infantry between Bunker Hill and Stephenson's Depot. Smith's force consisted of Imboden's brigade, led by the ill general's brother Col. George W. Imboden, and McCausland's brigade under Col. Milton J. Ferguson. Smith dismounted most of his troops and deployed them on the front line with a mounted regiment from each brigade in reserve. Averell opened the fight with Capt. Gulian Weir's 5th U.S. Artillery shelling the Southerners. The Union troopers then charged the dismounted Confederates and broke Ferguson's brigade on the right. As the confusion extended to the left, Col. Imboden ordered Lt. Col. David Lang to withdraw his 62nd Virginia. As Lang complied, a Union bullet severed his spine, mortally wounding him. The 18th Virginia of Imboden's brigade counter charged and blunted the blue onslaught long enough for the dismounted men to withdraw safely. Nevertheless, Averell's troopers soon had the entire Confederate force on the run. Having just returned from Early's jaunt to assist Anderson at Berryville, Rodes's division moved out and repulsed Averell's troopers. The loss of Lt. Col. Lang deeply affected Imboden's brigade. "He was a noble soldier," wrote Colonel Imboden, "and his loss is a heavy one to the service and we will miss him greatly in the brigade." Although mortally wounded, he was "perfectly rational & sensible to his fate. . . . He looked death in the face with as much coolness and resignation as he did the enemy." In the larger scope of things, Lang's loss symbolized a growing problem throughout the Confederate armies: the loss of irreplaceable veteran officers that sapped combat effectiveness.[5]

Lomax's inability to successfully confront Averell should have been yet another warning sign for Jubal Early to take corrective action with his cavalry. If the smallest, least experienced division of Sheridan's cavalry could have its way with Lomax on a daily basis, remedial action of some sort should have been attempted. Yet, just as Early ignored Maj. Gen. Robert Ransom's recommendations to reorganize and rejuvenate the Valley Cavalry in August, the Confederate commander continued to disregard Lomax's ineffective

---

156; William H. Beach, *The First New York (Lincoln) Cavalry, From April 19, 1861, to July 7, 1865* (New York: The Lincoln Cavalry Association, 1902), 417.

5   George Imboden to My Dearest Mother, September 7, 1864; USAMHI; Roger U. Delauter, Jr., *62nd Virginia Infantry* (Lynchburg, VA: H.E. Howard, 1988), 40-1.

leadership. Early had made his career in the infantry and lacked the ability and experience to rectify the cavalry crisis himself. He also refused to allow others to make any changes until it was too late.

On September 10, Early disrupted the routine and seized the initiative from Averell. Confederate infantry under Rodes and Ramseur marched north on the Valley Pike and drove the New Yorker from his position at Darkesville. Lomax then took up the pursuit and pushed the Federals through Martinsburg. The Confederate infantry promptly returned to Bunker Hill that evening and then to Stephenson's Depot the next day. Once again, Early had split his command right under Sheridan's nose, but the Union commander still did not react with any aggressive movement toward Winchester.

Sheridan steadfastly maintained a defensive posture, and did so with the full knowledge and approval of General Grant. On September 9, Grant wrote, "I would not have you make an attack with the advantage against you, but would prefer just the course you seem to be pursuing - that is, pressing closely upon the enemy, and when he moves, follow him up, being ready at all times to pounce upon him if he detaches a considerable force." In writing that, Grant did not realize that Sheridan had missed several opportunities to "pounce" on isolated portions of the Confederate forces in the Shenandoah Valley.[6]

Sheridan continued to probe Early's lines along Opequon Creek seeking weak points in the Confederate defensive perimeter. On September 12, he accompanied the 6th Michigan Cavalry to the vicinity of Locke's Ford and scouted the terrain. At 6:00 a.m. on the following morning, Sheridan led a combined force of infantry and cavalry back to Locke's Ford on Opequon Creek north of Winchester. Merritt's mounted men led the way and drove off the Confederate pickets on the east bank of the Opequon. He sent a detachment from the 2nd Massachusetts Cavalry across the stream "to develop the force of the enemy at the crossing in that vicinity." They drove back the Confederate pickets and ascertained the presence of Confederate infantry. Merritt's horse soldiers pushed Early's pickets back toward Brucetown, capturing a dozen soldiers from Gordon's division along the way. Brigadier General George Washington Getty's division of the Sixth Corps supported Merritt's move, advancing to Gilbert's Mill on the east bank of the stream near Locke's Ford. The appearance of such a large U.S. force on the Opequon alarmed Jubal Early. He personally led the divisions of Gordon and Ramseur

6 OR 43, pt. 2, 57.

through Brucetown toward the Opequon, and shoved Merritt's cavalry back across the creek. Confederate sharpshooters traded shots across the stream with Getty's infantry and Merritt's cavalry. As the opposing lines stabilized, the soldiers added some political humor to the engagement that highlighted the importance of the coming presidential election: the Southerners cheered for McClellan as they fired, and the Union boys responded with hurrahs for Abe Lincoln.

When Getty committed a six-gun battery to the combat, Early ordered Capt. John C. Carpenter's Alleghany Battery to drive the Federals from their position. In the ensuing artillery duel, the Federals temporarily disabled three of Carpenter's four guns and killed or seriously wounded a dozen artillerists and 17 horses. Incredibly, a Federal solid shot struck a twelve-pound Napoleon of Carpenter's Battery in the muzzle, flaring it out "like a trumpet." A Confederate gunner later recalled, "That frightful duel being so uneven . . . left us nothing to do but to withdraw, and leave the enemy his well earned field of glory." After learning that Early remained in force near Brucetown, Sheridan broke off the engagement and withdrew to Summit Point.[7]

Further south, Sheridan detailed one of Wilson's brigades to scout the Spout Spring crossing of the Opequon on the Berryville-Winchester Turnpike. Ironically, Dick Anderson was planning to leave the Valley that day only to have his plans interrupted by Sheridan's cavalry. The First Corps commander had already issued marching orders to Kershaw and Cutshaw, and the force was preparing for its departure from Winchester. Wilson, however, had detailed Brig. Gen. John B. McIntosh "to make a strong reconnaissance toward Winchester for the purpose of determining the enemy's position" on the Berryville Turnpike. McIntosh moved out with the 2nd Ohio, 3rd New Jersey, 2nd and 5th New York, 1st Connecticut, and a section of the 2nd U.S. Artillery.[8]

McIntosh's brigade rode west along the Berryville Pike and attempted to capture Confederate vedettes from Bradley Johnson's brigade posted upon Limestone Ridge east of the Opequon. The Virginians fled quickly to the west bank of the creek. Johnson dismounted his main force and deployed it in some woods on a high eminence that commanded the road. McIntosh crossed the

7   OR 43, pt. 1, 24, 68, 573; C.A. Fonerdon, *A Brief History of the Military Career of Carpenter's Battery* (New Market, VA: 1911), 49-50; OR 43, pt. 1, 467; Aldace Walker, *The Vermont Brigade in the Shenandoah Valley 1864* (Burlington, VT: The Free Press Association, 1869), 73-74.

8   Lt. Gen. Richard Anderson, Report of Operations, 1864, FSNMP; OR 43, pt. 1, 24, 517.

Spout Spring, where the Berryville Pike crossed Opequon Creek, looking west-northwest. The Spout Spring crossing saw much action throughout Sheridan's Campaign, including September 13 when Wilson's cavalry captured the 8th South Carolina a couple of miles west of the creek. *MOLLUS-USAMHI*

Opequon and advanced rapidly up the road in the ravine, and Johnson's Virginians fired upon McIntosh's lead regiment, the 2nd Ohio. They veered left to avoid the fire and simultaneously flanked the Virginians from their position.[9]

On the south side of the road, the Ohioans saw a strong line of infantry confronting them. McIntosh rode out to his skirmish line and scanned the situation. He was facing Col. John W. Henagan's 8th South Carolina of Kershaw's division performing picket duty while they waited to depart the Valley. McInstosh decided to continue his advance and ordered a squadron of the 3rd New Jersey to charge up the road "as hard as they could go." His skirmishers advanced on foot while the 2nd Ohio clawed its way through the woods toward Henagan's right flank.[10]

McIntosh rode furiously over to the left to see Col. George Purington, commander of the 2nd Ohio. "Exceedingly excited & pointing toward the enemy," McIntosh shouted, "Charge Col. Charge!" With only a dozen men at

9   Ibid., 529.

10   Ibid., 530.

hand, Purington demurred that his command was not ready, but the fiery McIntosh thundered, "Never mind, charge, charge immediately." Still Purington hesitated, and McIntosh exploded. He ripped off an oath at the Ohioan and ordered him to attack with the men he had on hand, "yelling out at the top of his voice, charge my men, charge them, see them running, go for 'em."[11]

Inspired by McIntosh's fervor, the Ohioans in the vanguard assailed the Carolinians who offered surprisingly little resistance. As more Ohioans emerged from the thicket, they joined in the attack against the Palmetto men's right flank. With the Buckeyes on the left and the 3rd New Jersey on the right, Henagan's Carolinians quickly retreated and took refuge in a thickly wooded ravine on the south side of the Berryville Pike. The advance elements of the 2nd Ohio worked around the west side of the shrouded declivity and sealed off the Confederate line of retreat toward Winchester. The 3rd New Jersey hit the Carolinians on their left flank and completely trapped the Southerners. Hemmed in on all sides, the Carolinians quickly realized their plight, poured out of the woods, and surrendered without fanfare. The prisoners were a dirty lot, prompting Corp. Roger Hannaford of the 2nd Ohio to complain, "A flock of ten year old billy-goats stirred up could not have stunk worse than these Johnnies." McIntosh captured Colonel Henagan, more than 100 officers and men, the colors of the 8th South Carolina, and several Virginians from Johnson's brigade. Concerned that a Confederate counterattack would soon be forthcoming, McIntosh "sounded the recall." He marched his men back to Berryville not only with his prisoners, but also with a thorough understanding of the landscape of the Berryville Canyon that he later put to good use.[12]

As McIntosh suspected, the balance of Kershaw's old South Carolina brigade advanced under the command of Brig. Gen. James Conner, who had only recently arrived and assumed command of the brigade. Advancing promptly to support Henagan, Conner found that McIntosh had already departed with his prisoners. That one of the "best fighting regiments" in the Confederate service could be so easily captured bothered Conner. He reported that the woods where the 8th South Carolina surrendered "could have been

11 Roger Hannaford Papers, CiHS.

12 Henagan died at Johnson's Island Prison Camp at Sandusky, Ohio, in April 1865; OR 43, pt. 1, 530; "From the Third New Jersey Cavalry," *Newark Daily Advertiser*, September 22, 1864; W. C. Hall Diary, Atlanta Historical Society.

held at least long enough for re-enforcements to arrive." Privately, however, the South Carolinian wrote his mother that the Union cavalrymen are "decidedly the best troops" in Sheridan's army. The dash and élan of the Union cavalry had once again impressed itself upon the minds of the Confederate infantrymen.[13]

McIntosh's aggressive reconnassaince convinced Anderson that Sheridan might soon attack. With a possible action in the offing, the South Carolinian suspended the order to march to Culpeper. Regarding the capture of the 8th South Carolina, Anderson complained, "The conduct of Col. Henagan and his regiment on this occasion is inexcusable. The post was one which might have been defended for some time against any odds." Anderson must have fumed privately, as losses to his command numbered more than 700 men since arriving in the Shenandoah on August 16. Even worse, all of the losses had occurred in engagements of no consequence and, for the most part, were inflicted by the Union cavalry. When no attack came on September 14, Anderson departed with Kershaw and Cutshaw, moved to Front Royal, and then through Chester Gap toward Culpeper. To compensate for Anderson's departure, Early shifted Ramseur's division into position to cover the eastern approaches to Winchester. Ramseur posted Brig. Gen. Robert Johnston's brigade on the Berryville Pike and Brig. Gen. Archibald Godwin's brigade to the south on the Millwood Pike. Brigadier General John Pegram's brigade covered the Senseny Road, a smaller track running between the two pikes.[14]

Sheridan did not learn immediately of Anderson's departure, and until he did, the Army of the Shenandoah remained firmly entrenched east of the Opequon. Rainy weather in the first two weeks of September had also dampened the prospects for a major movement by the Army of the Shenandoah. Nevertheless, with the presidential election drawing closer, Sheridan keenly felt the continued political pressure to avoid defeat in the Valley. In his memoirs, he explained:

> I knew that I was strong, yet, in consequence of the injunctions of General Grant, I deemed it necessary to be very cautious; and the fact that the Presidential election was impending made me doubly so, the authorities at Washington having impressed upon

13 Gen. James Conner to My dear Mother, September 20, 1864, Duke; OR 43, pt. 1, 592-593.

14 Anderson's assessment was verified by the 23rd North Carolina on September 19. The Tar Heels put up a tough fight in the same position. They not only escaped, but delayed the Union approach. Lieutenant General Richard Anderson, Report of Operations, 1864; FSNMP; George Q. Peyton Diary, Manassas Library 76; John D. Paris Diary, SHC-UNC.

me that the defeat of my army might be followed by the overthrow of the party in power, which event it was believed would at least retard the progress of the war, if indeed, it did not lead to the complete abandonment of all coercive measures . . .[15]

While the campaigning in August and early September produced no tangible military outcomes, the cumulative effect of the many small battles provided Sheridan with two important, perhaps decisive advantages. First, the constant engagements wore out Early's cavalry and overstretched the already strained Confederate remount system. "We cannot rely upon our cavalry to hold points," complained Major Hotchkiss of Early's staff. Second, "In these skirmishes," observed Sheridan, "the cavalry was becoming educated to attack infantry." The experience thus gained coupled with the wear and tear upon Early's army would be exploited to the fullest extent when Sheridan and Early finally clashed. Wesley Merritt agreed, adding "They [the engagements] gave the cavalry increased confidence, and made the enemy correspondingly doubtful even of the ability of its infantry, in anything like equal numbers, to contend against our cavalry in the open fields of the Valley."[16]

From the Confederate perspective, Jubal Early had played a masterful game of bluff. The constant shuffling of his forces had convinced Sheridan that "the difference of strength between the two opposing forces at this time was but little." While Sheridan had a field army of nearly 40,000, Early possessed no more than half that number at any point in the campaign, including Anderson's troops. Further, Old Jube's operations in the lower Shenandoah Valley successfully withheld 30,000 men from Grant's operations against General Lee at Petersburg. A Winchester correspondent wrote on September 10, "Now 'Old Jubal' has the confidence of the army and people of the Valley to a greater extent than any other officer of the army (Lee always excepted)." One historian of the campaign, Capt. L. W. V. Kennon, U.S.A., noted that Early had conducted his campaign "with conspicuous skill and judgment, although with audacity that bordered on rashness."[17]

Early would soon commit the one error he could ill-afford—that of underestimating his opponent. Sheridan's missed opportunities to crush

15 Sheridan, *Memoirs*, vol. 2, 499-500.

16 Hotchkiss to My Dear Sara, September 3, 1864, LC; OR 43, pt. 1, 46; Merritt, "Sheridan in the Shenandoah Valley," 500-521.

17 OR 43, pt. 1, 46; *Richmond Whig*, September 15, 1864.

isolated portions of the Confederate forces and his careful and restrained campaigning in the wake of Anderson's arrival in the Shenandoah convinced Early that Sheridan was a timid commander. "The events of the last month had satisfied me that the commander opposed to me was without enterprise and possessed an excessive caution which amounted to timidity," Jubal concluded. His Confederate troops were coming to the same conclusion. "The enemy is not far distant, though we have them so completely carved down it takes but short notice to disperse them," declared Sgt. Joseph J. Felder of the 4th Georgia.[18]

Early's assessment of his opponent was dead wrong. His army would soon pay the price for his miscalculation.

---

18 Early, *A Memoir of the Last Year of the War*, 80; Joseph J. Felder to Dear Sister, September 8, 1864, GDAH.

THE MOVE MEANS FIGHT

Prelude to Battle, September 15 - 18

By mid-September, Sheridan felt growing pressure to defeat Early in the Shenandoah Valley. Sherman's victory in Georgia had energized the northern political landscape in a way that had not been seen since the major victories at Vicksburg and Gettysburg in 1863. It also loosened the political constraints on Sheridan's campaign and placed him squarely in the cross-hairs of the War Department. Important business interests in Washington, D.C. complained loudly to the Lincoln administration about the negative economic impact of Jubal Early's continued presence in the northern Shenandoah Valley. Throughout the late summer, his troops raided the Baltimore and Ohio Railroad and the Chesapeake and Ohio Canal along the Potomac. Both were vital economic arteries to the U.S. capital. The Confederate raids on the B & O Railroad had so disrupted the flow of coal used for heating and lighting that supplies in the capital had dwindled to critically low levels. With winter lurking around the corner, John Garrett, president of the B & O, protested Sheridan's apparent inability to defeat Jubal Early and keep the railroad open.

President Lincoln addressed the matter quickly. On September 12, he observed that "Sheridan and Early are feeling each other at a dead lock." He asked Grant, "Could we not pick up a regiment here and there to the number of say ten thousand, and quickly, but suddenly concentrate them at Sheridan's camp and enable him to make a strike?" Grant responded that he would soon be on his way to visit Sheridan "and arrange what was necessary to enable him to start Early out of the Valley."[1]

On September 14, Halleck advised Grant of the growing chorus of complaints. "Reliable business men inform me that the long and continued disruption of the Chesapeake and Ohio Canal [sic] and Baltimore and Ohio Railroad is very seriously affecting the supply of provisions and fuel for public and private use in Baltimore, Washington, Georgetown and Alexandria," wrote Halleck. The businessmen urged that Sheridan drive Early "far enough south to secure these lines of communication from rebel raids. If Sheridan is not strong enough to do this he should be re-enforced." Halleck "respectfully submitted these representations" to Grant for his "consideration." Already grasping the situation, Grant notified Halleck, "I will leave here to-morrow morning for the Shenandoah Valley to see Sheridan," but, "[I] will not pass through Washington . . . unless it is the wish of the President or Secretary of War to do so." The Union commander later explained his reasons for avoiding the capital: "I knew it was impossible for me to get orders through Washington to Sheridan to make a move, because they would be stopped there and such orders as Halleck's caution (and that of the Secretary of War [Stanton]) . . . would be given instead, and would, no doubt, be contradictory to mine." Grant realized that Sheridan had taken Stanton's cautions too much to heart, and set out to invigorate Union operations in the Shenandoah Valley.[2]

Although Grant did not say it, he had good reason to be concerned about Sheridan's attitude toward guarding these vital transportation arteries. Only two days earlier, Grant had received a dispatch from Sheridan explaining the difficulties that confronted him in the Valley. It was essentially an explanation for his inaction with the added assurance that Sheridan would attack Early as soon as he detached troops to Richmond and Petersburg. Sheridan likely hit a nerve when he closed the communiqué by stating, "There is no interest suffering here except the Baltimore and Ohio Railroad, and I will not divide my

---

1   Abraham Lincoln to Lieut. Genl. Grant, September 12, 1864, Lincoln Papers, LC; U.S. Grant to A. Lincoln, September 13, 1864, Lincoln Papers, LC.

2   *OR* 43, pt. 2, 83-84; Grant, *Memoirs*, 620-621.

force to protect it." Grant, however, needed to impress upon Sheridan the true importance of the B & O Railroad.[3]

Aside from political pressure, Sheridan fully intended to strike Early the moment he detached troops to Petersburg. Ironically, Sheridan's operations had unwittingly thwarted Anderson's departure on September 13. Sketchy information and rumors filtered into headquarters, but Sheridan would only act on verified intelligence. "I always believed in fighting on information," recalled Sheridan. At the time, the information he wanted was not at his immediate disposal. He told Grant on September 15, "I have nothing new to report . . . . There is as yet no indication of Early's detaching . . ." The situation frustrated the Ohio general. He later recalled, "I wanted information of what was going on in the enemy's lines, and I wanted it awful bad. . . . But how I was going to get it, I didn't know."[4]

To find answers, he turned to his friend, Maj. Gen. George Crook. He had campaigned in the area since July, and many of his officers and men had served in the Valley since 1862. Crook had previously told Sheridan of a loyal Quaker school teacher who resided in Winchester. Crook had made her acquaintance when his Army of West Virginia briefly occupied Winchester in late July. One of Crook's officers, Lt. Col. Benjamin Franklin Coates of the 91st Ohio Infantry, had visited some relatives and old family friends who resided in and around Winchester. Coates's parents were Quakers who had lived near Winchester and had belonged to Hopewell Meeting, a Quaker community situated a few miles north of town. Before Benjamin was born in 1827, his parents left Winchester and moved west, settling in southern Ohio. Among those Coates visited in 1864 was the Wright family who were, for the most part, loyal Quakers and abolitionists.

In late July 1864, Crook dined at their residence and met Miss Rebecca L. Wright. Crook apparently visited the Wright family again in August during Sheridan's initial foray up the Valley. At that time, Rebecca, who considered herself "pretty well informed" on the general situation around Winchester, told Crook, "If Gen. Sheridan knew as much as I do he would capture Early's

---

3   George F. Pond, *The Shenandoah Valley in 1864* (New York: Charles Scribner's Sons, 1883), 150.

4   "A Heroine of the War: What General Sheridan Says of Her Work," Washington Correspondent of the Chicago Inter-Ocean, reprinted in the *Helena Independent*, April 3, 1884; *OR* 43, pt. 2, 89.

force." Her fidelity to the United States and knowledge of the situation impressed Crook. When Sheridan asked for assistance, Crook recommended the young Quaker as a trustworthy source of information.

The Civil War wounded and divided the Wright family as it had so many others across the United States. In 1861, Confederate authorities arrested and imprisoned their patriarch, Amos A. Wright, because of his fervent Unionist beliefs. Later freed from captivity, he spent the rest of the war away from home in hiding. According to Rebecca, her brother David had been conscripted into the Confederate ranks and died as a soldier fighting for a cause he opposed. Her two surviving brothers went into hiding to avoid conscription. When General Crook befriended the Wrights in the summer of 1864, only Rebecca, her mother Rachael, and sister Hannah were residing in the family home on Loudoun Street, the main thoroughfare in Winchester. Hannah, however, did not share her family's predominantly Unionist beliefs. Rebecca later recalled Hannah as a "Rebel," and didn't trust her. But in September 1864, Rebecca had no idea she would have any reason to fear her sister's loyalty to the South.[5]

Although Hannah was a Confederate sympathizer and David had served in the Confederate Army, the family still suffered for its convictions. The 24-year-old "Becky," as Rebecca was known, lost her job as a teacher because of her views, but she persevered by teaching the children of the few Unionists who remained in Winchester. Throughout the war, reminders of their minority status were never far away. Late at night on August 21, Confederate troops

5   Thanks to Ben Ritter of Winchester for his assistance with the Wright family research. Two men by the name of David Wright served in Virginia units. A David P. Wright served in the 20th Virginia Cavalry and died at Rock Island Prison Camp in Illinois. Burial records indicate David Paul Wright was buried there, making him the most likely candidate to be Rebecca's brother. However, if he was a Unionist forced into the Confederate ranks, it is strange that he was given a horse and placed in a cavalry. Secondly, he would have had the opportunity to swear allegiance to the United States and obtain his freedom when captured. It might be that while the family was Unionist, David, like his sister Hannah, was not. A second David Wright served in the 33rd Virginia Infantry until at least June of 1862. At some point after that time, he was discharged from a hospital but never returned to the regiment. He was born in Winchester; however, he did not die in Confederate service. He was married in 1867 in Winchester and died and was buried in Hampshire County, West Virginia. This Wright seems to better fit into the Wright family in question, but his sister claimed that he died in Confederate service in an interview in 1912. It may have been that she exaggerated the story to gain sympathy and enhance the plight of her family. The bottom line is that neither soldier's identity in relation to the Wright family is certain. Rebecca's brother was David H. Wright, and the soldier who died in prison was "David P." *New York Times*, July 28, 1912; *Winchester Death Book*, Winchester City Hall; 1850 U.S. Census – Frederick County, VA; Rock Island Prison Cemetery Register.

searched the home of the Wright women, a common occurrence for Winchester Unionists whenever Confederate forces held the town.[6]

In spite of their hardships, the Wright sisters maintained their social life as well as circumstances permitted. Despite political differences, many young people gravitated toward the Wright family's home, making it the scene of much socializing. In late summer 1864, a Louisiana officer was convalescing at the home of the Wrights' next door neighbor. The girls quickly caught his attention, and, as soon as his condition permitted, he made their acquaintance. On the evening of September 14, 1864, the officer, whose name Rebecca forgot ("nor would I tell it if I remembered"), called at the Wright house and spent the evening bantering with the girls. The conversation flowed freely and naturally gravitated toward military matters about Winchester. The Louisiana officer spoke about Early's force and dispositions, explaining that Robert E. Lee's situation at Petersburg was dire and that Anderson's troops would soon be leaving the Valley. "We spent a pleasant evening together," recalled Rebecca, "and our rebel friend left us without suspicion that he had placed in my hands information which, if in the possession of the Union General would enable him to crush General Early. . . . Nor did I myself realize the importance of the information I had obtained."[7]

On September 15, the day after Rebecca Wright conversed with the Louisiana officer, Sheridan asked Crook "for the name of that young lady in Winchester." Meanwhile, Sheridan's scouts had been constantly roving the countryside, making contacts and seeking information. Even before Crook had identified Wright as a loyal contact, these enterprising scouts became acquainted with Tom Laws, a free black man who lived near Millwood, just outside the Union lines. There he scratched-out a meager living growing vegetables on a small patch of land. More importantly, he possessed a pass from the Confederate military authorities that permitted him to enter Winchester three times a week to sell vegetables at the farmers' market. Sheridan's scouts "sounded" Laws and found him "both loyal and shrewd." He agreed to carry out the most dangerous part of Sheridan's effort to contact Rebecca Wright and carry the general's message through the enemy lines. Two scouts brought Laws to Sheridan's headquarters late at night on September 15. Sheridan first assured

6 Mahon, *Winchester Divided*, 165.

7 "Woman's Wit Turned Defeat into Victory for Sheridan," *New York Times*, July 28, 1912.

himself of Laws's loyalty and reliability. Then the general wrote a message for Miss Wright, which was rolled up in foil and given to Laws. The Union scouts instructed him to carry the message in his mouth and swallow it if he ran into any problems with Confederates. Scout James Campbell went to Laws's cabin inside the Confederate lines and awaited his return.[8]

On September 16, Laws successfully ventured through the Confederate lines to Winchester. Around noon, he showed up unexpectedly at the school where Rebecca taught. The young teacher was in her classroom when Laws walked in and "softly closed the door behind him." He asked to speak with "Miss Wright." Rebecca responded that she was Miss Wright but that she also had a sister. "Perhaps thee wants to see my sister Hannah," said Rebecca. "No, I don't," replied Laws. "Your sister is not on our side. I want to see Miss Wright the Unionist. I have a letter for her from Gen. Sheridan." Laws took the concealed note from his mouth and gave it to her and told her to wrap her reply in the foil. She instructed Laws to return for her response at three o'clock and then hurried home to read the message:

> I learn from Major Gen. Crook that you are a loyal lady and still love the old flag. Can you inform me of the position of Early and his forces, the number of divisions in his army, and his probable or reported intentions? Have any more troops arrived from Richmond, or are any more coming or reported to be coming?
>
> I am very respectfully, your most obedient servant.
>
> P. H. Sheridan, Maj. Gen. Commanding
> You can trust the bearer.

The letter "greatly troubled" Wright. "I realized what would be the consequences if I should give him this information which by some act of Providence, I had obtained from my Confederate friend only two evenings before." She quietly approached her mother for guidance on the matter. Rebecca told her she would ignore Sheridan's message for "[t]he rebels would kill us if they should find it out." Her mother agreed, but added, "Men are dying for their country, and thy life and my life may be needed too. I would not persuade thee. Settle it with thy conscience. Go to thy room and giveth thyself

---

8   Sheridan, *Memoirs*, 2:3-4; Letter of Arch Rowand, Sheridan's Scouts, to War Department, September 3, 1897, National Archives.

to prayer." Rebecca did just that, and, upon deep reflection, realized that the United States needed her help. She wrote back to Sheridan:

> I have no communication whatever with the rebels, but will tell you what I know. The division of Gen. Kershaw and Cutshaw's artillery, twelve guns and men, Gen. Anderson commanding, have been sent away, and no more are expected as they cannot be spared from Richmond. I do not know how the troops are situated, but the force is much smaller than represented. I will take pleasure hereafter in learning all I can of their strength and position, and the bearer may call again.

She rolled the letter up in the foil and waited for Tom Laws to return. He showed up promptly at three o'clock, retrieved the note, and delivered it to Scout Campbell, who was waiting at Laws's cabin.

Campbell's arrival at Sheridan's headquarters set the wheels of war in motion. The information was just what Sheridan needed. He concluded "this was my opportunity" and decided to throw his whole force south of Winchester the next day. Later that same evening, General Averell sent Sheridan a dispatch that confirmed Anderson's departure. Sheridan also learned that Grant was on his way to meet with him at Charlestown, so he deferred action until he could consult with his commander.

General Grant had independently concluded that the time for Sheridan to resume the offensive in the Shenandoah Valley had arrived, and that it was likewise time to destroy "that source of supplies for Lee's army." On September 17, the generals met at the Rutherford House in Charlestown and discussed their plans for the campaign. Grant asked Sheridan for a map showing the positions of both armies in the Valley. Sheridan immediately pulled one from his coat pocket and then outlined his plan to move to Newtown and capture Early's army. Grant recalled Sheridan saying that "if he had permission he would move so and so (pointing out how [on the map]) against the Confederates, and that he could 'whip them.'" Sheridan outlined a plan that called for most of his force to seize the Valley Pike at Newtown, nine miles south of Winchester. Averell's cavalry would push up the Pike from Martinsburg, and Merritt's division would march up the Berryville Pike, cross Opequon Creek, and strike Winchester. The movement would cut Early off from his communications and force him to fight for his life on ground of Sheridan's choosing. The little Irishman's plan impressed Grant. Although the supreme Union commander had brought a battle plan with him, he concluded that Sheridan "was so clear and so positive in his views and so confident of success, I said nothing about this and did not take it out of my pocket." Grant departed the Valley believing that the climactic battle for control of the Shenandoah Valley would be fought at Newtown.[9]

Grant's presence in the Valley told the perceptive veterans that something big was afoot. "Gen. Grant has been here two days," wrote Capt. Thomas Hyatt of the 126th Ohio to his wife. "I should not be surprised if there would be bloody work in this valley soon. God grant that we may all be able to do our part and be prepared for our fate. . . . Kiss the boys for me and may God bless you all." Major Aldace Walker of the 11th Vermont realized that Grant's presence "means something. Either this army is to be reduced for the sake of the Petersburg campaign, or we shall fight here . . ." A Vermont sergeant lamented the Union commander's presence: "I hate to see that old cuss around. When that old cuss is around there's sure to be a big fight on hand."[10]

On the day of Grant's arrival, Sheridan's cavalry again struck the Opequon crossings. At one o'clock that morning, Col. John B. McIntosh led three regiments toward the ford at Spout Spring. The 18th Pennsylvania Cavalry charged across the Opequon south of Spout Spring, knocked some of Brig. Gen. Bradley Johnson's Virginians back toward Winchester, and advanced for a mile before returning to camp. The 1st Connecticut Cavalry crossed at the spring and scattered the Confederate pickets there. The 5th New York Cavalry veered off to the north and followed a farm road that led to Tanquary's Ford at Burnt Factory. The New Yorkers crossed the stream and skirmished around the shops and houses that comprised the hamlet, routed more of Johnson's cavalry, and made a circuit back to the Berryville Pike. Before re-crossing the creek at Spout Spring and heading back to camp, McIntosh ordered the burning of two nearby mills. As part of Grant's effort to destroy Valley resources, the destruction alarmed the local citizenry. "What are we to do for bread," exclaimed Mrs. Lee, "God only knows, but He will protect us."[11]

Sheridan's cavalry also made contact with the Confederates at Locke's and Seiver's Fords, several miles to the north. New Yorkers from Devin's brigade

9   Grant, *Memoirs*, 620; Sheridan, *Memoirs*, 2:9-10.

10 Thomas J. Hyatt to Dear Wife, September 18, 1864, *The Ohio State Archaeological and Historical Quarterly*, April - June 1944; Aldace F. Walker, *Quite Ready To Be Sent Somewhere* (Victoria, Canada, 2002), 301; John W. DeForest, *A Volunteer's Adventures: A Union Captain's Record of the War* (Yale, 1946), 172.

11 Mrs. Hugh Lee Diary, WFCHS, Handley Library; Julia Chase Diary, WFCHS, Handley Library.

found the 17th Virginia Cavalry from Col. Milton Ferguson's brigade to be "very friendly, riding to the middle of the stream, shaking hands, exchanging tobacco for coffee, etc." Torbert also sent cavalry to the same crossings on September 18. He instructed Merritt and Wilson to send a regiment to each ford "to make a demonstration." Torbert emphasized, "Let them show themselves as much as possible, and then quietly withdraw and return to camp." By then, the Confederates had become so accustomed to the daily U.S. Cavalry appearances that the Southerner's sense of alarm had greatly diminished, further weakening Early's already feeble picket lines.[12]

Military campaigns are not fought in vacuums, and the best plans are often preempted by the action of the opponent. So it was that while Sheridan and Grant strategized at Charlestown on September 17, Jubal Early made another unexpected move that altered Sheridan's plans and the very nature of the coming battle. The B & O Railroad was the Federal supply line, and Early knew if he could compromise it, the interruption would ripple throughout the North.[13]

On the afternoon of September 17, Early assembled a force composed of his two largest infantry divisions, two small brigades from Maj. Gen. Lunsford L. Lomax's cavalry division, and Maj. Carter Braxton's artillery battalion. Early's force numbered approximately 7,500 men. He left approximately the same number of troops guarding the Opequon Creek line under Breckinridge and Fitz Lee. The latter protested the movement to Martinsburg, but Early still executed his plan. The detachment of such a large number of men from the defenses of Winchester left the town open to attack from Sheridan's forces at Berryville, but Early clearly accepted that risk in an effort to disrupt the vital B & O Railroad. He believed the risk was low due to Sheridan's perceived timidity. Early later wrote, "I knew my danger, but I could occupy no other position that would enable me to accomplish the desired object." Even Early's postwar nemesis, Maj. Gen. John B. Gordon, considered Early's judgment to be "good generalship to take just such risks under the circumstances." Although Early

---

12 J. W. Patton Diary, Tennessee State Library and Archives; The Civil War Diary of John Wilson Philips, *Virginia Magazine of History and Biography*, January 1954; Theophilus F. Rodenbough, *History of the 18th Regiment Cavalry Pennsylvania Volunteers* (New York, 1909), 57; Louis N. Beaudry, *Historic Records of the Fifth New York Cavalry* (Albany, 1865), 171; Hillman A. Hall, *History of the Sixth New York Cavalry*, 223; OR 43, pt. 2, 99.

13 John W. Daniel's incomplete manuscript on the Battle of Winchester, JWD Papers, UVA.

was belligerent and willing to take chances, he lacked the finesse that Stonewall Jackson often used to lure his opponents into traps.[14]

After the war, one of Early's former staff officers asked the aged Valley commander if he had ever reconsidered the decision to go to Martinsburg in light of Sheridan's immense numerical superiority. Early's eyes blazed with excitement as he looked at the officer and explained, "Major, I hope you will never have that thought again. You forget the whole scheme of the Valley Campaign. It was a bluff game from the beginning," insisted Early. "I had made Sheridan afraid of me. If once I showed him that I was afraid of him the case was gone, and he would have run me from one place to another."[15]

While Early was certainly engaged in a game of bluff with Sheridan, he need not have taken two full divisions of infantry to Martinsburg. Gordon's division, accompanied by an additional brigade of Fitz Lee's cavalry, would have been sufficient for the task at hand, leaving Rodes's large division available to render immediate support to Ramseur and Breckinridge.

The Confederate force moved north and reached Bunker Hill, where they camped for the night. Early the next morning, Lomax's cavalry encountered Col. James Schoonmaker's cavalry brigade from Averell's division posted just south of Martinsburg. Schoonmaker's Pennsylvania and Ohio men offered Lomax's horsemen stubborn resistance, but the Federal horsemen were forced to retreat through Martinsburg and eastward across Opequon Creek. Having cleared the way to Martinsburg and the railroad, Lomax did not attempt to drive the Federals any further.[16]

Early ordered Lomax to send a brigade to destroy the railroad bridge over Back Creek, six miles west of Martinsburg. Lomax dispatched Vaughn's small Tennessee brigade to do the job. Vaughn's brigade, now commanded by Lt. Col. Onslow Bean, had experienced rough times for the last year, and morale had plummeted accordingly. Much of the brigade was captured during Grant's Vicksburg campaign. In late 1863, Confederate authorities reconstituted Vaughn's brigade by combining the exchanged men with the odds and ends of

14 Ibid. Thomas G. Jones to J. W. Daniel, JWD Papers, Duke; Memoir of Randolf Barton contained in Margaretta Barton Colt, *Defend the Valley: A Shenandoah Family in the Civil War* (Oxford, 1994), 332.

15 John W. Daniel's incomplete manuscript on the Battle of Winchester, JWD Papers, UVA.

16 E. P. Goggin to L. L. Lomax, September 27, 1864, ChiHS; Samuel Clarke Farrar, *History of the 22nd Pennsylvania Cavalry and the Ringgold Battalion, 1861-1865* (Pittsburgh, 1911) 365; *OR* 43, pt. 498, 554, 610.

several other units. The brigade had suffered heavy losses in both officers and men at the battle of Piedmont on June 5, 1864. Vaughn's brigade had earned a poor reputation as a result of its poor discipline and high desertion rate. Not surprisingly, Lomax sent his assistant adjutant general, Edmund P. Goggin, with Bean to ensure that the Back Creek Bridge was burned as ordered.[17]

Bean's Tennesseans arrived at the designated bridge around half-past noon on the afternoon of September 18, after covering the six miles from Martinsburg. They fired the bridge, which crumbled in flames by 3:00 p.m. Afterward, they cut the telegraph wires, tore down the telegraph poles in several places, and tore up some track. Goggin recalled that the Tennesseans bent the rails so as to "render [them] unserviceable." Overall, Goggin reported to Lomax that Bean and his men performed their assigned tasks with "reasonable success and energy."[18]

When the work was finished, the Tennesseans headed back toward Winchester in accordance with Lomax's orders. Instead of returning to Martinsburg, they rode up the Back Creek Valley as quickly as the rugged terrain permitted them to move on their jaded horses. They covered about 10 miles before going into camp for the night at Ganotown, 19 miles north of Winchester.[19]

Meanwhile, Gordon's infantry and Jackson's brigade of Lomax's division carried out the work of destruction in and around Martinsburg. They tore up the railroad, and destroyed some bridges and culverts in the area. Unlike most towns in the Shenandoah Valley, Martinsburg had gained notoriety among the Confederates as being a "Union Town" with "Yank sticking out of everyone's face" and only a few "true hearted" Southerners to be found. The Confederate soldiers took what they wanted from Martinsburg just as they had done back in early July. Liquor was in abundant supply and discipline quickly eroded. "The men spread themselves, talked big, drank gallantly and took what they pleased and did what they pleased generally," wrote Capt. John Y. Bedingfield of the 60th Georgia Infantry to his mother two days later. The drinking apparently began even before the troops entered the town, as Col. James Schoonmaker, commander of the Union rear guard, reported capturing a few prisoners who

17 E. P. Goggin to L. L. Lomax, September 27, 1864, ChiHS.

18 Ibid.

19 Ibid.

were all "more or less intoxicated." One report claimed that Maj. Gen. Lunsford Lomax "manifested a very strong liking for the ardent spirit." Lomax took dinner at a private home and left his compliments for Averell in a "half drunken way."[20]

The breakdown in discipline came as no surprise to Jubal Early. A recent inspection revealed that Gordon's division in particular was breaking down. The inspecting officer concluded that discipline was "lax" and, in the case of Gordon's old Georgia brigade, orders "were not enforced" and officers were "inefficient." The inspector also noted that the command suffered greatly from a want of proper clothing, with the Louisiana brigade sorely needing pants.[21]

While in Martinsburg, Jubal Early personally supervised the search "of a private house in which Mr. Brenaman, the telegraph operator, had located his instruments." Early interrogated the Unionists about the strength and position of Sheridan's army. The lady of the house asked Early if he would again invade Maryland. Although "Old Jube" had no such intentions, he couldn't help but take advantage of the opportunity to spread confusion and confirmed the woman's fears. Early found the telegrapher's equipment and soon received the disturbing news that Lt. Gen. U. S. Grant was with Sheridan at Charlestown. Surely, Grant's presence presaged an aggressive movement on the part of the Union Army. Although Early claimed this knowledge enlightened him to the coming action, he never notified his commanders near Winchester. As a result, the commanders on the Opequon Creek line made no arrangements to meet the likely threat. "Gen. Early was surprised at Winchester," concluded Capt. James B. Clay, an aide-de-camp on Breckinridge's staff.[22]

Early quickly ordered Gordon's and Jackson's commands out of town and had them marching south back to Bunker Hill. Colonel Schoonmaker's Ohio and Pennsylvania troopers reoccupied the town later that night only to discover that not all of the Southerners had left. Captain Benjamin F. Keller of the 60th Georgia Infantry stayed behind and drank himself into a stupor, and was apprehended by the Federal cavalry when it reentered town. The horsemen took Keller to headquarters where the Georgian "addressed General Averill [sic] in a most extraordinary speech for a thoroughly drunk man." Even worse,

20 John Y. Bedingfield to Dear Ma, September 20, 1864, UVA; Theodore C. Wilson, "Additional Details of the Fight," *New York Herald*, September 22, 1864.

21 Inspection Report, Gordon's division, August 20, 1864, RG 94, National Archives.

22 James B. Clay to Gabriel C. Wharton, June 4, 1905, Clay Family Papers, LC.

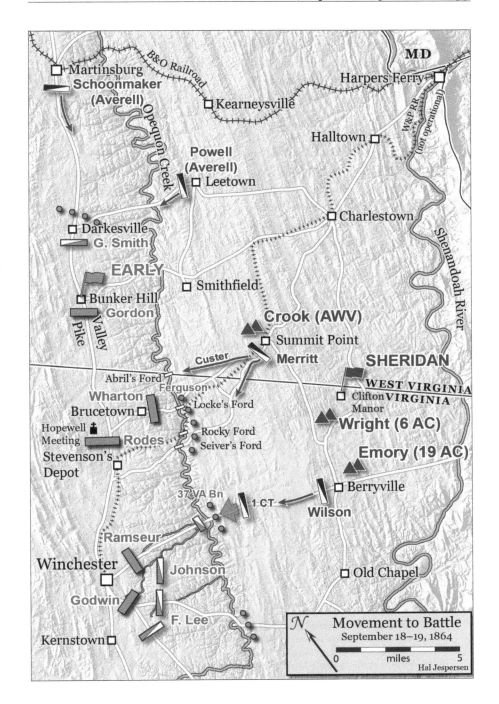

MD

Martinsburg
Schoonmaker
(Averell)

B&O Railroad

Kearneysville

Harpers Ferry

Halltown

W&P RR (not operational)

Opequon Creek

Powell
(Averell)
Leetown

Charlestown

Shenandoah River

Darkesville
G. Smith

EARLY

Smithfield

Bunker Hill
Gordon

Valley Pike

Crook (AWV)

Summit Point

Custer

Merritt

SHERIDAN

Abril's Ford

Ferguson

WEST VIRGINIA
Clifton VIRGINIA
Manor

Wharton
Brucetown

Locke's Ford

Wright (6 AC)

Hopewell
Meeting
Stevenson's
Depot

Rodes

Rocky Ford
Seiver's Ford

Emory (19 AC)

37 VA Bn

1 CT

Berryville

Wilson

Ramseur

Winchester

Johnson

Old Chapel

Godwin

F. Lee

N   Movement to Battle
September 18–19, 1864

Kernstown

0   miles   5

Hal Jespersen

Keller failed to comprehend his situation and mistook Averell for Gordon. To the humor of all present, the soused Keller looked at his guards and told them "stick by me," which they gladly did.[23]

Sheridan learned of Early's jaunt to Martinsburg after orders had already been issued for a move at nine o'clock that evening. At noon on September 18, Averell informed Sheridan that the divisions of Rodes and Gordon and a brigade of cavalry were at Martinsburg. That information caused Sheridan to change his battle plan. Instead of moving to Newtown and severing Early's line of retreat, Sheridan decided to make a night march and charge directly at Winchester to destroy the small force Early had left in place there. Sheridan and his staff drew up the orders and sent them out to his generals, but the commander just as quickly cancelled the night march and the army stood down.[24] Instead he ordered:

> This command will move to-morrow morning at 2 o'clock in the following order and on the following designated routes:
>
> 1. The cavalry division of Brigadier-General Wilson will move on Winchester via the Berryville pike and will drive in the enemy's cavalry on that pike and follow them up.
>
> 2. The Sixth Corps will move from its present camp across the country to the crossing of Opequon Creek by the Berryville pike, and will advance toward Winchester on said pike. As soon as it has reached the open county it will form in line of battle, fronting in the direction of Stephenson's Depot, unless the developments which may occur cause other dispositions to be made.
>
> 3. The Nineteenth Corps will march by the Berryville pike, and when the head of the column reaches the crossing of the creek the commanding officer will report to Major-General Wright for instructions. The line of battle of the Nineteenth Corps will be formed under direction of Major-General Wright. The utmost promptitude should be exercised in the formation of this line of battle.

---

23 The *New York Herald* named the officer as Captain Conrad Keller of the 60th Georgia Cavalry. However, Georgia rosters reveal a Captain Benjamin Keller of the 60th Georgia Infantry listed as captured on September 19, 1864. *New York Herald*, September 22, 1864; www.civilwardata.com/active/hdsquery.dll?soldierhistory?c&112938, as accessed October 14, 2009.

24 Sheridan, *Memoirs*, 2:9-10.

4. General Crook will march his command to the crossing of Opequon Creek by the Berryville pike, and be held there as a reserve to be marched to any point required.

5. The cavalry divisions of General Merritt and General Averell will be governed by such directions as they may receive from the chief of cavalry. Corps commanders will be required to furnish strong guards for the protection of their trains. Corps commanders will be notified of the location of army headquarters.

By command of Major-General Sheridan.[25]

Sheridan subsequently issued other orders that fleshed out the plan for the cavalry and explained some of his expectations of his subordinates. As such, Torbert wrote to Merritt:

The army will start at 2 o'clock to-night to Winchester via the Berryville and Winchester pike. General Wilson will be in advance of the infantry. The fords you go to are near the Winchester railroad, just to the left as you go out. Watch well the fords on the creek and the movements of the enemy. One division of infantry of the enemy was in Martinsburg to-day and another at Bunker Hill. Averell will be directed to watch them well, and follow them, if they move, so as to make a junction with you. You, of course, will have to be governed by circumstances, but the move means fight. They can't help but concentrate their infantry on Sheridan, and if you and Averell can join we will pitch into their rear. I will join you early in the morning. The greatest promptness will be exercised in the above.

Your, &c.,

A. T. A. Torbert, Chief of Cavalry[26]

The Confederate forces at Winchester remained in their previous defensive alignments. Ramseur's division had taken over the positions covering the eastern approaches to Winchester while Bradley Johnson's cavalry picketed his front. Brigadier General Archibald C. Godwin's brigade of Ramseur's division was on the Millwood Pike. These North Carolinians backed up Fitz Lee's division of cavalry under Brig. Gen. Williams C. Wickham. Camped southwest

25 OR 43, pt. 2, 102-103.

26 Ibid., 104-105.

of town, Wickham's troops had been picketing the area as far out as Berry's Ferry on the Shenandoah River in Clarke County. Wharton's division of Breckinridge's corps watched the Opequon crossings east of Stephenson's Depot in the vicinity of Brucetown. Two cavalry brigades from Lomax's division led by Col. Milton Ferguson (McCausland's) and Col. George Smith (Imboden's) guarded the Opequon crossings along Breckinridge's front.[27]

Early rashly divided his outnumbered army with Sheridan only 10 miles to the east. Staff officer Henry Kyd Douglas worried that "Gen. Early, in these bold movements seems to rely too much upon the timidity and caution of Sheridan." High ranking officers had recently discussed what they deemed to be Early's rash actions. Brigadier General William R. Cox shared his concerns with General Rodes. "I know," replied Rodes, "I can't get him to believe it." When September 18 passed without incident at Winchester, Douglas expressed his relief in his diary before adding, "I shall be glad if tomorrow passes away just as quietly." Such was not to be.[28]

Sheridan's orders for a movement and attack on September 19 initiated the largest and bloodiest battle ever fought in the Shenandoah Valley. Its scale would exceed several engagements considered major battles in the Western Theater, including Perryville, Champion Hill, Kennesaw Mountain, and Peachtree Creek.

27 Fitz Hugh Lee, Report of Operations, 1864, MOC; John C. Donahue Journal, Virginia Historical Society.

28 William R. Cox, "Address on the Life and Character of Maj. Gen. Stephen D. Ramseur, Ladies Memorial Association of Raleigh," contained in David Schenck, Sketches of Maj. Gen. Stephn Dodson Ramseur (n.p., 1892), 39-40; Henry Kyd Douglas, *I Rode With Stonewall: The Experiences of the Youngest Member of Jackson's Staff* (Chapel Hill, NC, 1940), 296.

A Good Prospect of Warm Work

The Battle of Opequon Creek, September 19

The sun had set behind the Allegheny Mountains; storm clouds churned in the twilight sky over the Valley. Under a light rain, men from both armies abandoned the warmth of their campfires and scurried like wispy shadows moving through the darkness for the shelter of their neatly arrayed dog tents. At Sheridan's headquarters in Clifton Manor, a woman of strong Southern proclivities appeared on the portico to politely bid goodnight to a group of officers smoking pipes around a fire. "Good night, Madam. Tomorrow we hope to let you hear of a victory," replied one. "It will never be on your side," she laughed. "If your army advances it will be whipped."[1]

When Sheridan changed his battle plan at the last minute, he shifted his approach from the rolling farmlands south of Winchester to the more rugged eastern approaches to the town and Stephenson's Depot. Here, Early's smaller force could utilize the rough ground created by the drainage of Opequon Creek to hold Sheridan's larger force at bay before slipping away as they had done in

1 "Sheridan's Great Victory," Correspondence of the *New York World* contained in the *Milwaukee Sentinel*, September 28, 1864.

Clifton Manor, Sheridan's headquarters prior to the Third Battle of Winchester.
Scott C. Patchan

August. Only one week earlier, Sheridan complained to Grant that "it was exceedingly difficult to attack" Early in his position behind that stream. "The Opequon Creek is a very formidable barrier; there are various crossings but all difficult; the banks are formidable," he noted. Because they had maneuvered on the same ground before, the Union leadership understood the terrain they would fight upon. Sheridan's gamble was that his army could rapidly negotiate the difficult ground and take advantage of Early's divided army.[2]

Sheridan's revamped battle plan was simple. Assuming the Rebels between his army and Winchester consisted of one division of infantry and Early's shaky cavalry, he planned to overwhelm them by sheer numbers. Some 27,000 men from the Sixth and Nineteenth corps and Brig. Gen. James Harrison "Harry" Wilson's cavalry division were on hand to attack 5,000 enemy. Torbert's two remaining cavalry divisions would cross the Opequon Creek at northern fords leading to Stephenson's Depot and Bunker Hill. Merritt's division would use Locke's and Seiver's fords to confront Wharton's division guarding the approaches to Stephenson's Depot and Brucetown. Averell would cross at the

2   OR 43, pt. 2, 69.

northern fords leading to Darkesville and Bunker Hill and gain the Valley Pike, where he would harass and delay the two divisions that Early had taken to Martinsburg, and Sheridan crushed the Confederates at Winchester. Crook's quick-marching Army of West Virginia would form a mobile reserve, which Sheridan intended to use south of Winchester, a remnant of his original plan.

Speed was the key to Sheridan's success. His forces needed to quickly seize Spout Spring where the Berryville Turnpike crossed Opequon Creek. A short distance beyond the ford, the road entered a narrow and rugged ravine about two miles long known as the Berryville "Canyon." Within the confines of this defile, there was little room to maneuver as both the Berryville Pike and Ash Hollow Run passed through it. This geography posed a serious obstacle for large bodies of troops attempting to traverse it, as Sheridan intended to accomplish. Conversely, it offered Winchester's Confederate defenders an opportunity to neutralize the Union numbers. Securing the Berryville ravine would be an early but primary objective for Sheridan. If he failed in this initial maneuver, his battle plan would be ruined by dawn's first light.

Sheridan assigned the task of securing the Spout Spring crossing and the Berryville Canyon to Wilson and his cavalry division. Wilson struck the first blow of the battle late at night on September 18 when he sent Maj. George O. Marcy's 1st Connecticut Cavalry to secure Limestone Ridge. The ridge commanded the ground to the east as well as Opequon Creek, so it was critical for launching an attack against the Rebels on the west bank. Marcy's men rode five miles in advance of the main body of Wilson's division, guided only by the luminescence of a full moon when the evening clouds dispersed. Brigadier General Bradley Johnson's brigade of Virginia and Maryland men guarded the Opequon crossings east of Winchester. Johnson posted Lt. Col. James R. Claiburne's 37th Virginia Cavalry Battalion at Spout Spring. Claiburne deployed his pickets on Limestone Ridge, where the Southerners waited for the routine appearance of the Union cavalry along the Berryville Pike.

Shortly before midnight, the 1st Connecticut bolted out of the inky darkness and scattered the Virginians from the ridge. The New Englanders gained their objective and consolidated their position just east of the creek. The routed Virginians fled to Spout Spring and informed Claiburne of the Federal movement. By this point in the campaign, Sheridan's cavalry crashing through a Confederate picket line had become such a regular part of the daily routine that the Confederate commanders thought little of this seemingly ordinary event. Bradley Johnson later recalled that he customarily had to "ride over to the Berryville Pike and re-establish my lines" every morning. Wilson's seizure of

Limestone Ridge, however, was anything but routine, and Sheridan would use this high ground to begin his operations early the next morning.[3]

About the same time the Rebel horsemen secured Limestone Ridge, bugles sounded in Wilson's camp "at an early hour" on the morning of September 19. A Union horse soldier vividly described the scene in a letter home:

> Thousands of fires were burning in field and grove; men and horses were placed in bold contrast by the bright fires to the deep darksome gloom beyond, and each little squad, as it gathered together about the burning pile and made preparations for the march, seemed magnified to tall and giant like spirits moving in a blazing vault formed by the curling smoke as it rolled upward and wreathed itself in the silver sheen of the green spreading branches above.[4]

Wilson's troopers rode out of camp near Berryville about 2:00 a.m. with Brig. Gen. John B. McIntosh's brigade in the van. McIntosh and his troopers knew the terrain well, having fought over that very ground during the successful reconnaissance of September 13 that captured the 8th South Carolina.

McIntosh was born in 1829 to a Regular Army family stationed near the site of modern-day Tampa, Florida. Death in battle had found his father during the Mexican War while a teenaged McIntosh was serving his country as a midshipman aboard the USS *Saratoga*. McIntosh resigned from the navy after the war and settled in New Jersey. When the Civil War broke out, his brother James sided with the South. An outraged John joined the 2nd U.S. Cavalry as a second lieutenant to wipe away the perceived dishonor that tarnished the McIntosh family name. He performed capably and was made colonel of the 3rd Pennsylvania Cavalry in late 1862. He commanded a brigade during the Chancellorsville and Gettysburg campaigns, and received a promotion to brigadier general for his services during the 1864 Overland campaign.[5]

McIntosh's brigade reached Opequon Creek before daylight with Maj. Walter Hull's 2nd New York Cavalry leading the 5th New York. Hull's New Yorkers splashed into the stream and easily scattered the startled Virginians

3   W. A. Croffut and John M. Morris, *The Military and Civil History of Connecticut During the War of 1861-65* (New York: Ledyard Bill, 1868), 718; Clement Evans, ed., *Confederate Military History* (Extended Edition), vol. 12, 257-258.

4   Robert B. Ware, "From the Second Ohio Cavalry," *Cleveland Herald*, October 22, 1864.

5   Warner, *Generals in Blue*, 300; Eric Wittenberg, "Brig. Gen. John B. McIntosh," www.civilwarcavalry.com/?p=639, accessed on September 22, 2010.

Spout Spring crossing looking east. McIntosh's Federals charged down the road you see here toward the stream in the foreground on September 19, 1864, driving the Rebel troopers back toward Winchester. *Dwight and Walter Briscoe, Photographers, 1885, DeGolyer Library, SMU*

picketing at Spout Spring. Daniel Wood's brick house and burned-out mill sat 400 yards west of the creek. Claiburne's 37th Virginia Battalion opened fire from the hill behind the house. The New Yorkers charged and pushed the Virginians into the Berryville ravine. The 18th Pennsylvania and 2nd Ohio led the main body of Wilson's division across the creek and joined the 2nd and 5th New York Cavalry in pursuit. The Rebels ended resistance, choosing instead to flee to the opposite end of the ravine where pickets from Col. Charles C. Blacknall's 23rd North Carolina Infantry of Brig. Gen. Robert Johnston's brigade of Ramseur's division waited along the edge of the same woods where the 8th South Carolina had surrendered to McIntosh on September 13. Before Blacknall's pickets comprehended the situation, the retreating Virginians ran through the Tar Heels closely pursued by McIntosh's brigade.[6]

Sleeping soundly beneath a simple fly tent, Blacknall was roused to action by the rattle of small arms fire echoing up the ravine. He fumbled with his boots, climbed upon his horse, galloped to the front, and took charge of his regiment. Although nearly surrounded by the 2nd and 5th New York, the 23rd

6   OR 43, pt. 1, 518; Louis N. Beaudry, *Historic Records of the Fifth New York Cavalry, First Ira Harris guard, Its Organization, Marches, Raids, Scouts, Engagements, and General Services During the Rebellion of 1861-1865* (Albany, NY: S. R. Gray, 1865), 171.

North Carolina fought tenaciously. Blacknall formed his troops into a hollow square, and his men cut their way out to Johnston's main line atop a hill overlooking the western end of the ravine. Their escape was not without loss. A bullet struck Blacknall in the ankle, inflicting a wound that eventually proved fatal. The Carolinians fell back under the covering fire provided by the balance of Johnston's brigade, carrying their wounded leader with them.[7]

Brigadier General Robert Johnston's simple field headquarters, established under a tree alongside the Berryville Pike on the Enos Dinkle farm, consisted of an old army wagon and a single camp stool in front of a fire. When Johnston heard the firing, he sprang into action and quickly placed his three remaining regiments into position behind wooden barricades. The 5th and 20th North Carolina regiments occupied the works on the Berryville Pike, while the 12th Regiment moved off to the left and occupied a barricade blocking a farm lane on Johnston's left. In front of his position, the Berryville Pike veered sharply to the left and rose out of the ravine. The Carolinians' position was perpendicular to the road and parallel with Ash Hollow, a ravine that crossed the pike. The works sat a few yards in front of the woods on the south side of the road and offered the Tar Heels a convenient secondary position should they be driven back. Johnston's troops had barely gotten into position when the New Yorkers charged up the Berryville Pike. The Southerners fired a volley that sent the Federals scurrying back to the safety of the Berryville ravine.[8]

With the morning sky brightening, McIntosh acted quickly to take the ground held by Johnston at the western end of the ravine. He rallied the repulsed New Yorkers and deployed them as skirmishers in front of Johnston's position. With their Spencer rifles, the Union horsemen kept the North Carolinians struggling to match their rate of fire. McIntosh then brought up Capt. Charles Peirce's battery of the 2nd U.S. Artillery to support a renewed attack and ordered Col. William P. Brinton's 18th Pennsylvania Cavalry into the fight. The Pennsylvanians came on "at a stretch gallop & like a torrent they burst on the rebs." The Union horsemen charged right up to the works, then turned and rode along the Confederate line, emptying the contents of their

7   Blacknall might have survived, but he insisted that the surgeons not amputate his foot. They attempted to save the limb, but Blacknall died as a result. E. A. Turner, "Twenty Third Regiment," *North Carolina Troops*, 2:251, 255; James O. Coghill to Dear Brother, October 6, 1864, Duke; George Wilfong to Mrs. Lovina Wilfong, October 3, 1864, Duke.

8   Bradley T. Johnson, "Tar Heels' Thin Grey Line," *Charlotte Observer*, May 19, 1895; George Wilfong to Mrs. Lovina Wilfong, October 3, 1864, Duke.

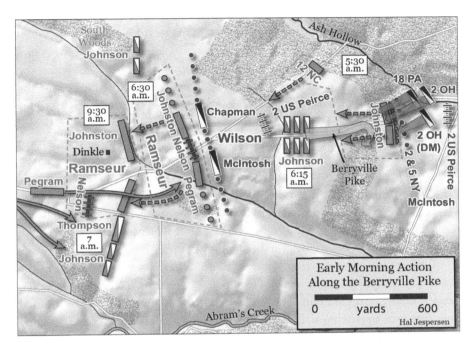

Early Morning Action
Along the Berryville Pike

0   yards   600

Hal Jespersen

carbines into the faces of the astonished North Carolinians. The Tar Heels fought back stubbornly in the closely contested fight as Brinton fed his regiment into the fight piecemeal by battalions. One Pennsylvanian described the contest as "doubtful." Brinton's horse was wounded, but he remained in the saddle and rallied his troopers under a heavy fire. He led a final charge that drove the 5th and 20th North Carolina regiments from their works and into the secondary position in the woods behind them. The Carolinians regrouped and resumed firing. The severe fire of the Tar Heels drove the horse soldiers from the captured works, and the unhorsed Brinton became a prisoner.[9]

Undaunted, McIntosh reacted quickly and put the 2nd Ohio Cavalry into the fight when it reached the front line. An Ohio horse soldier wrote, "Brave and grim, Gen. McIntosh, always foremost in a charge, was with us, and drawing his sabre, ordered us to charge their battle line." McIntosh dismounted seven Buckeye companies and advanced them through the woods on the south side of the road. These troopers climbed the hill toward the top of the bluff and opened fire on the North Carolinians. Then, under the personal leadership of

9 Rodenbough, *History of the Eighteenth Regiment of Cavalry Pennsylvania Volunteers*, 26; Roger Hannaford, Reminiscences, CiHS.

General McIntosh, the mounted Ohioans of Maj. Bayard Nettleton's battalion pounded up the pike toward Johnston's battle line and swept over the breastworks. The Buckeyes passed around the corner of the wood lot where the Carolinians had taken refuge and overlapped Johnston's right flank, driving the Tar Heels from their position. On Johnston's left, the 12th North Carolina withdrew as its position became untenable after the line on the pike broke. McIntosh quickly gathered Nettleton's Ohioans together and sent them off to pursue the retreating Carolinians as they withdrew toward Winchester. McIntosh's other regiments quickly advanced up the hill and occupied the captured works, thereby securing the vital starting point for Sheridan's attack. Nettleton's battalion attempted to follow up its success but encountered heavy resistance. "Balls were coming thick and fast," recalled an Ohio soldier, "and men fell like leaves before the winds of wild weather."[10]

Earlier that morning, Brig. Gen. Bradley Johnson was sleeping upon the ground in an open meadow when a frightened horseman from Johnson's own brigade nearly trampled him. The frightened horseman informed Johnson that Sheridan was advancing with a heavy force on the Berryville Pike. Watching from high atop a knoll behind General Johnston's position, Bradley Johnson observed "a thin gray line of North Carolinians" continually fire at the Federal horsemen and then march in retreat. The Maryland brigadier saw the 2nd Ohio break around the Tar Heels' right flank and threaten to cut the gray infantry off from Winchester. He immediately ordered his brigade to charge and save Johnston's men from destruction.[11]

Colonel Thomas F. Toon formed his 20th North Carolina into a hollow square and retreated under heavy pressure from McIntosh's horsemen. Peirce's gunners honed in their pieces on Toon's force. Almost immediately, a Yankee shell killed Toon's horse, and the situation deteriorated quickly for the retreating Carolinians. Fortunately for them, General Johnson's Marylanders and "wild Southwest Virginia horsemen" had deployed in columns of fours and charged headlong into McIntosh's brigade. The Virginians pounded up the Berryville Pike, yelling and churning large clouds of dust that magnified their numbers. With the cheers of the foot soldiers echoing in their ears, Johnson's

---

10 Robert B. Ware, "From the Second Ohio Cavalry," *Cleveland Herald*, October 22, 1864.

11 George Wilson Booth, *Personal Reminiscences of a Maryland Soldier in the War Between the States, 1861-1865* (Baltimore: For Private Circulation Only, 1898), 144; *Charlotte Observer*, May 19, 1895.

Virginia and Maryland horsemen swept past the North Carolinians, allowing them to withdraw to the safety of a ravine east of the Dinkle farm. According to a soldier with the 2nd Ohio, Johnson's hard-charging cavalry greatly impressed the Federals:

> I tell you it did look really frightful to watch them. They started toward us a full half mile distant from the extreme left of their line. First at a trot, but gathering momentum as they came, by the time they were half way toward us they were on a full gallop, nearer, nearer, they came . . .[12]

McInstosh's brigade fired several volleys into Johnson's charging wave of gray, but the Confederates advanced without pause. The Federal horsemen fell back into the woods as the Confederates rapidly approached. Captain Peirce quickly perceived the situation and aimed his guns at the approaching Southern cavalry. The U.S. gunners bravely held their fire until the last possible minute and then "treated" Johnson's troopers to several rounds of canister. The effect proved instantaneous as the head of Johnson's column disintegrated. McIntosh, in turn, called for a charge of his own, and Nettleton's battalion of the 2nd Ohio bolted toward the stunned Confederates, crashing into their right flank. The Confederate horsemen "turned and retreated faster than they came." Johnson's 8th Virginia Cavalry, however, regrouped, charged, and blunted the Federal pursuit. Although repulsed, the charge of Bradley Johnson's Southern troopers allowed Gen. "Bob" Johnston to safely extricate his brigade. For the Federals, McIntosh and Wilson had successfully secured the key ground at the western terminus of the Berryville ravine. They remained content to hold their ground as heavy skirmishing continued until the Union infantry reached the field. Meanwhile, Phil Sheridan and his staff had followed the cavalry onto the battlefield and watched much of the fighting. When it was over, Sheridan rode over to McIntosh, gave him an approving pat on the shoulder and said, "You have done nobly."[13]

Meanwhile, the sounds of combat echoed through the ravine back to Ramseur's headquarters at Mr. James H. Burgess's farm. Ramseur immediately ordered Brig. Gen. John Pegram to take his brigade to Johnston's assistance. Pegram's Virginians were already formed and waiting for their officers when

---

12 Roger Hannaford, Reminiscences, CiHS.

13 Ibid; *Charlotte Observer*, May 19, 1895; Tenney, Diary of Luman H. Tenney, 131.

Lt. Joel Abbott, 8th Virginia Cavalry, part of Brig. Gen. Bradley Johnson's brigade, Lunsford Lomax's division. *LC*

the orders arrived. They marched a short distance and went into position on the south side of the Berryville Pike. They spread out to cover as much ground as possible, and provided Johnston a bulwark upon which to regroup his brigade. Reinforcements from the cavalry quickly came to General Ramseur's aid. Colonel William L. Jackson's brigade of about 500 horsemen, led by Lt. Col. William P. Thompson, rode to the sound of the guns. Thompson's Virginians dismounted, deployed on Pegram's right, and joined the swaying battle between the opposing skirmish lines. The Southern cavalrymen drove back advancing Union troopers and captured several prisoners. Two regiments from Bradley Johnson's brigade deployed on Thompson's right flank, south of Abram's Creek. The Marylander also posted two regiments on Ramseur's left flank and used the balance of his command to extend the line on both flanks. Additional assistance came from the 12 guns of Lt. Col. William Nelson's battalion of artillery that went into battery at key points behind the developing Confederate line.[14]

---

14 Jubal Early places Jackson's (Thompson's) brigade in position guarding the Senseney Road well south of Ramseur's position. While Jackson's command ended up in that position by the early afternoon, it was only after much maneuvering. Johnson's brigade went to the right first and was later followed by Jackson and Wickham. While no official report survives from Jackson's brigade, the few sources obtained clearly indicate that it was in position along the Berryville Pike. A memorandum of Jackson's brigade from the John W. Daniel Papers at UVA places it on the left of that road supporting artillery. French Harding's more detailed account places Jackson first on the right of Ramseur's division south of the road and then moving to Ramseur's left to support artillery. While neither account renders a fully satisfactory description of the activities of Jackson's brigade throughout the battle, they do make it clear that Jackson

By now McIntosh had deployed all of his troopers into line of battle in front of Ramseur's position. Wilson then deployed Chapman's brigade in the large woodlot known as the First Woods on the north side of Berryville Pike. Chapman's troopers extended the cavalry screen northward to Red Bud Run. Skirmishing between both infantry and dismounted cavalry grew in intensity. Every knoll in front of the Union position was soon dotted by white puffs of smoke that marked the position of the Southern sharpshooters. Many Confederates concentrated their fire on Peirce's battery which sat upon an exposed elevation just north of the Berryville Pike. To make matters worse, Nelson's twelve-gun battalion opened fire and hammered the U.S. horse artillerists. Unable to endure the unequal contest, Peirce withdrew his guns about 200 yards behind a ridge that sheltered them from the Confederate gunners. Once established in the new position, Peirce fired his guns only sporadically in order to avoid the unwanted attentions of Nelson's powerful guns. Throughout the course of the early morning action, Peirce lost 10 men wounded, a substantial loss for a mounted battery.

Major General Fitzhugh Lee had his headquarters in Winchester and soon heard the sounds of heavy fighting along the Berryville Pike. Still recovering from a severe bout of influenza, Lee immediately rode out to assist Ramseur. When Lee arrived, Ramseur informed the veteran cavalryman that there was nothing in front but Federal cavalry. The North Carolinian hastily concluded that it was only the routine appearance of the Union cavalry and proposed to advance and drive the Federals off. The more cautious and experienced Fitzhugh Lee told the bold Ramseur, "Let us wait a while and see what's what." Ramseur's proposition had caused alarm among some of Pegram's men who overheard his proposal. They remembered all too well the consequences of Ramseur's rashness at Bethesda Church and Stephenson's Depot. General Lee's patient response, however, reassured the Virginians lying within earshot of the two generals.[15]

Soon after the fighting commenced, Fitzhugh Lee ordered Brig. Gen. Williams C. Wickham to take the division from its camp on the Millwood Pike.

was not in position on Ramseur's right until later in the battle. OR 43, pt. 1, 610-611; Mrs. Hugh Lee Diary, WFCHS, Handley Library, 684; Victor L. Thacker, *French Harding Civil War Memoirs* (Parsons, WV, 2000), 170-171; Diary of A Member of Jackson's Brigade, Filson Historical Society, Louisville; Account of Jackson's Brigade at Winchester, John W. Daniel Papers, UVA.

15 George Q. Peyton Diary, Typescript Copy, Manassas Library Relic Room; Thomas H. Carter to John W. Daniel, November 28, 1894; John W. Daniel Papers, Duke University.

The gray coated cavaliers, long the nucleus of Maj. Gen. J. E. B. Stuart's vaunted Cavalry Corps, numbered about 1,500 men by September 19, 1864. They rode down the Valley Pike, passed through Winchester, and then headed east toward Ramseur's far left flank near Red Bud Run. After crossing that stream, Lee posted Col. Thomas M. Munford's cavalry brigade and Maj. James Breathed's six-gun battery of horse artillery on the heights on the north bank of Red Bud Run near the Huntsberry House. Munford immediately dismounted his brigade and advanced his troopers all along the front astride Red Bud Run. These dismounted cavalrymen moved swiftly and engaged Wilson's men on the south bank, firing across the stream. Munford's Virginians relieved the pressure on Johnson's troopers covering Ramseur's left flank. Colonel William Payne's brigade went into line of battle on the south side of Red Bud Run, and his Virginians deployed in line of battle in a ravine on the Hackwood farm, where they were concealed from any approaching Federals. Because they were not immediately engaged, Payne's men hunted about and discovered a nearby orchard, and before long were consuming fresh apples for breakfast. On their left, a pond formed by a "spring of clear cold, sparkling water gushing out of a limestone ledge in volume sufficient to turn a mill" provided cold water for the men and horses.[16]

Captain Randolph Barton and Sgt. Robert Burwell of the 2nd Virginia Infantry, part of the Stonewall Brigade, had spent the night at Mrs. Hugh Lee's home near the eastern edge of Winchester. When the sounds of artillery fire first rolled into Winchester about 6:00 a.m., Barton, like most Confederates, assumed the distant thunder was nothing more than the customary daily "cavalry affair." He roused Burwell, and the two Winchester natives decided to ride to the sound of the firing, capture some much-needed equipment from the Yankees, and then return in time for breakfast. A mile and a half out of town, however, they found Generals Ramseur and Lee seriously engaged with Wilson's entire Federal division. When they tendered their services, Ramseur put them to work. Burwell dashed off to carry a message to one of Ramseur's subordinates when a Union bullet struck his leg, slicing it with a nasty 14-inch flesh wound. Somehow he managed to ride his horse back to Mrs. Lee's home

---

16 Fitzhugh Lee, Report of Operations, 1864, MOC; Jed Hotchkiss, Maps of Munford's Brigade on September 19, 1864; "Sketch Book of the Second Corps, Army of Northern Virginia in Engagements of 1864-5," LC; P. J. White, "The Battle of Winchester," *Richmond Times-Dispatch*, November 20, 1904.

where his sisters tenderly nursed the wound, a luxury very few soldiers had that day.[17]

Moving simultaneously with Wilson's early morning advance from Berryville, Merritt's division rode out of its bivouac at Summit Point seven miles to the north. Major General Alfred T. A. Torbert, Sheridan's Cavalry Corps commander, accompanied Merritt during the early stages of the battle. Torbert also had Averell's division under his command, but, unaccountably, it did not leave its camps at Martinsburg and Leetown, West Virginia, until 5:00 a.m. Torbert ordered Merritt to move his division to the fords on the Opequon to the left (south) of the Winchester and Potomac Railroad crossing site. Torbert explained the cavalry's mission to Merritt in a note written late on September 18:

> Watch well the fords on the creek and the movements of the enemy. One division of
> infantry of the enemy was at Martinsburg to-day, and another at Bunker Hill. Averell
> will be directed to watch them well, and follow them, if they move so as to make a
> junction with you. You, of course, will have to be governed by circumstances, but the
> move means fight. They can't help but concentrate their infantry on Sheridan, and if
> you and Averell can join, we will pitch into their rear.[18]

Merritt awoke his troops from their slumber to the stirring bugle call of "Boots and Saddles" at 1:00 a.m. His troopers immediately addressed the needs of their mounts, feeding and saddling their trusted horses before indulging themselves with a hasty soldier's breakfast. Brigadier General George A. Custer had his brigade ready to move by 1:30 a.m. and paced anxiously back and forth in front of his headquarters tent. The men in the ranks were unaware of the army's destination, and daily moves were routine in Sheridan's cavalry. One Michigan trooper recognized a member of Custer's staff riding past and called out, "What's up Captain? Where are we going? Prospect of a fight to-day?" He replied that they were off to the Opequon again and needed to arrive before daylight. Then he added, "There is a good prospect of warm work before night."[19]

---

17 Mrs. Hugh Lee Diary, WFCHS, Handley Library; Mahon, 167-168; Memoir of Randolph Barton contained in Colt, *Defend the Valley: A Shenandoah Family in the Civil War*, 332-333.

18 *OR* 43, pt. 1, 104-105.

19 C. C. Colbrath, "Custer at Winchester," *Detroit Free Press*, May 1, 1886.

Merritt's division broke camp shortly after 2:00 a.m. Torbert and Merritt rode with Col. Charles R. Lowell, the well regarded but inexperienced commander of the recently reorganized reserve brigade. The division's horse artillery, ordnance train, and ambulance wagons trailed Lowell. Brigadier General Thomas Devin's brigade brought up the rear of the division. Custer's brigade advanced independently toward Abril's Ford located three miles north of Merritt's destination. In front of the main column, Capt. Theophilus F. Rodenbough's 2nd United States Cavalry led the division through the early morning darkness. Rodenbough had just returned to duty after recovering from a serious combat wound suffered at the battle of Trevillian Station on June 11, 1864. Frequent operations along the Opequon during the preceding five weeks had familiarized the Union cavalrymen with the roads and rolling countryside of Clarke and Jefferson counties east of that stream. Merritt's men consumed several hours traversing the seven mile stretch between their camps at Summit Point and the Opequon crossings.[20]

Merritt quickly assessed the situation and ordered Custer to move his brigade upstream to Locke's Ford. There the road ran through Wade's Depot (or Wadesville) a whistle stop on the Winchester and Potomac Railroad, crossed the creek, ascended the opposite slope, and wound its way toward Brucetown and beyond it to the Martinsburg Pike. Merritt directed Lowell "to affect a crossing" at what Merritt termed Seiver's Ford. Actually, the spot where Lowell forded the Opequon was immediately to the left or south of the Winchester and Potomac Railroad bridge and not at Seiver's Ford. The actual crossing bears the name Rocky Ford and is located three-quarters of a mile downstream from Seiver's Ford. Lieutenant William Harrison of the 2nd U.S. Cavalry fittingly described the ground where his brigade was to operate:

> The opposite bank of the creek was steep and thickly wooded, and to the right of the ford was a deep cut, through which the Winchester and Potomac Railroad passed. The bridge, the roadway of which had been destroyed, crossed the creek diagonally. The stone abutments and piers were intact. The abutment and the adjoining pier on the

---

20 Custer's report is clear that he did not move directly to Locke's Ford. Instead, he initially advanced toward Abril's Ford. This is the crossing where Gen. Edward Braddock led the 44th and 48th Regiments of Foot from the British Army across Opequon Creek on his way to defeat and destruction at the battle of the Monongahela in 1755. This ford is also sometimes referred to as Carter's Ford. OR 43, pt. 1, 443, 454, 462.

enemy's side were at an angle with the wooded bluff, making the arch directly in the line of the deep cut.[21]

Primary responsibility for defending the ground on the Confederate side of Opequon Creek rested with Brig. Gen. Gabriel C. Wharton's division of 2,100 men. Cavalrymen from Brig. Gen. John C. McCausland's brigade screened Wharton's front and flanks. McCausland was absent for undisclosed reasons, so Col. Milton Ferguson had assumed command. Wharton retained Col. Thomas Smith's brigade in reserve near Stephenson's Depot to meet any emergencies. On Wharton's right flank, Col. George S. Patton's brigade guarded the Charlestown Road crossing (Seiver's Ford) and another to the south that led to Jordan Springs, a prewar resort and wartime hospital. Patton's area of responsibility included Seiver's, Clevenger's, and Tanquary's fords. On Patton's immediate left, a gap existed in the Confederate picket lines along the creek. At some point during the night, the commander of the cavalry unit in that sector withdrew his troops without notifying Wharton or his brigadiers. Three-quarters of a mile north of the Charlestown Road, Col. Augustus Forsberg's brigade defended nearly three miles of creek frontage that stretched from Rocky Ford near the railroad to a point across the state line into Berkeley County, West Virginia. "This weak line of defense must have been observed by the enemy's reconnoitering parties," commented Forsberg, "which during the 18th frequently made their appearance on the opposite bank and exchanged some few shots." The Swede noted that before Kershaw departed Winchester, Ramseur's entire division had guarded the same position that Forsberg now held with a single brigade.[22]

Captain Stephen Adams's 30th Virginia Sharpshooter Battalion held Forsberg's right flank at Rocky Ford near the Winchester and Potomac Railroad Bridge. The sharpshooters occupied a formidable defensive position behind a steep railroad embankment leading to the bridge. The path of the railroad curved slightly to the north as it crossed the Opequon, while the fordable section of the creek flowed parallel and south of the roadbed. This condition allowed the defenders to resist any attacks across the creek ensconced

21 Rodenbough, Theo. F., *From Everglade to Canyon with the Second Dragoons, etc., . . . 1836-1875* (New York: 1875), 348.

22 Augustus Forsberg Memoir, Washington and Lee University; Jed Hotchkiss, "Position of Wharton's Division September 19, 1864, Sunrise to 9 A.M." Sketch book showing positions of Second Corps, A.N.Va. in Engagements of 1864-5, LC.

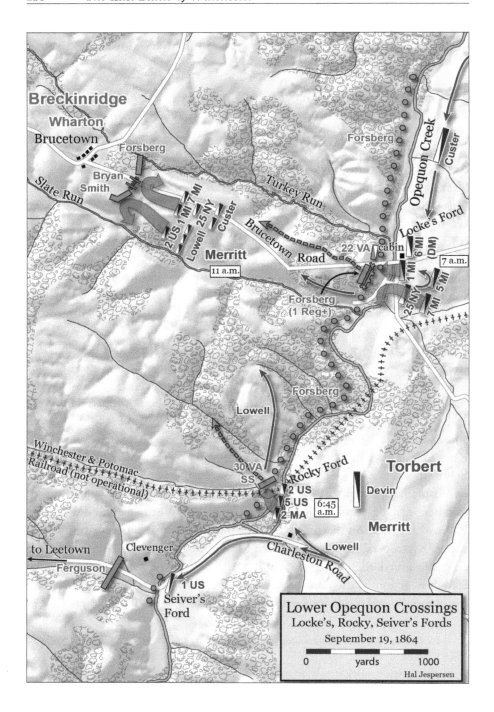

Breckinridge

Wharton

Brucetown

Forsberg

Bryan

Smith

Slate Run

Turkey Run

Forsberg

Opequon Creek

Custer

Locke's Ford

2 US

1 MI

7 MI

Lowell

25 NY

Custer

Brucetown Road

22 VA

cabin

1 MI

6 MI

(DM)

7 a.m.

Merritt

11 a.m.

25 NY

1 MI

7 MI

5 MI

Forsberg
(1 Reg+)

Forsberg

Lowell

Winchester & Potomac
Railroad (not operational)

30 VA
SS

Rocky Ford

Torbert

Devin

2 US

5 US

2 MA

6:45
a.m.

Merritt

to Leetown

Clevenger

Ferguson

Charleston Road

Lowell

1 US

Seiver's
Ford

Lower Opequon Crossings
Locke's, Rocky, Seiver's Fords

September 19, 1864

0   yards   1000

Hal Jespersen

behind the railroad embankment. To Adams's left, the 45th and 51st Virginia regiments extended Forsberg's line so that it covered nearly three miles and reached into Berkeley County. A complete lack of artillery support made Forsberg's situation even more precarious.[23]

When the Union cavalry reached the creek, General Merritt halted and dismounted Lowell's brigade at a farmhouse located between Rocky and Seiver's fords. Several scouts from the 2nd U.S. Cavalry crawled down to the creek concealed "by a heavy mist and the brawling of the creek over its rocky bottom." Through the mist, the scouts saw Confederate cavalry pickets on the east bank backed up by an infantry reserve on the opposite side of the Opequon. "The opposite bank," recalled one of the Regulars, "was precipitous and covered with timber." The fighting began when the U.S. troopers filtered down toward Rocky Ford in force. Shots rang out in the predawn darkness as the Virginia troopers from Colonel Ferguson's brigade fired their obligatory warning shots before hastily retreating across Opequon Creek. The Regulars fired back at the muzzle flashes with their Sharps breech-loading carbines, but soon heard the sound of the Virginians galloping rapidly away. Merritt dispatched the 1st U. S. Cavalry to secure his left flank against any Confederate attempt to cross the creek on the Charlestown Road at Seiver's Ford three-fourths of a mile south of Lowell's position. He then ordered Lowell's brigade to capture Rocky Ford and retained Devin's brigade in reserve on the east bank of the stream.[24]

On the west bank, Captain Adams, commander of the 30th Virginia Sharpshooters, sent word to Colonel Forsberg that the enemy had appeared in his front with a "threatening attitude." The Swede immediately rode to Adams's position at Rocky Ford to offer what assistance he could. Upon reaching Rocky Ford, Forsberg learned of Ferguson's withdrawal on his right flank during the

---

23 Rodenbough, *Second Dragoons*, 348. Additionally, the author has spent time on this obscure part of the battlefield, which is in almost the same condition as it was during the war. The embankment is very steep and affords excellent cover, but at the same time the railroad bed would limit the effective firing range of a man covered behind it. A Confederate soldier in position there would have an excellent field of fire at Federals descending the east bank into the stream, but as the Federals exited the stream and ascended the west bank, the width of the roadbed in conjunction with the height of the embankment limited the Confederate field of fire in regard to Federals who made it to the base of the embankment.

24 *OR* 43, pt. 1, 443, 454.

night. Watching the Federal activity on the opposite side of the Opequon, Forsberg termed the situation "critical."[25]

Captain Rodenbough dismounted a portion of his 2nd U.S. Cavalry and posted them in the outbuildings of a farm near the ford where they exchanged shots with the pickets of the 30th Virginia on the opposite bank of the creek. The balance of the 2nd U.S. Cavalry deployed on horseback on a grass covered hill overlooking the ford. Lowell sent dismounted troopers from the 5th U.S. and 2nd Massachusetts Cavalry Regiments across the creek in skirmish order. They quickly gained a lodgment on the west bank south of the tracks and engaged the 30th Virginia's pickets posted in some woods immediately south of the railroad. The Virginians soon withdrew to the shelter of the railroad embankment under an intensifying fire. From their cover, the rugged mountain men from southwest Virginia opened an accurate fire on the aggressive Federals and slowed the advance. The dismounted Regulars took shelter among the trees in the wooded terrain on the west bank. The situation stalemated briefly until Captain Rodenbough led the mounted section of the 2nd U.S. Cavalry in a headlong charge down the hill and into Opequon Creek. The Virginians opened up a galling fire that pinned down several officers and orderlies of the 2nd U.S. Cavalry "in the archway between the abutment and adjacent pier on the enemy's side." Lieutenant William Harrison recalled, "The bullets, hot from the muzzles of their guns, [struck] the abutment pier and water like leaden hail." Fortunately for Rodenbough's men, the rebels overshot most of their intended targets. Once across the creek, the horsemen of the 2nd U.S. urged their mounts forward and dashed straight up the steep railroad embankment. Their sudden appearance stunned the Virginians on the other side, and resulted in the capture of 40 Confederate defenders. Several officers and men of the 30th Virginia were shot down, including Captain Adams who was severely wounded. The rest of the rebel sharpshooters retreated up Rocky Ford Road toward a prominent height closer to Brucetown. Colonel Lowell quickly ordered the remainder of his brigade across the creek and formed his line to cover a wide front. Rodenbough's command continued its dash northward, threatening the right flank and rear of the troops resisting Custer's crossing at Locke's Ford.[26]

25 Forsberg, 35, WLU; Theo. F. Rodenbough, *Sabre and Bayonet: Stories of Heroism and Military Adventure* (New York: G. W. Dillingham Co. Publishers, 1897), 18.

26 OR 43, pt. 1, 443, 490; Rodenbough, *Second Dragoons*, 348-50; Forsberg, 35, WLU.

Brigadier General George A. Custer's Michigan brigade marched toward the Opequon, "conducted by the most direct route across the country, independent of roads." Custer reached the creek at Abril's Ford three miles north of Merritt before sunrise "unobserved by the enemy whose pickets were posted on the opposite bank." Here, the old French & Indian War era Braddock Road crossed the Opequon. He concealed his brigade behind a strip of woods and waited for orders.[27] Shortly after daylight, Custer received Merritt's orders for the Michigan brigade to secure Locke's Ford. He quickly moved his command to the designated area one and a half miles upstream (south). When Custer reached the ford, he concealed his brigade in a belt of woods behind a range of hills. The morning was still quiet, and one Michigan soldier described the day as "fresh and balmy" with birds twittering in the trees."[28]

The pickets of 51st Virginia Infantry from Forsberg's brigade and the 22nd Virginia Cavalry of Ferguson's brigade were on the alert as the Union horsemen arrived at the ford. Custer immediately ordered Col. James Kidd's 6th Michigan to dismount and take position on the hilltop overlooking the ford. Colonel Kidd, stricken with jaundice, led his regiment forward across the field leading to the crest. Across the creek, the rebel sharpshooters remained in their entrenchments and opened a telling fire that threw the dismounted Federals into confusion. Kidd and Custer ignored the bullets and urged the men toward the hilltop. At length, the Michigan troopers reached the crest and deployed around a log cabin, several outbuildings, and stone fences. The 6th Michigan settled quickly into its new position and rapidly fired Spencer repeating rifles into Virginians on the opposite bank.[29]

Custer organized the balance of his brigade to seize Locke's Ford. This crossing offered the Virginia defenders an excellent defensive position. A high tree-covered ridge sat just west of the Opequon, and the Confederates had strengthened the position with rifle pits and rail breastworks. The cleared ground on the east side of the creek sloped gently toward the Creek for about 100 yards until it reached the water, where it dropped off quickly. This sloping ground provided the defenders of Locke's Ford an excellent shooting range at

27 OR 43, pt. 1, 454.

28 Ibid.; *Detroit Free Press*, May 1, 1886.

29 OR 43, pt. 1, 454, 464; Walter S. Hough, "Braddock's Road Through the Virginia Colony," 18; J. H. Kidd, *A Cavalryman with Custer* (New York, Bantam Books, 1991), 280.

any Federals crossing the exposed turf. The only shelter available to the attackers was the farm house and several out buildings.

Custer selected Lt. Col. Melvin Brewer of the 7th Michigan to take his regiment and the 25th New York Cavalry, temporarily attached to his brigade, and prepare for a mounted charge across the creek. When the New Yorkers' commanding officer requested the honor of leading the attack, Custer readily assented to the inexperienced newcomer's request. With the Empire State boys in the lead, the two regiments moved toward the ford under cover of the hill held by Kidd's 6th Michigan. The eager New Yorkers burst into the open, but the concentrated fire of the Virginians blunted the effort. The 25th New York turned around and rushed to the rear through the 7th Michigan, throwing that unit into disorder as well. Custer ordered Brewer to reform both regiments behind the hill and brought up the capable Col. Peter Stagg and his 1st Michigan Cavalry. Stagg deployed two squadrons under Lt. Col. George R. Maxwell. Stagg was preparing for the charge when Custer rode up to his band and shouted, "Follow that regiment and when you see me wave my sword give them some music!" Maxwell's squadrons advanced under the same heavy fire that had greeted the New Yorkers a short while before, but his seasoned horsemen weathered the storm, splashed through the stream, and gained a foothold on the west bank, where they were promptly pinned down by Virginia sharpshooters.

The 1st Michigan's Maj. Thomas M. Howrigan saw Kidd's men on the ridge and concluded that they could do more to assist their comrades. He galloped up to the 6th Michigan and requested Kidd to increase his efforts, exclaiming, "They are shooting my men off their horses." As Howrigan was speaking, a rebel bullet struck his saddle bag. He reached inside and extricated the shattered remnants of what had been a flask of whiskey. The infuriated Irish major shouted, "God Damn their black souls, they have broken my whiskey bottle!" Howrigan then turned his horse around and raced back to his regiment with bullets whistling all around him.

Custer reinforced Stagg with the 7th Michigan Cavalry and renewed the advance, but Lowell's success on the left soon brought relief. Elements of the reserve brigade, after penetrating Colonel Forsberg's Confederate line at Rocky Ford, moved toward the right flank of the 51st Virginia and threatened its line of retreat. The stalwart defenders learned the 30th Virginia Sharpshooters had retreated and Union troopers were moving on them from the right and rear as well as in their front. With no support and the looming prospect of capture, the Confederates in front of Custer withdrew toward Brucetown. As they began to pull back, Colonel Stagg's 1st Michigan charged and captured several prisoners who lagged behind in their rifle pits. Custer's Wolverines then formed a junction on their left with Lowell's Regulars and cautiously followed Forsberg's Virginians towards Brucetown. Thus, by 7:00 a.m., two of Sheridan's cavalry divisions had successfully crossed Opequon Creek. The third, Brig. Gen. William Averell's command, was moving into action farther downstream.[30]

For the Confederates, Forsberg's retreat dashed any hopes that Breckinridge and Wharton had entertained toward stopping a Federal advance at the Opequon. Forsberg later recounted the situation: "By degrees the whole line was thrown into confusion and I had no other resource but to rally the brigade on higher ground near Brucetown, about 1½ miles from the river. There we took a stand . . ." Wharton reinforced the Swede with Col. Thomas Smith's brigade, and Breckinridge bolstered the Virginians with two guns from Capt. Thomas Bryan's Lewisburg battery of Maj. William McLaughlin's artillery battalion.[31]

Torbert and Merritt pursued Forsberg slowly and with a greater purpose than simply driving the Southerners from the battlefield. Instead, they sought "to prevent Breckinridge from sending his Corps to join the rest of Early's forces near Winchester." Their mission was to lock Breckinridge and Wharton in place at Brucetown while Sheridan dealt with the rest of Early's army. Lowell followed Forsberg toward Brucetown along the Rocky Ford Road, while Custer's brigade proceeded over the hill that dominated Locke's Ford and also headed toward Brucetown. Merritt dispatched Lt. Franck E. Taylor's Battery of the 1st U.S. Artillery when Custer encountered determined resistance at Locke's Ford. The guns now arrived at Custer's position and dropped trail on Jabber's Hill between the creek and Brucetown. The Regular Army gunners intermittently shelled Wharton's position near Brucetown, while Merritt advanced dismounted skirmishers from the brigades of Lowell and Custer. The steady staccato pop of carbines and repeating rifles soon rang out along the lines as the Union horse soldiers engaged Wharton's sharpshooters. For the next several hours, the situation at Brucetown changed little.[32]

30 OR 43, pt. 1, 455, 462, 464; Kidd, *Cavalryman With Custer*, 283; *Detroit Free Press*, May 1, 1886.

31 Forsberg, 35; U.S. War Department, *Atlas to Accompany the Official Records of the Union and Confederate Armies* (Washington: Government Printing Office, 1891-5), Plate LXXXI Map 12.

32 OR 43, pt. 1, 444, 454-455; Recollections of Mrs. Mary Becker Boden, Jerry Reid, Brucetown, VA.

Major General William W. Averell's mounted division broke camp at 5:00 a.m., several hours after Merritt departed Berryville. Averell had not, as his orders specified, followed Gordon's division when it withdrew from Martinsburg. Having reoccupied Martinsburg the night before, Col. James Schoonmaker's brigade was already in position west of the Opequon. Colonel William H. Powell's brigade camped two miles east of the Opequon at Leetown and five miles from Darkesville on the Martinsburg Pike. Averell rode with Powell's men that morning and Theodore Wilson, a journalist for the *New York Herald*, accompanied the division commander. Wilson observed that the day was "clear and bright. The sun shone warmly, and all nature seemed arrayed in holiday attire." Powell's brigade headed west to Burn's Ford, crossed the Opequon unopposed, and moved on to the Martinsburg Pike. Averell and Powell linked with Schoonmaker a short distance north of Darkesville.[33]

A detachment of Averell's highly effective scouts led by Lt. William H. Wakefield of the 14th Pennsylvania reconnoitered the area before moving forward with the rest of the division. Averell's scouts had gained a reputation for efficiency and stealth since the general arrived in West Virginia in 1863. They often disguised themselves as Confederates and slipped in and out of Confederate camps and formations unnoticed. The information they gained often provided Averell with the best and most timely intelligence of any commander in the Valley, including Sheridan and Early. Most recently, Averell used information garnered by his scouts to win lopsided victories against superior numbers at Rutherford's Farm on July 20 and Moorefield on August 7.

At 8:30 a.m., Wakefield's troopers encountered pickets from Lt. Col. Charles T. O'Ferrall's 23rd Virginia Cavalry of Colonel Smith's (Imboden's) brigade posted near Darkesville. The Union cavalrymen shoved the Virginians back toward Smith's main position at Bunker Hill. As Averell advanced, he heard the sounds of artillery barking at Brucetown to the south, prompting him to deploy his 2,500-man division into two columns with one on either side of the Martinsburg Pike. Powell took the left side of the road and Schoonmaker the right, with Lt. Gulian V. Weir's horse artillery rolling up the Pike. Mounted skirmishers preceded the division and steadily drove in the Confederate pickets until they reached a point north of Bunker Hill. There, Colonel Smith decided to make a stand. He deployed his small command of no more than 600 men

---

33 Theodore C. Wilson, "Additonal Details of the Fight," *New York Herald*, September 22, 1864.

from the 18th and 23rd Virginia Cavalry, the 62nd Virginia Mounted Infantry, and a tiny unauthorized battalion of Marylanders.[34]

The ground between Bunker Hill and Martinsburg was the scene of multiple engagements over the preceding weeks and bore the resultant scars. "All around were open fields and these well covered with new and old dead horses. Occasionally even a human body may be found partially exposed here," observed the *New York Herald's* imbedded reporter. Averell learned from local residents that only Smith's small brigade stood in front of Bunker Hill. Averell advanced slowly and attempted to conceal his strength from the Southerners until he could get in close and engage them. He knew from the experiences of the last few weeks that the Southern cavalry would flee when it saw a large force approaching. When his advance reached Bunker Hill, Averell deployed Weir's Battery L, 5th U.S. Artillery. At 10:00 a.m., the gunners opened fire and Averell's cavalry charged. The artillery fire in particular disrupted Smith's defensive efforts. His brigade quickly splintered and ran off toward Winchester without attempting to make a stand, living up to its derisive moniker of the "Mutual Life Insurance Company." The rout began so quickly that Averell could not bring most of his strength to bear upon the Confederates.[35] Private Norval Baker of the 18th Virginia described the quick collapse of Smith's brigade:

> The [U.S.] Sharpshooters were sending lead at us very fast, we could hear the lead whizzing over our heads. . . . By this time we were near the top of the ridge and several batteries opened on us and the air was full of flying lead and iron. The shells burst over and behind us, pieces tore up the ground and the horses plunged in every way and the fast horses left the slower ones and in less time than it takes to tell it, the regiment was scattered 300 yards wide.[36]

---

34 Although regimental historian Robert Driver places McClanahan's battery at Winchester, it is clear from both Union and Confederate accounts that Colonel Smith had no artillery support during the battle while commanding Imboden's brigade. If the battery was present on the battlefield, it was not with Imboden. Sutton, *History of the Second West Virginia Cavalry*, 159; Robert Driver, *The Staunton Artillery–McClanahan's Battery* (Lynchburg, VA: H. E. Howard, 1988), 103.

35 Imboden's brigade was jokingly referred to as the "Mutual Life Insurance Company" because of its tendency to retreat without engaging the Federal cavalry at close quarters, thereby avoiding casualties. *OR* 43, pt. 1, 442; *New York Herald*, September 22, 1864.

36 "Diary and Recollections of I. Norval Baker," Frederick County Historical Society.

As Smith's Virginians dashed away, Averell halted to reorganize his division before moving toward Winchester. Weir's battery shelled the Rebels as they rode away, but the Federals did not press their advantage aggressively. Lieutenant Colonel O'Ferrall of the 23rd Virginia recalled that Averell "seemed to be acting cautiously." Although Smith's command quickly fled, Averell later described the fighting at Bunker Hill as "a determined stand." Colonel Smith knew that if he attempted to confront Averell with his small brigade, the Union troopers would destroy it in the open country. With his men in headlong retreat, Smith withdrew steadily southward toward Stephenson's Depot. Only Averell's deliberate advance permitted Smith to regroup Imboden's brigade.[37]

Earlier that morning, Breckinridge detailed a section of the Lewisburg Artillery to Smith's assistance under the command of the Kentuckian's chief of artillery, Lt. Col. John Floyd King. The 22-year-old Georgian saw the fleeing Confederate cavalry, dashed into their midst, and "partly succeeded" in rallying the horsemen around his guns. Deploying on the right side of the Martinsburg Pike, the Lewisburg gunners fired at the approaching Union cavalry and slowed Averell's advance, but not for long. Weir's six-gun battery responded quickly and easily overmatched the Virginians' two rifled pieces. King withdrew the guns rearward to a sheltering hollow where they stood silently to avoid attracting unwanted attention from Weir's guns.[38]

Back at Brucetown, Lt. Col. Alexander Swift "Sandie" Pendleton, Early's adjutant general, rode up to Breckinridge and Wharton at 9:00 a.m. Pendleton ordered them to withdraw and "move to Winchester at once." Wharton objected: "Tell Genl. Early I have been hotly engaged since early dawn in the effort to prevent a large body of cavalry from crossing the Opequon . . . but if I withdraw my force, this large body of cavalry in the open country would have greatly the advantage of the infantry & certain disaster would follow." Pendleton replied, "I have given you Genl. Early's orders," and spurred his horse toward Winchester. Breckinridge and Wharton ignored the young staff

---

37 OR 43, pt. 1, 442; *New York Herald*, September 22, 1864; O'Ferrall, 115; Diary of Sergeant Henry Corbin, *Historical Magazine*, October 1873, 215.

38 The exact role of Lt. Col. J. Floyd King is uncertain. Breckinridge's artillery battalion was formally called King's Battalion, but Maj. William McLaughlin seems to have led the battalion at this time. King was transferred from battalion command on June 10, 1864, but remained with Breckinridge. Some historians refer to him as the deputy chief of artillery for Early's army. After two decades of studying this campaign, this author has concluded that King functioned as Breckinridge's artillery chief. Milton W. Humphreys Papers, "Autobiography," UVA.

officer and decided to hold their position. They believed that Early would have sanctioned their actions if he understood the state of affairs at Brucetown.[39]

Wharton deployed Smith's and Forsberg's brigades behind "a long line of rail barricades" at the edge of the woods, "protected in addition by a formidable cheval-de-frise." Smith's men formed on the south side of the Brucetown Road, their battle line angling to the right and rear so faced in a southeasterly direction. Bryan's guns sat at the angle in Wharton's line where the woods began on the south side of Brucetown. Forsberg's troops extended the line across the road and faced east toward Locke's Ford. Patton's brigade remained isolated off to the right covering the Charlestown Road near Leetown, while Ferguson's mounted Virginians covered the gap as well as Wharton's flanks.[40]

As the Union cavalry slowly approached Brucetown, they traversed a rolling country crisscrossed by rock walls and rail fences. On the hill in front of town, the Union troopers spied Wharton's infantry and marveled at how "the sunlight danced upon their polished musket-barrels, while the butternut of their well-worn uniforms blended with their neutral tinted breastwork." When the Southerners saw the approaching Union cavalry, they "waved their battle-flags defiantly, and by their actions plainly said, 'Take them if you dare!'"[41]

Merritt accepted the challenge about 11:00 a.m. and ordered Lowell and Custer to charge Wharton's troops. On the right, Custer directed the 1st and 7th Michigan and the 25th New York to "test the strength and numbers of the enemy." On the left, Lowell instructed Capt. Theophilus Rodenbough to advance the 2nd U.S. Cavalry to support Custer's pending charge. The handsome Lowell added, "I will go with you." The U.S. officers examined the terrain and selected "the best line of approach to the enemy's position." The officers bellowed, "Draw Sabre! Trot-March!" The tough Regulars of the 2nd U.S. Cavalry eagerly obeyed and rode toward the wooded ridge at Brucetown where the "stars and bars fluttered temptingly in the distance-just out of reach."

39 Four decades later Wharton claimed he held Merritt at the Opequon. He did not hold the horsemen east of the stream, but his division did block Merritt's path to Early's left flank and rear. Wharton to Clay, May 15, 1905, Clay Family Papers, LC.

40 This is not the same Leetown from whence General Averell began his movement near Martinsburg that morning. It is a small hamlet on the Charlestown Road, about midway between Opequon Creek and the Martinsburg Pike. OR 43, pt. 1, 444, 455; Rodenbough, *Sabre and Bayonet*, 21.

41 Ibid., 20-21; Rodenbough, *Second Dragoons*, 350.

As the Regulars and Custer's men neared the Confederate position, the order "Charge!" rang out along the lines and the blue formation surged forward.[42]

The sudden appearance of four Union cavalry regiments charging out of the Opequon bottom lands elicited heavy fire from Bryan's guns. Fortunately for the Federals, the iron missiles did little harm. The Virginia infantry fired their rifles, but their volleys were "not very effective, being as a rule too low," although a number of horses went down early in the advance. The cavalry aimed its charge at Bryan's artillery posted in the angle of the line. As the Regulars closed in on the rail works, Lowell shouted, "Go for the flag," but the Confederates withdrew the banner safely behind the guns. "It began to look as if we were going to capture a trophy," recalled Captain Rodenbough, "when a flash of fire burst in our faces, followed by a crashing sound." Wharton's men fired and repulsed the charge. Horses dashed about without riders, and the regimental bugler sounded "The Rally" as the Regulars withdrew.[43]

On the right, Custer led the 1st and 7th Michigan and 25th New York toward Bryan's guns with "his yellow locks floating in the breeze." Lieutenant Albert T. Jackson and Lt. Col. George R. Maxwell dashed ahead, followed by troopers from the 1st Michigan. A Rebel artillery round tore Jackson's arm from his body, inflicting a mortal wound. Despite the fire, the small band of Wolverines reached "within a few feet of their artillery," but could not sustain their advance. The Rebels blunted the charge and put Custer's men to flight.[44]

Torbert and Merritt realized the position's strength and halted offensive operations against Breckinridge. Instead, the dismounted troopers skirmished with Rebel infantry to hold them in place at Brucetown, "as great a display of our forces was kept up as circumstances would allow." Freezing Breckinridge fulfilled their role in Sheridan's battle plan. The curtain was about to rise on the battle's main act along the Berryville Pike, where the bloodiest combat ever fought in the Valley would soon rage.[45]

---

42 Ibid.

43 OR 43, pt. 1, 444, 455, 462, 490; Rodenbough, *Sabre and Bayonet*, 21-22.

44 OR 43, pt. 1, 455; Rodenbough, *Sabre and Bayonet*, 21.

45 OR 43, pt. 1, 444, 455.

POUR IT INTO 'EM

The Berryville Pike

Sheridan's sudden arrival in Maj. Gen. Stephen D. Ramseur's front on the Berryville Pike set the stage for a potentially quick and decisive victory. The Union army commander had followed Brig. Gen. James Wilson's division into the fight and left Maj. Gen. Horatio G. Wright to oversee the passage of the 24,000 Union infantrymen from both the Sixth Corps and Nineteenth Corps through the narrow confines of Berryville Canyon. If these foot soldiers could negotiate the ravine, deploy their battle lines, and quickly attack the vastly outgunned Confederates in front of Winchester, Sheridan might easily achieve the decisive victory that Lincoln and Grant desired.

Sheridan's orders formally placed Wright in command of both corps (the Sixth and the Nineteenth) for the march on Winchester that day. Sheridan's action implied that he lack a certain confidence in Bvt. Maj. Gen. William Emory. Furthermore, when Sheridan prepared the army's marching orders, he referred to all of his subordinates by name—with the sole exception of William Emory. The army commander directed that the Nineteenth Corps's "commanding officer will report to Major-General Wright for instructions." Sheridan never publicly expressed any particular dissatisfaction with Emory, but Wright's temporary elevation to lead both corps on the march, and his reluctance to personally reference him by name and rank, indicated otherwise.[1]

Emory's Nineteenth Corps arrived upon Limestone Ridge overlooking Opequon Creek shortly before 5:00 a.m. Wright's Sixth Corps had not yet appeared, so Emory sought out his designated superior for orders. Wright instructed Emory to "remain where I was until the Sixth Corps had passed with its trains." Emory protested "against the passage of his [Wright's] baggage in my front." Wright, however, "produced the orders of the march and insisted upon the orders being observed . . ." A short while later, the Sixth Corps reached the creek and began crossing. As the duly appointed commander of both corps, Wright had the authority to alter the original order of the march, but he strictly adhered to Sheridan's original instructions. He probably wanted the veterans of the Sixth Corps to lead the infantry onto the battlefield, but it became problematic when Wright allowed his trains across the creek before Emory's combat troops were permitted to move. The ensuing delay denied Sheridan and the Army of the Shenandoah a legitimate opportunity to destroy Jubal Early's army in detail.[2]

Although Wright finalized the deployment of the Sixth Corps's battle line by 9:00 a.m., two additional hours elapsed before the Nineteenth Corps completed its formation. The situation within the narrow confines of the Berryville Canyon was chaotic even before the Sixth Corps's wagons entered. Artillery, ambulances, wounded troopers, and stragglers from Wilson's division already crowded the ravine, and the arrival of Wright's trains quickly stretched the narrow ravine beyond its capacity. Traffic quickly backed up east of the creek beyond Limestone Ridge, blocking the path of the Nineteenth Corps. "By some stupendous oversight," wrote Capt. John DeForest of the 12th Connecticut, "the VI Corps was closely followed by its baggage train and thus the infantry column was cut in two parts by miles of wagons." In the Army of the Shenandoah, responsibility for compliance with Sheridan's general orders regarding limitations on transportation rested with each corps commander. In this case, Wright failed to ensure that the Sixth Corps wagons did not hinder the

---

1   OR 43, pt. 2, 103.

2   William H. Emory, Report of Service, NA, 352-353; OR 43, pt. 1, 149, 279, 318; *ibid.*, pt. 2, 179-180; Richard B. Irwin, *History of the Nineteenth Army Corps* (New York, 1892), 379-380; William H. Emory to Mr. Swinton, May 12, 1866, Handley Library, Winchester, VA.

deployment of Emory's infantry who had been subordinated to Wright and it cost the army dearly.[3]

Finally, Wright belatedly halted his trains and ordered them back across the creek; however, the maneuvering wagons only worsened the jam. Emory, who had joined Wright on the front line, dispatched a staff officer to Brig. Gen. Cuvier Grover ordering him to "hurry forward regardless of the order of march, and, so far as the trains were concerned, to pass them." After dispatching all of his staff officers on the same errand without effect, Emory rode to the rear and personally urged his troops forward. Sheridan fumed over the delay in the Nineteenth Corps's deployment, but when Emory returned to the front, he apprised Sheridan of the Nineteenth Corps's situation and his corrective actions, which Sheridan readily endorsed. Nevertheless, it would be some time before the troops reached the firing line. "But the defile," lamented Emory, "was long and narrow and the troops did not join me on the field until nearly 11:00 a.m." His soldiers pressed on through the gorge toward Winchester, "dodging around wagons and mules."[4]

The Union Army's appearance also caught Jubal Early off guard, a fact he vehemently denied in the postwar era. Only self-inflicted delays experienced by the Army of the Shenandoah during its subsequent passage through the narrow confines of the Berryville Canyon allowed Early to reassemble his forces and avoid disaster. Although Early's memoirs claimed that he had presaged Sheridan's attack by learning of Grant's presence at Charlestown on the 17th, Early's reactions to that information revealed no sense of urgency. Indeed, Maj. Gen. John B. Gordon observed, "The reports of the Federal approach, however, did not seem to impress General Early and he delayed the order for concentration until Sheridan was upon him." Early admitted as much in his

3   Sheridan issued general orders No. 2 which greatly limited the number and defined the type of wagons each unit could take on the campaign. These orders were reiterated on August 9 and 27 prior to the army's previous moves. On both occasions, Sheridan delegated the oversight of transportation to the corps commanders. On September 18, Sheridan issued a circular that reminded his subordinates that "all regimental and other wagons that will inconvenience the quick movement of troops will be parked at Summit Point with the supply wagons . . ." Based upon the series of orders and general practice, it appears that Wright was lax in allowing his wagons to accompany the troops onto the battlefield. Wright did make every effort to rectify the situation once he was apprised of it. OR 43, pt. 1, 149, 279, 318, 740, 941; Frank M. Flinn, *Campaigning with Banks in Louisiana, '63 and '64 and with Sheridan in the Shenandoah Valley, '64 and '65* (Boston, 1889), 177; DeForest, *A Volunteer's Adventures*, 173.

4   George Crook claims that Sheridan was furious with Emory. Schmidt, *Crook Autobiography*, 125.

after-action report to Gen. Robert E. Lee, writing that upon learning of Sheridan's approach that morning he simply ordered, "Rodes, Gordon, and Breckinridge to have their divisions under arms ready to move to Ramseur's assistance." At the time this order was issued, Early and the aforementioned commands were in the vicinity of Stephenson's Depot, nearly four miles from Ramseur's location on the Berryville Pike. Furthermore, Early issued that order only after he heard the guns at Winchester and received a message from the battlefield. Early placed these two events at "about the time of Gordon's arrival," which occurred at approximately 8:00 a.m. By Early's own admission to Lee, "Old Jube" then departed Stephenson's Depot and headed to Ramseur's position "to ascertain the extent and character of the demonstration," while Rodes and Gordon waited near Stephenson's Depot.[5]

General Early reached Ramseur's position near the Dinkle farm no earlier than 8:30 a.m. Although Fitz Lee had previously notified Valley District headquarters of Sheridan's advance via signal flags, Early reported that he did not understand the true nature of the "demonstration," as Early termed it, until he arrived at Dinkle's and found Ramseur's entire division "in line of battle, and the enemy evidently advancing with his whole force." Early immediately "ordered up" his other divisions and placed the army's wagon trains "in motion for their security." Gordon and Rodes finally received marching orders at 9:00 a.m. and promptly complied.[6]

If Early had truly surmised that Sheridan would launch an attack on September 19 because of Grant's presence at Charlestown on the 17th, it stands to reason that a responsible commander would have warned all of his division commanders of the likelihood of the impending attack. Although Early later claimed to have suspected "an early move" by Sheridan, he did not notify his division commanders of the pending danger. The evidence is clear that Fitz Lee, Ramseur, Gordon, Breckinridge, and Wharton received no prior warning or special instructions from Early regarding an impending attack. The remaining division commander, Robert Rodes, did not survive the battle, but the movements of his division early that morning did not invoke any sense of urgency. Rodes's division had camped at Hopewell Meeting house no more than six miles from the battlefield and two miles north of Stephenson's Depot.

---

5   OR 43, pt. 1, 554-555; Early, *Memoir of the Last Year of the War for Independence*, 84-86; Jones, ed., *The Civil War Memoirs of Captain William J. Seymour*, 138.

6   OR 43, pt. 1, 554.

At sunrise, Rodes marched his command to the depot in compliance with orders Early had issued on the previous evening. At Stephenson's Depot, Rodes's division remained stationary for at least one and possibly two hours before receiving Early's orders to march to Ramseur's assistance. If Early truly anticipated a fight at Winchester on September 19, 1864, why did he not rush Rodes to Ramseur's assistance at sunrise?[7]

Strangely, Gordon's division reached the battlefield before Rodes despite the fact that the Georgian had more than twice the distance to cover in marching from Bunker Hill. Acting under Early's orders of the previous evening, Gordon left Bunker Hill at sunrise and reached Stephenson's Depot at 8:00 a.m. Breckinridge likewise received no warning of the pending attack. Instead of preparing for battle early that morning, the Kentuckian sent a staff officer into Winchester to tell Breckinridge's wife that he would soon join her for breakfast in town. Early blamed the lack of communication with Gordon and Breckinridge on poor staff work but never addressed the question of what delayed Rodes. In the end, however, Early's scattered army was able to concentrate in time to meet the gathering storm thanks to a wagon-clogged road in the Berryville Canyon.[8]

Brigadier General George W. Getty's division led the Sixth Corps through the rolling countryside of western Clarke County. Reaching Spout Spring, the Union foot soldiers splashed across Opequon Creek without pause. They marched along the Berryville Pike which shared the narrow confines of the ravine with silvery waters of Abram's Creek. As the infantrymen trudged out of the bottomlands, dazed and bleeding cavalrymen from Wilson's division stumbled along in agony while others were borne to field hospitals upon stretchers, a visible reminder of what awaited the infantry at the front. As the Federal infantrymen marched out of the canyon, "which loses itself in the high and rolling country" east of Winchester, they saw the town's church spires

---

7   During the retreat from Washington in July, Early learned that the pursuing Federals under Horatio Wright were at Snicker's Gap on July 17. As a precaution, Early ordered his division commanders to have their men sleep on their arms and to be ready to move into action at a moment's notice. Because of Early's precautions, the next day saw a Confederate victory at the battle of Cool Spring. Stephen D. Ramseur to David Schenck, October 10, 1864, SHC-UNC; Gabriel C. Wharton to James B. Clay, May 15, 1905, Clay Family Papers, LC; James B. Clay to Gabriel Wharton, June 4, 1905; Clay Family Papers, LC; William R. Cox, "Major General Stephen D. Ramseur," 18, 247; Fitz Lee, Report of Operations 1864, Museum of the Confederacy; OR 43, pt. 1, 554, 605.

8   Samuel Clay to Gabriel Wharton, June 4, 1905, Clay Family Papers, LC.

rising in the distance. Unlike Sheridan's first advance up the Valley, Ramseur's infantry and Fitz Lee's cavalry stood firmly between Winchester and the Federals and showed no signs of leaving. When the Confederate artillerists saw the approaching blue column, they opened fire and rained iron down on the Union soldiers, hurrying them toward the shelter of the woods.[9]

As Getty's division filed into position, they found Sheridan "personally superintending from the commencement the operations of the day." The army commander's presence reassured both officers and men. A Vermonter wrote, "It was with great satisfaction that we found him in this early twilight at the very front, and under the fire of the enemy, carefully attending to details which we had been accustomed to see more celebrated commanders entrust to their staff." As Sheridan sat astride his black horse alongside the road, the soldiers broke their stride and turned to get a closer look at their commander. In doing so, they slowed the column, prompting Sheridan to urge them to hurry to the front.[10]

Getty posted Brig. Gen. Daniel Bidwell's brigade on the far left astride the Old Berryville Road with the unit's left flank anchored upon Abram's Creek. Brigadier General Frank Wheaton's Pennsylvania and New York regiments held the center, while Col. James M. Warner's Vermont brigade deployed on the right. Warner's right flank rested a short distance south of the Berryville Pike. As the Sixth Corps infantry arrived and deployed, Wilson withdrew most of his troopers and posted them south of Abram's Creek. They regrouped around Greenwood Church nearly a half mile south of Getty's left flank. The tired troopers, who had already seen several hours of action, replenished their cartridge boxes and prepared for further duty on Sheridan's left flank; however, they did not rejoin the fight until well into the afternoon.

Brigadier General James D. Ricketts's division followed Getty's men onto the battlefield. Most of Ricketts's men abandoned the crowded road and turned northward into the woods, stirring up a flock of wild turkeys that flew back over the soldiers' heads, startling some of the edgy troops as they moved toward the sounds of battle. Ricketts posted Col. J. Warren Keifer's brigade in a timbered area on the north side of the Berryville Pike. Ricketts placed Col. William Emerson's brigade across the Berryville Pike in the space between Keifer and

9   OR 43, pt. 1, 212.

10 Aldace F. Walker, *The Vermont Brigade in the Shenandoah Valley, 1864* (Burlington, 1869), 91-92; Lemuel A. Abbott, *Personal Recollections and Civil War Diary, 1864* (Burlington, 1908), 152.

Getty. With the Nineteenth Corps yet to arrive on the field, some of Wilson's dismounted cavalry remained in position to cover Ricketts's right flank.[11]

Brigadier General David Russell's division remained in reserve behind the center of the Sixth Corps front line, much to the dismay of its commander. Russell asked Sheridan, "Phil, why do you put me in the rear?" Having served under Russell in the Regular Army, Sheridan replied, "Because I know what I shall have there in a commanding officer if the line should break . . ." This division, perhaps the best in Sheridan's army, had gained a reputation as shock troops by their attacks at Rappahannock Station in late 1863 as well as at Spotsylvania's "Bloody Angle" back in May. Colonel Edward L. Campbell's 700-man New Jersey brigade supported Emerson's brigade on the left of the Berryville Turnpike while Col. Oliver Edwards's brigade moved even farther to the left behind Getty's division. Brigadier General Emory Upton's brigade remained in column on the Berryville Pike behind the New Jersey brigade.[12]

The Sixth Corps's artillery soon arrived on the battlefield. As the cannon rolled down the pike, General Sheridan ribbed Colonel Charles H. Tompkins, the Sixth Corps's Chief of Artillery, calling out, "I want to see some dead horses before night." He would not be disappointed. Tompkins quickly positioned his batteries along the battle line in key spots to support the infantry. The 1st New York Independent Battery unlimbered behind Keifer's right flank. The 5th Maine went into battery with a section on either side of the Berryville Pike. Battery M, 5th U.S. Artillery, rolled into position on the extreme left of Getty's line to support Bidwell's exposed brigade. Battery C, 1st Rhode Island, dropped trail in a cornfield to the right of the Regulars and behind Bidwell's infantry. The big guns of the Sixth Corps proved a welcome addition to the Federal battle line. Nelson's gunners had been firing into the blue infantry, unimpeded by Federal counter-battery fire to dissuade their efforts against the Union foot soldiers. Now, the Confederate gunners struggled to maintain their position against accurate counter-battery fire delivered by the experienced and well-armed gunners from the Army of the Potomac.[13]

Army correspondents gathered on the heights behind the Sixth Corps. The commanding position offered them an impressive view of the deploying armies

---

11 OR 43, pt. 1, 221.

12 Nelson Hutchinson, *History of the Seventh Massachusetts Volunteer Infantry*, 288.

13 OR 43, pt. 1, 271; Tompkins, 271, 273, 274-275.

that was greatly enhanced by the natural beauty of the lush Shenandoah Valley. "The sunshine was mild and the breezes were faint, the leaves scarcely swayed in their passing," wrote the *New York World's* correspondent. To the far west loomed the Allegheny Mountains beyond the town, while the Blue Ridge sat behind the U.S. position. Within the impressive viewshed sat the town of Winchester, its church spires faintly visible like "silver threads" against the dark hues of the Allegheny Mountains in the distance. The blue columns of U.S. infantry "debouched from the pike and woods upon the fields and plateaus; some waiting in the hollows behind the crest." Sheridan, Wright, and Emory rode "swiftly with their staffs along the lines, looking well to every point of advantage upon the ground" as they studied the Rebel positions through their field glasses. Officers and orderlies galloped across the "levels and hollows" as they carried orders to the skirmish lines and zipped back to their respective headquarters with fresh reports on enemy deployments. Union skirmishers plied their trade from behind rail fences and along the wood lines. Beyond the U.S. troops, the reporters saw the "faint columns" of the Confederate battle line. The Southern sharpshooters and skirmishers appeared as "white specs in the cornfields" with groups of them clustered around homes and barns. Smoke from the artillery fire hung in the air over the batteries as the Union Army deployed.[14]

In front of the Sixth Corps and concealed in a ravine, Ramseur's division waited for the Union attack. To cover this extended front with only two small brigades, Ramseur positioned his units behind rail breastworks with 20-yard gaps between each regiment. On the higher ground behind Ramseur's infantry, Nelson's artillery firmed up the Confederate defenses and fired over the Southern foot soldiers into the Sixth Corps. Brigadier General Robert Johnston had reformed his North Carolina brigade north of the Berryville Turnpike upon the farm of Enos Dinkle, a farmer from Pennsylvania with three sons in the Confederate cavalry including one killed at Gettysburg. Johnston's four regiments sheltered themselves behind rail breastworks on the western slope of the deep ravine immediately east of the Dinkle house. The North Carolinians' position was far enough down the slope that they remained partially concealed from the view of the approaching Union soldiers but still high enough to shoot into the advancing blue lines. On Johnston's right flank south of the pike, Brig.

---

14 "The Battle of Berryville," *New York World,* contained in *The Rutland Weekly Herald,* September 29, 1864.

Brig. Gen. Robert D. Johnston
LC

Gen. John Pegram's Virginians waited in line of battle. Brigadier General Archibald Godwin's North Carolina brigade was en route from its previous position on the Millwood Pike and had yet to rejoin the division, so Lt. Col. William Thompson's dismounted Virginia troopers remained in position between Pegram and Abram's Creek. Further south, part of Bradley Johnson's brigade of cavalry covered the Confederate Army's right flank. The balance of Johnson's brigade deployed on Ramseur's left flank, stretching out and screening the 1,600 yards between Robert Johnston's left and Red Bud Run, a stream that lined the northern edge of the main battlefield.[15]

Although the two Sixth Corps divisions confronting Ramseur outnumbered him almost four-to-one, the rough terrain and the chosen Federal formation partially negated that numerical advantage. The ground in front of the Sixth Corps was broken and choppy, especially in Getty's front on the south side of the Berryville Pike. Ravines flowing into Abram's Creek created several steep-sided chasms that bisected the Berryville Pike. For Union troops advancing along the axis of that road, it was akin to sailing upon a rough ocean where undulation precluded them from seeing what lay in front or to the rear. Ramseur's defenders took full advantage of the terrain to withstand the coming Union assault.[16]

15 Map of Ramseur's Position, September 19, 1864, Hotchkiss Papers, LC.

16 Readers can better understand the position of the advancing soldiers of the Sixth Corps by recalling a vacation day at a beach with heavy incoming surf. As one wades out into the water, larger waves immediately in front of the beach-goers block their vision of what lies beyond that

On Getty's left, Bidwell's brigade deployed on a high, open ridge, exposing this outfit to Confederate artillery fire. Bidwell quickly deployed a skirmish line in front while his regiments shook out their battle line under a rain of iron projectiles. Lieutenant Colonel Augustus W. Dwight's 122nd New York slithered through a cornfield and relieved some dismounted troopers who had been occupying rail breastworks erected after Wilson secured the position. Dwight rapidly deployed four of his companies on the skirmish line. The 77th New York followed Dwight's men into the field and deployed on his left flank. While they moved into position, the accurate fire of the Confederate sharpshooters and Nelson's artillery annoyed the New Yorkers. The 122nd New York soon lost Lt. Col. Dwight to a Confederate sniper's bullet. Angered by the rapid loss of four officers to Confederate fire, the 77th New York's commander, Lt. Col. Windsor B. French, advanced "twenty good shots" to suppress the Confederate sharpshooters and artillerists. The combined efforts of Bidwell's soldiers stifled much of the activity of the Confederate sharpshooters and gave the artillerists pause as they worked their pieces.[17]

Bidwell continued his deployment, placing the 43rd New York Infantry in echelon to the left and rear of the 77th New York. The 49th New York went into line of battle to the left of the 43rd New York but faced several left flank companies southward toward Abram's Creek to counter a harassing fire from Bradley Johnson's Virginians south of the stream. Next, the 7th Maine extended its line from the 49th New York's refused left flank toward the creek and likewise refused its left flank to the rear and braced it upon Abram's Creek. Bidwell retained the tiny 61st Pennsylvania Battalion in reserve behind his three left regiments.[18]

---

wave. This is the viewshed that Union soldiers would have had when they entered a ravine— they could see nothing but the opposite slope of the ravine. Also, the ravines do not cross the road at perfect perpendicular angles. Instead, they followed varied angles caused by the more meandering course of the water flows that created these topographical features. As a result, during the Sixth Corps' attack portions of the line were at varying points, with some troops in the bottom of a ravine while others were at the crest dependent upon the angles of the feature. In the end, this choppy terrain disjointed the cohesiveness of Wright's advance.

17 OR 43, pt. 1, 191, 212, 219; Unpublished Report of Lt. Col. Augustus W. Dwight and Charles H. Enos, "The Veteran's Column: September 19—Battle of Winchester," contained in the *Fayetteville Weekly Recorder*, http://www.rootsbweb.com/~nyononda?war/onondaga.htm, accessed on December 15, 2006.

18 OR 43, pt. 1, 212, 219.

A deep ravine with steep sides separated Bidwell from the rest of Getty's division to the north. On the opposite side of the ravine, a dense growth of young pines offered concealment to Wheaton's veteran brigade. The 139th Pennsylvania anchored Wheaton's left flank near the gully. The 102nd Pennsylvania, primarily a Pittsburgh outfit with a large contingent of men from the city's iron foundries and steel mills, continued the line northward with the 93rd Pennsylvania next in line. The 98th Pennsylvania, a predominantly German unit from Philadelphia, occupied Wheaton's right flank. In front of the battle line, Pennsylvania skirmishers swarmed over the cleared ground west of the woods and traded shots with Ramseur's sharpshooters. Wheaton deployed the small 62nd New York as flankers to cover the extensive ground to the north until other troops moved into position.[19]

North of Wheaton's position, the Army of the Potomac's stoic 1st Vermont Brigade solidified Getty's right flank. This rugged Green Mountain State outfit had lost 1,400 men in a heroic stand against Lt. Gen. James Longstreet's devastating counterattack on the second day of the battle of the Wilderness on May 6, 1864. As a result of continued combat losses and expiring enlistments, the Vermont Brigade was not the same sturdy and dependable unit that had followed Grant and Meade into the Wilderness. The enlistments of many veterans recently expired, depriving the outfit of experienced officers and men. Some of the losses were replaced when the 11th Vermont (1st Heavy Artillery) joined the brigade after the horrendous combat at Spotsylvania. Still, enough veteran leadership remained to carry on the brigade's reputation and inspire the newcomers to sustain the proud military tradition of the Green Mountain State.

Brigadier General Lewis Addison Grant, the brigade's usual commander, had taken a temporary leave of absence from the army, so Col. James M. Warner of the 11th Vermont took his place at the head of the brigade. Warner, a West Point graduate, advanced the 6th Vermont through a narrow strip of woods in skirmish order until they reached its western edge where they immediately engaged Ramseur's sharpshooters. Warner formed the rest of the brigade in line of battle on the eastern edge of the woods, concealing them from enemy view. Warner's right flank rested a short distance from the Berryville

---

19 Nine of ten companies in the 98th Pennsylvania were German. The remaining company was Irish. OR 43, pt. 1, 196, 204.

Turnpike, connecting with the left flank of Brig. Gen. James B. Ricketts's division just south of the road.[20]

Ricketts began the war as commander of a Regular Army battery that became the focus of the fighting upon Henry Hill at the First Battle of Bull Run. Four bullets pierced his body, and he fell into the hands of the Confederates. After his exchange, he commanded a division at Second Bull Run and Antietam where a fall from his horse disabled him. In the spring of 1864, Ricketts received command of his current Sixth Corps division and led it in all of its actions leading up to Winchester, including the hard fight against Early's veterans at Monocacy. This division originally joined the Army of the Potomac in the wake of the Gettysburg campaign as part of the devastated Third Corps. Already viewed as outsiders, Ricketts's troops transferred to the Sixth Corps during the reorganization of the Army of the Potomac in the spring of 1864. Prior to joining Meade's army, these troops had been part of the much-maligned command of Maj. Gen. Robert H. Milroy. Consequently, many long-time Sixth Corps veterans viewed Ricketts's division as a weak stepchild and were quick to find fault with its performance, often derisively referring to them as "Milroy's Boys."[21]

Ricketts placed his division in a double line of battle pursuant to General Wright's orders. Colonel Emerson's multi-state brigade extended the Union battle line northward across the Berryville Pike. The 151st New York relieved Wilson's dismounted troopers on the skirmish line, all the while taking fire from Ramseur's sharpshooters. Armed with breach-loading Sharps rifles, the New Yorkers shoved back the Confederate sharpshooters and secured a good position where a section of the 5th Maine Battery unlimbered in front of the infantry line. Behind these skirmishers Emerson deployed the 14th New Jersey astride the Berryville Pike with its left flank adjoining the Vermont Brigade. The 106th New York extended Emerson's front line onto the grounds of Enos Dinkle's farm on the north side of the Berryville Pike. Major Edwin Dillingham's 10th Vermont deployed on the pike behind the 14th New Jersey

20 Much of Brig. Gen. James Ricketts's division fought under Maj. Gen. Robert Milroy, whose command was devastated during the early stages of the Gettysburg campaign at Second Winchester in June of 1863 by Lt. Gen. Richard Ewell's Second Corps, including Jubal Early's division, which played a key role in that Confederate victory. OR 43, pt. 1, 207; Walker, *Vermont Brigade in the Shenandoah Valley*, 92.

21 Warner, *Generals in Blue*, 404.

with Col. John W. Schall's 87th Pennsylvania to its right behind the New Yorkers.[22]

Colonel Joseph Warren Keifer's brigade anchored the right flank of both Ricketts's division and the Sixth Corps. When the war broke out in 1861, Keifer closed the doors to his law office in Springfield, Ohio, and was appointed major of the 3rd Ohio Infantry. On September 30, 1862, Ohio's governor commissioned Keifer as colonel of the newly formed 110th Ohio. He had experienced combat in the Shenandoah Valley at the Second Battle of Winchester on June 15, 1863, leading a counterattack that enabled many Union soldiers to escape capture at that disastrous defeat. Keifer suffered a shattered forearm at the Wilderness and had only recently returned to duty. Doctors advised the 28-year-old Keifer against returning to active service. The young colonel ignored their advice and, after a lengthy convalescence, resumed command with his arm still in a sling. "He is a good, competent officer. The men have every confidence in him," asserted an Ohio soldier. "His only fault is he has star on the brain. Well, if he wins it, he will wear it worthily."[23]

Keifer posted his brigade in two lines of battle with the 122nd Ohio's Maj. Charles M. Cornyn leading the brigade's sharpshooters to the front of the woods. They engaged their Confederate counterparts, who were swarming in front of Johnston's North Carolina brigade. Lieutenant Colonel Aaron W. Ebright, a former county sheriff from Sherman's hometown of Lancaster, Ohio, deployed his 126th Ohio on Keifer's left flank, linking with the 106th New York on Emerson's right. On the Ohioans' right flank, Col. John W. Horn's 6th Maryland and 138th Pennsylvania held Keifer's left and right center positions respectively. The 67th Pennsylvania anchored Keifer's right flank. Its regimental adjutant, Lt. John F. Young, led the Pennsylvanians into battle because their colonel had been dishonorably discharged for failing to do his duty at the battle of Monocacy. Keifer's three remaining regiments deployed behind the front line, extending Emerson's rear line northward. The 9th New York Heavy Artillery, equipped as infantry, held the left and the 122nd Ohio manned the center, while the 110th Ohio anchored the right.[24]

22 OR 43, pt. 1, 231, 235-236, 238-239, 243.

23 Keifer had led a desperate counterattack at Second Winchester in June 1863 that allowed many Union soldiers to avoid capture during that disastrous Union defeat at the hands of Lt. Gen. Richard S. Ewell. Thomas Campbell Diary, USAMHI.

24 OR 43, pt. 1, 246, 258, 260, 263, 266, 269.

Col. Joseph Warren Keifer and wife.
Nicholas Picerno Collection

Once Ricketts's deployment was completed, it took Emory's Nineteenth Corps more than one hour more to reach the front. When it did, Wright posted it 40 yards north of the Sixth Corps's right flank. The small gap was caused by Ash Hollow Run, a stream that formed a natural divide between the two corps. Emory's corps completed its deployment within the sheltered confines of the First Woods by 11:00 a.m. Brigadier General Cuvier Grover's division formed a double line of battle supported by Brig. Gen. William Dwight's division, which deployed in a column of regiments behind the right of Grover's rear line. This

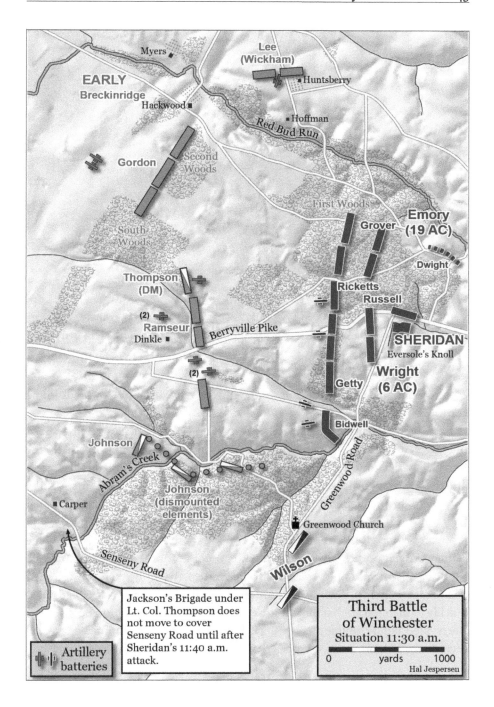

Myers

Lee
(Wickham)

Huntsberry

EARLY
Breckinridge
Hackwood

Hoffman

Red Bud Run

Gordon

Second
Woods

First Woods

South
Woods

Emory
(19 AC)

Grover

Dwight

Thompson
(DM)

Ricketts

Russell

(2)
Ramseur
Dinkle

Berryville Pike

SHERIDAN
Eversole's Knoll

Wright
(6 AC)

Getty

(2)

Bidwell

Johnson

Greenwood Road

Abram's Creek

Johnson
(dismounted
elements)

Carper

Greenwood Church

Senseny Road

Wilson

Jackson's Brigade under
Lt. Col. Thompson does
not move to cover
Senseny Road until after
Sheridan's 11:40 a.m.
attack.

Artillery
batteries

Third Battle
of Winchester
Situation 11:30 a.m.

0   yards   1000

Hal Jespersen

Brig. Gen. James B. Ricketts's division advancing through the woods north of the Berryville Pike. *A. R. Waud, LC*

corps would guide its advance upon the movements of the Sixth Corps in the coming attack.[25]

As the Union infantry finalized its dispositions for battle, Ramseur realized that Ricketts greatly overlapped General Johnston's left flank north of the Berryville Pike. Fortunately for Ramseur, Brig. Gen. Archibald Godwin's North Carolina brigade was just reaching the southern outskirts of the battlefield from its initial position on the Millwood Pike. Ramseur shifted Pegram's and Johnston's infantry northward the length of one brigade, and Godwin's troops took over the defenses on the south side of the Berryville Pike as they arrived on the battlefield. At some point before the Federals attacked, Thompson's dismounted cavalry also moved to the north side of the road where they went into position on Ramseur's left flank. Pegram's Virginians filed quickly to their left so that most of this brigade was now in position north of the Berryville Pike. Forming the center of Ramseur's line, the Virginians covered themselves behind some rail piles that Johnston's Carolinians had previously

25 The details of the Nineteenth Corps's deployment are discussed in the subsequent chapter.

erected. Lastly, Thompson's dismounted troopers hustled on foot into position on Johnston's left flank where they supported a Virginia battery from Nelson's battalion planted along the edge of a wooded hilltop. Once these last minute adjustments were in place, Ramseur's line barely covered the front of the Sixth Corps, albeit with gaps between the regiments. No sooner had these Confederates settled into their new positions than they spied the long blue lines of the advancing Sixth Corps. Ramseur's final adjustment had come not a moment too soon.[26]

Sheridan's attack began at precisely 11:40 a.m., a time nearly all participants agreed upon. Ricketts began the attack along the Berryville Pike with Getty on his left and the Nineteenth Corps on its right. Sheridan had directed Wright to guide his advance upon the Berryville Pike, this duty falling into the hands of Ricketts. His "blue patches," as the men of the Third Division were known for the color of the corps badges on their caps, set the pace of the advance for the rest of the army to follow. Moving first naturally placed Ricketts slightly ahead of all other units. Those on the far right and left flanks of the Union battle line lagged behind the center due to their distance from the guide.

Ricketts's assignment was not as simple as it seemed. No sooner did the veteran division commander begin the attack, than the path of the Berryville Pike impacted the course of the assault. The road veered sharply southward a short distance in front of the initial position of the Union battle line. As Ricketts advanced, his troops followed the course of the road which rapidly pulled them southward away from the Nineteenth Corps's left flank. That corps continued upon a more direct course as it approached the Confederates in its front. As a result, as the Sixth Corps veered southward with the road, the gap between the two corps soon expanded to dangerous proportions that would ultimately lead to the initial failure of Sheridan's attack.

Major Peter Vredenburgh's 14th New Jersey of Emerson's brigade straddled the Berryville Pike and served as the unit of direction for Sheridan's attack. Its color guard formed up in the very middle of the narrow dirt road, and their flags served as the guides for Union troops on both sides of the road to follow. These banners also attracted the unwanted attention of Nelson's Confederate artillery. Shells exploded all around the color guard as the Southern

26 George Q. Peyton, Journal 1864-1865, Virginia Room, Bull Run Regional Library; Joseph C. Snider Diary, WVU; Bumgardner, "Early's Little Black Captain," 158; "Jackson's Brigade at Winchester," JWD Papers, UVA; Harding, 170-171.

gunners honed in on the troops deployed in the open road. Moments before the attack began, Vredenburgh mounted his horse and ventured out in front of his regiment. A member of his staff suggested that Vredenburgh dismount and proceed on foot for his own safety, but the major refused, explaining, "I can manage the regiment much better mounted." Then, he turned to face his men and called out, "Boys, we are the guide on the left of the line in this charge. Advance on [the] double quick, keep your ears open to the orders, and I will do the best that I can for you." Vredenburgh then ordered the advance and his New Jersey soldiers stepped out of the woods and trudged toward Ramseur's line.[27]

As the Union troops moved along the open road toward Winchester, Nelson's artillery continued to pound the blue battle lines, firing "unmercifully" at the oncoming United States troops. The 14th New Jersey had barely reached the skirmish line when a solid shot struck Major Vredenburgh, who at that very moment was the most important man along the Union battle line. The iron projectile ripped into the left side of his neck and burrowed through his torso before exiting his right shoulder. His arms flung reflexively into the air, and he fell back headfirst onto the hard macadam surface of the pike. Lying in the middle of the road, Vredenburgh reflexively threw his hands over his face and took his last breath. The major's untimely death threw the 14th New Jersey into a confusion that quickly spread along the Sixth Corps's battle line in both directions. Captain Jacob Janeway immediately assumed command and struggled to reform the stunned regiment. Back at the edge of the woods, he ordered the men to lie down to avoid the heavy Confederate artillery fire. To the right of the New Jersey regiment, the 106th New York followed Janeway's example and dropped to the ground.[28]

When the rear line of Emerson's brigade reached the edge of the woods, the sweeping fire of the Confederate artillery likewise disrupted the advance of the 10th Vermont. Major Dillingham attempted to realign his regiment after it had fallen into some confusion "under the first shock of the enemy's fire," but a solid shot "twisted off" his leg and mortally wounded him. The situation was not any better in the 87th Pennsylvania on the right. The confusion among the

---

27 Lt. E. L. Corvasts to My Dear Wife, Vredenburgh Collection, Monmouth County Historical Association, Freehold, New Jersey; David G. Martin, *The Monocacy Regiment*, 162-163.

28 Ibid.

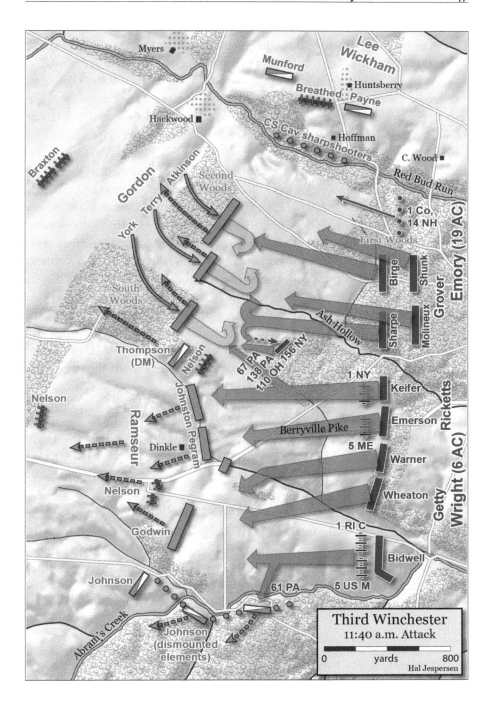

Myers

Munford

Lee
Wickham

Breathed

Huntsberry

Payne

Hackwood

CS cav sharpshooters

Hoffman

C. Wood

Braxton

Gordon

Second
Woods

Red Bud Run

Terry

Atkinson

First Woods

1 Co.
14 NH

York

Birge

Shunk

Emory (19 AC)

South
Woods

Ash Hollow

Sharpe

Molineux

Grover

Thompson
(DM)

Nelson

67 PA
138 PA
110 OH 156 NY

1 NY

Keifer

Ricketts

Nelson

Johnston Pegram

Ramseur

Dinkle

Berryville Pike

5 ME

Emerson

Warner

Wright (6 AC)

Nelson

Wheaton

Getty

Godwin

1 RI C

Bidwell

Johnson

61 PA

5 US M

Abram's Creek

Johnson
(dismounted
elements)

Third Winchester
11:40 a.m. Attack

0   yards   800

Hal Jespersen

Union troops near the Pike allowed Pegram's Virginians in front of Ricketts to direct their rifle fire at Getty's division as it attempted to advance on the left.[29]

South of the Berryville Pike, Getty's division encountered significant topographical challenges as it advanced against Ramseur. The terrain there was more broken than on the north side of the road, and Ramseur used that terrain to his advantage. A battery of Nelson's battalion deployed on a hill behind Godwin's brigade and pounded the advancing Federal lines. Making matters worse for the Union infantry, a section of Lomax's horse artillery at the Carper Farm on the Senseney Road just south of Abram's Creek poured an enfilading fire into Getty's left. On his right, Col. James M. Warner's Vermonters passed through some tangled woods with a dense undergrowth that "necessarily" threw their line "somewhat into confusion." When they sorted out their ranks and reached the far edge of the woods, Maj. Aldace Walker of the 11th Vermont scanned the terrain in front and determined that their chances for success were "appalling." A few hundred yards in their front, a deep ravine or hollow (the Dinkle Ravine hereafter) crossed the pike perpendicularly, flowing across the Dinkle farm toward Abram's Creek. A short distance south of the road, that hollow turned nearly 90 degrees eastward and then ran almost directly from Ramseur's line toward the Vermont brigade, though angling off slightly toward the Vermonters' left.[30]

As the Vermonters advanced, their predicament worsened. On Pegram's right flank, the 52nd Virginia slid into position at the head of the hollow where it veered sharply to the east along the south side of the road. The Virginians fired down the ravine, delivering an enfilading fire into the right flank of the Vermont brigade as it entered the ravine. Undaunted, Warner's troops raced into the ravine but quickly discovered its bottom was marshy, while the steep southern slope beyond was covered with small pines. The slope of the ground naturally caused the Vermonters to turn slightly to their left as they climbed the southern side of the hollow, further exposing their right flank. Pegram's Virginians quickly took advantage of the opportunity and raked the 11th Vermont's right flank with a blistering volley "at short pistol range." The Virginians fired "coolly, as rapidly as they could load, directly along our line,

29 Alanson Austin Haines, *History of the Fifteenth Regiment*, 114; Major Aldace Walker, "The Vermont brigade in the battles of Winchester and Fisher's Hill," *Vermont Chronicle*, October 15, 1864.

30 Walker, *Vermont Brigade in the Shenandoah Valley*, 93-94; OR 43, pt. 1, 207.

Brig. Gen. John Pegram
LC

thus enfilading us completely." The Vermonters broke for the pines on the slope to their left and all semblance of order disappeared. "We scrambled out of the gully in a hurry, losing severely, of course," wrote Walker. In veering leftward to avoid the enfilading fire of the Virginians, Warner's Vermonters pulled away from Ricketts's left flank, creating a small gap between the two Sixth Corps divisions. This was only one of several gaps that developed in the

Union battle line as the troops readjusted their position due to terrain or enemy activity during the initial Union attack. With Getty's division moving over the hill toward Godwin and out of sight, Pegram's men focused entirely upon Ricketts's renewed advance.[31]

In the center of Getty's line, Frank Wheaton's Pennsylvanians picked their way through the same briars and brambles that also hindered the Vermonters on their right. When they entered the open ground, Wheaton saw the confusion caused by the thick vegetation and stopped briefly behind a sheltering rise of ground to sort out his jumbled ranks. Before the Pennsylvanians perfected their alignment, the Vermonters "rushed forward with a shout." Wheaton's men joined the surging battle line, but, from that point, he realized that "it was impossible to preserve the order in the advance that was so desirable and important." It was not long before the fire of Godwin's Confederates "checked the advance and necessitated another readjustment" of Getty's line.[32]

On Getty's left flank, Bidwell's brigade struggled as much with the rough terrain in its front as it did with direct resistance from Confederate infantry. As a result Bidwell advanced alone, with a deep ravine separating his command from Wheaton to the right. On Bidwell's right, the 77th and 122nd New York moved ahead under heavy fire from a two-gun battery deployed in their front. As they moved forward, Godwin's sharpshooters fired with deadly accuracy. Bidwell's left wing encountered stiff resistance from the Confederate horse artillery and Bradley Johnson's cavalry posted on the commanding south bank of Abram's Creek. Johnson's dismounted Virginians (armed with Enfield rifles) charged Bidwell's flank guards on the south bank and shoved them back across the creek. From the elevated ground the Confederate troopers had just seized, they delivered a withering fire into Bidwell's left on the opposite bank and prevented it from moving forward. Instead, the 7th Maine and the 43rd and 49th New York halted and traded shots with Bradley Johnson's Virginians.[33]

With a hostile force menacing Bidwell's left flank, he dispatched his reserve, the tiny 61st Pennsylvania, to deal with the threatening Virginians. The Pennsylvania battalion waded through Abram's Creek and engaged Johnson's horsemen south of the stream. The Virginians resisted briefly, but the

---

31 Major Aldace Walker, "The Vermont brigade in the battles of Winchester and Fisher's Hill," *Vermont Chronicle*, October 15, 1864.

32 *OR* 43, pt. 1, 197.

33 *New York Herald*, September 22, 1864.

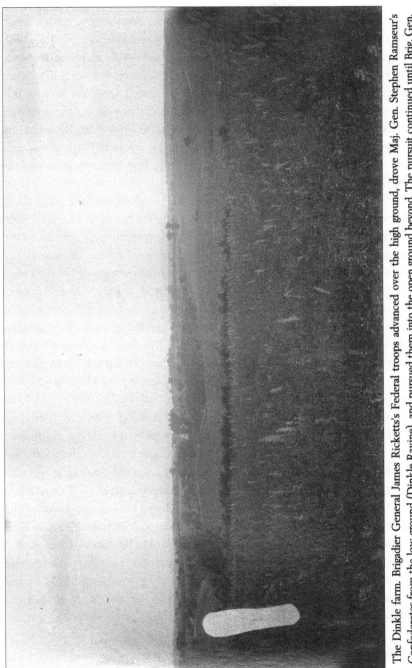

The Dinkle farm. Brigadier General James Ricketts's Federal troops advanced over the high ground, drove Maj. Gen. Stephen Ramseur's Confederates from the low ground (Dinkle Ravine), and pursued them into the open ground beyond. The pursuit continued until Brig. Gen. Bryan Grimes's Southern brigade on Robert Rodes's right flank swept over the open ground on the right and struck Ricketts's flank forcing him to fall back to the Dinkle Ravine. *Dwight and Walter Briscoe, Photographers, 1885, DeGolyer Library, SMU*

Pennsylvania infantry prevailed and cleared the Southerners away from Bidwell's flank. If Gen. James Wilson had pressed the Confederate cavalry with his 3,000 superbly armed troopers south of Abram's Creek, Johnson never would have been able to harass Bidwell's flank. Furthermore, only Johnson's 800-man brigade and a section of horse artillery defended Senseney Road at this point in the battle. Sheridan and Wilson missed an early opportunity to shatter the Confederate right flank and threaten Early's line of retreat. Between the terrain, Nelson's artillery, and Johnson's annoying cavalry, Getty's advance struggled to gain traction. A rejuvenated Ricketts, however, soon broke the deadlock on the Sixth Corps's right flank.[34]

After sorting through the confusing series of events along the pike, Capt. Peter Robertson's 106th New York resumed the advance on Emerson's right flank. On his immediate right, Col. Keifer's brigade immediately continued the movement, and soon Ricketts had his entire division moving forward. The open woods on the north side of the pike only partially sheltered Keifer's men from Nelson's shelling, and shells still screamed through the treetops, disheartening the men. The angle of the wood line caused Keifer's left wing to uncover first, and when it did, the Virginia artillerists "opened their batteries with splendid aim and fearful destruction." The 6th Maryland's color-bearer quickly went down mortally wounded, and Lt. William H. Burns snatched them up only to have his head torn off by a Rebel shell, leaving the flag stained with his blood. Johnston's and Pegram's men fired volley after volley into the approaching Union troops, but the soldiers kept coming. The 10th Vermont and 87th Pennsylvania from Emerson's rear line emerged from the confusion, passed over the prone 14th New Jersey and joined the attack on the road. Not to be left behind, the Jersey soldiers rose up and joined the assaulting force.[35]

Ricketts's division attacked the highest concentration of Confederate infantry and artillery that confronted the Sixth Corps during the assault. The Virginians and North Carolinians blasted away at the Federals from behind their rail barricades on the western slope of the Dinkle Ravine. A Confederate battery, posted on the high ground behind the infantry, rained death and destruction into the Federal ranks. A second battery posted on Ramseur's left flank partially enfiladed Ricketts's right from a ridge on the north side of the Dinkle Ravine. An embedded reporter with the Sixth Corps observed that the

---

34 *OR* 43, pt. 1, 212.

35 Grayson M. Eichelberger, "6th Maryland Infantry," USAMHI.

The Dinkle farm lane in 1893. This area where heavy combat took place between Ramseur's Confederates and Ricketts's Federals is now a shopping center. *Scott C. Patchan*

Southern "guns posted at first in well selected overlooking positions, never knew a moments rest."[36]

Jubal Early, his face aglow with a "look of fierceness" seldom seen by his soldiers, galloped up behind the battery and Thompson's dismounted Virginia cavalry on Ramseur's left to survey the scene and encourage the troops. "Pour it into 'em—give 'em hell—God damn their blue-bellied souls – pour it into 'em," roared Early in his "never to be forgotten nasal tones." Although the Confederate commander had ridden into the thick of battle he remained "cool as cucumber" while "the shrieking shells . . . and hissing minnies flew through the air." He watched the destruction the Confederate gunners wrought among the advancing Sixth Corps and Nineteenth Corps with "the fire of battle veritably flashing from his eyes." As quickly as he stormed onto the field, Early dashed off to examine the situation farther to his left.[37]

36 "Battle of Berryville," *New York World*, contained in *The Rutland Weekly Herald*, September 29, 1864.

37 William McDougal, "The Battle of Winchester and Fisher's Hill," *The Lancaster Gazette*, October 20, 1864; George Q. Peyton, Diary 1864-1865, Bull Run Regional Library; John H.

Ricketts's advance faltered intermittently under the intense Confederate fire, but ground inexorably closer to Ramseur's position in the Dinkle Ravine. With every step Ricketts's men took, however, the gap between the Sixth and Nineteenth Corps expanded to greater and more dangerous proportions. On Keifer's right flank, Col. Jacob Sharpe's Nineteenth Corps brigade advanced rapidly but quickly collapsed under the weight of a Confederate counterattack by Gordon's division. When the Sixth Corps shifted leftward to follow the pike, the gap expanded to about 400 yards. The defeat of Sharpe's brigade offered an opportunity and the Confederates promptly took advantage of it. A "large body" of Southerners attacked into the gap and threatened Keifer's right flank. York's Louisiana brigade turned its attention to Keifer's right flank after driving Sharpe back to the First Woods. Thompson's dismounted troopers on Ramseur's left flank may also have participated in this attack as well. Colonel Keifer reacted quickly to the threat and changed front to the right with his two Pennsylvania regiments on the right side of his front line. Ricketts personally shifted Lt. Col. William Ball's 110th Ohio out of the second battle line and into a covering position on the Pennsylvanians' right flank. Keifer's three-regiment demi-brigade fired into the Confederates and, as one witness remembered, drove "the enemy back for a time and kept them engaged." When Col. Edward Molineux's Nineteenth Corps brigade moved up from its supporting position and took up Sharpe's abandoned position, the Southerners slowly fell back. Keifer's regiments continued advancing, albeit detached from the balance of their division.[38]

At this point, Keifer's battle-thinned regiments extended well beyond Ramseur's left flank and rendered his infantry's position in the ravine untenable.

Gilson, *History of the 126th Ohio Volunteer Infantry*, 220-221, 249; "Battle of Berryville" account from the *New York World* contained in *The Rutland Weekly Herald*, September 29, 1864; Jackson's Brigade at Winchester, John W. Daniel Papers, UVA.

38 The identity of these Confederate troops is difficult to determine. Initial inquiry led to the belief that the counterattacking Confederates belonged to Robert Rodes' Confederate division. However, this action took place before Rodes appeared on the field (he clearly arrived on the scene after the discomfiture of Ramseur's and Gordon's divisions by the attacks of the Sixth Corps and Nineteenth Corps). Also, Rodes' troops were completely successful when they did counterattack, and were not repulsed until Union reinforcements entered the fight to turn the tide. After years of study, I have come to the conclusion that these attacking Southern troops included elements of Col. Zebulon York's brigade from Gordon's division and Thompson's dismounted horsemen. *OR* 43, pt. 1, 247; Keifer to My Dear Wife, September 20, 1864, Keifer Papers, LC; "Battle of Berryville" account from the *New York World* contained in *The Rutland Weekly Herald*, September 29, 1864.

Although Johnston's brigade had thus far steadfastly maintained its position, Keifer's movement beyond the flank forced the Tar Heels to abandon their position to avoid being cut off from Winchester. Keifer's Pennsylvanians and Ohioans on his right wing saw the breaking Confederates and set their sights on the same hilltop battery where Early had observed the progress of the battle on Ramseur's left flank. These guns had been enfilading Ricketts's main battle line as it approached Ramseur's position, but Keifer's men changed that. His Pennsylvania and Ohio men opened fire, driving off the supporting cavalry, and forcing the artillerists to retreat from their guns. The two Pennsylvania regiments closed in on the guns in anticipation of their capture while the 110th Ohio ascended an open hill on Ricketts's right flank.

The ground behind the Confederate position was wide open, and a soldier of the 12th North Carolina realized that this was an "awful time on our side to give back then, but we were forced to do it." The Union infantry had withheld its fire until they were within 50 yards of the Confederate works and the Southerners turned to run. "Then it came our turn to shoot," reported a Buckeye from the 126th Ohio. "We poured a volley into their rear, and then with a yell started after them on the double quick as they retreated in great confusion."[39] Confederate officers attempted to halt the retreat by oaths and with the flat of their swords, but the men had done all the fighting at Dinkle's Farm that they intended to do. The confusion soon spread to the units on the left flank of Pegram's brigade, and the Virginians joined their North Carolina comrades in retreat.[40]

The break continued along the line to Pegram's right near the Berryville Pike. They ran through a small but steep-banked stream and then ascended the western slope of the ravine which led directly to the Dinkle farmhouse. As the Virginians struggled across the stream, Pvts. William T. McDougle and Franklin C. King of the 126th Ohio sprinted ahead of their regiment and captured 16 prisoners, including the wounded Lt. Col. George A. Goodman and two other officers from the 13th Virginia Infantry. The fire of Ricketts's veterans had a deadly effect upon the Confederates. One North Carolinian

39 J. Warren Keifer to My Dear Wife, September 20, 1864, Library of Congress; George Wilfong to Lovina Wilfong, October 3, 1864, Duke; William McDougle, "The Battle of Winchester and Fisher's Hill," *The Lancaster Gazette*, October 20, 1864.

40 Member of the 12th North Carolina to Mr. Lovina Wilfong, October 3, 1864, Duke; William McDougle, "The Battle of Winchester and Fisher's Hill," *The Lancaster Gazette*, October 20, 1864.

wrote, "The balls came as thick as hail at us. It is a mystery to me how we got out." As George Peyton and some comrades of the 13th Virginia bolted past the white-washed Dinkle farmhouse, he saw "a cloud of what looked like feathers." They stopped briefly and quickly realized "that what we thought were feathers were scales of white wash that the bullets coming through the house were knocking off." The Virginians "hesitated about going through this flock of missiles but as there was no other way, we opened the gate, stooped down, and ran through the bullets into the yard." They evaded the bullets and raced through Dinkle's cornfield in their retreat.[41]

Major General Steven D. Ramseur dashed angrily into the midst of his retreating Virginians and North Carolinians as they did "some tall running" toward Winchester. Although he exhorted them to halt and make a stand, the mob continued rearward. The chaotic retreat brought back bad memories for Ramseur. On July 20 during the engagement at Rutherford's farm, Brig. Gen. William W. Averell had embarrassed the young Confederate general, and he was not about to let it happen again. He grabbed a discarded rifle and, in his own words, "knocked every man over the head who refused to halt." With the assistance of his staff and some "gallant" officers from his brigades, Ramseur succeeded in establishing some order among his men. Without reinforcements, the division commander knew they would be unable to stem the blue tide. As Ricketts's advance passed the Dinkle house, his line became overextended, allowing Ramseur's men to halt in jumbled groups and offer a pestering resistance against the advancing Federals. Although the Federals had been jumbled in their success, they pressed on toward Winchester.[42]

Those men who rallied and maintained the fight for Ramseur inflicted a toll upon the officer corps of the advancing U.S. troops. In Keifer's brigade, Lt. Col. Aaron Ebright had sent his horse to the rear to minimize his exposure to enemy bullets and consequently led the 126th Ohio forward on foot. He led his troops "with more than his usual coolness" until a .58 caliber bullet ripped into his chest and fulfilled his pre-battle premonition of death. Captain Thomas J. Hyatt and Lt. Rufus Ricksecker fell in rapid succession. The young lieutenant begged not to be left behind, but when several Ohioans tried to help him, Ricksecker said, "It's no use boys; I'm going to die, save yourselves." As two soldiers carried the wounded Hyatt toward the rear, a second bullet struck him,

41 George Q. Peyton, Diary 1864-1865, UVA.

42 Stephen D. Ramseur to Dear Brother, October 10, 1864, Ramseur Papers, UNC.

Maj. Gen. Stephen D. Ramseur
LC

killing him instantly. Three other Buckeye officers fell wounded, but Capt. George Washington Hoge assumed command and held the 126th Ohio steady. On the Ohioans' right flank, the 6th Maryland's Col. John Horn went down with a wound so horrendous that everyone who saw him assumed he would soon be dead. Fortunately, Capt. Clifton K. Prentiss kept the Marylanders in order, as both units passed by the Dinkle house and into the cornfield beyond.[43]

43 Julius Ricksecker, "First Lieutenant Rufus Ricksecker," and T. W. McKinnie to J. H. Gilson, September 18, 1882, in John H. Gilson, *History of the 126th Ohio Volunteer Infantry* (Salem, OH, 1883), 255, 257.

On the left flank of Ricketts's division, Col. Emerson's brigade enjoyed similar success as it moved in conjunction with the Ohioans and Marylanders to their right. Emerson's men pressed the advantage gained by Keifer and drove the Rebels in confusion, collapsing Pegram's line rapidly from left to right. With Keifer's men flanking Pegram's left, many of his Virginians fell back to their right rear (southwest) seeking safety behind Godwin's brigade. In an attempt to stem the blue tide, Godwin tried to extend his already attenuated line toward the Pike, but the pressure from Getty's division forced him to pull back or suffer the consequences of being outflanked and cut off if he stayed much longer.

In front of Godwin, Getty's division moved in for the kill. Warner's Vermont brigade renewed its advance after the successful rush of Ricketts's division eliminated the flanking fire from Pegram's brigade. The Vermonters raced pell-mell across a plateau and scooped up dozens of prisoners. Confederates hid in ravines and woodlots only to surrender when the Vermonters overran their hideouts. On Warner's right, the 11th Vermont chased a section of Nelson's artillery from three different positions each time it attempted to resist the Union attack. The most advanced portions of the brigade halted when they saw Godwin's North Carolinians rallying in their front. Major Aldace Walker of the 11th Vermont and several other officers from the brigade gathered 40 men and halted in a trench nearly one mile from where the attack began. "They were all tired out," wrote Walker, "but we fired away all we could . . . but our ranks were too much disorganized."[44]

On Warner's left flank, Frank Wheaton's Pennsylvania and New York regiments surged forward and drove Godwin's North Carolinians from their rifle pits, capturing almost 200 men from Ramseur's broken division. Sergeant Jacob A. Schmid of the 98th Pennsylvania raced ahead of his Key Stone comrades in an attempt to capture the flag of one of Ramseur's retreating regiments. Schmid closed to within 20 yards when a member of the Rebel color guard turned and fired. The bullet ripped the Pennsylvanian's haversack in half, but the sergeant continued his pursuit. The Rebels hid behind a lime kiln and attempted to ambush Schmid, who single-handedly captured five of them, including the culprit who ruined his haversack. Soldiers of the 102nd Pennsylvania rounded up more than 100 more with the assistance of their

44 "The Vermont brigade in the battles of Winchester and Fisher's Hill," *Vermont Chronicle*, October 15, 1864.

beloved canine mascot Jack, who barked and raced alongside with the soldiers throughout the battle.[45]

Captain James Bumgardner of the 52nd Virginia briefly stopped to watch his comrades retreat in confusion when the glint of sunlight reflecting off a musket on the ground caught his eye. He picked it up and carefully aimed at a mounted Federal officer riding in front of the line of battle. The Southern captain fired, and the Yankee tumbled from his horse. Bumgardner fled toward Winchester, but as he ascended a ridge, a squad of Wheaton's Pennsylvanians cut off his retreat and ordered him to surrender. A color-bearer sprinted up and politely requested his sword. The Virginian handed it over and told him that he would just as well give it to the color-bearer as to anyone else. The Pennsylvanian thanked a bemused Bumgardner graciously, acting as if the Virginian "had voluntarily made him a handsome present."[46]

On Getty's left flank, Bidwell's brigade advanced rapidly through "undulating fields, traversed by deep ravines, almost stripped of their timber" against the right wing of Archibald Godwin's North Carolina brigade. These Tar Heels held a "strong position on the crest of the hill and behind a fence" from whence they "desperately disputed every step" of Bidwell's assault. Godwin's left wing broke and ran toward the woods in his rear as Ramseur's line crumbled from left to right. Bidwell's brigade aimed for the woods and pursued the beaten Tar Heels under a heavy fire from a Confederate battery. Bidwell's success signaled the complete discomfiture of Ramseur's division. Unless something changed quickly, Wright's Sixth Corps would soon be on the outskirts of Winchester.[47]

It was only a few minutes after noon. The situation along the Berryville Pike was moving in Sheridan's favor. Ricketts and Getty had overwhelmed Ramseur's division, and thousands of jubilant Yankees were racing after his fleeing infantry. Keifer's men eyed the guns of Nelson's battalion and concluded it was only a matter of time before they overran the battery on

45 Story of Jacob A. Schmidt, 98th Pennsylvania, Civil War Miscellaneous Collection, USAMHI; John H. Niebaum, *History of the Pittsburgh Washington Infantry 102nd (Old 13th) Regiment Pennsylvania Veteran Volunteers and Its Forebears* (Pittsburgh, 1931), 116.

46 James Bumgardner, "Early's Little Black Captain," no date, copy in possession of author.

47 Thomas W. Hyde, *Following the Greek Cross or Memories of the Sixth Army Corps* (Cambridge, 1894), 398-399; W. B. French, "From the 77th, Late Battles in the Shenandoah," contained in The Saratogan, October 13, 1864; OR 43, pt. 1, 212, 219.

Ramseur's left. Sheridan's attack was only 30 minutes old. Success seemed to be well in hand. Not only had Wright's Sixth Corps put Ramseur to flight on the Berryville Pike, but Emory's Nineteenth Corps attained similar success on the right against Gordon's recently arrived division.

THE PRETTIEST STAND UP, FAIR, OPEN FIELD FIGHT

The Middle Field and the Second Woods

Major General William H. Emory's Nineteenth Corps did not finalize its deployment until 11:00 a.m. as a result of the traffic jam in the ravine. After Emory's troops struggled along the side of the road, they eventually halted on the north side of the Berryville Pike about 300 yards to the rear of the Sixth Corps. Brigadier General Cuvier Grover's 8,000-man division led the corps onto the field and rolled out its battle lines between Ash Hollow and Red Bud Run in terrain that one soldier aptly described as "a rolling farm interspersed with woods." Grover's troops deployed into a double line of battle and then advanced through the woods to move on line with the Sixth Corps posted on the south side of Ash Hollow. The use of this massed formation negated much of the Federal numerical advantage and also created thick targets for the Confederate artillery. Missiles that overshot their mark in the front line often struck soldiers in the second line of battle.

The commander of the largest division in Sheridan's army was a dapper, 34-year-old 1850 West Point graduate from Maine. Brigadier General Cuvier Grover had served in the Regular Army on frontier duty and along the

Northern Pacific Railroad for 12 years. He was promoted from captain to brigadier general on April 14, 1862, and capably led an infantry brigade under "Fighting Joe" Hooker during the Peninsula campaign and at Second Bull Run. In 1863, the War Department transferred Grover to the Department of the Gulf where he commanded a division under Maj. Gen. Nathaniel P. Banks during the Port Hudson and Red River campaigns. Grover's most intense combat experience occurred at Second Bull Run where his lone brigade smashed through Stonewall Jackson's line along the unfinished railroad only to be bloodily thrown back by fresh Confederate units that struck his unsupported flanks.

Grover posted Col. Jacob Sharpe's brigade on the left flank of the Nineteenth Corps. Sharpe had attended West Point but transferred out and subsequently graduated from Dartmouth in 1856. He later married the daughter of Union general Philip St. George Cooke, making him the brother-in-law of two Confederate generals, J. E. B. Stuart and John R. Cooke. Sharpe began the war as a lieutenant in the 56th New York, but in 1862 he received a promotion to lieutenant colonel in the freshly recruited 156th New York. He quickly rose to full colonel and participated in the Port Hudson and Red River campaigns, a shared experience among many Nineteenth Corps officers. Sharpe posted the 156th New York on the left of his line, 40 yards from Keifer's right flank. The 128th and 176th New York occupied the brigade's left and right center positions respectively with the 38th Massachusetts on the brigade's right.[1]

On Sharpe's right flank, Brig. Gen. Henry W. Birge's brigade deployed and extended Sheridan's battle line toward Red Bud Run. Birge was a quintessential political general. Prior to the war, he had served on the staff of Connecticut Governor William A. Buckingham, and in 1861 received a major's commission in the 4th Connecticut Infantry. He subsequently organized the 13th Connecticut and became its colonel. He had served at Port Hudson and was promoted to brigadier general exactly one year before the Third Battle of Winchester. Aside from service during the Red River campaign, Birge had limited combat experience as he led his troops into battle against Maj. Gen. John B. Gordon and his battle-hardened veterans.[2]

---

1   Michael S. Franck, *Elmwood Endures, History of a Detroit Cemetery* (Detroit: Wayne State University Press, 1996), 173; Massachusetts Adjutant-General's Report, January 1865, 837.

2   Warner, *Generals in Blue*, 33.

Musician Sam Doble, 12th Maine, Nineteenth Corps. LC

Birge deployed the 75th New York on his left to connect with Sharpe's brigade. The 14th and 12th Maine and the 26th Massachusetts extended the line to the right. The 14th New Hampshire, an inexperienced regiment going into its first battle, anchored Birge's right flank. Birge also posted the Irish 9th Connecticut Infantry on the north bank of Red Bud Run to guard the right flank of the army during the advance. The Irishmen's enlistments expired soon, and, not surprisingly, they maintained a passive posture throughout the day and failed to adequately protect Grover's right flank.

Grover formed his two remaining brigades behind the front line. Colonel David Shunk's Iowa and Indiana soldiers formed in line of battle behind Birge's brigade. Shunk was a 42-year-old carriage builder who had organized and led a company of Hoosiers during the War with Mexico. During the Civil War he fought at Pea Ridge, Port Gibson, and participated in Grant's "Forlorn Hope" Assaults on Vicksburg, where he bravely led his troops against the massive Confederate fortifications. By the summer of 1864, Shunk's interest in the military had waned. He informed the adjutant general of Indiana, "I want to come home to vote this fall. Can't you find some duty for me to perform about election time and get me ordered home to do it?" The relatively young Shunk died only a few months after the Valley campaign in February 1865, so perhaps illness was silently sapping his strength and weakening his resolve. Regardless of his personal situation, Shunk remained with the army. At Winchester, he posted the 28th and 24th Iowa on his left and the 18th and 8th Indiana on the right.[3]

On Shunk's left, Col. Edward L. Molineux's brigade deployed. An English immigrant from London, Molineux had been active in the Brooklyn militia since the 1850s. In the summer of 1862, he raised the 159th New York and became its colonel. He led the regiment during the Port Hudson campaign until he was wounded at Irish Bend in 1863. Throughout his service, Molineux developed into a dependable and natural leader of men who could be counted on to make quick decisions and take decisive action, qualities that were put to good use at Winchester. He posted the 22nd Iowa on his left with the 159th New York, 13th Connecticut, 3rd Massachusetts Cavalry (dismounted), 131st New York, and the 11th Indiana extending the line to the right where it linked with Shunk's brigade.[4]

After Grover deployed his troops, they maneuvered through a hardwood forest christened the First Woods in the after-action reports. Across Grover's front, skirmishers, including a few companies that specialized in sharp shooting, relieved flankers from the Sixth Corps who had been screening the ground prior to the arrival of the Nineteenth Corps. The skirmishers filtered through the First Woods, and, after deploying in the open fields beyond the trees, traded shots with dismounted Confederate cavalry and Gordon's sharpshooters when the latter arrived.

Brigadier General William Dwight's division deployed in the open ground behind the woods that sheltered Grover's command. Emory instructed Dwight to place his division behind Grover's right "as a reserve" and deploy it "in

3 Daniel Shunk to Adj. Gen. Lazarus Noble, July 6, 1864, Indiana State Archives.

4 *OR* 43, pt. 1, 330.

column of regiments." Emory told Dwight that he should be prepared "to move promptly in any direction, and particularly to be ready to wheel into line to the right in case the right flank of the army should be assaulted." Dwight had this assignment because Sheridan inexplicably did not provide even a small contingent of cavalry to serve as the army's eyes and ears on either flank of the infantry. Dwight placed Col. George L. Beal's brigade so that its lead regiment, the 114th New York, was positioned to the right and rear of Grover's second line of battle. The balance of the brigade deployed in a column of regiments behind the New Yorkers as Emory had ordered. Brigadier General James W. McMillan deployed his lead unit in echelon to the left and rear of Beal's last regiment with each successive unit taking position in the same manner behind the one that had preceded it. Dwight also relieved skirmishers from the Sixth Corps who had been guarding the army's right flank. Their commander explained the nature of the ground on the right to Dwight, but inaccurately told him that Federal cavalry was screening the Union right flank well in advance of any portion of his skirmish line. This information gave the Nineteenth Corps false assurances about the safety of their right flank as Wilson's cavalry had departed this area before Dwight arrived on the field. The only horsemen on the north side of Red Bud Run were Confederates from Wickham's division. Dwight deployed skirmishers and flankers from the 47th Pennsylvania to cover the ground. He also ordered them to "move forward parallel with the column when it should advance."[5]

Emory had difficulty deploying his artillery in the heavily wooded terrain. After the attack began, he ordered a section of Capt. Milton L. Miner's 17th Indiana Light Battery into position on the left of Grover's division. Two of Emory's remaining batteries remained limbered behind the infantry and did not deploy until after the infantry advanced. Only three of Emory's batteries made it to the front. Lieutenant John V. Grant's 5th New York Battery found the woods so rough that he reversed course and cut his way out to the rear. The end result of these difficulties was that Grover's division went in without artillery support during the initial assault.[6]

Shortly before Sheridan's attack began, General Emory conferred with Grover, his brigadiers, and his regimental commanders. This last minute

5 It is more likely that the cavalry the Sixth Corps officer saw in advance of his line was Confederate. OR 43, pt. 1, 288.

6 Ibid., pt. 1, 286, 317, 356.

council laid out Emory's expectations of his command. He explained that the guide would be on the Sixth Corps to the left. In an unpublished after-action report, Col. Thomas W. Porter of the 14th Maine detailed their final instructions:

> After passing through the timber in our immediate front the line would be rectified and we would advance across an open space of about equal width (in which were our sharpshooters). The farthest edge of this latter space was bounded by timber in which the enemy was supposed to be posted; we were to advance to the near edge of the timber to ascertain the enemy's force & position. I was also told that the dispositions of troops had been made to protect our flanks & afford the necessary support; & further that as our supplies were reported to be cut off by the enemy we were expected to cut our way through any & all opposition.[7]

Emory's false assertion about being cut off by the enemy created a sense of desperation in Grover's command. When the officers returned to their regiments, word of the situation filtered down the chain of command to the enlisted men. It created a sense of urgency that disrupted the measured advance that Emory desired.

Even before the main attack began, the intensity of the skirmishing flared on Emory's right flank and provided a glimpse into the severity of the developing engagement. Lieutenant John Sturtevant's company of the 14th New Hampshire found itself in a hot spot in the Middle Field near Red Bud Run. As Sturtevant's men shoved Bradley Johnson's Virginians back across the field, Major Breathed's Confederate horse artillery opened fire from its position near the Huntsberry farm house on the opposite side of the stream. The New Hampshire men were close enough to actually hear Breathed's officers calling out commands to their gunners. Only the deep chasm formed by Red Bud Run separated the Southern artillery from the Federal infantry. When Birge's skirmish line reached the point about halfway across the Middle Field, Breathed's gunners opened fire "with telling effect." One shell exploded in the air above the skirmish company of the 14th New Hampshire. The force of the

---

7 Report of Colonel Thomas W. Porter, 14th Maine, Yale University. This report was not included in the published *Official Records*. Francis H. Buffum, *A Memorial of the Great Rebellion: Being a History of the Fourteenth Regiment New Hampshire Volunteers, Covering Its Three Years of Service, With Original Sketches of Army Life, 1862-1865* (Boston: Franlin Press: Rand, Avery & Co., 1882), 208-209.

blast slammed Sturtevant to the ground with a shell fragment in his arm, but the rugged officer from New Hampshire crafted a makeshift sling and doggedly remained in charge of the regiment's skirmish line.[8]

The sudden explosion of hostile artillery at such close range startled the Federals. Emory's battle plan had called for Col. Thomas W. Cahill's 9th Connecticut to cover Grover's right flank on the north bank of Red Bud Run, but that outfit failed to fulfill its orders. Had the Irish regiment from Connecticut advanced, Fitz Lee's presence would have been known to Grover and remedial measures likely taken. Some Union officers asserted that the Irishmen could have easily driven off or captured the lightly supported guns. As it was, Sturtevant's men could do no more than hug the earth and pray for Divine protection. To make matters worse, the Confederate sharpshooters halted at the edge of the Second Woods and opened an accurate sniping fire into the ranks of Birge's skirmish line. Troopers from Munford's brigade filtered along the opposite bank of Red Bud Run and sought out eligible positions to ply their ability as marksmen.

Major General John B. Gordon's division of 2,600 men arrived on the battlefield "just before" the Nineteenth Corps advanced. His troops universally describe reaching the field and almost immediately deploying for action. The Georgian posted his division on the farm land south and east of Hackwood, a 1777 stone mansion constructed by Hessian prisoners captured by George Washington during the Revolutionary War at the battle of Princeton in 1776. Brigadier General Zebulon York posted his Louisiana Tigers on Gordon's right flank, deploying them along the eastern edge of the Second Woods. Brigadier General William Terry's Virginians, including the remnants of the Stonewall Brigade, went into position to the left and rear of York's brigade in a ravine immediately west of the Second Woods. Colonel Edmund N. Atkinson's Georgia brigade slid into position on Terry's left flank and relieved Payne's cavalry, allowing the horsemen to rejoin Wickham north of Red Bud Run. The Georgians shook out their battle line immediately east of the Hackwood barn with their left flank resting near a swampy stretch of Red Bud Run. The ground on the eastern face of the ravine rose to such a height that the Georgians could not see more than 30 feet ahead of them. Gordon immediately deployed a skirmish line in front of his division, the men rushing out of the ravine, through the Second Woods, and into the Middle Field. There, they encountered their

Union counterparts from Grover's division posted in the field and opened a lively skirmish.[9]

Early's chief of artillery, Col. Thomas H. Carter, had previously posted seven guns from Maj. Carter M. Braxton's artillery battalion upon a prominent hill behind Gordon's right flank. From the high ground, Braxton's seven guns covered a field 250 yards in width between the two wood lots. This position allowed the gunners to see beyond the woods to their right and left and fire into the larger field (the Middle Field) beyond as well as to help cover the extensive ground on Ramseur's left flank. On the north bank of Red Bud Run, Fitz Lee deployed Wickham's cavalry division and Maj. James Breathed's six-gun battery of horse artillery upon the heights which overlooked the stream. The position of the horse artillery and its supports projected significantly forward from Gordon's left. As Rodes's division was still marching across the open ground between the Martinsburg Pike and the Confederate battle line, Gordon and Lee had only 4,200 troops between them to weather the coming storm. Although Grover outnumbered Gordon and Lee by a nearly two-to-one margin, the Southerners had at least 13 strategically positioned cannon between their commands. These guns proved to be a balancing factor in the coming action, and their impact was magnified as Grover completely lacked artillery support during his advance.[10]

While the troops deployed, Jubal Early conferred with Gordon and Rodes, hastily developing a strategy to confront the massive Union force that was at

---

9   John Worsham of the 21st Virginia Infantry placed General Gordon's divisional alignment as follows: Terry on the right, York in the center, and Atkinson on the left. However, both Captain Seymour of the Louisiana Brigade and Jed Hotchkiss placed York's brigade on Gordon's right flank and Terry in the center of the line. Worsham's account, however, has generally been accepted by most historians. Hotchkiss sketched a drawing of Gordon's alignment that clearly favors Seymour's version of events. "Sept. 19," contained in Sketch Book of Positions 2nd Corps, A. N. Va., Campaign of 1864, Hotchkiss Map Collection, Library of Congress; G. P. Ring to My Dear Darling, September 21, 1864, Tulane; Terry L. Jones, *The Civil War Memoirs of Captain William J. Seymour: Reminiscences of a Louisiana Tiger* (Louisiana State University Press, 1997), 140; I. G. Bradwell, "Early's Valley Campaign, 1864," *Confederate Veteran*, 1920, vol. 23, 218-220; I. G. Bradwell, "With Early in the Valley," *Confederate Veteran*, 1914, vol. 22, 504-506; I. G. Bradwell, "Sheridan at Trevillian," *Confederate Veteran*, 1929, vol. 37, 452-455; Charles S. Arnall to John W. Daniel, November 30, 1904, JWD Papers, UVA; OR 43, pt. 1, 554-5.

10   Gordon's division numbered roughly only about 2,600, and Fitz Lee's about 1,600 present for duty. http://www.co.frederick.va.us/historical_markers.aspx, accessed on June 10, 2009; William R. Cox, *Address on the Life and Character of Maj. Gen. Stephen D. Ramseur* (Raliegh: 1891), 39-40.

Maj. Gen. John B. Gordon
LC

that very moment picking its way through the First Woods. "It was a moment of imminent and thrilling danger," recalled Early. The Southern generals realized that remaining on the defensive might prove futile against so large a force. General Early ordered Gordon and Rodes to attack the Federal infantry on its right flank as it approached. Time was in short supply. Gordon's division was still completing its deployment, and Rodes had just reached the battlefield near the Valley Pike, well to the right and rear of Gordon. One of Rodes's brigades, Brig. Gen. Cullen Battle's Alabamians, had yet to even reach the battlefield.[11]

Although Jubal Early did not know it, he had an important ally in the topography of the battlefield. The geometric configuration in the Nineteenth Corps's area of operations worked against Sheridan. That sector of the battlefield essentially formed a large, triangle shape with Sheridan's assault launching from the apex. The Union battle line would attack from the narrow point of the triangle across an ever-widening field as it approached the base, which was the Confederate battle line. In fact, the width of the space between the Berryville Pike and Red Bud Run increased from six-tenths of a mile at the initial point of assault to one full mile at the point of contact with the enemy. This was a 700-yard increase of battle frontage that Sheridan had not considered in his planning. Not surprisingly, as the Federal line advanced, it pulled apart in at least three places, two of them several hundred yards in width. Conversely, Early's advancing Confederates concentrated their strength as they moved across the ever-narrowing battlefield toward the point of the triangle. If the Confederates forced the Federals back in confusion, the attackers would once again be packed into the tight confines of the Berryville Ravine. Although often discussed, such a scenario was unlikely as Sheridan had two infantry divisions in reserve that equaled Early's available manpower on the field.[12]

By 11:30 a.m., hours of incessant skirmishing and artillery fire made the atmosphere "stifling and hazy." A staff officer of the Nineteenth Corps dashed up to Lt. Col. Alfred Neafie, commander of the 156th New York on Sharpe's (and the Nineteenth Corps's) left flank. The aide instructed Neafie, "Col. you have the post of honor; you are the battalion of direction. You will advance with and be guided by the movements of the 6th Corps." At 11:45 a.m., Neafie saw Ricketts's division moving 40 yards to his left. He joined the movement promptly, and the balance of Grover's division joined the advance en echelon from Sharpe's right. The battle line advanced through the First Woods under fire from the Confederate artillery that was shooting blindly into the woods. Sharpe's New York and Massachusetts men soon emerged from the timber and entered the Middle Field which consisted of ploughed fields, fences, and rough

11 Early, *Autobiography*, 422; *Mobile Advertiser and Register*, October 12, 1864; *Richmond Whig*, October 5, 1864.

12 *OR Atlas*, 99, pt. 1; GIS Measuring Tool at www.ShenandoahGIS.org accessed on June 9, 2009; Whitney Maps, LC Map Division.

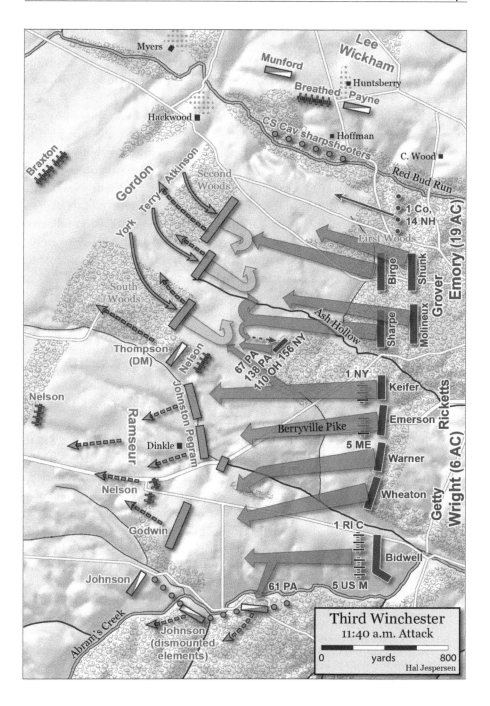

Myers

Munford

Lee
Wickham

Breathed
Payne

Huntsberry

Hackwood

CS Cav sharpshooters
Hoffman

C. Wood

Braxton

Gordon

Atkinson
Terry

Second
Woods

Red Bud Run

1 Co,
14 NH

York

First Woods

Emory (19 AC)

Birge

Shunk

Grover

South
Woods

Ash Hollow

Sharpe

Molineux

Thompson
(DM)

Nelson

67 PA
138 PA
110 OH 156 NY

Nelson

Ramseur

Johnston Pegram

1 NY

Keifer

Emerson

Ricketts

Dinkle

Berryville Pike

5 ME

Warner

Nelson

Wheaton

Getty

Wright (6 AC)

Godwin

1 RI C

Bidwell

Johnson

61 PA

5 US M

Abram's Creek

Johnson
(dismounted
elements)

Third Winchester
11:40 a.m. Attack

0   yards   800

Hal Jespersen

broken country, and quickly descended into the Ash Hollow ravine as it wrapped around their front. The hollow naturally bore Sharpe's brigade to the right and away from the Sixth Corps, which increased the isolation of Grover's attacking force.[13]

As the Nineteenth Corps advanced, the aforementioned topography and the heavy growth of trees came quickly into play as the Federals struggled to cover the increasing width of the battlefield. The trees limited visibility between Keifer's brigade on the Sixth Corps's right and Sharpe's brigade on the left of the Nineteenth Corps. On Grover's left flank, Neafie's 156th New York advanced straight ahead toward the western edge of the South Woods with its left flank resting near Ash Hollow. Off to his left, Ricketts's division followed the southward course of the Berryville Pike and pulled farther away from the Nineteenth Corps. Officers of both corps could not see what was occurring with the other. Both commands firmly believed that the other had failed to advance. Neafie recognized the danger posed from the growing gap and angled the 156th New York "very much" to the left. In doing so, Neafie lost his connection with the rest of Sharpe's brigade as that unit continued moving straight ahead. Although under a heavy fire form the Confederates in the woods, the New Yorkers plunged ahead with their pet eagle screeching above the roar of battle. To his right, the 128th and the 176th New York, together with the 38th Massachusetts, pressed toward the woods where York's Louisiana brigade awaited.[14]

On Grover's right, Birge's brigade advanced obliquely to the right to confront Gordon's Confederates who soon appeared along the edge of the Second Woods, and to cover the extensive ground between Sharpe's right flank and Red Bud Run. Birge's rightward drift created a second, larger gap in Grover's line about 400 yards wide. This growing fissure sapped the inertia of the attacking force, spreading out the advancing Union forces as they neared the point of contact. Cuvier Grover instantly perceived the peril posed by the large gap in the center of his battle line and galloped back to Col. Edward

13 George W. Powers, *The Story of the Thirty-Eighth Regiment of Massachusetts Volunteers* (Boston: Dakin and Metcalf, 1866), 165; Alfred Neafie to Benjamin Benson, July 4, 1888, USMA at West Point, NY; David H. Hanaburgh, *History of the 128th Regiment New York Volunteer* (New York: Enterprise Publishing Co., 1894) 146; Berry J. Benson, Record of Service of the 128th New York Volunteers, USMA at West Point.

14 OR 43, pt. 1, 318, 344; Report of the 38th Massachusetts 1864-1865, Contained in Massachusetts Adjutant General's Report, Public Document No. 7, 1865, 837-838.

Looking north from the Berryville Pike. The Nineteenth Corps fought on the high ground in the distance. Much of the ground was wooded at the time of the battle. *Dwight and Walter Briscoe, Photographers, 1885, DeGolyer Library, SMU*

Sketch of Brig. Gen. Cuvier Grover's division in action. *A. R. Waud, LC*

Molineux's brigade. He instructed the Englishman to move his brigade to the right and fill the gap, but the maneuver took time to accomplish.[15]

Gordon's division finalized its deployment almost simultaneously with the start of Grover's advance. When Sharpe's brigade first appeared in the Middle Field, "Old Jube" personally galloped over to Brig. Gen. Zebulon York's Tigers posted near the eastern end of the Second Woods. Early extended a brittle arm, pointed at Sharpe's approaching blue battle line, and urged the Louisiana soldiers to advance and "meet them half way" across the field. York's brigade of 650 men strode out of the woods and entered the Middle Field. "The beautiful and rare sight was presented of two opposing lines charging at the same time," recalled Louisiana Capt. William J. Seymour. Captain George P. Ring of the 6th Louisiana declared this encounter "the prettiest stand up fair open field fight" that he witnessed during the war.[16]

15 *OR* 43, pt. 1, 318, 330.

16 G. P. Ring to Wife, September 20, 1864, Tulane University; Jones, *Seymour Memoirs*, 140; Peter Eltinge to Father, September 26, 1864, Duke.

Brigadier General William Terry's Virginia brigade of 800 men likewise moved forward on York's left flank, lagging behind as a result of starting farther to the rear. York's brigade ultimately occupied the high ground at the western end of Ash Hollow, which gave them a significant advantage over the advancing Federals. Even more decisive was the fire of Braxton's artillery battalion posted upon the high ground overlooking the field between the Second and South Woods. These guns fired over the Confederate line and into the ranks of Sharpe's brigade. The two sides traded volleys until the Confederate rifle fire directed at the 38th Massachusetts on Sharpe's right became too much for the New Englanders to withstand. Officers urged the regiment forward under the blistering fire, but only a small part kept pace with the colors. Ten minutes from the time that the close range fighting began, the 38th Massachusetts began to fall back. Lieutenant Colonel James P. Richardson of the 38th recalled, "We came to close quarters with them, but under the tremendous fire of ten times of our number, the line melted away and the Regiment went to pieces." Sharpe's entire battle line then crumbled from right to left and rushed back to the cover of the First Woods. York's brigade fired into the backs of the retreating Federals and "made the ground black with their hateful bodies," according to Captain Ring. Private George W. Powers of the 38th Massachusetts noted that Sharpe's brigade had "advanced too fast, leaving its right flank exposed; and, [was] unable to withstand the heavy fire concentrated upon it."[17]

Colonel Sharpe worked feverishly to stem the tide of his retreating troops until the Confederates shot his horse out from under him. Undaunted, the colonel continued his exertions while on foot, recklessly exposing himself until he went down with a hideous groin wound that would cause him pain for the balance of his life. Lieutenant Colonel Richardson of the 38th Massachusetts, the brigade's next ranking officer, had barely assumed command when he, too, fell severely wounded. The battered and leaderless brigade floundered under the intense fire of Terry's and York's men and streamed back to the First Woods.[18]

The Southerners followed Sharpe's broken troops, firing as they went. The 1st Maine Battery's timely arrival at the edge of the First Woods gave pause to the jubilant Confederates and blunted their pursuit. On the far left of the Nineteenth Corps's line, Lt. Col. Neafie maintained the integrity of the 156th New York but lacked support on both flanks. He led his troops back to the First Woods where they halted and fired at the attacking Confederates. When the advancing Southerners opened fire on the right flank of the Sixth Corps, Col. Keifer led three regiments from Ricketts's division forward on Neafie's left flank.

While Sharpe battled York and Terry, Brig. Gen. Henry Birge's brigade was moving directly toward Atkinson's Georgians. Before the attack began, Birge halted his battle line along the western fringe of the First Woods for five minutes to dress his lines. Colonel Willoughby Babcock, commander of the 75th New York Rifles, used the time to gallop along his battle line yelling, "Boys, I only ask you to follow me!" Birge soon gave the command, and the brigade entered the field. Their appearance attracted the attention of Major Breathed's horse artillery, which was unlimbered near the Huntsberry house on the north side of Red Bud Run. The Virginia horse gunners opened fire, raking the Federal right flank as it advanced. Despite the sharp fire, the Union battle

17 Report of the 38th Massachusetts 1864-5, Contained in Massachusetts Adjutant General's Report, Public Document No. 7, 1865, 837; Statement of Lieutenant Colonel James P. Richardson contained in the Medal of Honor File for Alphonso M. Lunt, National Archives.

18 Sharpe's wound was exactly where any male would most dread injury. *OR* 43, pt. 1, 344-345; *New Paltz Times*, December 31, 1886; Massachusetts Adjutant General's Report, January 1865, 837.

Brig. Gen. Zebulon York, the commander of the Louisiana Tigers, fell with a serious wound that required the amputation of his left arm. The injury ended his field service. *LC*

line, wrote one eyewitness, "steadily advanced in good order without wavering or returning the fire."[19]

Birge's men dealt with significantly less disruption than Sharpe because the Second Woods screened their advance from Braxton's guns. Atkinson's Georgians and Col. John Stover Funk's Stonewall brigade on Terry's left opened a "galling" fire from the Second Woods, reaping a deadly windfall among Birge's entire brigade. In spite of the losses, the disciplined Yankees closed ranks and weathered the storm in "the best possible order," continuing across the meadow "with perfect coolness." On the right flank of the Union line, Col. Alexander Gardner's 14th New Hampshire received a volley that sailed just over the heads of its troops but riddled the regiment's battle flag. The regiment slowed down to return fire, starting on the right flank and quickly gained the advantage, outflanking Gordon's left. The 60th Georgia held Atkinson's left flank and soon buckled under the enfilading fire from the New Hampshire troops. The 26th Massachusetts pressed forward on Gardner's left, and in a matter of minutes Atkinson's entire brigade unraveled from left to right. Birge's troops jubilantly quickened their pace and raced toward the Second Woods pursuing the retreating Virginians and Georgians. The break

19 Henry Hall and James Hall, *Cayuga in the Field: A Record of the 19th N.Y. Volunteers, all the batteries of the 3d New York Artillery, and 75th New York Volunteers*, 2 vols. (Truair, Smith & Co. 1873), vol. 2, 202; "The Recent Victory in the Valley—From the Twelfth Maine," September 22, 1864, and "Another Letter from Sheridan's Army—From the Fourteenth Maine," both contained in the *Bangor Daily Whig and Courier*, October 3, 1864; William E. S. Whitman and Charles H. True, *Maine in the War for the Union: A History of the Part Borne By Maine Troops in the Suppression of the American Rebellion*, 297, 329; Willie Root Papers, USAMHI.

quickly extended to the balance of Terry's brigade, which had briefly engaged with Molineux's newly arrived brigade. On Gordon's right flank, the Louisiana Tigers found themselves "far in advance" and wholly unsupported. With three regiments from Colonel Keifer's Sixth Corps' brigade and Neafie's 156th New York confronting him, York slowly withdrew his men in good order to avoid being cutoff by the advancing Union forces. The battle ended badly for York when a Yankee bullet shattered his left arm. Colonel William R. Peck assumed command of the consolidated Louisiana brigade in place of the stricken York. Peck, a giant of a man at six-and-one-half feet tall and 330 pounds, developed his military knowledge on most of the Army of Northern Virginia's famous battlefields. He was well prepared to handle the sudden increase in command responsibility.[20]

From the rear of the Federal line, General Grover watched as Birge's advance became "somewhat irregular" while pursuing the retreating Confederate troops. Grover galloped over and ordered Birge to halt and regroup at the eastern edge of the Second Woods. Birge issued orders to that effect, but the exultant soldiers saw no reason to stop with the Confederates finally on the run. Colonel Thomas W. Porter of the 14th Maine attempted to stop his troops, but "such was their impetuosity that, in one word, it was impossible. They were intent on driving the masses of the enemy in their front & the firing was so heavy it was not possible to make any command heard."[21] On Birge's left flank, the 75th New York's bugler blew the call to halt, but the men in their enthusiasm mistook it for an order to charge and plunged headlong into the timber. On the opposite end of the line, a drunken staff officer dashed upon the scene and ordered the 14th New Hampshire to "Charge bayonets! Forward! Double Quick!" Gardner's rookies eagerly complied and excitedly chased the Georgians into the woods. Grover's plan to regroup disintegrated as the New Yorkers and New Englanders let out a victorious yell and entered the trees.[22]

---

20 G. P. Ring to My Dear Darling, September 21, 1864, Tulane; Jones, *Seymour Memoir*, 140; Early, *Autobiography*, 422. York's wound required the amputation of his arm and effectively ended his service with the Army of Northern Virginia.

21 Report of Colonel Thomas W. Porter, 14th Maine, of the Battle of Winchester, Civil War Manuscripts, Yale University Library.

22 Willie Root Papers, CWTI Collection, USAMHI; Report of Colonel Thomas W. Porter, 14th Maine, of the Battle of Winchester, Civil War Manuscripts, Yale University Library; Buffum, 210.

Birge's regiments pressed on through the timber, stopping only now and then to deliver a volley at pockets of Confederate resistance. The Southerners "skipped from tree to tree" as they fired back at their pursuers, but so great was their rout that each Confederate standard had only a handful of men defending it. The most effective Southern resistance came from Breathed's artillery, which sent its shells crashing into the treetops above the Federal soldiers. "The shells came screaming through the trees, lopping off branches, crippling the line and destroying organization," explained a New Hampshire soldier. Nevertheless, Birge's disordered but jubilant brigade chased the panic-stricken Confederates from the Second Woods and pursued them into the open fields of the Hackwood farm. The rapid advance through the timber placed Birge well beyond the supporting distance of Molineux on his left and Shunk in the rear. For the moment, Birge was succeeding in grand style as Gordon's division was falling back, much of it in considerable disorder.[23]

Gordon and Ramseur were retreating in varying degrees of confusion. The situation on the battlefield was now exceedingly fluid. The Union attack had hammered back both Confederate flanks. In the center, however, progress had been checked first by York's and Terry's brigades, and then three of Rodes's brigades moving forward to bolster the retreating Louisiana and Virginia soldiers. "While Rodes was moving in column up the Martinsburg road near Winchester," Brig. Gen. William R. Cox later recalled, "we were unexpectedly called to attention, faced to the left and moved forward to engage the enemy."[24] When Rodes's division left the pike, Gordon was moving to engage Grover's Union command nearly one mile east of that road. As Gordon's men withdrew, Rodes arrived within striking position of the attacking Federals. Brigadier General Bryan Grimes's 900-man North Carolina brigade led the division onto the battlefield and moved to assist the left wing of Ramseur's broken command. Cox's 800 or so North Carolinians moved up on Grimes's left flank and entered the South Woods to strike the junction of the Sixth and Nineteenth Corps. Brigadier General Philip Cook's Georgia brigade of 600 men advanced into the narrow clearing between the Second and South Woods that was about 800 feet wide. Brigadier General Cullen Battle's Alabama brigade brought up the rear of

23 Buffum, *Memorial of the Great Rebellion,* 210; "Recent Victory in the Valley—From the Twelfth Maine," September 22, 1864, contained in the *Bangor Dailey Whig and Courier,* October 3, 1864.

24 William R. Cox, Major-General Stephen D. Ramseur, 250.

The Hackwood farm with house in distance on the right. This ground was fought over throughout the day. Major General John Gordon's Confederate division initially deployed in the ravine prior to advancing into the Second Woods. Brigadier General Henry W. Birge's Federal brigade (from right to left in this image) drove back Gordon. During the later stages of the battle, Maj. Gen. George Crook's Federals advanced past the Hackwood house and across the terrain shown here. *Dwight and Walter Briscoe, Photographers, 1885, DeGolyer Library, SMU*

Rodes's column and did not enter the fight with the rest of the division. The Alabama outfit was only then arriving near Hackwood when Gordon's men poured out of the Second Woods in confusion.[25]

While his infantry was moving toward the combat, Rodes directed a passing battery into position behind Cox's brigade and then turned to watch his division plunge into the woods. "Charge them, boys! Charge them," he shouted amidst the din of battle. His normally placid black stallion became jittery. Rodes was struggling to keep his trusted mount under control when a Union bullet or shell fragment (the record is unclear which) struck him just behind the ear. The blow tumbled the general head first from his saddle to the ground while his horse galloped off in a panic. Several staff officers and orderlies rushed to his aid, but within a few minutes Rodes was dead. His staff placed him in a nearby ambulance, which carried his body into Winchester. Although Brig. Gen. Cullen A. Battle was the division's senior brigadier, he was not present with the three brigades Rodes had just fed into battle. At the moment it mattered little because his capable brigadiers executed his plans. Staffers kept the news of his death quiet because they worried about the negative impact upon morale with the division locked in mortal combat with Sheridan's army.[26]

Rodes's death notwithstanding, his division changed the tactical situation on the battlefield. Just as the 75th New York and the 14th Maine chased the last vestiges of Rebel resistance from the Second Woods, Cook's Georgia brigade wheeled promptly to the right and raked them with a blistering rifle fire. "We were still advancing & had cleared the timber of the enemy in our front when I observed a strong force of the enemy moving perpendicularly to our line & upon our flank," wrote Colonel Porter of the 14th Maine. "This force was nearly in rear of our line." The Northern officers ordered their regiments to change front to meet the new threat, but the roar of combat drowned out their commands. Birge seemed detached from the reality of the situation and twice ordered his officers to "halt for they were exposing the brigade's flank." Porter

---

25 OR 43, pt. 1, 605, 1,002, 1,011; *Macon Telegraph*, October 6, 1864; Diary of Captain James M. Garnett, *SHSP*, 5; Julius Schaub, Diary and Memoir, Troupe County, Georgia Historical Society; Hotchkiss, "Winchester 11 a.m.," Sketches for Battle Maps, LC.

26 Early issued a congratulatory order to Cullen Battle on September 20, 1864, complimenting the Alabamian for the way he handled the division at Winchester. Jed Hotchkiss to Wife, September 20, 1864, LC; Major Green Peyton, "Robert E. Rodes," *Virginia Military Institute Memorial*, 456-457; Marcus D. Herring, "Rodes at Winchester," *Confederate Veteran*, vol. 28, 184; *Richmond Whig*, September 24, 1864; *Mobile Advertiser and Register*, October 4, 1864.

politely informed Birge's courier that "I had attempted to halt in vain, & that our flank must be protected, as checking the advance at this time would be to lose all we had gained." Birge's rapid pace placed his brigade well beyond timely supporting distance of Shunk's Midwesterners in Grover's second line.[27]

On Birge's right, the 12th Maine, 26th Massachusetts, and 14th New Hampshire pursued the Confederates out of the trees and into the rolling grounds of the Hackwood farm. The 14th New Hampshire halted briefly to gain some semblance of order in the same ravine that held Atkinson's Georgians prior to the battle. After a momentary pause, the New Hampshire troops fired a volley into the running Rebels and continued the chase. In the center of Birge's ragged and dangerously uneven line, the 12th Maine and 26th Massachusetts joined the reckless pursuit, driving the fleeing Confederates past Hackwood toward a rocky ledge west of the Second Woods.

Jubal Early and Col. Tom Carter, his chief of artillery, sat astride their horses on the eminence where seven guns of Maj. Carter Braxton's artillery battalion were deployed. They had watched the situation deteriorate as Gordon's men tumbled out of the Second Woods and into the open ground directly in their front and left. When Birge's jubilant brigade emerged from the woods in pursuit, Early dourly told Carter and Braxton that their guns would soon be captured and galloped away to avoid sharing their fate. The gunners' role left them no choice but to stay and fight it out. Carter and Braxton realized they had a perfect opportunity to shred the Union attackers with canister if the retreating Confederates could get out of the way before the Federals were on top of the guns. "To open fire upon the enemy would kill our own troops," worried Carter, "as they filled the space between us and the enemy, and both were in canister range." Braxton did not fret but turned to Carter and calmly suggested that their artillerists fill their cannon with double loads of canister. Carter assented and the two men "rode down the line giving the order." Once the guns were loaded, the artillerists bravely waited for the gray mob to clear the way so the gunners could fire at the jubilant Federals unimpeded.[28]

---

27 Report of Colonel Thomas W. Porter, 14th Maine, of the Battle of Winchester, Civil War Manuscripts, Yale University Library.

28 Carter did not intend to accuse Early of cowardice in leaving the guns, pointing out instead that he left the scene properly. His capture would have proven nothing but bravado and would have caused even more confusion than already existed. Early was probably not yet aware of the death of Rodes. Thomas H. Carter to John W. Daniel, November 28, 1894, Duke.

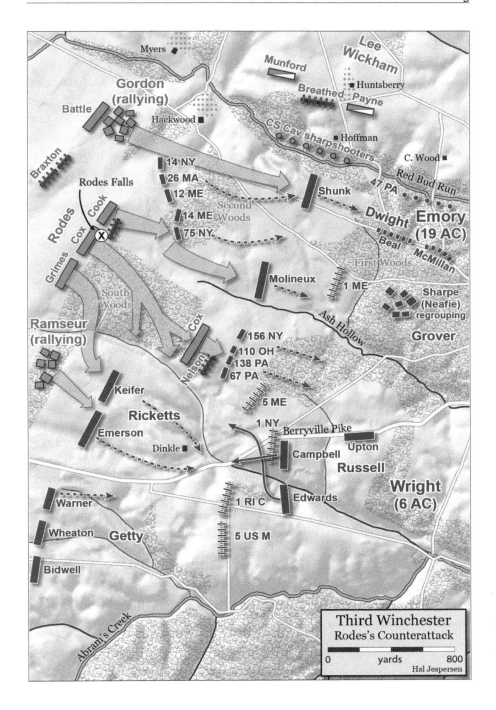

Myers
Munford
Lee
Wickham
Gordon (rallying)
Huntsberry
Breathed
Payne
Battle
Hackwood
CS Cav sharpshooters
Hoffman
C. Wood
Braxton
Rodes Falls
14 NY
26 MA
12 ME
Red Bud Run
Shunk
47 PA
Rodes
Cook
Second
Woods
Dwight
Emory
(19 AC)
Cox
14 ME
75 NY
Beal
McMillan
Grimes
South
Woods
First Woods
Molineux
1 ME
Sharpe
(Neafie)
regrouping
Ramseur (rallying)
Cox
Ash Hollow
Grover
Nelson
156 NY
110 OH
138 PA
67 PA
Keifer
5 ME
Ricketts
1 NY
Berryville Pike
Upton
Emerson
Dinkle
Campbell
Russell
Wright
(6 AC)
Warner
1 RI C
Edwards
Wheaton
Getty
5 US M
Bidwell
Abram's Creek

Third Winchester
Rodes's Counterattack

0   yards   800
Hal Jespersen

The situation looked doubtful at best for the Confederates, but Braxton's Virginians and Georgians stood by their guns and did not flinch. "The Lieutenants sat on their horses like equestrian statues," recalled Colonel Carter, "save that they drew their pistols for close quarter combat." At the last possible moment, the Confederate infantrymen cleared out, allowing Braxton to fire. The approaching Union infantry did not expect the pending onslaught as Braxton had masked his guns behind haystacks. The gunners held their fire until Birge's men were close enough "to feel the flame of the powder," and then the Confederate guns belched forth their double loads of canister in deadly unison. A dense cloud of heavy sulfuric smoke prevented the Confederate artillerymen from immediately seeing the results of their handiwork. When the smoke dissipated, the Virginians "had the joy to see . . . a field of flying, disorganized men . . . scudding [scooting] to the woods." The lethal doses of canister staggered Birge's New Englanders and inflicted a horrific loss of life and limb. "The rebels poured such a deadly fire of grape and canister into our ranks that it was impossible for any troops to stand such a fire," reported Sgt. Charles C. Messer of the 26th Massachusetts.[29]

Granted a reprieve by Braxton's artillery, Gordon's retreating infantry finally halted when they reached the rocky ledge. The men poured into the midst of Battle's Alabama Brigade ranks while it was "marching by the flank to take its position, and not suspecting the close proximity of the enemy." A body of "terror stricken" Confederate cavalry had already raced through the Alabamians, but Battle and his officers kept their men out of the temporary confusion. Jubal Early had spotted Battle, galloped over, and ordered him to advance and drive back the approaching Federals. The Alabamians cheered Early as he rode off to examine the situation over on the Berryville Pike. Cullen Battle had earned his promotion to brigadier general on the bloody first day at Gettysburg and had proven his worth in every fight thereafter. Now, with a great sense of urgency, he bellowed out, "By the right flank—Charge!" The Alabamians advanced directly toward the shattered New England regiments composing Birge's right wing and opened fire. Officers vainly tried to stem the retreat at the western edge of the Second Woods, hoping that Shunk's brigade would soon come to their aid. Some of the Yankees resisted for a few minutes,

29 Charles C. Messer Memoirs, Civil War Misc. Collection, USAMHI; Ezra Farnsworth, Jr., "Reminiscences of the Shenandoah Valley in 1864," *MOLLUS-Minnesota*, vol. 5, 327; Col. Thos. H. Carter to John W. Daniel, November 28, 1894, JWD Papers, UVA.

but Battle's men elicited the piercing "Rebel Yell" and furiously attacked Birge's right, driving it back into the Second Woods in confusion like a flock of sheep hounded by a pack of wolves.[30]

In the woods on Birge's left, Col. Willoughby Babcock bravely led the 75th New York Rifles in a futile fight against Cook's Georgians. Although two horses were shot out from under him, Babcock remained in the fight until an iron ball from Rebel case-shot shattered one of his thighs, mortally wounding the New Yorker. Birge's left fell to pieces when Battle's brigade charged past the right flank of the 14th Maine. Officers attempted to reform the 75th New York and 14th Maine along the western edge of the Second Woods, but "so close was the enemy that it was impossible to check the retrograde movement." Colonel Porter of the 14th Maine declared, "The position of affairs presented the plain proposition with three alternatives: annihilation, capture, or retreat." Shattered beyond repair, Birge's brigade streamed through the woods back toward the Middle Field.[31]

Retreat provided Birge's men little relief from their ordeal. As the battered Federals retreated through the timber, Breathed's horse artillery pummeled the dispirited mob. The horse gunners fired round after round into the stymied, confused mass of retreating Federals, and the situation worsened as they reached the Middle Field. Fitz Lee's sharpshooters took careful aim from their perches along Red Bud Run and dropped many with their unerring fire. The chaos of the retreat became so great that Birge and his officers were unable to rally their demoralized troops even after they reached the First Woods. Birge's command lost 107 men killed outright, 349 wounded and 69 missing, which was the most of any brigade in Sheridan's army that day.

As Birge's men retreated through the Second Woods, Col. David Shunk's advancing brigade of Indiana and Iowa troops marched out into the field loaded down with full backpacks, camp equipment, and their bayonets still ensconced in their scabbards. An enlisted man of the 8th Indiana questioned his commander, "Why in the name of the Lord don't we get orders to unsling the knapsacks?" The officer casually remarked that there was no need to worry as

30 "Diary of Capt. Robert E. Park, Twelfth Alabama Regiment," *SHSP*; *Mobile Advertiser and Register*, October 12, 1864; *Richmond Whig*, October 5, 1864.

31 Report of Colonel Thomas W. Porter, 14th Maine, of the Battle of Winchester, Civil War Manuscripts, Yale University Library; Willie Root Papers, USAMHI; John Y. Bedingfield to Dear Ma., September 20, 1864, Bedingfield Letters, UVA; Hall, *Cayuga in the field*, vol. 2, 202-204.

there was "a line [Birge] in our front." Such reassurances quickly dissipated as the brigade entered the Middle Field and encountered the accurate fire of Breathed's horse artillery and Fitz Lee's sharpshooters. Although smoke and trees concealed Birge's fate from Shunk's view, "the frantic yells and terrific uproar told of a desperate struggle."[32]

Shunk's brigade halted behind a worm fence in the center of the Middle Field where they laid down under fire from the Confederates. Birge's battered command soon appeared and raced out of the Second Woods with Battle's Alabamians hot on their trail. Shunk's men couldn't fire at the attacking Southerners without hitting their own troops, so they opened their ranks to allow the New Englanders to pass to the rear. Cullen Battle's Alabamians followed right at the heels of Birge's retreating men, shouting "Surrender! Surrender! Surrender! You sons-of-bitches!"

Already rattled by Lee's force along Red Bud Run, the Westerners joined the retreat, their line collapsing like dominoes from right to left. On the right, the 8th Indiana managed to fire one wild volley before racing back to the First Woods, with the 18th Indiana quickly joining their fellow Hoosiers. Sergeant Nicholas Miller later joked about the hasty retreat when he wrote, "Our brigade soon found that we had business about a half mile to the rear . . ." The 24th Iowa, holding Shunk's left-center position, managed to unleash two volleys into the oncoming Alabamians before likewise withdrawing to the First Woods. On the brigade's left, the 28th Iowa stood firm until the collapse of the units on its right left the Hawkeyes with no choice but to join the expanding retrograde movement. The sheer intensity of the fire from the Army of Northern Virginia veterans stunned the westerners. "Every available gun was brought into action and the very air was made to groan with its weight of lead and iron," related Pvt. Michael W. Cook of the 28th Iowa. "The timber was constantly crashing and falling, and the smoke arose like from one dense forest on fire."[33]

Meanwhile in the clearing at the edge of the First Woods, Capt. Albert W. Bradbury planted four pieces of the 1st Maine Battery on the left side of Hackwood Lane. These guns opened fire at the Confederate infantry holding

32 N. Miller, Civil War Memoir, Western Historical Manuscript Collection-Columbia, 49; James B. Black, *The Soldier of Indiana*, 686-687; *American Tribune*, March 3, 1892.

33 OR 43, pt. 346, 350, 355; N. Miller, Civil War Memoir, Western Historical Manuscript Collection-Columbia, 49; *American Tribune*, March 3, 1892; Diary of Michael W. Cook, Iowa Historical Society.

the edge of the opposing woods. With the Confederates routing the brigades of Birge and Shunk on the right, Grover yelled, "Bradbury, you must push a section into that gap. We must show a front there." Bradbury immediately rushed his remaining section to the threatened portion of the line on the right. The gunners galloped into position and unlimbered where a triangular point of trees jutted out of the woods and into the Middle Field. They fired into the Alabama brigade and at a Southern battery that unlimbered on the northern edge of the Second Woods. Bradbury slowed the Confederates, but no infantry support appeared. The lieutenant commanding the section fell wounded, and the Nineteenth Corps chief of artillery ordered Bradbury to send his caissons to the rear, fearing they would be captured.[34]

Out of the smoke and chaos and death appeared Capt. William T. Rigby leading a dozen men from the 28th Iowa back to Bradbury's position "with great coolness amid much confusion." Bradbury saw this small but organized squad and shouted to Rigby, "Captain, you are not going to retreat any further I hope!" "Certainly not," retorted Rigby, "Halt, front. Three cheers men. Hip Hip Hurrah!" The Iowans cheered lustily, and then fired at the opposing Alabamians, who had slowed their advance. Captain Bradbury reported that a respectable force quickly assembled around Rigby and "many men were induced to halt and reform who might otherwise have been still more demoralized." Most notably, Lt. Col. Bartholomew W. Wilson rallied the entire 28th Iowa on Rigby's left and solidified the infantry support that Bradbury needed to maintain his position.[35]

On Grover's left, Col. Edward L. Molineux's brigade finally had an opportunity to make its presence felt on the battlefield. When his brigade initially moved through the First Woods, the Confederate artillery fired "with all the engines of war they could concentrate upon our lines." Grover directed Molineux to move from his position behind Sharpe and fill the 400-yard breach that developed between Sharpe and Birge. Molineux followed the axis of Ash Hollow, with the stream dividing the center of the brigade's battle line. By the time Molineux's brigade reached the front line, Sharpe's brigade was falling

34 OR 43, pt. 1, 356-357; John W. DeForest, "Sheridan's Battle of Winchester," Harper's New Monthly Magazine, vol. 30, 197.

35 OR 43, pt. 1, 357-358; Alfred Rigby Diary, Emory University (Alfred Rigby was an enlisted man and his relationship to Captain Rigby is uncertain); Lurton D. Ingersoll, "24th Iowa," Iowa in the Rebellion (Philadelphia, 1866), 501-514.

back in confusion on Molineux's left and Birge was reaching the apex of his wild attack on the right.

Molineux's left wing, composed of the 22nd Iowa and 159th New York, had passed through Ash Hollow ravine directly in front of the opening between the Second and South Woods. The rest of the brigade had moved over the more level area of Middle Field north of the hollow. At the opposite end of that clearing sat Braxton's Confederate artillery, which was shelling the Federals "as fast as the pieces could be loaded and fired." The artillery fire was so intense that the 22nd Iowa shifted to the right behind the New Yorkers to gain some cover from the trees. When the brigade marched up out of the low ground formed by the ravine, Terry's Virginians greeted Molineux's command with a volley. A brief exchange of musketry ensued until Birge's success forced Terry to retreat in haste.[36]

However, it was not long before the Confederates regained the advantage. Once Birge's brigade was driven out of the Second Woods, Cook's Georgians moved against Molineux's brigade. After pushing through the timber the Georgians attacked Molineux's right flank, which was manned by Col. Daniel Macauley's 11th Indiana. This Zouave-attired regiment had experienced hard combat in the Western Theater under Maj. Gen. U. S. Grant at Fort Donelson, Shiloh, and Vicksburg. Now, the Hoosier veterans found themselves bearing the brunt of Cook's sharp attack. Macauley reacted quickly and ordered his two right companies to deliver an oblique fire into the attacking Southerners. This timely maneuver, combined with the fire of Bradbury's artillery and confusion among the suddenly surging Confederates, prevented the Southerners from quickly crushing the Hoosier's right flank. At the same time, North Carolinians from the left of Cox's brigade confronted Molineux's left. Cook's Georgians ground to a temporary halt and the battlefield became crowded in this sector, especially when Col. Peck quickly shoved York's brigade back to the attack against Molineux. At the same time, artillery rounds from Braxton's and Breathed's batteries crashed among the Federals with unabated fury. The

36 Col. Edward L. Molineux sketched a map that clearly shows his brigade never made it into line with Birge and Sharpe. In this map, the gap between Birge and Sharpe does not appear as large as Grover reported. It appears that the gap was largely caused by the quick collapse of Sharpe's brigade, excepting the 156th New York on his extreme left. OR 43, pt. 1, 330, 337; Jacob Switzer, "Reminiscences of Jacob C. Switzer," *Iowa Journal of History*, 56-58; Homer B. Sprague, *History of the 13th Regiment of Connecticut Volunteers During the Great Rebellion* (Hartford, 1867), 228.

situation deteriorated rapidly for Molineux because Shunk's brigade had completely collapsed on the right. The Southerners sorted out their ranks, with Cook's Georgians quickly regrouping and passing behind York's resurgent brigade to attack Molineux's left wing with help from Cox's brigade. Grover saw the danger and promptly ordered Molineux to retreat before his command was trapped and destroyed.[37]

Molineux dispatched a staff officer to ride along his brigade line and order his regiments to withdraw. With no time for formality, the officer galloped behind the line from right to left shouting at the top of his lungs, "Retreat! Retreat!" On the right, "Colonel Dan," as the soldiers of the 11th Indiana affectionately called Macauley, had his horse shot from under him, but still managed to lead his regiment and the 131st New York in a fighting and, given the situation, a relatively well-organized withdrawal. By the time the retreat order reached Molineux's left wing, however, Cox's North Carolinians were driving back Neafie's 156th New York and the three Sixth Corps regiments of Keifer's brigade on Molineux's left.

Cook's Georgians were now poised to overrun Molineux's left wing. Some officers and men from the 13th Connecticut, 22nd Iowa, and 159th New York did not hear the order to retreat, while others stubbornly refused to withdraw because they believed the order to be a serious mistake. This cadre of Federal soldiers remained in Ash Hollow ravine, where they steadfastly battled the Southerners directly to their front. Unfortunately for these Federals, they were completely oblivious to the approaching danger. Cook's Georgians surged forward, overran their position, and captured about 200 men along with the battle flag of the 22nd Iowa and another unidentified banner. Those who retreated did so under a rain fire of musketry and artillery and sustained heavy casualties.

With Molineux swept from the Middle Field, the situation looked dire for General Emory's Nineteenth Corps. Colonel Keifer, who had been positioned on high ground in the center of the Union line, "could tell the progress of the battle everywhere," he later wrote, "I plainly saw the Rebel masses pressed forward until they seemed to outnumber the 19th Corps three to one." The fate

---

37 OR 43, pt. 1, 330; Theo T. Scribner, *Indiana's Roll of Honor*, 2 vols. (Indianapolis, 1866), vol. 2, 233; S. D. Pryce, "Vanishing Footprints: The 22nd Iowa Volunteers," *Iowa Historical Society*, 542; William F. Tiemann, *The 159th Regiment Infantry New York State Volunteers in the War of the Rebellion, 1862-1865*, 98.

of Phil Sheridan's effort at Winchester now rested in the hands of the Army of the Shenandoah's battlefield reserves.[38]

38 Several acts of heroism occurred during this chaotic retreat. Private Peter J. Ryan of the 11th Indiana saw a comrade fall into the hands of the Confederates, rushed back into the fray, and not only rescued his friend, but also captured 14 Confederates in the "severest part of the battle." Ryan hustled the Confederates to the rear and then rushed back to the edge of the woods where he rejoined his regiment battling the Southerners. *OR* 43, pt. 1, 330; Theo T. Scribner, *Indiana's Roll of Honor*, vol. 2, 238; D. A. Hills to Dear Mother, September 26, 1864, Haviland-Heigend Historical Collection, Elting Memorial Library, New Paltz, New York.

HAVE THIS THING STOPPED

Russell and Dwight Restore the Union Line

The difficulties that ruptured the Nineteenth Corps's battle line also impacted the Sixth Army Corps. Just as Brig. Gen. James B. Ricketts's division reached the apex of its assault, the gaping hole on the Sixth Corps's right flank ended any successful advance. Troops from both corps bickered for years over which corps broke first and caused the setback. The truth is that terrain and ground cover prevented the respective units from maintaining both physical and visual contact with each other, particularly when the Sixth Corps pulled to the left as its advance adhered to the Berryville Pike. The Nineteenth Corps, or more specifically Sharpe's brigade, collapsed first as it struggled to fill the gaping hole in the Union line under heavy artillery fire.[1]

On the Berryville Road, the divisions of Ricketts and Brig. Gen. George W. Getty of Maj. Gen. Horatio G. Wright's Sixth Corps had driven Ramseur's

---

1 Sharpe's brigade broke because it found itself facing the heart of Confederate resistance at the same time that the developing gaps in the Union battle line pulled his battle line in two directions, separating his regiments as they neared contact with the Confederates. Readers should note that the activity described in this chapter relating to the repulse of the Sixth Corps occurred almost simultaneously with the actions of the Nineteenth Corps discussed in the preceding chapter.

brigades from their positions around the Dinkle farm. As the U.S. forces advanced over the farm, the gap on Ricketts's right flank grew and dispersed his troops over a wider front. The three regiments that Col. Joseph W. Keifer had led into the gap now moved against two of Nelson's batteries, closing to within 200 yards of the guns and disconcerting the Confederate gunners.[2]

Some of the gunners struggled to withdraw their guns by hand while others simply abandoned them and fled to the rear, pleading for infantry support. Lieutenant Thomas W. Stephenson of the 4th North Carolina of Cox's brigade rushed his company to aid the artillery, but a Union bullet mortally wounded him. Keifer's men closed on the battery, but Cox's brigade arrived and charged Keifer's front and right. The Ohio and Pennsylvania troops fired a wild volley that sailed harmlessly over the Carolinians' heads. In response, the cool Tar Heels leveled an accurate, broadside volley into the Federals that effectively broke Keifer's command. "Successful resistance was no longer possible," lamented Keifer, whose Ohioans and Pennsylvanians broke and ran for the rear in wild disorder, which exposed the left flank of the 156th New York of the Nineteenth Corps. At that moment, remembered Keifer, "all seemed lost."[3]

While Keifer moved off to the right and advanced on the Rebel guns with three regiments, the larger portion of his brigade on the left pursued Ramseur's retreating division creating a smaller gap within his brigade's battle line. The senior officer in Keifer's rear line, Col. William H. Ball, readily perceived the situation and led the 122nd Ohio and 9th New York Heavy Artillery into the growing breach. Ball soon lost sight of Keifer as the brigadier plunged into the woods and learned nothing of where his commander had gone. Nevertheless, Ball's troops hustled through the Dinkle Ravine, passed by the house and barn, and entered the cornfield to the right and rear of the 6th Maryland.

Some of Cox's North Carolinians moved into the woods on the north side of the Dinkle cornfield after they defeated Keifer and fired at Ball's command. After wheeling his regiments to confront Cox's Confederates in the woods, Ball

---

2   *OR* 43, pt. 1, 246-247, 266, 344.

3   North Carolinian Tom Watkins stated that his command battled Ohio troops. The only Ohio troops in the line during Sheridan's initial attack belonged to Keifer's brigade. Additionally, Capt. Seaton Gales of Cox's brigade staff recorded in his journal, "we first attacked the enemy, the left of the Nineteenth Corps and the right of the Sixth Corps." Thomas J. Watkins Reminiscences, 1864-1865, William A. Smith Papers, Duke, 181-182; R. Lee Hadden, 4th Regiment, North Carolina State Troops, Members of Co. C, 4th North Carolina to Family of Lieutenant Thomas W. Stephenson, February 19, 1865, Mr. William Curry Private Collection; Seaton Gales Journal, *Our Living and Our Dead*, March 4, 1874.

spied a body of troops bearing what he thought was the U.S. flag taking position in a strip of woods at the western edge of the Dinkle farm. Colonel Ball thought they were Union troops firing at Confederates in the woods, so he ordered the 122nd Ohio and 9th New York to advance and offer their support. As it turned out, the line was actually Brig. Gen. Bryan Grimes's North Carolina brigade.[4]

Grimes's Tar Heels easily recognized the Federals and fired into them at long range. Despite this, Ball still believed that Grimes's men were friends, and that the bullets striking his troops came from Confederates posted in the woods beyond. As he drew closer, the Ohioan realized his mistake and halted his advance. Grimes was now in Ball's front, and Cox was on his right, threatening his command's line of retreat. Under fire from both directions, the Federals perceived the danger and rushed toward their left rear to evade capture. Ball halted his jumbled command back in the Dinkle Ravine, where the waiting bayonets of Maj. Lambert Boeman's 4th and 10th New Jersey Regiments from Russell's division deterred any further retreat.

With Ball falling back, Grimes saw Ricketts's remaining troops still battling the rapidly regrouping remnants of Ramseur's division. "We had been in line but a short time when muskets began to crack on our left," recalled a Virginian of Ramseur's division. "I don't think I ever heard such a noise as was made when Rodes started in. It sounded as if every tree in the woods was falling down and that a terrific thunder storm was raging in the woods." These sounds ended Ramseur's retreat and revitalized his troops who turned and rejoined the fight.[5]

Ricketts's remaining troops were unsupported on both flanks, and Grimes readily perceived his opportunity to strike. He excitedly called to Col. John R. Winston of the 45th North Carolina, "Colonel Winston, look yonder! Look Yonder!" Winston instantly comprehended the situation and moved the 45th North Carolina to the right until it was opposite the right flank of the 6th Maryland. Simultaneously, an officer of the 12th North Carolina of Johnston's

---

4 Some historians have positioned Cullen Battle's brigade attacking into the gap between the Sixth Corps and Nineteenth Corps. This was not the case. The Alabamians clearly faced off against the extreme right of the Union battle line. Captain May of the 3rd Alabama tended to the wounded color bearer of the 26th Massachusetts in the Second Woods, and his command remained in that position until driven out late in the day. At the same time, Capt. Ira Berry of the 14th New Hampshire, the far right regiment of the Union line, was captured by the Gulf City Guards of Mobile, Alabama—part of Battle's brigade. OR 43, pt. 1, 260; Buffum, *A Memorial*, 214; William May Memoirs, Alabama Department of Archives and History.

5 George Q. Peyton, Manassas Library Relic Room, 80.

brigade grabbed his colors and shouted, "Forward Boys, forward," as Ramseur's reconstituted line joined in the attack to the right of the 45th North Carolina. To the left of the Marylanders, the soldiers of the 126th Ohio focused intently upon the stiffening resistance from Ramseur's troops in their front, as Grimes's entire brigade struck like a hammer. Suddenly, recalled an Ohioan, "The rebels . . . came sweeping back like an avalanche," shoving the Ohio and Maryland men back toward the Dinkle Ravine.[6]

On Ricketts's left flank, the balance of Emerson's brigade found itself in an advanced position with Ramseur's men offering stiffer resistance with each passing minute. On Emerson's right, the 10th Vermont advanced through the cornfield "somewhat unmindful of discipline in their eagerness, rushed across the field toward the enemy's line and battery . . ." Captain Lucius Hunt halted the 10th Vermont and was "rectifying" his line when a staff officer informed him that Keifer's brigade was retreating on the right. Hunt's men pulled back in good order at first, but the 10th Vermont soon got caught up in the chaos of the retreating troops. The Vermonters "shared in the general confusion which then occurred for a time in consequence of disorder on our right and a flank fire from that direction" from Grimes's and Cox's North Carolinians. The rest of Emerson's line quickly unraveled, and his troops sought safety by retreating to the left and rear under an enfilading fire from his right.[7]

South of the Berryville Pike, Getty's division encountered trouble even before Grimes and Cox defeated Ricketts. The soldiers of Warner's Vermont Brigade had already fallen into some disorder as they chased Godwin's brigade toward Winchester. Godwin rallied a number of his men in some old rifle pits and found support from one of Nelson's batteries. The combined fire from these two sources "considerably scattered" the Vermont Brigade. Only the 2nd Vermont on Warner's left flank avoided the confusion, advancing alongside of Frank Wheaton's Pennsylvanians. The Confederate artillery in front of Wheaton's brigade limbered up and pulled out, but the cannon in front of Bidwell's brigade continually enfiladed Wheaton's line. Wheaton saw that Bidwell had not kept pace on his left and the Vermonters were falling back on the right. Without support on either flank, Wheaton made "every effort to halt the troops and form a new line, to hold the ground we had gained," but the

6 OR 43, pt. 1, 266, 605; *Lancaster Gazette*, October 20, 1864; *Philadelphia Weekly Times*, July 25, 1885.

7 OR 43, pt. 1, 20, Report of the 10th Vermont.

unrestrained Pennsylvanians plunged ahead, isolated and heading directly toward Godwin's stiffening battle line.[8]

Wheaton looked to the right and saw Grimes's well organized brigade 600 yards off to his right and on the same line as his Pennsylvanians. Upon ascending the next crest, he finally comprehended the precariousness of his command's situation. The Pennsylvanians halted and engaged Godwin's Tar Heels, but, as expected, Grimes threatened his right and rear. Wheaton ordered a hasty retreat, collecting scattered groups of Vermonters as he fell back. Bidwell, on Wheaton's left, did not advance nearly as far and assisted in covering the Pennsylvanians' retreat.[9]

As the situation deteriorated, the Sixth Corps's veteran officers kicked into action. When Brig. Gen. David Russell saw the Confederates shatter Ricketts's right flank, the 1st Division's commander turned to an aide and said, "Somebody must go in there at once." Before Russell even gave the command, his battle-seasoned brigades were already moving to restore Ricketts's broken battle line. Brigadier General George W. Getty witnessed Wheaton's plight and galloped over to Lt. Col. Edward L. Campbell's New Jersey Brigade of Russell's division. Campbell's men had been trailing Ricketts's division along the Berryville Pike. Getty ordered Campbell to take the 15th New Jersey to the north side of the road and advance into the cornfield beyond the Dinkle Ravine to slow the attacking Confederates. As Campbell led the 15th New Jersey forward, Russell galloped up and shouted above the din of battle, "Clear the enemy out of that cornfield," as he pointed at Grimes's approaching brigade. Campbell then led the Jersey troops to edge of the contested cornfield and opened fire at the approaching Carolinians.[10]

Suddenly the "Rebel Yell" rang out as North Carolinians from Cox's brigade charged out of the woods on the right of the Jersey men. The Confederates halted behind a rail fence running along the north side of the cornfield, rested their rifles on the top rail, and delivered a devastating volley into the Federals. As Grimes's brigade commenced firing into the Jersey soldiers from the front, the regimental commander, Capt. William T. Cornish, hesitated before giving the order to return fire. Cox's men used the time to file

8   Ibid., pt. 1, 197-198, 207-208.

9   Ibid., pt. 1, 197-198, 212.

10   *Boston Daily Advertiser*, October 4, 1864; OR 43, pt. 1, 169, 197, 212.

Brig. Gen. David Russell gave his life sealing the breach
in the Union battle line. *LC*

down the Dinkle Ravine toward the rear of the New Jersey troops. Under heavy
fire from Grimes and with Cox threatening his rear, Cornish belatedly ordered a
retreat. His regiment fell back through the Dinkle Ravine and up the opposite
slope in considerable disorder. For now, the regiment was left hors de combat,
and the victorious Confederates surged across the Dinkle farm.[11]

11 S. P. Halsey Journal, USAMHI.

While Campbell and the 15th New Jersey were in the cornfield, the 4th and 10th New Jersey regiments found themselves swamped by fugitives from Ricketts's division. Boeman ordered his troops to fix bayonets and forcibly halt Ricketts's disordered troops in the ravine. On the south side of the road, General Getty galloped up to Battery C, 1st Rhode Island Light Artillery and directed its fire at Grimes's North Carolinians advancing through the cornfield. From the far left of the Union line, Bidwell also ordered Capt. James McKnight's Battery M, 5th U.S. Artillery to open fire on the Confederates swarming over the plateau. The effective shelling by the Union guns slowed the Tar Heels' advance and gained crucial minutes.[12]

The situation remained tense because the balance of Russell's division had not yet reached the scene of the action. The task of stopping the North Carolinians of Rodes's division rested with Col. Charles Tompkins's Sixth Corps Artillery, as his batteries had followed up the advance of the infantry. The 1st New York Battery had deployed in its advanced position behind Ricketts's division, but its commander was immediately wounded. The 1st New York Battery held its advanced position until the Nineteenth Corps collapsed and exposed Ricketts's right flank. The New Yorkers withdrew their guns by hand behind a protective rise of ground. They hitched the guns to their horses and withdrew 200 yards to a second rise immediately south of the road where they redeployed and fired again at the advancing Confederate infantry.[13]

With seemingly everyone wearing blue in full retreat on the north side of the Berryville Pike, Capt. Greenleaf T. Stevens's 5th Maine Battery became the focal point of the Federal resistance. General Wright lost heart and rushed a staff officer who ordered Captain Stevens to withdraw, as the battery was in great danger of being overrun by Cox's Tar Heels. However, a cool and determined Colonel Tompkins "sat upon his horse with a loaded revolver close behind the battery, and ordered it not to move." Despite the threat of Cox's brigade in their front, the Maine gunners were "loading and firing with the regularity and precision of a field day." Tompkins also brought up the guns of

---

12 It is interesting to note that when the veteran officers of Horatio Wright's Sixth Army Corps saw the break in the line and took instant action without waiting for any orders. General George Getty reported that he ordered the 1st New York Battery to open fire, but the New Yorkers were positioned on the north side of the Berryville Pike. OR 43, pt. 1, 169, 197, 212; Robert R. Proudfit, "The Jersey Troops in the Shenandoah," *Newark Daily Advertiser*, September 27, 1864.

13 Ibid., pt. 1, 271, 275.

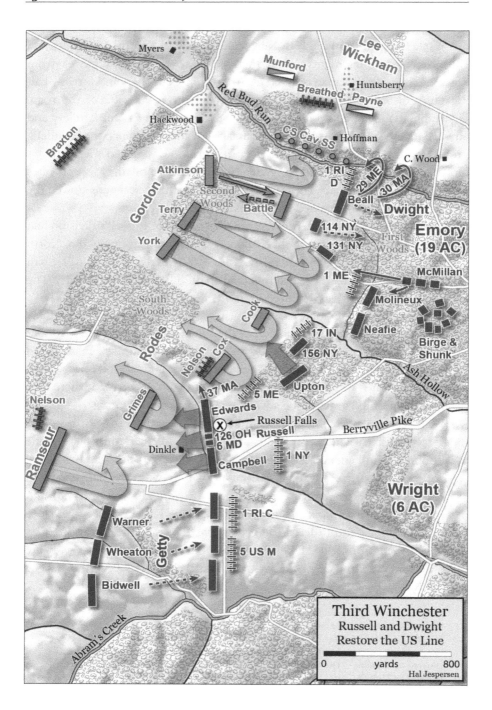

Third Winchester
Russell and Dwight
Restore the US Line

0   yards   800

Hal Jespersen

Capt. George W. Adams's Battery G, 1st Rhode Island Light Artillery, and Capt. William H. McCartney's 1st Massachusetts battery. He deployed these batteries on the south side of Berryville Pike where they unlimbered and fired at Confederate infantry. The Union infantry may have turned and run, but these blue-coated gunners were not going anywhere.[14]

Colonel Oliver Edwards, commander of Russell's 3rd brigade, had watched Ricketts's division fall into confusion and took immediate action. "It was no time to await orders," recounted Edwards, "and I moved my brigade at a run by the right flank across the turnpike." As the brigade marched to the right, Capt. Henry H. Young, a daring officer on Edwards's staff who would soon become Sheridan's chief of scouts, rode ahead of the brigade to a rise of ground, coolly smoking a cigar as he surveyed the situation on the battlefield. Captain Young noticed Edwards's movement had left the batteries on the south side of the pike unsupported and that regrouped elements of Ramseur's division were setting their sights on the suddenly unsupported guns. The Confederates approached too close for the comfort of Captain McCartney, and he limbered his guns to withdraw. Captain George Adams's Battery G, 1st Rhode Island, however, stood firm. As the Confederates closed in to capture the guns, he loaded all four with canister and blasted directly into their ranks. Captain Young galloped after Edwards's column and snared Col. Baynton J. Hickman and his 49th Pennsylvania Infantry to save the artillery from capture. Hickman immediately about faced his Pennsylvanians back across the road toward the endangered guns. They fired, charged, and drove the Southerners back, blunting the threat to the artillery. In doing so, Young and the 49th Pennsylvania also secured Wheaton's line of retreat by driving off the Confederates threatening his rear.[15]

While the detachments moved to save the batteries, Edwards led his brigade farther to the right to close the breach in the Union battle line. His brigade approached the Dinkle farm with the 119th and 82nd Pennsylvania, 2nd Rhode Island, 5th Wisconsin, and 37th Massachusetts manning the line from left to right with signficant gaps between the regiments to cover the ground formerly held by Ricketts's division. As the brigade advanced through the Dinkle Ravine in front of the 5th Maine Battery, Edwards's soldiers forced

14 *Providence Daily Journal*, October 1, 1864.

15 *OR* 43, pt. 1, 185, 187; Robert Grandchamp, *The Boys of Adams's Battery G.*, 184-185.

the fleeing Union troops to lay down. As the line moved forward, Edwards looked to his right and saw that a large force of Confederates were surging through the gap in the line and heading toward the pike to his right and rear. He detached Lt. Col. George L. Montague's 37th Massachusetts up the ravine to deal with that threat, shouting, "The 37th with its Spencer rifles can do it!" Meanwhile, the balance of Edwards's brigade ascended the western slope of the ravine, and, reaching the top, opened fire at Grimes's North Carolinians who had advanced farther than any other Confederate command. At 150 yards, Edwards's sudden appearance and firepower forced the Southerners to halt their advance and return fire.[16]

Moments later, General Russell advanced the 4th and 10th New Jersey regiments out of the same ravine on the left of Edwards's brigade. Two small regiments from Ricketts's division that had retained their cohesion, the 6th Maryland and 126th Ohio, deployed on the left of the New Jersey soldiers. Almost immediately after they got into position, Tar Heels from Ramseur's division and Grimes's brigade attacked, and the battle escalated with a renewed fury across the Dinkle farm land. "We went on through blood and fire a mile in advance of the army," wrote Private Thomas P. Devereux of the 43rd North Carolina. With no support on either flank however, Grimes' attack ran out of steam.[17]

As the Southerners pressed their attack, General Russell rode up to Colonel Edwards and ordered him to charge. Russell was giving the order when Edwards heard the sickening thud of a bullet striking the general. The round pierced his side. "Good God General, are you badly hurt?" exclaimed Edwards. Although Russell realized the seriousness of the wound and that it was likely mortal, he stuffed his shirt into the gash, withdrew his saber, and announced, "It makes no difference at such a time as this. Order your brigade to charge!" Just moments after the injured Russell finished speaking, a shell burst in the air above the two men and a large fragment tore through the general's body, killing him instantly. Edwards called Russell's orderly over and then galloped ahead to lead the blue line forward, carrying out his fallen leader's final orders. Grimes and his men were in an exposed situation under heavy fire, and his regimental

---

16 Oliver Edards, "Memorandum," 191, Illinois State Historical Library; "Their Heroic Past Recalled by Survivors of the 37th Regiment. Addresses by Gen. Edwards and Lieut Gov," *Springfield Republican*, September 20, 1893.

17 Thomas P. Devereux to his mother, September 20, 1864, NC State Archives.

Looking north from the Berryville Pike at the Dinkle Ravine and high ground beyond. Brig. Gen. John Pegram's Rebel brigade held the low land (the immediate foreground) and Brig. Gen. James Ricketts's Federal division attacked from right to left during the initial attack. After Maj. Gen. Robert Rodes repulsed Ricketts, Brig. Gen. David Russell's Federal division assaulted over the same ground and solidified the Union line west of the Dinkle farm. According to the postwar farm owner, Russell was killed by the "two trees." *Dwight and Walter Briscoe, Photographers, 1885; DeGolyer Library, SMU*

commanders gave the order to fall back to the woods at the western edge of the Dinkle farm.[18]

Russell's counterattack achieved its goal, but it cost him his life. Sheridan later wrote, "In the early days of my army life, he was my captain and my friend, and I was deeply indebted to him, not only for sound advice and good example, but for the inestimable service he had just performed, and sealed with his life." Colonel Edwards described Russell as "the purest, truest, ablest soldier I ever knew; had he risen to the command of an army he would have proved himself second to no commander in the Union army." Brigadier General Emory Upton assumed command of the division, but on the field, Russell's competent brigade commanders rose to the occasion and continued the restoration of the Union battle line without interruption.[19]

While Edwards dealt with Grimes and Ramseur, Montague's 37th Massachusetts, armed with Spencer repeating rifles, rushed up the Dinkle Ravine. Montague halted his regiment and formed it behind the ravine's crest at a right angle to Edwards's main line, facing northwest. Cox's brigade advanced southward, but failed to see the 37th Massachusetts as the crest concealed their presence. Stevens's guns were also partially screened by some woods behind the gully. As the surging Tar Heels neared the crest, Stevens's battery belched forth a volley of canister into the gray clad troops. Simultaneously, Montague ordered a charge, and the 296 men of the 37th Massachusetts advanced and emptied their Spencer repeating rifles into the stunned Confederates.[20]

Sergeant Julius L. Schaub of the 14th North Carolina recalled that, "We ran into a masked battery which opened on us with grape and canister and enfilade fire." The North Carolinians sought refuge behind stumps and ruts and attempted to hold their position. Major Joseph H. Lambeth of the same outfit

---

18 Traditionally, the time between Russell's first wounding and his death has been interpreted as longer in duration. However, the after-action report of Maj. Henry Dalton, Russell's adjutant general, stated that just before he received his fatal wound, Russell "had just before received a bullet wound." Russell was wounded and killed while with Colonel Edwards, who provides the most in-depth description of the event. In addition to showing how little time elapsed between Russell's wounding and death, Edwards asserted that it was a shell fired by a Union battery that killed the general. OR 43, pt. 1, 164; Oliver Edwards, "Memorandum," Illinois State Historical Library, 192; "Brigadier General David A. Russell," *Boston Daily Advertiser*, October 4, 1864.

19 Sheridan, *Memoirs*, 23; Edwards, Memorandum, Illinois State Historical Library, 192.

20 OR 43, pt. 1, 169, 177, 184-185; Oliver Edwards, "Their Heroic Past Recalled," *Springfield Republican*, September 20, 1893; Bowen, *History of the Thirty Seventh Massachusetts Volunteers*, 377, 379; Mason Whiting Tyler, *Recollections of the Civil War*, 278.

went down with a serious wound. The Tar Heels soon received an order to fall back to the South Woods. Not everyone heard the command amidst the roar of cannon and rifles, so some held their ground to the bitter end. The Bay State soldiers rushed forward with fixed bayonets and captured 150 Confederates who had thrown themselves on the ground to avoid the terrible fire. Among the captured Confederates was Col. Risden Tyler Bennett, the young commander of the 14th North Carolina. The 37th Massachusetts continued its charge across the field for a good distance until it found itself far in advance of any other Union troops. Somehow along the way, the New Englanders captured the battle flag of the 2nd Virginia Infantry, which had gotten mixed up with Rodes's men during the counterattack. The Southerners fell back "fighting more or less" until they reached the safety of the woods. Isolated and alone, Montague halted his regiment in a ditch and maintained an incessant firefight with the Confederates posted in the South Woods. The situation remained troublesome for the Union cause. Cook's Georgians had yet to be checked as they ventured farther east than Cox's brigade had.[21]

Major General Horatio Wright was watching the combat and saw the Confederates surging toward the Berryville Pike. Wright ordered Brig. Gen. Emory Upton to the right about the same time that Edwards detached the 37th Massachusetts on the same mission. Upton promptly marched his command across the pike and plunged into the open woods well to the rear of Edwards's brigade and the 5th Maine Battery. Upton's men swung into a line of battle in the woods with the 121st New York on the left, the 65th New York in the center, and the 2nd Connecticut Heavy Artillery serving as infantry on the far right. Upton faced the line obliquely to the right to face Cook's approaching Georgians. The brigadier ordered his troops to fix bayonets and hold their fire until the enemy was in close range. When the Georgians closed to within 200 yards, Upton's New Yorkers fired "a few volleys at short range" and deterred the Southerners from making any further advance. On the right, the 2nd

<hr/>

21 Edwards and Bowen disagree on when the 2nd Virginia's battle flag was captured. Bowen places it during the repulse of the Rodes-Gordon counterattack, while Edwards claims it was taken during the final charge. It would appear that only a portion of Terry's brigade was in the movement confronted by the 37th Massachusetts. When Gordon's division hastily withdrew after its initial success, the 300-man remnant of the Stonewall brigade joined with Rodes's division when it swept forward. Oliver Edwards, Memorandum, Illinois State Historical Library, 191-192; Bowen, *History of the Thirty Seventh Massachusetts Volunteers*, 376-377; *Springfield (MA) Daily Republican*, September 29, 1864; *National Tribune*, May 28, 1925; Julius L. Schaub, Memoir, Troupe County Georgia Historical Society.

Connecticut advanced and opened fire. Followed by the rest of the brigade, they drove the Rebels back in disorder to the woods across the field. During the fighting, the 2nd Connecticut's commander, Col. Randal S. Mackenzie, rode his horse slowly back and forth along some rising ground in front of his regiment, "in a very reckless manner, in plain sight and easy range of the enemy." The Georgians fired briskly from the woods at the bold colonel, who simply commented, "I guess those fellows will get tired of firing at me by and by."[22]

Like the Sixth Corps on its left, the Nineteenth Corps worked hard to restore its line and solidify the army's right front. As Col. Edward Molinuex's brigade retreated before the attack of Cook's Georgians and York's Louisiana brigade, Molineux raced back to the western edge of the First Woods, grabbed a battle flag, and held it aloft. His courage and example rallied the men, and his veterans halted and rapidly shook out a battle line. General Emory deployed a section. Farther to the right where the brigades of Birge and Shunk had been completely shattered, Emory and Grover "rode hither and tither through the fire, endeavoring by threats, commands, and entreaties to halt and re-form the panic-stricken stragglers." To one pack of fugitives, Emory yelled, "Here is good cover. Halt and form a line here . . . . Never mind your own regiments. Never mind if you belong to fifty regiments. Make a regiment here."[23]

Colonel Dan Macauley reformed the 11th Indiana around its battle flag as Color Sgt. George Seston waved the banner high in the air to inspire the men. In doing so, he attracted the unwanted attention of York's attacking Louisiana men who promptly shot the Hoosier. Seston tossed the flag into the air as he dropped and cried, "Catch the colors!" He died on the ground where he fell, never speaking another word. On Macauley's left, the 3rd Massachusetts Cavalry (dismounted) and remnants of Molineux's other regiments regrouped. The 156th and 176th New York of Sharpe's brigade rallied farther to the left and joined the resistance. To the right of the Hoosiers, Emory and Col. Nicholas Day rallied the 131st New York along the southern face of a "slim strip of wood projected from the center of my line for 200 or 300 yards into the open field." He deployed the New Yorkers into a line that was nearly perpendicular to the 11th Indiana. The New Yorkers faced toward the left flank of the attacking Confederates heading toward Bradbury's four guns and the

---

22 OR 43, pt. 1, 173, 180; Vaill, *The County Regiment*, 52-53.

23 J. W. Carmichael, "Battle of the Opequon," *National Tribune*, October 10, 1918; John W. DeForest, "Sheridan's Battle of Winchester," *Harper's New Monthly Magazine*, vol. 30, 196.

11th Indiana. When they saw the backs of the Southerners from York's and Terry's brigades, the blue line "poured a fire into the enemy that made them oblique farther to the right." There, the 11th Indiana and the mixture of troops from Sharpe's and Molineux's brigades triggered a volley, charged, and drove the Confederates back. They did not get far. The gritty Southerners halted in ravines and timber, turned, and opened fire at the approaching Northerners. A vicious and prolonged firefight ensued, and the Union advance halted, but Emory and Molineux had restored the line.[24]

On Emory's right, Brig. Gen. William Dwight and his division ran into a grinding wheel operated by Cullen Battle's Alabamians. When the Union attack began, Dwight led his division forward in a column of regiments behind Grover's second line. Dwight anticipated that Grover's large division would rout the Confederates, so he closely followed the second line to observe the situation. As he moved through the woods, the sounds of the battle told Dwight that Grover was "stoutly opposed and that great difficulties were in front of us." Dwight reached the edge of the woods and watched as Grover's second line charged across the field "in great disorder." Suddenly, when the cheers of Grover's men stopped, Dwight sent an aide to hurry his division to the front. Within five minutes, Grover's men retreated "in a panic of terror, having been repulsed, apparently with more than ordinary effect," according to Dwight. Before long, one of Emory's staff officers dashed up to Dwight and exclaimed, "The running away of the 2d division must be stopped." Moments later, Emory personally appeared, joining Dwight near the western edge of the First Woods. The commander of Dwight's lead brigade, Brig. Gen. George Beal, rode with his staff ahead of his troops and joined the assembled officers.

General Emory turned to Beal and bellowed, "Have this thing stopped at once!"

Beal asked, "What will you have me do?"

<hr />

24 Precise Confederate dispositions are difficult to ascertain because of the dearth of detailed accounts and after-action reports. General Gordon's men were in retreat when Rodes took over the offensive, and Gordon's men soon regrouped to join in the fight. The rapid forward and backward movements of Gordon's troops, coupled with Rodes's advance, meant that there was considerable confusion along substantial parts of the Southern line of battle. The standard Confederate account is that the Southern forces were driving back the Federals in defeat until the Union cavalry appeared on the Confederate left flank. It is now clear that significant action transpired before that occurred, including the repulse of the Confederate counterattack. OR 43, pt. 1, 280; Scribner, *Indiana's Roll of Honor*, 284; Irwin, *Nineteenth Corps*, 385-386.

Col. Samuel R. Per Lee of the 114th New York was severely wounded when a Confederate bullet struck him in the throat.
Nicholas Picerno Collection

Dwight interjected with the reply, "Throw one of your regiments straight to the front, beyond that point—we must hold it at all hazards."[25]

Colonel Samuel R. Per Lee's 114th New York led Dwight's column through the First Woods, with an occasional Confederate shell hurtling through the treetops. One of these rounds exploded under Lee's horse but spared both horse and rider, so he wisely dismounted and led his regiment on foot. As the New Yorkers neared the western limits of the woods, bullets whistled by with ever increasing frequency and shells exploded all around them. Officers and sergeants shouted orders to the men in the ranks in a manner that would have "had the spice of the ludicrous, under any other circumstances, coming from twenty throats all at once." Captain James F. Fitts recalled the cries of "Guide right, I tell you!" "Brown, fix your bayonet, damn you!" "Steady in the centre!" "Keep up there on the left—guide right you villains!" "Keep cool men—don't flinch from those devils in front of you!"

When the 114th New York neared the edge of the timber, Lee wheeled his men into line of battle. General Dwight yelled, "You must drive back the enemy." Dazed survivors from Grover's division joined the New Yorkers, and Emory barked as the battle line advanced. The 350 soldiers of the 114th New

---

25 The "point" referred to by Dwight was a strip of woods that projected into the Middle Field between the two farm tracks that combined to form Hackwood Lane near the eastern edge of the Second Woods. William Dwight, Report of Service, NA, 197-198; Gould, *29th Maine*, 492; Gould, *Journal*, 399-400; James F. Fitts, "The Last Battle of Winchester," *The Galaxy*, 1866, vol. 2, 328.

York marched out of the woods into a meadow that formed "a sort of bay with woods running out on either side" before opening into the vast Middle Field. As the New Yorkers advanced, they weathered a storm of Confederate bullets and fleeing foot soldiers from Grover's broken division. "Many ran thro' our line, some attached themselves to our ranks, but all was confusion and defeat," recounted Maj. Oscar C. Curtis. In the distance, the New Yorkers saw Battle's Alabamians waving their battle flags and firing mercilessly into Grover's defeated legions.[26]

Per Lee led the 114th New York into the bay and several rods beyond the point of woods where Rigby's Iowans and Bradbury's artillery section were holding out on the left. The Alabama brigade "came out of the opposite wood, banners flying, and opened on us with a murderous fire," recalled Curtis, whose New Yorkers fired "fast and thick" into the advancing Alabamians, who outnumbered the New Yorkers almost three-to-one. Complicating matters, Fitz Lee's sharpshooters and horse gunners fired directly into the New Yorker's right flank from the north bank of Red Bud Run. "The enemy taking advantage of the fact that our flanks were exposed," wrote a New York soldier, "got an enfilading fire on us – on the left with musketry, on the right with artillery and musketry." The regiment wavered, but Per Lee strode up and down the regimental line shouting words of encouragement. A rebel bullet to his neck soon felled him, and Maj. Oscar Curtis took command of the regiment. He ordered the New Yorkers to quickly lay down upon the ground to avoid the storm of projectiles.[27]

The New Yorkers fired from their prone position, rolled onto their backs to reload, and turned back over to fire again. In spite of being outnumbered and flanked, the 114th New York somehow blunted the victorious surge of the Alabamians until Dwight brought up additional troops. Captain Fitts explained their situation: "There was no concealment, no shelter; the ground was open; the position of each [side] was well understood; our business [was] simply to withstand the Rebel advancing, punishing him to our utmost, and receiving his blows as long as they could be endured. Most literally were these orders obeyed." The deadly Confederate fire killed and wounded 190 men from the

26 Dwight, Report of Service, 203, NA; *Oxford Times*, October 12, 1864; James F. Fitts, "The Last Battle of Winchester," *The Galaxy*, 1866, vol. 2, 327.

27 *Chenango Union*, October 5 & 12, 1864; *Oxford Times*, October 12, 1864; *Chenango Chronicle*, July 6, 1865; James Sherwood Diary, Civil War Misc. Collection, USAMHI.

114th New York in this sacrificial stand. The scene was horrendous, as the regimental historian recalled:

> The veterans of Stonewall Jackson fired amazingly low, so that the grass and earth in front of the Regiment was cut and torn up by a perfect sheet of lead. Their bullets sought the hiding places of the men with fatal accuracy, and by ones and twos and threes, they went crawling to the rear, with their blue clothes defaced with streaks and lots of crimson gore. Blood was on everything—was everywhere . . . was spattered upon bushes—was gathered in ghastly puddles upon the ground.[28]

While the 114th New York shed its life blood holding the line, the remaining four regiments of Beal's brigade approached the edge of the First Woods. Beal asked Dwight where he wanted them positioned, and the division commander shouted, "Deploy it to the right!" Beal quickly deployed into line of battle with his left flank resting upon Hackwood Lane. The 153rd and 116th New York arrived first with Col. Edwin P. Davis of the former outfit ushering them into position. Major William Knowlton deployed the 29th Maine next in line, and Capt. Samuel D. Shipley's 30th Massachusetts rounded out the brigade formation with his right flank resting upon the ravine through which Red Bud Run flowed. Beal's command did not dally at the wood line, but advanced into the Middle Field at the double quick, except on the right, where the 30th Massachusetts moved through the dense woods along Red Bud Run. The brigade halted when it reached a rail fence that extended across the field. The position was located about 150 yards to the right and rear of the 114th New York. The troops quickly tore it down, constructed a hasty barricade, and opened fire at the Rebels across the field who were posted in some low ground. Major Curtis saw the reinforcements coming up on his right rear and pulled the 114th New York back into line on the brigade's left. Once in position on Beal's left, the survivors of the battered New York regiment again opened fire.[29]

The deployment of the balance of Beal's brigade came not a moment too soon as more of Gordon's men streamed back into the fight on the Confederate left. Atkinson's Georgia brigade came up on Battle's left, extending the Southern battle line toward Red Bud Run. From the protection of the Second

28 James F. Fitts, "The Last Battle of Winchester," *The Galaxy*, 1866, vol. 2, 329; Beecher, *114th New York*, 423.

29 Maj. Oscar H. Curtis to Mr. Editor, "From the 114th New York," September 27, 1864, *Oxford Times*, October 12, 1864.

Maj. William Knowlton of the 29th Maine was killed while his regiment fought in the Middle Field to solidify the Union right flank. *Nicholas Picerno Collection*

Woods, some gullies, and makeshift fortifications between the woods and the run, the Georgians raked Beal's brigade with a blistering fire. Simultaneously, Maj. Carter Braxton moved some guns to a position immediately north of the Second Woods near Hackwood Lane and also opened fire on Beal. Major William Knowlton, a veteran who had found himself on the wrong end of Stonewall Jackson's First Battle of Winchester in 1862, raised himself up part way from the ground and saw the Georgians moving into position in his front. He shouted at soldiers of his 29th Maine to fire at the Southerners, and they complied readily with their veteran leader's command. In raising himself up, however, Knowlton exposed himself to the unerring fire of the Georgians "and was almost instantly hit." He died the next day. From the north side of Red Bud Run, Major Breathed advanced two guns to the east on the grounds of the Huntsberry farm. From this new location, his gunners fired into Beal's brigade from its right rear. At the same time, Gordon attempted to turn Beal's right flank, but the 30th Massachusetts charged up on the right and deployed in the thick woods under a "very brisk fire," stabilizing the line.[30]

While the fighting raged in the Middle Field, Dwight turned his attention to the brigade of Brig. Gen. James W. McMillan of Kentucky, which had followed Beal through the First Woods. With Beal's men holding the Confederates in check, Dwight intended to put McMillan's brigade into the battle on Beal's right

30 Gould, *Twenty-Ninth Maine*, 495; James Sherwood Diary, Civil War Misc. Collection, USAMHI.

and attack the Confederate left flank. When McMillan failed to arrive on a timely basis, Dwight rode back into the First Woods to retrieve his lost brigade. He found three of McMillan's regiments far to the left and rear of Beal's brigade "surrounded by fugitives from the 2nd Division." The fourth unit, the 47th Pennsylvania, had been assigned skirmish duty covering the right flank. The original five companies assigned that task had failed to advance with the division, so McMillan deployed the remaining Pennsylvanians to cover the right flank along Red Bud Run. Dwight ordered the balance of McMillan's brigade to halt and march toward the right to carry out his planned attack. He also urged the fugitives from Grover's division to join McMillan's ranks and return to the fight. Shortly after McMillan's brigade moved, Dwight learned that Emory had previously ordered the Kentuckian to the left without notifying the division commander. Dwight quickly halted McMillan's brigade and sought out Emory to clarify the matter. The erratic movements of the brigade only confused the officers and men. The 12th Connecticut's Capt. John W. DeForest quipped that they moved back and forth "until our heads were half turned by the confusion." He concluded, "We were apparently wanted in many places at once."[31]

Finding Emory, Dwight presented his case for using McMillan's brigade to attack on the right flank "as that was the point to continue the attack . . ." Indeed, Atkinson's brigade formed the Confederate left, and Early had no more reserves to put in. Emory demurred because Molineux's brigade was struggling to hold its own on the Nineteenth Corps's left. Instead of attacking, Emory ordered McMillan to relieve the remnants of Molineux's brigade on the left, deflating Dwight's hopes. In his report, Dwight summarized, "Under all these circumstances, and through the directions of the brevet major-general commanding the corps, the position of the First division now became a purely defensive one . . . . All thought of continuing the attack on the right with the 1st division was out of the question." Emory's Nineteenth Corps had been repulsed by fighting more ferocious than anything he or his troops had previously experienced, and, in his mind, any thoughts of attacking again were pure nonsense.[32]

McMillan deployed the 12th Connecticut and 8th Vermont on the left of Emory's line, relieving Molineux's exhausted holdouts whose ammunition was

31 OR 43, pt. 1, 289-290, 312; John W. DeForest, "Sheridan's Battle of Winchester," *Harper's Weekly*, 30:197-198.

32 OR 43, pt. 1, 290; Dwight, Report of Service, 209, NA.

running out. McMillan's command had already suffered casualties as it maneuvered through the First Woods. A shell fragment mortally wounded Lt. Col. Frank H. Peck, commander of the 12th Connecticut. When the regiment reached the edge of the woods, Capt. DeForest from the same regiment gazed across the Middle Field and observed, "No ranks of enemies were visible athwart those undulating fields, but there were long light lines of smoke from musketry and great piles of smoke from batteries while the rush and crash of shell tore through the forest." Amidst the roar of battle, General Emory mounted his gray horse and rode in front of McMillan's troops with the bridle reign in one hand and sword carried "at attention" in the other. He sauntered past "like a statue of stone" in front of McMillan's New Englanders, "his eyes keenly scanning the ranks as he passed from one end of the line to the other, while the terrible storm of death pelted pitilessly about him." The measured action of the "Old Man" firmed the men's resolve for their coming trial. The weakest man among us felt that he could and would dare anything after this brave act of the old soldier," recalled a Vermonter.[33]

McMillan then led the New England men onto the field at the double-quick. The Confederates lining the Second Woods and laying in gullies fired at the approaching Union troops and pinned them down a mere 200 yards into the Middle Field. The Federals hit the ground and stretched out in the tall grass, an action which completely concealed them from the Confederates. "We had not been in position five minutes before we felt how coolly and surely Lee's veterans could aim," recalled DeForest. McMillan's band lay upon a "very gentle slope and aimed upward" toward Gordon's Confederates in the Second Woods. After 15 minutes of firing from a prone position, Capt. Sidney Clarke ordered the 12th Connecticut to fire a volley. "Steady men! Wait for the word. Aim low," yelled the officers over the din. At Clarke's command, the New Englanders rose up, closed ranks, and "poured in a splendid crash of musketry," before dropping back to the ground. Although the Confederates briefly paused in their fire, both sides resumed a "steady file firing." "For two or more hours the bullets whizzed through the grass," reported DeForest.[34]

Ammunition ran low, and officers warned the men to "spare the cartridges, for we were a long way from our supports, or any chance of replenishing . . ."

---

33 OR 43, pt. 1, 289-290, 314-315; J. W. DeForest, "Sheridan's Battle of Winchester," *Harper's Weekly*, 30:197-198; Carpenter, 8th Vermont, 79-80.

34 DeForest, *A Volunteers Adventures: A Union Captain's Record of the Civil War*, 198.

Clarke instructed his men to cease firing when he learned that each man had only ten cartridges left in their boxes. The situation was the same over in Col. Stephen Thomas's 8th Vermont. One of his Green Mountain boys gathered up a haversack full of cartridges from the numerous dead and wounded laying in the field. He then walked along the line of prone Vermonters and distributed the cartridges, "throwing them down just as if he were salting cattle, a handful or two in a place." Private Francis Forbes's rifle broke, so he handed it to his lieutenant for repair. The officer scoffed, "Throw it away. There's one right over there under that dead man." McMillan's men hunkered down in the grass, husbanding their last rounds in case Gordon renewed his attack.[35]

Back on the right, Beal's brigade maintained its struggle with Battle's Alabamians and Atkinson's Georgians, who were still attempting to turn Emory's right flank. Additionally, signs of the Confederate forces arriving from the neighborhood of Stephenson's Depot on the far right added to fears that the Confederates might be concentrating against Emory's right to attempt a major attack. To counter the danger, Dwight led the 160th New York of McMillan's brigade to refuse Beal's right flank behind Red Bud Run. While they were in motion, Dwight discovered that the withdrawal of the 114th New York from its advanced position in front of the Second Woods had created a gap in the Union line to the left of Beal's command. Dwight promptly posted Lt. Col. John B. Van Petten's 160th New York into the open ground on Beal's left. Van Petten's regiment did not advance as far as the 114th New York, but halted in the Middle Field with its left flank resting on the projection of woods. The 160th New York came under immediate and heavy fire from the Alabamians in front and an enfilading fire on its right from Breathed's artillery firing from the north bank of Red Bud Run. Van Patten was wounded early, but refused to leave the field and remained with his regiment.[36]

Beal and his officers struggled to hold their troops in position under the intense fire of Gordon's infantry and Breathed's artillery. Gordon's advancing line extended nearly to Red Bud Run, and Fitz Lee's sharpshooters were in a strong position on the opposite side of the stream. The adjutant of the 30th Massachusetts reported that the position along the fence line was maintained

35 Ibid., 198; Francis C. Forbes, "A Soldier of Sheridan," Vermont Historical Society, 21; Carpenter, *8th Vermont*, 180-181.

36 OR 43, pt. 1, 289-291, 314; A Sergeant of the 160th New York, "From the 160th," September 22, 1864; *Auburn Advertiser and Union*, October 5, 1864.

with difficulty "from the detachments of various regiments breaking to the right and rear." The combined enfilading fire from the Southern infantry and artillery forced Beal's troops to withdraw to the safety of the First Woods. With the rest of the brigade falling back to the woods, Major Curtis ordered the 114th New York to follow. "It was only at that moment," noted one of the New Yorkers, "that our fearful destruction became apparent."[37]

Their work, however, was not done as Gordon persisted in his efforts to force Emory's right flank. "The enemy brought up line after line and seemed determined to turn our right," wrote Beal. Dwight directed Beal to refuse his right flank, and the Maine brigadier promptly shifted the 30th Massachusetts and 29th Maine into position facing northward and looking across Red Bud Run. Dwight reinforced Beal with the 47th Pennsylvania, solidifying the Union right. Beal personally commanded the three regiments on his right flank and placed Col. Edwin Davis in command of the 116th and 153rd New York, which, at that time, were laying down along the edge of the woods. Davis's New Yorkers sprang forward "with a yell" under a heavy fire from the same Confederate infantry in front and the horse artillery across Red Bud Run. Major Oscar Curtis rallied the remnants of the 114th New York around their battle flag and charged after Davis, coming up on his right flank. Lieutenant Edward E. Breed seized the colors of the 114th New York and rushed ahead of the small band until he was fatally shot in the chest. At the fence line, Davis's New Yorkers dropped down on the ground and opened fire at the Confederates who had likewise assumed a prone position.[38]

While Davis battled the Rebel infantry, Beal determined to neutralize the enemy horse artillery posted near the Huntsberry House north of Red Bud Run. The 30th Massachusetts, supported by elements of the 29th Maine, struggled through a swampy stretch of the stream and reinforced Lt. Col. Alexander Strain and the right flank skirmishers of the 153rd New York. Fitz Lee's

37 Massachusetts Adjutant General's Report, 1865, 30th Massachusetts, 733-743; Record of Events, 30th Massachusetts Infantry, NA, RG, 594.

38 These Rebels were likely detachments from Atkinson's Georgia brigade. OR 43, pt. 1, 312; George Beal to William W. Virginia, September 27, 1864, Nicholas Picerno Collection, Bridgewater, Virginia; Capt. James F. Fitts to Editors of the *Chenango Chronicle*, September 26, 1864, New York State Military Museum; James F. Fitts, "The Last Battle of Winchester," *The Galaxy*, 1866, vol. 2, 329-330; "Part Taken by the 114th N.Y. Vols.," *Chenango Union*, October 12, 1864; A Sergeant, "From the 116th Regiment," October 16, 1864, *Buffalo Morning Express*, October 25, 1864.

troopers, Breathed's gunners, and some assisting infantry saw the struggling Bay State regiment and opened fire, killing a lieutenant and several others. With the battery "strongly supported," the Union troops ended the effort against Breathed's guns and returned to their position south of Red Bud Run.[39]

At General Emory's request, Capt. Elijah D. Taft, Nineteenth Corps Chief of Artillery, deployed Battery D, 1st Rhode Island Light Artillery on the right of the corps line. The Rhode Islanders roared into action and silenced the two advanced guns of Breathed's Battery that were firing into the rear of Beal's line. The Rhode Island battery then turned its attention to the rest of the Confederate horse artillery posted near the Huntsberry House. This effort failed. Back over at the fence line in the middle field, Davis's New Yorkers began to run out of ammunition. At 2:30 p.m., cries of "More cartridges!" rang out along the line, and the soldiers rifled through the cartridge boxes of the dead and wounded to scavenge a meager supply of bullets that was soon expended. With no resupply alternative, Colonel Davis withdrew his troops back to the edge of the First Woods, which allowed Gordon to advance his left.[40]

Captain Taft instructed the commander of the Rhode Island battery to hold his position as long as possible "but to look out and not lose his pieces." When Gordon's men appeared, the gunners showered them with canister, forcing them to take shelter under the bank of Red Bud Run. Still under heavy fire from Breathed's battery, the Rhode Islanders struggled to withdraw. The Southern gunners disabled one of the Rhode Island guns, and its section promptly withdrew to the rear. The battery's remaining section stayed only a short while longer under Breathed's fire and then it too limbered up and headed to the rear. The last gun was about to pull out when a shell killed its two lead horses halting its withdrawal. Some of Gordon's men had crept forward under cover of the steep bank. One Rhode Islander later recalled that Gordon's men "now commenced to give us some trouble and we began to think that we had stayed too long." The gunners had fired away all of their canister, so they fired solid shot along the bank, slowing the Confederates.[41]

---

39 William Dwight, Report of Service, National Archives; 30th Massachusetts, Record of Events, National Archives; Massachusetts Adjutant General's Report, January – 1865, 733-734; John M. Gould, Journal, 400.

40 James F. Fitts, "Last Battle of Winchester," *The Galaxy*, October 1866, 322-332.

41 The Rhode Islanders claimed Rebel infantry was moving up on the right flank. Accounts from the 30th Massachusetts of Beal's brigade verify that claim. It appears that elements of

Fortunately, Davis's New Yorkers marched into the woods and halted when in a place of "comparative safety." With Gordon's men presenting "a bold front once more in the open field," the troops smashed open the wooden ammunition boxes and stuffed 40 rounds into their cartridge boxes. The bloodied New Yorkers ran back to the edge of the timber and opened a sharp fire into the Confederates across the field, forcing them back to the woods from whence they had come. The Confederate threat to the Union right had ended.[42]

While fighting raged across the field, Sheridan dispatched most of his staff officers and orderlies along the lines, rallying troops and obtaining situational reports. As General Dwight put the 160th New York into the line, one of those aides galloped up and inquired, "How things stood?" Dwight replied, "We had the worst of it." Emory sent Sheridan multiple reports warning that the Confederates were trying to turn his right flank. This information all factored into Sheridan's decision on how to utilize Crook's Army of West Virginia in the battle. Sheridan summoned Crook's command to the battlefield at noon, but only to place his reserves near the front for deployment in battle. At the time, Crook had nearly persuaded Sheridan to send the Army of West Virginia on a march around Early's right flank to sever his line of retreat south of Winchester. Rodes's successful counterattack dashed Crook's hopes. With the reports coming in on the dire situation confronting the Nineteenth Corps, multiple officers suggested that Sheridan send Crook to reinforce the right. He initially resisted these, still hoping to implement Crook's plan, but the worsening situation on the right forced Sheridan's hand. In addition to Emory's dire reports, Torbert had not yet reported to army headquarters. According to Sheridan's plans, Torbert's cavalry should have arrived on the northern outskirts of the battlefield in position to support Emory's right, yet there was no sign of the cavalry. Ultimately, Sheridan's uncertainty over Torbert's status

Confederate infantry might have assisted in the protection of Breathed's guns and moved up Red Bud Run to fire on the Union right flank. Or, it could have been that what the gunners thought was infantry was actually dismounted cavalry from Lee's division on the north bank of Red Bud Run. OR 43, pt. 1, 286; Sumner, *Battery D, 1st Rhode Island Light Artillery in the Civil War, 1861-1865*, 136-137; Massachusetts Adjutant General's Report, 1865, 30th Massachusetts, 733-743; Record of Events, 30th Massachusetts Infantry, NA, RG, 594; James Bowen, *Massachusetts in the War, 1861-1865*, 461; William H. Emory, Report of Service, National Archives, 357.

42 "Part Taken by the 114th N.Y. Vols," September 17, 1864, *Chenango Union*, October 12, 1864; A Sergeant, "From the 116th Regiment," October 16, 1864, *Buffalo Morning Express*, October 25, 1864; Capt. James F. Fitts to Editors of the *Chenango Chronicle*, September 26, 1864, New York State Military Museum.

tilted the scales in favor of sending Crook to bolster Emory. Sheridan did so in the mindset of renewing his attack once Crook was in position. A member of Sheridan's staff carried the welcome news to Emory and Dwight, saying "Gen. Sheridan wanted us to hold on a while longer as Gen. Crook was on his way up." Dwight responded, "Tell Gen. Sheridan we should be able to hold on, and that if Gen. Crook came in we should easily flank and beat the rebels."[43]

The intensity of the battle action subsided when the two sides fought to a standstill. Firing along the lines, however, remained heavy. Jubal Early had stopped Sheridan's massive assault. Some 8,000 Confederates had withstood the onslaught of nearly three times their number. Thus far, the experience, leadership, and élan of Early's Second Corps had neutralized Sheridan's numbers, but the Irishman remained undaunted and did not consider himself defeated. Most Union generals would have been content to await Early's next move or withdraw after the rough handling Old Jube's veterans had given the Army of the Shenandoah. Sheridan, however, was cut from a different bolt of cloth. He readied his army for another round of battle. Unfortunately for Jubal Early, his reserves were on their way back to Richmond.[44]

---

43 OR 43, pt. 1, 47, 361; Schmidt, *Crook, Autobiography*, 126; William Dwight, Report of Service, National Archives, 214.

44 There are many examples where Federal generals with the advantage of numbers did not (for many reasons) counterattack after a hard fight that inflicted at least equal casualties on their opponent. Some examples include: McClellan at Malvern Hill, Hooker at Chancellorsville, Meade at Gettysburg, Buell at Perryville, and Sherman in front of Atlanta in July 1864 (Peachtree Creek, Atlanta, and Ezra Church). Stephen W. Sears, *To the Gates of Richmond: The Peninsula Campaign* (New York, 1996), 335-336; Stephen W. Sears, *Landscape Turned Red: The Battle of Antietam* (New York, 1983), 342-343, 346-347; Kenneth W. Noe, *Perryville: This Grand Havoc of Battle* (Lexington, KY, 2002), 318-321, 340-342; Stephen W. Sears, *Chancellorsville* (New York, 1996), 420-424; Albert Castel, *Decision in the West: The Atlanta Campaign of 1864* (Lawrence, KS, 1992), 379-380, 413-414; Jeffry D. Wert, *Gettysburg: Day Three* (New York, 2001), 253-254.

A MAGNIFICENT SIGHT TO OBSERVE

The U.S. Cavalry Advance

While the battle raged at Winchester throughout the early afternoon hours of September 19, the Union cavalry moved slowly toward the battlefield. Under the bright rays of the late morning sun, Brig. Gen. William W. Averell and his troopers leisurely traversed the six miles between Bunker Hill and the Brucetown Road. Since about 10:00 a.m. when he routed Col. George Smith's brigade at Bunker Hill, Averell had little contact with the Rebel cavalry aside from skirmishing by his advance scouts. The Southerners lacked the manpower to resist Averell in the open ranges of the lower Valley and studiously avoided direct contact. That changed when Averell encountered Maj. Gen. John C. Breckinridge's infantry and artillery posted on a rise along the edge of some woodlots, blocking the approach to Stephenson's Depot.[1]

Lieutenant General Jubal A. Early had waited all morning for Breckinridge to arrive at Winchester with Brig. Gen. Gabriel C. Wharton's division and Maj. William McLaughlin's artillery battalion. When they failed to appear, Early sent

---

1 "Position of Wharton's Division at Noon, Battle of Winchester," Hotchkiss Sketchbook, LC.

Lt. Col. Sandy Pendleton back to Brucetown to reiterate his instructions. Pendleton reached the Kentuckian's position at noon and ordered him to "hasten" his command to Winchester. Both Breckinridge and Wharton attempted to point out the presence of Brig. Gen. Wesley Merritt's cavalry division in their front, but Pendleton cut them off and quickly clarified the situation. "If you remain here your force will be surrounded and captured," explained Pendleton. "Averell was then three miles in your rear on the north side of the turnpike." The Kentuckian instantly recognized the gravity of the situation and gave the necessary orders to put Wharton's command in motion for Winchester.[2]

Breckinridge also realized that the extrication of Wharton's division was easier ordered than done, and that it must be conducted covertly. If not, Merritt's division could seize the opportunity to pounce upon the Confederate infantry as it marched away in vulnerable column formation. Wharton ordered Cols. Augustus Forsberg and Thomas Smith to "withdraw quietly and, if possible, unobserved by the enemy who was massing on our left." Smith's Virginians rapidly improved the rail barricades in front of their position to give the impression that they were digging in for an extended stay. Breckinridge instructed Col. John T. Radford of the 22nd Virginia Cavalry to dismount his men, hide their horses in the woods, and deploy in front to allow the infantry to move quietly back into the woods. The ruse worked, and Wharton's division slipped away from Brucetown undetected by the U.S. cavalry. "From the configuration of the ground," explained Brig. Gen. George A. Custer, "the enemy was enabled to move or mass troops in rear of his position, unseen by my command . . . he abandoned the position in our front and withdrew toward our left."[3]

When the vanguard of Wharton's infantry division neared Stephenson's Depot, he discovered that his troops were "just opposite the line of attack of Averill's [sic] Cavalry" as it slowly forced back Col. George Smith's cavalry and its supporting artillery. Wharton quickly deployed his troops to assist their mounted comrades. Forsberg's brigade formed a line of battle in some woods between the Martinsburg Pike and the railroad bed. Thomas Smith's brigade deployed to the right of the Swede on the east side of the tracks. McLaughlin's artillery battalion, meanwhile, solidified the Southern line of battle by galloping

2   Wharton to Clay, May 15, 1905, Clay Family Papers, LC.

3   Ibid., Augustus Forsberg Memoir, Washington and Lee University; *OR* 43, pt. 1, 455-456.

The Stephenson family home. Union and Confederate forces swept past this house during the fighting on September 19, 1864. *Scott C. Patchan*

up and dropping trail. Captain William M. Lowry unlimbered his Wise Legion battery upon an elevation immediately northeast of the depot on Wharton's right flank and opened fire. Captain George B. Chapman's Monroe Battery and a section of Bryan's Lewisburg Battery rolled into position on Wharton's left flank and deployed behind a stone wall on the west side of the pike near the Stephenson house. A sizeable contingent of Smith's horseless cavalrymen armed with Enfield rifles spread out behind the wall and opened fire at Averell's approaching Federal horsemen.

As the Federals closed in, the entire Confederate line opened fire. On the left, Bryan's gunners cut their timing fuses so short that the shells exploded almost as soon as they exited the barrels. The solid shot from Lowry's guns struck the ground immediately in front of Averell's line. Faced with this sudden Confederate resistance, the Union horsemen sized-up the situation, about-faced, and retired to a position about one-half mile north of Stephenson's Depot, where they took shelter behind a rise in the ground. Captain Bryan of the Lewisburg battery advanced "a man who had the courage to go to the top of the elevation." He watched the impact of this battery's projectiles fall among the Federals and signaled the gunners so they would know how to adjust their range.[4]

Averell moved quickly to neutralize the Confederate cannon by ordering up Capt. Gulian V. Weir's Battery L, 5th U.S. Artillery to fire back at the Southern gunners. For a while, both sides remained content with the artillery duel, and their relative positions remained unchanged. The slowdown in the action played into Sheridan's strategy as his goals for the cavalry included holding Confederate forces away from the main battlefield as long as possible. The Union cavalry's success at keeping Breckinridge's infantry and artillery off the battlefield during Sheridan's initial attack proved to be of inestimable value, especially considering the damage Early's troops inflicted without Breckinridge's presence.

Breckinridge held the line covering the pike near Stephenson's Depot until Col. George S. Patton's brigade safely withdrew from its position on the Charlestown Road and rejoined Wharton's division near the depot. Colonel George Smith used this respite to regroup Imboden's brigade on the west side of the pike behind the artillery. When Patton arrived, his brigade deployed behind Wharton in some woods near the railroad bed on the east side of the Martinsburg Pike. Once Patton was in position, McLaughlin's artillery limbered up and moved toward Winchester with the brigades of Smith and Forsberg. Patton remained in position to cover the retreat until Wharton had safely withdrawn the balance of his division. Patton then slowly fell back, following the broken railroad toward Winchester. Colonel George Smith's dismounted cavalry and a couple of cannon now covered the Martinsburg Pike in the vicinity of Stephenson's Depot without any support.[5]

Averell cautiously maneuvered his division against Smith's small brigade of Virginians. Perhaps the infantry rifles that most of Smith's men carried deceived the Federal general into thinking that he was still facing Southern infantry. At length, Averell extended his right beyond the Lewisburg gunners

4 Milton Humphreys of the Lewisburg artillery believed that the Union horsemen thought that Smith's dismounted troopers, armed with cumbersome infantry rifles, were in fact infantrymen. Humphreys: "they might have easily ridden over our battalion." Milton Humphreys, Memoir, UVA, 358; Hotchkiss Sketchbook, LC.

5 While Col. George S. Patton was the grandfather of America's World War II hero, Col. George Smith was the World War II general's step-grandfather. Wharton to Clay, May 15, 1905, Clay Family Papers, LC; Augustus Forsberg Memoir, Washington and Lee University; Jed Hotchkiss Papers, "Noon—Stephenson's," Sketch Book Showing Positions of Second Corps, A. N. Va. in engagements of 1864-65, LC.

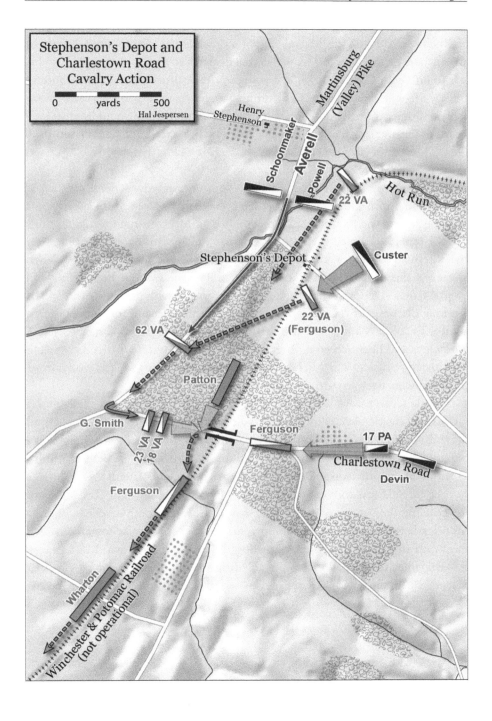

Stephenson's Depot and
Charlestown Road
Cavalry Action

0   yards   500

Hal Jespersen

Martinsburg
(Valley) Pike

Henry
Stephenson

Schoonmaker

Averell

Powell

22 VA

Hot Run

Stephenson's Depot

Custer

62 VA

22 VA
(Ferguson)

Patton

G. Smith

23 VA

18 VA

Ferguson

17 PA

Charlestown Road

Devin

Ferguson

Wharton

Winchester & Potomac Railroad
(not operational)

on the west side of the Martinsburg Pike, while the dismounted Northern skirmishers pressed Smith's front. Averell dispatched a party of his scouts to his left to link with Custer's brigade coming up from Brucetown and reconnoiter the Confederate dispositions on Smith's right flank. Averell's scouts soon reported that "the enemy seemed confused and that firing could be distinctly heard in the enemy's rear." The firing heard by the scouts emanated from Brig. Gen. Thomas Devin's brigade as they drove Col. Milton Ferguson's outgunned cavalry back upon Smith's right flank and rear.[6]

At 1:30 p.m., Maj. Gen. Alfred T. A. Torbert ordered a general advance of Merritt's division. The Union horsemen had belatedly realized that Wharton's division had slipped away from Brucetown. On Merritt's right flank, Custer's brigade remained directly in front of Wharton's old position for some time after the Virginian's infantry and the covering cavalry abandoned their lines. When Custer realized that he had been duped, he hurried his brigade toward Stephenson's Depot, claiming to have done so without any orders. His commander's report did not agree with that assertion. Custer soon encountered Radford's 22nd Virginia on the far left flank of Ferguson's brigade. These Virginians had been screening Breckinridge's withdrawal but proved no match for Custer's brigade. The Michigan men opened fire, charged, and easily drove the Virginians back toward the Martinsburg Pike.[7]

While Custer advanced, Col. George Smith had to address dual threats facing his brigade. Averell outnumbered him at least four-to-one in front, and Devin's brigade was shoving the remaining three regiments of Ferguson's brigade up the Charlestown Road toward the Martinsburg Pike behind Smith's position at Stephenson's Depot. Simultaneously, Col. Charles R. Lowell's reserve brigade was moving cross-country between Custer and Devin toward the pike. As the sounds of combat drew near, Colonel Smith quickly withdrew his brigade from its exposed position at the Stephenson House toward Carter's farm near the junction of the Martinsburg Pike and Charlestown Road.[8]

Brigadier General Thomas Devin's brigade traversed Opequon Creek at Seiver's Ford, the Charlestown Road crossing, at 1:00 p.m. Merritt ordered the

---

6 OR 43, pt. 1, 456, *Richmond Daily Whig*, October 12, 1864; *New York Herald*, September 22, 1864.

7 *Richmond Daily Whig*, October 12, 1864.

8 OR 43, pt. 1, 456; *Richmond Daily Whig*, October 12, 1864; *New York Herald*, September 22, 1864; O'Ferrall, *Forty Years of Active Service*, 115.

Col. George S. Patton
LC

New Yorker to "cross on the left, advance, and, if possible gain the Winchester pike, and endeavor to affect a junction with Lowell and Custer." On the west side of the stream, Col. Milton Ferguson guarded the Charlestown Road with the 14th, 16th, and 17th Virginia cavalry regiments about a half mile west of Opequon Creek. Ferguson's mountaineers were skirmishing with troopers from the 1st U.S. Cavalry on the far left flank of Colonel Lowell's reserve brigade when Devin crossed the creek and arrived at the Clevenger farm.

Major Coe Durland's 17th Pennsylvania Cavalry led Devin's brigade across the creek. Emerging from the stream on the west bank, the Union troopers trotted past the picturesque and well-manicured Clevenger estate on their right. A short distance west of the Opequon, the Pennsylvanians joined the Regulars, and the combined force drew sabers and charged. Ferguson's mounted Virginians opened a scattering fire with their Enfield rifles, but failed to check the charging Federals. Lacking sabers and pistols, Ferguson's men did not wait around to engage in close quarters combat. Instead, they fled up the Charlestown Road toward the Martinsburg Pike more than one mile away.[9]

Durland's Pennsylvanians and the 1st U.S. Cavalry, supported by Devin's entire brigade, chased the Virginians across the bridge that carried the road over the Winchester and Potomac railroad bed. The Pennsylvanians shoved Ferguson's routed troopers into Col. George Smith's brigade, which by then had fallen back to the Carter farm. Smith's troopers jeered and taunted the panicked troopers, while Ferguson struggled in vain to rally his command. The 17th Pennsylvania's rapid advance also cut off the withdrawal of Patton's brigade, which was following the railroad bed southward on the east side of the pike. Patton saw Devin's cavalry on the Charlestown Road, deployed, charged,

9   *OR* 43, pt. 1, 482.

Pvt. Levi Hocker of the 17th Pennsylvania Cavalry made it through the fighting at Third Winchester unscathed, only to be captured by John Mosby's men at Berryville five days later. He survived imprisonment and was exchanged in February 1865. *LC*

and swept the Union horsemen off the road. With the path clear, Patton continued his withdrawal toward Winchester. Devin described the confusion as "momentary," but it was long enough for Ferguson to regroup and Smith to send assistance.[10]

George Smith sensed confusion among the Union cavalry after Patton's sweep and quickly took advantage of the rare opportunity for his outgunned cavalry to strike back. Up to this point, Smith was holding Averell "pretty well in check," and the New Yorker seemed to be acting cautiously toward the

10 Devin reported: "[H]aving crossed a bridge and a run, I was suddenly attacked on my right flank by a column of the enemy's infantry, which I had broken through as they retired from Custer's front." Lieutenant Henry Morrison of the 23rd Battalion Virginia Infantry, Patton's brigade, reported that during the withdrawal, the Virginians had to charge to clear the cavalry off the road. No Union troopers aside from Devin's men engaged Rebel infantry at this stage of the battle. In addition, Hotchkiss's maps and sketches show Patton besieged by Union horsemen north of Red Bud Run. Henry Morrison to Brother, September 20, 1864, USAMHI; OR 43, 1, 482.

outgunned Southerners. Leaving the 62nd Virginia Mounted Infantry to confront the momentarily docile commands of Averell and Custer, Smith led the 18th and 23rd Virginia cavalry regiments to the right and charged Devin's command. The Virginians struck the disorganized Pennsylvanians and Regulars before they fully regrouped from Patton's blow. The mounted Southerners fired their revolvers into the Yankees and knocked Devin's advance back across the bridge. Ferguson used the opportunity to rally some of his men along the west side of the railroad cut. From there, his troopers made cogent use of their Enfields, effectively holding Devin's brigade in check while Patton made his escape toward Winchester.[11]

Devin reacted quickly to the setback and ordered Col. Alfred Gibbs's 1st New York Dragoons into action. The Dragoons shook out a battle line across the road, blunted Smith's charge, and engaged the Virginians in a "sharp fight." Smith's and Ferguson's Virginians held their ground and "kept up a lively fusillade" that held Devin at bay for several minutes. Devin sent the 9th New York Cavalry to the right and soon flanked the Virginians out of their positions. The Southern troopers rapidly withdrew under the pressure from the flank movement, but halted at the southern edge of the field several hundred yards from the Federals and prepared to offer further resistance. While Devin was occupied, Averell attacked from the front and Custer shoved the 22nd Virginia back upon the 62nd Virginia. The combined pressure easily drove the 62nd Virginia Mounted Infantry back. Although the Union cavalry had routed Ferguson and Smith from the field, the fast-moving combat operations disrupted the victorious Union cavalry formations. Torbert halted to regroup his horsemen on either side of the Martinsburg Pike before making his next push.[12]

Although Jubal Early had withstood Sheridan's main assault along the Berryville Pike axis, bad news poured in from both of his flanks. When Breckinridge reached the battlefield, he told Early of the threat posed by Torbert's two divisions near Stephenson's Depot. If the situation on the left wasn't enough to trouble the Rebel commander, Maj. Gen. Lunsford L. Lomax reported that a potentially precarious situation was developing on the

11 O'Ferrall, *Forty Years of Active Service*, 115; OR 43, pt. 1, 482; Bowen, *History of the Thirty Seventh Massachusetts Volunteers*, 229.

12 OR 43, pt. 1, 482; Bowen, *History of the Thirty Seventh Massachusetts Volunteers*, 230; O'Ferrall, *Forty Years of Active Service*, 115; *Richmond Daily Whig*, October 12, 1864.

Confederate right flank south of Abram's Creek. There, Wilson's skirmishers probed Lomax's position around 1:00 p.m. Prior to that time, Wilson had remained docile south of Abram's Creek. Although this was only a tentative movement that soon subsided, Lomax realized the danger confronting him. At that time, only Brig. Gen. Bradley Johnson's 800 troopers and a section of horse artillery guarded the Confederate line of retreat. For Jubal Early, the time for decision had arrived.[13]

Early possessed few viable tactical options to deal with the dual threats to his flanks. His right flank protected the Army of the Valley District's line of retreat up the Shenandoah Valley. If Wilson broke through Lomax and reached the Martinsburg Pike, Early's army would be cut off from its line of retreat up the Shenandoah Valley. Having no other choice, Early shifted Lt. Col. William Thompson's brigade to his right. Shortly thereafter, Early sent Col. Thomas T. Munford's brigade and Capt. John J. Shoemaker's two-gun battery from Fitz Lee's division on the left to Lomax, who now commanded more than half of the effective Confederate cavalry on the field. He had no more than 2,200 cavalrymen and four pieces of artillery with which to secure Early's vital line of retreat against Wilson's 3,000 horsemen and six rifled cannon. However, the terrain on Senseney Road helped to balance the odds. The steep banks of Abram's Creek and the high ground on the stream's west bank helped offset Wilson's numerical advantage. Given the limited resources at Early's disposal and the situation he faced across the full spectrum of the battlefield, there was little more that the Confederate commander could do at this point. His prior jaunt to Martinsburg had put his army in a no-win situation.[14]

To confront Torbert on the Martinsburg Turnpike, Early had tasked Fitz Lee with a virtually impossible assignment. The Confederate commander ordered Lee to take charge of all cavalry on the Confederate left. He also ordered Breckinridge to leave Patton's brigade on the left to assist Fitz Lee. Lee had only about 2,000 cavalrymen in the four brigades on hand to confront the 6,000 men in Torbert's two divisions. Lee's situation was exacerbated by the

---

13 Wilson, *Under the Old Flag*, Roger Hannaford Memoir, Cincinnati Historical Society; Robert B. Ware, "From the 2d Ohio Cavalry," Oct. 1, 1864; *Cleveland Herald*, October 22, 1864; Old Pokeepsie, "From the 2nd Ohio Cavalry," October 2, 1864; *Painesville Telegraph*, October 20, 1864.

14 T. T. Munford, "Reminiscences of Cavalry Operations," *Southern Historical Society Papers*, 13 (1885), 450; Fitzhugh Lee, Report, Museum of the Confederacy; James D. Ferguson Journal, UNC; Robert T. Hubard, UVA.

fact that less than half his force was properly equipped for mounted combat. Nevertheless, General Lee mounted his mare "Nellie Gray" and galloped out to Rutherford's farm at the extreme left of the Confederate line along the Martinsburg Pike. In the distance to the north, he saw Torbert's massive force driving the brigades of Smith and Ferguson. "Every man we had was already contending against fearful odds," observed Lee, "and though the pending disaster, was from the very open nature of the country clearly perceptible, the means of remedying it was not." Although already skirmishing with Crook's infantry at the eastern edge of the Huntsberry farm, Lee "suddenly called away" most of Col. William Payne's 600-man brigade and Captain Johnston's four-gun battery. Lee led the cavalry "at full speed" across the fields toward the Valley Pike while the artillerists moved to a safer location more suitable for artillery.[15]

While Payne headed toward the pike, Smith and Ferguson rallied their commands at Rutherford's farm one mile south of Carter's farm. Fortunately for the Southern cause, Torbert moved slowly in following up his successes at Stephenson's Depot and on the Charlestown Road. Lee later asserted that Torbert's "moving at a walk preserving their alignment" prevented him from destroying Early's army. This brief respite provided Smith with enough breathing room to keep Imboden's brigade together during the hectic retreat from Carter's farm. His men halted in an open stand of pines on Rutherford's farm astride the Martinsburg Pike. Considering the circumstances, Smith's men were in good order; however, Colonel Ferguson struggled to reassemble his

---

15 While Crook's movement was underway, Union cavalry began driving the Confederates from the environs of Stephenson's Depot. (Crook's actions will be discussed in detail later as a lead up to his most significant contribution to the battle's outcome so that his story can be told without interruption.) Lieutenant Colonel James Comly and Capt. Russell Hastings of the 23rd Ohio, Duval's division, confirmed that their skirmishers engaged Payne's cavalry during Crook's flank march. Payne apparently left a squadron behind to cover the withdrawal, perhaps the small 15th Virginia Cavalry. As far as Breathed's artillery is concerned, it is certain that Shoemaker's two-gun battery departed and went with Tom Munford to the right at 1:00 p.m. The exact disposition of Johnston's four guns after their withdrawal from Huntsberry farm is uncertain. Given the effectiveness of the Southern artillery in preventing a complete disaster for Early, and the volume of artillery fire that would be directed at Crook's infantry and Torbert's cavalry, it is reasonable to assume that these guns assisted in covering the army's retreat to Winchester. James Comly Journal, RBHPC; F. Lee, Report, MOC, 48; Lieutenant Colonel Alexander Strain, Statement on Nineteenth Corps Action North of Red Bud Run, contained in letter to John M. Gould, Nicolas Picerno Collection; Grief Lamkin Diary, VHS; John C. Donohoe Diary, VSLA.

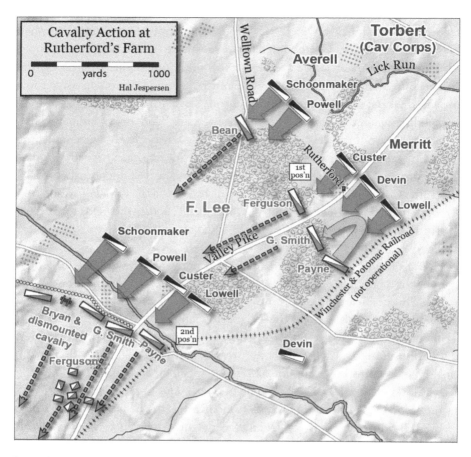

brigade and consequently deployed only a portion of his command with Smith's Virginians.[16]

West of Smith's left flank, Lt. Col. Onslow Bean's small brigade slid into position on the Welltown Road after a roundabout route to the battlefield. On September 18, Bean's men accompanied Early to Martinsburg. Lomax sent Bean's command on the raid that destroyed the B & O Railroad bridge over Back Creek west of Martinsburg. They returned along the small valley formed by that stream and spent the night at the mountain hamlet of Ganotown. On the morning of the battle, Bean's mounted infantry rode their weary mounts for 15 miles over the rough ground of the Back Creek Valley and the passage through Little North Mountain, arriving at their old camp in the vicinity of White Hall,

Union cavalry advancing toward Rutherford's farm. Alfred R. Waud wrote on the back of the drawing, "The cavalry advancing to the attack of Fitz Hugh Lee and Lomax. There were five brigades—regiments by squadrons in line. I have drawn but a portion of the line in the sketch. The bands played and but for the firing it resembled a review." *A. R. Waud, LC*

five miles northwest of Winchester, at 11:00 a.m. Like other Rebel commanders, Bean did not hear the sounds of combat raging on the Berryville Pike, so the tired men went into camp. Captain Edmund P. Goggin of Lomax's staff had ridden with Bean on his mission. When the Tennesseans went into camp, Goggin rode on to Winchester. He did not hear any signs of the combat there until he reached town at noon. When he realized the situation, Goggin sent a courier back to hasten Bean's small command to the field. Bean's Tennesseans and Georgians rode up the Welltown Road which angled into the Martinsburg Pike from the northwest about a half mile south of Rutherford's farm. The tiny brigade was riding south when Bean saw that Averell's Union cavalry had reached the Welltown Road south of his position, cutting off Bean's men from the rest of the Rebel army. Bean filed his brigade to the right and avoided the Federals. The Southerners worked their way around Averell's right flank in plain sight of Col. James Schoonmaker's brigade. A Georgia trooper considered it "mysterious" that the Federals did not attack them, concluding that the Northerners must have mistaken them for Union troops. In actuality, it was Averell's innate cautiousness materializing at an inopportune time. Bean's command detoured westward around Averell's right flank until it was safely past the Federal cavalry. Bean then filed back to the left (east) and formed a line of battle opposite Schoonmaker's brigade on Averell's right flank.[17]

17 E. R. Goggin to L. L. Lomax, September 27, 1864, CHS; John W. Lee, "Memories of the Virginia Valley Campaign of 1864," *The Georgia Enterprise*, February 19, 1904.

Alfred R. Waud sketch of Gen. George Custer and his command before the cavalry charged the Confederates. *A. R. Waud, LC*

By 3:00 p.m., Torbert's cavalry was riding south toward Rutherford's farm on the Valley Pike. Five brigades of the Army's finest horse soldiers moved in spectacular fashion as they rode southward in columns of squadrons. Merritt redeployed his division and placed Col. Charles R. Lowell's reserve brigade on the extreme left flank of his line with orders to make contact with Crook's infantry. Custer's brigade straddled the Pike, and Devin formed on his left. The line swept toward the Rutherford farm and the open woods where the Confederate cavalry had assembled. Averell's division occupied the right side of the Martinsburg Pike. Colonel William Powell's West Virginia brigade manned Averell's left and Col. James Schoonmaker's Ohio and Pennsylvania troopers held the far right. An embedded reporter described the scene as "a magnificent sight to observe," but no one could match Custer's vivid portrayal:

> One continuous and heavy fire of skirmishers covered the advance, using only the carbine, while the line of brigades as they advanced across the open country, the bands playing the national airs, presented in the sunlight one moving mass of glittering sabers. This combined with the various bright-colored banners and battle-flags, intermingled here and there with the plain blue uniforms of the troops, furnished one of the most inspiring as well as imposing scenes of martial grandeur ever witnessed upon a battlefield.[18]

18 *OR* 43, pt. 1, 546.

Col. William H. F. Payne led his men in a daring but futile charge against Torbert's cavalry. *LC*

Though awed by the display, Fitz Lee understood that if he waited for the Union cavalry to attack, his outnumbered and outgunned troopers stood no chance of withstanding the approaching juggernaut. Lee led Payne's brigade toward the pike and, without stopping, ordered a charge; he would compensate for his weakness with shear audacity. Payne dashed out in front of his 600 Virginians and raced across the Rutherford fields to the right of the men rallied by Colonel Ferguson. These veterans of Lt. Gen. J. E. B. (Jeb) Stuart's Cavalry Corps headed straight for the 2nd Massachusetts troopers covering the left of Merritt's skirmish line. Although relatively few in number, the Southern troopers came on with "their sabers flashing in the sunlight with hideous yells, cursing and swearing, and scattering themselves so as to make their line of attack as fierce as possible," wrote an eyewitness. The attack's ferocity shoved the Massachusetts cavalry and 1st New York Dragoons in front of Devin back upon Merritt's main body. The attack hit the Bay State troopers so hard they were unable to reorganize and rejoin the fight as a cohesive unit.

The Virginians continued their daring assault, driving the Federals three-quarters of a mile across the ground toward Carter's farm before the mounted charge finally expended its momentum. The offensive scattered the Virginians and seriously disrupted unit cohesion. On the Confederate left, Bean's brigade achieved similar success against the advance of William Averell's division by stalling Colonel Schoonmaker's advance. The lightly regarded Tennesseans and Georgians held their ground against Averell's half-hearted advance until events unfolding on their right prompted them to finally pull back.[19]

19 *New York Herald*, September 22, 1864; *Richmond Daily Whig*, October 12, 1864; John W. Lee, "Memories of the Virginia Valley Campaign of 1864," *The Georgia Enterprise*, February 19, 1904.

When the Rebels closed to within pistol range of the Michigan brigade, Devin instantly struck back at Payne with the 9th New York. Moments later, Custer launched the 1st Michigan at the charging Virginians. The Union horseman crashed into the Confederates and "a short closely contested struggle ensued." Custer noted that the Southerners "relied wholly upon the carbine and pistol, but my men preferred the saber," not comprehending that many of the ill-equipped Southern horsemen lacked sabers altogether. On Custer's right flank, Col. William H. Powell's West Virginians joined the fight and found that the Confederates were oriented toward Merritt's command. The 2nd West Virginia fired repeating rifles into the flank and rear of Payne's Virginians while the 3rd West Virginia raced for the Rebel cavalry's left flank. Fitz Lee's "Nellie Gray" was shot out from under him, but he escaped on an orderly's mount. The Virginians fled, but quickly discovered that the 3rd West Virginia of Powell's brigade was now blocking their path of escape. With no other choice, Payne charged to the rear and cut his way out toward the pine woods at Rutherford's farm, barely extricating his command from its tenuous predicament.[20]

The 9th New York and 3rd West Virginia pursued the Virginians toward Rutherford's woods. Virginians from the brigades of Smith and Ferguson lined the timber's edge to fire at the oncoming Yankees, but fled before the Federals made contact. Fitz Lee attempted to rally Payne's brigade, but his situation had become futile. Private Joseph C. Donohoe of the 6th Virginia Cavalry related, "The scene now beggared description, an entire division being in wild flight, all efforts to rally them proving unavailing." The Union cavalry chased after the Virginians "all bent on securing a battle flag." The *New York Herald's* reporter, Theodore C. Wilson, reported that Brig. Gen. Wesley Merritt's brightly colored headquarters flag could be seen fluttering at the front "in the thickest of the fight." Merritt and his brigadiers urged their men to "keep steady and not be too reckless; for it was not urging forward the men needed, but constant orders not to go too far." More than one overly ambitious U.S. trooper became a prisoner as the Union cavalry stormed toward Winchester.[21]

Farther west, Col. James Schoonmaker's brigade bolted toward Bean's Confederates near the northwestern fringe of Rutherford's woods. Before the

20 OR 43, pt. 1, 456, 462, 482; *New York Herald*, September 22, 1864; Fitz Lee, Report, MOC; Ferguson, Itinerary, SHC-UNC; P. J. White, "General Early's Valley Campaign," *Richmond Times-Dispatch*, September 23, 1906.

21 Joseph C. Donohoe Journal, The Library of Virginia.

Federals closed, Bean withdrew his brigade after the Confederate cavalry collapsed on the Martinsburg Pike. Payne's men retreated three-quarters of a mile on the east side of the pike before regaining any semblance of order. Lee and Payne reassembled the shaken command as rapidly as possible without regard for company designations. Lee halted and placed as many troopers from Payne's and Smith's brigades as he could behind what Custer termed "a ditch" (likely the headwaters of Red Bud Run), hoping to check the pursuing Federals from behind this natural obstruction. Payne's Virginians blasted away at Merritt's approaching horsemen with their carbines, but the Federals jumped their horses over the ditch and scattered Payne's men once more. This time, Lee was unable to rally his troopers until they fell back behind the protection of Patton's brigade of infantry along the line of the Winchester and Potomac Railroad. The Virginia infantry opened fire and bought Lee time to regroup his horsemen. While the men rallied, Lee and Patton discussed Torbert's cavalry pounding up the pike and Crook's infantry advancing along Red Bud Run. According to Lt. Henry P. Morrison, a staff officer with Patton's brigade, Lee "promised to attend to their cavalry" while Patton marched to the right to confront Crook's advance.[22] Meanwhile, at Eversole's Knoll on the Berryville Pike, a messenger arrived at Sheridan's headquarters at 2:00 p.m. bearing the long-awaited news that Torbert's cavalry was approaching Winchester. The report energized Sheridan, who thus far had assumed the traditional role of a Civil War army commander. After closely overseeing the deployment of his troops, he had remained near his headquarters and observed the battle's progress. His deportment changed when he learned of Torbert's approach. Sheridan reverted to the combat persona that staved off defeat in the Round Forest at Stones River and darted up Missionary Ridge at Chattanooga.[23]

Sheridan mounted his steed "Rienzi" and galloped to the right to personally examine the situation on that flank. When he arrived, General Dwight noticed that the Irish general was "a good deal excited, and his manner was that of the cavalry general rather than of the calm military head." Emory expounded upon the brutal repulse his corps had suffered and exclaimed, "My dead are

---

22 Henry P. Morrison to Brother, September 20, 1864, USAMHI; P.J. White, "The Battle of Winchester," *Richmond Times Dispatch*, November 20, 1904; F. Lee Report, MOC; Jed Hotchkiss, Wharton's Positions at Winchester, Sketch book showing positions of Second Corps, A.N.Va. in engagements of 1864-5, LC.

23 Sheridan, *Memoirs*, vol. 2, 24.

Lt. John M. Gould, adjutant, 29th Maine Infantry. *Nicholas Picerno Collection*

everywhere!" Unfazed by his histrionics, Sheridan fired back, "You haven't begun to fight yet! I've got Crook here with 10,000 men, and I am going to throw them in and whip these fellows as they haven't been whipped lately." Sheridan's verve failed to sway Emory, who continued to fret about withdrawing the army without further loss. His corps's rough handling that morning had convinced him that he was participating in another Red River-style defeat. In his mind, Sheridan needed a successful rearguard action like the one "Old Brick Top" had delivered at Pleasant Hill, Louisiana, earlier that year. General Dwight, however, took confidence in Sheridan's words and readied his division for more combat.[24]

Sheridan quickly turned and rode through the First Woods toward the rear to await Crook's arrival at the eastern end of the timber. Lieutenant John M. Gould of the 29th Maine stumbled upon the army commander, who mistook Gould for a messenger from the front. "Well! What is it?" barked the little Irishman. Gould explained that he had been sent to the rear in search of ammunition for General Beal's brigade. Having just been spurned by an ordnance officer from another command, the young officer slyly added, "Too bad that a wagon now in there but belonging to another command should have been sent out when our brigade was in such need." The last words had barely rolled off Gould's tongue when Sheridan bellowed, "Take that damn wagon to the front quicker than hell. Damn quick, I say, damn it. If the driver won't go, you seize it, damn it. Get that ammunition in there, and damn quick too."

Sheridan's attitude proved contagious. The same vim and vigor that sent Gould on his new mission would soon be applied to dealing with the Rebels.[25]

---

24 Brigadier General William Dwight, Report of Serve RG 594, NA.

25 Gould, Journal, 497.

Chapter 18

A CONTINUOUS, DEAFENING
WAIL OF MUSKETRY

Crook's Attack

In accordance with General Sheridan's battle plan, Maj. Gen. George Crook's Army of West Virginia broke camp at Summit Point at 5:00 a.m., three hours after Maj. Gen. Horatio B. Wright's Sixth Corps departed Berryville. The command arrived at Opequon Creek around 9:00 a.m. where it waited in reserve, guarding the army's "wagon train and other impedimenta." Crook's men had experienced arduous campaigning and combat throughout the summer and welcomed the opportunity to sit this battle out. The troops brewed coffee from the cool creek water and consumed a leisurely breakfast along its banks while the battle raged at the front. As the command relaxed in a lush field of clover, Capt. Russell Hastings of the 23rd Ohio expressed his hope that Wright's infantry could win the fight unaided. Crook smiled and said, "I cannot find a four leaf-clover, so I suppose we will have to go in."[1]

---

1 Russell Hastings Papers, "For My Children," RBHPC; L. W. V. Kennon Papers, Interview with George Crook, September 28, 1888, USAMHI; Schmidt, *Autobiography*, 125; DuPont, *Shenanandoah*, 109-110.

His comment prompted an outpouring of similar adages from other officers that portended hard fighting for the Army of West Virginia. With the sounds of battle reverberating back from the front lines, Crook grew frustrated at his lack of orders, and rode with his staff to Sheridan's headquarters. Crook arrived there just as Sheridan was issuing his final orders to the corps and division commanders of the Sixth and Nineteenth Corps. When the conference broke up, Crook requested "to be with General Sheridan and remain on the battlefield with him."[2]

George Crook's soldiers knew the Shenandoah Valley better than most men in Sheridan's command. Kernstown, Cross Keys, Port Republic, Winchester, New Market, Piedmont, Snickers Gap, and other bloody fields traced their path through the war. Foremost among the Valley veterans was Col. Joseph Thoburn. Born in County Antrim, Ireland, in 1825, Thoburn's family immigrated to Canada later that year and subsequently settled on a farm near St. Clairsville, Ohio. After studying medicine, he opened a practice in Wheeling, Virginia, where he was living when the war erupted in 1861. He enlisted as the surgeon of the 1st West Virginia Infantry, a three month regiment, but was appointed colonel when the regiment reorganized under three-year enlistments. In 1862, he led his troops at Kernstown, Port Republic, and Second Manassas before returning to campaign in the mountains of West Virginia. He remained there until spring 1864 when he returned to the Shenandoah Valley as an acting brigadier, leading his command in the thick combat at New Market, Piedmont, and Lynchburg. When Crook rose to command the Army of West Virginia, Thoburn ascended to division command. He performed capably against long odds at Snicker's Gap and covered Crook's retreat after the latter's debacle at Kernstown. Thoburn was a true leader of men who had modestly earned the sobriquet "Cool Joe" from his troops for his calm demeanor under fire.[3]

---

2 Crook wrote at least two versions of how he ended up at Sheridan's headquarters. In one, he said that he requested to be with Sheridan. In the other, he claimed that Sheridan requested his presence. Captain Henry A. DuPont, Crook's chief of artillery, confirmed that Crook left the crossing after growing frustrated while waiting for orders. L. W. V. Kennon Papers, Interview with George Crook, September 28, 1888, USAMHI; Schmidt, *Autobiography*, 125.

3 Colonel Rutherford B. Hayes is perhaps the most celebrated officer of Crook's command. While Hayes was a capable officer, his reputation is more an outgrowth of his subsequent political career that culminated with his questionable election to the presidency of the United States in 1876. His overall combat experience paled compared to that of Cols. Joseph Thoburn and Isaac Duval. Hayes had a few significant combat experiences, including his service and wounding at South Mountain in September 1862, leading a successful attack at Cloyd's

Col. Joseph Thoburn
Nicholas Picerno Collection

The commander of Crook's 2nd division, Col. Isaac Harding Duval, was born the son of a glassmaker and textile manufacturer in Wellsburg, Virginia, on September 1, 1824. The adventuresome lad grew up in the northern panhandle of what is now West Virginia, exploring along the banks of the Ohio River. Its churning waters and the shrill whistles of the paddle wheelers beckoned the young Virginian westward. At 13 years old, Duval boarded a steamboat and headed west where he spent his next 14 years as a frontiersman in the untamed

Mountain as a brigadier, and having his brigade routed at the Second Battle of Kernstown. Caldwell, *12th West Virginia.*

West. He often served as a scout, and participated in John C. Fremont's explorations along the Oregon Trail and into California. In 1851, Duval sailed to Cuba and took part in an attempt to liberate the island from Spain. When the insurrection failed, Duval fell into Spanish hands and narrowly escaped execution. His wanderlust satisfied, he returned to Wellsburg and established himself in the mercantile business until war came to the border town. Duval fought alongside Thoburn as the major of the 1st West Virginia at Kernstown and Port Republic before resigning later in 1862 to accept the colonelcy of the 9th West Virginia. He led that regiment in action at Cloyd's Mountain on May 9, 1864, rose to brigade command during the ensuing Lynchburg campaign, and led it to victory under Averell against a larger force at Rutherford's farm on July 20. By the end of that month, Duval was commanding a division in Crook's army.[4]

Earlier in the battle, Crook had approached Sheridan during the initial success of the 11:40 a.m. infantry assault. He begged Sheridan, "Give me a division of cavalry, and with my troops I would turn the enemy's right and cut off his retreat up the Valley . . ." Sheridan had been on the verge of endorsing Crook's proposal when Maj. Gen. Robert E. Rodes's division smashed into the Federal line and drove the divisions of Grover and Ricketts into confusion. The path to Early's right flank was lightly guarded at that time; however, the desperate situation on the battlefield nixed any movement to the left. Instead, Sheridan rushed staff officers off to check the movement to the rear of the broken troops of the Sixth and Nineteenth Corps. Although the situation seemed desperate, Sheridan's reserves from the Sixth and Nineteenth corps already outnumbered all of the Confederates Lt. Gen. Jubal Early had on the battlefield. An outright defeat appeared very unlikely; however, the shattered condition of the Nineteenth Corps and reported additional threats against his right flank required Sheridan's attention. He turned to his old West Point roommate and ordered him to bring his Army of West Virginia forward to the battlefield.[5]

Crook's troops were listening intently to the guns and watching the smoke rise above the trees. The sounds of battle "brought to us the impression that our

---

4   Betty Caldwell, "Wellsburg's Harding Duval Left Mark on Fronteir American," Historical Society of Brooke County (WV).

5   George Crook, Memoirs, Crook-Kennon Papers, USAMHI; Schmidt, DuPont, *Shenandoah*, 126; Sheridan, *Memoirs*, vol. 2, 24.

troops were not advancing, possibly not holding their line," recalled Captain Hastings of the 23rd Ohio. They also noticed that the signal flags upon a nearby hilltop signal station were fluttering "in a quick nervous way as though the information and orders must be passed on as quick as thought." When a staff officer galloped from the signal station toward a group of officers gathered around Col. Rutherford B. Hayes, one officer turned to Hastings and said, "I wonder if that damn fool isn't coming over here to tell us to go in."[6]

Thoburn led the brigades of Cols. George D. Wells and Thomas M. Harris up the Berryville Pike as quickly as the narrow confines of the Berryville Ravine would permit. Lieutenant Colonel Robert S. Northcott's brigade, about 900 men, remained at Spout Spring Crossing to guard the wagons east of the Opequon. Duval's division followed Thoburn across the creek and up the Berryville Pike.[7]

Reaching the front proved to be a difficult task for the Army of West Virginia. Thoburn reported that he encountered "wagons, artillery, ambulances, and stragglers running back from the scene of action, very seriously impeding my progress." Lieutenant Elmer Husted of the 123rd Ohio described it as "a tide of wounded men and stragglers going to the rear . . ." As Thoburn's men neared the battlefield, "the tide" almost completely blocked the road. The sight of the wounded provided grim reminders of the firing line. Husted lamented, "Men wounded in almost every possible shape being carried off in every possible way, some on stretchers, some in blankets, others leaning on the arm of a comrade, covered with blood, minus an arm or hand. Oh! Such sights." Some of the wounded pleaded with Crook's men, "Hurry up, boys, they need you up there; they are giving our boys hell!" Hundreds of shirkers spread exaggerated tales of woe to the approaching reinforcements. "We are whipped; the Rebels are at our heals [sic]," claimed those who had not remained on the battlefield long enough to learn that Russell and Dwight had restored the line. William B.

6 Hastings mistakenly believed that this signal station was Sheridan's headquarters. In fact, Sheridan was at the front. Russell Hastings Memoir, RBHPC, 25.

7 According to an upublished report of the 36th Ohio, the lead regiment of Duval's division, Duval used the Old Berryville Road to the south, saving time instead of filing two divisions one after the other through the Berryville Canyon. This path was neglected when the Sixth Corps and Nineteenth Corps deployed that morning. *OR* 43, pt. 1, 368; A West Virginia Officer to Editors, *Intelligencer*, October 10, 1864, *Wheeling Daily Intelligencer*, October 19, 1864; DuPont, *Shenandoah*, 120-1; Draft of Col. W. H. C. Adney's Report on part taken by 36th [Ohio] at the Battles of Opequon and Fisher's Hill, October 4, 1864, John T. Booth Papers, Ohio Historical Society.

Stark of the 34th Massachusetts considered it "very poor encouragement for us to see so many going to the rear and hearing the remarks they made." Crook recalled, "There seemed to be fully as many men fleeing back from the battle field as I had in my command, spreading the report that our army had all been cut to pieces & to say the least the effect was demoralizing."[8]

The Army of West Virginia reached the front around 2:00 p.m., and its soldiers found Sheridan and Crook anxiously awaiting their arrival on the field. Lieutenant Colonel Thomas F. Wildes of the 116th Ohio saw the army commander and called for "three cheers" for Sheridan, and the soldiers responded heartily with a thunderous cheer for their fellow Ohioan. General Sheridan waved and shouted back, "Go for 'em boys," eliciting even more enthusiastic cheers from the soldiers. Sheridan instructed Crook to take position "on the right and rear of the Nineteenth Corps, and to look out for our right, as the enemy was reported to be moving in that direction." Crook wasted no time and moved his divisions into an open field behind the First Woods. When Thoburn reached the meadow, he found the Nineteenth Corps fighting the enemy on the opposite side of the woods. He deployed his division into two lines of battle. Duval's troops soon reached the field behind Thoburn's division and deployed likewise.[9]

While Thoburn and Duval marshaled their forces behind the First Woods, Crook headed to the front. As he rode through the woods, General Dwight joined him. The two men shook hands, and Dwight explained the tactical situation and voiced his opinion that the attack should be continued from farther to the right. Crook personally assessed the state of affairs, scouted the terrain, and learned the disposition of the troops already on the ground. While so engaged, he spotted a captain from the 29th Maine perched in a tree near Red Bud Run. Crook asked him if this was the right flank of the army, and the officer said that he thought it was. Crook retorted that his orders were imperative to go

8   First Draft of Crook's Autobiography, Crook-Kennon Papers, USAMHI; OR 43, pt. 1, 368; Lt. Elmer Husted to Friends, September 28, 1864, *Norwalk Reflector*, October 15, 1864; William B. Stark Journal, typescript copy in possession of author; Jonathan Wishon, "One Day's Fighting," *National Tribune*, 1924.

9   Contrary to the memoir of Capt. Henry DuPont published 62 years after the battle, both Sheridan and Crook agree that the army commander met Crook and issued orders to him when his men arrived on the battlefield. Russell Hastings Memoir, RBHPC; OR 43, pt. 1, 361; John M. Gould; *Wheeling Daily Intelligencer*, October 19, 1864; William T. Patterson Journal, Ohio Historical Society; OR 43, pt. 1, 361-362, 368; Schmidt, *Autobiography*, 126; *New York Herald*, September 21, 1864.

in on the right and he had to be certain. The captain assured him he had seen no other Federal troops to his right. Crook quickly saw that the open ground on the north side of Red Bud Run offered a prime opportunity to strike the Confederate flank. "I felt morally sure that if the enemy were to renew their assault on the Nineteenth Corps and succeed in driving them back," recalled Crook, "they would carry me with them." He decided to take Duval's division and personally lead it across Red Bud Run, "intending, if possible, to turn his [Gordon's left] flank."[10]

Crook galloped back through the trees to the staging area behind the First Woods. He outlined his plans to Thoburn and ordered him to advance his division through the woods and take position on the right flank of the Nineteenth Corps. Crook next explained his intentions to Colonel Duval. As Crook passed along Duval's ranks, his troops acknowledged their leader with the "most vociferous cheering." They vowed to "wipe out Winchester," a reference to their embarrassing July 24 drubbing at Kernstown a few miles to the south. Crook had misread the situation that day and was largely responsible for the magnitude of the defeat, but now faced an opportunity for redemption. He felt that "the fate of the day depended upon the conduct of his command, and most earnestly did he labor, not only to impress his division and brigade commanders, but his whole command with the importance of unflinching courage and indomitable determination on their part."[11]

Crook left nothing to chance on his flank march. He led Duval's division and Capt. Henry A. DuPont's artillery brigade northward along an old country road. The blue column followed the track a short distance, passing by a "primitive manufacturing establishment" known locally as the Factory. The Mountaineers and Buckeyes crossed a mill race from nearby Morgan's Mill, and then easily splashed through Red Bud Run. Once on the north bank, Crook encountered the 9th Connecticut of the Nineteenth Corps. These troops had been ordered to screen Grover's advance from the north side of the stream, but

10 Dwight, Report of Service, 217, NA; Schmidt, *Autobiography*, 127; Russell Hastings, Memoir, RBHPC; *OR* 43, pt. 1, 361; *Wheeling Daily Intelligencer*, October 19, 1864; Sheridan, *Memoirs*, vol. 2, 24-25.

11 Thoburn's report and a letter from an officer of Crook's command make it clear that Crook fully briefed Thoburn on the plan prior to taking Duval's division to the north side of Red Bud Run. These sources completely erode Sheridan's claims about having conceived and ordered Crook's subsequent attack. *Wheeling Daily Intelligencer*, October 19, 1864; *New York Herald*, September 21, 1864.

they failed to move forward with the main battle line. They informed Crook they had not seen any Confederates all day. Nevertheless, Crook detailed Capt. William S. Wilson's company of the 36th Ohio to scout the ground out toward the north on Crook's right flank. Duval deployed his division into a double line of battle with Col. Rutherford B. Hayes's brigade in front and Col. Daniel Johnson's brigade in a supporting line. Crook instructed DuPont to hold his artillery in readiness to support Duval should an opportunity arise. Crook ordered his troops "to walk fast, keep silent, until within about one-hundred yards of the guns [on Gordon's left], and then with a yell to charge at full speed."[12]

Thoburn's division had remained on the south bank of Red Bud Run and advanced into the First Woods. He saw that the Nineteenth Corps's right flank extended all the way to Red Bud Run, which blocked him from deploying his division. The situation rectified itself when General Emory appeared in person. He told Thoburn, "My lines are very much extended and very weak," and asked him to relieve Beal's brigade. Thoburn readily agreed, and Emory pulled Beal's brigade out of the line and shifted it to the left to strengthen the center of the Nineteenth Corps, which created enough room for Thoburn to fulfill his original instructions. He promptly advanced his division to the western fringe of the First Woods and placed the brigade of the hard-nosed Harvard Law graduate, Col. George D. Wells, in the front line. The brigade of another West Virginian physician turned soldier, Col. Thomas M. Harris, manned the second line.

The previous Confederate efforts against Emory's right flank triggered concern that the next Confederate attack might hit Thoburn's right as well. The West Virginian deployed three regiments in a line of battle that ran perpendicularly to his main battle line. These troops deployed in the fringe of woods paralleling Red Bud Run and facing northward. Thoburn's skirmishers soon found themselves engaged with their Southern counterparts from Gordon's infantry in front and Col. William Payne's cavalry sharpshooters on the opposite side of the run. Jittery nerves flared among the soldiers as they waited in line of battle under fire from the Southern artillery and sharpshooters. Officers steadied their men by example in those most trying moments before

12 Given that the 9th Connecticut remained well to the rear and did not advance with the Nineteenth Corps, it is not surprising that its members had not seen any Confederates all day. Sheridan, *Memoirs*, vol. 2, 24; OR 43, pt. 1, 361-362; Rutherford B. Hayes to Wife, September 21, 1864, R. B. Hayes Presidential Center.

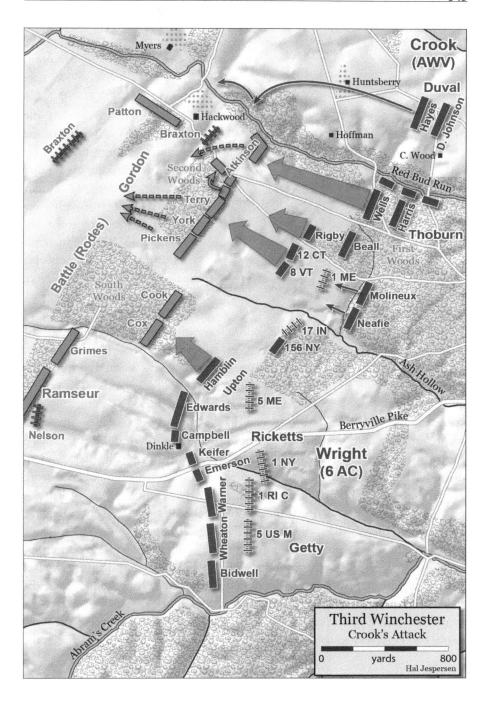

Myers

Crook
(AWV)

Huntsberry

Duval

Hayes

D. Johnson

Patton

Hackwood

Hoffman

Braxton

Braxton

C. Wood

Red Bud Run

Gordon

Second
Woods

Atkinson

Wells

Harris

Thoburn

Terry

York

Rigby

Beall

First
Woods

Pickens

12 CT

8 VT

1 ME

Battle (Rodes)

South
Woods

Cook

Molineux

Cox

Neafie

Ash Hollow

17 IN

Grimes

156 NY

Ramseur

Hamblin

Upton

5 ME

Nelson

Berryville Pike

Edwards

Campbell

Ricketts

Dinkle

Keifer

Wright
(6 AC)

Emerson

1 NY

Wheaton

Warner

1 RI C

5 US M

Getty

Bidwell

Abram's Creek

Third Winchester
Crook's Attack

0   yards   800

Hal Jespersen

Capt. William McKinley of Maj. Gen. George Crook's staff, Army of West Virginia. NA

the attack. In the ranks of the 123rd Ohio, Lt. Elmer Husted rode calmly amongst his men, nonchalantly smoking his pipe as if he was taking a Sunday afternoon stroll through the streets of his hometown of Norwalk, Ohio. The lieutenant's cool demeanor helped to settle his troops as they anxiously awaited the oncoming storm sure to break around them.[13]

Looking out across the Middle Field, a somewhat jumbled Confederate line waited for the next wave of Union attackers to appear. Colonel Harris observed that the Southerners "on this part of the field, occupied a stone wall some 300 yards distant in our immediate front and wood on our left flank." The several advances and retreats by Maj. Gen. John B. Gordon's command had considerably mixed the various regiments and brigades. According to a wounded Iowan who was trapped behind the Southern lines, the enemy used the precious lull in the action to their advantage, "generally making their position better and stronger." All across Gordon's front, soldiers from Alabama, Georgia, Louisiana, and Virginia took the opportunity to fortify their position, digging in as best they could behind stone and rail fencing, constructing breastworks, or simply taking shelter behind trees. The swampy stretch of Red Bud Run on Gordon's left flank still provided the Southerners with a large degree of security, and the Georgian considered his position safe from attack in that direction. A wounded Iowa soldier lying helplessly in the field between the Second and South Woods thought the same. "It looked to me as though their position could be held against any odds and I was fearful the battle had been lost to us." A soldier of the 31st Georgia observed that in the

---

13 *Norwalk Reflector*, October 18, 1864.

woods, "every man had the advantage of a big oak to protect his body to some extent."[14]

With the fluid nature of the combat in Gordon's section of the battlefield and a paucity of official Confederate reports, it is difficult to ascertain the precise location of each brigade, let alone individual regiments. Confederate memoirs and letters offer little detail in that regard as well. Post-action and postwar writings focused on the successful counterattack, but relayed painfully little information describing the battle as it turned badly for the Confederates. Furthermore, it is highly likely the regiments and brigades had become intermixed during the see-saw contest. It is clear from multiple U.S. sources that a substantial Confederate force, most likely Atkinson's Georgia brigade or elements thereof, held the ground from Hackwood Lane at the northeast corner of the Second Woods. Their line extended northward to a steep ridge overlooking a swampy stretch of Red Bud Run. On Atkinson's right, Brig. Gen. Cullen Battle's Alabama brigade, now under Col. Samuel Pickens, lined the eastern edge of the Second Woods immediately south of Hackwood Lane. Brigadier General William Terry's Virginians held the ground on Pickens's right, and Brig. Gen. Zebulon York's Louisiana soldiers held the far right of the woods. Given the casualties and leakage of men to the rear during the back and forth action, Gordon now commanded no more than 2,500 men along the Second Woods front. Major Carter Braxton beefed up Gordon's position by deploying some of his artillery in an open field between the Second Woods and the edge of Red Bud Run. The balance of his artillery battalion remained in position on the knoll behind Gordon's right flank.[15]

14 Captain DeForest of the 12th Connecticut, McMillan's brigade, described the Confederates as "striving to hold this wood [the Second Woods] and the adjacent field. Jacob Switzer was wounded during the initial Nineteenth Corps attack and remained behind the Confederate front line throughout the day." OR 43, pt. 1, 388; Cullen Battle, Memoir ADAH; Mildred Throne, ed., "Reminiscences of Jacob C. Switzer of the 22nd Iowa," Iowa Journal of History, vol. 56, 60-62; I. G. Bradwell, Under the Southern Cross, 46.

15 Jubal Early stated that Atkinson's brigade was put in on the left when Crook attacked. The alignment of the Confederate battle line described above is based upon known alignments along Gordon's front at the time of the Confederate counterattack. Its location is also based upon archeological studies, both formal and informal, conducted on that section of the battlefield. Battle's brigade restored Gordon's left when Atkinson's brigade broke during Grover's assault. All Alabama brigade sources confirm their placement and a straight-ahead movement into the woods with no shift rightward to rejoin the division. I. G. Bradwell of the 31st Georgia stated that most of the Alabamians remained at the edge of the Second Woods. Robert L. Jolley, "An Archeological Survey of the Confederate Left Flank, Third Battle of

Rodes's division, now firmly commanded by General Battle, remained in the South Woods on Gordon's right flank. As the senior brigadier in Rodes's division, Battle formally assumed command after the heavy combat subsided. The eastern front of this wooded area extended at least 100 yards closer to the Federal position than that occupied by Gordon's division. From the northern face of this woodlot, the Confederates could deliver an enfilade fire into the left flank of any Federals attacking Gordon's position in the Second Woods. Brigadier General Philip Cook's Georgians manned the line in the open field between the Second and South Woods, sheltering themselves behind rail fences and other obstacles hastily assembled into crude breastworks. The North Carolina brigades of Brig. Gen. William R. Cox and Brig. Gen. Bryan Grimes held the South Woods opposing Upton's division. Ramseur's division had regrouped in the fringe of woods at the western edge of the Dinkle cornfield and maintained a firm foothold on its position. Brigadier General Archibald Godwin's brigade now formed the nucleus of Ramseur's regrouped line and deployed across the Berryville Pike. Brigadier General Robert Johnston rallied on his left flank, and Brig. Gen. John Pegram held the right, with Lt. Col. William Nelson's artillery supporting from key elevations along and behind the line.[16]

Meanwhile, Crook made good progress north of Red Bud Run and sent Capt. William McKinley to inform Thoburn of the situation and order him to attack when Duval's men charged on the right. McKinley first encountered Sheridan, who sent McKinley back to Crook to inform him that Torbert's cavalry was advancing to his support along the Valley Pike and to attack as soon as Duval's division was in position. Sheridan then rode through the woods, located Thoburn, and ordered him to attack as soon as he heard Duval's troops advancing on his right flank. The commanding general used "the most

Winchester September, 19, 1864," *Archeological Society of Virginia Quarterly Bulletin*, December 2007, 4:197, 204-206; Jed Hotchkiss, 1864 Sketchbook, LC; George P. Ring Letter, September 20, 1864, Tulane; Worsham, *Foot Cavalry*, 167.

16 Although some have incorrectly written that Brig. Gen. Bryan Grimes assumed command of Rodes's division, post-battle orders and pronouncements regarding that command clearly state that Brig. Gen. Cullen Battle took command of the division. Even Grimes makes no mention of commanding the division in a letter home to his wife after the fighting ended. Battle remained in command until Early appointed Ramseur as Rodes's successor at Fisher's Hill. "Map of Ramseur's division, September 19, 1864," Jed Hotchkiss Papers, LC; *Richmond Daily Whig*, October 5, 1864; "The Command of the Late Gen. Rodes," *Mobile Advertiser and Register*, October 12, 1864.

enthusiastic terms" to impress upon Thoburn the importance of his advance. Sheridan remained with Thoburn, deeming "that portion of our lines formed by the 1st division of Gen. Crook's command, as being the point of highest importance."[17]

Over on the north bank of Red Bud Run, Crook and Duval joined forces with Lt. Col. Alexander Strain. General Dwight had ordered Strain to lead several companies of the 153rd New York and cover the Nineteenth Corps's right flank on the north side of the run. Strain presumably shared his knowledge of Lee's position with Crook and the New Yorkers were joined on the skirmish line by sharpshooters from the 23rd Ohio of Duval's division. The advancing Union soldiers quickly brushed aside the dismounted troopers Payne left behind to screen Gordon's left flank, and similarly drove away the remaining guns of Major Breathed's artillery. Duval's division now advanced unopposed along the north bank of Red Bud Run. Lee lamented, "The withdrawal of troops [Payne's brigade] from the front of Crook's right allowed him to advance it . . ." At 3:00 p.m., Duval's division reached the point opposite Thoburn's right flank. Crook ordered a charge, and his men cheered vociferously, announcing their approach to all. Thoburn's men heard the roar to their right and attcked on the bank of Red Bud Run.[18]

Crook's rugged Ohio and West Virginia men stepped quickly and quietly through the fields of Mr. Huntsberry's farm. Upon reaching a point opposite Gordon's line, Crook swung his right flank around to the left in order to strike Gordon's left flank and rear. Atkinson's Georgians, however, saw the threat and reacted quickly when Duval came into view on the opposite side of the run. Atkinson shifted part of his brigade into position along a commanding ridge that overlooked Red Bud and faced the approaching Unionists. From the higher ground on the south bank, the Georgians fired their rifles at the blue formation as it came into range. From the open ground immediately north of the Second Woods, Lt. Col. Carter Braxton trained his guns on Duval's division and showered it with case shot and exploding shells. "Everything on the

17 William T. Patterson Journal, Ohio Historical Society; "A West Virginia Officer to Editors," October 10, 1864, *Wheeling Daily Intelligencer*, October 19, 1864; DuPont, *Shenandoah*, 120-1; *OR* 43, pt. 1, 368.

18 Statement of Alexander Strain to John M. Gould, August 5, 1870, Nick Picerno Collection; *Wheeling Daily Intelligencer*, October 19, 1864; Lt. Col. James Comly Papers, RBHPC; Crook, *Autobiography*, 126-127; William S. Wilson to R. B. Hayes, April 9, 1887, RBHPC.

Col. Isaac Duval's Federal division charged down the brush-covered distant slope to the right and unexpectedly stumbled upon Red Bud Run, which prevented their capturing a Confederate battery on the south bank of the swampy run. *Scott C. Patchan*

enemy's left was turned on us," recalled Capt. Russell Hastings of the 23rd Ohio. "Bullets, shot, shell and shrapnel rained on us like hail."[19]

Crook's men saw Braxton's guns fewer than 400 yards away and believed that the artillery would soon be in their grasp. With Hayes's brigade in the lead, the Union battle lines passed over a ridge and reached a thick fringe of underbrush that girded Red Bud Run. Crook's "Mountain Creepers" dashed down the slope through the tangled foliage, shouting "Go for that battery!" They plied their way through the thickets only to discover an even greater impediment that completely checked their advance. Although a shallow narrow creek where Duval's division initially passed over to the north bank, Red Bud Run turned into a deep and miry swamp with steep banks. The 23rd Ohio's Lt. Col. James Comly aptly described the obstacle as, "A deep slough, twenty or thirty yards wide, and nearly waist deep, with deep soft mud at the bottom, and the surface overgrown with a thick bed of moss, nearly strong enough to bear

19 Manuel and George Semples of Winchester have been relic-hunting the Third Winchester battlefield since the hobby became a popular pastime. Their findings and those of professional archeologists verify Hastings's assertion about the volume of Confederate fire that was directed at Duval's division as it traversed the ground on the north side of Red Bud Run. Russell Hastings Memoir, RBHPC; J. W. Delay to R. B. Hayes, January 7, 1886, RBHPC; Jesse Tyler Sturm, *Remembrances*, 93.

the weight of a man." On the hill beyond that "morass," Braxton's gunners limbered up their cannon and raced away while Crook's men struggled through the muck and mud.[20]

The two lines of Duval's division quickly intermingled, as the second line did not stop in time to avoid the confusion in front of the swamp. From the high ground south of Red Bud Run, Rebel gunners rained fire and iron down upon the Federals as they crowded together on the opposite bank of the swamp. Duval's situation quickly worsened when Colonel Patton's 700 Virginians arrived near Hackwood and joined some of Gordon's men already in position among several buildings about the Hackwood farm. Patton's men deployed behind a stone wall along Hackwood Lane, between the house and Martinsburg Pike. The Southern infantry opened fire and staggered the Ohioans and West Virginians struggling along Red Bud Run. Lieutenant Morton L. Hawkins of the 34th Ohio described the fire of the Georgians and Virginians as "simply murderous." Acting brigadier, Col. Daniel Johnson of the 14th West Virginia, went down seriously wounded near the edge of the swamp. The Confederates also shot down three color bearers of the 34th Ohio before 18-year-old Pvt. Jonathan Harlan caught the flag at the edge of the slough. Immediately struck by a spent shell fragment, the force of the blow cut through his blanket roll and rendered him helpless for a moment or two.[21]

Out of the confusion rode Col. Rutherford B. Hayes. He plunged his horse into the murky waters in an effort to inspire his troops. Hayes's horse quickly mired in the soft, muddy swamp bottom. The horse struggled "frantically" and carried him to the middle of the quagmire but could go no farther. "I jumped off, and down on all fours, succeeded in reaching the rebel side-but alone," wrote Hayes two days later. Lieutenant Colonel Comly saw his commander's valiant struggle and ordered the 23rd Ohio to follow Hayes. "It was a work of almost incredible difficulty," reported Comly. "Men were drowned or suffocated in the slimy mud or tangled in the moss, wounded and could not be got out. But still the men plunged through." Hayes's example proved contagious and the 13th West Virginia plunged into the muddy water and struggled through the swamp. When the soggy soldiers of the 23rd Ohio finally crawled out of the swamp, Hayes deployed them behind a stone wall and waited

20 James Comly Papers, Journal, OHS.

21 Morton L. Hawkins, "Sketch of the Battle of Winchester, September 19, 1864," *Ohio-Mollus*, vol. 1, 158; Jonathan Harlan to R. B. Hayes, July 8, 1887, RBHPC.

The veterans of the 23rd Ohio who followed Rutherford Hayes across Red Bud Run at Third Winchester, pictured at muster-out in Cleveland in 1865. *R. B. Hayes Presidential Center*

for reinforcements. Pinned down by the Confederate rifle and artillery fire, he waited for help before attempting to advance.[22]

Soldiers of Col. Hiram T. Devol's 36th Ohio and Lt. Col. William H. Enoch's 5th West Virginia entered the swamp to the right of Hayes, "but after a vain struggle had to be helped out by their comrades so that comparatively few men succeeded in crossing at this point." Devol ordered the 36th Ohio and 5th

22 R. B. Hayes to Wife, September 21, 1864, RBHPC; James Comly, Journal, RBHPC; Frank, "From the Thirteenth V. V. I., September 20, 1864," *Point Pleasant, WV Weekly Register*, October 13, 1864.

West Virginia to march upstream toward Hackwood, where the two regiments crossed with less difficulty. Lieutenant Jacob Reasoner of the 36th Ohio made it across about the same time as Hayes. Although the water rose up to his armpits, Reasoner muscled his way through the "soft and slimy" mud and emerged on the Hackwood side of Red Bud. Soaked to the bone, Hayes and Reasoner sat down upon a large rock and poured the water out of their boots.[23]

Although popular history told of a future president of the United States leading a division through the "slough" at Red Bud Run and on to victory, the movement was not a singular charge. Instead, it took time for a significant

23 Jacob Reasoner to J. T. Booth, September 18, 1887, RBHPC; Draft Report of Lt. Col. W. H. C. Adney 36th Ohio at Battles of Opequon and Fisher's Hill, October 4, 1864, John Booth Papers, OHS.

Col. Hiram Devol of the 36th Ohio was a veteran of Antietam, Chickamauga, and Chattanooga prior to the 1864 Shenandoah Valley Campaign. *Larry Strayer Collection*

portion of Duval's division to get into action. Most of Duval's troops either retraced their steps downstream and came up behind Thoburn's division or moved west along the run searching for a more practical fording site. A few days later, Hayes admitted to his wife that "my line above and below me crossed it (Red Bud Run) easily thus separating still more the different parts of my line. No one knows a battle except the little part he sees."[24]

On the south bank of Red Bud Run, Thoburn's division made its presence felt and provided relief for Duval's struggling soldiers. Thoburn's men had waited anxiously for the cheers of Duval's division to signal their assault. Bullets were already whizzing among Thoburn's troops as they stood along the edge of the First Woods waiting to attack. His skirmishers maneuvered into the Middle Field and traded shots with Gordon's men. In Thoburn's front line, Col. George D. Wells arrayed his regiments with the 116th Ohio on the left, 5th New York heavy artillery in the center, and the 123rd Ohio on the right. Behind Wells, Col. Thomas M. Harris deployed the 10th West Virginia on his left, the 54th Pennsylvania in the center, and the 15th West Virginia manning the right. The 34th Massachusetts, 11th West Virginia, and 23rd Illinois remained in a line facing north along the margins of the run.[25]

24 *Ironton Register*, December 2, 1886; R. B. H. to Dearest [Wife], September 21, 1864, RBHPC.

25 OR 43, pt. 1, 369; *Wheeling Daily Intelligencer*, October 19, 1864; *Norwalk Reflector*, October 15, 1864.

At 3:00 p.m., the shouts of Duval's men announced their approach on the north bank of Red Bud Run. Simultaneously, Thoburn's soldiers stepped out of the First Woods and charged Gordon's troops posted across the field. An Ohio soldier reported that the Confederates responded by waving their "dirty emblems of treason" and unloading a withering volley into the Federals when they were about 300 yards from Gordon's position. Undaunted, Wells's troops let out a wild yell and continued the advance without stopping to return fire. The fortitude of Thoburn's troops in withstanding this fusillade drew praise from the Nineteenth Corps. "The broad blue wave surged forward with a yell which lasted for minutes," wrote Capt. John W. DeForest. "In response there arose from the northern front of the woods a continuous, deafening wail of musketry without break or tremor. For a time I despaired of the success of the attack, for it did not seem possible that any troops could endure such a fire."[26]

Thoburn's lead regiments, the 116th Ohio, 5th New York, and 123rd Ohio, raced across the field toward the Georgians on Gordon's left flank. Off to Thoburn's left front, several companies of gritty Iowans from the 24th Regiment who had rallied with Capt. William T. Rigby opened fire at the Confederates across the field. As the blue battle lines neared the center of the Middle Field, Atkinson's Georgians and Pickens's Alabamians delivered heavy volleys into Thoburn's assault force. Terry's Virginians, not then under any direct attack in their front, angled their rifles toward Thoburn's left flank and laced it with a biting crossfire. Still, the rugged "Buzzards" or "Mountain Creepers" did not stop to return fire, but rather closed ranks and surged through the field. The Georgians now found themselves threatened on two fronts by both Thoburn and Duval. They could no longer exclusively confront Duval's division coming in on their left flank and rear. Attacked in both front and flank, the Georgians facing the Middle Field began to fall back toward the northern face of the Second Woods.[27]

Colonel Wells's brigade halted briefly when it reached the makeshift breastworks that the Southerners had just abandoned, and his veterans emptied their rifles into the retreating Confederates before renewing the advance. On Wells's right flank, the 5th New York and 123rd Ohio delivered a deadly enfilade fire into the right and rear of the Georgians who had turned toward

26 DeForest, *A Volunteer's Adventures: A Union Captain's Record of the Civil War*, 186-188.

27 *OR* 43, pt. 1, 350, 368, 376; Charles A. Lucas, "A Soldier's Letter from the Field," *Iowa Historical Record*, January 1902, 438-439; Wildes, *116th Ohio*, 170-171.

Alfred R. Waud's sketch of the charge of the 8th Vermont Infantry, part of Brig. Gen. William Emory's Nineteenth Corps, at Third Winchester. *A. R. Waud, LC*

Red Bud Run to confront Duval. Firing all the while, the Georgians fell back slowly through a ravine and the woods bordering Red Bud Run. On Wells's left flank, the 116th Ohio pursued the Georgians through the open ground north of the Second Woods. Confederates from Gordon's center and right flank shifted into position in Hackwood Lane along the northern fringes of the Second Woods and delivered an effective enfilading fire into Thoburn's left flank. These Southerners had likely shifted into this position when Duval first made his appearance known across Red Bud Run. Thoburn took quick action to alleviate that situation. He directed Lt. Col. Thomas F. Wildes's 116th Ohio to change front and attack the Southerners who now lined the northern edge of the Second Woods. Amidst the din of battle, however, Wildes's excited Buckeyes continued chasing the wavering Georgians and did not stop to carry out the change of front. Thoburn next grabbed the 10th West Virginia Infantry from his second line and Colonel Harris's brigade. Major Henry H. Withers's 10th West Virginia changed front to the left and attacked the Confederates delivering the enfilading fire from the northern front of the Second Woods. The rifle fire from the Southern troops rocked Withers's Mountaineers with a deadly fusillade. The 10th West Virginia suffered horribly under this barrage of lead which brought the regiment to a standstill. The regiment's colors toppled to the ground several times and dozens of West Virginians fell dead or wounded. Already, the Union attack began to falter.[28]

Fortunately for the West Virginians, help was on the way from several directions. Wildes belatedly turned the 116th Ohio to the left and attacked the Confederates lining the northern face of the Second Woods. Captain Rigby's Iowans continued to support the attack from Thoburn's left, and Duval's men emerged from the Red Bud bottom lands on the Hackwood farm, threatening to cut off any Confederates lingering too long in the Second Woods. The Confederates along the northern edge of woods withdrew deeper into the timber and battled the pursuers from the 116th Ohio and 10th West Virginia. The Virginians, Louisianans, and Alabamians struggled valiantly against the Federals. Under the heavy pressure, Gordon ordered his men to retire to a stone wall located in a vast open field a few hundred yards to his right and rear. At some point in the combat, Colonel Pickens of the Alabama brigade went down wounded, and Col. Charles M. Forsyth assumed command. He maintained a steadfast position, but was unaware of the threat that Duval's force posed to his escape route from the woods. Fortunately, Brig. Gen. Cullen A. Battle perceived the peril to his Alabama brigade. He rode rapidly into the Second Woods and ordered Forsyth to pull his brigade back toward Winchester. Captain William H. May of the 3rd Alabama recalled that once the order to fall back was given, the brigade began "a disorderly retreat."[29] Although Crook had driven Gordon's division from its position on Early's left flank, Gordon's predicament could have been much worse. The swampy stretch of Red Bud Run and Col. George S. Patton's brigade prevented substantial elements of Duval's division from quickly enveloping the Confederate line and the Southerners escaped to fight again that day.[30]

In the Middle Field, Col. Stephen Thomas of the 8th Vermont detected the slackening Confederate fire and suggested to Capt. Sidney E. Clark of the 12th Connecticut that the two regiments join the advance. Although their ammunition was literally exhausted, the two officers ordered their men to fix bayonets. Colonel Thomas rode out in front of his Vermonters and shouted,

28 OR 43, pt. 1, 368, 387-388; *116th Ohio*, 170-171.

29 William May Memoir, FSNMP.

30 OR 43, pt. 1, 368, 376-377.

"Boys, if you ever pray, the time to pray has come. Pray now, remember Ethan Allen and old Vermont, and we'll drive 'em to hell. Come on old Vermont!" Thomas raised his sword over his head and spurred his horse toward the woods. His 8th Vermont followed closely behind, cheering as they went.[31]

On Thomas's right flank, Captain Clark called out to the men of the 12th Connecticut, "The 8th Vermont is going to the devil, but they shan't go ahead of us." Then the 12th Connecticut surged forward and joined Thomas's advance toward the position just abandoned by the Confederates. As the two New England regiments neared the woods, their brigade commander, Brig. Gen. James W. McMillan, rode up behind them and ordered them to halt as the jittery Emory had strictly forbidden his troops from advancing into the woods. Caught up in the spirit of the charge, the men ignored McMillan's plea and entered the timber. By the time they entered the trees, Thomas's men only found "lots of dead rebels," and halted their advance to avoid Emory's ire. The "Old Man" remembered all too keenly the fate that Birge's brigade had met when it ventured beyond the Second Woods earlier that day, and feared that McMillan might endure the same result.[32]

While Thoburn attacked Gordon, Patton's brigade kept Duval's straggling advance at bay in the low ground along Red Bud Run and prevented the West Virginian from quickly severing Gordon's line of retreat. Patton was born in Fredericksburg, Virginia, in 1833 and graduated from the Virginia Military Institute in 1852, ranked second out of a class of 24. Although he was a lawyer by trade and preferred the close-knit company of his family, he possessed a "peculiar aptitude for a soldier's duty and a soldier's life." His character is somewhat obscured by the "Old Blood and Guts" persona of his historically more significant grandson, Gen. George S. Patton III. A fellow officer recalled, "Graceful and elegant as a speaker," Colonel Patton "enforced discipline without exciting dislike, and commanded his men without diminishing their self respect."[33] A well-trained officer corps had honed Patton's brigade into a capable combat unit as demonstrated on many battlefields in the Allegheny

---

31 Carpenter, *8th Vermont*, 181.

32 Pvt. Francis C. Forbes, "A Soldier of Sheridan," VTHS, 21; Carpenter, *8th Vermont*, 182.

33 Ironically, the historical image of Patton's grandson is inaccurately ingrained in the American populace by the gravelly voice of actor George C. Scott. Green Peyton, *Virginia Military Institute Memorial*, "George S. Patton," 422-424.

The Hackwood farm: Thoburn's Federal division advanced across the immediate right foreground while Duval's division emerged from the bottom ground in the right distance and then passed the Hackwood house. Devin's cavalry swept in through the open ground in the distance to the left. These forces converged on Patton's Confederate brigade as it attempted to escape through the ground on the far left of the picture and out of the image. *USAMHI*

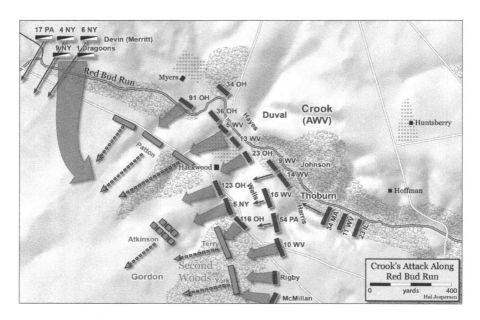

Mountains as well as the bloody fields of New Market, Cold Harbor, and Kernstown.

Like Patton, Lt. Col. George M. Edgar, commander of the 26th Battalion Virginia Infantry, had graduated from the Virginia Military Institute. The leader of the 23rd Battalion Virginia Infantry, Lt. Col. Clarence Derrick, attended West Point but resigned a few months shy of graduation when Virginia seceded from the Union. Patton's Virginians had already performed a critical duty for Jubal Early with the assistance they provided to the Southern cavalry along the Charlestown Road and Martinsburg Pike. Now, they anchored themselves behind the stone wall that lined Hackwood Lane west of the house and trained a blistering musketry at Duval's struggling division.

In marching around the morass, Duval's division had lost much of its organizational cohesiveness and was spread out over a frontage of about 500 yards. Nevertheless, the dogged determination of his Ohio and West Virginia soldiers, combined with Gordon's eventual withdrawal, increased the pressure on Patton's brigade. As the Georgians withdrew, Hayes's comingled advance of the 23rd Ohio and 13th West Virginia charged up the same ravine where the Georgians were stationed earlier that morning. The 36th Ohio and 5th West Virginia marched westward along the run until they "affected a very difficult crossing some three hundred yards further up [from Hayes] and in face, too, of the fire of a brigade of rebels posted behind stone walls" and among the Hackwood buildings. As the troops climbed out of the stream, officers hurried them forward to the shelter of a stone wall "without respect to regiments" to confront Patton's Virginians.[34]

Hayes's men charged out of the bottomland, still hoping to capture Braxton's repositioned artillery. From their hilltop position, however, the gunners had an excellent view of the events in the field. As Federal pressure mounted, the artillerists hitched their guns to the limbers and fell back several hundred yards. Hayes's Ohioans and West Virginians doggedly advanced, but they, too, found themselves under fire from the Confederates posted around Hackwood. The Georgians and Virginians raked the right flank of the 23rd Ohio with a "galling" enfilade fire that stunned the Buckeyes. The Ohio troops dropped to the ground and took cover among the numerous rock outcroppings and undulations in the rolling fields.[35]

Although Patton's brigade held its line, the pressure from Duval continued to build. Colonel Daniel D. Johnson's brigade initially deployed behind Hayes's brigade and extended farther to the right. When Johnson's men reached the Red Bud swamp, they encountered a most demoralizing situation watching Hayes's men struggle to deal with the obstruction. Johnson went down soon after, and Lt. Col. Benjamin F. Coates of the 91st Ohio took command of the brigade.

34 At the heart of this line was the veteran 36th Ohio. Few regiments in Sheridan's army could lay claim to the combat effectiveness of the 36th. George Crook molded the unit along the lines of a Regular Army infantry regiment. As a result of Crook's discipline and training, the 36th Ohio quickly earned a reputation as a hard-hitting offensive unit. Crook's rigorous training paid its first dividends in May 1862 when the 36th Ohio led a sweeping counterattack against Confederate Brig. Gen. Henry Heth's brigade of Virginians at Lewisburg, West Virginia. This victory netted the Federals four cannon, 157 Confederate prisoners, and halted a Confederate attempt to retake West Virginia. Ironically, most of the same Confederate troops routed at Lewisburg now lay concealed behind the stone wall in front of the 36th Ohio. In September 1862, the 36th Ohio stormed the Confederate position at Fox's Gap during the battle of South Mountain and helped stem the tide of Confederate Maj. Gen. A. P. Hill's counterattack at Antietam. In 1863, Crook's Ohioans joined the Army of the Cumberland and served with distinction at Chickamauga and Chattanooga. In spring 1864, the 36th Ohio returned to West Virginia at the request of now Bvt. Maj. Gen. George Crook. They accompanied Crook's Army of West Virginia into southwest Virginia and once again played a key role in an offensive during the Union victory at Cloyd's Mountain on May 9 and continued on with Crook throughout the Valley campaigns of that year. As fate would have it, the troops Crook had routed at Lewisburg in 1862 delivered a decisive flank attack upon the 36th Ohio at the Second Battle of Kernstown on July 24, 1864. There, the Ohioans suffered the loss of 112 men killed and wounded with another 24 missing, or nearly 50 percent of its total manpower. This defeat weighed heavily upon the shoulders of Crook's proud Ohioans, and they looked expectantly for an opportunity to wash away the stains of Kernstown. Tappan Adney, "History of the 36th Ohio," Booth Papers, OHS, 28.

35 James Comly Diary, OHS.

The Hackwood home, 2012.
Scott C. Patchan

The 14th West Virginia marched to the left and crossed downstream where the Red Bud narrowed. Some of the Mountaineers went over the swamp upon a felled tree. On Johnson's extreme right flank, the 91st Ohio avoided much of the confusion and sent skirmishers out toward the Valley Pike. They saw momentarily that Torbert's cavalry was sweeping up the pike to cover Crook's right flank. The 91st Ohio crossed the creek farther west near the Meyer farm, where Red Bud Run was a clear stream, fed by the cool, clean waters of vibrant springs. The Buckeyes charged toward Patton's position, but fell in heaps under the unerring aim of the Virginians. Like Hayes's men on the left, the troops took shelter wherever they could. In the ranks of Patton's brigade, Lt. Col. Edgar saw the struggling Federals and cried out, "Isn't it glorious to see them piled up that way?"[36]

Although Patton kept Duval's straggling advance pinned down, the withdrawal of Gordon's division on Patton's right and rear quickly changed the dynamic of the entire situation along Red Bud Run. Lieutenant Henry R.

---

36 John Weed Memoir, USAMHI; Jesse Tyler Sturm, Whirlpool, 93; Henry P. Morrison to My Dear Brother, September 20, 1864, USAMHI.

Morrison of the 23rd Virginia Battalion wrote home that "Gordon's men . . . fled in confusion far to the rear, leaving us to be enfiladed on the flank and rear." Patton received "order after order" from Maj. Gen. John C. Breckinridge to fall back and rejoin Wharton's division closer to Winchester, but his brigade was locked in combat with Duval's troops and could not be safely extricated. Patton's situation quickly worsened when Hayes led the muddy men of the 23rd Ohio and 13th West Virginia forward through the open ground immediately east of Hackwood and threatened Patton's right flank. In his front, more and more Federals hunkered down behind rock outcroppings and inequities in the ground and shot back at the Virginians. Toward the pike, the Union cavalry was moving beyond his left flank. Patton determined that his position was untenable and hurriedly withdrew his brigade from its position behind the rock fence lining Hackwood Lane. Patton began his retreat through a small wooded lot in some disorder, but his men fell into confusion as they were literally besieged from three sides.[37]

As Hayes's small command and elements of Thoburn's division advanced through the fields east of Hackwood, they opened fire into the flank and rear of Patton's retreating command. The Virginian attempted to change front and meet these attacks, but the situation deteriorated quickly as George Crook's men increased their deadly pressure. The bullets from Crook's rifles flew picked their way through Patton's ranks because Gordon's infantry was no longer protecting his rear. Lieutenant Colonel Adney of the 36th Ohio took advantage of the situation and advanced a throng of men from his own regiment and the 5th West Virginia. These Unionists leapt over the wall that had been sheltering them and closed to within 25 yards of Patton's embattled Virginians. At the same time, the Union cavalry menaced Patton's left flank. He was attempting to shift his Virginians to meet the attack when a jagged chunk of iron shell ripped into his thigh, inflicting a wound that would ultimately prove fatal. Patton was carried back to the home of a relative in Winchester where he died several days later. Under pressure on three sides, his brigade quickly lost its cohesion and retreated toward the town. Their troubles, however, had only just begun.[38]

37 Ibid.; Draft of Col. W. H. C. Adney's Report on part taken by 36th [Ohio] at the Battles of Opequon and Fisher's Hill, October 4, 1864, John T. Booth Papers, Ohio Historical Society.

38 James Comly Papers, OHS; F. Lee, Report, MOC; Booth Papers, OHS; Morrison, USAMHI; A. T. Ward Diary, OHS.

Lt. Col. Willam C. Adney
Larry Strayer Collection

While George Crook battled Gordon and Patton, Torbert's cavalry thundered up the Valley Pike on the heels of the retreating Rebel cavalry and into the area behind the Southern infantry. During his approach to the main battlefield, Torbert's command separated into separate columns, "each with its own special and select object in view." Merritt and Devin spied Patton's brigade as it withdrew in disorder from its position along Hackwood Lane. Merritt ordered Devin to charge at once, but the New Yorker had already comprehended the situation and readied for the appropriate course of action. He aimed the 1st New York Dragoons and 9th New York Cavalry toward the retreating Virginians, whom they struck at precisely the right time. Under assault from three different directions, Patton's men were completely unprepared to resist the mounted attack. Lieutenant Morrison of the 23rd Virginia Battalion wrote, "We found ourselves cut off by the converging columns of infantry and cavalry."[39]

"A terrible scene" ensued as the saber-wielding New Yorkers exploded into the midst of Patton's troops. The Union troopers hacked their sabers to the left and right, creating a veritable panic among Patton's men. Although Morrison was on the receiving end of this attack, he considered the ensuing melee to be "the most exciting scene I ever beheld." Sandwiched between Crook's infantry and Devin's cavalry, Patton's Virginians suffered

39 OR 43, pt. 1, 457; Henry P. Morrison to My Dear Brother, September 20, 1864, USAMHI.

Confederate Col. George S. Patton led a brigade of infantry in Jubal Early's army at the battle of Third Winchester, where a shell fragment mortally wounded him when it struck him in his leg. He was carried here, the home of his cousin Philip Williams, where he died several days later. *Scott C. Patchan*

horrendously in the fiercely contested, hand-to-hand encounter. When the melee ended, Devin's New Yorkers had captured 300 prisoners and all three battle flags from Patton's regiments. As the Union horsemen corralled the prisoners, Confederate artillery closer to Winchester fired into the mass of humanity, killing friend and foe alike, but preventing the Federal cavalry from advancing any farther for the time being.[40]

Patton's Virginians did not go down without a fight, and not all were captured. Major Conway W. Ayres of the 9th New York and Capt. Raymond L. Wright of Devin's staff lost their lives in the melee. Lieutenant Morrison picked up a wooden fence rail and knocked at least one New Yorker off his horse. Some Federal horsemen ordered the Virginians to halt and surrender only to be blasted from their saddles. Patton's survivors raced to the rear and halted

40 Ibid.; August T. Ward Diary, Booth Papers, OHS.

behind a second stone fence where Gordon had already reformed elements of his division. The sacrificial stand of Patton's brigade blocked Duval's flanking force and allowed Gordon to rally his division unmolested by Devin's horsemen. The larger portion of Patton's survivors deployed on Gordon's left flank and, once again, opened fire at the approaching Union infantry. As his division fell back before Crook's attack, Maj. Gen. John B. Gordon stood firm in the maelstrom and attempted to rally his men. A 16-year-old private from the 12th Georgia Battalion grabbed the bridle reins of Gordon's horse and attempted to lead the fiery commander to safety. Gordon ordered the soldier to release the horse and then continued to shout orders to his broken troops.[41] The young soldier then stood in front of his commander ready to defend him to the death. The battalion's color-bearer joined them and "instantly" Gordon's troops rallied behind the stone wall and gave "shot for shot" to the Union attackers.[42] Gordon's efforts to rally the broken Confederate infantry greatly impressed Capt. George Ring of the 6th Louisiana who wrote home the next day: "I never saw as fine a sight in my life as our noble Gen. Gordon presented as he galloped down the line with a stand of colors in his hand, his hat off and his long hair streaming in the wind. I had the colors of Stafford's brigade with a few men and as he passed [he] sang out to me, 'Form your men Captain, I know they will stand by me.'"[43]

The situation looked bleak for Jubal Early. Gordon's, Patton's, and Battle's brigades were all driven from their initial positions and had absorbed heavy losses. Inspired by Gordon's gallantry, most of the men from these battered legions sheltered themselves behind another stone wall running perpendicularly to the Valley Pike and resumed their fire on Crook's men as they pursued across the undulating plain. Hundreds, however, did not rally but continued their retreat into Winchester. When the infantry first wavered, Braxton's guns fell back to a position closer to Winchester. Fortunately for Early, the balance of Battle's (Rodes's) and Ramseur's divisions maintained a strong line in front of Wright's Sixth Corps. The situation for the Confederate Army of the Valley District would have been much more precarious if Emory had permitted his

41 OR 43, pt. 1, 482; George M. Edgar Papers, UNC; Hotchkiss, "[Wharton's Positions] "Winchester, Sept. 19, 1864," Sketchbook showing positions of Second Corps, A.N.Va. in engagements of 1864-5." Library of Congress Map Division.

42 *Louisville Morning Herald*, November 1, 1904.

43 George P. Ring to Wife, September 21, 1864, Tulane.

Nineteenth Corps to join in the attack on Crook's left flank. Emory's reluctance to do so granted Gordon enough time to rally his division and resist the continuation of Crook's assault.

When the Second Woods fell to Crook's Federals, Sheridan and some officers of the Nineteenth Corps rode to the front and discussed the unfolding situation from atop some high ground at the western edge of the woods. Sheridan watched Crook's Army of West Virginia and Devin's brigade decimate the Confederates on the Hackwood farm. General Dwight described Sheridan as being "in the height of excitement" as he witnessed the heretofore unprecedented event of the Army of Northern Virginia's Second Corps being driven from a battlefield. The officers were speaking when one of General Averell's aides galloped up to the Irish general and reported that Averell had "been chasing the rebels in from Martinsburg and Bunker Hill all the day." Sheridan ordered Averell to charge, but the aide protested that Averell's "horses couldn't move faster than a walk," as they had "been out many days and nights." Sheridan abruptly cut off the staff officer's excuse with a litany of profanity. "Tell him to charge. Tell him I say charge!" shouted Sheridan. "We've got the rebels on the hip. Tell him we have whipped them on our left and front and that he must charge [on] the right. Do it quick. I don't care a —— for horse flesh today!"[44]

Compared to Merritt, Averell had encountered significantly less resistance throughout the day. Spurred on by Sheridan's orders, he now aggressively advanced on the west side of the Pike against light opposition from the remnants of Smith's, Ferguson's, and Bean's brigades. Colonel James Schoonmaker's brigade advanced with the 22nd Pennsylvania on the right, the 8th Ohio in the center, and the 14th Pennsylvania on the left. When Schoonmaker's men emerged from some woods and saw Confederate troopers in their front, they let out a cheer and charged. Lieutenant Colonel Andrew Greenfield of the 22nd Pennsylvania called out, "Hold on Boys! Hold on," but could not restrain the eager troopers. They surged toward the Confederates and the whole field was "covered with men on horses going at utmost speed at the enemy." The Southerners did not wait to confront the Federal horsemen but

---

44 Gould, *The Civil War Journals of John Mead Gould 1861-1865*, 401; Dwight, Report of Service, NA; George Beal to My Dear General, September 27, 1864, Nick Picerno Collection, Bridgewater, VA.

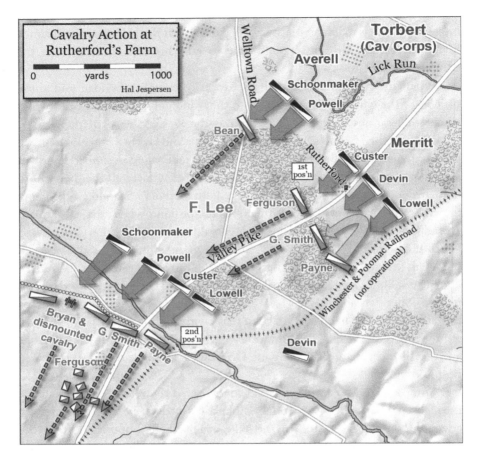

Cavalry Action at
Rutherford's Farm

0   yards   1000
Hal Jespersen

fled and scattered. Schoonmaker's troopers pursued, but many of the Southern horsemen escaped over the heights to the west.[45]

On Schoonmaker's left flank, Col. William H. Powell's West Virginians advanced along the immediate west side of the Pike with Custer on the opposite side of the road. Powell's three West Virginia regiments charged Payne's brigade, leaving the 1st New York Lincoln Cavalry in reserve with Averell. The rapid charges and pursuit had spread Averell's division over a wide front and left him with few organized troopers at hand. The Southerners were nearby, and their bullets flew around Averell. He spotted a section of Bryan's battery deployed behind a stone wall in an open field west of the Pike supported by

45 Samuel C. Farrar, *22nd Pennsylvania*, 374; Colonel George Smith, "Imboden's brigade," October 4, 1864, *Richmond Daily Whig*, October 12, 1864.

rallied elements of George Smith's brigade. Averell summoned a squadron from the 1st New York and quickly charged the guns.[46]

The New Yorkers reported to their general at the front where "bullets were flying thickly about, and every few seconds a shell came plunging through." Averell ignored the danger and attentively watched the Confederate movements. The New Yorkers readied themselves for the charge, battling a strong impulse to rush the gun alone before Averell had finalized his dispositions. The general sensed their restlessness and wisely warned, "Wait, wait; they are too many for you." Averell ordered the squadron commander to dismount his troopers and position them along a stone wall that allowed them to enfilade the Confederate position. The New Yorkers rushed to the position and promptly raked the dismounted Confederates with a hot enfilading fire while the mounted troopers of Powell's and Schoonmaker's brigades exploded into the midst of the Southerners, capturing one cannon, a caisson, and 80 prisoners.[47]

After overrunning Smith's position at the stone wall, Averell quickly regrouped his troopers and got them moving toward Winchester once again. Schoonmaker's brigade raced toward the Star Fort, an earthen fortification on a commanding height about one-half mile from the wall. Some of the Confederate cavalry from Bean's and Smith's brigades had regrouped in and around the bastion. The Tennesseans and Virginians attempted to rally there, but their stand proved short-lived. When Averell gave the order, Schoonmaker led his men in a charge up the ridge that forced the Tennesseans out of the stronghold. The Pennsylvanian did not occupy the fort, choosing instead to regroup his command to continue the attack against the next obstacle: Fort Jackson on the next height immediately west of Winchester.[48]

---

46 William H. Beach, *First New York Cavalry*, 426-7, 429; *OR* 43, pt. 1, 498.

47 West Virginians, Pennsylvanians, and New Yorkers claimed the capture of this gun. Averell attributed the capture to his division. It seems that the 22nd Pennsylvania seized the gun, but that its capture was achieved by the combined actions of Averell's command. *American Tribune*, February 13, 1891; *New York Herald*, September 22, 1864; William H. Beach, *First New York*, 426-7, 429; *OR* 43, pt. 1, 498, Samuel C. Farrar, *22nd Pennsylvania*, 374, 376.

48 James F. Hays, "Battle of Opequon," *National Tribune*, October 24, 1918; William D. Slease, *14th Pennsylvania*, 131-132; Samuel C. Farrar, *22nd Pennsylvania*, 375-377; Schoonmaker was from a wealthy family in Pittsburgh and would become a postwar industrialist. He was awarded the Medal of Honor in 1899 for the charge on Star Fort. Lt. Col. G. L. Gillespie, Map of the Battlefield of Winchester (Opequon), September 19, 1864; *Richmond Whig*, October 12, 1864; Sutton, *2nd West Virginia*, 159-160; Reuben Clark, Memoir, GDAH.

The Tennessee and Virginia horsemen did not stop to offer resistance after abandoning the fort. Instead, these troopers raced out the Pughtown Road and along the backside of the ridge pursued by part of Schoonmaker's brigade. A squad of 25 men from the 14th Pennsylvania Cavalry pursued a group of Confederates behind Winchester past Milroy's Fort toward Tidball's Spring before an officer recalled them.[49]

On Averell's left flank, meanwhile, Powell's West Virginians and Custer's Michigan troopers attacked the remnants of Payne's and Ferguson's Southern brigades along the axis of the Valley Pike. When the blueclad horsemen thundered into effective range, the Virginians triggered a volley, but the effort failed to arrest the determined Yankee horse soldiers. The Virginians refused to wait and engage in hand-to-hand combat, choosing instead to whirl their mounts in the opposite direction and bolt toward Winchester. Some of Custer's and Powell's troopers, although scattered in their burst of success, chased Ferguson's men and the 62nd Virginia Mounted Infantry of George Smith's brigade right into the outskirts of town.[50]

Hundreds of hatless, unarmed, and panic-stricken Confederate cavalrymen rushed "in the wildest disorder" into Winchester closely followed by advance elements of Union cavalry. The Virginians raced down the streets crying, "The Yankees are coming!" to anyone within earshot. Rather than halting to regroup, the horsemen haphazardly surged out of the southern end of Winchester. The appearance of the routed cavalrymen created a panic in the town. "Skulkers, teamsters, drivers, negroes, boys, and fools all fled in wild dismay," confirmed Chaplain John D. Paris. While the disheartened troopers spread panic, Maj. Gen. Robert E. Rodes's body was being prepared for impromptu viewing at the home of Frederick W. M. Holliday, a former colonel who had lost an arm fighting with the Stonewall Brigade at Cedar Mountain in 1862. An Alabama soldier from the quartermaster's department stopped at the home to pay his respects to his fallen commander and found "a great many ladies around his body with tears in their eyes." The soldier struggled vainly to fight back his own tears, but his mourning abruptly ended when the Confederate cavalry rushed through the streets. Several women ran into the house to exclaim, "The Yankees were right in town!" The news prompted the Alabamian and his

49 James F. Hays, "Battle of Opequon," *National Tribune*, October 24, 1918; William D. Slease, *14th Pennsylvania*, 131-132; Samuel C. Farrar, *22nd Pennsylvania*, 375-377.

50 OR 43, pt. 1, 457; *Richmond Daily Whig*, October 12, 1864.

Maj. Gen. John C. Breckinridge, the former Vice President of the United States, led an infantry corps in Jubal Early's Army of the Valley. *LC*

commander to run into the street and mount their horses, where they "witnessed the grandest stampede I ever saw in my life." Bolder elements of Custer's and Powell's brigades had entered the northern outskirts of town and fired "several volleys" down the streets. Officers corralled about 300 Confederates from the wagon guards, stragglers, and other rear echelon troops and deployed them to resist the Federal cavalry. This motley force opened fire and repulsed the Union horsemen. The panic, however, was on.[51]

---

51 Shaffner Diary, 51-52; Mrs. Hugh Lee Diary, WFCHS, Handley Library; G. Ward Hubbs, *Voices*, 313.

When Torbert's horsemen appeared, Jubal Early quickly recognized the threat that the Union cavalry posed to his left flank and rear. Left with little choice, the Virginian committed his last infantry reserves to the fight. Major General John C. Breckinridge led the two remaining brigades of Brig. Gen. Gabriel C. Wharton's division toward the Pike to stave off the disaster developing with the Union horsemen lurking in the rear. Breckinridge had at most only 1,500 men in the small brigades of Col. Thomas Smith and Col. Augustus Forsberg. Breckinridge's men awaited orders behind Cullen Battle's division just outside the western edge of the South Woods. When Early's orders arrived, Breckinridge about-faced Wharton's division with Smith on the left and Forsberg on the right, and headed toward the victorious Federal cavalry bolting up the Pike. The situation facing the Confederates was grim when Wharton's brigades moved forward. Forsberg later recalled that the Valley Pike and the adjoining fields were littered with "wagons, caissons, ambulances, straggling cavalry and infantry, all in a disorderly mass flying before the rapidly approaching cavalry of the enemy."[52]

Breckinridge, Wharton, and some staff officers rode in front of the two brigades as they headed toward the Pike. The command, wrote an observer, swept behind the regrouping survivors from Gordon's and Patton's commands in "splendid style." Breckinridge's move interposed Wharton's division between the retreating Confederates and the approaching Union cavalry, and Wharton's mountaineers "opened a deadly fire on the enemy."

The loud crash of musketry announced to the rest of the army that Wharton's men had joined the battle as Merritt attempted to capitalize on his prior success. Custer's men were closing in on a retreating Confederate battery when Wharton's appearance brought their pursuit to a sudden halt. A soldier in Devin's 4th New York recalled that Wharton's men "got up from behind a stone wall and opened a fearful cross fire upon us, when the enemy in front poured into us volley after volley." The 7th Michigan was pounding up the pike when Wharton's men rose to rake the Federals with a close range volley that ended their charge. Wharton's sudden onslaught caught Merritt's division by surprise. Wharton had his horse shot out from under him, but quickly climbed on his cousin's mount and continued the fight. Braxton's Southern gunners turned their pieces about and fired toward what was once their rear, directly into

---

52 Augustus Forsberg Papers, W&LU; W. W. Stringfield, "69th North Carolina," in Clark, *History of the Several Regiments,*" vol. 3, 753-754; OR 43, pt. 1, 482; Early, *Autobiography,* 425.

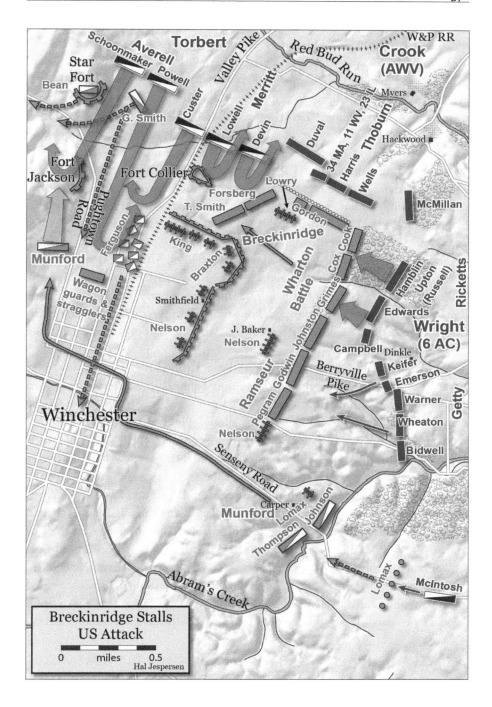

Breckinridge Stalls
US Attack

0   miles   0.5

Hal Jespersen

the midst of the successful but now expended Union cavalry formations. McLaughlin's (King's) artillery battalion also shelled the Union cavalry. Struck by Wharton's men and well-aimed artillery fire, the stunned troopers quickly fell into disorder and withdrew to the shelter of a slight ridge about 1,000 yards from the Confederate line, where they regrouped. Their work was not yet done.

The Union repulse was not limited to Merritt's cavalry division. His withdrawal exposed Averell's left flank to a galling flank fire from part of Wharton's command. Captain Chapman's battery rolled forward with Wharton and deployed in Fort Collier, an old redoubt at the western end of the fence near the Valley Pike. Once unlimbered, Chapman's guns opened fire at Averell's troopers falling back after their mad dash on Winchester and the heights farther west. This Confederate enfilading fire forced the New Yorker to pull back his advance and consolidate his position west of the Pike. Although Breckinridge's advance and the quick action of the troops in Winchester had checked the Union cavalry, the sound of this heavy gunfire in their rear rattled the soldiers of Ramseur's and Battle's divisions, who were still busy confronting the Sixth Corps. Some of these Confederates wavered, and their officers were barely able to maintain order.[53]

With the Union cavalry stalled, at least temporarily, Breckinridge slid Wharton's two small brigades into position behind the stone wall between Patton's remnants and Fort Collier. Wharton's Virginians joined the fight against Crook's infantry. Lieutenant Colonel George Edgar recalled that Gordon's "men took on fresh courage and energy" when Wharton's men moved at the double-quick into a battle line behind the stone wall on Gordon's left. Officers of the broken Confederate infantry and cavalry units used the respite gained by Wharton's advance to regroup. Edgar and Lt. Col. Clarence Derrick rallied a few survivors from the 23rd and 26th Virginia Battalions near the Fort Collier redoubt, while Fitz Lee reformed Payne's brigade near the fort on the Valley Pike. Lee assumed command of the ad hoc force around Fort Collier and assembled as many men as he could. A new Confederate line began to solidify after dodging a catastrophe that only a few minutes before seemed imminent and inevitable. Breckinridge and Wharton, claimed Edgar, had "saved the army from immediate disaster." Without their timely arrival,

53 OR 43, pt. 1, 457, 465, 498; Gabriel C. Wharton to James B. Clay, May 15, 1908, Clay Family Papers, Library of Congress; Early, *Memoir*, 425; William O. Lee, *Personal and Historical Sketches and Facial History of the Seventh Regiment Michigan Volunteer Cavalry, 1862-1865*, 168; *New York Irish American*, October 8, 1864; Wharton to Clay, May 15, 1905, Clay Family Papers, LC.

Torbert's cavalry would have gained the rear of the Second Corps and cut it off from Winchester.[54]

From the heights containing Star Fort, Lt. Col. Andrew Greenfield gathered several hundred scattered troopers from the 14th and 22nd Pennsylvania regiments. Schoonmaker ordered Greenfield to charge the Rebel horsemen regrouping in Fort Jackson atop Fort Hill northwest of Winchester. The Pennsylvanians put spurs to their horses, raced down the eminence, across the Pughtown Road, and galloped up the next hill toward Fort Jackson. The horses struggled up the steep incline, but the troopers gained the crest and, again, routed the Confederate troopers from the weathered earthwork. The rapid advance over the rugged ground, however, scattered Schoonmaker's men in the wake of their success. Unfortunately for them, a fresh and organized Confederate force was on its way to contest Schoonmaker's advance.[55]

When Torbert's cavalry first smashed up the Martinsburg Pike, Jubal Early ordered Col. Thomas Munford to take Wickham's brigade back to the far Southern left to keep the line of retreat open for the Confederate infantry. First, Munford carefully extricated his troops from the Seneseny Road sector without attracting the attention of Brig. Gen. James H. Wilson's division. Although Wilson's docile command displayed some signs of life, Munford successfully pulled out of line without drawing attention and led his four Virginia regiments and a section of horse artillery around the west side of Winchester to the heights known as Fort Hill. When Munford reached the top of the hill, he found Schoonmaker's and Greenfield's troopers in possession of the heights. A small group of Pennsylvanians already occupied Fort Jackson and the rest of the Federal horsemen were scattered across the hill in disorganized fashion.[56]

Munford ordered a saber charge, and the 1st, 2nd, and 3rd Virginia cavalry bolted toward the Pennsylvanians. The Rebels surprised the Federals, ejected them from Fort Jackson, and drove the rest off the hill. Munford dismounted

54 Augustus Forsberg Papers, W&LU; George M. Edgar Papers, "The Battle of Winchester," SHC-UNC.

55 George B. Sanford, Rebels and Redskins, 268-269; William H. Powell, "The Battle of Opequon," *American Tribune*, February 13, 1891; *New York Times*, September 22, 1864; G. L. Gillespie, *Official Atlas of the Civil War* (Gramercy Books, 1983), Map of Battlefield of Winchester, September 19, 1864, Plate 1, page XCIX.

56 Munford, "Reminiscences of Cavalry Operations," 450; Hotchkiss, Sketch and Narrative, "[Munford's Brigade] Winchester—Sept. 19, 1864," in "Sketch book showing positions of Second Corps, A.N.Va. in engagements of 1864-5," Library of Congress Map Division.

the three regiments, leaving the horses with the 4th Virginia. The 1st and 2nd Virginia occupied the fort and surrounding rifle pits and waited for the next Federal attack. Captain John J. Shoemaker followed the cavalry up the hill with two guns from Stuart's Horse Artillery, which he promptly deployed and fired into the thick masses of Union infantry and cavalry on the plains below. Although Shoemaker had only two pieces, his men fired rapidly and disrupted the advance of both Torbert's cavalry and Crook's infantry.

After ejecting Schoonmaker from Fort Jackson, Munford deployed the 3rd Virginia cavalry into position to the right of the fort to cover the gap between the ridge and Smithfield Redoubt, a breastwork covering the northern edge of Winchester. There, the 3rd Virginia prevented Powell's brigade from severing Munford's cavalry on Fort Hill from the rest of Early's army. Schoonmaker attempted to dislodge Munford, but lost several officers from the 14th Pennsylvania in the process, including its commander Capt. Ashbell Duncan.[57]

Soon, Jubal Early galloped up Fort Hill to survey the situation. As he rode along the heights, he realized his army had narrowly avoided destruction. Still, his forces remained dangerously exposed due to his reallocation of forces from his right flank to his left and rear. Cullen Battle sent his division's sharpshooter battalion to Smithfield Redoubt behind Wharton's position. As previously discussed, Early had ordered Lomax to send Munford's brigade and Shoemaker's artillery to Fort Jackson on the heights behind Winchester to keep it out of the hands of Averell. These moves were not without risk, as Munford's departure left Lomax with only Lt. Col. William Thompson's (Mudwall Jackson's) and Brig. Gen. Bradley Johnson's brigades to guard the army's line of retreat on the right. Jubal Early had no other choice as Averell might very well cut off the Confederate line of retreat from the back side of Winchester if the vital heights had remained unoccupied. Early had to take chances, as he simply lacked the assets needed to address the multiple threats confronting his army. And now that Sheridan's infantry renewed its efforts, "Old Jube" could do little more than watch and wait for the inevitable.

---

57 Fort Hill is best known as the site of Brig. Gen. Robert H. Milroy's extensive earthen fortifications. However, the commanding heights also contained Fort Jackson, which the Rebels built on the northeastern part of the hill in 1861. Munford, "Reminiscences of Cavalry Operations," *Southern Historical Society Papers*, XIII (1885), 450; Hubard, Memoir, UVA.; John J. Shoemaker, *Shoemaker's Battery*, 79; Hotchkiss, Sketch and Narrative, "[Munford's Brigade] Winchester—Sept. 19, 1864," contained in "Sketch book showing positions of Second Corps, A.N.Va. in engagements of 1864-5," Library of Congress Map Division.

Chapter 19

PRESS THEM GENERAL ... I KNOW THEY'LL RUN

The Final Union Attack

As soon as Colonel Thoburn initiated his attack, Phil Sheridan rushed to throw his entire army into the contest. Sheridan dispatched staff officer Maj. George "Sandy" Forsyth with orders for Maj. Gen. Horatio Wright, commander of the Union Sixth Corps, to "act in concert with Crook." As Forsyth rode from Thoburn's position toward the Berryville Pike, he saw Brig. Gen. Emory Upton, now commanding Russell's division, and told him that General Crook was advancing on the right. Hearing this, the combative Upton leapt into action. His division occupied an advanced position on the left of the Nineteenth Corps and was within rifle range of the Confederate line. However, Upton devoted his primary attention to his right wing during the initial stages of the renewed assault because that area was the focal point of the attack. Upton was a man who knew where the action was and made sure that he would be in on the kill.[1]

---

1 OR 43, pt. 1, 162, 169; Sheridan, *Memoirs*, vol. 2, 24-25. Emory Upton's creative tactical plan at Spotsylvania, where he urged his superiors to use a column-based formation rather than linear tactics, pierced the Confederate line on May 10, 1864, but was ultimately unsuccessful because of a lack of support.

Upton's brigades had become considerably intermixed during Russell's fateful counterattack. The 2nd Connecticut and 65th New York of Col. Joseph Hamblin's (Upton's) brigade held on the extreme right of the line. Then Col. Oliver Edwards's 37th Massachusetts and 2nd Rhode Island Battalion continued the line to the left where it linked with the 121st New York of Hamblin's brigade. The aforementioned stretch of Upton's battle line operated as an informal brigade under his direct command. Here the position stretched from a triangular patch of scrub and brush pines that formed the southwestern point of the First Woods into the open grasslands of the Middle Field. The line rested within easy rifle range of the Confederates posted in the South Woods, and his right flank extended in advance of the Nineteenth Corps, which remained in the First Woods to Upton's right and rear.

The balance of Upton's division deployed on the south side of the Dinkle Ravine and operated under the effective control of Col. Oliver Edwards, the division's senior brigadier. The 15th New Jersey of Lt. Col. Edward Campbell's brigade manned the right of this line, with the 5th Wisconsin Battalion and the 49th, 82nd, and 119th Pennsylvania regiments of Edwards's brigade extending the line to the left across the open grounds of the Dinkle farmstead. The few hundred remaining men of Campbell's New Jersey brigade manned the division's left flank. Brigadier General James Ricketts's division filled out the line between Campbell's left and the Berryville Pike.

The portion of the division operating with Edwards held a difficult position during the coming attack. In its immediate front, the North Carolina brigades of Brig. Gens. Bryan Grimes and Robert Johnston presented a solid front with a thick line of sharpshooters posted in Mr. Dinkle's fields. The main Confederate battle line rested several hundred yards away at the far end of the Dinkle farm. Two Confederate batteries were in position behind the infantry in the fringes of a narrow strip of woods that separated the Dinkle and Baker farms. On Edwards's right front, Cox's brigade occupied a position in the western portion of the South Woods with a heavy line of skirmishers nearer the eastern edge of the timber. This gave Cox the ability to enfilade Edwards's right flank if he advanced too far into the open field.

When Thoburn charged the First Woods, Upton pushed Hamblin's brigade into action in front of the South Woods. His regiments attacked in echelon beginning on the right flank. Colonel Ranald Mackenzie placed his hat on the point of his sword and rode out in front of the 2nd Connecticut and ordered a charge. He led the unit through the Middle Field toward Cook's Georgians who were posted behind a fence running along the eastern face of

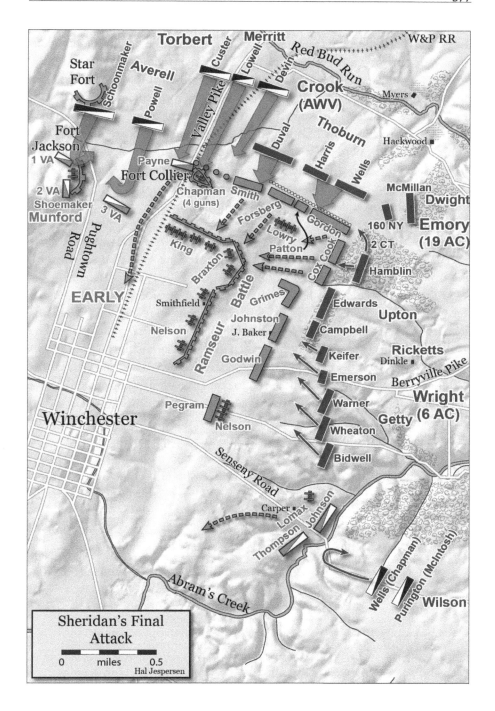

Star Fort
Schoonmaker
Torbert
Averell
Powell
Custer
Merritt
Lowell
Devin
Red Bud Run
W&P RR
Crook
(AWV)
Myers ∙
Valley Pike
Thoburn
Fort Jackson
1 VA
Payne
Fort Collier
Chapman
(4 guns)
Smith
Duval
Harris
Wells
Hackwood ∙
McMillan
Dwight
2 VA
Shoemaker
Munford
3 VA
Forsberg
Lowry
Gordon
160 NY
2 CT
Emory
(19 AC)
King
Patton
Cox
Cook
Hamblin
Pughtown Road
EARLY
Braxton
Battle
Grimes
Edwards
Upton
Smithfield ∙
Johnston
Campbell
Nelson
Ramseur
J. Baker ∙
Keifer
Dinkle ∙
Ricketts
Godwin
Emerson
Berryville Pike
Pegram
Warner
Wright
Winchester
Nelson
Wheaton
Getty (6 AC)
Bidwell
Senseny Road
Carper ∙
Lomax
Johnson
Thompson
Abram's Creek
Wells (Chapman)
Purington (McIntosh)
Wilson

Sheridan's Final
Attack

0   miles   0.5
Hal Jespersen

the South Woods. As the regiment marched across the field, the rifle fire from Cook's troops took a heavy toll on the Connecticut men. Mackenzie's troops pressed forward and charged up to the fence line, firing at Cook's Georgians as they went. On Mackenzie's left, Col. Joseph Hamblin continued the attack with the 65th New York. The New Yorkers encountered heavy initial resistance from the right wing of Cook's brigade, but kept up a rapid fire of their own. Company C of the 65th New York carried repeating rifles and plied them with vigor against the Georgians. Mackenzie saw Hamblin's struggles in the Middle Field and swung the right battalion of the 2nd Connecticut to the left. The realigned battalion unleashed a deadly enfilade fire that pried the Georgians from their position. Private Lewis Bissell from Mackenzie's regiment told his father that the Confederates were soon "running for dear life—that is, those who did not fall." The 65th New York felt the pressure ease, charged forward, and captured a large number of Cook's Georgians.[2]

After Crook launched his attack, Sheridan rode along the Army of the Shenandoah's battle line toward the Berryville Pike. He dashed behind the engaged troops in Hamblin's brigade at a full gallop and then rode along the line of Edwards's brigade, swinging his sword in the air and exhorting his troops onward. "It was a most inspiring scene," related Capt. Mason W. Tyler of the 37th Massachusetts. "We were not used to seeing a commanding general on the front line of battle, and the exploding shells and whistling bullets added excitement to the scene." A Rhode Island captain recalled that "the whole army cheered and shouted itself hoarse," when Sheridan appeared.[3]

Spurred on by Phil Sheridan's inspiring presence, the stretch of Upton's line comprised of the 37th Massachusetts, 2nd Rhode Island, and 121st New York now entered the fray. Shortly before 4:00 p.m., this sector of Upton's

2   OR 43, pt. 1, 162, 164, 179; Lewis Bissell to Dear Father, September 21, 1864; William R. Cox, *Address on the Life and Character of Maj. Gen. Stephen D. Ramseur* (Raleigh: E. M. Uzzell, 1891), 38-41; Julius L. Schaub, Memoir, Troupe County, GA Historical Society; "The Battle of Winchester," *Providence Daily Journal*, September 30, 1864.

3   As Sheridan rode along the battle line, his neckerchief fell off and was picked up by a Wisconsin officer of Edwards's brigade. Captain Miles L. Butterfield of the 5th Wisconsin returned the neckerchief or "necktie" to Sheridan after the active campaign ended with a note asking Sheridan's permission to retain the souvenir. Sheridan sent it back, saying "I will be glad if you will keep it." Rhodes, *All For the Union: The Civil War Diary and Letters of Elisha Hunt Rhodes*, 185-186; Mason Whiting Tyler, *Recollections of the Civil War*, 278; *Springfield Daily Republican*, September 29, 1864; Miles L. Butterfield, "Personal Reminiscences with the VI Corps," Wisconsin MOLLUS, 4:86-87; OR 43, pt. 1, 189.

division advanced directly toward the South Woods and attacked Cox's North Carolinians. The 37th Massachusetts already occupied an advanced position in the Middle Field that gave them an enfilading fire on Cox's troops who were posted in an advanced portion of the South Woods. Armed with Spencer rifles, these Bay State soldiers and the men in the adjacent 2nd Rhode Island Battalion did the bulk of the work against Cox's brigade.

When Upton's division advanced, the North Carolinians found themselves in a salient, vulnerable to attack on three sides. Cox further complicated his situation by clinging stubbornly to his position even after his commander, Brig. Gen. Cullen Battle, urged a withdrawal. Instead, Cox held his position until the break in the Confederate line extended right up to his brigade. His men resisted Upton's assault behind fences, thickets, and rifle pits along the edge of the South Woods. Cox realized the urgency of Battle's order when Lt. Col. George Montague's 37th Massachusetts raked the Tar Heels' left flank. Simultaneously, the 2nd Rhode Island and 121st New York volleyed into the front of the Confederate line. Flanked and having already suffered heavy casualties during Rodes's earlier counterattack, Cox's brigade fell back fighting through the timber. As the Federals moved through the woods in the wake of Cox's withdrawal, Montague's 37th Massachusetts cut off and captured several groups of Confederates fleeing southward.[4]

On the Berryville Pike, Maj. Gen. Horatio G. Wright's Sixth Corps's officers had reorganized the jumbled ranks of Ricketts's and Getty's divisions as well as the situation allowed. Both of these divisions had lost heavily in the late morning assault. In particular, Ricketts's division and Getty's Vermont brigade had fallen into considerable disorder. When Ricketts's command rejoined the final battle line, it occupied only a fraction of the space it had held during the opening assault due to casualties and stragglers. For those troops on the firing line, the corps's ordnance department distributed a fresh supply of ammunition, all while lying under a heavy artillery fire from the Confederate

---

4 As noted earlier in Chapter 16, Edwards and Bowen disagree on the timing of the capture of the 2nd Virginia's battle flag. Bowen places it during the repulse of the Rodes-Gordon counterattack, while Edwards recalled its loss during the final charge. It may be that the flag was captured in the woods at this time. *OR* 43, pt. 1, 169, 177, 184-185; Oliver Edwards, "Their Heroic Past Recalled," *Springfield Republican*, September 20, 1893; Bowen, *History of the Thirty Seventh Massachusetts Volunteers*, 377, 379; *Our Living and Our Dead*, March 4, 1874; Mason W. Tyler, *Recollections of the Civil War*, 278; Isaac O. Best, *History of the 121st New York State Infantry*, 182l; William R. Cox, *Address on the Life and Character of Maj. Gen. Stephen D. Ramseur* (Raleigh: E. M. Uzzell, 1891), 38-41.

gunners. To protect the infantry, Col. Charles C. Tompkins strategically deployed his artillery along open ground on either side of the Berryville Pike. His gunners demanded instant attention from their Confederate counterparts of Nelson's Battalion.

Wright reported that when he saw Crook's successful advance on the right, he "at once ordered forward the Nineteenth and Sixth Corps," even before he received Sheridan's orders to do so via Major Forsyth. However, when Sheridan arrived on the line about 40 minutes after Crook attacked, the Sixth Corps, with the exception of Upton's right wing, had not moved. What might have seemed swift to Wright paled in comparison to the rapid work of Crook and Upton. It took significant time and the impetus of Phil Sheridan before the divisions of Getty and Ricketts of the Sixth Corps launched into action.[5]

Sheridan crossed the Dinkle Ravine and entered the farmstead bearing the same name. A multitude of troops from both Upton's and Ricketts's divisions were lying in line of battle trading shots with Ramseur's and Grimes's Confederates. The army commander streaked past the infantrymen, waving his hat overhead and yelling, "Give them hell, my men!" The invigorated Wisconsin, Pennsylvania, and New Jersey riflemen responded with thunderous cheers. When he reached the soldiers of the 49th Pennsylvania, he yelled, "The only way to do [it] is kill every son of a bitch," before he bolted away "like a streak of lightning." Even more, noted John C. Arnold of the 49th Pennsylvania, Sheridan "seemed to be smiling all the time and such cheering I had never heard before." Sheridan didn't stop but swept past the Dinkle house and came upon Ricketts's motionless division. "We are in a fair way to win the day," shouted Sheridan to some fellow Ohioans. His rousing appearance in the midst of the troops on the firing line "put the men in good spirits, and show[ed] us that he was not afraid of bullets." The foot soldiers again responded with vociferous cheers, and their officers gave the order to attack.[6]

Sheridan continued along the front lines with "his face aglow with excitement, the perspiration rolling down his forehead." His horse galloped along the Sixth Corps's skirmish line "at a terrible speed" until he crossed the Berryville Pike. He then turned to his left and raced back toward the main battle

---

5 Emory Upton, it should be remembered, plunged into the fight with General Crook on his own without any instructions from Generals Wright or Sheridan to do so. OR 43, pt. 1, 150.

6 *Lancaster Gazette*, October 20, 1864; Report of Lt. Col. Otho H. Binkley, 110th Ohio; OR 43, pt. 1, 258; John C. Arnold to Dear Wife and Family, September 23, 1864.

line, exhorting his cheering men as he went. The army commander dashed up to Brig. Gen. George W. Getty and stated firmly, "General, I have put Torbert on the right, and told him to give 'em hell, and he is doing it. Crook too is on the right and giving it to them. Press them General, they'll run!" Sheridan added more of his spicy, inspirational profanity, then stared intently at Getty with his piercing black eyes and added with conviction, "Press them, General, I know they'll run!"[7]

Wright soon had the entire Sixth Corps tramping toward the Confederates posted astride the Berryville Pike. The advance began from a line that rested a few yards west of the Dinkle barn. Building upon Upton's initial advance on the right, Wright's forward movement started on the right flank of Edwards's brigade with the 15th New Jersey. Edwards's Wisconsin and Pennsylvania troops conformed to the advance and were soon joined on the left by Campbell's two small New Jersey battalions, the entire line sweeping over the undulating farm fields. The South Woods on the opposite side of the chasm were cleared when Upton drove off Cox's brigade, so Edwards advanced without worry for his right flank. He headed directly toward Grimes's North Carolinians posted at the far end of the field on some high ground in front of a thin strip of woods. The Carolinians fired, but the collapse of Cox's brigade on the left rendered their resistance futile. Under pressure in his front, Grimes withdrew his brigade by 4:30 p.m. and fell back through the woods. When they entered the open ground around the Baker house, Grimes's Carolinians saw the chaos and "began to show symptoms of alarm." A furious Bryan Grimes grimly rode among his troops with a drawn revolver and assured them that he would "blow the brains out of the first man who left the ranks." The bold move worked, and his brigade deployed around George Baker's brick house to resist the Union assault.[8]

Moving forward in conjunction with Edwards, the balance of the Sixth Corps attacked Ramseur's division posted astride the Berryville Pike. Brigadier General Robert Johnston's brigade and the left wing of Brig. Gen. Archibald Godwin's brigade waited for Ricketts to attack at the western end of the field. At least eight cannon backed up the infantry from a position along the edge of a narrow strip of woods that separated the Dinkle and Baker farms. Just before

---

7 "The Vermont Brigade in the Battles of Winchester and Fisher's Hill," *Vermont Chronicle*, October 15, 1864; George T. Stevens, *Three Years in the VI Corps*, 401.

8 Bryan Grimes, *Extracts of Letters*, 68-70.

Confederate Brig. Gen. Bryan Grimes led a brigade in Jubal Early's
Army of the Valley. *LC*

the attack began, Ricketts galloped up to some of his troops and told them that
all he needed them to do was "to sweep over the hill in our front and then the
Rebels "will run like the devil." With Col. J. Warren Keifer's brigade on the right
and Col. William Emerson's command on the left, Ricketts's division picked up
the general advance and extended it to the Berryville Pike. Unlike Upton's

advance, Ricketts's command received a destructive fire from the Rebel batteries that Nelson had in position at the far end of the line. Nevertheless, his troops closed in, and Johnston's brigade and Godwin's left wing had no choice other than to withdraw and conform to Grimes's movements. As the North Carolinians hastily abandoned their position in the field, Ricketts's men opened fire. "We pressed close after them," reported Corp. William T. McDougle of the 126th Ohio, "and poured cold lead in their rear as fast as powder would drive it."[9]

Just before Getty advanced, Sheridan continued his ride along the battle line all the way to the far left infantry position. Along the way he roused the Pennsylvanians of Brig. Gen. Frank Wheaton's brigade and stopped in front of Bidwell's brigade. Sheridan took off his cap and shouted, "Boys go in . . . I have the cavalry in their rear, and now, boys, give them h—l." Wrote Capt. Samuel Davidson of the 43rd New York, "Away we went, as if the lower regions were actually let loose, and I tell you we drove them mighty lively." Getty's three brigades moved against the right wing of Godwin's brigade and the Virginians of Pegram's brigade south of the Berryville Pike. Tompkins's artillery had pounded the Southern position incessantly prior to the attack. His twelve-pound Napoleon cannons shelled Ramseur's infantry, while the rifled guns focused their attention on the Rebel batteries in order to suppress the enemy fire against the U.S. infantry. Although the Southern infantry was vastly outgunned by Getty's legions, the rugged terrain and skillful support of the Confederate artillery evened the odds on this sector of the battlefield.[10]

The Southern artillery proved to be the biggest obstacle to Getty's success. Several hundred yards off to Getty's left flank, two rifled cannon from Lomax's horse artillery sat upon a hillock at Carper's farm on the Senseney Road, supported by Thompson's Confederate cavalry brigade. A lack of threatening activity on the part of Wilson's cavalry division in front of Lomax permitted the gunners to devote their full attention upon Getty's lines. They "fearfully enfiladed" his division from the left as it advanced over the rough ground. At the same time, Nelson's battalion pounded the Sixth Corps from the front. Nelson and his battery commanders operated their gun crews so as to create a crossfire that enfiladed the advancing lines of Getty and Ricketts. Lieutenant

9 *Lancaster Gazette*, October 20, 1864.

10 OR 43, pt. 1, 162, 197-198; *Providence Daily Journal*, September 30, 1864; *Daily Knickerbocker*, September 28, 1864.

Colonel John B. Koehler of the 98th Pennsylvania wrote how the Confederate shells, "with a hellish voice, plunged into our lines, tore up the ground and in bursting scattered death among the men."[11]

Although the Southern artillery slowed Wright's assault, the collapse of the line north of the Berryville Pike ultimately forced Godwin and Pegram to fall back toward Winchester. The advancing U.S. battle line presented a daunting spectacle to the Southerners. Private George Q. Peyton of the 13th Virginia of Pegram's brigade admired the approaching blue ranks "moving forward in grand style, their flags were all unfurled, and the officers were all riding in front of their line hearkening them on." He even spotted a dog barking and running excitedly back and forth along the front of one of Getty's regiments as the blue line closed in.[12]

While Ramseur's men held their position in Dinkle's Woods, the sounds of the battle closing in on their left and rear began to unnerve them. To Private Peyton, the "artillery sounded like thunder and the musketry like artillery." When "great crowds of stragglers" from Gordon and Battle ran from the left, Ramseur and his men knew "the jig was up." They fell back through the woods and into the open plain in front of Winchester. Pegram called for volunteers to slow the advancing Federals and deployed them on a sacrificial skirmish line on the Burgess farm. Ramseur personally positioned one of Nelson's cannon and directed its fire into the approaching blue ranks to cover the retreat. Before the Yankee gunners could get the range, Ramseur led the piece to another position and resumed shelling.[13]

As Ramseur's troops withdrew, Brig. Gen. Archibald A. Godwin rode up to Maj. John Beard and praised his handling of the 57th North Carolina, Godwin's old command, in stemming the Union advance along the Berryville Pike. While the two men spoke, a shell burst overhead and killed Godwin instantly. Beard saw a "convulsive movement of the General's limbs," caught him as he fell, and laid him on the ground. Godwin's adjutant had him carried to the home of Mrs. Octavia Long, who had accompanied the General to church on the previous evening. He was later buried in Winchester's Mount Hebron

---

11 J. B. Kohler to My Dear Son and Daughter, October 4, 1864, Handley Library, Winchester, VA.

12 George Q. Peyton, "A Civil War Record for 1864-1865," Bull Run Regional Library, Manassas, VA, 82-83.

13 Ibid.

Cemetery only a few hundred yards from where he fell. Lieutenant Colonel Anderson Ellis assumed command and kept the troops in line. At Ramseur's direction, he placed them on the right flank of Early's line along the eastern and southeastern fringes of Winchester.

While the Sixth Corps pushed ahead along the Berryville Pike, Crook's Army of West Virginia hammered Jubal Early's left flank back at a 90-degree angle for three-quarters of a mile. Breckinridge's counterstrike bought time for survivors from John Gordon's division and George Patton's brigade to regroup on Gabriel Wharton's right flank behind a rock fence that ran perpendicularly to the Martinsburg Pike. It also formed a right angle with the main portion of the Confederate line that faced the Sixth Corps. Lieutenant Colonel Carter Braxton skillfully posted his guns at intervals along the wall with the infantry. On Breckinridge's left flank, four guns from Capt. George B. Chapman's Monroe (Virginia) Battery fired away from behind formidable earthen ramparts at Fort Collier. The ad-hoc force of horsemen and foot soldiers under the direction of Fitz Lee continued to support Chapman's cannon. Behind Gordon's division, Capt. William M. Lowry's guns of the Wise Legion Artillery deployed in a lunette constructed upon a slight rise of ground and blasted away at the approaching Union foot soldiers.[14]

Colonel George D. Wells's brigade of Thoburn's division had enthusiastically spearheaded the pursuit of Gordon's troops through the Second Woods and over the open fields of Hackwood. On his left, the 10th West Virginia and 116th Ohio chased pockets of Confederates through the Second Woods toward the Sixth Corps. With the 5th New York and 123rd Ohio, Wells led the Union forces into the open ground. When the Union troops charged straight ahead toward Hackwood, Breckinridge's Confederates peppered Thoburn's left flank with an accurate enfilading fire, but the Unionists did not falter. Thoburn ordered his command to change their direction toward the source of the incoming fire, but he instantly saw that his men already understood the situation. "The instincts of the soldier prompted the proper movement before my commands could be conveyed," reported Thoburn, "Each man was marching and facing toward the enemy's fire." Wells's brigade moved against the new Southern position, but Gordon's rapidly regrouping Georgians, Louisianans, and Virginians blasted the Federal brigade with a

---

14 OR 43, pt. 1, 376; George Edgar Papers, "Third Battle of Winchester," SHC-UNC; Milton Humphreys, Reminiscences, UVA; Hotchkiss Sketchbook, Library of Congress Map Division.

deadly rifle fire. At the same time, Wharton's Virginians, North Carolinians, and Tennesseans aimed their guns to their right and laced Wells's right flank. The focused Confederate fire stalled Wells's advance as his troops dropped to the ground behind a low stone fence in front of Gordon's position.[15]

On Wells's left flank, Lt. Col. Thomas F. Wildes's 116th Ohio exited the woods and attempted to jumpstart the advance. Again, blistering rifle fire from Gordon's men forced the Buckeyes to halt their advance and seek shelter behind the same wall that covered Wells's other troops. The 116th Ohio's color-bearer, Corp. Henry T. Johnson, raced out in front of the wall under the galling fire, waved the regimental colors, and challenged his comrades to follow him. Wildes ordered Johnson back to the regiment, but he defiantly yelled, "Bring your regiment to the colors, Colonel Wildes, for I'll be [damned] if this flag retreats while I carry it." A Rebel bullet shattered one Johnson's arms, but he tenaciously clung to his advanced position. His comrades always remembered the "rage in every fine feature of his beardless, blood-stained, and begrimed face" as he stood between the opposing battle lines urging his comrades forward "with the battle-scarred and riddled banner streaming over his bare head" and blood soaking his coat and streaming down his pants. Eventually, several comrades sprinted out and hauled him to safety where they waited for the stalemate to break.[16]

Colonel Thomas M. Harris's brigade had followed Wells during the initial advance across the Middle Field. After the 10th West Virginia swung into the woods on Wells's left, the 54th Pennsylvania and 15th West Virginia trailed Thoburn's vanguard into the fields of Hackwood farm. These regiments swept behind Wells's line, swung around his right flank, and charged toward Wharton's position. Once again, the Virginians rose up behind the stone wall and delivered a devastating volley into the Federals that stopped them cold and seriously wounded Lt. Col. John Linton, commander of the 54th Pennsylvania. The Pennsylvanians and West Virginians could go no farther and sank behind the protective shelter of the low wall in front of Breckinridge's position.[17]

In spite of the heavy resistance from Breckinridge's corps, Crook's soldiers continuously piled into the fight and ratcheted up the pressure on the

15 OR 43, pt. 1, 368-369.

16 James M. Dalzell, *Private Dalzell: His Autobiography, Poems and Comic War Papers* (Cincinnati: Robert Clarke & Co., 1888), 97.

17 *OR*, 43, pt. 1, 389.

Confederates. When the Federals plunged into the Second Woods, Harris realized that the three regiments which Thoburn had fronted northward along Red Bud Run had not advanced. The West Virginian galloped back toward the creek and pulled up in front of the 11th West Virginia, 23rd Illinois, and 34th Massachusetts "like a mad man shouting 'come on boys' and swinging his broadsword over his head." "Come on we have routed them," yelled Harris, "the day is ours. Charge boys charge!" The regiments followed him through the woods as quickly as the dense tangle along Red Bud Run permitted. They soon encountered a deep ravine on their left flank that separated them from the rest of Thoburn's division to their left. The gully eventually wrapped around their front where it drained into Red Bud Run, further slowing their advance; however, Harris and the regimental officers kept moving them ahead enthusiastically. As they trudged forward, Harris observed "large portions" of Duval's command retracing its steps along the north bank of Red Bud Run in search of a place to cross the mire. These troops found a suitable ford at the point Harris's troops had just passed and crossed to the south bank of Red Bud Run. There, they reformed their ranks and followed Harris's column into the fight.[18]

The three regiments with Harris emerged from the woods, swung around to the left, and tried to extend the Union battle line toward the Martinsburg Pike. Heavy rifle fire from Breckinridge's corps and the exploding projectiles from the Rebel artillery stalled Harris's advance 150 yards shy of Thoburn's line. The 34th Massachusetts ascended a hill and absorbed a tremendous volley from the opposing Confederates. One Bay State soldier never forgot the "vivid sheet of fire, like the burning, blinding lightning's glare, [that] ran along the front [of the wall] and a deadly storm of grape and bullets." Major Harrison W. Pratt of the 34th Massachusetts called out, "I don't know about standing under such a fire without orders," as the Bay State soldiers hit the ground.[19]

Harris pushed the 11th West Virginia and the 23rd Illinois battalion forward on the right of the Bay State regiment only to be predictably pinned down by Wharton's Confederates. Colonel Isaac Duval's division then rolled into position on Thoburn's right flank. Wharton's men greeted them with the

18 Ibid., pt. 1, 386; William B. Stark Diary, Typescript copy in possession of author.

19 William S. Lincoln, *Life with the 34th Massachusetts Infantry in the War of the Rebellion* (Worcestor, MA: Noyes, Snow and Co., 1879), 356; J. Chapin Warner to Dear Father and Mother, September 21, 1864, Massachusetts Historical Society.

This Alfred Waud sketch depicts the combat with John Gordon's and Gabriel Wharton's Southern divisions reformed behind the stone wall running perpendicular to the Berryville Pike. George Crook's Federals are attacking in the foreground, with Horatio Wright's Sixth Corps advancing on the distant left. *A. R. Waud, LC*

same withering rifle fire from the front and the enfilading fire from Chapman's battery at Fort Collier.[20]

Breckinridge's infantry and Carter's artillery took a deadly toll on Crook's troops as they struggled to continue their attack. In McLaughlin's (King's) battalion, Lowry's gunners fired so rapidly that they soon used up all their ammunition and then retired from the field. In Braxton's battalion, Carpenter's battery likewise expended so much of its ammunition that its captain sent two guns to the rear. As a result of these efforts, the resilient Army of the Valley District stopped Crook cold after his initial success. As of 4:30 p.m., Jubal Early still had a chance to hold the field and withdraw his army under cover of the approaching darkness.

In spite of the tremendous Confederate fire, Crook, Thoburn, and Duval bravely urged their men forward. They rushed small squads of soldiers to

---

20 William Adney, Report of the Battle of Winchester, John T. Booth Papers, OHS.

shallow hollows and rock ledges in advance of the Army of West Virginia's position. From their newfound cover, they fired on Breckinridge's Confederates, drawing the Confederate fire away from the main line and permitting more of their comrades to advance. In this way, Crook steadily closed in and increased the pressure on Breckinridge. Under heavy fire, Crook and his officers galloped up and down his battle line "as cool as if he was sitting at home." Unlike Sheridan, Crook said little, but his calming presence charged the men with electricity. Regardless of bravery, it was clear that the blue line was going nowhere without help. The optimism that dominated Crook's ranks only moments before began to wane. "We was too weak to advance further without assistance," admitted a volunteer from the 9th West Virginia Infantry. The effect of the fire on Duval's men was not lost on the Confederates. They noted how their "showers of leaden hail" had dropped hundreds of Federals in front of the stone wall. A Virginia officer of Patton's brigade recalled that the fire of Breckinridge's Corps made "the hills blue" with the dead and wounded of Crook's command.[21]

21 George M. Edgar, "The Battle of Winchester, September 19, 1864, called also the Battle of the Opequon," UNC; *Springfield Daily Republican*, September 29, 1864.

Breckinridge had Crook pinned down and in need of assistance. The very man to provide the sorely needed aid was already on the move. Emory Upton's division had cleared Cook and Cox from the South Woods and reached the western edge. There they came under fire from Confederate artillery posted in Smithfield Redoubt on the outskirts of Winchester. The Confederate guns rained fire and iron on the Union troops in the woods and severely hampered their movement. Undaunted, Upton peered out across the plain in front of the woods and saw the damage that Breckinridge's corps was inflicting upon Crook. Upton perceived that the solution to the problem was already in position off to his right and rear in the southwest corner of the Second Woods. Colonel Stephen Thomas and the 8th Vermont and 12th Connecticut of Brig. Gen. James McMillan's brigade had halted in the Second Woods. If Thomas advanced again, he would strike the right flank of the Confederate line directly. Unfortunately, Maj. Gen. William H. Emory peremptorily forbade McMillan's men from advancing any farther. Memories of Grover's ill-fated attack had apparently dampened Emory's enthusiasm for a further advance. Upton dashed up to Colonel Thomas and urged him to attack the exposed Confederates in his front. Thomas refused, and Upton flew into a rage.[22]

General Crook simultaneously spied Thomas's opportunity to break the stalemate and rode over to confer as well. When the Ohioan arrived, he found Upton "nearly crying, he was so mad" at Emory's senseless orders. Upton begged Crook to lodge formal charges against Emory and referred to him as "a damned old coward." The demure Crook simply urged Thomas to help resuscitate the stalled attack. Neither Upton's ranting nor Crook's gentle persuasion moved the Vermonter to action. His lack of ammunition and fear of Emory's retribution exceeded his desire to aid comrades from another corps. Upton returned to his troops, stewed briefly, then turned around and raced over to Crook and raved that Thomas was "a damned coward."[23]

Crook rode back to Thomas and attempted to use Upton's charge of cowardice to motivate the New Englander. Thomas bristled at the accusation, and his face flushed red in anger. Crook calmly reassured the Vermonter that he doubted Upton's charge, and added that an immediate advance by Thomas would eliminate any doubts about his personal bravery. A startled Thomas shot back, "Do you want me to go in without my Generals?" Crook coolly told

22 Schmidt, *Crook*, 128; See Upton's report, OR 43, pt. 1, 162-165.

23 Schmidt, *Crook*, 128.

Thomas, "This is no time to be hunting up generals," and rode off without saying another word, leaving Thomas clinging to his orders. Unbeknownst to Upton, Crook, and Thomas, General McMillan was at that very moment bringing up reinforcements to assist Crook.[24]

Brigadier General Emory Upton was not a man to sit back and watch his comrades in arms die needlessly if he could do something about it. He took the matter into his own hands and promptly notified Crook that the Sixth Corps would come to his aid. He assigned 24-year-old Col. Ranald "Band Hand" Mackenzie to the task. This fearless Regular Army officer was the son and brother of naval officers and a great-great-grandson of William Alexander (aka Earl of Stirling, or Lord Stirling), who served as a major general in the Continental Army during the American Revolution. Mackenzie rode out in front of the 2nd Connecticut, led it to the right, and marched through the open field in front of Thomas's resting brigade. Mackenzie's troops quickly slid into position behind a rail fence. He ordered them to open fire and "for ten minutes they had the privilege of pouring an effective fire into the rebels who were thick in front." Mackenzie's men enfiladed Gordon's right flank and loosened the Georgian's grip on the stone wall. General McMillan brought up the 160th New York with replenished cartridge boxes. The New Yorkers rushed through the Second Woods, crossed the open ground to the south, and then entered the South Woods. There, Col. Van Patten's New Yorkers deployed to Mackenzie's right flank and further damaged Gordon's right flank with a concentrated enfilade fire. When Thoburn's division saw the Rebels retreating, they leapt the wall and attacked. Crook's entire corps took up the charge from left to right. His left joined Upton's right, effectively sealing the recalcitrant Nineteenth Corps out of the fight.[25]

Gordon's discomfiture occurred as Battle's division withdrew toward Winchester in varying states of confusion and disorder. As the Southerners retreated, Upton pushed his division into the fight, shouting, "Come on gallant fellows, we are whipping them at every point." As Upton passed the western edge of the woods, a rebel bullet unhorsed him, but he quickly mounted another. As his troops entered the open ground, they encountered a heavy fire directed at their left flank by Bryan Grimes's Carolinians posted upon the high

24 Ibid.

25 OR 43, pt. 1, 162, 164, 177; Vaill, *The County Regiment*, 53-54; www.williamsclub.org/artlit/index.html.

ground containing the Baker house. Upton reacted instantly by instructing Col. Joseph Hamblin and Mackenzie to change front to the left so that Mackenzie's right flank joined Crook's left and faced toward the Berryville Pike. "Gain the ridge and open [fire] on them right and left," shouted Upton to Hamblin. The six-foot-four-inch tall Hamblin led his command up the ridge and urged his men to "Give it to them." Hamblin lost his horse but "rider-less studs galloped hither and thither," and the colonel quickly remounted and continued fighting. The fire from Hamblin's brigade forced Grimes to abandon his position and withdraw into Smithfield Redoubt with the remnants of his brigade.[26]

At the same time that Upton attacked Breckinridge and Gordon's right flank, Torbert's cavalry assaulted the Kentuckian's left near the Martinsburg Pike. Fitz Lee's ad hoc force and Capt. George B. Chapman's Monroe artillery defiantly manned Fort Collier and its surrounding area. The Confederate gunners steadily shelled the Union cavalry on both sides of the Martinsburg Pike and held it at bay. Torbert and Merritt recognized the need to counter the Confederate artillery and quickly rolled their own batteries into position. Lieutenant Cuyler's battery of the 3rd U.S. Artillery unlimbered on the road and sent its iron missiles at the Confederates manning the imposing fortification. This heavy relentless pounding from the U.S. Regular Artillery killed 34 horses in and around Fort Collier. Captain Chapman went down mortally wounded when a shell fragment struck him in his back. Just moments later, his second in command suffered a similar gruesome fate. The Virginians incurred heavy casualties and struggled under the terrific firestorm to withdraw two of the battery's cannon with the few remaining horses. As the fort's defenders wavered under the destructive Union fire, Fitz Lee received a serious leg wound that incapacitated him and robbed the Southerners of a key leader at a critical point in the battle.[27]

The revitalized Union cavalry now joined the assault on Fort Collier. From the west side of the pike, Averell's division swept forward once again against scattered resistance from regrouped remnants of Ferguson's, Smith's, and Bean's brigades and turned the Confederate left. Brigadier General Wesley Merritt used the consternation created by Upton and Averell to resume the

---

26 OR 43, pt. 1, 162-163; *Providence Daily Journal*, September 30, 1864; Grimes, *Extracts of Letters*, 67-8.

27 OR 43, pt. 1, 407; Rodenbough, *From Everglade to Canon with the Second Dragoons*, 351; Johnston, *Chapman's Battery*, 51.

offensive. Colonel Charles R. Lowell's reserve brigade of 600 Regulars waited in column of squadrons while sheltered behind a small rise of ground. With Confederate shells whizzing through the air about them, the U.S. troopers had dismounted and were waiting for orders. Merritt scanned the horizon and saw the confusion among the hard-hit Southerners in and around Fort Collier. He sensed an opportunity and ordered the Regulars to charge. Lowell sauntered resolutely out in front of his brigade and the U.S. cavalrymen climbed into their saddles. The brigade deployed into column of squadrons with the 2nd U.S. in the lead. Lowell raised his hand in the air and motioned forward, and the small but determined band moved toward Fort Collier. The bugler soon sounded the call to pick up the pace, and the Regulars quickened their advance to a trot. Individual horsemen grew anxious and tried to increase the speed of the attack, but their officers worked to "restrain the inclination of some of the men to force the pace."

As they closed in, Lowell ordered the charge and the horsemen bolted for the earthen fort. The supporting cavalry from Payne's brigade and Edgar's infantry fired a volley that staggered the head of the column, but the officers urged the Regulars on with shouts of "Forward! Forward!" The 2nd U.S. quickly regained composure, and the attack continued. The Union horsemen leaped their mounts over a ditch and obliterated the Confederate skirmish line. Scattered Confederate cavalrymen fired parting shots and then fled, their color-bearer showing off a "remarkably bright set of horseshoes" to the Yankees as he raced into Winchester. Simultaneously, Powell's West Virginians flanked the fort and surged past it on the opposite side of the Martinsburg Pike, and Lowell's Regulars overwhelmed the fort, capturing two of Chapman's guns.[28]

Chapman's remaining guns fired one shot at the oncoming United States cavalry, but the shells sailed harmlessly overhead. The remaining Confederate infantry and dismounted cavalrymen fired a few rounds into the oncoming blue mass. One bullet seriously wounded Capt. Theophilus F. Rodenbough, commander of the 2nd U.S. Cavalry. As Union horsemen charged, their formation broke apart and the men became scattered. Only a few men remained in the charge when a Rebel detachment on Wharton's left flank turned and

---

28 Rodenbough, *From Everglade to Canon with the Second Dragoons*, 355-356; William H. Powell, "Sheridan in the Shenandoah: The Battle of Opequon," *The American Tribune*, February 13, 1891.

opened fire at the attacking Union troopers, killing the horse of Lt. W. H. Harrison of the 2nd U.S. Cavalry. A crowd of awed Confederates gathered around the unhorsed Regular Army officer. The mounted charge astonished the Southerners who marveled, "Great God! What a fearful charge! What brigade? What regiment?" Harrison proudly responded, "Reserve Brigade, 2nd United States Cavalry." His bursting pride subsided quickly when the Confederates stole every item of value and utility before hauling him off as a prisoner of war.[29]

Beyond the fort, the Union cavalry surged around the guns of Captain Carpenter's battery; however, the Alleghany Roughs stood firm and fought back with hand pikes and sponge staffs. A body of horsemen halted 100 yards beyond the guns and turned around to charge the battery from the rear. Captain Carpenter shouted to the Roughs, "Load with canister and fire to the rear." The Federals shot toward the Confederate gunners with "reckless intrepidity." Carpenter's Virginians swung their guns around to the rear in the nick of time and rammed home their last load of canister. The Virginians fired and shattered the Federal formation, limbered up, and raced away to safety, barely evading capture.[30]

The successful charges of Upton's infantry and Torbert's cavalry loosened the bolts that had anchored Breckinridge's flanks. Thoburn had already raced along his line and instructed his officers to advance as soon as Wright's Sixth Corps moved on the left. After failing to persuade Colonel Thomas to advance, General Crook rode up to Col. Isaac Duval and implored, "It all depends on you. If you can take that position the day is ours!" Similar orders went out in Thoburn's command. Crook's line advanced with a cheer, but encountered heavy fire from the Confederates still in position. Lieutenant Elmer Husted of Thoburn's division "never expected to reach that fence alive, for the bullets flew around my head like hail and their artillery was pouring grape and canister into us most unmercifully." The 23rd Ohio's Capt. Russell Hastings shouted, "Follow me," to his troops as he leapt his horse "Old Whitey" over the stone wall that sheltered his men. The Buckeye soldiers clambered over the wall, and Hastings led them in pursuit of Breckinridge's retreating Southerners. With similar scenes occurring all along Crook's front, his troops surged forward and

29 Rodenbough, *From Everglade to Canon with the Second Dragoons*, 352.

30 Fonerdon, *History of Carpenter's Battery*, 50-52.

forced Breckinridge's command to hastily retreat toward the Smithfield Redoubt.[31]

When the Union cavalry first thundered in on George Patton's brigade, Jubal Early ordered Brig. Gen. Cullen Battle to send the sharpshooter battalion of Rodes's division to the imperiled Confederate left. Colonel Hamilton Brown led the marksmen "at a double quick" to the extreme left. The sharpshooters arrived in the open plain as Breckinridge's infantry were retreating in confusion before assaulting Crook's infantry and Merritt's thundering cavalrymen. The sharpshooters never had a chance, as Sgt. Sam Collier afterward told his parents: "They came pouring down upon us like a thousand bricks which of course we could not stand. We fell back when everything at this moment began to run, wagons, ambulances and every thing mired up together. The whole face of the earth was literally alive with rebels running for their lives."[32]

With utter chaos ruling the hour, it was Col. Tom Carter's artillery that saved Early's command from certain destruction. Carter's gunners hitched drag ropes from the limber wagons to the gun trails and moved the artillery pieces from one position back to another as the Confederate line withdrew. Every time the Confederate left was forced back, Carter's artillery took up a new position farther to the rear and opened fire, slowing the Union advance just long enough for the remnants of Southern infantry to align on his position. "In all my experience," Carter proudly remembered, "I never saw artillery so effectively operated." From the weathered earthen ramparts of Smithfield Redoubt, Carter's gunners showered the approaching Unionists with iron. Nelson's battalion covered the eastern approach to Winchester along the Berryville Road and helped keep the Sixth Corps at a respectable distance. The battalions of Lt. Cols. Carter Braxton and J. Floyd King (McLaughlin's) faced northward and fired with reckless abandon into the jumbled masses of Union cavalry and Confederate infantry. Captain Shoemaker's horse gunners from Fort Jackson on the commanding heights behind the town also added their firepower. According to Custer, this fire killed as many Southerners as Northerners, but it stalled the advance of the Union horsemen and gave Early

31 OR 43, pt. 1, 374-375; *Norwalk Reflector*, October 18, 1864; Russell B. Hastings Papers, For My Children, RBHP; James Findley to Dear Brother, September 22, 1864, James G. Findley Papers, Western Pennsylvania Historical Society.

32 Sam Collier to My Darling Parents, September 21, 1864, NCDAH.

and his subordinates the time needed to fashion a piecemeal battle line at the edge of town.[33]

The majority of the Confederate troops did not rally, but rather retreated into the town of Winchester. In front of Mrs. Lee's house near the eastern side of town, Capt. George Williamson, a Marylander on Gordon's staff, drew his sword and tried to rally the beaten Confederates. To Mrs. Lee, he "looked like a knight of olden times, his face stern and eyes blazing." As the gray coated troops fled the battlefield and streamed through the streets, the patriotic Southern women of the town rushed out of their houses and into the streets. They cried and pleaded with the retreating fugitives to return to the battlefield. Some linked arms and attempted to block the way. Mrs. Fannie Gordon, the general's wife, specifically called out the men of her husband's division. She stood in the street "with uplifted hands and pleading words" as she vainly tried to urge them back. "I shall never forget the appalling spectacle which I that day witnessed for the first time of Confederates retreating in disorder," she later wrote.[34] His soldiers pleaded with her to go inside the house for her own safety as Union artillery shells were already striking in the town. She persisted and succeeded in gathering 200 men and sent them back toward the battlefield before she saw to her personal well-being. By the time the men reached the outskirts of town, they were swept up in the confusion and chaos of the final Confederate retreat.[35]

33 Thomas H. Carter to John D. Daniel, November 28, 1894, UVA; *OR* 43, pt. 1, 458.

34 The quote from Mrs. Gordon is from the dedication of the 8th Vermont Infantry monument on the Winchester battlefield. Herbert E. Hill, 6.

35 Mrs. Hugh Lee Diary, WFCHS, Handley Library.

Every Damn Thing in the Shape of
a Rebel Is on the Run

Confederate Collapse

When morning dawned on September 19, 1864, Maj. Gen. Stephen Dodson Ramseur's Confederates fired the first volleys of the battle at Phil Sheridan's approaching cavalry along the Berryville Pike east of Winchester. Now, as the sun set on the Shenandoah Valley, these hardened Rebel veterans were doing their best to slow the Federal onslaught long enough for Jubal A. Early to escape with what was left of the Confederate Army of the Valley District. For "Old Jube," an outright battlefield defeat was now a forgone conclusion. The extent of the damage Phil Sheridan could inflict upon Early's remaining troops remained to be determined—with Ramseur's division facing more than four times its numbers while everything on his left collapsed and melted away into the distance.

As Ramseur's line of battle turned and marched in retreat toward Winchester with the Sixth Corps following, Brig. Gen. William R. Cox mistook the organized line of Southerners for a Union flanking column on the Confederate right flank and began to withdraw. Early recognized the mistake and rushed what was left of Cox's brigade back into its position in Smithfield Redoubt, and Ramseur's division deployed immediately south of it. Elements of his division took up positions in Mount Hebron Cemetery where they made their final stand. Indeed, some of his men would ultimately be buried there. Ramseur's infantry, Lt. Col. William Nelson's artillery, and two brigades of Maj. Gen. Lunsford L. Lomax's much maligned cavalry had the vital task of keeping Early's line of retreat open long enough for the rest of the army to withdraw safely through town. At this point, "Old Jube" could hope for no more than survival. Given the odds against him, he viewed that as a melancholy victory of sorts, and remained incredulous for the rest of his life that Sheridan had not completely crushed his Valley Army.[1]

On Ramseur's left, the battered remnants of Brig. Gen. Cullen A. Battle's and Maj. Gen. John C. Breckinridge's commands holed up for their last stand at Smithfield Redoubt. General Joeseph E. Johnston had constructed this two-sided earthwork in 1861 prior to the battle of Manassas. Although weatherworn, it suited Early's needs as one side faced north and ran perpendicular to the Valley Pike, and the other fronted eastward at a right angle to the Berryville Pike. Early, Breckinridge, John Gordon, and others galloped among the retreating infantry and implored them to stand and fight. Gordon's efforts in particular succeeded to a large degree, aided by his innate heroic stature. When Cox's brigade wavered, Gordon snatched up the colors of the 4th North Carolina and urged the men to fight on. Sheridan was tightening his vice around the Rebel remnants; Gordon needed to find a way to gain time to escape. "Get into the ditches and fight for fifteen minutes and you save the army," shouted Gordon to survivors of his old Georgia brigade. Breckinridge rode up to the color bearer of the 37th Virginia and asked him to hand over his flag. The Virginian denied the Kentuckian's request, telling him, "I just came off the skirmish line and could carry the flag anywhere anyone else could."[2]

The Southern army had little time to rally as the Union infantry slowly but steadily followed the retreating Confederates to their final position. Horatio Wright's Sixth Corps doggedly closed in on the Smithfield Redoubt. In the heat of combat, Wright lost sight of sealing off the enemy right flank. Instead, he guided the divisions of Brig. Gens. William R. Getty and James Ricketts to the right (north) and ordered that the battle lines be kept tightly together at all

---

1　"Battle of Winchester: September 19, 1864," *Our Living and Our Dead*, New Bern, NC, October 29, 1873; Clarence R. Hatton, "Gen. Archibald Campbell Godwin," *Confederate Veteran*, vol. 28, 133-134.

2　G. P. Ring to Wife, September 21, 1864, Tulane University; Worsham, *One of Jackson's Foot Cavalry*, 169; *The Sunny South*, May 11, 1901; "Reminiscences of George C. Pile," *Bristol Courier* (TN-VA), Jan. 23 - Feb. 27, 1921.

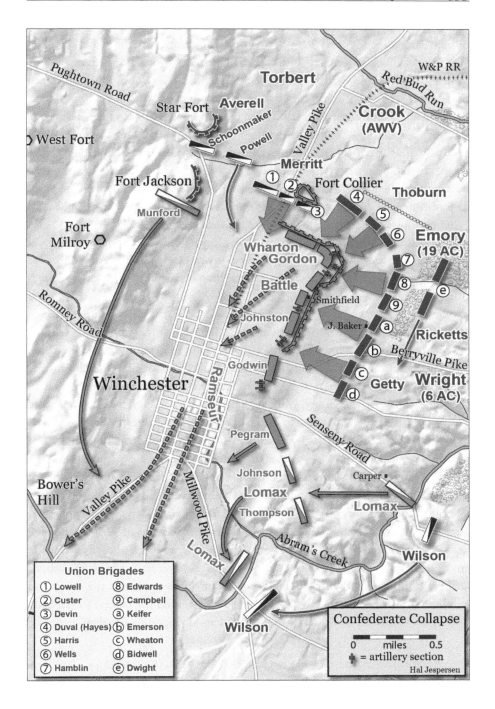

Pughtown Road

Torbert

Star Fort Averell

West Fort

Fort Jackson

Munford

Fort
Milroy

Romney Road

Winchester

Bower's
Hill

Valley Pike

Schoonmaker

Powell

Valley Pike

W&P RR

Red Bud Run

Crook
(AWV)

Merritt

① ② Fort Collier   Thoburn
      ④
③   ⑤
               ⑥ Emory
Wharton   ⑦ (19 AC)
Gordon   ⑧
             ⑨   ⓔ
Battle
          Smithfield
Johnston   J. Baker ⓐ
                         ⓑ Ricketts
Godwin   ⓒ Berryville Pike
                         ⓓ Getty Wright
                                   (6 AC)
Ramseur

Pegram

Johnson   Carper

Lomax
Thompson   Lomax

Abram's Creek   Wilson

Senseny Road

Millwood Pike

Lomax

Wilson

Union Brigades

① Lowell	⑧ Edwards
② Custer	⑨ Campbell
③ Devin	ⓐ Keifer
④ Duval (Hayes)	ⓑ Emerson
⑤ Harris	ⓒ Wheaton
⑥ Wells	ⓓ Bidwell
⑦ Hamblin	ⓔ Dwight

Confederate Collapse

0   miles   0.5
⚑ = artillery section
Hal Jespersen

points. Brigadier General Emory Upton's movement to the right to assist Crook was the likely cause. With Gens. George Crook and Alfred Torbert pouring in from the right and advancing toward the left, Wright's movement made little sense considering that all the Confederates were retreating toward the Federal left. Wright might have been overcompensating for the fateful gaps that developed in the Union battle line during Sheridan's initial attack. Unfortunately, his measured and well-ordered advance could not deliver the rapid, crushing blow needed to smash Early's right. As the situation warranted a prompt and decisive thrust at the retreating Southerners, an amazed Virginian of Ramseur's division later opined, "If they came straight at us, they would have caught a lot of our stragglers who were running to the rear."[3]

On the right flank of the Sixth Corps, Upton wasted no time fretting over orderly alignments and pressed his division toward the redoubt. The Smithfield Redoubt provided Col. Thomas Carter's massed artillery with an excellent platform from where they performed their deadly work. The Southern gunners fired canister and case shot "with terrible accuracy" into the blue lines. A single shell burst killed the 2nd Connecticut's Maj. James Q. Rice, ripping his arm off and "tearing his body asunder," and seriously wounding acting Lt. Col. Jeffrey Skinner. One fragment wounded Colonel Mackenzie but he remained on the battlefield. The intense Confederate artillery fire forced Mackenzie's men to seek shelter in a dry creek bed while iron projectiles shrieked overhead. Private Lewis Bissell wrote, "Shells exploded over our battle line. Four struck and exploded so close to me that I was covered with dirt. One struck our line while the men were lying down—exploded blowing men to atoms and throwing bodies everywhere." Mackenzie pulled his dazed soldiers back and sheltered them behind a rise of the ground where they remained until the battle ended.[4]

Similar experiences occurred all along the Sixth Corps battle line as it attempted to advance over the open ground. Some portions of Wright's line fell back under the terrible storm of iron. When Col. Oliver Edwards's brigade emerged from the west side of the Dinkle farm and South woods, the Southern artillery pounded his Pennsylvania and Wisconsin troops from the front and left. The fire became unbearable, and Edwards ordered the troops to fall back "fifty paces" and lie down. As the foot soldiers dropped to the dirt, a smiling

---

3   OR 43, pt. 1, 212-213; George Q. Peyton, *A Civil War Record for 1864-1865*, 83.

4   Mark Olcott, *The Civil War Letters of Lewis Bissell, A Curriculum* (Washington, D.C., 1981), 304.

Brigade commander Col. Oliver Edwards, one of the unsung Union heros of the Third Battle of Winchester. *LC*

Phil Sheridan appeared on the field and raced over to the right to confer with Crook and Torbert. Lieutenant Colonel Gideon Clark of the 119th Pennsylvania reported that "the enthusiasm of the men became unbounded" upon Sheridan's appearance. More importantly, they resumed their advance and closed in on the final Confederate line.[5]

5   John C. Arnold to My Dear Wife and Family, September 23, 1864, Library of Congress; *OR* 43, pt. 1, 189.

Brig. Gen. Emory Upton
LC

The army commander had no monopoly on inspiration that day. When Emory Upton saw his division foundering under the terrible fire of the Confederate artillery, he galloped to the center of his battle line and pulled up his mount in front of the 37th Massachusetts. There, the young general exclaimed, "I want to fight with this regiment, give me your colors and I will place them where you will get more rebs in three minutes than you can here in a week." Upton grabbed the flag, spurred his horse, and galloped across the open plain in front of Smithfield Redoubt. The Massachusetts boys trailed Upton toward the Southern line, and were soon joined by the 65th New York on the right and 121st New York on the left.[6]

Upton's entire division took up the charge with "officers and men cheering, shouting, swearing, each striving to be the first to reach their destination." All the while, Upton waved the flag of the 37th Massachusetts and urged the troops forward in their "mad race" until a shell fragment ripped into this thigh. The iron gouged a wound one inch deep and three inches long but spared his bone. In spite of his injury, the wounded general refused to leave the battlefield and watched the closing scenes of the battle from a stretcher. Colonel Oliver Edwards arrived moments after Upton went down and took over active command of the division. He galloped up to his old Massachusetts regiment, seized the colors, and shouted, "Come on my boys; I am going to fight with the old 37th."[7]

To Upton's left, the balance of Horatio Wright's Sixth Corps slowly approached the thin Confederate line on the eastern outskirts of Winchester. When Ricketts's division advanced on Upton's left flank, the earth "shook and trembled" beneath the feet of the advancing Union troops with "shells bursting and flying in all directions." When Ricketts's line closed to within 500 yards of the Confederates, it halted and the men "commenced firing as fast as we could."[8]

On James Ricketts's left flank, William Getty's division continued its forward movement toward Jubal Early's final line of battle. Two of Getty's brigades actually crossed over to the north side of the Berryville Pike as the line inexorably closed in on embattled Winchester. Getty's troops moved through an open plain and then ascended with relative ease the ridge containing Mr. Baker's brick mansion. As the Union men were seizing that position, Ramseur's and Battle's remaining troops opened fire at the Northerners from in and around the redoubt. Southern artillery joined in, adding canister to the ordnance being hurled into the advancing blue ranks. The steady fire brought the line to a fitful halt. Although they had suffered severely and could drive forward no

6   *National Tribune*, May 28, 1925; "Their Heroic Past Recalled; Addresses by Gen. Edwards and Lt. Gov. Matle," *Springfield Republican*, September 20, 1893; Best, *History of the 121st New York State Infantry*, 181-182.

7   *Springfield Republican*, September 29, 1864; *Otsego Republican*, December 3, 1864.

8   *Lancaster Gazette*, October 20, 1864; John R. Rhoades to Sarah A. Rhoades, September 20, 1864, Rutherford B. Hayes Presidential Center.

farther, the Union infantry somehow managed to cling to their advanced position.[9]

Colonel James Warner's Vermont brigade pushed past the Baker house and into the garden beyond. His troops took position behind "a paling fence of hard wood boards" and encountered "the hottest fire of the day, being exposed to a withering musketry fire in front and . . . from a battery which enfiladed the line." The Vermonters looked to the left and saw the Union battle line bowed back "with the extreme left retired and the rebs pressing it." Brigadier General Frank Wheaton's Pennsylvanians pushed their way forward on Warner's left flank, but they, too, could go no farther once they reached the Baker house line. Wheaton requested artillery support, and Getty promptly rushed Captain Greenleaf Steven's Fifth Maine Battery to the front and deployed on Wheaton's left flank.[10]

On the far left of the Sixth Corps, Brig. Gen. Daniel D. Bidwell's brigade struggled to keep pace with the rest of Getty's division as it inclined to the right. As a result of diverging to the right, Bidwell complained that Confederates began "accumulating in large numbers" in the woods off to his left as they were no longer under direct attack. Bidwell deployed the 43rd New York to reinforce his skirmish line to cover the ground, but was continually pulled to the right allowing the Confederates to escape. Bidwell's brigade also faced the difficulty of advancing over the roughest terrain on the battlefield at this point in the conflict. Fortunately, he did not encounter as much direct resistance from the Southern infantry as did his comrades on the right.[11]

To assist the stalled Sixth Corps infantry, Col. Charles Tompkins advanced the Sixth Corps's batteries and pounded back at the Confederates in the redoubt. At the same time, DuPont's battery and the horse artillery hammered away from the north. The combination of the various Union batteries placed

9 The role of this portion of the army was to serve as the anvil to George Crook's and Alfred Torbert's hammer. Unfortunately, surviving accounts detailing the movements and actions of the various units comprising Getty's and Ricketts's divisions are frustratingly generic. Most of the surviving records from these divisions focus upon the combat that began at 11:40 a.m. Additionally, there is little diversity among the activities of the various brigades and regiments in detailing what happened during the final attack. Tales of Phil Sheridan's appearances along the battle line shortly before the advance began, heavy artillery firing, and the final collapse of the Southern line summarize the typical account of the last advance from these troops in this part of the army at that time of the battle.

10 *OR* 43, pt. 1, 208; Aldace Walker to Mr. Editor, *Vermont Chronicle*, October 15, 1864.

11 *OR* 43, pt. 1, 212-213.

the entire Confederate position in crossfire, and casualties mounted quickly. A Georgia soldier from Gordon's division recalled, "All the artillery horses were killed and the men fell dead every moment, but I never saw guns served so magnificently, and every discharge plowed furrows in the enemy." Colonel Tom Carter was wounded by a shell fragment and left the field leaving the Southern artillery under the control of Lt. Col. William Nelson.[12]

The rapid shell fire from Braxton's and McLaughlin's battalions pinned down Crook's advance along the northern front of the redoubt. Thoburn's command halted briefly, but regrouped quickly under fire at the stone wall recently abandoned by Gordon's men. Eschewing the dubious protection that the rocks offered against artillery fire, Thoburn advanced his command into a ravine that provided a natural refuge from the punishing Confederate artillery fire. On the extreme left of Thoburn's line, one Confederate battery in particular honed in on the 116th Ohio. Lieutenant Colonel Thomas F. Wildes responded by moving his Buckeyes closer to the Confederate works. The Ohioans crawled up the ravine's forward slope until they reached its crest where the terrain better protected them from the Confederate fire. They could now place the Southern artillery in their sights and opened fire. At first, the Buckeyes found the range too great, so they loaded their rifles with double shots of gunpowder. Men and horses began to drop within the redoubt, reducing the volume of fire from the Confederate gunners. Colonel George D. Wells praised the Confederates manning the artillery at the redoubt. "The enemy's guns were served with great precision," wrote Wells, "and with wonderful nerve and pluck in the face of our fire at short rifle range."[13]

On Crook's right, a group of officers from Duval's division had crawled to the crest of the ridge and peered over the top at the Confederates manning the redoubt. "A half a dozen batteries were playing upon us, & it required the strenuous efforts of their officers to induce the men to remain under such a murderous fire," wrote the wounded adjutant of the 91st Ohio, James G. Findley.[14] Lieutenant Colonel James Comly of the 23rd Ohio watched

12 Fred R. Laubach Diary, Civil War Misc. Collection, USAMHI; *The Sunny South*, May 11, 1901.

13 OR 43, pt. 1, 376-377; *Athens Messenger*, October 13, 1864; Wildes, *Record of the 116th Regiment, Ohio Infantry Volunteers in the War of the Rebellion*, 172.

14 James G. Findley to Dear Brother, September 22, 1864, Historical Society of Western Pennsylvania.

Maj. Gen. George Crook's command attacking the Smithfield redoubt position.
A. R. Waud, LC

quizzically as his counterpart from the 91st Ohio, Benjamin F. Coates, maneuvered around so that his feet rested at the top of the hill next to the other men's heads. When asked what he was doing, Coates stated that he was placing all of his vital organs as far away from the Confederate fire as possible. The men chuckled, but the mounting casualties in front of Smithfield Redoubt quickly returned them to the grim reality of their situation. Lieutenant Lyman H. McBride of the 23rd Ohio crawled forward leading a party of men armed with Dresden rifles. McBride's Buckeyes took careful aim and began to pick off Rebel artillery horses at long range.[15]

Crook's infantry received timely support from Capt. Henry A. DuPont's Battery B, 5th U.S. Artillery. The Regulars galloped up to the front line and deployed their six rifled guns on the right flank of Duval's division manned by the 91st Ohio. The lieutenant in command sighted one of the guns and aimed it at a particular Confederate cannon in the works that had been wreaking havoc among Crook's command. The first shot fired struck the embrasure and

15 James Comly Diary, OHS.

A sketch of the 5th Michigan Cavalry in the final charge at Third Winchester.
A. R. Waud, LC

exploded, knocking out the Confederate piece and sending the nearby troops scurrying away.[16]

Sheridan now rode up behind the stalled Army of West Virginia and consulted with George Crook. The quiet Crook understood that the overall situation favored the Union, but readily perceived that there was little pressure against the Confederate right. Crook pointed toward the Union left and told Sheridan, "There is where we need to put some troops." The Army commander immediately turned to General Emory and ordered Dwight's division to the left. The Nineteenth Corps troops quickly marched behind the Sixth Corps in an attempt to sweep around Early's right and cut off his line of retreat south of Winchester. The move, however, occurred much too late to have any impact on the battle's outcome.[17]

After sending Dwight to the left, Sheridan and Crook galloped behind the Union battle line as they headed toward the Valley Pike. Along the way, Crook

16 A. C. Soley, "Sheridan at Winchester," *Springfield Republican*, February 14, 1887.

17 William Dwight, Report of Service, National Archives.

Col. Rutherford B. Hayes
Generals in Blue

gave his officers instructions for the final assault, and Sheridan encouraged the men in his typical fashion. As he rode among the infantrymen, Sheridan's fiery demeanor caught the attention of Lt. Frederick Whitaker of the 6th New York Cavalry. The horse soldiers were amazed as Sheridan "treated the infantrymen to a taste of the tallest swearing that they had ever heard." "None in the cavalry corps had heard him vituperate in such a manner," observed Whitaker, "the general impression there being that he was a kind indulgent chief." Sheridan the hellfire spewing infantryman had reemerged and now dashed off to energize the cavalry. Duval then raced along his lines waving his sword and urging the men to "stand their ground." Duval, whose leadership and bravery throughout the course of the battle was cited by many officers and enlisted men of the Army of West Virginia, would not finish the fight. He soon received a severe bullet wound to the thigh, placing Col. Rutherford B. Hayes in command of the division.[18]

Sheridan left Crook's infantry and continued toward the Valley Pike where the cavalry regrouped for another charge in the vicinity of Fort Collier. Along the way, he encountered Lt. William C. Cuyler, a frustrated young officer from Georgia who was struggling to free a gun belonging to the 3rd U.S. Artillery from a deep rut, all the while under a heavy fire from the Confederate cannon. Sheridan jumped from his mount and eagerly assisted Cuyler and his men in freeing the piece. Sheridan smiled and nodded at Cuyler, saying "That's the way to do it, my boy," before he galloped away. He located Maj. Gen. Alfred T. A. Torbert and instructed him "to collect his cavalry and charge." With artillery

18 Frederick Whitaker, *The Complete Life of General George A. Custer*, 235; Sturm, 94.

Maj. William Yonce of the 51st Virginia fell mortally wounded during the final stages of the Winchester battle. *John Milgrim Collection*

pounding the Union troops and Schoonmaker's brigade reeling from its repulse at Fort Jackson, Sheridan met with Col. William H. Powell and ordered him to hold his position at all hazards. Powell did more than fulfill his instructions, and his West Virginians and New Yorkers darted up the west side of the Martinsburg Pike and twice charged Munford's Virginians in and around Fort Jackson. Elements of Schoonmaker's brigade again charged from the heights of Star Fort, but the Virginians held firm. Munford had sealed off Averell from interdicting Early's retreat through Winchester.[19]

Under the "fearful" fire of Captain Shoemaker's horse artillery firing down from Fort Jackson, Merritt culled together a force spearheaded by Custer's Michigan brigade and deployed them in column of squadrons. Colonel Thomas C. Devin moved into position on Custer's left flank with a few hundred men from the 4th and 6th New York in the same formation. Colonel Charles Lowell formed the "fragment of the Reserve Brigade" on Custer's right, likewise in column of squadrons. As the Union cavalry prepared to charge, Confederate gunners in Smithfield Redoubt spied the gathering blue mass and began to pull back to escape the coming storm.[20]

19 Lt. William C. Cuyler was a native of Savannah, Georgia. His father was Col. John M. Cuyler, a 30-year Regular Army veteran and surgeon who was serving as the Medical Inspector for the United States Army in the War Department at the time of the Third Winchester battle. *New York Herald*, September 22, 1864; *New York Times*, September 21, 1864; Theo F. Rodenbough, *Sabre and Bayonet*, 26; William H. Powell, "Sheridan in the Shenandoah: The Battle of the Opequon," *American Tribune* (Indianapolis, IN), February 13, 1891; Munford, *Reminiscences of Cavalry Operations*, 450; Munford, "Reminiscences," 450.

20 *OR* 43, pt. 1, 445.

Merritt's cavalry quietly advanced to within 500 yards of Smithfield Redoubt. The maneuver was, noted Custer, "entirely unobserved" by Gabriel Wharton's Confederates as they focused on the heavy lines of the approaching Union infantry off to Custer's left. In the opposing Confederate ranks, Col. Augustus Forsberg, commander of the brigade on Wharton's left, "thoughtlessly" exposed himself as he anxiously stared at the hypnotic movements of the Union cavalry. Union troops fired at him from multiple directions, and a bullet struck his right hand as he pointed at Merritt's approaching horsemen. A second bullet brought him to his knees, and a staff officer assisted the wounded Forsberg into Winchester. Major William A. Yonce of the 51st Virginia took command of the brigade only to be mortally wounded minutes later.[21]

Wesley Merritt ordered the charge with less than 1,000 horsemen. The fiery Tom Devin rode out in front of his New Yorkers manning the left column and shouted, "Draw sabres, forward!" Custer's band played and the cheers of the horsemen could be heard above the din of the battle. His troops soon thundered up the fields on the immediate east side of the Pike. Merritt, Devin, and Custer led from the front and the entire line of cavalry columns "advanced with a steady gate until within short range of their line." Then they charged at the double quick and burst into the very midst of the Rebels.

Breckinridge saw the New Yorkers coming and ordered some of his Virginians to hold their fire until the horsemen were only 80 yards away. His Southerners "turned and delivered a well-directed volley of musketry" but could not halt the onrushing Union troopers. The Southerners "stood like demons" to receive the charge but before they could reload and fire a second volley, Merritt's horsemen "swung around their flank, cutting them down like thistles." The Union troopers exploded into the midst of the defenders "sabering right and left, capturing prisoners more rapidly than they could be disposed of." Many of Wharton's troops sought shelter in a large stone house and offered stout resistance from its doors and windows. Lieutenant Colonel Melvin Brewer of the 7th Michigan Cavalry fell mortally wounded, but Custer's cavalrymen soon surrounded the house and quickly subdued those who had sought refuge inside. Between the last charge, Lowell's assault on Fort Collier, and Devin's flattening of Patton's brigade, Merritt's division decimated Wharton's infantry. The Southern division lost 1,200 men, nine battle flags, two

21 Ibid., 457; Augustus Forsberg Memoir, W&L.

brigade commanders, and dozens of officers. The division had been effectively destroyed and ceased to exist as an effective combat unit. Private Thomas W. Fisher of the 51st Virginia told his parents, "not to make a short story long, I will just say that we got pretty badly whipped & even routed somewhat." Although the cost was tremendous, Breckinridge and Wharton's stand provided enough time for the rest of Early's army to avoid the same fate and continue the campaign.[22]

Colonel James R. Love II led the Thomas Legion (composed of men from western North Carolina and eastern Tennessee) of Col. Thomas Smith's brigade in a desperate rearguard action. Love deployed and fought his men in a formation he later called a "squad drive," which held the Union horsemen in check long enough for their comrades to escape. Love's men fought until they were surrounded, and in doing so lost 75 men out of the 165 the Legion carried into the fight. The loss of nearly half the unit—which effectively gutted the outfit—included Lt. Col. James A. McKamy, four captains, and several lieutenants. East of Winchester, Col. John R. Winston's 45th North Carolina was among the last of the organized troops to leave the battlefield. The regiment had the unenviable distinction of losing more men than any other unit in the Second Corps that day at Winchester—and the Tar Heels were not yet done fighting. With a bullet hole already venting his hat, Colonel Winston watched with no little consternation as the mixed collection of Federal cavalry and Confederate infantry rolled in mass confusion toward Winchester. The colonel fronted his 45th North Carolina to face north, and once so aligned the Carolinians "fired rapidly into the moving mass of friends and foes," aiming high in hopes of missing their comrades and hitting their mounted foes.[23]

To the observers in the Union infantry, the charging cavalry proved to be one of the most spectacular sights they ever saw. Custer's trademark blond hair flowed in the wind and identified him to all who watched the brilliant charge.

---

22 James Comly Journal, OHS; *Northampton Free Press*, October 11, 1864; *New York Herald*, September 22, 1864; T. W. Fisher to Dear Father and Mother, September 20, 1864, *Southwest Virginia Today*, March 13, 2011; "Bahlman Gives History of Men Serving in '61," *Charleston Gazette*, September 22, 1922.

23 W. W. Stringfield, "Sixty Ninth Regiment," contained in Clark, *Histories of the Several Regiments and Battalions from North Carolina*, vol. 3, 754; Inspection Report of Wharton's division, September 29, 1864, National Archives; Col. John R. Winston, "A Spirited Campaign: General Early's Struggle Against Generals Hunter and Sheridan," *Philadelphia Weekly Times*, July 25, 1864.

The Berryville Pike between the lines of the last attack at Third Winchester. The Sixth Corps formed for the final assault on the ridge in the distance. *Dwight and Walter Briscoe, Photographers, 1885, DeGolyer Library, SMU*

Merritt, Devin, and many other officers participated, but Custer's locks ensured that he stood out. The final charge of the Union cavalry was so impressive that the awed Federal infantry "involuntarily paused a moment to watch them." A Massachusetts officer reported, "Down they come where the rebels have partly reformed their line, fairly riding them into the ground . . . how the sabres glisten in the sun as they cut right and left."[24]

Crook's infantrymen were mesmerized at the sight of Custer sweeping around the Confederate left flank "and almost into the earth-works" with his band playing the entire time. "It was the most magnificent thing that was ever

24 Fred, Letter from the 34th Regiment, September 28, 1864, *Northampton Free Press*, October 11, 1864.

seen," recorded Lt. Col. Comly of the 23rd Ohio. Crook's entire line stood up "with a tremendous yell" and "rushed pell-mell for the breastworks." Crook's mass of soldiers "each tried to outstrip his neighbor, cheering like mad and rushing for the breastworks." On Crook's left, Lt. Col. Thomas F. Wildes's 116th Ohio followed, with the balance of Wells's brigade just behind. The Confederates loosed a "feeble and irregular fire" at the charging U.S. soldiers then abandoned their guns and fled in haste. The Ohioans scaled the Rebel redoubt and jubilantly waved their colors over a twelve-pounder Napoleon cannon and its accompanying caisson loaded with ammunition. Fourteen dead and wounded horses littered the ground, a macabre testament to the Ohioans' marksmanship.[25]

25 James Comly Diary, OHS; Wildes, 172-173; Alexis G. Soley, "Sheridan at Winchester, How the 34th Massachusetts Had a Hand in the 'Whirling,'" *Springfield Republican*, February 14, 1887.

When Merritt's cavalry poured around the Confederate left, Col. Oliver Edwards saw that there was no time to issue orders to his brigade and regimental commanders. He dashed up to the 37th Massachusetts, and, with their battle flag in hand, ordered it to charge bayonets against the hilltop fortress. The troops hesitated, so Edwards yelled, "Boys, your colors are going to that hill. Will you follow?" The men cheered and Edwards dashed off toward the redoubt, while Upton's entire division took up the charge and surged forward. Only a few colors, their guards, and a skeletal line of infantry remained in the works. Edwards's infantry easily drove them out and captured some prisoners while the rest fled toward the town in confusion. Edwards' troops then clambered into the breastworks and found some abandoned artillery pieces "yet in position, hissing hot with action, with their miserable rac-a-bone horses attached." While Edwards led the troops in the final assault, Emory Upton demanded that his stretcher bearers carry him to the top of a hill "that he might see with his own eyes the retreat of the foe." With victory assured, Upton finally allowed the orderlies to carry him to the Sixth Corps field hospital. A wounded but still-jubilant sergeant from the 121st New York was being carried past a surgeon on his way to the rear when he exclaimed, "'Oh! Doctor, I am willing to go now. You cannot find them,' and with a toss of his cap and a lusty hurrah he continued on his way."[26]

On Edwards's left flank, Ricketts's division made its final push of the battle. As Colonel Keifer led his brigade forward, he scanned the scene toward Winchester and realized that he was partaking in the "most stirring and picturesque" charge of the war. The setting sun shone through the church spires that hung above the town, and "its rays glistened upon the drawn sabers of the thousands of mounted warriors." The soldiers of his brigade, indeed of Ricketts's entire division, saw the success attained by Merritt's cavalry and

---

26 Claims abound that a large number of artillery pieces were captured during the final charge by the Union infantry. Reality suggests that only two pieces (at the most) were captured during this phase of the combat. George Crook's men were the first to enter Winchester; the "hissing hot with action" pieces some in the Sixth Corps claimed to have captured were almost certainly the same guns that members of Crook's command had already seized. The Union army captured a total of just five guns at Winchester—and this minimal claim is disputed by Jubal Early, who admitted only to the loss of three pieces (though he left open the possibility that the cavalry may have lost some guns, of which he was never informed). Dudley Landon Vaill, *The County Regiment*, 55-56; Oliver Edwards Memorandum, Illinois State Historical Library, 193; *Otsego Republican*, December 3, 1864; James Comly Diary, OHS; Daniel M. Holt, *A Surgeon's Civil War: The Letters and Diary of Daniel M. Holt, M.D.*, edited by Janet L. Coryell, James M. Greine, and James R. Smither (Kent, OH, 1994), 250.

"rushed with yells of triumph." Similar scenes occurred all along the Union line.[27]

The unprecedented collapse of the Confederate forces at Winchester was truly chaotic. "Old Jube" attempted to put the best face on the affair in his reports and memoirs, but the scene was beyond redemption. Sergeant Richard W. Waldrop of the 21st Virginia, Gordon's division, considered it "the most disorderly retreat I ever saw." His comment is noteworthy, as the old Stonewall division had helped put Federals to rout at or near Winchester on several occasions. "The road was filled with fugitives from all commands," admitted Waldrop, "and kept in a run until we reached Newtown." An artillery sergeant labeled the scene "a sickening sight." Sergeant Sam Collier of the 2nd North Carolina, Cox's brigade wrote home, "I never ran so fast in all my life. To come out and tell the truth I ran from two miles the other side of Winchester to Newtown a distance of ten (10) miles and I can assure you I had good company from Brig Genls [sic] down to privates."[28]

For Sheridan's soldiers, the rout of Early's army was a long time in coming. Many of the Unionists had been on the losing end of such battles, but it did the troops good to see the Confederates running away. "Every damn thing in the shape of a rebel is on the run," declared John Beech of the New Jersey brigade. The surgeon of the 77th New York, Sixth Corps declared, "For once in their lives they know they are whipped—yes skinned alive."[29]

As the Confederate army withdrew through the town, officers paused briefly at the home of Winchester socialite Mrs. Hugh Lee and assured her "they would be back in a few days," as they had always returned in the past. General Breckinridge, whose wife had been staying in town, told Lee that Kershaw's division "was still in striking distance." General Gordon dashed up to Lee's door to arrange for the safety of his wife, and then ran back into the street. He grabbed the flag from a passing Confederate and shouted for the men to "rally and follow [me]." Mrs. Lee and the other women encouraged the soldiers to follow Gordon, "but to little purpose," as she lamented in her journal. Gordon finally managed to assemble a small rear guard composed of

27 Keifer, *Slavery and Four Years of War*, vol. 2, 114; *Perry County Weekly*, October 14, 1864.

28 Richard W. Waldrop, Diary, SHC-UNC; Humphreys, Memoir, UVA, 361; Sam Collier to Parents, September 21, 1864, NC Dept Archives and History.

29 "The John Beech Story," *Newark Sunday News Magazine*, January 29, 1961; Holt, *A Surgeon's Civil War*, 253.

100 men from the 60th Georgia of Atkinson's brigade. Gordon ordered Capt. John Y. Bedingfield to "skirmish with the Yanks until our army could get some distance south of Winchester." The Georgians tried their best but the Union cavalry nearly captured them and compelled a precipitous retreat.[30]

Sergeant Milton Humphreys of the Lewisburg Artillery had stopped to clear a clogged gun just inside the Winchester town limits. He ordered Pvt. John Wallace and "another strong man" to ram the jammed shell down the tube by striking the protruding end of the rammer with a sledgehammer. Although shells from Union batteries were exploding and damaging the homes all around them, several women stood nearby watching and asked the gunners what had happened on the battlefield. Humphreys vainly urged them to go inside for their own safety. Panicked infantrymen, ignorant of what the gunners were doing, told the women that the gunners were about to "kill themselves and them too . . ." The women screamed and ran back into their house with a single exception. One terrified woman and a panicked infantryman "tried by force" to stop the gunners from their task. Humphreys grabbed the woman by her arm and "dragged her away." He then turned toward the soldier who quickly "resumed his flight." Just then Jubal Early rode up and shouted, "Stop that you damn fools, you'll kill yourself and everybody about you!" The strapping John Wallace cast an angry glance at Early and unwittingly shouted, "Go to hell, you damned old clodhopper and tend to your own business." The profane Early took no offense, but simply smiled, perhaps approvingly, and rode away.[31]

Brigadier General Gabriel Wharton led the last organized remnants of his Southern division away from the battlefield. Together with a staff officer, Wharton rode behind the small command as it retreated through the town in the hope of finding safety and breathing room beyond. During his journey a woman emerged from her house with a pot of coffee and a pair of cups. With shells whizzing overhead, Wharton warned her to go back inside. The woman refused. "You are the last Confederate soldiers I will ever see in Winchester," Wharton recalled her saying, "and that she wanted to give us the coffee." Just after she spoke, a solid shot ripped through a tree and severed a limb. According to the general, the tree limb "struck her and came near losing all the coffee [but]

30 Mrs. Hugh H. Lee, Diary, WFCHS, 635-636; John Y. Bedingfield to Dear Ma, September 20, 1864; Bedingfield Letters, UVA.

31 Private Wallace's comrades were unsure whether he realized that he was speaking to the Confederate army commander. Milton Humphreys, Memoir, UVA, 361-362.

Capt. Augustus F. Ward, 36th Ohio
Larry Strayer Collection

the woman did not move a muscle." The heroics moved the hardened combat veteran. "If you are brave enough to stand there," he told her, "I could certainly stay to drink her coffee." The unlikely pair were drinking their coffee when Wharton looked around and realized they were the last Confederates in sight. Winchester had changed hands scores of times during the war; Wharton's final departure symbolized the end of the last Confederate occupation.[32]

As the Confederates fled south out of Winchester, General Crook's old command, the 36th Ohio, had the honor of carrying its flag into town ahead of any other U.S. troops. These Buckeyes were soon joined by throngs of Crook's Ohioans and West Virginians. With the dim twilight illuminating the way, the infantrymen advanced through the town and cleared out isolated pockets of Confederate skirmishers as they went. As bullets zipped down the streets, the band of the 14th West Virginia struck up some music until a cannonball bounded down the street and scattered the men to the sidewalks. The Confederates had thrown away rifles, knapsacks, and other perceived impediments, and the streets were littered with the "usual debris of a defeated and rapidly retreating army."

As the Union troops reached the southern end of town, the resistance stiffened. "We had some regular street fighting," reported the 36th Ohio's Capt. Augustus T. Ward. Their situation became especially dangerous when a section of Capt. Thomas Bryan's Lewisburg Artillery joined Capt. Shoemaker's guns on the heights west of Winchester. The Rebel gunners opened fire and enfiladed the cross streets of the town as the Union troops advanced. The gunners fired round shot that struck the hard road and bounded over the heads of the Union troops, "inflicting more damage on the houses than to our columns." The

32 Gabriel C. Wharton to James B. Clay, May 15, 1905, Clay Family Papers, LC.

continued advance of the Federals flanked the Southerners and forced them to abandon their position. Crook's soldiers halted their advance near Milltown where, as several of them noted, they had last camped on July 24, the day that Early had crushed Crook at the Second Battle of Kernstown. The men now cheered in earnest as they had fulfilled their pledge to "Wipe out Winchester."[33]

On the Confederate right flank, General Ramseur began to slowly withdraw his division now that the bulk of Early's army had retreated through Winchester. Although the Tar Heel's command had been badly battered by the Sixth Corps during Sheridan's late morning assault, Ramseur proudly boasted how he "brought up the rear, division organization unbroken. I was the rearguard and repulsed several attacks and saved our wagons and artillery." He prudently avoided the potential confusion of a retreat through Winchester and sidled his division along the southeastern outskirts of town. He also reoriented his battle line so that it gradually faced in a more northerly direction to confront any pursuit by the Union infantry. When Ramseur's men drew near the Front Royal Road southeast of Winchester, they witnessed and heard an unprecedented and haunting scene for the Army of Northern Virginia. "We could see Yanks by the thousand marching towards the town," recalled Pvt. George Q. Peyton of the 13th Virginia, "while cheer upon cheer rent the air from victorious Yanks."[34]

On Ramseur's right flank, Maj. Gen. Lunsford L. Lomax bluffed Wilson into passivity even though his two brigades holding the line contained fewer than 1,400 shoddily armed and mounted troopers. Their accomplishment is often overlooked considering that they guarded Jubal Early's vital line of retreat against more than 3,000 Union horse soldiers armed with Spencer repeating rifles and a six-gun rifled battery. In the distance to the east, Ramseur's soldiers saw these "great columns of cavalry moving along parallel with us." They moved cautiously thanks to the presence of Abraham's Creek and Lomax's horsemen protecting Ramseur's right flank. At one point, Col. Sandy Pendleton rushed over and ordered Ramseur to deploy skirmishers in case Wilson's

33 Report of Lt. Col. William H. S. Adney, 36th Ohio at Battles of Opequon and Fisher's Hill, October 4, 1864, John Booth Papers, OHS; *Journal History of the 23rd Ohio*, RBHPC, 31; Capt. A. T. Ward Diary, John Booth Papers, OHS; Alexis G. Soley, "Sheridan at Winchester, How the 34th Massachusetts Had a Hand in the 'Whirling,'" *Springfield Republican*, February 14, 1887; Sturm, *Civil War Remembrances*, 97.

34 Stephen D. Ramseur to Dear Brother, October 10, 1864, Ramseur Papers, SHC-UNC, George Q. Peyton, Memoir, UVA.

Federals broke through Lomax's thin screen. When Ramseur reached the Millwood Pike, he reoriented his battle line so that it faced northeast with Lomax covering the right.[35]

The cavalry that moved menacingly off to Ramseur's right flank belonged to Brig. Gen. James H. Wilson's division. Situated on the far left of the Union battle line, this command played a minimal role in the final outcome of the battle. After moving south of Abram's Creek that morning, Wilson failed to closely engage Lomax's horsemen on the Confederate right. Instead, the division picketed the army's left and observed developments with the infantry battle. Major John Wilson Phillips of the 18th Pennsylvania Cavalry noted that the division had moved to "a range of hills completely overlooking the field and then for two and a half hours, our batteries playing, we witnessed the bloody conflict," a typical description of Wilson's activities for that afternoon. A trooper from the 22nd New York reported that it took Wilson until 3:00 p.m. simply to drive in Lomax's skirmish line.[36]

Brigadier General John B. McIntosh led a dismounted battalion of the 5th New York Cavalry against a party of Confederate skirmishers concealed in some woods along the Senseny Road. The New Yorkers flushed the Butternuts from the trees and chased after them, but the New Yorkers ran into Lomax's dismounted horsemen posted behind rails and rock walls. The Virginians opened fire and repulsed the enemy battalion. McIntosh attempted to halt the retrograde movement by dashing amongst the retreating troopers. A Confederate bullet drilled into his right lower leg. He was carried from the field and the amputation that night six inches below his knee ended his career as a field officer. "His loss cast a gloom over all who knew him," lamented Major Phillips. "In camp and in field . . . he was the same kind brave man, & gallant officer. His brigade loved him and would follow him wherever he led." Unfortunately, the elimination of McIntosh and his leadership severely hindered the usefulness of Wilson's division the rest of that afternoon. McIntosh's fall left the brigade under the untested leadership of Lt. Col. George

35 Ramseur to My Dear Brother, October 10, 1864, Ramseur Papers, SHC-UNC; George Q. Peyton, Memoir, 83; Hotchkiss Papers, "Pegram's Div. at Winchester," September 19, 1864, LC.

36 Civil War Diary of John Wilson Phillips, *Virginia Magazine of History and Biography* (January 1954), 112; Report of Service, Brigadier General John B. McIntosh, NA; Wilson, 555.

Brig. Gen. John McIntosh, pictured here after his leg was amputated.
Months later his wound was still unhealed and suppurating. *LC*

Purington. Any hopes Sheridan had held that Wilson's division would severely
hamper Jubal Early's retreat died when McIntosh went down.[37]

Lieutenant Albert C. Houghton of McIntosh's staff dashed back to the 2nd
Ohio Cavalry on the far left of Wilson's division in search of Purington. When
he learned that he was now in command of the brigade, his countenance
revealed "feelings of horror and surprise." Private Roger Hannaford of the 2nd
Ohio knew right away that Purington "did not want the position" and, even
worse, feared that he "might not be able to fill it." Hannaford's assessment was

37 Ibid.

quite accurate. After a few weeks of tentative, uninspiring leadership, Purington surrendered command of the brigade.[38]

On Wilson's right, Brig. Gen. George H. Chapman's brigade advanced along the Senseny Road in an effort to move up on the immediate left flank of the Sixth Corps and strike into the hordes of Confederates fleeing the battlefield. This half-hearted movement by a small fraction of Wilson's command appears to have been a token move to satisfy Sheridan's order "to push along the Senseny Road and, if possible, gain the valley pike south of Winchester." If Wilson could have broken through Lomax's attenuated battle line here, the Union cavalry might have damaged Ramseur's division in the same manner that Merritt wrecked Wharton's command.

Almost simultaneously with McIntosh's wounding, Chapman rode out to his skirmish line to study the Confederate dispositions in front of his command. As he scanned the Confederates through his binoculars, a Southern sharpshooter posted in some pines off to his left fired. The lead ball struck a glancing blow on Chapman's sword belt but nevertheless "partially disabled" him for several hours. Colonel William Wells became active commander of the brigade, even though the stricken Chapman remained on the field. At 4:00 p.m., Wells dismounted the 22nd New York, deployed it in front of the brigade, and proceeded to advance up the Senseny Road. The attack shoved Confederate horsemen from Lt. Col. William Thompson's brigade back beyond Abraham's Creek. On the commanding heights of the west bank, the Virginians made a determined stand from behind breastworks on Carper's farm and forced the Federals to retire back across the creek. As they withdrew, the Confederate artillery near the Carper house opened fire and shelled the Federals as they climbed up the east bank of the stream, killing and wounding several of them.[39]

With both brigade commanders down wounded, Wilson ceased his efforts to smash through Lomax's thin line and initiated a sweep around Lomax's southern flank. He ordered Purington to head for the Millwood Pike and attempt to hit the retreating Confederates on the Valley Pike at Kernstown, four miles south of Winchester. Although Wilson had 3,000 rested and fully

38 Roger Hannaford, Memoirs, Cincinnati Historical Society; Bradley Johnson to Wife, September 29, 1864, Duke.

39 OR 43, pt. 1, 518; Benedict, *1st Vermont Cavalry*, 658; Sheridan, *Memoirs*, vol. 2, 25; William N. Pickerill, *History of the Third Indiana Cavalry*, 162; Elliot Hoffman, *A Vermont Cavalryman in War and Love*, 329.

equipped troopers, Lomax managed to hold the Illinois general at bay with less than half as many men and two guns. Wilson waited until he saw the Confederates on the main battlefield breaking in confusion before he moved. Wilson made a lengthy, cross-country end run around the Confederate right flank. He looped southward and gained the Millwood Pike, but Lomax simply moved Bradley Johnson's troopers directly south to the junction of the Millwood and Front Royal Pikes. The direct route allowed Lomax to easily interpose his troopers in front of Wilson's division by 6:00 p.m. Wilson's lack of aggressiveness amazed the Confederates. "What caused me the greatest wonderment," testified Capt. George W. Booth of Bradley Johnson's staff, "was the inertness of the Federal pursuit." Colonel Tom Munford watched the inactivity on the Confederate right from the heights of Fort Hill on the opposite side of Winchester and mused, "Why this great body of horse were not hurled upon General Early's army is a mystery to me."[40]

The opportunity to intercept Early's retreat had been lost, but Wilson nonetheless continued his looping course. When Johnson's Virginians and Marylanders blocked the way, Purington ordered an attack. Twenty-three-year-old Capt. Walter Hull led the 2nd New York Cavalry in a saber charge directed at Johnson's front while a squadron of Wilson's scouts under Capt. Theodore A. Boice of the 5th New York struck the Marylander's command on its right flank and rear. As had become routine in the Valley, the New Yorkers scattered Johnson's men "in all directions," just as they might have done two hours earlier if Wilson had only made the effort along the Senseny Road. Wilson continued on his way toward Kernstown, moving across the country and running into "stone fences and rough ground" in the darkness.[41]

Although Munford had sealed off the Confederate left flank and prevented Averell from interdicting the retreating Confederate rabble, the Virginian's work was not done. He still had to extricate his own brigade from the fracas. He abandoned his position on Fort Hill and retired around the western and southern outskirts of Winchester. When he reached Milltown where the Valley Pike spanned Abraham's Creek one mile south of Winchester, Munford assumed that he would have found his brigade in "the ugliest kind of place." By

---

40 George Wilson Booth, *Personal Reminiscences of a Maryland Soldier in the War Between the States, 1861-65*, 146; Munford, *Reminiscences of Cavalry Operations*, 450.

41 *OR* 43, pt. 1, 518.

then, Munford's brigade had reached Bower's Hill well behind the army's rear guard in darkness that grew deeper with each passing minute. Some Union cavalry advancing up the Valley Pike out of Winchester struck Munford's flank, and the Virginian changed front and drove the Federals from the Pike and then proceeded to withdraw up the Middle Road to Newtown, six miles to the south where he joined the rest of Early's army later that night.[42]

Wilson gained the Valley Pike near dusk, but ran into a section of Capt. Thomas Bryan's Lewisburg artillery deployed on a nearby ridge with the last brilliant rays of sunlight shining directly toward the approaching Union horsemen. The gunners fired several shells, fell back to the next ridge, and redeployed to fire a few more shells before again withdrawing. As the Confederate cavalry withdrew over the hill, they passed through the fading sunlight as they moved and then descended in the darkness beyond and disappeared from the sight of the Unionists. They continued on a southwest course until reaching the Middle Road, which carried them toward Newtown, where the scattered remains of Early's army gathered that night.[43]

Wilson halted his division one mile south of Winchester and sent one battalion each from both the 2nd Ohio and 3nd New Jersey Cavalry up the Valley Pike "with orders to advance as far as possible." The troopers cheered as they galloped up the pike toward Kernstown. There, Ramseur had deployed his division behind stone walls running perpendicular to the road. Johnston's brigade crossed the road with Pegram on his right and Godwin's command on the left, all facing toward Winchester and waiting for the Union cavalry. A Virginian of Pegram's brigade recalled the scene: "The horses sounded like thunder and the air was filled with all sorts of sounds."[44]

The Union troopers attempted to stampede the Southerners "by making all sorts of hideous sounds. Some barked like dogs, some bellowed like bulls, some brayed like jackasses, and here they came to ride over the Rebels." The Federals captured a few stragglers in their advance and scattered others into the darkness as they neared Kernstown. Ramseur's skirmishers fired a "pattering" volley to warn their comrades waiting in line of battle of the approaching Union cavalry.

42 Munford, *Reminiscences of Cavalry Operations*, 450.

43 Roger Hannaford, Memoirs, Cincinnati Historical Society, 162; Humphreys, Memoir, UVA, 363.

44 Some elements of John B. Gordon's division took part in the rearguard as well. George Q. Peyton, Memoir, 83-84.

The Confederates broke their ranks and allowed the 3rd New Jersey to pass beyond their lines. The Southerners then sealed off their line and delivered several "stunning volleys" into the Jersey men, killing and wounding several. The Confederates also fired into the trailing battalion from the 2nd Ohio and sent them scattering back down the pike. The trapped troopers from the 3rd New Jersey galloped southward up the pike and "then flanked off & safely rejoined their command toward sunrise the next morning."[45]

Wilson's actions on the Federal left did not accomplish any of Sheridan's goals. He was too cautious and allowed himself to be intimidated by the thin line of ill-equipped and poorly disciplined "Valley Cavalry" the Union troopers had run through on a daily basis leading up to the battle. Colonel William Wells of the 1st Vermont Cavalry, an acting brigade commander at the close of the battle, wrote home, "Our Div might have taken a great many prisoners had we been commanded by a superior Genl." Within two weeks Wilson was relieved of command, sent to Georgia, and replaced by Custer. When that happened, Wells noted, "The Div feel very much pleased at the change. Think you will hear better accounts of us now we have a gallant leader."[46]

As the sun set behind the Allegheny Mountains, it became abundantly clear that Sheridan's army had attained an unprecedented success. For the first time in the war, a major portion of the Army of Northern Virginia had been routed from a battlefield. Winchester, which had changed hands more than 70 times, would never again be controlled by Southern forces. The losses suffered by Jubal Early's Army of the Valley District crippled it effectiveness; Southern morale and confidence plummeted. Conversely, the Union army's confidence in both Sheridan and themselves climbed to an unprecedented level.

Early and his army survived to fight another day. Their valiant attempt to reverse their fortunes the following month at Cedar Creek aptly demonstrated as much. But the Union victory along Opequon Creek sowed the seeds of the Confederacy's ultimate demise in the Shenandoah Valley.[47]

---

45 Ibid., 83-84; Hannaford, Cincinnati Historical Society, 162.

46 Hoffman, *A Vermont Cavalryman in War and Love*, 340.

47 Although an argument can be made that part of the Army of Northern Virginia had been routed off South Mountain on September 14, 1862, the bulk of that force comprised a single Southern division under Maj. Gen. D. H. Hill. At Third Winchester two years later, the defeated Rebels consisted of a large portion of Gen. Robert E. Lee's command operating independently as an army in the Shenandoah Valley.

Chapter 21

NEVER A VICTORY SUCH AS THIS
Winchester to Fisher's Hill and Beyond

On the outskirts of Winchester, the Union Army of the Shenandoah celebrated its unprecedented victory. Generals Phil Sheridan, Horatio Wright, William Emory, and George Crook galloped along the Sixth Corps's line of battle. "The men were wild with joy," wrote Capt. Elisha H. Rhodes of the 2nd Rhode Island, "I cried and shouted in my excitement and never felt so good before in my life." "Hurrah for Sheridan," the troops shouted, as their enthusiasm "seemed to carry them away as they broke out in cheer after cheer and heard the words of praise" from Sheridan. When he halted in front of the cheering Vermont brigade, Sheridan shouted, "I guess we'll go to Winchester." Then he turned and rode into Winchester with Crook, following the Army of West Virginia into town. One of Alfred Torbert's aides rode up to Sheridan with a message, and the Ohioan slapped him on the shoulder, saying, "Well isn't this bully!" As Sheridan and Crook continued up the main street of town, three loyal Union girls gave the generals "the most hearty reception."[1]

---

1 Sanford, in his *Experiences in Army Life*, 268, noted that Sheridan's manner at the time "was not at all in Sheridan's line but he was feeling unusually happy, and well he might." Mark, Penrose G. Mark, *Red, White, and Blue Badge: Pennsylvania Volunteers: A History of the 93rd Regiment,*

The girls told the generals how they had watched the battle from the roof of their home "with tears and lamentations" when Sheridan's initial assault faltered. But now they joyfully exalted the Union victory and "indulged in the most unguarded manifestations and expressions." Crook knew the girls from his previous visits to Winchester and did not want to see them harmed should the Union fortunes at Winchester change once more. He reminded them "that the Valley had hitherto been a race-course—one day in possession of friends, and the next enemies," and advised them to be cautious in their words. The girls replied that they had no such fears as "Early's army was so demoralized . . . that it would never be in condition to enter Winchester again."[2]

As was to be expected, the arrival of the victorious Union troops did not sit well with the town's secessionist majority. Soldiers of the 37th Massachusetts paraded the captured flag of the 2nd Virginia Infantry through town, much to the displeasure of many of Winchester's women, who only days earlier had presented the new banner to the men. Laura Lee described September 19, 1864, as "the most dreadful day we have ever spent." Her house mate, Mrs. Hugh Lee, agreed, and stayed awake most of the night worrying that Sheridan would burn them out. Her fears never came to pass, but hungry Federals prowled the town seizing chickens and any food they could lay their hands upon. The dreaded Yankees even surprised her by sharing supplies for the wounded Confederates in town.

After the generals calmed the girls, Crook led Sheridan to the home of Rebecca Wright. When the sounds of battle rolled into Winchester that morning, she couldn't help but wonder if the information about Anderson's departure that she had supplied to Sheridan had caused it. At one point during the day her mother said, "Becky, this must be thy battle." She denied it but wondered if her mother was correct. Shells exploded all around the Wright home, and Rebecca later recalled, "It was the most terrible day of all our experience in old Winchester." The shelling grew fiercer as the day progressed, and the Wright women sought safety in their cellar.[3]

390; Rhodes, *All For the Union: The Civil War Diary and Letters of Elisha Hunt Rhodes*, 185; Haines, *The History of the Fifteenth Regiment New Jersey Volunteers*, 264; Sheridan, *Memoirs*, vol. 2, 27-28;

2 Ibid.

3 Proudfit, "The Jersey Troops in the Shenandoah," *Newark Daily Advertiser*, September 27, 1864; Mrs. Hugh Lee Diary and Laura Lee Diary, Handley Library; "Woman's Wit Turned Defeat Into Victory For Sheridan," *New York Times*, July 28, 1912.

As the daylight waned, the roar of battle faded and then ceased altogether. Rebecca grew restless and went upstairs to observe the situation. Seeing nothing from the first or second floor windows, she went to the attic window. "I saw the old flag waving and, it was coming into town." She dropped to her knees and thanked "the Giver of all good." Rushing to the cellar, she jubilantly shouted to her mother and sister, "The old flag is coming in! Come on up, now, all will be safe! The fires will be put out, and everything will soon be all right. The dear old flag is coming back again."[4]

Later that evening, Rebecca heard the rattle of swords clanging against the steps of the front porch. She opened the door, saw two officers, and reached out her hands to both, "welcoming them as Union officers." Sheridan introduced himself and confirmed that he had fought the battle based upon her information. The news startled Rebecca, who asked Sheridan "to swear on his sabre that he would not mention until after the war that I had given him the information." She knew her family members' "lives would be worthless" if the Winchester secessionists learned that she had played a role in Jubal Early's defeat. Then Sheridan sat down at her desk and composed a dispatch to Lt. Gen. U.S. Grant. Sheridan wrote, "I have the honor to report that I attacked the forces of General Early on the Berryville pike at the crossing of Opequon Creek, and after a most stubborn and sanguinary engaged, which lasted from early in the morning until 5 o'clock in the evening, completely defeated him, driving him through Winchester, captured about 2,500 prisoners, five pieces of artillery, nine army flags and most of their wounded."[5]

Official news of Sheridan's victory did not reach Washington until the following day. Brigadier General John D. Stevenson, the commandant of the post at Harpers Ferry, had telegraphed Secretary of War, Edwin Stanton, at noon on September 19 to inform him that a battle was underway. Stevenson reported that "heavy and continuous firing" could be heard all the way to Harpers Ferry. At 1:45 p.m., the anxious Stanton replied, "Spare no pains or effort to obtain the earliest and most reliable information, and telegraph

4 Ibid.

5 Sheridan's post-battle dispatch quoted in the text was written at 7:30 p.m. in the Wright house. The more famous dispatch that ended with, "We have just sent them whirling through Winchester, and we are after them tomorrow," was composed by Sheridan's chief of staff, Lt. Col. James W. Forsyth, at 1:00 a.m. on September 20. It was directed to Brig. Gen. John D. Stevenson at Harpers Ferry who, in turn, forwarded it to Secretary of War Edwin M. Stanton in Washington. OR 43, pt. 1, 24.

immediately. . . . Leave nothing undone to get accurate information." Stanton evidently expected the worst. He instructed the president of the Baltimore and Ohio Railroad to "Be ready to move troops from Washington to Harpers Ferry rapidly on short notice." Stevenson sent several more updates to Stanton throughout the afternoon and into the early evening hours. At 5:50 p.m., Stevenson updated Stanton with the reports of an officer who had left the battlefield at 1:00 p.m. Stevenson added that he still heard heavy firing from Winchester, and closed by saying, "Every indication is most favorable to us." At 1:00 a.m. on September 20, Sheridan's chief of staff, Lt. Col. James W. Forsyth, penned the famous telegram, "We have just sent them whirling through Winchester, and we are after them tomorrow." Stevenson sent a summary of the battle results to Stanton at 7:40 a.m. Exactly four hours later, Stevenson forwarded Forsyth's message to Stanton, precisely 24 hours after Sheridan's infantry assault began.[6]

The news was received with great joy in Washington and at Grant's headquarters in City Point near Petersburg. President Abraham Lincoln telegraphed Sheridan, "Just heard of your great victory. God bless you all, officers and men. Strongly inclined to come up and see you." When Grant heard the news, he congratulated Sheridan and urged him to "push your success and make all you can of it." Sheridan's victory at Winchester created "much rejoicing" for Grant, for it was he who first brought Sheridan to Virginia and then subsequently assigned him command in the Shenandoah Valley "amid the doubts of some of the principal officials at Washington." In the immediate aftermath of Sheridan's victory at Winchester, Grant recommended that Sheridan be promoted to brigadier general in the Regular Army and that his appointment as commander of the Middle Military Division be made permanent. Lincoln readily agreed and made the appointment that very day.[7]

Celebrations abounded in the wake of Sheridan's victory at Winchester. Grant ordered the firing of 100 guns in Petersburg, and Stanton did the same in Washington. The Union victory in the Shenandoah Valley gave a shot in the arm to sagging Union morale. Although Sherman had captured Atlanta at the beginning of September, the Confederates had remained defiant in Virginia, the primary source of the Union's frustrations throughout the war. While steady progress could be measured in the Western Theater with a string of Federal

---

6   Ibid., pt. 2, 114-115, 123-124.

7   Ibid., 117; Porter, *Campaigning With Porter*, 298.

triumphs from Mill Spring and Fort Donelson in early 1862 through Atlanta, Sheridan's victory provided the first solid evidence that the course of the war in Virginia was turning in favor of the north. The battle clearly continued the political momentum that Lincoln and the Republican Party had gained with the fall of Atlanta.[8]

Celebrations among the soldiers and the army unleashed a new confidence in the Union troops, especially those who had served in the Army of the Potomac and had experienced years of disappointment. Dr. Daniel M. Holt of the 121st New York likely summed up the feelings of many. "For forty-eight hours my eyes have scarcely known sleep; but I cannot sleep," explained the surgeon. "Every fibre of my body and every nerve of my system is alive to the fact that at last we have done something to call out the praise and gratitude of the nation, and it has been acknowledged."[9]

Back at Winchester, the jubilation soon died down as the exhausted soldiers bedded down for the night in the fields surrounding the town. Colonel Windsor B. French of the 77th New York recalled that when his regiment halted its advance, his right flank rested near the grave of Gen. Daniel Morgan, the Revolutionary War hero of the battle of Saragota, Cowpens, and several other important fields. This proximity was meaningful for the men of the 77th New York, as their regiment had been raised in Saratoga, New York, and they were intimately familiar with the details of that battle in 1777. The soldiers of the Vermont brigade quickly realized that they had halted near a large vineyard and promptly went to work eating grapes.[10]

The victory had been costly to both armies. Sheridan lost more than 5,000 men, most of them killed and wounded. Jubal Early lost nearly 4,000 irreplaceable soldiers, five guns, and perhaps as many as 15 battle flags. Ironically, Cook's Georgians captured three Union colors during Rodes's counterattack, which they successfully carried from the field along with several hundred prisoners. The loss of Robert Rodes was an irreparable blow to Early's army. In addition to Rodes, the Confederate Army of the Valley District lost the services of Maj. Gen. Fitzhugh Lee as a result of his severe wound. Early also

---

8 John G. Nicolay and John Hay, *Abraham Lincoln, A History*, 305; "Another Glorious Victory," *Marysville Tribune*, September 28, 1864.

9 Holt, *A Surgeon's Civil War*, 252.

10 W. B. French to Messrs. Potter & Judson, September 28, 1864, "The Late Battles in the Shenandoah," *The Saratogian*, October 13, 1864; Walker, *Vermont Brigade*, 106.

lost several capable brigade commanders: Brig. Gen. Archibald Godwin, killed; Brig. Gen. Zebulon York, wounded; Col. George S. Patton, mortally wounded; and Col. Augustus Forsberg, wounded. Scores of field and line officers were also lost. The battle of Opequon Creek gutted Early's officer corps, a blow from which his army never recovered.[11]

Early withdrew his men to the perceived safety of their fortified position at Fisher's Hill the next day. Most of his army had marched through the night until 2:00 a.m. to get ahead of Sheridan and was on the road again by 4:00 a.m. They reached Fisher's Hill at noon where the men cooked rations and slept off the effects of their recent exertions. "I have never exerted myself so much in my life and my voice was completely gone," wrote Brig. Gen. Bryan Grimes to his wife. "I was as sore as a boil all over, had to have Polk (his body servant) to rub me over with liniment." At Fisher's Hill, Early had held Sheridan at bay back in August until Anderson arrived in the Valley, forcing the Ohioan to withdraw toward Harpers Ferry. The army's arrival at Fisher's Hill provided the troops a slight boost in morale. "We are in a very strongly fortified position," observed an officer of the Louisiana Tigers. "The enemy are now in plain sight on the heights of Cedar Creek. . . . We have just received orders to man the breastworks and we are anxious for them to come at us here as we think we can get even with them for the repulse of Monday." William F. Brand of the Stonewall Brigade wrote, "We are strongly fortified & have a commanding position. I think by the blessing of God, we may be able to give them a sound thrashing." Ohio Col. J. Warren Keifer agreed with the strength of Early's position, but with a newly found confidence in Union arms he added, "I think we can whip the enemy even there."[12]

Sheridan wasted no time in following up his victory. He ordered the army to move out in pursuit of the Confederates at 5:00 a.m. the next morning. Torbert sent William Averell's division southward on the Back Road while Merritt led the main column up the Valley Pike. Wilson's division headed east out of Newtown and gained the Front Royal Road. Wright's Sixth Corps marched in the open fields on the west side of the Pike, and Emory's Nineteenth Corps did the same to the east. The ordnance train, ambulances,

---

11 Jed Hotchkiss to wife, September 21, 1864, Library of Congress.

12 George Ring to My Own Darling, September 21, 1864, G. P. Ring Papers, Tulane; William F. Brand to Kate Armentrout, September 22, 1864, Brand Civil War Collection, UVA; J. W. Keifer to My Dear Wife, September 20, 1864, Keifer Papers, LC.

and wagons moved on the Pike, while Crook's Army of West Virginia followed in reserve. Sheridan left Col. Oliver Edwards's Sixth Corps brigade and the 17th Pennsylvania Cavalry in Winchester to garrison the town.[13]

Brigadier General Thomas C. Devin's reduced strength brigade encountered elements of Lomax's division at Middletown and shoved them across Cedar Creek through Strasburg to Fisher's Hill. Devin occupied the town and deployed pickets to confront Jubal Early's pickets south and west of town. Custer's and Lowell's brigades arrived and took up positions on some high ground overlooking the town. On the Back Road, Averell drove some of Lomax's advance pickets across Cedar Creek and chased them back toward Fisher's Hill. Wilson reached Cedarville a few miles north of Front Royal without encountering any Confederates.

Sheridan rode toward Strasburg escorted by the battle-scarred remnants of the 2nd U.S. Cavalry and arrived early in the afternoon with his horsemen. They passed through Strasburg and surveyed the heights of Fisher's Hill from the narrow flood plain that held the Valley Pike. They quickly realized that Early held a position impregnable to direct assault and that "the situation, at least, required some deliberation." Sheridan and his escorts withdrew to safer environs on the northern outskirts of Strasburg. Orderlies pitched Sheridan's headquarters tent in front of a stone mansion just outside of Strasburg, and the army commander deliberated over the challenge at hand.[14]

Sheridan convened his generals and discussed the situation. Every private in the army knew that a frontal assault would be sheer madness. The army commander initially proposed that Crook attack Early's right flank by marching along the base of Massanutten Mountain. The officers hashed over the idea, but Sheridan realized the impracticality of the plan as it would entail two river crossings. Instead, he "resolved to use a turning-column against his [Early's] left," an arrangement proposed by Crook. With that plan in mind, Sheridan moved Crook's Army of West Virginia into a heavy growth of timber north of Cedar Creek and out of sight of the Confederate lookouts posted atop Signal Knob at the northern extreme of Massanutten Mountain. Sheridan also decided to send Torbert with Wilson's and Merritt's divisions into the Luray Valley "with a view to reentering the Valley of the Shenandoah near New Market." If

13 *OR* 43, pt. 2, 110-111.

14 John Price Kepner Diary, Virginia Historical Society; Theo Rodenbough, *From Everglade to Canyon with the Second Dragoons, 1836-75*, 357.

all went as planned, Torbert's divisions would be in position to intercept Early's army as it retreated up the Valley.[15]

By 5:00 p.m., the Union infantry arrived and relieved Merritt's horsemen from the town and surrounding heights. While Merritt shifted most of his troopers two miles to the right on the Capon Road, the infantry went into camp on the outskirts of Strasburg. The Nineteenth Corps extended leftward from the town almost as far east as the road running between Strasburg and Front Royal. Emory detached a regiment to picket that road. The Sixth Corps went into position on the right of the pike with Merritt's shifting cavalry division filling the gap between the infantry and Averell's division on the Back Road. Crook's Army of West Virginia halted atop Hupp's Hill north of Cedar Creek "in fair view of the rebel lookouts," but moved into a heavily wooded ravine after dark. Crook's troops moved "slowly and quietly" through the night made darker than normal by heavy cloud cover that blotted out the stars. In the distance on Fisher's Hill, Crook's men saw "far-off in the front the enemy's camp-fires gleaming and the intervening fires of the Sixth Corps and Nineteenth Corps [that] lighted up the heavens . . . a grand sight." Although Crook had officially forbidden camp fires, "there was many a little fire built and a blanket held over it to hide the light while the boys made their cup of coffee."[16]

On the morning of September 21, Torbert departed for the Luray Valley with Merritt's division and left Devin's small brigade with Averell's division to support Sheridan's efforts at Fisher's Hill. Before leaving, Torbert passed orders for Averell to "Move out as far on the Back and Middle roads as far as you can until stopped by superior force." Sheridan wanted "to know as soon as possible whether the left of the enemy's infantry can be forced." At 7:45 a.m., Averell advanced up the Back Road and forced the Confederate pickets back to Lomax's entrenched position at Fisher's Hill. Sheridan soon joined the cavalryman and his brigadiers on the skirmish line to personally inspect the dispositions and terrain on Jubal Early's left. Averell warned Sheridan that "cavalry could not carry the position without cooperative movements of infantry." Averell suggested that "an infantry corps, by hugging the base of the

---

15 OR 43, pt. 1, 48; Sheridan, *Memoirs*, 34; Martin F. Schmitt, ed., *Crook*, 129.

16 OR 43, pt. 1, 48, 152; Jesse Tyler Sturm, *Civil War Remembrances*, 99; W. T. Patterson Diary, Ohio Historical Society.

[Little] North Mountain, might break around the enemy's left and render his position untenable."[17]

Early that same morning at Guard Hill, Wilson's division readied to force a crossing of the two forks of the Shenandoah River immediately north of Front Royal. Torbert passed to Wilson Sheridan's instructions to "make a strong demonstration in the morning to ascertain what infantry are in or near Front Royal. If the enemy develops cavalry only he desires you to run them off." Sheridan worried about Maj. Gen. Joseph B. Kershaw's Confederate division, which had departed Winchester on September 15 and passed through Front Royal on its way east across the Blue Ridge. With Early's defeat at Winchester, Sheridan correctly concluded that Kershaw would soon rejoin Early. However, Kershaw's division was near Culpeper and did not rejoin Early until September 24.[18]

When Wilson reached the Shenandoah River early on the morning of September 21, a thick blanket of fog concealed the landscape and the Confederate positions on the far bank of the southern fork of the river. Brigadier General Williams C. Wickham had posted Col. Thomas Munford with three regiments numbering no more than 600 men to cover the river crossings. These Virginians, the very men who saved Early's left flank from disaster at Winchester, dismounted and deployed behind breastworks to even the odds. The fog aided Munford as "One could not see fifty steps ahead, but could hear everything."[19]

While Wilson attempted to scan the situation, his troopers deployed in line of battle, dismounted, and shivered in the cold, damp fog for more than an hour. Though Wilson was unable to accurately measure the Confederate strength and position at Front Royal, he ultimately attacked straight up the Front Royal Pike with Lt. Col. George Purington's brigade. He also sent a detachment under Col. William Wells upstream to Kendrick's Ford to charge across the river and strike the 4th Virginia Cavalry.

When Purington attacked, Wilson ordered every bugler in his division to sound the charge. Munford's troopers repulsed the first charge from their position in and around a mill on the south bank of the South fork of the

---

17 OR 43, pt. 2, 136-137; pt. 1, 499.

18 Ibid., pt. 2, 121-122.

19 OR Atlas, 85:19; T. T. Munford, "Reminiscences of Cavalry Operations," 451-452.

Shenandoah River. The checked Federals scrambled from their horses, hit the dirt along the north bank of the South fork, and fired their seven-shot Spencer repeating carbines at the Virginians. Wilson soon ordered the 18th Pennsylvania and 2nd Ohio into the attack. After heavy resistance from Munford, the Union horsemen forced the Virginians from their positions. At Kendrick's Ford, Wells managed to force a crossing that rendered Munford's position completely untenable. With the fog lifting and his lines crumbling, Munford withdrew through Front Royal to the Luray Valley road. There, Wickham advanced the 3rd Virginia Cavalry to cover the retreat of Munford's three regiments. Pursued gingerly by Wilson, Wickham withdrew six miles into the Luray Valley and halted behind Gooney Run, a substantial creek that flowed across the valley. Wilson approached Wickham's position but did not press the issue, allowing the Confederate cavalry to regroup and move to a stronger position unmolested. Soon after, Torbert arrived at Front Royal with Merritt's command and camped for the night.[20]

Back at Fisher's Hill, Sheridan used September 21 to feel out Early's position. The Sixth Corps ground inexorably forward against several lines of Confederate skirmishers posted upon rises on the plateau between Strasburg and Fisher's Hill. The intervening high ground made it difficult for Sheridan to gain a precise understanding of Early's position. Although Early had taken refuge at Fisher's Hill in August, Sheridan did not venture beyond Strasburg at that time, so as the Army of the Shenandoah closed in on Early's position, they were covering new ground. Skirmishers from Brig. Gen. Frank Wheaton's division drove off Confederate sharpshooters, securing an advanced position. Sheridan rode forward with Wheaton's advance. The army commander dismounted and walked through a pine grove to the skirmish line beyond followed by Wright, Emory, Wheaton, two unnamed brigadiers, and Col. Charles Tompkins, the Sixth Corps's chief of artillery. The assemblage of brass took in the situation and soon ordered the Napoleons of the 1st Massachusetts Battery forward to the skirmish line. The guns roared into action, knocking Confederate skirmish reserves and work details back to the main Southern fortifications on Fisher's Hill. Meanwhile, Sheridan continued to study the landscape and Southern dispositions. He observed a commanding height

20 OR 43, pt. 1; J. W. Patton Diary, Tennessee State Library and Archives; W. N. Pickerill, *History of the Third Indiana Cavalry*, 163; Roger Hannaford Memoir, Cincinnati Historical Society; B. J. Haden, *Reminiscences of Jeb Stuart's Cavalry*, 37; Munford, "Reminiscences of Cavalry Operations," 452.

known as Flint Hill to the right front "which it was desirable to obtain." However, Confederate sharpshooters from Pegram's and Ramseur's divisions manned wooden rail pens on the hill and clung to their position with dogged tenacity, repulsing the skirmishers from Maj. Gen. George W. Getty's Sixth Corps division. This commanding height had "a fine view of the enemy's works," so Sheridan ordered Wright to take it around 4:00 p.m. Getty bolstered his skirmish line with Major Robert Munroe's 139th Pennsylvania from Pittsburgh. Two companies deployed to the right in skirmish order. They linked with Averell's horsemen whose position was centered along the Back Road. Munroe charged and routed a detachment of Confederate riflemen from a house in front of Getty's position. Munroe then pressed up the hill and attacked the Confederates in their rail pens, but the accurate fire of the Southern sharpshooters sent the Pennsylvanians reeling back down the hill.[21]

Munroe soon ran into heavy resistance from Confederates of Pegram's division who drove 139th Pennsylvania back. Horatio Wright quickly spied Keifer's nearby brigade and promptly ordered Ricketts to reinforce Getty with one of Keifer's regiments. The unlucky lot fell to the 126th Ohio but Captain George W. Hoge led his Buckeyes forward to aid the beleaguered Union skirmish line. The left of Hoge's line advanced through a thick wood, which sheltered it from the Confederate gunfire. However, his right moved over open ground and came under heavy fire from the front and right flank. The Ohioans, many of them recent recruits and conscripts drafted into the army, stopped to return fire, sapping the advance of its momentum. The Ohioans moved to within a few rods of the Confederate rail pens but "being much exposed and suffering terrible without the ability to inflict much loss on the enemy," temporarily fell back in confusion. The 126th Ohio lost 21 men in a matter of a few minutes and withdrew behind a hill a short distance to their rear. There, Hoge rallied his men and waited for assistance. Keifer saw the 126th Ohio needed help and ordered the 6th Maryland into the fight. Some of the Confederates had left their works and chased after the Ohioans but they ran into the Marylanders who herded the Confederates back into their bullpens. Like the preceding Pennsylvanians and Ohioans, however, the Marylanders could not drive the Southerners from their fortifications.[22]

21 OR 43, pt. 1, 152, 192.

22 Ibid., 152, 254, 264; Sheridan, *Memoirs*, vol. 2, 36.

Finally, about 6:00 p.m., Wright ordered Col. James M. Warner to attack with his entire brigade of Pennsylvanians and a small New York outfit, with the 6th Maryland and 126th Ohio supporting on the right. The U.S. soldiers fixed bayonets and advanced up the hill without stopping to fire. The renewed assault drove the Southerners from the position and secured for Sheridan this valuable piece of real estate. With Flint Hill secured, Union skirmishers advanced beyond the crest, halted on the southern face of the height and opened fire at the Confederates in their main trenches atop Fisher's Hill. Although the entire affair cost Sheridan only 66 men killed and wounded, it provided the Army of the Shenandoah with a valuable vantage point to examine Early's position and placed its infantry and artillery in range of the Confederate line.[23]

During the night, the soldiers of the Sixth Corps moved forward and to the right in order to occupy the newly gained position. They worked feverishly through the night constructing earthworks and lunettes, which artillery soon occupied. The darkness and "intricacies of the ground, cut up by ravines and covered by dense woods" slowed progress and it took "nearly all night to accomplish." Although Flint Hill had fallen, Early's sharpshooters reconstituted a second skirmish line a short distance north of Tumbling Run.[24]

On September 22, Torbert continued his push up the Luray Valley. Sheridan would be sadly disappointed in the results of those operations. Although Torbert had at his disposal 5,000 horsemen and several batteries of horse artillery, Brig. Gen. Williams C. Wickham's 1,500 cavalrymen and six guns used the rugged terrain behind Overall Run to block Torbert's half-hearted advance. Wickham had gone across the Massanutten to see Early and left Col. Tom Munford in command at Milford. On the hill overlooking the creek, Munford positioned his troopers in "loop-hole breast-works which extended clear across the Valley." Torbert arrived in front of this position at 11 a.m. and probed the Confederate line. "The length of their line was very short, and the banks of the creek so precipitous it was impossible for the men to get across in order to make a direct attack." At first, Torbert's artillery shelled the Confederates, but Maj. James Breathed's Virginians responded in kind. Torbert's troopers feigned an attack up the road toward the bridge over the run and ran into Col. William Payne's well-positioned brigade. Torbert then initiated a tentative flanking effort against Munford's right.

23 OR 43, pt. 1, 192, 199.

24 Ibid., pt. 1, 152.

Munford reacted quickly, sending a dismounted squadron supporting Breathed's battery into the threatened sector. Munford blunted the hesitant effort with the one squadron, reinforced only by noisy buglers from several regiments. Munford ordered the buglers to sound the charge as he led the dismounted troopers to meet the Federal flanking threat, which was driven back quickly. Of Torbert's efforts to break through the Confederate force at Milford, Munford retorted, "The idea of two divisions, six thousand strong, of magnificently mounted cavalry, allowing two skeleton brigades and a battery 'in poor condition' to hold them for three days needs no commentary." After being bluffed by Munford, Torbert withdrew his force toward Front Royal, "not knowing that the army had made an attack at Fisher's Hill, and thinking that the sacrifice would be too great to attack without that knowledge." Torbert lost only 30 or so men in the Luray Valley actions, not all of them at Milford. In all of the operations relating to Fisher's Hill, Col. Thomas Munford and his outgunned Virginians once again proved themselves to be saviors of Jubal Early's army.[25]

Fisher's Hill offered Early a place to regroup his battered legions two miles south of Strasburg and 20 miles up the Valley Pike from Winchester. In July and August, Early's army had fortified Fisher's Hill, and those earthworks now provided the Southerners a second chance to stop Sheridan. If Early had not stretched out his army by going to Martinsburg on September 18, he very likely would have withdrawn to Fisher's Hill upon Sheridan's approach. Whereas the Valley was 20 miles wide near Winchester, its breadth slimmed down to four miles at Fisher's Hill. To the east, Massanutten Mountain abruptly emerges from the valley floor between Strasburg and Front Royal, separating the Shenandoah into two distinct valleys—the Luray to the east and Shenandoah proper to the west.[26]

A series of hills or rises stretching westward from the Shenandoah River to Little North Mountain composed the high ground collectively known as Fisher's Hill. On the northern face of this chain, the sparkling waters of Tumbling Run descended out of the Alleghany Mountains from the west and flowed across the base of Fisher's Hill until emptying into the Shenandoah River. The eastern end of this chain of hills anchored firmly upon the river and

25 Munford, "Reminiscences of Cavalry Operations," 454-455; OR 428-429.

26 James O. Coghill, October 6, 1864, Duke.

provided a commanding, cliff-like bluff that dominated the Valley Pike. As the range extends westward, however, it gradually loses much of its natural strength as a defensive position. There, a relatively level stretch of land spanned the ground between the last hillock and Little North Mountain. Additionally, the Luray Valley east of Massanutten Mountain offered Sheridan a ready avenue to flank Fisher's Hill via New Market Gap, which opened 30 miles behind Early's position. Nevertheless, if Early was going to confront Sheridan in the more northerly reaches of the Shenandoah Valley, Fisher's Hill was "the only position in the whole Valley where a defensive line could be taken against an enemy moving up the Valley." He understood that the line had "several weak points" but did not want to fall back to the gaps in the Blue Ridge located in the upper valley as Stonewall Jackson had done in 1862. "I determined therefore to make a show of a stand here," explained Early, "with the hope that the enemy would be deterred from attacking me in this position, as had been the case in August."[27]

Fisher's Hill also provided Jubal Early the opportunity to establish a defensive position with great depth. In addition to the chain of hills that formed Early's main position, a series of crests and ridges on the north side of Tumbling Run screened the main Confederate position from Sheridan's view. The Confederate commander posted his dependable sharpshooters upon these eminences to force Sheridan to battle for every inch of ground as he moved toward Early's main line. An ordnance train from Staunton arrived early on the morning of September 22 to supply the Southern troops with much needed arms, accouterments, and ammunition. Ammunition boxes were distributed along the trenches and limber chests were removed from the wagons and placed near the guns on the firing line. Early's men had dug in and meant to stay.[28]

Jubal Early's Confederate army worked non-stop throughout September 21 and 22 to strengthen and improve its defenses. Brigadier General Gabriel Wharton's decimated division held a formidable bluff near the Shenandoah River on the right of the Confederate line. Wharton lost 1,200 men at Winchester, and every regiment but one lost its battle flag. Two of his three brigade commanders went down wounded, one mortally. On Wharton's left, Maj. Gen. John B. Gordon's division contained 2,000 troops at most but had

---

27 Jubal Early, *A Memoir of the Last Year of the War*, 93.

28 Diary of Captain James M. Garnett, *Southern Historical Society Papers*, XXVII, 8.

emerged from the Winchester fight in much better condition than Wharton. Major General Stephen D. Ramseur's division, now under the command of Brig. Gen. John Pegram, held the works to Gordon's left. Ramseur replaced the lamented Maj. Gen. Robert E. Rodes and held the left of Early's infantry battle line with the largest division in the army.[29]

Across the swale on Ramseur's left, Early deployed four of Lomax's small dismounted cavalry brigades. As the line ranged westward along Lomax's line, the declivity of the hills lessened, diminishing the position's defensive value. By the time the line intersected the Back Road, the ground was virtually level compared to the rest of the terrain. Dismounted horsemen picketed the side of Little North Mountain to provide the Southerners advanced warning of any threat from that direction. Lomax's horse artillery deployed in gun emplacements at three locations along his battle line, including one on his left flank atop a 900-foot hill. This last position commanded the relatively level ground leading up to the base of Little North Mountain.

Sheridan began his operations on September 22 at 4:00 a.m., advancing the Nineteenth Corps closer to Early's position. One hour later, Sheridan ordered Crook to march his Army of West Virginia under cover to a wooded position between the right-rear of the Sixth Corps and Little North Mountain. Crook moved promptly and arrived at his destination by mid-morning. Once again, his men waited patiently in the woods, still unable to ignite fires to cook rations or brew some hot coffee. While Crook's men sat, Sheridan initiated a series of maneuvers in front of Fisher's Hill designed to attract the attention of the entrenched Confederates and secure key positions from which to launch the coming assault. At 11:30 a.m., he instructed General Emory "to press the enemy, to mask an attack on their left." After some brisk skirmishing, Emory's Nineteenth Corps moved forward and captured some of Early's advanced rifle pits.[30]

---

29 *OR Atlas*, 82:11; Anderson and Associates, "Survey and Mapping of Fisher's Hill Battlefield Earthworks, Shenandoah County, Virginia," Blacksburg, 1994. Uncertainty exists as to the precise disposition of Ramseur's division. However, Jed Hotchkiss produced a well drawn battle map of the action. Some Confederate accounts place Cullen Battle's brigade on the far left of Ramseur's line. Clearly, Bryan Grimes's brigade held that position. Judging from the very light casualties absorbed by Battle's brigade at Fisher's Hill, his location on the far right, as depicted by Hotchkiss after he had a chance to review the post-battle accounts, seems very likely. Hotchkiss map is located in the Library of Congress.

30 John Mead Gould, *Civil War Journals*, 405; OR 43, pt. 1, 283, 293, 319, 320.

While Emory feinted on the left, Sheridan ordered Horatio Wright to march Ricketts's division toward the Back Road to "carry two hills & push the enemy into their main forts." Ricketts's division moved into position by noon, driving off the Southern sharpshooters as they went. Ricketts halted the march around 2:30 p.m. when his troops reached George Noss's farm, only one-third of a mile from the Back Road. While the Confederates on Fisher's Hill watched Ricketts march toward the Back Road, Sheridan instructed Crook "to move my troops, still unobserved, to the eastern slope of North Mountain, and to pass around the enemy's extreme left and get on his flank and rear and drive him from his works." Crook moved out at 2:00 p.m., with his line nearly three-fourths of a mile behind Ricketts.[31]

Averell's division joined in the action upon Ricketts's success in securing the heights in front of Lomax's center. Averell had been pressing against Lomax's advance line since the previous day, but had been unable to make any progress against the sheltered Confederates without any support on his left flank. Ricketts's successful attack allowed Averell's dismounted troopers to storm the ridge in their front, drive off the Confederates, and chase them to their main line on the smaller ridge that sufficed for Fisher's Hill in this sector of the battlefield. While Crook moved behind Averell's position, the main body of the New Yorker's mounted division swept up the Back Road and went into position on Ricketts's right flank by 4:00 p.m.

The visual impact of the martial activity of 20,000 United States troops arrayed in line of battle with flags flying and supported by 75 pieces of artillery preyed upon the minds of Early's soldiers. Still stunned from the defeat at Winchester, the Confederate infantrymen and artillerists on Fisher's Hill watched the mesmerizing maneuvers of the Union infantry against Early's advanced outposts. Compounding the already intimidating scene, Ricketts's division marched off through gullies and woods, only to reappear opposite the Confederate left. Then, in a scene that mirrored Sheridan's victory at Winchester, Averell followed up Ricketts's successful advance with a cavalry sweep from the Union Army's right flank. Sheridan reported that Confederate signalmen atop Massanutten Mountain mistook Ricketts's column for the flanking attack. While Crook's flanking march would not go entirely undetected, the more immediate threat and enthralling spectacle of martial

---

31 Ibid., 223; J. Warren Keifer to My Dear Wife, September 23, 1864, Library of Congress.

grandeur directly in front of Fisher's Hill beckoned the attention of the Confederates and lulled them into a false perception of the developing events.[32]

While Ricketts skirmished in front of Lomax and Ramseur, Sheridan ordered Crook to move his troops, "still unobserved, to the eastern slope of North Mountain, and to pass around the enemy's extreme left and get on his flank and rear and drive him from his works." The march was difficult, but Crook's men were experienced mountain campaigners. "Very silently and very gently, we marched along the side of [Little] North Mountain, crossing ravines, climbing declivities, clambering over rocks," related one of Crook's officers, "Until we were exactly opposite the rebel works and on their immediate flank, which, strange to say, was entirely unprotected." Concealed by the diversionary movements of Ricketts and Averell, Crook's flank march caught the Confederates off guard. The next day, a Confederate artillery officer admitted that Crook's movement "was not discovered till it had been actually accomplished, and the columns had not only reached the rear of our lines but had actually charged upon the rear of our position."[33]

Crook's command "rushed with unwonted fury down the mountainside, a living avalanche with an impetuosity that was useless to resist," recalled Capt. William Patterson of the 116th Ohio. The attack promptly rolled up Lomax's division and herded the troopers back toward the Confederate infantry.[34]

When sounds of gunfire announced Crook's attack, Ricketts's infantry and Averell's cavalry joined the attack. After Lomax collapsed, the Federals moved against Ramseur's division. Not only did the Tar Heel face the threat from Crook on his left and rear, but Ricketts's division also moved from a hilltop to his left front. Further complicating the situation, Maj. Gen. Horatio Wright ordered the balance of the Sixth Corps into the fray. Ramseur began to shift his brigades to the left to meet the coming attack and offered the first serious resistance encountered by Crook. He achieved some initial success in stalling

32 OR 43, pt. 1, 48.

33 Micajah Woods to My Dear Father, September 23, 1864, UVA; Thomas F. Wildes, One Hundred Sixteenth O.V.I., 181; OR 43, pt. 1, 363; Henry DuPont, The Campaign of 1864 in the Valley of Virginia, 136; J. Q. Howard interview with R. B. Hayes, R. B. Hayes Papers, "Fisher's Hill," RBH Presidential Center; William B. Stark Diary, Massachusetts Historical Society. This diary contains a sketch drawn of the battlefield that clearly shows the location where Crook's men were discovered.

34 OR 43, pt. 1, 370, 390; W. T. Patterson Diary, OHS; M. S. Watts, "General Battle and the Stolen Colt," Confederate Veteran, May 1922, 169.

Crook's approach, but the converging Union forces soon put Ramseur's division to flight. From then on, it was only a matter of time for the Confederates as Crook and Ricketts joined forces and swept along the left flank and rear of Early's rapidly disintegrating battle line. As the balance of the Sixth and Nineteenth Corps pressed from the front, Early ordered Wharton to shift his troops from the extreme right near the Shenandoah River to the far left of the army. Unfortunately for the Confederates, the attack progressed too swiftly and Wharton simply became caught up in the confusion before he could get anywhere near the left.

The scene at the pike was one of confusion and joyous celebration, but there was work yet to be done. The 34th Massachusetts led Crook's jubilant throng to the Valley Pike. Colonel Wells rode up to his New Englanders, laughed, and called out, "34th were you never going to stop?" The "Buzzards" poured in by the hundreds with Crook and Thoburn soon joining on the happy scene. A Bay Stater asserted, "Such cheering one hears only once in a lifetime." Men celebrated and fired guns into the air when they reached the pike and attempted to sort out their jumbled ranks. The jubilant Union troops cheered first for "Old Abe," then for Sheridan and all the officers on down to the regimental commanders. Demoralized Confederates surrendered in droves. Some Southerners "took off their hats" to the Stars and Stripes and told their Yankee captors, "Boys, ye done that well." In the midst of the jubilation and cheering, the chaplain of the 10th New Jersey called his men together. He offered God a prayer of thanksgiving "for the victory and praying for the future success of our army without much further effusion of blood."[35]

The victory at Fisher's Hill was Sheridan's tactical masterpiece of his 1864 Shenandoah Valley Campaign. Once again, George Crook played a decisive role in the victory, although Averell contributed to it as well. It was a fitting capstone to the deadly slugfest at Winchester three days previous. It solidified the hard-fought gains from that battlefield and further wrecked Early's army. The outstanding maneuvering of Sheridan's forces at Fisher's Hill prompted some Confederates to believe "that Grant Commanded in Person." Captain Bedingfield of the 60th Georgia concluded, "But be that as it may, I never saw anything managed better in my life." Losing only 509 men killed and wounded

---

35 Letter from the 65th New York, September 24, 1864, in possession of author; Bradley M. Gottfried, *Kearney's Own: The History of the First New Jersey Brigade in the Civil War* (Rutgers University Press, 2005), 220; Edmund Halsey Diary, USAMHI; Stark Diary, MHS.

with 19 missing, Sheridan inflicted losses upon Early's army at a minimum of 300 killed and wounded and nearly 900 prisoners. The Army of the Shenandoah captured at least 16 pieces of artillery, with claims as high as 25. The loss of the guns stung the pride of the Valley Army's gunners. Major Carter Braxton reported the loss of his guns to Early "with tears in his eyes." Jubal Early admitted the loss of a dozen guns, but Jed Hotchkiss put the figure at 18. At least three battle flags were captured, two by Thoburn's division and another by Bidwell's brigade.[36]

When Sheridan penned his memoirs, he concluded that:

Fisher's Hill was, in a measure, a part of the battle of the [Battle of] Opequon [Third Winchester] . . . it was an incident of the pursuit resulting from that action. In many ways, however, it was much more satisfactory, and particularly so because the plan arranged on the evening of September 20 was carried out to the very letter by Generals Wright, Crook, and Emory, not only in all their preliminary maneuvers, but also during the fight itself.

36 A careful review of Federal accounts, which studiously avoided double counting captures, found that Thoburn's division seized at least three guns from Lomax; Keifer captured four pieces posted along Ramseur's stretch of the line; Bidwell captured four at Pegram's position and one on the pike; and the Nineteenth Corps captured four guns, for a total of 16 pieces. A loss of at least 15 guns can be substantiated from Confederate accounts, and looking at pre- and post-battle numbers of guns per the tri-monthly returns of Early's army. Unfortunately, the horse artillery is not included in these returns. On August 31, 1864, Early's three artillery battalions had 35 guns. Only three guns were lost from these battalions at Winchester, leaving 32 for the fight at Fisher's Hill. In late September, Carpenter's Battery was reconstituted with four guns that were added at Brown's Gap. The return for September 30 at Waynesboro shows these same three battalions with only 23 pieces of artillery, including four added after Fisher's Hill, meaning that Early had only 19 of the 32 guns remaining with his army at the end of September. Although not conclusive, this indicates a loss of at least 13 guns from his three artillery battalions at Fisher's Hill. This total is buttressed by the detailed journal of Confederate artillerist Henry Berkeley, who states that Braxton lost nine guns, Nelson three, and King one, for a total of 13 at Fisher's Hill. His allocation of the losses among the battalions also computes perfectly with the comparison between the August 31 and September 30 returns. Adding in the known loss of a minimum of two guns from the horse artillery at Fisher's Hill produces a minimum of at least 15 pieces. However, Federal accounts suggest that at *least* three guns were taken from the horse artillery, and as many as five may have being captured. It should be noted that George Crook's command may rightfully claim a stake in the capture of the guns credited to the Sixth Corps and Nineteenth Corps. These guns were abandoned because of Crook's and (subsequently) Ricketts's attack and flanking movements. In some cases, Crook's men physically overran the guns, but Crook refused to post guards, choosing instead to allow other units coming up behind him to move into position and later claim the captures. John W. Bedingfield to Dear Ma, September 26, 1864, UVA; Berkeley, *Four Years in the Confederate Artillery: The Diary of Private Henry Robinson Berkeley*, 100; *OR* 43, pt. 1, 1,011, 2:883.

Sgt. Peter Lauck Kurtz of the 5th Virginia, Stonewall Brigade, survived the fighting at Winchester but was captured at Fisher's Hill on September 22. *LC*

Dr. J. T. Webb of the 23rd Ohio proudly declared, "We have whipped the flower of the Rebel army." Never before in Virginia had Union troops achieved such decisive back-to-back victories over the Confederates, let alone within 72 hours. Early would attempt to retrieve his fortunes, but after Fisher's Hill, the balance of power in the Shenandoah Valley had shifted decisively and permanently to the Union forces.[37]

37 Sheridan, *Memoirs*, vol. 2, 41; Letter of J. T. Webb, September 28, 1864, RBH Presidential Center.

Though the campaign continued in the Valley for nearly a month longer, Sheridan had inflicted irrevocable damage upon Early's force at Opequon Creek and Fisher's Hill. The loss of 5,000 veteran Confederate officers and enlisted men along with 20 guns would have serious repercussions for Jubal Early at Cedar Creek the next month. The men would fight on but their organizations had been ripped asunder, and the élan that had previously characterized their actions had evaporated along with their confidence in "Old Jube." Sheridan would maneuver Early back into Brown's Gap where he licked his wounds and regrouped. Amazingly, Sheridan backed off and gave Early the time he needed to refresh his army. After Fisher's Hill, the Confederates were amazed at the slowness of the pursuit and believed that Sheridan would soon finish them off, given that his immense army was flushed with victory. The Union cavalry ranged as far south as Staunton, destroying crops, barns, mills, and any supplies that could be of any use to the Confederate Army in what became known as "The Burning." Sheridan then decided that the campaign had ended, turned around, and headed back toward Winchester, burning out the Valley as he went. The U.S. troopers drove off most of the Valley's livestock, leaving little for valley residents. Winchester and Fisher's Hill were the beginning of the end of the Confederacy's domination of the Shenandoah Valley.

General Robert E. Lee immediately returned Kershaw's division and an artillery battalion to the Shenandoah Valley. Lee also dispatched Brig. Gen. Thomas Rosser's cavalry brigade to Early. Rosser replaced Maj. Gen. Fitzhugh Lee as Early's cavalry chief, and closely pressed the Union cavalry as it withdrew down the Shenandoah Valley covering Sheridan's incendiary operations. Sheridan fumed at his cavalry's seeming inability to harness Rosser, and, on October 9, ordered Torbert to "whip him or get whipped trying." The Union horsemen went out and promptly routed Rosser at the battle of Tom's Brook, capturing 300 prisoners and 11 artillery pieces.

At that point, everyone in the Union Army believed that Early's force had been wrecked and was incapable of posing a serious threat. "Old Jube" proved them all wrong. Sheridan had actually sent the Sixth Corps back toward Washington when Early's entire army showed up at Fisher's Hill. The Confederates punished a reconnaissance force under Crook on October 13 near Strasburg, so Sheridan recalled the Sixth Corps. Early determined to attack Sheridan's force in its camps at Cedar Creek and sent Gordon and Hotchkiss to Signal Knob where they studied the Union deployments and developed a plan of attack.

Early implemented the plan and hit Sheridan's army before dawn on the morning of October 19. The attack was a smashing success, but discipline broke down in the Confederate Army and men drifted away from the firing line after hours of combat. Sheridan, who had been at Washington and spent the night in Winchester, returned in mid-morning to rally his forces. At 4:00 p.m., Sheridan counterattacked. Early's army broke again, and Sheridan earned his most famous victory in the Shenandoah Valley. The seeds of that victory were planted along the Opequon Creek at Winchester on September 19 with the heavy losses sustained by Confederate officer corps and the devastating impression that Sheridan's cavalry embedded upon the minds of the rank and file of "Old Jube's" army.

THE LAST BATTLE OF WINCHESTER

One of the Hardest Fights on Record

Of all the participants of the Third Battle of Winchester, no single individual received more accolades or saw his career rise higher as a result of that decisive engagement than Maj. Gen. Phil Sheridan.

The army commander rightfully deserves much credit for that unprecedented Union victory, not only in the Shenandoah Valley but also in Virginia at large. He achieved success through his patient approach to the campaign and remaining true to his and Grant's conviction that the Union offensive in the Valley had to wait until Jubal Early detached troops back to the Army of Northern Virginia. He understood not just the military but the political realities of his command in the Shenandoah. Sheridan's victory at Winchester was the beginning of the end of Confederate military power in Virginia. Early never recovered from the devastating losses his army suffered. Major General Fitzhugh Lee went so far as to state, "It occasioned the fall of Richmond by ultimately liberating a large army, flushed with victory, whilst we could only use as a counter active element, the small remnant of a dispirited band."[1]

---

1 Fitzhugh Lee, "Report of the Operations, May 4, 1864 to September 19, 1864," MOC.

Sheridan's patience and cautiousness, contrary to his popularly perceived image as a reckless hard-riding cavalryman, set the stage for his victory. Although much of that initial prudence was based upon political constraints due to the pending presidential election, he utilized the time to prepare his army and lull his opponent into a false sense of confidence. Through daily mounted reconnaissance attacks at multiple points along Early's lines, Sheridan allowed the Confederates to grow accustomed to the regular appearance of Union horse soldiers crashing through Southern picket lines, driving back the rebel horse, and pressing forward until the Confederate foot soldiers ended the Federal jaunt. In his *Memoir of the Last Year of the War for Independence*, Early opined of the time leading up to the fight at Winchester, "The events of the last month had satisfied me that the commander opposed to me was without enterprise and possessed an excessive caution which bordered on timidity." Early's intent was to denigrate Sheridan. Ironically, the embittered Early unwittingly revealed just how completely Sheridan's pre-battle tactics had lulled "Old Jube" to sleep prior to Winchester.[2]

Not only had Early slipped into a false sense of comfort with the military situation in the Shenandoah Valley, but even after Wilson's cavalry stormed up the Berryville Canyon, Early and many of his subordinates also did not readily acknowledge the magnitude of what was occurring on the morning of September 19, 1864. Major General Stephen D. Ramseur reacted as if Wilson's appearance was the daily Union cavalry breakthrough, and he wanted to counterattack. Breckinridge sent word to his wife that he would soon be in town for breakfast. Early himself held Rodes's and Gordon's divisions near Stephenson's Depot for at least one hour before committing them to the main battlefield at Winchester. Sheridan's daily movement tactics leading up to the battle had created complacency within the Confederate ranks. And so it was that when Sheridan's horse soldiers appeared intent on initiating the battle on September 19, their appearance brought little immediate alarm in the Southern army.

During the Third Battle of Winchester, or Opequon Creek as most Union soldiers dubbed it, Sheridan's dogged persistence and inspirational battlefield leadership spurred the Army of the Shenandoah on to victory. Union forces often enjoyed substantial manpower advantages during the course of the war in Virginia, yet Federal generals proved unable to translate that advantage into

2 Early, *A Memoir of the Last Year of the War*, 80.

victory. Sheridan fully utilized his army, feeding his reserves into the fight to continue attacking. His unprecedented personal leadership during the combat thoroughly inspired his soldiers. Seeing an army commander ride along not only the line of battle but also the skirmish line in the thick of the fight astonished most of the troops. They could hardly believe that their army commander was right there with them with shells crashing all around and bullets whizzing past. Yet Sheridan rode among them, shouting, cursing, and inspiring his men onto victory. "He came on the field like a whirlwind, riding the proud black pacer which afterward carried him to Cedar Creek," recalled Capt. James F. Fitts of the 114th New York. "He was himself, a living inspiration." A Massachusetts soldier recalled, "The men saw their leader and went wild with excitement," when Sheridan rode down the line.

The ride Sheridan made along his battle line at Winchester on September 19, 1864, set the stage for his more famous and dramatic ride at Cedar Creek exactly one month later. There, after being driven back in wild flight, his men turned back to fight and win a victory when they saw their commander—the very man who had ridden along the combat line at Winchester—galloping back toward Cedar Creek urging his troops on to victory. In some ways, his men reciprocated at Cedar Creek what Sheridan had previously earned at Winchester. If Sheridan was going to the front to attack Jubal Early, that was surely the place to be. After September 19, Sheridan was the hero of his army. Men who prided themselves on never cheering for a commanding general since the day Maj. Gen. George B. McClellan was relieved of command now hurrahed for Little Phil. The victory at Winchester invigorated the rank and file of the Army of the Shenandoah. "I never saw the troops in better spirits or more enthusiastic," recorded one staff officer. "The Gen. was cheered everywhere he went."[3]

Sheridan's victory at Winchester proved to be of immense political value to Abraham Lincoln. General Grant wrote that Sheridan's decisive victory at Winchester "electrified the nation." Indeed, it further convinced the Northern voters that the war effort was moving in the right direction, even in the Union's heretofore "Valley of Humiliation" in Virginia and against some of the best troops from Lee's Army of Northern Virginia. Lincoln's personal secretaries John B. Nicolay and John Hay observed that Sheridan "by restraining his own

3 James F. Fitts, "The Last Battle of Winchester," *The Galaxy*, vol. 2, 330; Ewer, *The Third Massachusetts Cavalry*, 204.

A sketch of Federal troops cheering Phil Sheridan as they pursue Jubal Early up the Shenandoah Valley after Third Winchester. *A. R. Waud, LC*

spirit, which was naturally ardent and enterprising, until he saw a prospect of almost certain success, and then by striking with all his might he rendered inestimable service, at a time it was much needed." Just as Sheridan's ride along his battle line had inspired his men to make one final push toward Winchester, the battle's outcome fired the Unionist cause in the North and increased the momentum that Maj. Gen. William T. Sherman had created with the capture of Atlanta 18 days earlier. The political and moral impact of the victory was not lost upon the Southerners. "Considering the effect this affair will no doubt have on the election in the North," wrote Capt. John Y. Bedingfield of the 60th Georgia, "it is certainly unfortunate." Major General Stephen D. Ramseur opined, "This is sad also, coming as it does, on the heels of the Affair at Atlanta."

In Philadelphia, citizens erected flags on all public buildings to celebrate the victory at Winchester. The *New York Times* reported, "The whole city is rejoicing over the news, and anxiously awaiting news of a similar character from GRANT." The *National Daily Republican* noted that, "When Sheridan advances, McClellan goes backward." The victory, combined with the fall of Atlanta and Farragut's operations in Mobile Bay, squelched talk of a negotiated peace, as called for in the Democratic platform upon which McClellan was running. Instead, trumpeted the *New York Times*, "Peace is being negotiated now every day, and by every victory, and it will receive its definite surety and sanction by the reelection of ABRAHAM LINCOLN." Of course, Abraham Lincoln rejoiced in the news. On the day after the battle, the president wrote Sheridan, "Have just heard of your great victory. God bless you all, officers and men. Strongly inclined to come up and see you." After a long summer of defeat and failure, events now shifted in Lincoln's favor.[4]

The *New York Times* correspondent in Nashville eloquently summed up the boost in morale that the Northern populace and soldiery received from Sheridan's victory at Winchester:

> The brilliant victories of SHERIDAN in the Shenandoah are the themes of all tongues. Our diligent little extras give us the telegraphic news as promptly as you get it there. We rejoice at a great victory as heartily and loudly as our Union friends do in the North. The cannon at the capital thundered forth the people's joy that the "Valley of Humliation" had become at length the "Delectable Mountains," affording the people a delightful prospect of the "promised land" of peace and rest for the war-wearied and war-worn, their toils and sufferings triumphantly ended.
>
> The prospect, in truth, is brightening all around us. There is no longer a pretext for craven despondency. The country has got what the popular heart was sighing and panting for—great and repeated successes. The moral effect of them is greater than the material effect. A few more such successes and the great work is done. These will be sure to come, for the mind and heart of the people are fully in this work of saving the country, and they will save it, in spite equally of the arts of false friends and the arms of open enemies.[5]

Although Sheridan won an important and rousing victory at Winchester, his tactics on the battlefield did not become a model for cadets to study at West Point. Sheridan's first mistake entailed funneling the entire Sixth Corps and Nineteenth Corps through the narrow confines of Berryville Canyon. This decision delayed his deployment and, as noted in the narrative, could have been avoided by using other nearby routes to get his troops to the front more quickly.

---

4 John G. Nicolay and John Hay, *Abraham Lincoln: A History*, 306; John Y. Bendingfield to Dear Ma, September 20, 1864, Bedingfield Letters, UVA; *The New York Times*, September 20, 1864; *Daily National Republican*, September 28, 1864; S. D. Ramseur to My own darling wife, September 25, 1864, Ramseur Papers, SHC-UNC; Roy M. Basler, *Collected Works of Abraham Lincoln*, 7:13.

5 *New York Times*, October 9, 1864.

Second, Sheridan's cautiousness that morning prevented him from defeating Early in detail. Once the Sixth Corps deployed, Sheridan's available force exceeded 15,000 fighting men to attack Ramseur's division and the four understrength Confederate cavalry brigades, together numbering no more than 5,000 men. Instead, Sheridan chose to wait for the 12,000-man Nineteenth Corps to negotiate the traffic jam in the Berryville Canyon. By the time Sheridan attacked two hours later, Early's strength increased by nearly 6,000 men and 11 pieces of artillery via the arrival of Gordon's and Rodes's divisions. Some historians postulate that if Sheridan had not significantly outnumbered Jubal Early, the Confederate Army of the Valley District would have been victorious that day. In reality, Sheridan's overall operational strategy of waiting for Early to detach Kershaw's division and its accompanying artillery ensured that "Little Phil" had the odds well in his favor.[6]

Although Sheridan deserved praise for his battlefield presence and successful operational planning, his inexperience showed at times. The positive fallout from the victory notwithstanding, Sheridan's campaign prior to Third Winchester revealed his inexperience as an army commander. When Sheridan took command of the Army of the Shenandoah, he utilized his cavalry as a mobile strike force just as he had brazenly suggested to Maj. Gen. George G. Meade, commander of the Army of the Potomac. When Sheridan came east in the spring of 1864, he chastised Meade for assigning his troopers the seemingly mundane duties of guarding flanks and other traditional cavalry roles. Although using cavalry as a strike force paid dividends for Sheridan at Winchester, his failure to assign cavalry the traditional role of guarding the flanks of the advancing infantry contributed substantially to his initial battlefield setback. This omission allowed Maj. Gen. Fitz Lee to get a division of dismounted troopers and six pieces of artillery on the right flank of the Nineteenth Corps at the outset of the fight. Had Sheridan positioned one of Wilson's brigades to cover Emory's right flank north of Red Bud Run, Lee would not have been able to harass the infantry unimpeded, and may have been forced back along with

---

6 It is often speculated that if Joseph Kershaw's Confederate infantry and artillery had been present at Third Winchester, Jubal Early would have emerged victorious. However, Sheridan's strategy was predicated upon Early detaching troops back to Petersburg. If that had not occurred, the battle would have developed much differently and may have consisted of maneuvering to flank Early out of the lower Valley to free up the B & O Railroad from Early's destructive raids, rather than an outright battle, or, Grant could have reinforced Sheridan or launched an attack of his own at Petersburg to force Lee to recall troops from the Valley.

Gordon's infantry. On the opposite flank, Bradley Johnson's Southerners annoyed and delayed the advance of Bidwell's Union brigade with only two small dismounted cavalry regiments. Just as they could have on the Union right, some of Wilson's troopers positioned here on the left could have easily kept Bidwell's flank safe.

He missed two good opportunities during the campaign. On August 25, Early left Richard Anderson with fewer than 6,000 men to confront Sheridan's 30,000 infantrymen at Halltown. While an attack on Anderson might not have ended the campaign, Sheridan certainly failed to take advantage of this beckoning opportunity. Instead of overwhelming Anderson, Sheridan focused on Torbert's cavalry, which had gone out on a reconnaissance in force that day. Similarly, Sheridan missed a chance to attack Early and Anderson with their backs to the Opequon on September 4, the day after the engagement at Berryville. Early split his force in half right in front of Sheridan's entire army to reconnoiter the strong Federal position. With the waters of the Opequon flowing behind the Confederates, Sheridan missed a rare occasion to cripple the Confederate forces in the Valley and bring the campaign to an early close. Seldom did Early place his army in such a vulnerable formation in open ground. However, when he learned that Anderson was dangerously exposed in front of Sheridan, Early had no choice but to go to the South Carolinian's assistance.

Sheridan also let Early escape after defeating him at Fisher's Hill on September 22 (three days after Third Winchester) by allowing him to fall back unmolested to Brown's Gap in the Blue Ridge to recover, reorganize, and most importantly to receive reinforcements from Lee's army. The lack of pursuit amazed soldiers in Early's army. Even after Cedar Creek, Sheridan did not finish off the Confederates in the Valley. Although victorious, Sheridan had yet to carry his determination and zest on the battlefield to his management of campaigns. By the spring of 1865, Sheridan's newly honed instinct to deal a devastating blow played the critical role in running Lee's army to ground at Appomattox. Perhaps Sheridan's reflection on lost opportunities to completely finish off Early and threaten Richmond from the Valley motivated the Ohioan during the war's final days in Virginia.

While Sheridan emerged the victor at Winchester, another general's contributions loomed large in the Union's changing fortunes in the Valley. General Grant trusted Sheridan to carry out his designs in the Shenandoah. Grant recognized the organizational problems that plagued the Valley and the Potomac region, and he took action to rectify it. Further, Grant gave Sheridan the resources he needed to accomplish his mission. Sending two cavalry divisions away from the Army of the Potomac impeded his own ability to conduct operations against Lee at Richmond and Petersburg, but Grant did so because President Lincoln could not afford another Chambersburg or Washington raid. While Sheridan's victories at Third Winchester and Fisher's Hill pleased General Grant, the Union commander in chief hoped that Sheridan would finish off Jubal Early once and for all, cross east over the Blue Ridge, and capture Charlottesville and Gordonsville on the Virginia Central Railroad. Such a move would have threatened Richmond from the west and potentially ended the fighting in 1864. (Sheridan did not make the move, largely because of logistical considerations.)

Sheridan's subordinates played important roles during the campaign and battles. For the Sixth Corps commander, the battle at Winchester provided Maj. Gen. Horatio G. Wright with a learning opportunity from which he profited immeasurably. His mediocre performance after taking over for the lamented Maj. Gen. John Sedgwick at Spotsylvania called into question his suitability for corps command. At Winchester, Wright displayed a degree of pettiness at Spout Spring in his dealings with Maj. Gen. William Emory and the Nineteenth Corps. Wright's actions exacerbated Sheridan's decision to funnel 24,000 troops through the narrow confines of Berryville Canyon. Wright also claimed credit for the independent actions of his subordinates, including Russell, Getty, and Upton. Wright's strict adherence to tight formations and a measured advance during the final stages of the battle against the rapidly collapsing Rebel lines allowed hundreds of Confederates to escape what should have been certain capture. It should be noted that most of Wright's shortcomings were emblematic to the Army of the Potomac, his home for most of the war.

Still, Wright's Winchester experiences did not pass without profit. It is fair to say he underwent something of a transformation that day that would reap benefits to the Union cause for the balance of the war. At Winchester Wright witnessed the vigor that Sheridan applied to his movements on the battlefield and the stunning end result. Exactly one month later, Wright stepped to the forefront at Cedar Creek, where he kept the Army of the Shenandoah intact when Jubal Early surprised it in its camps. Wright uncharacteristically exposed himself on the front lines and even led an impromptu counterattack. Although wounded and bleeding profusely, he remained on the battlefield and had much of the army well in hand when Sheridan reached the front. Wright continued his emergence as a combat leader in 1865 during the Union breakthrough of Lee's lines at Petersburg in early April and again a few days later at the battle of Sailor's Creek.

George Crook played a hero's role at Winchester. The army commander's loyal friend also achieved redemption for his and the Army of West Virginia's debacle at Second Kernstown and the ensuing burning of Chambersburg, Pennsylvania. Although Wright was the senior officer in the army and therefore the official second in command, Crook's friendship with his fellow Buckeye gave him influence and status beyond his rank. His prior experience in the Valley and his knowledge of Winchester's Unionist citizens (the critical access to Rebecca Wright, for example, who provided knowledge of Kershaw's departure from Winchester), proved invaluable to Sheridan. As an experienced Indian fighter, Crook adeptly carried out the reconnaissance missions that Sheridan assigned to the Army of West Virginia throughout the campaign. No other single officer contributed as much to Sheridan's success at Winchester and Fisher's Hill as did George Crook.

Years after the war ended, Sheridan's old friend felt short-changed for what he perceived to be Sheridan's failure to fully credit his efforts in the victories at Winchester and Fisher's Hill. When Sheridan wrote his report of the campaign after the war, he did not credit Crook for his significant contributions. Nor did Sheridan correct the record when he wrote his memoirs years later. However, Sheridan did credit Crook shortly after the battle. At that time, Crook pointed out to Sheridan that the cavalry had gotten credit for the capture of many prisoners that Crook's Army of West Virginia had actually captured. Sheridan, Crook wrote, replied that he "had seen it all & for me to say nothing about it & he would see that I got justice."[7] On September 23, Sheridan followed up on his promise on Crook's role in the recent battles. "I have the honor to request the promotion of Brevet Major-General George Crook to the full rank of major-general," Sheridan wrote General Grant. "His good conduct, and the good conduct of his command, turned the tide of battle in our favor at both Winchester and Fisher's Hill."[8]

Whether or not Crook was aware of this message is uncertain because he did not mention it when he penned his critique of Sheridan many years later. However, a very close friend and ardent admirer of Crook, Rutherford B. Hayes, thought that Crook "had received very substantial recognition for his services in his promotion." Crook's military career progressed steadily during

---

7   Draft of Crook's Manuscript, Crook-Kennon Collection, USAMHI.

8   It should be noted that Sheridan did not have access to his subordinates' reports when he wrote his own report long after the battle. OR 43, pt. 2, 153.

From left to right: Brig. Gen. Merritt, Maj. Gens. Sheridan and Crook, Col. James Forsyth, and Brig. Gen. Custer. (Officers' ranks as of Third Winchester.) LC

his postwar years in the Regular Army. It is difficult to explain how it would have done so without recognition of his Civil War associations with Phil Sheridan. Although Sheridan did indeed recognize Crook in the form of career advancement, he certainly did not praise him the same way that he did the flamboyant cavalrymen Wesley Merritt and George Armstrong Custer. Given Crook's continued close association and advancement in the postwar Regular Army, it is difficult to believe that Crook emerged from the Civil War with feelings of resentment and bitterness toward Phil Sheridan. The true break between these men came years later over differences in Indian policy, and was cemented into place when Sheridan accepted Crook's resignation over the Geronimo affair.[9]

Throughout the Valley Campaign, William Emory played the role of the dutiful veteran that he was. Expectations for Emory never seemed high to begin with, and he did not disappoint. He clearly failed to grasp Sheridan's tenacity and victorious resolve, especially when the commander continued to attack at Winchester even after his initial setback. Where Sheridan saw an opportunity to press the offensive on the battlefield, Emory could not move beyond the bloody repulse of Grover's division. Although the veteran officer had participated in previous combat, he and his commands had never experienced anything like the losses they suffered at Third Winchester. In fact, Grover's failure rattled Emory to such a degree that he forbade his command from advancing into the Second Woods when Crook advanced later in the afternoon. Instead, only a few individual units joined Crook's attack. Then, Sheridan belatedly shifted Emory's Nineteenth Corps to the left flank, but the battle ended before it could accomplish anything. Some veterans of the Sixth Corps disparaged the Nineteenth Corps in their memoirs and histories. At Winchester, Emory's command proved its fortitude on the battlefield and joined the large fraternity of Union commands that came out on the short end of the stick against the Army of Northern Virginia's Second Corps. It was an initiation of sorts, but Emory and his command proved their worth at Cedar Creek, both during Early's predawn attack and again during Sheridan's counterstrike later that afternoon.

In the aftermath of Winchester, Emory chastised Brig. Gen. William Dwight for his brutally honest report on the battle. The account included accurate descriptions of the chaos that ensued upon Grover's repulse. Emory, who favored Grover, refused to accept the facts that Dwight presented in his report and ordered him to rewrite it. When Dwight refused, Emory relieved him of command and placed him under arrest. In truth, Dwight played a significant role in restoring the Union line and ending the Southern counterattack at Winchester. When the army found itself in a tight situation at

---

9 According to historian D. Scott Hartwig, "It was Crook's command of the Department of Arizona which he assumed in 1882, that destroyed the once strong friendship of these men and turned Crook into a bitter enemy of Sheridan." Contained in "Commentary," Edward J. Stackpole, *Sheridan in the Shenandoah*, Harrisburg: Stackpole, 1992, 413-414; Hayes Interview, December 17, 1889, L. W. V. Kennon Journal, USAMHI.

Cedar Creek, Sheridan restored Dwight to command and ordered him to take charge of his division during the counterattack. After that battle Emory and his command spent the rest of the war in the backwaters of the Middle Military Division and on the South Carolina coast. The 30 days between Winchester and Cedar Creek proved to be the most eventful month of their collective military experiences.[10]

Sheridan's most celebrated heroes of the Third Battle of Winchester were the members of his already famous Cavalry Corps. The corps commander, Maj. Gen. Alfred Torbert, functioned more as an administrative head than an actual decision-maker. It is likely that Sheridan placed Torbert in that position because of his familiarity with the Delawarean and the need to place the more qualified Brig. Gen. Wesley Merritt in permanent command of the First Cavalry Division. Torbert also suffered from leading a corps filled with more renowned and experienced cavalry officers than him. Merritt, Brig. Gen. William W. Averell, Brig. Gen. Thomas Devin, and the outlandish Custer attracted the attentions of the newspaper writers and the public. A loyal subordinate, Torbert did the duty that was asked of him efficiently. Although he oversaw the massive cavalry attack that closed out the fight at Winchester, Merritt, Custer, Devin, and Averell grabbed the headlines with their dash and vigor on the battlefield. The unprecedented attack became the template that Sheridan used to close out the war. On battlefields from the Shenandoah Valley to Five Forks, Sailor's Creek, and Appomattox, Sheridan's horse soldiers rode down the proud veteran infantry of the Army of Northern Virginia. Unfortunately, Torbert did not have the dash that Sheridan wanted in a cavalry corps commander. When Sheridan left the Valley to join Grant at Petersburg, he placed Merritt in command of the Cavalry Corps and began the campaign while Torbert was absent.

Sheridan's officer corps suffered heavy losses at Winchester. The loss of Brig. Gen. David Russell struck hardest. Russell provided a steadying hand for Wright and the Sixth Corps and provided more combat experience and leadership ability than almost any other division commander in Sheridan's army. "Had he risen to the command of an army," Col. Oliver Edwards declared of Russell, "he would have proved himself second to none in

---

10 Brig. Gen. William Dwight attended West Point but did not graduate. He left the academy to engage in business at home in Boston. He also had three brothers who died for the Union cause during the course of the war. Paul Andrew Hutton, *Phil Sheridan and His Army* (University of Oklahoma Press, 1999), 364-368.

command in the Union army." Brigadier General Emory Upton's wounding during the latter stages of the battle robbed the Sixth Corps of Russell's able replacement for the balance of the campaign. In the Nineteenth Corps, Emory lost the services of Col. Jacob Sharpe (who was acting in the capacity of a brigadier) to serious injury. Isaac Duval, an unsung division commander from Crook's command, fell in front of the final Confederate line outside of Winchester. The loss of Brig. Gen. John B. McIntosh to a career-ending wound robbed Sheridan of one of the army's most underrated Union horsemen. McIntosh often energized Wilson's division on the battlefield and would be sorely missed. In addition to McIntosh, Brig. Gen. George Chapman fell with a minor wound as the battle was winding to a close.[11]

While George Crook chafed over his perceived lack of recognition at Winchester, many other officers throughout the ranks of the Army of the Shenandoah could validly make similar claims. After the fallen Russell, Upton received the lion's share of the credit for restoring the Union battle line on the right flank of the Sixth Corps. In truth, the actions of Upton's brigade might be better described as "mopping up" the last vestiges of Confederate resistance. Upton's heavy losses came in the final attack and his subordinates reported firing only a few volleys during the action to restore the Union line. The unheralded Col. Oliver Edwards of the 37th Massachusetts, then commanding another of Russell's brigades, delivered the key counterattack that ensured the maintenance of the Sixth Corps battle line when Ricketts fell back in confusion before Grimes and Cox. Edwards later explained, "It was the service of the 37th and the brigade to which it was attached that saved the battle to the Union cause that day, for had they not held the ground vacated by the 19th Corps and 3rd division of the 6th there would have been nothing left for Sheridan except to withdraw from the field."[12]

Upton's claims also detracted from the efforts of the Nineteenth Corps. When Upton arrived on the battlefield, he reported as if his were the only troops in the area. In truth, Colonel Molineux's brigade was resisting the Confederates from the western edge of the First Woods when Upton's brigade came up from the south and opened fire into the right flank of Cook's attacking Georgians. Colonel Ranald Mackenzie's report of the 2nd Connecticut of

11 Oliver Edwards, Memorandum, Illinois State Historical Library, 192.

12 "Their Heroic Past Recalled by Survivors of 37th Regiment, Addresses by Gen. Edwards and Lieut. Gov," *Springfield Republican*, September 20, 1893.

Upton's brigade described more maneuvering than fighting at this point of the battle. Colonel Joseph Hamblin of the 65th New York simply reported, "A few volleys at short range repulsed the enemy." Upton's men charged and formed on the left of the 37th Massachusetts, which had held its advance position unaided the entire time. Molineux's brigade lost 507 men resisting the Confederate attack with more than 80 percent of the casualties killed and wounded. Certainly, Emory Upton played an important role in the action, but others—such as Edwards and Molineux—did as much or more than the ambitious Upton.[13]

* * *

Jubal Early's star plummeted after the defeat at Winchester. His ensuing disaster at Fisher's Hill just three days later cemented his misfortune. Sadly for Early's sake, his own overconfidence and misreading of Sheridan's abilities and demeanor led to the crotchety Virginian's downfall in the Valley. Major Robert Stribling of Cutshaw's battalion offered an opinion on the matter:

> It is clear that Early, after Kershaw left, should have drawn his army well in hand and made all necessary preparations to fall back, and take position where the Valley narrowed, and then arranged to strike Sheridan when he exposed himself on following after or in passing by as was suggested to him by General Lee in his letter of the 17th instant.[14]

A couple of years before Early died, one of his staff officers and admirers, Senator John W. Daniel, sat down and spoke to the general about the 1864 Valley Campaign. "Let me ask if you do not now think it would have been better to have retired before Sheridan, instead of making [a] fight at Winchester, and prepared for battle on your own terms?"

The aging warrior's dark eyes lit up upon hearing Daniel's query. "Major, I hope you will never have that thought again," declared Early. "You forget the whole scheme of the Valley Campaign. It was a bluff game from the beginning.

13 OR 43, pt. 1, 177, 179; Isaac O. Best, *History of the 121st New York State Infantry*, 181.

14 Col. Robert M. Stribling, Statement on Early at Third Winchester, John W. Daniel Papers, UVA.

I had made Sheridan afraid of me. If once I showed him that I was afraid of him, the case was gone and he would have run me from one place to another." Daniel also recorded that "Early was touching the sensorium of the Federal nervous system at Martinsburg when Early advanced; and was playing successfully his oft repeated play."[15]

Early's reasoning for remaining at Winchester and marching half his army to Martinsburg was true. His error was in gambling his entire force on a mere bluff. Robert E. Lee made himself into a legend taking calculated risks throughout the war, but he rarely resorted to rashness. When Early marched the larger portion of his infantry 20 miles north of Winchester to Martinsburg with Sheridan's force less than nine miles away, he placed the entire army in jeopardy.

Early effectively guided his small force against Sheridan for six weeks prior to his defeat. He kept his army well in hand and did not overextend it and move his units beyond supporting distance. Even when Anderson remained at Charlestown, Early did not venture more than seven miles away, and the South Carolinian retained a clear route of retreat in the event of trouble. Major General Bryan Grimes related Early's prudence during that part of the campaign:

> The enemy have a large force between us and Harper's Ferry, which Early is demonstrating upon, and are contesting the ground most stubbornly. This is a mere feint to frighten them and cover some important move on our part. I have no idea we will fight here, for the enemy outnumber us three to one, and Early knows too well the importance of preserving his army.[16]

Unfortunately, Early's understanding of that fact soon diminished and led to his defeat at Winchester. Although no major battles were fought during the six-week period derisively referred to as the "mimic war," maneuvering furnished Early with a blueprint for how he could successfully cope with Sheridan's superior numbers in the Shenandoah. Early campaigned across a theater 40 miles in length, and he used it to his utmost advantage. Careful to keep his troops from becoming exposed, he remained a step ahead of Sheridan.

15 Conversation between J. E. Early and J. W. Daniel, J. W. Daniel Papers, UVA.

16 Emphasis added by author. Early certainly forgot about that by mid-September. Grimes, *Letters*, 62.

His men moved quickly and gave his army the appearance of a much larger force. When the situation called for it, Early did not hesitate to retreat to the safety of Fisher's Hill until reinforced by Anderson. Unfortunately for the South, Early's success made him overconfident, and he crossed the line from taking a calculated risk to venturing into the territory of recklessness.

Things broke down when Anderson departed with Joe Kershaw's infantry and Cutshaw's artillery. Instead of husbanding his forces to keep a wary eye on Sheridan, Early truly believed that Sheridan was "afraid" of the Virginian. "Old Jube" believed his jaunt to Martinsburg in the face of Sheridan's large army was audacious and justified by military necessity. According to Brig. Gen. John B. Gordon, Early's move to Martinsburg likely resulted from a character flaw. He noted that Early, though brave and imperturbable in battle, lacked what the Georgian termed "official courage, or what is known as the courage of one's convictions—that courage which I think both Lee and Grant possessed in an eminent degree." When writing of the lead-up to the Third Battle of Winchester, Gordon added of Early:

> The rash officer's boldness is blind. He strikes in the dark, madly, wildly, and often impotently. The possessor of the courage which I am trying to describe is equally bold, but sees with quick, clear, keen vision the weak and strong points in the adversary, measures with unerring judgment his own strength and resources, and then, with utmost faith in the result, devotes his all to its attainment—and wins.[17]

In 1862, Stonewall Jackson pressed on toward Harpers Ferry on the heels of his victory at First Winchester; a proper degree of prudence and judgment governed his movements. When he learned of Federal reinforcements under Maj. Gens. John Fremont and Irvin McDowell moving in force to cut Jackson off in the Lower Valley, he immediately turned his army around and headed to the Upper Valley. There, he maneuvered his army into a position that resulted in victories at Cross Keys and Port Republic on June 8 and 9, defeating elements from both Federal columns. Whereas Jubal Early judged the situation as either Sheridan or Early being afraid of the other, Stonewall carefully assessed the tactical and strategic consequences of the situation and enhanced his chances against long odds by maneuvering to a position that favored the Confederates.

---

17 Gordon, *Reminiscences*, 317-318.

Had Jubal Early possessed Jackson's barometer for measuring the appropriate course of action, he would not have taken his two largest infantry divisions to Martinsburg on September 17. The prudent move dictated keeping his army well in hand around Winchester and retreating to Fisher's Hill when Sheridan moved. The outcome of a fight at Fisher's Hill before Early lost nearly 4,000 men, five guns, and much of the army's confidence at Third Winchester might have been significantly different than the battle that actually developed on September 22. However, in the aftermath of Winchester, Early lacked the manpower to adequately man the position at Fisher's Hill. Ultimately, Early's march to Martinsburg placed his army in an untenable position where it had to fight an unnecessary battle simply to survive.

The defeat at Winchester filled Capt. Seaton Gales, a veteran staff officer from Cox's North Carolina brigade, "with equal mortification and pain." He also believed that the disaster need not have occurred. He analyzed the situation and concluded:

> They (Federals) really exceeded us in proportion of at least three or four to one . . . but even in the face of such odds, I feel confident that we would in this engagement have held our own, but that the advance of Sheridan was in the nature of a surprise, and caught us at great disadvantage in the scattered disposition of our forces, which prevented general and simultaneous co-operation, and that selection of position, without which under ordinary circumstances no inferior force can cope with one that is vastly superior. I attribute then our disaster mainly to the objectless expeditions to Bunker Hill and Martinsburg on the two preceding days. But for them, the enemy, when they advanced, would have found us in a situation where we could have countervailed their advantage of numbers and successfully resisted them.[18]

Ultimately, the Third Battle of Winchester initiated the campaign's twilight for Jubal Early and the Army of the Valley District. His army simply could not overcome the heavy loss of officers and men and regain the Valley. Early valiantly worked to retrieve Confederate fortunes in the Shenandoah Valley. When he recouped 70 percent of his Winchester and Fisher's Hill losses through the arrival of Kershaw's division and Brig. Gen. Thomas Rosser's cavalry, Early launched a daring surprise attack against Sheridan at Cedar Creek exactly one month after Winchester. It was one of the most daring plans of the

18 *Our Living and Our Dead*, New Bern, NC, March 4, 1874.

war, and it almost succeeded. In the end, however, Sheridan's victory at Winchester sowed the seeds of Early's defeat at Cedar Creek. At Winchester, Early lost hundreds of veteran officers and thousands of men. The resulting fragility of his army, combined with Early's own loss of decisiveness in the face of success, resulted in another embarrassing defeat in the Valley.

Early's failures at Winchester and Fisher's Hill severely damaged his reputation with wild gossip taking flight throughout the South. Though unsubstantiated, rumors quickly spread that "Applejack," a local variety of whiskey, led to his twin defeats. The *Charleston Mercury* reported, "We have two enemies to contend with in the Valley—one of whom has never been beaten since Noah drank too much wine and lay in his tent." In response to the rumors, General Early wrote to Col. A. R. Botelor to set the record straight. "Capt. Page," Early related, "informs me that he was told in Richmond that it is reported that I was very drunk at Winchester & advanced to rally my men with a bottle in my hand." The charge stunned Early, and he told Botelor, "I think Colonel you have seen enough of me to know how utterly false is the imputation alluded to."[19] The straight-laced Jed Hotchkiss, who was not present at Winchester but knew Early and those around him intimately, was stunned by the accusation. "There is not one word of truth in it. A baser slander was never circulated," Hotchkiss told his brother. "It is true that Gen. Early is a drinker of spirits, is too fond of it, but I have never seen him under the influence of liquor since we started on this campaign. He is sober enough to know his duty and attend to it at all times."[20]

Unfortunately, these rumors circulated for years after the war ended. Perhaps they helped ease the pain of defeat in Stonewall's Valley among a few of the old veterans, but they were untrue, nevertheless. The rumors deeply upset Early. In a letter dated October 19, 1864, the exasperated general declared, "God only knows how & faithfully I have labored for success in this campaign."

A more immediate concern, however, was that Early's officers and men exhibited a waning confidence in their general. Victory and success throughout the summer kept spirits high and the men believing in "Old Jube." However, his unprecedented defeats in the Shenandoah steadily eroded the support of

19 Jubal Early to Col. A. R. Botelor, Fisher's Hill, October 19, 1864. The letter appears to have been written early in the morning before the battle of Cedar Creek occurred.

20 Hotchkiss to brother, Oct. 3, 1864, LC; *Charleston Mercury*, September. 30, 1864.

many of his officers. One wrote to Virginia Governor William "Extra Billy" Smith with a litany of complaints on Jubal's generalship. The governor passed the note on to General Lee (without revealing the author's identity), saying only that it was from "an officer who has my entire confidence." Not coincidentally, Governor Smith's son, Col. Thomas Smith, commanded a brigade in Wharton's division and was the only brigadier of that command to escape the debacle at Winchester. The letter read:

> The army once believed him a safe commander, and felt that they could trust to his caution, but unfortunately this has proven a delusion and they cannot, do not, and will not give him their confidence. He was surprised at Winchester. He did not expect a general engagement that day. This destroyed the confidence, which the reputation for safety once gave the army in him, and Fisher's Hill was the terrible sequence. . . . I believe the good of the country requires that General Early should not be kept in command of this army; that every officer with whom I have conversed upon the subject is of the same opinion, and I believe it is the sentiment of the army.[21]

Unlike the drinking rumors, this officer rooted his allegations in fact. Early was clearly surprised, and many in his army subsequently lost confidence in "Old Jube" after Winchester and Fisher's Hill. Despite this erosion in support Early retained some support among the officers and men even after his loss at Cedar Creek on October 19. "All have the greatest confidence in General Early," opined General Grimes. "No blame can be attached to him for our failures." William F. Brand of the Stonewall Brigade asserted, "All want to wipe out the old stain of Fishers Hill & Winchester. I think the people are entirely too hard on Early. The army has not entirely lost confidence in our old leader." Brand's next statement revealed the extent to which the rumors about Early's drinking had taken hold. Brand wrote, "I fear he uses too much of the poisoned water but don't think he is ever past tending to his duty."[22]

Early was aware of his tenuous grip on the reins of command in the Valley in the wake of his defeats. To Robert E. Lee, Early lamented, "I deeply regret the present state of things, and I assure you everything in my power has been done to avert it." Fortunately for Early, Lee remained in his corner in spite of

21 *OR* 43, pt. 2, 894.

22 Bryan Grimes, *Letters*, 79; William F. Brand to Catherine Armentrout, October 15, 1864, UVA.

the defeats and Governor Smith's damning letter. Perhaps suspecting that Smith's son was the source of the information, Lee asked the governor to name the officer so that a formal investigation might be conducted and allow Early to face his accuser. In dealing with Early, Lee chose to coach rather than dismiss the loyal subordinate. "I very much regret the reverses that have occurred to the army in the Valley, but trust they can be remedied," Lee wrote his subordinate on September 27. "The arrival of Kershaw will add greatly to your strength, and I have such confidence in the men and officers that I am sure all will unite in the defense of the country. . . . One victory will put things right. You must do all in your power to invigorate your army." After telling him that Brig. Gen. Thomas L. Rosser's cavalry was en route to the Valley, Lee made it clear to Early that he expected victory: "I have given you all I can; you must use the resources you have so as to gain success. The enemy must be defeated and I rely upon you to do it." At the same time, Lee doubted Early's assessment of Sheridan's strength. Lee concluded that Sheridan's "effective infantry, I do not think, exceeds 12,000 men." Lee's estimate was off by some 18,000 bayonets in the infantry alone. He assured Early that "A kind Providence will yet overrule everything for our good." Early gave his best effort at Cedar Creek, to no avail.[23]

While it is easy to criticize Early for his decisions, he largely succeeded in carrying out the mission that Lee needed. He saved Lynchburg from capture by Maj. Gen. David Hunter's Army of West Virginia in June, and successfully invaded Maryland and raided to the very gates of Washington, D.C. After that raid, Lee permitted Early to remain in the Valley in order to draw troops away from Grant's army at Petersburg. From July to December, Early's activities in the Valley kept 30,000 Federal troops away from Grant's operations against Petersburg and Richmond, the primary theater of war in Virginia. Even after Early's defeats, his army's presence in the Shenandoah Valley kept the reinforcements there until December. Without Early's operations in the Shenandoah Valley in the latter half of 1864, Robert E. Lee's survival at Petersburg would have been in doubt, especially if Sheridan, his cavalry, and Wright's Sixth Corps had been available for Grant's operations against Lee. In many ways Early accomplished more with his command in the Valley than he would have had he remained with Lee.

---

23 For the definitive work on Cedar Creek, see Ted Mahr's *The Battle of Cedar Creek: Showdown in the Shenandoah*. OR 43, pt. 2, 880-881, and *ibid*, pt. 1, 559.

Senator John W. Daniel noted that the end result of Early's mission in the Valley was that he served two opposing interests. Lee's interest (and that of the Confederacy in general) came first. It necessitated that Early draw as many Federals into the Valley as possible. Early's own interests were subordinate to Lee's. Fewer Federals in the Valley could have allowed him to achieve tactical success. Lee's goal, however, was to win the war and not battles in the Valley. Early was nothing if not devoted to General Lee. "He served Lee first of all with stern unselfishness, letting Kershaw leave when his own need was sore," explained Daniel, "because he believed Lee's need more sore and more important." Lee recognized and appreciated the personal sacrifices that Early made in the Valley.[24]

The defeats in the Valley ruined Early's military reputation. As Lee observed, the government and the public judged Early's generalship on the end result—multiple and devastating defeats in a region previously known for Confederate success. After the rout of his fragmented remains of an army at Waynesboro on March 2, 1865, Lee finally relieved Jubal from command. "Your reverses in the Valley of which the public and the army judge chiefly by the results, have I fear impaired your influence," Lee explained. "While my own confidence in your ability, zeal and devotion to the cause is unimpaired, I have nonetheless felt that I could not oppose what seems to be the current of opinion, without injustice to your reputation and injury to the service." Lee closed the message thanking Early "for the fidelity and energy with which you have always supported my efforts and for the courage and devotion you have manifested in the service of the country."[25]

That the Army of the Valley District lived to fight another day after Winchester is itself a testament to the inherent combat abilities of the Army of Northern Virginia's old Second Corps. The fighting men of Rodes's, Gordon's, and Ramseur's divisions and the artillery conducted what might have been their toughest, albeit most futile, fight of the war. Although usually castigated, even Early's cavalry played critical roles at important points during the battle. "The escape of General Early's army on that day from destruction was marvelous," declared P. J. White of the 5th Virginia Cavalry, "and can only be explained by the valor of his men." Ramseur's infantry fought for nearly a dozen hours,

24 John W. Daniel Papers, Misc. Notes, UVA.

25 Robert E. Lee to Jubal A. Early, March 30, 1865, Tulane.

confronting Wilson at sunrise, battling Wright's Sixth Corps throughout the afternoon, and then beating off Wilson's mounted pursuit in the darkness at Kernstown. Rodes arrived on the battlefield at the very moment Early's destruction seemed inevitable. The division commander's counterattack into the gap in the Federal line saved the day, an accomplishment purchased at the cost of Rodes's own life and the lives of hundreds of others. Gordon's division showed tremendous resiliency, returning to the fight in full force and vigor after its initial discomfiture.[26]

Breckinridge's division, which was under the immediate command of Brig. Gen. Gabriel Wharton, likewise played a critical role in saving Early's army when the Union cavalry stormed up the Valley Pike. Wharton's command essentially sacrificed itself to slow the overwhelming forces under Torbert and Crook, allowing the rest of the army to retreat safely through Winchester. The cost was high. Wharton lost two of his three brigadiers, nine of ten regimental or battalion battle flags, and almost 1,200 men out of the 2,200 who went into battle—an astounding casualty rate of at least 55 percent. Although the division was small, prior to Winchester it possessed the most complete organizations and officer corps in the entire army. After its sacrificial stand it ceased being an effective combat unit. Wharton and his command would go on to participate in the battles of Cedar Creek and Waynesboro, but the division never regained the soul and the strength it left behind in the open fields north of Winchester.

Among the Confederate officer corps, the loss of Maj. Gen. Robert E. Rodes was a crippling blow to the Army of the Valley District. "We have never suffered a greater loss save in the Great Jackson," lamented Maj. Jed Hotchkiss of Early's staff. "Rodes was the best Division Commander in the Army of N. Va. and was worthy of and capable for any position in it." Such words coming from a man who served side-by-side with Jackson on a daily basis cannot be taken lightly. Similar sentiments echoed throughout the army at the loss of this universally beloved leader. The loss of Rodes probably impacted Early more than he ever admitted. A long time fellow division commander with Jubal in the Second Corps, Rodes's relationship with Early appears to have been collegial, unlike the tenuous relationship between the army commander and the ambitious Gordon. Early more readily accepted advice and suggestions from

---

26 P. J. White, "General Early's Valley Campaign," *Richmond Times Dispatch*, September 23, 1906; S. D. Ramseur to My Dear Brother, October 10, 1864, S. D. Ramseur Papers, SHC-UNC.

Rodes as well as he listened to anyone. When Rodes died, Early had no one capable of stepping into Rodes's position.[27]

Rodes's eventual replacement, Maj. Gen. Stephen D. Ramseur, went into combat on September 19, 1864 with a stigma hanging over his head. Ramseur's aggressiveness got him into trouble at Bethesda Church back in May and at Rutherford's farm on July 20. There, he violated Early's orders to remain on the defensive and cover the removal of wounded men and supplies from Winchester when the army was retreating from Snicker's Gap to Fisher's Hill. Instead, Ramseur went on the offensive, and a greatly outnumbered Brig. Gen. William Averell routed the North Carolinian with a lightning quick attack. Ramseur lost hundreds of men, four artillery pieces, and two brigadier generals. His misdirected aggressiveness nearly reared its head again on September 19, but the presence of the prudent Fitz Lee prevented the Tar Heel from lashing out blindly at the massive Federal force bearing down on Winchester. Thus restrained, Ramseur led his division through some of the toughest combat of the day. The first shots of the battle fired by Confederate infantry came from Ramseur's men near sunrise against Wilson's cavalry. The North Carolinian's foot soldiers rallied after being overwhelmed by the Sixth Corps and participated in the counterattack. They kept that corps at bay during the final attack, and covered Early's critical southern flank during the withdrawal. Fittingly, Ramseur's men fired the final shots of the battle at Kernstown when Wilson's men attempted a night pursuit. As Ramseur duly noted, "I made Early's old division do splendid fighting at Winchester and held my position unaided from early dawn until 9 o'clock."[28]

General John B. Gordon performed admirably in a tough situation at Winchester. Birge struck his left flank as his division was still advancing, triggering a near-disaster. When Rodes's counterattack turned the tables, Gordon quickly rallied his broken troops and returned them to the attack. He kept the pressure on Dwight's Nineteenth Corps division throughout the early afternoon hours. Gordon did not initially fear the results when Crook's flank attack struck, but that soon changed, as he later recalled:

27 Jed Hotchkiss to wife, September 21, 1864, Library of Congress.

28 George Q. Peyton, Memoir, UVA; Fitz Lee, Report, MOC; Thomas H. Carter to John W. Daniel, November 28, 1894.

When we first saw Hayes and his men coming over the hills, we rather laughed the movement to scorn, knowing of this morass on our left, but when on you came, plunging into the morass as though it was mere pastime, we began to wonder of what metal such men were made. One of my staff officers remarked, 'they must be devils', and as you rose to the brink of the bank away went my boys as though ten thousand devils were after them. After that charge my men always spoke of your Corps as 'Crook's devils.'[29]

Although forced back, Gordon kept his men well in hand and rallied them behind the stone wall that finally allowed the Georgian to confront Crook's attack. One Confederate officer told John W. Daniel of a captured Union cavalryman who had pursued too far ahead of his command. "Who was that man that was constantly galloping along the line during the fight," asked the prisoner.

"That was General Gordon," replied the lieutenant.

"Our Generals do not do [it] that way," declared the thoroughly impressed cavalryman.[30]

The aftermath of the Shenandoah Valley fighting, including the failed Confederate effort at Cedar Creek, brought about a final break between Gordon and Early over the conduct of the campaign. The two men remained lifelong enemies. Many Confederate veterans took sides in the feud, and their writings tended to reflect the man behind whom they had aligned themselves. For example, Col. Thomas H. Carter, Early's chief of artillery, believed the presence of Gordon's division on the Confederate left (the initial breaking point) at both Winchester and Cedar Creek might have had something to do with Early's defeats. "Gordon in the defense is not Gordon in attack," wrote Colonel Carter. "In the latter capacity he was unequaled; in the former he had superiors. . . . The creator molded him for the rush of the onset & put in him that subtle magnetic influence that strikes the electric chain wherewith we are darkly bound." While Carter's observation is insightful, the large odds arrayed against Gordon in both battles left the Georgian with no options to rectify the situation once the break started.[31]

29 Conversation between Gordon and Capt. Russell Hastings of Hayes's staff, Russell Hastings Papers, RBHPC.

30 Narrative on Third Winchester, John W. Daniel Papers, UVA.

31 Thomas H. Carter to John W. Daniel, November 19, 1894, J. W. Daniel Papers, UVA.

Maj. Gen. John C. Breckinridge's role at Winchester remains perplexing. Although he was a corps commander assigned to lead Wharton's and Gordon's divisions, Early split the command when he took Gordon and Rodes to Martinsburg prior to the battle. This left the Kentuckian with only Wharton's division and King's (McLaughlin's) artillery battalion. Breckinridge's immediate presence made Wharton somewhat of a supernumerary on the battlefield with a superior who had little else to command. Breckinridge and Wharton defied Early's 9:00 a.m. instructions to come to Winchester in order to hold Wesley Merritt's cavalry division at bay near Brucetown. The impact of the Union cavalry upon the Confederate infantry increased steadily, and Breckinridge understood the importance of keeping Merritt's command away from the main battlefield. However, when Averell's approaching division threatened the Kentuckian's left flank and rear, there was no choice but to pull back and allow Merritt to advance. When the Federal cavalry crashed into the rear of Early's battle line, Breckinridge and Wharton counterattacked and threw back the Federal horsemen after their initial approach. Reunited with Gordon's division, Breckinridge strove valiantly among the men as they struggled to hold off the Union attackers. Gordon later recalled the scene:

> General Breckinridge, who had scarcely a corporal's guard of his magnificent division around him, rode to my side. His Apollo-like face was begrimed with sweat and smoke. He was desperately reckless—the impersonation of despair. He literally seemed to court death. Indeed, to my protest against his unnecessary exposure, by riding at my side, he said: "Well, general, there is little left for me if our cause is to fail." Later, when the cause had failed, he acted upon this belief and left the country, and only returned after long absence, to end his brilliant career in coveted privacy among his Kentucky friends.[32]

As the army retreated south through the dark night, Gordon recalled that Jubal Early "could not resist the temptation presented by the conditions around us; and, at a time when the oppressive stillness was disturbed only by the dull sound of tramping feet and tinkling canteens, Early's shrill tones rang out, 'General Breckinridge, what do you think of the rights of the South in the Territories' now?'" The Kentuckian offered no reply. Orders soon arrived that sent Breckinridge to Southwest Virginia, where he assumed command to

32 John B. Gordon, *Reminiscences*, 322.

defend against a pending Union raid on Saltville. Early lost another accomplished general.[33]

Although the Confederates were outgunned and outmanned, no duty equaled the difficulties faced by Maj. Gen. Fitz Hugh Lee. Having just returned to command after suffering from serious illness for much of September, Lee confronted Torbert's advance up the Valley Pike. He clearly saw the outcome, but, as he admitted, lacked any resources to confront the impending charge. Bravely leading Payne's brigade in a futile countercharge, Lee stayed in the fight until seriously wounded. His most significant contribution to the survival of Early's army came in the morning. After keeping the impetuous Ramseur in check, Lee posted Breathed's horse artillery in position to dominate the northern portions of the Middle Field. Breathed's guns proved to be the bane of the Nineteenth Corps throughout the day as it battled Gordon and Rodes. Lee's vision in posting the guns was a key element in limiting the magnitude of Sheridan's victory at Winchester. His wounding deprived Early of an experienced cavalry chief; Lee did not return to duty until early 1865.

If any portion of Early's army was universally blamed for the Confederate loss at Winchester, it was the unfortunate cavalry. The standard post-battle reasoning stated that the Confederate infantry defeated the Union infantry and had it on the run, until the Southern cavalry failed to do its duty on the left flank. In truth, the Confederate counterattack was repulsed at least two hours before Torbert's horsemen thundered up the pike. Even more, the Confederate infantry already began retreating before Crook's attack when the Union horse soldiers arrived on the scene, complicating the reasoning behind the simple excuse for the defeat. Jubal Early lamented to Robert E. Lee, "The enemy's immense superiority in cavalry and the inefficiency of the greater part of mine has been the cause of all my disasters." While Early was technically accurate in his statement, the dispersal of his army over such a wide front from Winchester to Martinsburg placed his cavalry in desperate situations. Early struggled to simply reunite his army when Sheridan surprised him on September 19. About the only thing that Early could have done to prevent the rout of his army was to have better utilized the substantial earthen fortifications around Winchester. Based on the effectiveness of Shoemaker's two guns at Fort Jackson after the Union cavalry stormed up the pike, the judicious posting of a battery in Star

---

33 J. S. Johnston of Breckinridge's staff has Early making that statement during the retreat from Winchester on August 11. Ibid, 325.

Fort as a precautionary measure might have allowed the Confederate infantry to retreat from the battlefield with a semblance of order.[34]

Considering the circumstances of the Southern cavalry at Winchester, the outcome should have surprised no one. Early knew of that arm's weakness long before the battle, but took few if any corrective measures. In the end, the Southern horsemen were simply outnumbered and, as Fitz Lee accurately observed of the situation on the Martinsburg Pike, the Confederates simply had no more resources available to mitigate the situation. Other than break and run, 2,200 cavalrymen could only do so much when Torbert attacked them with nearly three times their number. At the same time, elements of the cavalry performed spectacularly at Winchester and beyond. Tom Munford's brigade shut the back door to Winchester when Averell tried to get around Early's left flank. Munford did the same in the Luray Valley when Sheridan tried to do an end run around Massanutten and come up behind Early's retreating army after Fisher's Hill. On the Senseney Road, Lunsford Lomax, with the small brigades of Brig. Gen. Bradley Johnson and Lt. Col. William Thompson (Jackson's), kept Wilson from interdicting Early's line of retreat southeast of Winchester. Without those covering movements, the damage to Early's army would have been infinitely worse.

In contrast to the Southern mounted arm, the Confederate artillery emerged from Winchester with widespread praise. Lt. Thomas B. Cabaniss of Cook's Georgia brigade opined, "Our artillery acted throughout most nobly, frequently driving back lines of the enemy, when entirely unsupported." A North Carolinian from Cox's brigade held the gunners up as an example for the rest of the army: "Had all done their duty as unflinchingly as the artillery troops, our colors would not now be drooped in dishonor." Early's veteran artillery chief Col. Tom Carter agreed. "In all my experience, I never saw Artillery so effectively operated," boasted the colonel, who was wounded by a shell fragment near the end of the battle and forced to relinquish command. Colonel Thomas M. Munford testified to the effectiveness of Major Breathed's battery: "The handling of our six guns of horse artillery, was simply magnificent." Union reports likewise praised the effectiveness of the Southern gunners, with Brig. Gen. Wesley Merritt describing it as a "fearful fire of artillery." Private Henry R. Berkeley of Nelson's battalion noted that his battery "fired 1,600 rounds of ammunition, about four times as much as we have ever used in a fight

34 *OR* 43, pt. 1, 558.

before." He properly asserted, "This was a great artillery fight, and the artillery covered itself with honor and glory, but its loss has been very heavy. My battery was engaged from sunup until 9 p.m., with short intervals of cessation between fierce engagements at close quarters."[35]

* * *

The Third Battle of Winchester was the largest and bloodiest battle ever fought in the Shenandoah Valley. Although its place in history has been somewhat eclipsed by Jubal Early's dramatic predawn attack and Sheridan's famous ride and ultimate victory a month later at Cedar Creek, Winchester's climactic struggle stood as the hardest ever waged in the Valley.

The unsurpassed tenacity of the day-long slugfest at Winchester convinced many Confederates that U. S. Grant was commanding the Union forces in person. "It was one of the hottest times I ever seen," declared North Carolinian Nathan R. Frazier of Grimes's brigade. "Gettysburg could not hold it a light while it lasted." Another Confederate agreed, describing Winchester as "one of the hardest fights on record; almost as heavy as the 12th of May [at Spotsylvania]." Union men saw it the same way. Sergeant Chester Ballard of the 37th Massachusetts declared Winchester "the hardest days fighting I ever saw, and I have seen some hard days this summer."

From a soldier's perspective perhaps Private Frazier from North Carolina summed it up best when he wrote, "For it was the hottest fighting I ever was in and I have bin in 21 batles and i hope i never will be in another."[36]

---

35 Letter Thomas B. Cabaniss, September 22, 1864, "Battle Near Winchester," *Macon Telegraph and Confederate*, October 6, 1864; 3rd North Carolina, Letter, "Battle of Winchester No. 3," *Wilmington Daily Journal*, October 26, 1864, Thomas H. Carter to John W. Daniel, November 28, 1894, John W. Daniel Papers, UVA; Munford, "Reminiscences of Cavalry Operations," 448; OR 43, pt. 1, 445; Henry R. Berkeley, *Four Years in the Confederate Artillery*, 97.

36 Nathan R. Frazier to Much Beloved Wife, September 28, 1864, Nathan R. Frazier Papers, ECU; Thomas P. Devereux to Mother, September 20, 1864, NC State Archives; Jones, ed., *Memoirs of Captain William J. Seymour*, 141; Chester H. Bardwell to Dear Father and Mother, September 20, 1864, William L. Clements Library, Michigan; Nathan R. Frazier to Much respected and dear wife, September 21, 1864, Nathan R. Frazier Papers, ECU.

Union and Confederate Orders of Battle
Shenandoah Valley Campaign
August 7 - September 19, 1864

U.S. ARMY OF THE SHENANDOAH
Maj. Gen. Philip H. Sheridan

Sixth Army Corps
Maj. Gen. Horatio G. Wright

First Division
Brig. Gen. David Russell, KIA Sept. 19
Brig. Gen. Emory Upton, WIA Sept. 19
Col. Oliver Edwards

First Brigade
Col. William Penrose
Lt. Col. Edward L. Campbell
4th New Jersey
10th New Jersey
15th New Jersey

Second Brigade
Brig. Gen. Emory Upton
Col. Joseph E. Hamblin
2nd Connecticut Heavy Artillery
65th New York Infantry
121st New York Infantry
95th/96th Pennsylvania Battalion

Third Brigade
Col. Oliver Edwards

37th Massachusetts
49th Pennsylvania
82nd Pennsylvania
119th Pennsylvania
2nd Rhode Island Battalion
5th Wisconsin Battalion

Second Division
Brig. Gen. George W. Getty

First Brigade
Brig. Gen. Lewis A. Grant
Col. James M. Warner
2nd Vermont
3rd Vermont
4th Vermont
5th Vermont
6th Vermont
11th Vermont (1st Heavy Artillery)

Second Brigade
Brig. Gen. Frank Wheaton
62nd New York
93rd Pennsylvania
98th Pennsylvania
102nd Pennsylvania
139th Pennsylvania

Third Brigade
Brig. Gen. Daniel Bidwell
7th Maine
43rd New York
29th New York
77th New York
122nd New York
61st Pennsylvania

Third Division
Brig. Gen. James B. Ricketts

First Brigade
Col. William Emerson
14th New Jersey
106th New York
151st New York
87th Pennsylvania
10th Vermont

Second Brigade
Col. Joseph Warren Keifer
6th Maryland
9th New York Heavy Artillery
110th Ohio
122nd Ohio
126th Ohio
67th Pennsylvania
138th Pennsylvania

Artillery Brigade
Col. Charles H. Tompkins
5th Maine Light Battery
1st Massachusetts Light Artillery, Battery A
1st Rhode Island Light Artillery, Battery C
1st Rhode Island Light Artillery, Battery G
1st New York Independent Battery
5th United States, Battery M

Nineteenth Army Corps
Bvt. Maj. Gen. William H. Emory

First Division
Brig. Gen. William Dwight

First Brigade
Brig. Gen. George L. Beal
29th Maine
30th Massachusetts
114th New York
116th New York
153rd New York

Second Brigade
Brig. Gen. James W. McMillan
12th Connecticut
160th New York
47th Pennsylvania
8th Vermont

Artillery
5th New York Independent Battery

Second Division
Brig. Gen. Cuvier Grover

First Brigade
Brig. Gen. Henry W. Birge
9th Connecticut
12th Maine
14th Maine
26th Massachusetts
14th New Hampshire
75th New York

Second Brigade
Col. Edward L. Molineux
13th Connecticut
11th Indiana
22nd Iowa
3rd Massachusetts Cavalry (dismounted)
131st New York
159th New York

Third Brigade
Col. Jacob Sharpe, WIA Sept. 19
Lt. Col. James P. Richardson, WIA Sept. 19
Lt. Col. Alfred Neafie
38th Massachusetts
128th New York
156th New York
175th New York (3 companies)
176th New York

Fourth Brigade
Col. David Shunk
8th Indiana
18th Indiana
24th Iowa
28th Iowa

Artillery
1st Maine Light Battery

Reserve Artillery
Capt. Elijah Taft
17th Indiana Light Battery
1st Rhode Island, Battery D

Army of West Virginia
Bvt. Maj. Gen. George Crook

First Division
Col. Joseph Thoburn

First Brigade
Col. George D. Wells
34th Massachusetts
5th New York Heavy Artillery
116th Ohio
123rd Ohio

Second Brigade (not engaged)
Col. William G. Ely[1]
Lt. Col. Robert S. Northcott
18th Connecticut[2]
2nd Maryland Eastern Shore[3]
1st West Virginia
4th West Virginia
12th West Virginia

Third Brigade
Col. Thomas M. Harris
23rd Illinois
54th Pennsylvania
10th West Virginia
11th West Virginia
15th West Virginia

Second Division
Col. Isaac H. Duval, WIA Sept. 19
Col. Rutherford B. Hayes

First Brigade
Col. Rutherford B. Hayes
Col. Hiram F. Devol

23rd Ohio
36th Ohio
5th West Virginia
13th West Virginia

Second Brigade
Col. Daniel D. Johnson, WIA Sept. 19
Lt. Col. Benjamin F. Coates
34th Ohio
91st Ohio
9th West Virginia
14th West Virginia

Artillery Battalion
Capt. Henry A. DuPont
Battery L, 1st Ohio Light Artillery
Battery I, 1st Pennsylvania Light Artillery
Battery B, 5th U.S. Artillery

Cavalry Corps
Maj. Gen. Alfred T. A. Torbert

First Division
Brig. Gen. Wesley Merritt

First Brigade
Brig. Gen. George A. Custer
1st Michigan
5th Michigan
6th Michigan
7th Michigan
25th New York

Second Brigade
Bvt. Brig. Gen. Thomas C. Devin
4th New York
6th New York
9th New York
19th New York
17th Pennsylvania

1   Departed the army sometime after September 3 and resigned his commission on September 20.

2   Ordered to garrison Charlestown and escort wagon trains on September 11.

3   Ordered to garrison Charlestown and escort wagon trains on September 11.

Reserve Brigade
Col. Alfred Gibbs
Col. Charles R. Lowell, Jr.
2nd Massachusetts
1st New York Dragoons[4]
6th Pennsylvania[5]
1st United States
2nd United States
5th United States

Second Division
Brig. Gen. William W. Averell

First Brigade
Col. James M. Schoonmaker
8th Ohio
14th Pennsylvania
22nd Pennsylvania

Second Brigade
Col. William H. Powell
1st New York (Lincoln Cavalry)
1st West Virginia
2nd West Virginia
3rd West Virginia
5th United States, Battery L, Lt. Gulian V. Weir

Third Division
Brig. Gen. James H. Wilson

First Brigade
Brig. Gen. John B. McIntosh
Lt. Col. George A. Purington
1st Connecticut
3rd New Jersey
2nd New York
5th New York
2nd Ohio
18th Pennsylvania

Second Brigade
Brig. Gen. George H. Chapman
3rd Indiana (3 companies)
1st New Hampshire Battalion
8th New York

22nd New York
1st Vermont

Horse Artillery
Capt. La Rhett L. Livingston
1st U.S., Batteries K and L, Lt. Franck E. Taylor
2nd U.S., Batteries B and L, Capt. Charles H. Peirce
2nd U.S., Battery D, Lt. Edward B. Williston
3rd U.S., Batteries C and F,
Capt. Dunbar R. Ransom
4th U.S., Battery C, Lt. Terrence Reilly

* * *

ARMY OF THE VALLEY DISTRICT
Lt. Gen. Jubal A. Early

Breckinridge's Corps
Maj. Gen. John C. Breckinridge

Breckinridge's Division
(Department of Southwest Virginia)

Brig. Gen. Gabriel C. Wharton

Smith's Brigade
Col. Thomas Smith
36th Virginia
60th Virginia
45th Virginia Battalion
Thomas Legion (69th North Carolina)

Forsberg's Brigade
Col. Augustus Forsberg, WIA Sept. 19
45th Virginia
51st Virginia
30th Virginia Battalion Sharpshooters

Patton's Brigade
Col. George S. Patton, MW Sept. 19
22nd Virginia, Lt. Col. John C. McDonald
23rd Virginia Battalion
26th Virginia Battalion

4 Gibbs and his 1st New York Dragoons transferred to Devin's brigade on September 9.

5 Ordered to remount camp in Pleasant Valley, Maryland on September 8.

Gordon's Division
Maj. Gen. John B. Gordon

Evans' Brigade
Col. Edmund N. Atkinson
13th Georgia
26th Georgia
31st Georgia
38th Georgia
60th Georgia
61st Georgia
12th Georgia Battalion

Terry's Brigade
Brig. Gen. William Terry
2nd, 4th, 5th, 27th, 33rd Virginia
Col. John H. S. Funk, MW Sept. 19
21st, 25th, 42nd, 44th, 48th and 50th Virginia
Col. Robert H. Dungan
10th, 23rd, 37th Virginia
Lt. Col. Samuel Saunders, WIA Sept. 19

York's Brigade
Brig. Gen. Zebulon York, WIA Sept. 19
Col. William R. Peck
5th, 6th, 7th, 8th, and 9th Louisiana
Col. William Monaghan, KIA Aug. 25
Col. William R. Peck
1st, 2nd, 10th, 14th, and 15th Louisiana
Col. Eugene Waggaman

Rodes Division
Maj. Gen. Robert E. Rodes, MW Sept. 19
Brig. Gen. Cullen Battle
Maj. Gen. Stephen D. Ramseur[6]

Battle's Brigade
Brig. Gen. Cullen Battle
Col. Samuel B. Pickens, WIA Sept. 19
Col. Charles Forsyth
3rd Alabama
5th Alabama
6th Alabama
12th Alabama
61st Alabama

Grimes Brigade
Brig. Gen. Bryan Grimes
2nd North Carolina Battalion
32nd North Carolina
43rd North Carolina
45th North Carolina
53rd North Carolina

Cox's Brigade
Col. William R. Cox
1st North Carolina
2nd North Carolina
3rd North Carolina
4th North Carolina
14th North Carolina
30th North Carolina

Cook's Brigade
Brig. Gen. Phillip Cook
4th Georgia
12th Georgia
21st Georgia
44th Georgia

Ramseur's Division
Maj. Gen. Stephen D. Ramseur
Brig. Gen John Pegram

Pegram's Brigade
Brig. Gen. John Pegram
Col. William Hoffman
13th Virginia
31st Virginia
49th Virginia
52nd Virginia
58th Virginia

Hoke's Brigade
Brig. Gen. Archibald Godwin, KIA Sept. 19
Lt. Col. Anderson Ellis, WIA Sept. 19
Lt. Col. William S. Davis
6th North Carolina
21st North Carolina
54th North Carolina
57th North Carolina

---

6   Assumed command of Rodes's division on September 20.

Johnston's Brigade
Brig. Gen. Robert D. Johnston
5th North Carolina
12th North Carolina
20th North Carolina
23rd North Carolina

Artillery (35 guns)
Col. Thomas H. Carter

Maj. Carter M. Braxton's Battalion
Allegheny Battery, Capt. John C. Carpenter
Lee Battery, Capt. William W. Hardwick
Stafford Battery, Capt. Raleigh Cooper

Maj. William McLaughlin's Battalion[7]
Lewisburg Battery, Capt. Thomas Bryan
Monroe Battery, Capt. George B. Chapman
Wise Legion Battery, Capt. William M. Lowry

Maj. William Nelson's Battalion
Amherst Battery,
Capt. Thomas J. Kirkpatrick
Fluvanna Artillery, Capt. Charles G. Snead
Georgia Regular Battery,
Lt. Thomas A. Maddox

Cavalry Corps
Maj. Gen. Fitz Hugh Lee

Lee's Division
Brig. Gen. Williams Wickham

Lomax's Brigade
Col. Reuben Boston
Col. William Payne
5th Virginia
6th Virginia
15th Virginia

Wickham's Brigade
Col. Thomas Owen
Col. Thomas Munford
1st Virginia
2nd Virginia

3rd Virginia
4th Virginia

Horse Artillery (6 guns)
Maj. James Breathed
1st Stuart Horse Artillery,
Capt. Phillip P. Johnston
Lynchburg Beauregard Battery,
Capt. John J. Shoemaker

Lomax's Division
Maj. Gen. Lunsford L. Lomax

Imboden's Brigade
Col. George H. Smith
18th Virginia
23rd Virginia
62nd Virginia Mounted Infantry

Johnson's Brigade
Brig. Gen. Bradley Johnson
1st Maryland Battalion
2nd Maryland Battalion
8th Virginia
21st Virginia
27th Virginia Battalion
36th Virginia Battalion
37th Virginia Battalion

McCausland's Brigade
Brig. Gen. John C. McCausland
Col. Milton Ferguson
14th Virginia
16th Virginia
17th Virginia
22nd Virginia

Jackson's Brigade
Col. William L. Jackson, WIA Aug. 25
Lt. Col. William P. Thompson
19th Virginia
20th Virginia
46th Virginia Battalion
47th Virginia Battalion

7   This battalion is sometimes referred to as Lt. Col. J. Floyd King's Battalion. King seemed to have served as Breckinridge's Chief of Artillery. Breckinridge was the official commander of the Confederate Department of Southwestern Virginia.

Vaughn's Brigade
Col. Gillespie, WIA Aug. 11
Lt. Col. Onslow Bean
16th Georgia Battalion
1st Tennessee Cavalry
12th Tennessee Battalion
16th Tennessee Battalion
39th Tennessee Mounted Infantry
43rd Tennessee Mounted Infantry
59th Tennessee Mounted Infantry
60th/61st/62nd Tennessee (fragments)

Horse Artillery (4-8 guns)
Charlottesville Battery, Capt. Thomas Jackson
Roanoke Battery, Capt. Warren Lurty
Staunton Battery, Capt. John H. McClanahan

First Corps (detachment)
Lt. Gen. Richard H. Anderson

Kershaw's Division
Maj. Gen. Joseph B. Kershaw

Kershaw's Brigade
Col. William D. Rutherford
Brig. Gen. James Connor[8]
2nd South Carolina
3rd South Carolina
7th South Carolina
8th South Carolina
15th South Carolina
20th South Carolina
3rd South Carolina Battalion

Wofford's Brigade
Brig. Gen. William Wofford, WIA Aug. 16
Col. Joseph Armstrong
16th Georgia
18th Georgia
24th Georgia
3rd Georgia Battalion
Cobb's Legion
Phillip's Legion

Humphrey's Brigade
Brig. Gen. Benjamin Humphreys, WIA Sept. 3
Col. Daniel Moody

13th Mississippi
17th Mississippi
18th Mississippi
21st Mississippi

Bryan's Brigade
Col. James P. Simms
10th Georgia
50th Georgia
51st Georgia
53rd Georgia

Maj. Wilfred E. Cutshaw's Battalion

Orange Battery, Capt. Charles W. Fry
Staunton Artillery, Capt. Asher Garbe
Richmond Howitzers, Capt. Lorraine F. Jones

8   Assumed command September 10, 1864.

The Army of the Shenandoah
Strength Reports

Present for Duty, Enlisted Men	Pre-August 17, 1864	August 31, 1864	September 10, 1864
Wright's Sixth Corps	11,144[1]	11,333[5]	12,028[7]
Emory's Nineteenth Corps	5,815[2]	12,068[5]	12,150[7]
Crook's Army of West Virginia	6,500[3]	7,029[6]	6,834[7]
Total Infantry	23,459	30,430	31,012
Merritt's Division	3,500[3]	3,434[5]	3,424[7]
Averell's Division	Not Present	1,500[5]	2,500[8]
Duffie's Division	800[3]	Not Present	Not Present
Wilson's Division	Not Present	2,957[5]	2,702[7]
Total Cavalry	4,300	7,891	8,626
Artillery	1,405[4]	2,025[4]	1,535[4]

Present for Duty, Enlisted Men	Pre-August 17, 1864	August 31, 1864	September 10, 1864
Army of the Shenandoah	29,164	40,346	41,173

1. OR 43, pt. 1, 743.

2. Ibid., 37, pt. 2, 547. One brigade of the present force of the Nineteenth Corps was detached to the Harpers Ferry garrison as wagon guards. The actual strength on July 31, 1864 for the corps was 7,315 enlisted men present for duty. A total of 1,500 men has been deducted from the Nineteenth Corps to account for the absence of that brigade.

3. Estimate based upon prior/subsequent strength reports and known gains/losses in strength.

4. Artillery totals are compiled from the same source as the main command to which they were attached.

5. OR 43, pt. 1, 974.

6. Record Group 393, Pt. 1, Entry 2418, Middle Military Division, Monthly Returns, August 1864.

7. OR 43, pt. 1, 61.

8. Ibid., 60.

The Army of the Valley District
Strength Reports

Present for Duty, Enlisted Men	August 20, 1864	August 31, 1864	September 10, 1864[2]	September 30, 1864
Gordon's Division	2,823	2,883	2,690	1,750[4]
Rodes's Division	3,386	3,305	3,244	2,345
Ramseur's Division	2,060	2,045	2,010	1,449
Second Corps Total	8,269	8,233	7,944	5,544
Wharton's Division	2,000*	2,100	2,172	1,071
Kershaw's Division	3,500*	3,445	—	—
Infantry Total	13,769	13,778	10,116	6,615
Lomax's Division	4,091	3,900*	3,215	2,000
Fitz Lee's Division	1,500*	1,400*	1,370[3]	1,000*
Cavalry Total	5,591	5,300	4,585	3,000

Present for Duty, Enlisted Men	August 20, 1864	August 31, 1864	September 10, 1864[2]	September 30, 1864
Artillery	1,000*	1,000	813	720
Army Total	20,360	20,078	15,514	10,335

The Army of the Valley strength reports are drawn from the *Official Records*, 43, Pts. 1 and 2.

* Estimate derived from prior and subsequent returns.

1. Second Corps artillery numbered 780 men present for duty. The balance is an estimate for Cutshaw's battalion.

2. September 10 strength is from the consolidated return of the Army of Northern Virginia, OR 42, pt. 2, 1,243.

3. Captured return for Lee's cavalry division for September 1864. It is not clear if this is from September 10 or 30. The assumption is that it is the former. *War Diary of Luman Harris Tenney*, 1861-1865, 132.

4. Estimate from Ted Mahr, *Battle of Cedar Creek*, 367.

Summary from Appendices 2 and 3:

	Available	Engaged
Sheridan's Strength on September 10, 1864	41,173	37,000
Early's Strength on September 10, 1864	15,514	15,514
Sheridan/Early Odds at Third Winchester	2.7 to 1	2.4 to 1

Casualties in the Army of the Shenandoah at Third Winchester, September 19, 1864

	Killed	Wounded	Captured or Missing	Total
SIXTH ARMY CORPS				
Maj. Gen. Horatio G. Wright				
First Division: Brig. Gen. David A. Russell, Brig. Gen. Emory Upton, Col. Oliver Edwards				
Field and Staff	1	2	0	3
First Brigade: Lt. Col. Edward L. Campbell				
4th New Jersey	2	19	1	22
10th New Jersey	1	14	1	16
15th New Jersey	4	44	7	55
Total First Brigade	7	77	9	93

	Killed	Wounded	Captured or Missing	Total
Second Brigade: Brig. Gen. Emory Upton				
2nd Connecticut Heavy Artillery	20	118	0	138
65th New York	6	26	0	32
121st New York	2	13	0	15
Total Second Brigade	28	157	0	185
Third Brigade: Col. Oliver Edwards				
37th Massachusetts	12	79	0	91
49th Pennsylvania	11	33	0	44
82nd Pennsylvania	7	55	0	62
119th Pennsylvania	2	21	0	23
2nd Rhode Island Battalion	0	6	0	6
5th Wisconsin	4	13	0	17
Total Third Brigade	36	207	0	243
Total First Division	72	443	9	524
Second Division: Brig. Gen. George W. Getty				
Field and Staff	0	0	0	0
First Brigade: Brig. Gen. Frank Wheaton				
62nd New York	0	4	0	4
93rd Pennsylvania	7	32	0	39
98th Pennsylvania	4	22	4	30
102nd Pennsylvania	7	51	4	62
139th Pennsylvania	3	37	0	40
Total First Brigade	21	146	8	175

	Killed	Wounded	Captured or Missing	Total
Second Brigade: Col. James M. Warner				
2nd Vermont	3	29	1	33
3rd Vermont	0	26	3	29
4th Vermont	1	15	0	16
5th Vermont	6	22	0	28
6th Vermont	5	45	0	50
11th Vermont (1st Heavy Artillery)	8	85	6	99
Total Second Brigade	23	222	10	255
Third Brigade: Brig. Gen. Daniel D. Bidwell				
7th Maine	1	17	0	18
43rd New York	2	6	0	8
49th New York Battalion	1	10	0	11
77th New York	2	38	2	42
122nd New York	6	28	0	34
61st Pennsylvania Battalion	0	16	0	16
Total First Brigade	12	115	2	129
Total Second Division	56	483	20	559
Third Division: Brig. Gen. James B. Ricketts				
Field and Staff	0	0	0	0

	Killed	Wounded	Captured or Missing	Total
First Brigade: **Col. William Emerson**				
14th New Jersey	6	56	0	62
106th New York	6	45	3	54
151st New York	3	14	0	17
87th Pennsylvania	7	47	0	54
10th Vermont	11	53	1	65
Total First Brigade	33	215	4	252
Second Brigade: **Col. J. Warren Keifer**				
6th Maryland	7	32	3	42
9th New York Heavy Artillery	6	36	0	42
110th Ohio	7	48	0	55
122nd Ohio	6	53	1	60
126th Ohio	12	40	2	54
67th Pennsylvania	9	28	4	41
138th Pennsylvania	3	48	3	54
Total Second Brigade	50	285	13	348
Total Third Division	83	500	17	600
Artillery Brigade: **Col. Charles H. Tompkins**				
5th Maine Battery	0	6	0	6
1st New York Independent Battery	0	6	0	6
1st Rhode Island Light Artillery, C	0	4	0	4
Total Artillery Brigade	0	16	0	16

	Killed	Wounded	Captured or Missing	Total
Total Sixth Army Corps	211	1,442	46	1,699

NINETEENTH ARMY CORPS				
Bvt. Major Gen. William H. Emory				
First Division: Brig. Gen. William Dwight				
Field and Staff	0	0	0	0
First Brigade: Brig. Gen. George Beal				
29th Maine	0	24	0	24
30th Massachusetts	5	17	0	22
114th New York	21	164	0	185
87th Pennsylvania	9	39	0	48
10th Vermont	10	59	0	69
Total First Brigade	45	303	0	348
Second Brigade: Brig. Gen. James McMillan				
12th Connecticut	10	60	1	71
160th New York	15	61	1	77
47th Pennsylvania	1	8	0	9
8th Vermont	9	28	0	37
Total Second Brigade	35	157	2	194
Total First Division	80	460	2	542

	Killed	Wounded	Captured or Missing	Total
Second Division: **Brig. Gen. Cuvier Grover**				
Field and Staff	0	0	0	0
First Brigade: **Brig. Gen. Henry W. Birge**				
9th Connecticut	0	0	1	1
12th Maine	14	83	15	112
14th Maine	7	52	3	62
26th Massachusetts	38	80	21	139
14th New Hampshire	31	88	19	138
75th New York Rifles	17	45	11	73
Total First Brigade	107	348	70	525
Second Brigade: **Col. Edward L. Molineux**				
13th Connecticut	6	39	32	77
11th Indiana	8	58	4	70
22nd Iowa	11	63	31	105
3rd Mass. Cavalry (dismounted)	19	87	0	106
131st New York	9	65	0	74
159th New York	5	50	20	75
Total Second Brigade	58	362	87	507
Third Brigade: Col. Jacob Sharpe **Lt. Col. Alfred Neafie**				
38th Massachusetts	8	47	8	63
128th New York	6	51	0	57

	Killed	Wounded	Captured or Missing	Total
156th New York	5	33	9	47
176th New York	20	91	0	111
Total Third Brigade	39	222	17	278
Fourth Brigade: Col. David Shunk				
8th Indiana	2	5	2	9
18th Indiana	6	32	0	38
24th Iowa	10	57	8	75
28th Iowa	10	56	21	87
Total Fourth Brigade	28	150	31	209
Total Second Division	232	1,082	205	1,519
Nineteenth Corps Artillery Reserve: Capt. Elijah D. Taft				
17th Indiana Light Battery	0	1	0	1
1st Maine Light Artillery, A	2	6	0	8
1st Rhode Island Light Artillery, D	0	4	0	4
Total Artillery Reserve	2	11	0	13
Total Nineteenth Army Corps	314	1,553	207	2,074

	Killed	Wounded	Captured or Missing	Total
ARMY OF WEST VIRGINIA				
Bvt. Maj. Gen. George Crook				
First Division: **Col. Joseph Thoburn**				
Field and Staff		2		2
First Brigade: **Col. George D. Wells**				
34th Massachusetts	6	96	0	102
5th New York Heavy Artillery	11	32	0	43
116th Ohio	4	30	0	34
123rd Ohio	6	42	0	48
Total First Brigade	27	200	0	227
Third Brigade: **Col. Thomas M. Harris**				
23rd Illinois	3	19	0	22
54th Pennsylvania	6	39	4	49
10th West Virginia	17	78	2	97
11th West Virginia	3	18	0	21
15th West Virginia	11	38	0	49
Total Third Brigade	40	192	6	238
Total First Division	67	392	6	467
Second Division: **Col. Isaac H. Duval**				
Field and Staff		1		1

	Killed	Wounded	Captured or Missing	Total
First Brigade: **Col. Rutherford B. Hayes**				
23rd Ohio	3	43	0	46
36th Ohio	4	33	0	37
5th West Virginia Battalion	4	22	1	27
13th West Virginia	2	23	0	25
Total First Brigade	13	121	1	135
Second Brigade: **Col. Thomas M. Harris**				
34th Ohio Battalion	10	37	0	47
91st Ohio	11	95	0	106
9th West Virginia	2	16	0	18
14th West Virginia	1	19	0	20
Total Second Brigade	24	167	0	191
Total Second Division	37	288	1	327
Total Army of West Virginia	**104**	**680**	**7**	**794**
CAVALRY CORPS **Bvt. Maj. Gen. Alfred Pleasonton**				
First Division: **Brig. Gen. Wesley Merritt**				
Field and Staff		1		1

	Killed	Wounded	Captured or Missing	Total
First Brigade: **Brig. Gen. George A. Custer**				
1st Michigan	6	33	0	39
5th Michigan	5	17	2	24
6th Michigan	2	16	2	20
7th Michigan	3	18	2	23
25th New York	1	3	3	7
Total First Brigade	17	87	9	113
Second Brigade **Brig. Gen. Thomas C. Devin**				
4th New York	0	13	4	17
6th New York	3	9	6	18
9th New York	3	16	0	19
1st New York Dragoons	2	7	4	13
17th Pennsylvania	0	4	1	5
Total Second Brigade	8	49	15	72
Third Brigade: **Col. Charles R. Lowell**				
1st United States Cavalry	4	14	6	24
2nd United States Cavalry	2	19	8	29
5th United States Cavalry	5	12	12	29
2nd Massachusetts	3	11	6	20
Total Third Brigade	14	56	32	102
Total First Division	39	193	56	288

	Killed	Wounded	Captured or Missing	Total
2nd Cavalry Division **Brig. Gen. William W. Averell**				
Field and Staff	0	0	0	0
First Brigade				
Col. James M. Schoonmaker				
8th Ohio	2	0	1	3
14th Pennsylvania	1	12	1	14
22nd Pennsylvania	0	2	0	2
Total First Brigade	3	14	2	19
Second Brigade				
Col. William Powell				
1st New York	0	4	0	4
1st West Virginia	2	1	1	4
2nd West Virginia	1	3	0	4
3rd West Virginia	1	2	1	4
Total Second Brigade	3	14	2	19
Total Second Division	7	24	4	35
Third Division **Brig. Gen. James H. Wilson**				
Field and Staff				
First Brigade				
Brig. Gen. John B. McIntosh				

	Killed	Wounded	Captured or Missing	Total
1st Connecticut	1	2	0	3
3rd New Jersey	4	6	11	21
2nd New York	2	5	0	7
5th New York	2	13	2	17
2nd Ohio	1	14	3	18
18th Pennsylvania	7	13	0	20
Total First Brigade	17	53	16	86
Second Brigade				
Brig. Gen. George Chapman				
3rd Indiana (2 companies)	0	1	2	3
8th New York	2	4	0	6
22nd New York	2	5	0	7
138th Pennsylvania	1	8	0	9
Total Second Brigade				
Total Third Division	22	73	18	113
CAVALRY CORPS				
Horse Artillery Capt. La Rhett L. Livingston				
1st United States, K and L	0	5	0	5
2nd United States, B and L	0	10	0	10
Total Horse Artillery	0	15	0	15
Total Cavalry Corps	68	305	78	451
Total Army of the Shenandoah	697	3,980	338	5,018

Casualties in the Army of the Valley District at Third Winchester, September 19, 1864

Confederate Summary	Killed / (mw)	Wounded / (Died)	Wounded & Captured / (Died)	Captured / Missing	Total*
Rodes's Division	151	426	248	289	1,150
Gordon's Division	77	235	146	186	660
Ramseur's Division	71	244	102	218	641
Wharton's Division	44	96	58	813	1,171
Total Infantry	343	1,001	554	1,506	3,622
Artillery	25	85	12	17	139
Lomax's Division	18	53	12	73	193
Wickham's Division	10	31	1	15	57
Horse Artillery (part of cavalry arm)	1	2	1	0	4
Total Cavalry	29	86	14	88	254
Grand Total	397	1,172	580	1,611#	4,015

* The total column figures exceeds the actual sum of the reported casualties because the total includes reported regimental details that sources, such as correspondence or a regimental history, provided only in total. In those cases, the details are provided from muster rolls, newspapers, and correspondence to the extent available. Overall, it is generally concluded that these totals are slightly underestimated in the killed and wounded category. Most of the details were provided by decades of study by researcher Alfred Young, who has compiled the names of virtually all of the infantry casualties in the Army of Northern Virginia for 1864. His work will be published by LSU press. The grand total is 255 higher than reported.

The Second Brigade, First Division, Nineteenth Army Corps reported that it escorted 125 officers and 1,380 men on a march from Winchester to Harpers Ferry on September 22, 1864. This means that at least 1,505 unwounded Confederates became prisoners of war out of the 1,611 men listed as captured or missing. It has been assumed that the remaining 106 men unaccounted for were unknown dead, deserters, and/or later returned to their units. OR 43, pt. 1, p. 78.

Confederate Summary	Killed / (MW)	Wounded / (Died)	Wounded & Captured / (Died)	Captured / Missing	Total*
Rodes's Division					
Field and Staff	1	0	1	0	2
Battle's Brigade					
F&S	0	0	0	0	0
3rd Alabama	6 (2)	49 (1)	9 (1)	13	77
5th Alabama	5 (1)	10	8	23	46
6th Alabama	5	10 (1)	7 (2)	16	38
12th Alabama	9 (3)	19 (1)	7	14	51
61st Alabama	8 (1)	14	8 (1)	14	64
Total	33 (7)	102 (3)	41 (4)	80	276
Cook's Brigade					
F&S	0	1	0	0	1
4th Georgia	9 (1)	25	12 (1)	9	55
12th Georgia	8 (1)	32	9 (1)	10	69
21st Georgia	11 (2)	31	24	16	82
44th Georgia	5 (2)	36	8	10	59

Confederate Summary	Killed / (MW)	Wounded / (Died)	Wounded & Captured / (Died)	Captured / Missing	Total*
Total	33 (6)	125	53 (2)	45	256
Cox's Brigade					
Field and Staff	0	1	0	0	1
1st North Carolina	5 (1)	10	4	8	27
2nd North Carolina	5 (2)	10	19 (2)	16	50
3rd North Carolina	5	5	5 (2)	11	26
4th North Carolina	8 (3)	16	16 (3)	34	74
14th North Carolina	8 (3)	28	25 (4)	17	78
30th North Carolina	3	12	4 (1)	3	22
Total	34 (9)	82	73 (12)	89	278
Grimes's Brigade					
Field and Staff	0	1	0	0	1
2nd North Carolina Battalion	6 (2)	17	11	7	41
32nd North Carolina	7	13	8 (2)	16	44
43rd North Carolina	16 (4)	38	26 (5)	21	101
45th North Carolina	12 (2)	19	10 (2)	23	64
53rd North Carolina	9 (2)	29	25 (4)	8	89
Total	50 (10)	117	80 (13)	75	340
Division Totals	151	426	248	289	1,150
Gordon's Division					
Field and Staff					

Confederate Summary	Killed / (MW)	Wounded / (Died)	Wounded & Captured / (Died)	Captured / Missing	Total*
Evans's Brigade					
Field and Staff	0	0	0	0	0
12th Georgia Battalion	5	14	12 (3)	5	36
13th Georgia	15 (4)	30	23 (6)	25	93
26th Georgia	4 (1)	21	7 (2)	4	51
31st Georgia	7 (2)	23 (1)	8	13	44
38th Georgia	3	16	8 (2)	17	58
60th Georgia	7 (2)	15	17 (1)	19	38
61st Georgia	3 (1)	4	9 (2)	17	36
Total	44 (10)	123 (1)	84 (16)	100	351
Terry's Brigade					
Field and Staff	0	0	0	0	0
2nd Virginia	0	1	1	0	2
4th Virginia	1	6	5	3	15
5th Virginia	2 (1)	5 (1)	2	5	14
27th Virginia	0	2	1	0	3
33rd Virginia	2	5	1	2	10
10th Virginia	1	3	1	6	11
23rd Virginia	0	7	5	3	15
37th Virginia	1	3	3	0	7
21st Virginia	2 (1)	11	3	8	24
25th Virginia	1	1	0	2	4
42nd Virginia	4 (1)	11	4	3	22
44th Virginia	1	1	2	2	6
48th Virginia	1 (1)	3	1	7	12

Confederate Summary	Killed / (MW)	Wounded / (Died)	Wounded & Captured / (Died)	Captured / Missing	Total*
50th Virginia	1	2	3	4	10
Total	17 (4)	58 (1)	32	47	155
York's Brigade					
Field and Staff	0	1	0	0	1
1st Louisiana	1	2	1	7	11
2nd Louisiana	2	6	0	2	10
10th Louisiana	4	4	0	8	16
14th Louisiana	2	0	2	1	5
15th Louisiana	0	0	0	1	1
5th Louisiana	NA	NA	NA	NA	20
6th Louisiana	NA	NA	NA	NA	17
7th Louisiana	NA	NA	NA	NA	20
8th Louisiana	NA	NA	NA	NA	23
9th Louisiana	NA	NA	NA	NA	19
Total	17	54	30	42	154
Division Totals	77	235	146	186	660
Ramseur's Division					
Field and Staff					
Lilley's Brigade					
Field and Staff	0	1	0	0	1
13th Virginia	6 (2)	5	12	31	54

Confederate Summary	Killed (mw)	Wounded / (Died)	Wounded & Captured / (Died)	Captured / Missing	Total*
31st Virginia	4	23	3	4	34
49th Virginia	2 (1)	17	2	8	29
52nd Virginia	7	0	18	11	36
58th Virginia	8 (1)	19	6	18	51
Total	26 (8)	75	29	69	205
Johnston's Brigade					
Field and Staff	0	0	0	0	0
5th North Carolina	4	15	10 (1)	37	66
12th North Carolina	4	12	6 (2)	14	36
20th North Carolina	4	20	16 (4)	15	55
23rd North Carolina	5	21	10 (2)	43	79
Total	17	68	42 (9)	109	236
Godwin's Brigade					
Field and Staff	1	1	0	0	2
6th North Carolina	10 (5)	17	12 (3)	7	46
21st North Carolina	9 (2)	34	11 (2)	17	71
54th North Carolina	5 (2)	24 (2)	3 (2)	8	40
57th North Carolina	3 (1)	25	5 (3)	8	41
Total	28 (10)	101 (2)	31 (10)	40	200
Division Totals	71	244	102	218	641

Breckinridge's Division					
Field and Staff					
Patton's Brigade					
Field and Staff	1 (1)	0	0	0	1
22nd Virginia	10	18	8 (2)	181	217
23rd Virginia Battalion	3	20	16	126	165
26th Virginia Battalion	4	7	6 (2)	68	115
Total	18	45	30 (4)	375	498
Forsberg's Brigade					
Field and Staff	0	1	0	0	1
30th Virginia Battalion	3	5	8 (1)	53	69
45th Virginia	4	6	4 (1)	79	93
51st Virginia	5	39	16 (1)	74	134
Total	12	51	28 (3)	206	297
Smith's Brigade					
Field and Staff					
36th Virginia	4	30	0	150	184
60th Virginia	9	0	32	70	101
45th Virginia Battalion	1	0	3	12	16
Thomas Legion	NA	NA	NA	NA	75
Total	14	30	35	232	376
Division Totals	44	96	58	813	1,171

Confederate Summary	Killed (mw)	Wounded / (Died)	Wounded & Captured / (Died)	Captured / Missing	Total*
Wickham's (Lee's) Division					
Field and Staff	0	0	0	0	0
Munford's Brigade					
Field and Staff		1			1
1st Virginia Cavalry	2	5	0	1	8
2nd Virginia Cavalry	1	7	0	1	9
3rd Virginia Cavalry	0	1	0	1	2
4th Virginia Cavalry	0	1	0	1	2
Total	3	15	0	4	22
Payne's Brigade					
Field and Staff	0	0	0	0	0
5th Virginia Cavalry	5	5	1	2	13
6th Virginia Cavalry	2	10	0	9	21
15th Virginia Cavalry	0	1	0	0	1
Total	7	16	1	11	35
Lee's Division Totals	10	31	1	15	57
Lomax's Division					
Field and Staff					

Confederate Summary	Killed (mw)	Wounded / (Died)	Wounded & Captured / (Died)	Captured / Missing	Total*
Johnson's Brigade					
1st Maryland Cavalry			1	2	3
2nd Maryland Cavalry					
8th Virginia Cavalry	3	7	0	2	12
21st Virginia Cavalry	2	1	0	17	20
25th Virginia Cavalry	3	5	0	3	11
36th Virginia Battalion					0
37th Virginia Battalion	1	0	0	5	6
Total	9	13	1	29	52
Thompson's (Jackson's) Brigade					
Field and Staff	0	0	0	0	0
19th Virginia Cavalry	0	4	0	5	9
20th Virginia Cavalry	0	1	0	0	1
46th Virginia Battalion	0	1	0	0	1
47th Virginia Battalion	1	1	0	1	3
Total	1	7	0	6	14
Smith's (Imboden's) Brigade					
Field and Staff	0	0	0	0	0
18th Virginia Cavalry	1	0	1	1	40
23rd Virginia Cavalry	2	4	2	11	19

Confederate Summary	Killed (mw)	Wounded / (Died)	Wounded & Captured / (Died)	Captured / Missing	Total*
62nd Virginia Mounted Infantry	1	14	3	7	25
Total	4	18	6	19	84
Ferguson's (McCausland's) Brigade					
Field and Staff	0	0	0	0	0
14th Virginia Cavalry	0	7	1	5	13
16th Virginia Cavalry	1	2	0	2	5
17th Virginia Cavalry	2	6	0	0	8
22nd Virginia Cavalry	1		4	12	17
Total	4	15	5	19	43
Lomax's Division Total	18	53	12	73	193
Corps Artillery: Col. Thomas Carter					
Nelson's Battalion					
Milledge's (Georgia)	2	9	0	0	11
Massie's (Virginia)	4	10	1	0	15
Kirkpatrick's (Virginia)	0	13	2	0	15
Total	6	32	3	0	41
Braxton's Battalion					
Hardwicke's (Virginia)	3 (1)	4	2	1	10
Carpenter's (Virginia)	10 (2)	16	5	1	32
Cooper's (Virginia)	2 (1)	6	1	0	9
Total	15	26	8	2	51

Confederate Summary	Killed (mw)	Wounded / (Died)	Wounded & Captured / (Died)	Captured / Missing	Total*
King's Battalion					
Chapman's (Virginia)	4	11	0	15	30
Bryan's (Virginia)	0	12	0	0	12
Lowry's (Virginia)	0	4	1	0	5
Total	4	27	1	15	47
Carter's Total	25	85	12	17	139
Horse Artillery					
Jackson's (Virginia)	0	0	1	0	1
Lurty's (Virginia)	0	0	0	0	0
McClanahan's (Virginia)	0	1	0	0	1
Shoemaker's (Virginia)	1	1	0	0	2
Johnston's (Virginia)	0	0	0	0	0
Total	1	2	1	0	4
Artillery Totals	26 (4)	87	13	17	143

Medals of Honor Awarded for Distinguished Service, August 16 to September 19, 1864

Recipient	Unit	Awarded For	Date of Action	Date of Award
Pvt. Frank Leslie and Sgt. Harry Mandy	4th New York Cavalry	Capture of flag from 3rd Virginia Cavalry	August 16, 1864	August 26, 1864
Pvt. Thomas Kelly	6th New York Cavalry	Capture of Cobb's Legion (GA) flag	August 16, 1864	August 26, 1864
Cpl. Issac Gause	2nd Ohio Cavalry	Capture of flag of 8th South Carolina	September 13, 1864	September 19, 1864
Corp. Chester B. Bowen	1st New York Dragoons	Capture of unidentified flag from Patton's brigade	September 19, 1864	September 27, 1864
Corp. Gabriel Cole	5th Michigan Cavalry	Capture of flag from 45th Virginia	September 19, 1864	September 27, 1864
Sgt. Henry M. Fox	5th Michigan Cavalry	Capture of flag form 60th Virginia	September 19, 1864	September 27, 1864
Sgt. Andrew J. Lorish	1st New York Dragoons	Capture of flag from unidentified unit of Patton's flag	September 19, 1864	September 27, 1864
Farrier George E. Meach	6th New York Cavalry	Capture of flag of Wharton's division	September 19, 1864	September 27, 1864

Recipient	Unit	Awarded For	Date of Action	Date of Award
Sgt. Patrick H. McEnroe	6th New York Cavalry	Capture of flag from 36th Virginia	September 19, 1864	September 27, 1864
Pvt. George Reynolds	9th New York Cavalry	Capture of 22nd Virginia or 23rd Virginia Battalion state flag from Patton's brigade	September 19, 1864	September 27, 1864
Pvt. Peter J. Ryan and Pvt. John Sterling	11th Indiana	With one companion captured 14 of the enemy in the severest part of the battle.	September 19, 1864	April 4, 1865
Sgt. Charles H. Seston	11th Indiana	Gallant and meritorious services in carrying the regimental colors	September 19, 1864	April 6, 1865
Surgeon Henry R. Tilton	8th Vermont	Tilton fearlessly risked his life and displayed great gallantry in rescuing and protecting the wounded men.	September 19, 1864	September 30, 1877
Sgt. Alphonso Lunt	38th Massachusetts	Lunt carried his flag to the most advanced position where, left almost alone close to the enemy's lines he refused their demand to surrender, withdrew at great personal peril, and saved his flag.	September 19, 1864	March 10, 1894
Sgt. Joel H. Lyman	1st New York Dragoons	In an attempt to capture a Confederate flag he captured one of the enemy's officers and brought him within the lines.	September 19, 1864	August 20, 1894
Sgt. Conrad Schmidt	2nd United States Cavalry	Went to the assistance of his regimental commander, whose horse had been killed under him in a charge, mounted the officer behind him, under a heavy fire from the enemy, and returned him to his command.	September 19, 1864	March 16, 1896

Recipient	Unit	Awarded For	Date of Action	Date of Award
Col. James Schoonmaker	14th Pennsylvania Cavalry	At a critical period, gallantly led a cavalry charge against the left of the enemy's line of battle, drove the enemy out of his works, and captured many prisoners.	September 19, 1864	May 19, 1899
Other Flag Captures at Winchester, September 19, 1864				
Lt. Robert Laughlin	9th West Virginia Infantry	Capture of a Confederate battle flag	September 19, 1864	
No soldier named	37th Massachusetts	Capture of flag from the 2nd Virginia	September 19, 1864	
No soldier named	49th Pennsylvania	Fitz Lee's Signal Flag	September 19, 1864	

Select Soldier Accounts of Third Winchester
and the Shenandoah Valley Campaign

Battle of Guard Hill or Crooked Run
Anonymous Trooper of the 5th Michigan Cavalry
Custer's Brigade
Merritt's Division
Source: *Detroit Advertiser & Tribune*, Sept. 2

Author's Note: This letter captures an up close and personal account of the evolving nature of cavalry tactics under Maj. Gen. Philip H. Sheridan. Under his leadership, the U.S. Cavalry took on a more aggressive role in combat operations, often going toe-to-toe with Confederate infantry. In the operations of August and early September of 1864, Sheridan's horse soldiers developed an élan that proved decisive in critical contests from the Shenandoah Valley all the way to Appomattox Courthouse. He also offers thoughts on the partisan war with Mosby's band.

*   *   *

Shepherdstown, Va. Aug. 22

Since writing you last we have seen something, felt something and experienced a sad change. On the 16th we moved from "Middletown to near Luray." on the north branch of the Shenandoah. Go with me, "their battery is throwing shell into the camp of the Michigan Brigade." 'Tis now time to saddle and right lively do the boys step around—our battery goes out and an artillery duel is had between them. The Regular and Second Brigades are at work already—'Tis time for Custer and his Michigan Brigade. Do you see that brigade of the rebels charging? They are coming for our battery; "Dismount to fight" is the order we receive, and in less than ten seconds we are "going in on our muscle." Do you see those rebel battle flags? Well—they are doomed to lose them—there are three of them. On we marched with a yell like so many mad devils. We are soon amongst them—hand to hand, foot to foot. Do you notice Corporal F.A. Pond—see him strive and fight for that flag, but no use, they tear it from the staff and not a piece is left as large as your finger nail, but the staff is ours. Corporal Pond is wounded. Ah, but he is a brave man, though no braver than any other of the 5th. But the rebel ranks are broken and the day is ours. All who are not killed or wounded fall into our hands as prisoners.

Wofford's Brigade, CSA, is known no more, although the General himself and a few escaped by swimming the river. Your humble servant has the pleasure of riding his saddle and wearing his rubber coat.

As Col. Alger sat on a stone wall waiting for the boys to re-mount, Gen. Merritt and staff rode up. Merritt remarked to the colonel that 'twas the nicest fight of the season, because neither party had any protection, as far as rifle pits and entrenchments were concerned; the open field and the best blood told the story. The 5th had the pleasure of capturing and turning over more prisoners than it had live men. Many of the Johnnys were killed—83 I believe were counted where we fought, including one colonel, one lieutenant colonel, two captains and three lieutenants—but from prisoners we learned that Longstreet had too many men lying back for us to presume to stay in that country. So the next morning we fell back to Berryville and took position on the pike leading to Snicker's Gap. On the night of the 18th we were on picket on the road leading to Shepard's Ford. Here is where our trouble commences: two of Co. A are captured by guerillas, as the boys call them. Corp. Day, Co. G is shot dead on post, and another wounded. A skirmish line is kept up all night. The moon shines so brightly that it is dangerous to ride along the lines. The bushwhackers are continually creeping up and "blazing away," but our boys get scattered along the line, hid also, and their fun is played out. In the morning a report goes in to the General. He orders that for each offense a dwelling house shall be burned. Capt. Drake's squadron is detailed to carry out the order into effect. How shall I proceed? how shall I tell you that a gang of Mosby's guerrillas took them unawares, as they were scattered around—captured 16 and then murdered them—took their arms from them, and then shot them with their own pistols. Fourteen were killed and two left for dead. Some of them had their throats cut. The two who were found were shot in three or four places, and left for dead, but came to and were able to tell the particulars. The men killed belonged to Companies C, G and M. The regiment immediately started after them, but to no purpose. We scoured the country for a long distance around, and could find nothing, only that Mosby left word that all men whom he caught he would kill. Pleasant thoughts to sleep with, and to stand picket with, knowing that death is the alternative if caught. But there must surely be a remedy for all these things.

> For they who do the Union save
> Ought ne'er to be buried in the grave.

When I cannot ask for "Lex Talionis," [an eye for an eye retaliation] then may be reason be stung senseless, and may destiny take her scissors and cut my thread of mortal life. That fate may hurl me on the rocky shore of "life's troubled sea." where all the anguish of mothers, the prayers of maidens, and tears of fathers and brothers drive the demon of demons from his hiding place. But enough. We are here on the banks of the Potomac near Shepherdstown. The rebels are in our front, and I hear they are fighting at Harper's Ferry. We have no infantry here; the trains are still on the north side of the river; and generally things are quiet. But seven officers are now present with the regiment. Health generally is good. The men for duty number 158.

A. Bugler

*   *   *

Sergeant Sam Collier
2nd North Carolina Infantry
Cox's Brigade
Rodes's Division
Source: North Carolina State Archives

Authors's Note: Collier's letter on Third Winchester provides one of the most honest accounts written by a Confederate in the wake of that unprecedented disaster. His account is rich with succinct details on the combat, but his vivid description of the retreat and a heartfelt encounter with a mortally wounded Federal captures the real emotion these men experience that is often overlooked in writing and presenting military history.

*   *   *

September 21, 1864
My Darling Parents,

I have been spared once more. On the morning of the 19th inst we left our camp six miles this side of Bunker Hill and came on within two miles of Winchester, when we found the "Yankees" drawn up in line of battle and advancing rapidly towards our rear. Genl. Rodes immediately formed line of battle and commenced to move forward, the sharpshooters in the advance. We (the sharpshooters) moved forward at a run & a to a piece of woods five yards in advance or rather forward when we ran into a strong line of battle of Yankee who were pouring a tremendous fire into a Brigade to our left. We halted until our line of battle came up when we all charged and drove the yanks about half a mile when they being reinforced charged us in term and drove us back two or three hundred yards.

Cousin John Goff was wounded just as we began to fall back. I did not see him when he was struck, but as I was going back across the field I saw three men carrying him off, one of the men had him on his back when I ran to him and had him laid on a tent and we four carried him off the field. We call very near being captured. I never saw minnie balls and grape shot rain so in all my life. We succeeded in getting him to the field hospital when Dr. Cobb came up and examined his leg which was broken just above the ankle. He seemed very cheerful the whole time.

Well after we got him back in the ambulance, we started back to the line, which we reached in safety. After being in there a few minutes we heard very heavy firing to our rear. Col. Brown of the 1st N.C. Regt but now commander of the Division sharpshooters, called for them and carried us at a double quick to where our cavalry were fighting both Yankee infantry and cavalry. They came pouring down upon us like a thousand bricks which of course we could not stand.

We fell back when everything at this moment began to run, waggons, ambulances and every thing mixed up together. The whole face of the earth was literally alive with rebels running for their lives. I would run a while and stop and laugh at others and think what fools we were making of ourselves, when some shell would come tearing among us and every thing would start off again. I would be among them. I never ran as fast in all my life. To come out and tell the truth, II ran from two miles the other side of Winchester to Newtown a distance of ten miles and I can assure you I had company from Brig Genl down to privates. But this is one thing that I did not do that was to throw away my gun and things. I always hold on to them let what may happen. It was equal to the 1st Manassas stampede. I never saw anything like it before. They never captured any of our wagons or ambulances. That was the only difference.

Cousin John was left in Winchester so he could not be brought off. We lost 49 in all from the Regt. A yankee gave me a watch for a drink of water. I will tell you about it. As I was walking along firing, one who was wounded in the side asked me for a drink of what which I could not refuse a wounded man if he was a yankee. After I gave it to him he pulled out his watch and said, "God bless you!, take this." I told him no, but he insisted and I took it. He was quite young and very intelligent. He told me his name was Caine and that he was from Penn. When we fell back I though I would pass by and see him, but he was dead having been struck by another ball. Poor boy, I could not help but feeling sorry for him.

As I have no more paper, I will close and finish in my next in a day or two. Love to all. Write soon.

Son,

Saml.

* * *

Brig. Gen. George Beal
Commanding First Brigade
Dwight's Division
Nineteenth Corps
Source: George L. Beal Letters, Nicholas Picerno Collection

Author's Note: Beal had campaigned under Nathaniel Banks in the Shenandoah Valley, where he experienced defeat at the hands of Stonewall Jackson at the First Battle of Winchester. His letter offers a detailed account of not only Third Winchester, but his role in the battle of Fisher's Hill and Sheridan's pursuit of Early's army into the upper Valley.

* * *

Harrisonburg, Va, Tuesday, September 27, 1864

My Dear General,

You have probably hear form us much oftener than I have heard form you as we have not had a mail for some time.

We have had a very fine trip from Berryville to this place and has really been one of the finest operations I have ever made in the valley.

At the Winchester fight, we went in as usual two lines in front of us broke and let the enemy back upon us with a rush before we had formed lines, we deployed into line and took position under a murderous fire and maintained the position, checked and held the enemy from 12 until 3 o'clock. The worked like good ones brought in line after line and seemed determined to turn our right. I had 3 regt in front and two at right angles enemy directly across our right flank. The enemy came on to us and planted a battery so as to rake the rear of the front line and the shot and shell was fearful but every one stood their ground manfully and held the key of our position for 4 long hours. At that time Genl. Crook came in and relieved us and then the charge was ordered and all hands went in for Winchester town. It was a splendid sight as we could see the whole thing and every body pushing ahead as fast as possible. I saw Custer's Cavalry charge when he took so many prisoners and it was and it was a charge that goes into history. I never saw so fine a thing and never expect to again.

Genl. Sheridan was right by my Brigade when he gave the order. I heard him his words was something like this: "I have got them this time and will drive them to h——l. Pitch in that cavalry and don't spare horse flesh."

In about 15 minutes they did pitch in with a vengeance drawn sabre! Hats off a yelling like so many devils nothing could stop such a shock and the rebs got out of the way as fast as they could. I thought then the copperhead stock was falling tremendous fast and and McClellan was standing a fine chance for an election.

We carried in about 18 hundred [men] and lost 396. I think my loss is the largest of any brigade compared with the numbers carried in.

We fought along side of the 6th Corps and had a good chance to compare as far as I could judge we beat them and can do it every day. We had the hardest fighting and saved the day and I think our losses are is much heavier than theirs however we are perfectly satisfied to compare notes with them or any other corps in the army.

Fishers Hill was a different kind of a battle and showed what a man of judgement can do with can do with a small loss.

Our Boys took a rifle pit or rail pen as we call them which was the most gallant thing done that day they had built in front of the hill. Pens measuring across a large open field covering their front entirely and in the rear was thick woods. Word came to me to make a detail and drive them out so as to get the position myself and hold it. I ordered the 116th N.Y. and 4 companies of the 30th Mass. And with the skirmish line charged with a yell a distance of a quarter of a mile. Johnny left immediately for the woods. I should judge they had 2 regiments behind those works and they tried a number of times to rally and retake them but – no go. They then opened their artillery and made it pretty hot, but we held the position and built breast-works ourselves and remained in that position until the final charge was made and in that we got the front seat as usual.

From that time to this we have been in one place of excitement. Our corp on the right had side of pike and the 6th on the left the lines joining and all in plain sight of one another. My Brigade had our Corps advance all the way, one regiment ahead as skirmishers and the rest in line of Battle, form Edinburg to New Market. We skirmished all the way with the enemy his lines being in sight and retiring as fast as we struck them. There was the excitement between the two corps to see who would get ahead; Sheridan had all he could do to keep them back. The artillery would rush for the hills to get the first shot and the side that got it first would let out a big yell. The rifle balls would come back thick and fast but no one ntoiced them no more than as though they had been... We went 18 miles that day without hardly a stop until and no one thinking at night fall that it was dinner time. It was the greatest gunning execution I ever saw.

The results of our weeks work you know better than I can write. We are all in the tip top shape and every man weights a ton. Bust your old cannon and charge the powder to me. My regards to Sarah and all inquiring friends.

Yours Truly, George

*   *   *

Lt. Elmer Husted
123rd Ohio Infantry
Thoburn's Division
Army of West Virginia
Source: *Norwalk Reflector*, October 18, 1864.

Author's Note: Husted spent much of his military service in the Shenandoah Valley and well understood why it was the Union's "Valley of Humiliation." He participated in Robert Milroy's debacle at Second Winchester in June of 1863, fought hopelessly under Franz Sigel at New Market in May of 1864, and experienced defeat with George Crook at the Second Battle of Kernstown in late July 1864. His letter captures a soldier's raw emotion, including the trepidation he felt as he moved toward combat, the exhilaration of the charge, and jubilation at final victory—all while providing vibrant descriptions of the scenes he witnessed on the Winchester battlefield.

*   *   *

September 28, 1864

On the afternoon of the 18th inst. We received orders to pack up and be ready to move. Lieut. Gen. Grant paid a flying visit the day before and everybody appeared to think that his visit meant work for us. All appeared to be anxious to get at the rebels who had been so near us for such a long time, and I think none were more so than Gen. Sheridan himself. It has been generally understood here that Gen. Sheridan's orders were, not to bring on an engagement, but to amuse the rebel Gen. Early, and keep him away from Gen. Lee as long as possible. But the order at last came to attack, and we did attack.

Early the next morning we could plainly hear cannonading and musketry firing in the direction of Winchester. Soon we were on the march towards that place, striking the Pike that runs east from Opequon Creek, being about five miles from Winchester. Here we halted and took dinner, and could distinctly see the smoke rising from the battlefield. The roar of the artillery and rattle of musketry had now become incessant. Still we could hear nothing of how the battle was going.

At last we received orders to move up, and had hardly got under way before we met a tide of wounded men and stragglers going to the rear. The tide increased as we neared the battlefield, almost blocking up the road, men wounded in every possible shape and being carried off in every possible way, some on stretchers, some in blankets, others leaning on the arm of a comrade, covered with blood, minus an arm or hand. Oh! Such sights.

This being my first great battle, I will try to give you some idea of my feelings and actions on that occasion, but you will never be able to comprehend the thing as it occurred to me. While we were passing this stream of wounded and stragglers, I was so busy trying to keep our men in the ranks that I hardly had time to think of what was soon to come, and then I felt like appearing calm, to keep the men in the same condition. I therefore rode along smoking my pipe, apparently as unconcerned as if walking the streets of Norwalk. We at last reached our position and formed in line of battle just behind a piece of woods, where we could not see the enemy.

At last, we were ordered to move forward through the woods and charge the enemy. When this order came, I began to feel a little weak in the knees and a kind of fainting sensation came over me so that I could hardly move. As we came in sight of the nemy, and stray bullets began to whiz around, this feeling wore off, and my greatest desire was to get at those rebs who were shaking their dirty emblem of treason at us from their breastworks. As we gained the edge of the woods we halted a moment to rest and reform. Then the order was given to charge.

A wild yell was the only answer as our whole corps (with our brigade in front) charged towards the rebel works, and as we reached the first one, we halted a little, and gave them a taste of our metal. We had not reached this position without the loss of many a brave fellow, as I could plainly see by looking over the ground in our rear. We soon charged again and gained the next stone fence, driving the rebels from it in every direction. I never expected to reach that fence alive for the bullets flew around my head like hail, and their artillery was pouring grape and canister into us move unmercifully.

I did not feel the least bit afraid; on the contrary, I was almost frenzied with excitement and was perfectly reckless as regarded my own safety. One of the boys who was wounded and making his way off the field was carrying his gun with him. I begged him to give me his gun, which he did, and not having any sword with me, I done the best execution that I could with that, and carried it through the fight. After resting a moment at the last fence, we were ordered to make the final charge.

The men rushed forward with determination to do or die. And they did do and they did die. After we had got about half the distance, were obliged to lie down again on account of the severe fire. It was but a moment, and our men with such a yell as I never heard before, started up and forward. Now the rebels being to waver, and as we get near, they ran. Oh what a shout went up – the shout of victory.

*   *   *

Captain John Y. Bedingfield
60th Georgia Infantry
Atkinson's (Evans) Brigade
Gordon's Division
Source: Special Collections, Alderman Library, University of Virginia

Author's Note: Bedingfield's letter provides a rare and sincere glimpse into the actions of Atkinson's Georgia Brigade at the time of the Third Battle of Winchester. Not only does this letter offer important information regarding the conduct of the soldiers during that time frame, but it provides important documentation of the Georgia Brigade's movements on the battlefield from the contemporary view point of an officer who ended the battle in command of his regiment.

*   *   *

September 20, 1864

Dear Ma,

Before you receive this you will have heard that a great battle was fought near Winchester yesterday. It was the severest battle ever fought in the Valley: indeed for the numbers engaged it has not been excelled during the war at any point. I was in the thickest of it but thanks to a Kind Providence I escaped unhurt. I will give you a brief account of the fight, and the moves preceding it.

On Saturday morning (the 17th) we received orders to be in readiness to march at 2 P.M. At the appointed time we started, marched 6 miles to Bunker Hill & camped for the night. At 4 A.M. Sunday started again and at 9 marched into Martinsburg without encountering opposition. This is notoriously a Union Town. You can see Yank sticking out of every body's face. I should not say every body, for like angels' visits a true hearted Southerner may now & then be found. We remained there until about 3 P.M. when we deliberately marched out again & at night camped on the ground we occupied the night before. I would like if time allowed it, to give a full account of the raid on Martinsburg, but simply say now, that the men spread themselves, talked big, drank gallantly and took what they pleased & did what they pleased generally.

At daylight yesterday (Monday) morning we were on the march again. As we proceeded in the direction of Winchester, cannonading could be distinctly heard and none of your Madison thunder is a circumstance of comparison with it. We marched on leisurely little dreaming of the exciting scenes soon to be enacted, thinking the firing was caused by the ordinary Cavalry clash on the part of the enemy. At about 12 M we came where the music was more distance, and were formed in line of battle. Skirmishers were thrown forward, brisk firing ensued & soon the line of battle was moving forward in quick time. Our line of battle soon met a Yankee line of battle, each advancing upon the other. The battle was now joined in good earnest & the shock of arms was awful in the extreme. Our brigade was on the extreme left & to prevent being flanked we were forced to retire. A retreat always creates confusion, no matter what may be the object, or cause of the retrograde move. We fell back some 300 yards when reinforcements coming up, our left was strengthened and forward we moved again; Then came the tug of war. It was soon decided, however, for the enemy seeing that we were in earnest this time, fled before us.

We drove them about a mile & halted. Notwithstanding our success on this occasion, a want of success in other parts of the field, necessitated another retrograde move on our part. I can not even expect to give you an intelligent account of the battle in all parts of the field but will merely state that we were outnumbered, & finally overwhelmed & compelled to retire in confusion leaving our dead and wounded in the hands of the enemy. I was left in command of about 100 men to skirmish with the Yanks until our army could get osme distance south of Winchester; we were compelled then to fall back precipitately & narrowly escaped capture by the cavalry which closely pursued us. During last night and this morning the entire army has fallen back to this point. We are now in line of battle on what is called Fisher's Hill, 2 miles south of Strasburg. Whether the enemy will follow up his advantage remains to be seen. This is a strong position & we can hold it. In killed & wounded our Brigade lost heavily. Major Jones, commanding the Regt. (60th) & Capt Russel—the only Capt. Present who ranks me—were both wounded.

The Major was slightly wounded and was brought off. Capt. R. lost an arm & is a prisoner. I am in command of the Regiment. Jos. Watson & Joe Going—my cook—were mortally wounded. Many more are known to be wounded, and many others missing whose fate we are ignorant of.

Considering the effect of this affair will no doubt have the election in the North, it is certainly unfortunate. But too much importance should not be attached to it by Southerners. Our army is intact, unconquered & unconquerable. We inflicted heavier loss on the enemy yesterday then he did on us. In killed and wounded theirs was no doubt three to our one. How many prisoners they took from us I am hardly able to conjecture; but I presume it will not fall short of

2,000. William young was struck by a piece of shell on the ankle. The wound is painful but not serious. He was brought off & will doubtless soon be at home. His gallant conduct yesterday elicited the praise of all beholders.

I will send this to Staunton by a wounded man, who is waiting for it.

As ever & c

John

*   *   *

Anonymous Trooper
4th New York Cavalry
Devin's Brigade
Merritt's Division
Source: *The Irish-American* (New York, NY)

Oct. 8, 1864

Camp 4th N Y Cavalry
Strasburg, Va. Sept. 25, 1864

To the Editors of *The Irish American*:
Gentlemen—Since the date of my last letter, great things have transpired in this department, and one of the most glorious battles, if not the greatest, of the war came off Saturday the 19th.

We were on picket in front of Smithfield, and were expecting to be relieved; but a movement being in progress, we received orders to stop until daylight, and drawing in our pickets under cover of night, to fall back to Summit Point, a distance of four miles, on reaching which we found all hands preparing which took place at 1 p.m. Ere this you have the particulars of the great and glorious battle which was fought on that eventful day. The gray dawn had scarcely lighted the far East until booming of cannon could be heard on our left, which soon spread to the centre, and thence to the entire right, and before the sun had risen to throw a light upon the scene, there could be heard the battle cry and charge after charge was made by our cavalry. The enemy we found in force on the south side of the Opequon Creek. We the 4th NY Cavalry were supporting a battery when the battle began in earnest from right to left, and about 1 p.m. the rebels began to run; and until that time I believe they even did not realize that we meant a general engagement.

As the day advanced we kept going more to the right of the line, and about 2 p.m. succeeded in cutting off three regiments of rebel cavalry. Then the skedaddle began in earnest. We left the battery to follow up; deployed in line of skirmishers in connection with the Averill forces; then all the bugles sounded "forward," and from right to left that sound was the order of the day. The country was open, affording no cover for the enemy, and giving a splendid view of the advancing columns. In this way we drove them to the fortifications at Winchester—12 miles in two hours—where they made a fierce stand. Never has this bloody war afforded such an opportunity to see both armies in the same field in hostile array. At charging we went on in the double quick, and the rebel infantry being unable to get out of the way quick enough, lay down at the back of a stone wall, which was running at left angles with our advancing columns. Most of our boys discovered the move; but a great number believed them to be our infantry, coming to our support. The order to charge could be heard above all the confusion—we charging the whole line for a distance of about one and a half miles, our batteries sending forth their fiery vengeance over our heads into the enemy's lines and fortifications—while they were not behind, in return, in throwing shell, grape, and canister into our lines.

As we charged at the speed of six minutes a mile, we repulsed two brigades of rebel infantry, concealed on our left flank, who got up from behind a stone wall and opened a fearful cross fire upon us, when the enemy also in front poured into us volley after volley. Their many ordinances were manned with telling effect. We were obliged to retire and rally; which we did in a style which is characteristic of the glorious first division of cavalry. Now, our determination to cut up and capture all the rebel crew was redoubled; and our brave General, riding in front of our line of battle gave the orders "draw sabres," "forward!" Then the whole line again advanced with a steady gait until within short range of their line, when we again took up the "double quick," and with cheers echoing above the continued roar of artillery and small arms, we charged them. They stood like demons to receive us; but we swung around their flank, cutting them down like thistles, capturing 900 men, 5 battle flags, 1 State of Virginia flag, and 1 Confederate national flag, 4 cannon, with numberless small arms. Thus ended and completed one of the grandest victories ever won by cavalry over double their number of infantry.

Now the sun's red glare began to kiss the distant mountain, and the fury of the battle ceased; but the cannonading was kept up by the enemy, for they could not get away fast enough; and in clearing out of the town, the stampede was a terrible one, running over women and children alike. As we marched across the battle ground, the sight was an awful one—the dead laying in heaps for a space of forty or fifty acres. We could not ride through without skipping over the dying, and the dead horses and men shared the same fate. The number of rebels killed and wounded were terrible. There was, without exaggeration, two to one of our loss, and that was heavy. We went in 100 men, and came out 40, losing the major commanding and a lieutenant. At daylight, we marched through the town, capturing rebels by the hundred. We then advanced out of the town two miles, and halted for the night. In passing through the town, many Union ladies waved their handkerchiefs, and showed little flags and other tokens of welcome to the Yankee army. The rebels kept up their retreat all night, and by noon of the 20th, we came up with them behind Strasburg, 180 miles, thus making 30 miles since the previous day, and in the meantime fought one of the greatest battles on record.

The Lost Child

Bibliography

Newspapers

The Alleghanian (Ebensburg, PA)
Advertiser and Union (Auburn, NY)
American Tribune
Army and Navy Journal
Ashtabula Sentinel
The Athens Messenger (OH)
Auburn Daily Advertiser (NY)
Augusta Daily Constitutionalist (GA)
Augusta Daily Chronicle & Sentinel
Aurora Commercial (IN)
Bristol (TN-VA) *Herald Courier*
Baltimore American
Bangor Daily Whig and Courier
Beaufort Journal (NC)
Belmont Chronicle (OH)
Boston Daily Advertiser
Buffalo Morning Express
Cadiz Republican
Charlotte Observer
Chenango American (NY)
Chenango Chronicle (NY)
Chenango Union (NY)
Chicago Times
Chicago Evening Journal
Cincinnati Daily Commercial
Cleveland Morning Leader
Cleveland Herald
Clinton Republican
Columbus Times (GA)
The Confederate Union (Milledgeville, GA)
Confederate Veteran (Nashville, TN)
Daily Chronicle and Sentinel (Augusta, GA)
The Daily Courier (Zanesville, OH)
Daily Knickerbocker (Albany, NY)

Detroit Advertiser and Tribune
Detroit Free Press
Fayetteville Observer (NC)
Gallipolis Journal
The Gazette (Rhineback, NY)
Fayette County Herald (OH)
Illinois Daily State Journal
The Independent
Ironton Register
Lancaster Gazette (OH)
Lynchburg Virginian
Macon Telegraph & Confederate
Mahoning Register
Mobile Register
Montgomery Advertiser and Register
National Defender (Brookeville, IN)
National Tribune
Norwalk Reflector
Newark Daily Advertiser
New York Herald
New York Irish-American
New York Mail and Express
New York Tablet
New York Times
New York World
New Paltz Times (NY)
Nicholas Chronicle (Summersville, WV)
Northampton Free Press
The Ohio Soldier
Otsego Republican
Our Living and Our Dead (New Bern, NC)
Orleans American (NY)
Oxford Times (NY)
The Painesville Telegraph (OH)

The Perry County Weekly (OH)
Philadelphia Weekly Times
Picayune (New Orleans, LA)
Pittsburg Evening Chronicle
Poughkeepsie Daily Eagle
Providence Daily Journal
Raleigh Confederate
Richmond Daily Whig
Richmond Dispatch
Richmond Sentinel
Richmond Times Dispatch
Richmond Whig
The Saratogan
Southern Recorder (Milledgeville, GA)

Springfield Republican
The Sunbury American
The Sunny South
The Transcript (Danielsonville, CT)
Trenton State Gazette
The Vermont Chronicle
Wabash Dealer (IN)
Wabash Transcript
Weekly Register (Point Pleasant, WV)
Wheeling Daily Intelligencer
Wilmington Daily Journal (NC)
Winchester News
Wyandot Pioneer
Zanesville Daily Courier

Government Records

Confederate States of America Inspections Reports, Microfilm #935, National Archives

Davis, Major George B., U.S. Army, Leslie J. Perry, Joseph Kirkley, compiled by Capt. Calvin C. Cowles, 23rd U.S. Infantry. *The Official Military Atlas of the Civil War.* Avenel, NJ: Gramercy Books, 1983.

U.S. War Department. *The War of the Rebellion: A Compilation of the Official Records of the Union and Confederate Armies.* 128 vols. Washington, D.C.: U.S. Government Printing Office, 1880-1901.

Archival Resources

Alabama Department of Archives and History
Cullen Andrew Battle, "The Third Alabama Regiment"
Henry Beck Diary, MSS 422f
John J. Tucker Diary
Henry F. Wilson Mobile Rifles Diary, 1860-1865

American Antiquarian Society, Worcester, Massachusetts
David Cushman Diary and Letters

American Jewish Archives
Alexander Hart Diary

Birmingham Public Library Archives
W. A. Parson's Letters, 12th Alabama

Atlanta History Center
W. C. Hall Diary, 20th South Carolina

Keith Bohanan, Carrollton, Georgia
David Lumpkin Eubanks Memoir, Typescript, 22nd Virginia Cavalry

Bucks County Historical Society
Helen H. Ely Papers, Samuel Ely Diary 1864

Bull Run Regional Library
George Quintus Peyton, "A Civil War Record for 1864-65," 13th Virginia

Ben Ritter Collection
James W. Adams, Letter-Diary

Bull Run Regional Library
George Quintus Peyton, A Civil War Record for 1864-1865

Bulloch County Historical Society
Martin W. Brett, "Experiences of a Georgia Boy in the Army of Northern Virginia"

Center for Archival Collections, Bowling Green State University, Bowling Green, Ohio
James J. Wood Diary
Perry D. Layland, Letter August 1, 1864

Chicago Historical Society
Field Return of Gordon's Division, Sept. 10, 1864
E. P. Goggin to Gen. L. L. Lunsford, Sept. 24, 1867, Lomax's Staff
Martin J. Russell, "Recollections of Col. Mulligan and the Irish Brigade," 23rd Illinois
Joseph F. Ward Letters, 34th Massachusetts
Gabriel C. Wharton to John C. Breckinridge, October 5, 1864

Cincinnati Historical Society
Roger Hannaford Memoir, 2nd Ohio Cavalry

Connecticut Historical Society
Fred Palmer Letters, 13th Connecticut
Henry G. Tray Collection, 18th Connecticut

Davidson College Archives
William Erskine Ardrey Collection, 30th North Carolina

Duke University Special Collections Library, Durham, North Carolina
R. Alfred Allen Diary, 22nd New York Cavalry
Thomas J. Watkins, Reminiscences in the William Alexander Papers, 14th North Carolina
John A. Bates Papers, 3rd Massachusetts Cavalry, Dismounted
Robert Boyd Papers, 7th South Carolina
Samuel D. Buck Papers, 13th Virginia
James O. Coghill Papers, 23rd North Carolina

James Connor Papers, Kershaw's Brigade
John W. Daniel Papers
Nathan G. Dye Diary and Letters, 24th Iowa
Eltinge-Lord Family Papers, 156th New York
John M. Gould Diary, 29th Maine
S. P. Halsey Papers, 21st Virginia Cavalry
Bradley T. Johnson Letters
James Madison Murphy Papers, 5th Maine
Isaac V. Reynolds Papers, 17th Virginia Cavalry
Robert S. Rodgers Papers, 2nd Maryland Eastern Shore, U.S.
Horace Smith Papers, 8th Vermont
John Wilfong Papers, 12th North Carolina

East Carolina Manuscript Collection, Greenville, North Carolina

Nathan R. Frazier Papers, 45th North Carolina
Hugh Harrison Mills Collection, 54th North Carolina
George Duncan Wells Letter book, 1864, 34th Massachusetts

East Tennessee State University

James W. McKee Papers, R. A. Spainhour Diary

Fredericksburg, Spotsylvania National Military Park Archives

Richard H. Anderson, Report of the 1864 Valley Campaign
Martin W. Brett, "Experiences of a Georgia Boy in the Army of Northern Virginia," 12th Georgia
J. L. Johnson Letter, October 4, 1864, 4th Georgia
E. A. Patterson Memoir, 57th North Carolina
J. F. Roser Letters, 110th Ohio

Georgia Department of Archives and History, Atlanta

Reuben Grove Clark, "War Experience of . . ." Memoir
Joseph Jackson Felder Letters, 4th Georgia
William H. May, 3rd Alabama, "Remembrances of the War Between the States"

Greensboro Historical Museum

Samuel Hutchinson Diary, 2nd Virginia Infantry

Hagley Museum, Wilmington, Delaware

Henry A. DuPont Papers

Handley Library, Winchester, Virginia

Charles M. Barritt Diary, 114th New York
I. Norval Baker, Diary and Recollections, 18th Virginia Cavalry
James M. Cadwallader Diary, 1st Virginia Cavalry
Edward Davis Diary, 1864, 114th New York
Petre Jennings Diary, 1864, Lewisburg Battery

O.H.P. Kite Diary, 33rd Virginia
John B. Kohler Letters, 98th Pennsylvania
Jacob Lemley Diary, 48th Virginia
W. H. Wampler, "Reminiscences of the War Between the States," 51st Virginia

Historical Society of Pennsylvania

William Stackhouse Diary
James Blain Collection
"Life of James S. Blain," by J. E. Dart, 26th Georgia

Illinois State Historical Library

Oliver Edwards Memorandum
Powell, William H., "General P. H. Sheridan, U. S. A., First Engagement with General Jubal Early, C. S. A., In the Battle of Opequon Creek"

Iowa Historical Society

Michael Cook Diary, 28th Iowa
Alfred Rigby Diary, 24th Iowa
B. F. Wilson, Letter of September 26, 1864, 28th Iowa

James Creed Collection

H. Nott Jr. to My Dear Father, July 29, 1864

Library of Congress, Washington, D.C.

John C. Arnold Letters, 49th Pennsylvania
James B. Clay Papers, Breckinridge's Staff
Jedediah Hotchkiss Papers, Early's Staff
Joseph Warren Keifer Papers
William Old Diary, Early's Staff
Howard M. Smith Diary and Letters, 1st New York Dragoons
Gabriel C. Wharton to James B. Clay, May 15, 1908
James H. Wilson Papers

Massachusetts Historical Society, Boston

Saregent Lorenzo Dow Letters, 3rd Massachusetts Cavalry, Dismounted
J. Chapin Warner Papers, 34th Massachusetts

McClung Collection, Lawson-McGhee Library, Knoxville

William W. Stringfield, "Memoirs of the Civil War"

Marshall University, Huntington, West Virginia

Andrew J. Jones Diary, 1864

Monmouth Historical Society (NJ)

Peter Vredenburgh Papers, 14th New Jersey
William Burroughs Ross Papers, 14th New Jersey

Linda Meeneghan Collection

William Armstrong Letter, 5th New York Heavy Artillery

Museum of the Confederacy

Report of Maj. Gen. Fitzhugh Lee of the Operations of His Cavalry Division from May 4, 1864 to September 19, 1864

The National Archives, Washington, D.C.

George Beal, Report of Service
George Chapman, Report of Service
Alfred N. Duffie Headquarters Letters
William Dwight, Report of Service
William Emory, Report of Service
Moses Harris, Medal of Honor File
Alphonso M. Lunt, Medal of Honor File, 28th Massachusetts
Confederate States of America Inspections Reports
John R. Kenly, Report of Service
John B. McIntosh, Report of Service
Edward Murray, Pension File
Record of Events for Union and Confederate Regiments
Jacob Sharpe Pension File
Report of Col. D. H. Strother, Chief of Staff to Major Gen. Hunter, Operations of the Army of West Virginia, May 21 – August 9, 1864
William B. Tibbits, Report of Service
Thomas M. Harris, Circumstances attending the death of Col. James A. Mulligan

New York Historical Society

Edward Sentell Diary, 160th New York
J. Stoddard Johnston, "Notes of the March of Breckinridge's Corps . . ."

New York State Library

Edward P. Davis Papers, 153rd New York

North Carolina Division of Archives and History, Raleigh, North Carolina

C.C. Blackwell Letters, 23rd North Carolina
Augustus Clewell Papers, 21st North Carolina
Samuel Collier Papers, 4th North Carolina
David Herman Diary, 87th Pennsylvania
Elias F. Hicks, "My War Reminscences," 20th North Carolina
William G. Lewis, "Sketch of the Life of W. G. Lewis, Brigadier General"
Thomas Pollock Devereux Letterbook, 43rd North Carolina

H. H. Smith Diary, 5th North Carolina
W. W. Stringfield, Diary and Memoirs, Thomas Legion
John C. Young Diary, 4th North Carolina

Pearce Civil War Collection, Navarro College, Corsicana, Texas

Michael Reilay, Letter August 3, 1864, 15th New York Cavalry
David I. Sample, Letter September 30, 1864, 53rd North Carolina

Pennsylvania Division of Archives and Manuscripts

John J. Carter Diary

Rockbridge County Historical Society, Lexington, VA

James R. McCutchan to Miss Kate, September 22, 1864, 14th Virginia Cavalry

Rodger Lemley Collection

Elmore Wilkinson Diary

Ohio Historical Society

John T. Booth Papers, 36th Ohio
William McVey Diary, 126th Ohio
William T. Patterson Diary, 116th Ohio
Rufus Ricksecker Letters, 126th Ohio

Nicholas Picerno Collection, Bridgewater, Virginia

George Beal Letters
John M. Gould Letters, 29th Maine
George Nye Letters, 29th Maine
29th Maine Regimental Collection

Rome-Floyd County Library (Georgia)

E. A. Hightower Letters

Rutherford B. Hayes Presidential Center

Benjamin F. Coates Papers, 91st Ohio
James M. Comly Diary and Journal, 23rd Ohio
Russell Hastings Papers, 23rd Ohio
Rutherford B. Hayes War Diary
John R. Rhodes Letters, 110th Ohio

Tennessee State Library and Archives

Abel Crawford Letters, 61st Alabama
J. W. Patton Diary, 18th Pennsylvania Cavalry

Troupe County, Georgia Archives

John T. Gay Letters, 4th Georgia
Julius L. Schaub Papers, 14th North Carolina

Tulane University

Robert E. Lee Papers
George P. Ring Papers, 6th Louisiana

United States Army Military History Institute, Carlisle, Pennsylvania

Allen Baker Diary, 1st Rhode Island Cavalry
Eugene Blackford Letters
Thomas Campbell Diary, 122nd Ohio
George Crook, L. V. Kennon Papers
Edmund Halsey Journal, 15th New Jersey
Grayson Eichelberger Memoir
George Imboden Papers, 1864, 18th Virginia Cavalry
Henry Kaiser Diary, 96th Pennsylvania
Frederick R. Laubach Journal, 93rd Pennsylvania
Andrew Lorish Letters, 1st New York Dragoons
Lewis Luckinbill Diary, 96th Pennsylvania
Charles C. Messer Memoir, 26th Massachusetts
Henry P. Morrison Papers, 26th Virginia Battalion
James W. Mulligan Letters, 1864, 15th New York Cavalry
Charles R. Paul Diary, 15th New Jersey
David Powell Memoirs, 1861-1865, 12th West Virginia
Willie Root Papers, 75th New York
Lewis Rosenburger Diary, 6th Maryland
Jacob A. Schmidt, Story of, 98th Pennsylvania
James Sherwood Diary, 114th New York
Ezra L. Walker Diary, 116th Ohio
Benjamin Warner Diary, 26th Massachusetts
John W. Weed Memoir, 91st Ohio

United States Military Academy

Benjamin F. Benson Papers, 128th New York

University of Alaska Archives, Anchorage

Alfred T. A. Torbert Letters

University of Michigan

Russell Alger Papers
Chester H. Ballard Letters, 37th Massachusetts
George H. Bates Letters, 2nd Connecticut Heavy Artillery
Isaac Oliver Best, "Sheridan in the Shenandoah," 121st New York
Walter Jackson Diary, 1st New York Dragoons

University of North Carolina, Chapel Hill, NC; Southern Historical Collection

J. Kelly Bennette Diary 1864, 8th Virginia Cavalry
George M. Edgar Papers
William Gaston Lewis Papers
James E. Green Diary, 53rd North Carolina
James D. Ferguson Journal, Fitz Lee's Staff
Bryan Grimes Papers
Benjamin G. Humphreys, "The Sunflower Guards," contained in Claiborne Papers
Samuel J. C. Moore Papers, Early's Staff
John Paris Diary and Letters, 54th North Carolina
Leonidas L. Polk Papers, 43rd North Carolina
Stephen D. Ramseur Papers
John A. Stikeleather, "Recollection of Life During the Civil War," 4th North Carolina
Achilles James Tynes Papers, 14th Virginia Cavalry
Richard W. Waldrop, Diary and Letters, 21st Virginia Infantry
Cary Whitaker Diary, 43rd North Carolina
George Whitaker Wills Letters, 43rd North Carolina

University of Notre Dame Archives

David Moriarity, "The Last Days of Colonel Mulligan in Virginia"
James A. Mulligan, Diary

University of Oregon

Hazard Stevens Papers

University of Virginia

John Y. Bedingfield Letters, 60th Georgia
William Franic Brand Letters, 5th Virginia
E. E. Bouldin Reminiscences
John Warwick Daniel Papers
Henry Pruitt Fortson Letters (Barnes Family Papers), 31st Georgia
Washington Hands Civil War Notebook, Baltimore Battery
Robert T. Hubard, Reminiscences, 3rd Virginia Cavalry
Milton Humphreys Papers, Lewisburg Battery
Thomas T. Munford Papers
Irving Whitehead, "Campaigns of Thomas T. Munford and History of the 2nd Virginia Cavalry"
B. K. Whittle Notebook, 1st Virginia Cavalry
Micajah Woods Papers, Charlottesville Battery, Horse Artillery

Vermont Historical Society

Francis Charles Forbes, "A Soldier of Sheridan," 8th Vermont
Virginia Historical Society, Richmond, Virginia
John C. Donohoe Diary, 6th Virginia Cavalry
Jubal A. Early Papers
Thomas T. Green Letters, 61st Alabama
Joseph Harrison Lambeth Diary, 1864, 14th North Carolina

John Price Kepner Diary, 6th Pennsylvania Cavalry
Grief Lampkin Diary, 5th Virginia Cavalry

E. L. Hobson Letters, 5th Alabama

Samuel J. C. Moore Papers, Early's Staff

William Barksdale Myers, Letters, Breckinridge's Staff

John Wilson Phillips Diary, 18th Pennsylvania Cavalry

William F. Tiemann, "Prison Life in Dixie," 159th New York

Rufus J. Woolwine Diary, 1864, 51st Virginia

Virginia Military Institute

William J. Black Diary, Shoemaker's Battery

John J. Shoemaker, Report of Operations September 3, 1864 to December 23, 1864

Virginia Tech Special Collections Department

Archibald Atkinson Memoir, 31st Virginia

Isaac White Letters, 62nd Virginia Mounted Infantry

Washington and Lee University

Augustus Forsberg Memoir

West Virginia University, Morgantown, West Virginia

Jacob M. Campbell Diary, 54th Pennsylvania

John S. Cunningham Letters, 13th West Virginia

William B. Curtis Papers, 12th West Virginia

Field History of the 13th Regiment West VA. Vol. Infantry for the Year 1864

John Mastin Diary, 22nd Virginia

H. E. Matheny Papers

Jewett Palmer Journal, 36th Ohio

Joseph C. Snider Diary, 31st Virginia

John V. Young Diary and Letters, 11th West Virginia

West Virginia State Archives, Charleston, West Virginia

Samuel C. Jones, Diary

James D. Sedinger, "Diary of a Border Ranger"

Cunningham Letters, 13th West Virginia

Western Historical Manuscript Collection, Columbia, Missouri

Nicholas Miller Civil War Memoir, 8th Indiana

The Historical Society of Western Pennsylvania

James G. Findley Letters, 91st Ohio

Walter R. DeGroot Collection, Arlington, Virginia

William DeGroot Letters, 5th New York Heavy Artillery

Yale University

William H. Emory Papers

Col. Thomas W. Porter, Report of the Battle of Winchester, 14th Maine

Personal Narratives, Memoirs, Diaries, and Letters

Abbott, Lemuel Abija, *Personal Recollections and Civil War Diary, 1864*. Burlington, VT: Free Press Printing Co., 1908.

Adams, John R., *Memorial and Letters of Rev. John R. Adams. D. D.* Privately Published, 1890.

Adams, John R., "Soldier's Letter," November 17, 1864, in *Otsego Republican*. December 3, 1864.

Anderson, D. C., "The Nineteenth Corps: An Amended Story of Gen. Emory's Command in the Valley Campaign." *National Tribune.* November 24, 1887.

Ball, John H., "From the Twelfth Regiment," *The Connecticut War Record*. New Haven, CT: Morris & Benham, Pub., Nov. 1864.

Berkeley, Henry Robinson, *Four Years in the Confederate Artillery: The Diary of Private Henry Robinson Berkeley*. Raleigh: University of North Carolina Press, 1961.

Betts, A. Q. *Experiences of a Confederate Chaplain, 1861-1864*. North Carolina Conference Methodist Episcopal Church.

Booth, George Wilson. *Personal Reminiscences of a Maryland Solider in the War between the States, 1861-1865*. Baltimore, MD: privately published, 1898.

Bowen, James L., "The 37th Mass. At the Opequon Fight," *National Tribune*. May 28, 1925.

Bradwell, I. G. "The Fight at Winchester, VA." *Confederate Veteran*. Volume 15, 1907.

———. "Sheridan and Trevillian Station," *Confederate Veteran*. Volume 37, 1929.

———. "Early's Valley Campaign, 1864," *Confederate Veteran*. Volume 28, 1920.

———. "With Early in the Valley," *Confederate Veteran*. Volume 22, 1914.

———. "With Early in the Valley, 1864," *Confederate Veteran*.

Brewer, A. T., *History of the Sixty-First Regiment Pennsylvania Volunteers 1861-1865*. Pittsburgh: Art Engraving & Printing Co., 1911.

Brown, James Alleine, *The Memoirs of a Confederate Soldier*. Abingdon, VA: Forum Press, 1940.

Buck, Samuel D. *With the Old Confeds: Actual Experiences of a Captain in the Line*. Baltimore, MD: H. E. Houck, 1925.

Buell, Augustus, *'The Cannoneer.' Recollections of Service in the Army of the Potomac*. Washington: The National Tribune, 1890.

Bumgardner, James, Jr., "Early's Little Black Captain, Memoirs of Capt. James Bumgardner, Jr.," 1916.

Butterfield, M. L., "Personal Reminiscences with the Sixth Corps, 1864-5," *War Papers Read Before the Commandery of the State of Wisconsin, Military Order of the Loyal Legion of the United States*. Milwaukee: Burdick & Allen, 1914.

Carmichael, J. W., "Battle of the Opequon," *National Tribune*. October 10, 1918.

Casler, John O. *Four Years in the Stonewall Brigade*. Edited by James I. Robertson Jr. Dayton, OH: Morningside Press, 1982.

Chase, Julia. *War Time Diary of Miss Julia Chase, Winchester, Virginia 1861-1864*. Winchester, VA: Handley Library, 1931.

Chittick, Geraldine F., Compiler, *In the Field: Doctor Melvin John Hyde Surgeon, 2nd Vermont Volunteers*. Newport, VT: Vermont Civil War Enterprises, 1999.

Clark, Orton S., "Sheridan's Shenandoah Valley Campaign," *MOLLUS-Minnesota*. Vol. 6, 1903.

Commager, Frank Y. "The Sixth Corps, Personal Reminiscences of General Wright," *National Tribune*. February 28, 1889.

Conway, William B., "From the Wilderness to the Shenandoah Valley of Virginia, 1864," *Atlanta Journal*. February 8, 1902.

Corbin, Henry, "Diary of a Virginian Cavalry Man, 1863-1864," *Virginia Historical Magazine*. October, 1873.

Corson, William Clark. *My Dear Jennie*. B. W. Corson, 1982.

Cowper, Pulaski, *Extracts of Letters of Major-General Bryan Grimes to His Wife, Written While in Active Service in the Army of Northern Virginia*. Raleigh: Alfred Williams and Co., 1884.

Cox, William R. *Address on the Life and Character of Maj. Gen. Stephen D. Ramseur*. Raleigh: 1891.

Crawford, W. J., "In the Valley with Sheridan at Winchester and Cedar Creek Against Early," *The National Tribune*. July 10, 1913.

Crockett, Edwin, "Fierce Frenzy of Battle," *National Tribune*. April 18, 1901.

Crowell, Kathy, compiler, "The Onondagas: A History of the 122d Regiment, New York Volunteers," accessed at www.rootsweb.com/~war/onondaga.tm.

Curtis, Oscar H., "From the 114th Regiment," September 27, 1864, *Oxford Times*. October 12, 1864.

Daniel, John W. "General Jubal Early: Memorial Address." *Southern Historical Society Papers*. Vol. 22, 281-323.

Dawson, Francis W. *Reminiscences of Confederate Service, 1861-1865*. Baton Rouge: Louisiana State University Press.

Dawson, Henry B., pub. "Diary of a Virginian Cavalryman, 1863-1864." *The Historical Magazine and Notes and Queries Concerning the Antiquities, History and Biography of America*. 2:210-215.

Dearborn, Valorus, "Diary of," accessed at www.2mass.reunioncivilwar.com/References/dearborn.htm

DeForest, John W. *A Volunteer's Adventures: A Union Captain's Record of the Civil War*. New Haven, CT: Yale University Press, 1946.

Douglas, Henry Kyd, *I Rode with Stonewall*. Chapel Hill: University of North Carolina Press, 1940.

Drickamer, Lee C. and Karen D. Drickamer, eds. *Fort Lyon to Harper's Ferry: On the Border of North and South with "Rambling Jour."* Shippensburg, PA: White Mane Publishing, 1987.

Duncan, Richard R., ed. *Alexander Neil and the Last Shenandoah Valley Campaign*. Shippensburg, PA: White Mane Publishing, 1996.

Dupont, Henry A. *The Campaign of 1864 in the Valley of Virginia and the Expedition to Lynchburg*. New York: National American Society, 1925.

Durkin, Rev. Joseph T. *Confederate Chaplain: A War Journal of Rev. James B. Sheeran, 14th Louisiana, and C.S.A*, Milwaukee: Bruce Publishing, 1960.

Early, Jubal A. *Autobiographical Sketch and Narrative of the War between the States*. Philadelphia and London: J. B. Lippincott, 1912.

————. *A Memoir of the Last Year of the War for Independence in the Confederate States of America*. Lynchburg, VA: C. W. Button, 1867.

————. "Early's March to Washington in 1864," Clarence Buel and Robert U. Johnston, (editors). *Battles and Leaders of the Civil War*, Volume IV, New York: Thomas Yoseloff, Inc., 1956.

————. "Winchester, Fisher's Hill and Cedar Creek," Clarence Buel and Robert U. Johnston, (editors). *Battles and Leaders of the Civil War*, Volume IV, New York: Thomas Yoseloff, Inc., 1956.

Eby, Cecil D., ed. *A Virginia Yankee in the Civil War: The Diaries of David Hunter Strother*. Chapel Hill: University of North Carolina Press, 1961.

Edwards, Oliver, "Their Heroic Past Recalled by Survivors of the 37th Regiment," *Springfield Republican*. September 20, 1893.

Elwood, John W. *Elwood's Stories of the Old Ringgold Cavalry, 1847-1865, The First Three Year Cavalry of the Civil War.* Coal Center, PA: Published by the author, Sergeant John W. Elwood, 1914.

Emerson, Edward W., *Life and Letters of Charles Russell Lowell.* Boston: Cambridge Press, 1907.

Farnsworth, Ezra, "Reminiscences of the Shenandoah Valley in 1864," *MOLLUS-Massachusetts.* Vol. 5, 1901.

Fish, Chauncy, "Wounded in the Back," *The National Tribune.* March 20, 1884.

Fitts, James F., "Letter from the 114th Regiment," September 26, 1864, *Chenango Chronicle.* October 1864.

———. "The Fight at Fisher's Hill," *Galaxy,* Vol. 5.

———. "The Last Battle of Winchester," *Galaxy,* Vol. 2, 1866.

Fisk, Wilbur, *Hard Marching Every Day: The Civil War Letters of Private Wilbur Fisk, 1861-1865.* Lawrence, KS: University Press of Kansas, 1992.

Flinn, Frank M., *Campaigning with Banks in Louisiana 1863 & 1864 and with Sheridan in the Shenandoah Valley in 1864 & 1865.* Lynn, MA: 1887.

French, W. B. "From the 77th: The Late Battles in the Shenandoah," September 28, 1864 in *The Saratogan.* October 13, 1864.

Frye, Dennis E. *The Second Virginia Infantry.* Lynchburg, VA: H. E. Howard, 1984.

Gaines, Samuel M., "Just Before the Battle: An Incident of the Battle of Winchester or Opequon," *Richmond Times-Dispatch.* September 3, 1905.

Gallaher, Jr. Dewitt Clinton, Ed. *A Diary Depicting the Experiences of Dewitt Clinton Gallaher in the War Between the States while Serving in the Confederate Army.* Charleston, WV: 1945.

Gallinger, C. E., "At Opequon," *The National Tribune.* December 15, 1892.

Garnett, James M. "Battle of Winchester," *Southern Historical Society Papers.* Volume 30, 1903.

———. "Diary of Captain James M. Garnett," *Southern Historical Society Papers.* Volume 27, 1899.

Gause, Isaac, *Four Years with Five Armies.* New York: The Neale Publishing Co., 1908.

Gilmor, Harry. *Four Years in the Saddle.* New York: Harper and Brothers, 1866.

Goerlich, Shirly, compiler, *Historical Address of Sergeant Major H. C. Hammond, Delivered at the Reunion.* Bainbridge, NY: RSG Publishing, 1995.

Gordon, John B. *Reminiscences of the Civil War.* New York: Charles Scribner's Sons, 1903.

Grant, Ulysses S. *Personal Memoirs of U. S. Grant.* New York: Charles L. Webster, 1889.

Grosvenor, Chauncey F. *The War of the Rebellion.* Bowiem MD: Heritage Books, 1994.

Hagemann, E. R., Ed., *Fighting Rebels and Redskins: Experience in Army Life of Colonel George B. Sanford.* Norman, OK: University of Oklahoma Press, 1969.

Hamblin, Deborah. *Brevet Major-General Joseph Eldridge Hamblin, 1861-1865.* Boston: 1902.

Harris, Moses, "With the Reserve Brigade," *Journal of the United States Cavalry Association.* Vol. 3, No. 8, March, 1890.

Harris, Nathaniel E. *Autobiography; the Story of an Old Man's Life, with Reminiscences of Seventy-Five Years.* Macon, GA: J. W. Burke, 1925.

Hassler, Frederick W. B., "A Military View of Passing Events from Inside the Confederacy (22nd Virginia)," *The Historical Magazine and Notes and Queries Concerning the Antiquities, History and Biography of America.* Vol. 4, 1869.

Hastings, Smith, "The Cavalry Service and Recollections of the Late War," *Magazine of Western History.* Vol. 11, 1890.

Hatton, Clarence, "Gen. Archibald Campbell Godwin," *Confederate Veteran.* Volume 28, 1920.

———. "The Valley Campaign of 1864," *Confederate Veteran.* Vol. 27, 1919.

Hawkins, Morton L., "Sketch of the Battle of Winchester, September 19, 1864," *Ohio MOLLUS*. Vol. 1, 1888.

Hayes, James F., "Battle of Opequon," *National Tribune*. October 24, 1918.

Herring, Marcus D. "General Rodes at Winchester," *Confederate Veteran*. Volume 28, 1919.

Hodam, Robert P., ed., *The Journal of James Harrison Hodam*. Eugene, OR: West Printers, 1995.

Holt, Daniel M. *A Surgeon's Civil War: The Letters and Diary of Daniel M. Holt M.D.* Kent, OH: Kent State University Press, 1994.

Hotchkiss, Jedediah. "Early's Lynchburg and Valley Campaigns," Evans, Clement A., ed. *Confederate Military History*. 12 vols. Atlanta: Confederate Publishing, 1899.

Howe, Henry Warren, *Passages from the Life of Henry Warren Howe*. Lowell, MA: Courier-Citizen Co., 1899.

Hubbs, G. Ward, ed. *Voices from Company D: Diaries by the Greensboro Guards, Fifth Alabama Infantry Regiment, Army of Northern Virginia*. Athens: University of Georgia Press, 2003.

Humphreys, Charles A., *Field, Camp, Hospital and Prison in the Civil War, 1863-1865*. Free Port, NY: Books for Libraries Press, 1971.

Hyatt, Hudson, "Captain Hyatt: Being the Letters Written During the Years 1863-1864 to His Wife, Mary by Captain T. J. Hyatt, 126th Ohio Volunteer Infantry," *The Ohio State Archaeological and Historical Quarterly*. Vol. 54, No. 2, April-June 1944.

James, James R., ed. *To See the Elephant: The Civil War Letters of John A. McKee*. Leawood, KS: Leathers Publishing, 1998.

Johnson, W. Gard, "Prison Life at Harpers Ferry and on Johnson's Island," *Confederate Veteran*. Volume 2, 1894.

Johnston, A. S., "Captain Beirne Chapman and Chapman's Battery: An Historical Sketch." Union, WV: n.p., 1903.

Johnston, J. Stoddard. "Sketches of Operations of General John C. Breckinridge."*Southern Historical Society Papers*, vol. 7.

Jones, Terry L., ed., *The Civil War Memoirs of Captain William J. Seymour, Reminiscences of a Louisiana Tiger*. Baton Rouge: Louisiana State University Press, 1991.

Jordan, William B., *The Civil War Journals of John Mead Gould, 1861-1866*. Baltimore: Butternut and Blue, 1997.

Kaufman, Jonas B. "Jonas Kaufman Diary." In *History of Cambria County, Pennsylvania* by Henry Wilson Storey, with Genealogical Memoirs. New York: Lewis Publishing, 1907.

Keifer, Joseph Warren, *Slavery and Four Years of War*. New York: The Knickerbocker Press, 1900.

Kidd, James H., "Charge of the First Cavalry Division At Winchester," *Ionia Daily Sentinel*. June 5, 1866.

Lang, Theodore F. *Loyal West Virginia from 1861 to 1865*. Baltimore: Deutsch Publishing, 1895.

Ledford, P. L. *Reminiscences of the Civil War, 1861-1865*. Thomasville, NC: News Printing House, 1909.

Lee, William O., *Personal and Historical Sketches and Facial History of and by Members of the Seventh Regiment Michigan Volunteer Cavalry, 1862-1865*. Detroit: 7th Michigan Cavalry Association.

LeFevre, Johannes, "The Fight at Winchester, September 21, 1864," *New Paltz Times*, May 6, 1887.

Long, A. L., "General Early's Valley Campaign,"*Southern Historical Society Papers*. Vol. 3, 1877.

Love, Solomon F., "Battle of the Opequon," *National Tribune*. March 9, 1911.

Lynch, Charles H. *The Civil War Diary, 1862-1865, of Charles H. Lynch, 18th Conn. Vol's*. Hartford, CT: Case, Lockwood, and Brainard, 1915.

McKim, Randolph H., *A Soldier's Recollections: Leaves from the Diary of a Young Confederate*. Washington: Zenger Publishing Co., 1983.

Meade, George, ed. *The Life and Letters of George Gordon Meade, Major General U.S. Army*. 2 vols. New York: 1913.

Merritt, Wesley, "Sheridan in the Shenandoah Valley," *Battles and Leaders of the Civil War*. Vol. 4.

Milling, James Alexander, *Jim Milling and the War, 1862-1865*. n.p., n.d.

Mont, Noah, "The Campaign in the Shenandoah Valley," *New Paltz Times*. December 31, 1886.

Montgomery, Asbe. *An Account of R. R. Blazer and His Scouts, Operations in West Virginia and in Loudoun and Shenandoah Valleys, against William and Philip Thurman and Mosby, the Great Guerrillas; by Asbe Montgomery, One of the Scouts Belonging to Captain Blazer's Company, Marietta, Ohio.* Marietta, OH: Printed at the Registry Office, 1865.

Morse, John T. ed., *Diary of Gideon Welles, Secretary of the Navy Under Lincoln and Johnson.* New York: Houghton Mifflin Co., 1911.

Moulton, Charles H. *Fort Lyon to Harpers Ferry: On the Border of North and South with "Rambling Jour."* 1987: Shippensburg, PA: White Mane Publishing, 1987.

Munford, Thomas T., "Reminiscences of Cavalry Operations," *Southern Historical Society Papers.* Vol. 13, 1885.

Neal, Basil L. *A Son of the American Revolution.* Washington, GA: Washington Reporter Print, 1914.

Newell, T. F. "General Early's Motto: Fight Em!" *Confederate Veteran*, 594.

O'Ferrall, Charles T. *Forty Years of Active Service.* New York: Neale Publishing, 1904.

————. "Official Diary of the First Corps, A.N.V. While Commanded By Lt. Gen. R. H. Anderson," *Southern Historical Society Papers.* Volume 7.

Olcott, Mark, ed. *The Civil War Letters of Lewis Bissell: A Curriculum.* Washington, D.C.: Field School Educational Foundation Press, 1981.

Opie, John N. *A Rebel Cavalryman with Lee, Stuart, and Jackson.* Chicago: W. B. Conkey, 1899.

O'Reilly, Private Miles. [Charles G. Halpine, pseudo.]. *Baked Meats of the Funeral. A Collection of Essays, Poems, Speeches, Histories, and Banquets.* New York: Carleton, 1866.

Park, Robert E. "Diary of Robert E. Park, Late Capt. Twelfth Alabama Reg't." *Southern Historical Society Papers.* vol. 1, (1875) and vol. 2, (1876).

Paxton, Alex, "Some Recollections of the War in the Great Shenandoah Valley," *Richmond Times-Dispatch.* September 4, 1904.

Peacock, Jane Bonner, "A Georgian's View of War in Virginia: The Civil War Letters of Arthur Benjamin Simms," *Atlanta Historical Journal.* Summer 1979, Volume 23, No. 2.

Poe, David. *Reminiscences of the Civil War.* Buckhannon, WV: Upshur Republican Print, 1911.

Porter, C., "In the Valley: Reconnaissance of the Second Division, Sixth Corps," *The National Tribune.* July 4, 1889.

Rhodes, Elisha Hunt. *All for the Union: The Civil War Diary and Letters of Elisha Hunt Rhodes.* Edited by Robert Hunt Rhodes. 1st Vintage Civil War Library Edition. New York: Vintage Books, 1992.

Rodenbough, Theo. F., *Sabre and Bayonet: Stories of Heroism and Military Adventure: Collected and Edited.* New York: G. W. Gillingham Co., 1897.

Runge, William H., ed. *Four Years in the Confederate Artillery: The Diary of Private Henry Robinson Berkeley.* Chapel Hill: University of North Carolina Press, 1961.

S. E. G., "Grovers Division at Winchester," *American Tribune.* November 21, 1890.

Schaub, J. L., "Gen. Robert E. Rodes," *Confederate Veteran.* Volume 16, 1908.

Schmidt, Martin F., ed. *General George Crook: His Autobiography.* Norman: University of Oklahoma Press, 1946.

Scott, W. W., Ed., "Diary of Capt. Henry W. Wingfield, 58th Virginia," *Bulletin of the Virginia State Library,* Volume 16, July 1927.

Shackelford, F. G., "My Recollections of the War 36th Virginia," *Nicholas Chronicle.* September 21, 1895.

Shaffner, C. L., ed. *Diary of Dr. J. F. Shaffner, Sr.* n.p., n.d.

Sheridan, Philip H. *Personal Memoirs of P. H. Sheridan.* 2 vols. New York: Charles L. Webster, 1888.

Smith, George H., "Imboden's Brigade," October 4, 1864, contained in *Richmond Whig,* October 12, 1864.

Smith, J. Soule, "A Young Confederate Veteran." *The Sunny South.* May 11, 1901.

———. "Sad News to Judge Smith; He Served Under Gordon," *Louisville Morning Herald.* January 11, 1904.

Sorrell, Gen. G. Moxley, *Recollections of a Confederate Staff Officer.* Jackson, TN: McCowat-Mercer Press, 1958.

Sprague, Homer B., "Sheridan's Battle of Winchester," *National Tribune.* January 8, 1914.

Stevens, George T. *Three Years in the Sixth Corps.* Albany: S. R. Gray, Publisher, 1866.

Stutler, Boyd B., ed. "With a Mountain Lad from Muddlety to Appomattox, A First Person Account by Peter H. Craig." *Civil War Times,* February 1967.

Summer, Merlin E., *The Diary of Cyrus B. Comstock.* Dayton, OH: Morningside Press, 1987.

Swift, Eben, "General Wesley Merritt," *Journal of the United States Cavalry Association.* Vol. 21, No. 83, March, 1911.

Taylor, James E. *With Sheridan up the Shenandoah Valley in 1864: Leaves from a Special Artist's Sketchbook and Diary.* Dayton, OH: Morningside Press, 1989.

Taylor, Oliver, "Memoirs of George Pile," *Bristol Herald Courier,* February 27, 1921.

Tenney, Francis Andrews, ed., *War Diary of Luman Harris Tenney, 1861-1865.* Cleveland: Evangelical Publishing House, 1914.

Thacker, Victor L., ed. *French Harding: Civil War Memoirs.* Parsons, WV: McClain, 2000.

Thoburn, Joseph. *Hunter's Raid 1864. From the Diary of Colonel Joseph Thoburn.* n.p.: Published by Thomas Beer, 1914.

Throne, Mildred, "Reminiscences of Jacob C. Switzer of the 22nd Iowa," *Iowa Journal of History.* Iowa City: The State Historical Society of Iowa, 1958.

Turner, Charles W., *The Allen Family of Amherst County, Virginia Civil War Letters.* Berryville, VA: Rockbridge Publishing Company, 1995.

———. *Civil War Letters of Arabella Spears and William Beverley Pettit of Fluvanna County, Virginia, Volume II, February 1864-March 1865.* The Virginia Lithography & Graphics Company, 1989.

Tyler, Mason Whiting, *Recollections of the Civil War.* New York: G. P. Putnam's Sons, 1912.

Watt, M. S. "General Battle and the Stolen Colt," *Confederate Veteran.* volume 33, 1922.

Wellman, Wade Manly. *Rebel Boast: First at Bethel—Last at Appomattox.* New York: Henry Holt, 1956.

Whitaker, Frederick, *A Complete Life of Gen. George A. Custer.* New York: Sheldon & Co., 1876.

White, P. J., "General Early's Valley Campaign," *Richmond Times-Dispatch.* September 23, 1906.

———. "The Battle of Winchester," *Richmond Times Dispatch.* November 20, 1904.

———. "Recollections of Winchester Battle," *Richmond Times Dispatch.* October 6, 1907.

Williams, Charles Richard, ed. *Diary and Letters of Rutherford Birchard Hayes.* Vol. 2. Columbus: Ohio State Archaeological and Historical Society, 1922.

Worsham, John H. *One of Jackson's Foot Cavalry.* Wilmington, NC: Broadfoot Publishing, 1987.

Yeary, Mamie, *Reminiscences of the Boys in Gray, 1861-1865.* Dayton: Morningside, 1986.

Unit Histories

Baquet, Camille, *History of The First Brigade, New Jersey Volunteers from 1861 to 1865.* Trenton: The State of New Jersey, 1910.

Bates, Samuel P. *History of Pennsylvania Volunteers, 1861-65.* Harrisburg, PA: B. Singerly, 1871.

Beach, William, *The First New York (Lincoln) Cavalry from April 19, 1861 to July 7, 1865.* New York: Lincoln Cavalry Association, 1902.

Beecher, Harris H., *Record of the 114th Regiment, N.Y.S.V., Where It Went, What It Saw, and What It Did*. Norwich, NY: J. J. Hubbard, Jr., 1866.

Best, Isaac O., *History of the 121st New York State Infantry*. Chicago: Lt. Jas. H. Smith, 1921.

Bidwell, Frederick David, *History of the Forty-Ninth New York Volunteers*. Albany: J. B. Lyon Company, Printers, 1916.

Blake, Ephraim E., *A Succint History of the 28th Iowa Volunteer Infantry*. Belle Plain, IA: Union Press, 1896.

Bonnell, John C., Jr. *Sabres in the Shenandoah: The 21st New York Cavalry, 1863-1866*. Shippensburg, PA: Burd Street Press, 1996.

Bowen, J. R., *Regimental History of the First New York Dragoons*. Published by the author, 1908.

Bowen, James, *Massachusetts in the War, 1861-1865*. Springfield, MA: Bowen & Son, 1893.

Bowen, James L., *History of the Thirty-Seventh Mass. Volunteers in the Civil War of 1861-1865*. Holyoke, MA: Clark W. Bryan and Co. Publishers, 1884.

Brooks, Thomas Walter, and Michael Dan Jones. *Lee's Foreign Legion: A History of the 10th Louisiana Infantry*. Gravenhurst on: T. W. Brooks, 1995.

Buffum, Francis H., *A Memorial of The Great Rebellion Being a History of The Fourteenth Regiment New Hampshire Volunteers*. Boston: Franklin Press: Rand, Avery & Co., 1882.

Campbell, E. L., *Historical Sketch of the Fifteenth Regiment New Jersey Volunteers*. Trenton: Wm. S. Sharpe, Printer, 1880.

Carpenter, George N., *History of the Eighth Vermont Volunteers, 1861-1865*. Boston: Press of Deland and Barta, 1886.

Casler, John O., *Four Years in the Stonewall Brigade*. Dayton, OH: Morningside Press, 1971.

Chapla, John D. *The 48th Virginia Infantry*. Lynchburg, VA: H. E. Howard, 1983.

Cheney, Newel, *History of the Ninth Regiment New York Volunteer Cavalry, War of 1861 to 1865*. Jamestown, NY: Martin Merz & Son, 1901.

Clark, Orton S., *The One Hundred and Sixteenth Regiment of New York State Volunteers*. Buffalo: Printing House of Matthews & Warren, 1868.

Clark, Walter, ed. *Histories of the Several Regiments and Battalions from North Carolina in the Great War—1861-65*. Vol. 3. Written by members of the respective commands. Published by the State. Raleigh: E. M. Uzzell, Printer, 1901.

Croffut, W. A. and John M. Morris, *The Military and Civil History of Connecticut During the War of 1861-65*. New York: Ledyard Bill, 1868.

Delauter, Roger U. *The 18th Virginia Cavalry*. Lynchburg, VA: H. E. Howard, 1985.

———. *McNeill's Rangers*. Lynchburg, VA: H. E. Howard, 1986.

———. *62nd Virginia Infantry*. Lynchburg, VA: H. E. Howard, 1988.

Denison, Frederic, *Sabres and Spurs: The First Regiment Rhode Island Cavalry in the Civil War*. Published by the First Rhode Island Cavalry Association, 1876.

Dickert, D. Augustus, *History of Kershaw's Brigade*. Dayton, OH: Morningside Press, 1976.

Dickinson, Jack L. *8th Virginia Cavalry*. Lynchburg, VA: H. E. Howard, 1986.

———. *16th Virginia Cavalry*. Lynchburg, VA: H. E. Howard, 1989.

Driver, J. Robert, Jr. *The 52nd Virginia Infantry*. Lynchburg, VA: H. E. Howard, 1985.

———. *The Staunton Artillery – McClanahan's Battery*. Lynchburg, VA: H. E. Howard, 1988.

———. *14th Virginia Cavalry*. Lynchburg, VA: H. E. Howard, 1988.

Ewer, James K., *The Third Massachusetts Cavalry in the War for the Union*. Maplewood, MA: Historical Committee of the Regimental Association, 1903.

Farrar, Samuel C. *The Twenty-Second Pennsylvania Cavalry and the Ringgold Battalion, 1861-65*. Pittsburgh: Twenty-Second Pennsylvania Ringgold Cavalry Association, 1911.

Fonerden, C. A., *A Brief History of the Military Career of Carpenter's Battery*. New Market, VA: Henkel & Co. Printers, 1911.

Gilson, John H. *Concise History of the 126th Ohio Volunteer Infantry from the Date of Organization to the End of the Rebellion*. Salem, OH: Walton, Steam, Job, and Cabel, 1883.

Gottfried, Bradley M., *Kearny's Own: The History of the First New Jersey Brigade in the Civil War*. New Brunswick, NJ: Rivergate Books, 2005.

Gould, John M., *History of the First-Tenth-Twenty-Ninth Maine Regiment*. Portland, ME: Stephen Berry, 1871.

Hadden, R. Lee, *Fourth Regiment North Carolina State Troops, 1861-1865*. R. Lee Hadden (Private), Centreville, VA, 1999.

Haines, Alanson A., *History of the 15th New Jersey Volunteers*. New York: Jenkins & Thomas, Printers, 1883.

Hale, Laura Virginia. *History of the Forty-Ninth Virginia Infantry*. Lanham, MD: S. S. Phillips, 1981.

Hall, Henry and James Hall, *Cayuga in the Field, A Record of the 19th N. Y. Volunteers, All the Batteries of the 3rd New York Artillery, and 75th New York Volunteers*. Auburn, NY: Truair, Smith & Co., 1873.

Hanaburgh, D. H., *History of the One Hundred and Twenty-Eighth Regiment, New York Volunteers (U.S. Infantry) in the Late Civil War*. Pokeepsie, NY: Regimental Association, 1894.

Harris, Nelson, *17th Virginia Cavalry*. Lynchburg, VA: H. E. Howard, 1994.

Haynes, E. M., *A History of the Tenth Regiment Vermont Volunteers*. Lewiston, ME: Journal Steam Press, 1870.

Hewitt, William. *History of the Twelfth West Virginia Volunteer Infantry: The Part It Took in the War of the Rebellion, 1861-1865*. n.p.: Published by the Twelfth West Virginia Infantry Association, 1892.

Hill, Herbert E., *Campaign in the Shenandoah Valley, 1864*. Boston: Rand Avery Company, Printers, 1886.

Hillman, Hall, *History of the Sixth New York Cavalry (Second Ira Harris Guard)*. Worcester, MA: The Blanchard Press, 1908.

Howell, Helena Adelaide, *Chronicles of the One hundred fifty-first regiment New York state volunteer infantry, 1862-1865, Contributed by Its Surviving Members. Compiled by Helena Adelaide Howell*. Albion: A. M. Eddy, printer, 1911.

Hubbs, G. Ward, *Voices from Co. D: Diaries by the Greensboro Guards, Fifth Alabama Infantry Regiment, Army of Northern Virginia*. Athens, GA: University of Georgia Press, 2003.

Iobst, Richard W. *The Bloody Sixth: The Sixth North Carolina Regiment, Confederate States of America*. Raleigh: North Carolina Centennial Commission, 1965.

Jones, Samuel C., *Reminiscences of the Twenty-Second Iowa Volunteer Infantry*. Iowa City: 1907.

Jones, Terry L. *Lee's Tigers: The Louisiana Infantry in the Army of Northern Virginia*. Baton Rouge: Louisiana State University Press, 1987.

Keyes, C. M., ed. *The Military History of the 123rd Regiment, Ohio Volunteer Infantry*. Sandusky, OH: Register Press, 1874.

Ledford, P. L., *Reminiscences of the Civil War 1861-1865*. Thomasville, NC: New Printing House, 1909.

Lewis, Osceola, *History of the One Hundred and Thirty-Eighth Regiment, Pennsylvania Volunteer Infantry*. Norristown, PA: Wills, Iredell & Jenkins, 1866.

Lillard, J. J. "Third Confederate." In *The Military Annals of Tennessee, Confederate*, edited by John Berrien Lindsley. Nashville: J. M. Lindsley, 1886.

Lincoln, William S. *Life with the 34th Massachusetts Infantry in the War of the Rebellion*. Worcestor, MA: Press of Noyes, Snow, and Company, 1879.

Maier, Larry B. *Leather and Steel: The 12th Pennsylvania Cavalry in the Civil War*. Shippensburg, PA: Burd Street Press, 2001.

Mark, Penrose G., *Red, White, and Blue Badge: Pennsylvania Volunteers A History of the 93rd Regiment*. Harrisburg: The Aughinbaugh Press, 1911.

Martin, David G. *The Fluvanna Artillery*. Lynchburg, VA: H. E. Howard, 1992.

Moore, Alison. *The Louisiana Tigers; or, The Two Louisiana Brigades of the Army of Northern Virginia, 1861-1865*. Baton Rouge: Ortlieb Press, 1961.

Moyer, H. P., *History of the Seventeenth regiment, Pa. Volunteer Cavalry*. Lebanon, PA: Sower's Printing Co., 1911.

Murray, Thomas Hamilton, *History of the Ninth Regiment Connecticut Volunteer Infantry, 'The Irish Regiment,' in the War of Rebellion, 1861-65*. New Haven: The Price, Lee & Adkins Co., 1903.

Nichols, George W. *A Soldier's Story of His Regiment and Incidentally of the Lawton-Gordon-Evans Brigade, Army of Northern Virginia*. Jessup, GA: Private, 1898.

Niebaum, John H., *History of the Pittsburgh Washington Infantry 102nd (Old 13th) Regiment Pennsylvania Volunteers and Its Forebears*. Pittsburgh, PA: Burgum Printing Co., 1931.

Norton, Chauncey S. *"The Red Neck Ties"; or, History of the Fifteenth New York Volunteer Cavalry*. Ithaca, NY: Journal Book and Job Printing House, 1891.

Norton, Henry, *Deeds of Daring: History of the Eighth N. Y. Volunteer Cavalry*. Norwich, NY: Chenango Telegraph Printing House, 1889.

Pellet, Elias Porter. *History of the 114th Regiment, New York State Volunteers*. Norwich, NY: Telegraph & Chronicle power press print, 1866.

Pickerill, W. N., *History of the Third Indiana Cavalry*. Indianapolis, 1906.

Powell, William H., "Sheridan in the Shenandoah, Battle of the Opequon," *American Tribune*. February 13, 1891.

Powers, George W., *The Story of the Thirty Eighth Regiment of Massachusetts Volunteers*. Cambridge Press: Dakin and Metcalf, 1866.

Prowell, George R., *History of the 87th Pennsylvania Volunteers*. York, PA: Press of the York Daily, 1901.

Rankin, Thomas H. *The Twenty-Third Virginia Infantry*. Lynchburg, VA: H. E. Howard, 1985.

Ray, Neill W. *Sketch of the Sixth Regiment, N.C. State Troops (Infantry)*. n.p., n.d.

Reed, Thomas J. *Tibbits' Boys: A History of the 21st New York Cavalry*. Lanham, MD: University Press of America, 1997.

Robertson, James I., Jr. *The Fourth Virginia Infantry*. Lynchburg, VA: H. E. Howard, 1982.

Rodenbough, Theo. F., *From Everglade to Canon with the Second Dragoons, 1836-1875*. New York: Van Nostrand, 1875.

———. *History of the Eighteenth Regiment of Cavalry Pennsylvania Volunteers*. New York: Wynkoop, Hallenbeck, Crawford, Co., 1909.

Roe, Alfred Seelye, *The Ninth New York Heavy Artillery*. Worcester, MA: Published by the Author, 1899.

Schmidt, Lewis G., *A Civil War History of the 47th Regiment of Pennsylvania Veteran Volunteers*. Allentown: Lewis G. Schmidt, 1986.

Scott, J. L. *36th and 37th Battalions Virginia Cavalry*. Lynchburg, VA: H. E. Howard, 1986.

Shaffner, J. F. Sr., *Diary of Dr. J. F. Shaffner, Sr.* North Carolina State Library Raleigh.

Shoemaker, John J. *Shoemaker's Battery: Stuart Horse Artillery, Pelham's Battalion, Army of Northern Virginia*.

Slease, William D. *The Fourteenth Pennsylvania Cavalry in the Civil War*. Pittsburgh: Art Engraving and Printing, n.d.

Smith, W. A. *The Anson Guards, Company C, Fourteenth Regiment North Carolina Volunteers, 1861-1865*. Charlotte, NC: Stone Publishing, 1914.

Sprague, Homer B., *History of the 13th Infantry Regiment of Connecticut Volunteers During the Great Rebellion*. Hartford: Case, Lockwood & Co., 1867.

Stevenson, James H. *Boots and Saddles—A History of the First Volunteer Cavalry of the War Known as the First New York (Lincoln) Cavalry*. Harrisburg, PA: Patriot Publishing, 1879.

Sumner, George C. *Battery D., First Rhode Island Light Artillery in the Civil War, 1861-1865.* Providence: Rhode Island Printing Company, 1897.

Sutton, Joseph J. *History of the Second Regiment West Virginia Cavalry Volunteers during the War of the Rebellion.* Portsmouth, OH: Joseph J. Sutton, 1892.

Thomas, Henry W. *History of the Doles-Cook Brigade, Army of Northern Virginia, C.S.A.* Atlanta: Franklin Publishing, 1903.

Tiemann, William F., *The 159th Infantry New-York State Volunteers in the War of the Rebellion, 1862-1865.* Brooklyn, NY: William F. Tiemann, 1894.

Underhill, Charles Sterling, '*Your Soldier Boy Samuel,' Civil War Letters of Lt. Samuel Edmund Nichols, Amherst, '65 of the 37th Regiment Massachusetts Volunteers.* Privately Printed, 1929.

Vaill, Dudley Landon, *The County Regiment: A Sketch of the Second Regiment of Connecticut Heavy Artillery.* Litchfield County, CT: University Club, 1908.

Vaill, Theodore F. *History of the Second Connecticut Volunteer Heavy Artillery, Originally the Nineteenth Connecticut Volunteers.* Winsted, CT: Winsted Printing, 1868.

Wainright, R. P. Page Wainwright, "History of the 1st U. S. Cavalry" contained in T. F. Rodenbough's *The Army of the United States, Historical Sketches of Staff and Line with Portraits of Generals in Chief.* New York: Maynard, Merrill & Co., 1896.

Walker, Aldace F., *The Vermont Brigade in the Shenandoah Valley.* Burlington, VT: The Free Press Association, 1869.

Walker, William C. *History of the Eighteenth Regiment Conn. Volunteers in the War for the Union.* Norwich, CT: The Committee, 1883.

Wall, H. C. *Historical Sketch of the Pee Dee Guards (Co. D, 23d N.C. Regiment,) from 1861 to 1865.* Raleigh, NC: Edwards, Broughton, 1876.

Weaver, Jeffrey C., *22nd Virginia Cavalry.* Lynchburg, VA: H. E. Howard, 1991.

Wellman, Manley Wade, *Rebel Boast: First at Bethel-Last at Appomattox.* New York: Henry Holt and Company, 1956.

West, Michael, *30th Battalion Virginia Sharpshooters.* Lynchburg, VA: H. E. Howard, 1995.

Westbrook, Robert S., *History of the 49th Pennsylvania Volunteers.* Altoona, PA: 1898.

Whitman, William E. S. and Charles H. True, *Maine in the War for the Union: A History of the Part Borne by Maine Troops.* Lewiston, ME: Nelson Dingley, Jr. & Co., 1865.

Wildes, Thomas F. *Record of the 116th Regiment, Ohio Infantry Volunteers in the War of the Rebellion.* Sandusky, OH: I. F. Mack and Brothers, Printers, 1884.

Williams, Capt. George T. *Company A, 37th Battalion Virginia Cavalry, C.S.A.* Roanoke, VA: R. H. Fishburne, 1910.

Windsor, A. H. *History of the Ninety-First Regiment, O.V.I.* Cincinnati: Gazette Steam Printing House, 1865.

Woodbury, Augustus, *The Second Rhode Island Regiment: A Narrative of Military Operations.* Providence: Valpey, Angell and Company, 1875.

Secondary Sources

Bartlett, Napier. *Military Record of Louisiana.* New Orleans: L. Graham, 1873.

Beck, Brandon, and Charles S. Grunder. *The First Battle of Winchester: Jackson's Valley Campaign.* Lynchburg, VA: H. E. Howard, 1992.

Benedict, G. G., *Vermont in the Civil War, A History of the Part Taken by the Vermont Soldiers and Sailors in the War for the Union.* Burlington, VT: The Free Press Association, 1886.

Berigner, Richard E., Herman Hathaway, Archer Jones, William N. Still Jr., eds. *Why the South Lost the Civil War*. Athens: University of Georgia Press, 1986.

Brown, James E. "Life of General John McCausland." *West Virginia History*, 4:239-293.

Bushong, Millard K. *Old Jube: A Biography of General Jubal A. Early*. Boyce, VA: Carr Publishing, 1955.

Castel, Albert. *Decision in the West: The Atlanta Campaign of 1864*. Lawrence: University Press of Kansas, 1992.

Coffy, David, *Sheridan's Lieutenants: Phil Sheridan, His Generals, and the Final Year of the Civil War*. Oxford: Rowman and Littlefield Publishers, 2005.

Colt, Margaretta Barton, *Defend the Valley: A Shenandoah Family in the Civil War*. New York: Oxford University Press, 1994.

Cook, Roy Bird, *Lewis County [WV] in the Civil War, 1861-1865*. Charleston, WV: Jerret Printing, 1924.

Cooling, Benjamin F. *Jubal Early's Raid on Washington 1864*. Baltimore: The Nautical and Aviation Publishing Company of America, 1990.

———. *Monocacy: The Battle that Saved Washington*. Shippensburg, PA, 2000.

Couper, William. *History of the Shenandoah Valley*. Vol. 2. New York: Lewis Historical Publications, 1952.

Croffut, M. A., *The Military and Civil History of Connecticut during the War of 1861-1865*. New York: Ledyard Bill, 1869.

Current, Richard N., ed. *Encyclopedia of the Confederacy*. 4 vols. New York: Simon and Schuster, 1993.

Davis, Major George B., U.S. Army, Leslie J. Perry, Joseph Kirkley. Compiled by Capt. Calvin C. Cowles. 23rd U.S. Infantry. *The Official Military Atlas of the Civil War*. Avenel, NJ: Gramercy Books, 1983.

Davis, William C., *The Battle of New Market*. New York: Doubleday and Co., 1975.

———. *Breckinridge: Statesman, Soldier, Symbol*. Baton Rouge: Louisiana State University Press, 1974.

Delauter, Roger U. and Brandon H. Beck, *Early's Valley Campaign: The Third Battle of Winchester*. Lynchburg, VA: H. E. Howard Co., 1997.

Duncan, Richard R. *Lee's Endangered Left: The Civil War in Western Virginia Spring of 1864*. Baton Rouge: Louisiana State University Press, 1998.

Ecelbarger, Gary L. *"We Are in for It!" The First Battle of Kernstown*. Shippensburg, PA: White Mane Publishing, 1997.

Foote, Shelby. *The Civil War: A Narrative*. 3 vols. New York: Random House, 1958-74.

Freeman, Douglas S. *Lee's Lieutenants: A Study in Command*. 3 vols. New York: Charles Scribner's Sons, 1942-44.

Gale, Edwin O. *Reminiscences of Early Chicago and Vicinity*. Chicago: Revell, 1902.

Gallagher, Gary W. *Stephen Dodson Ramseur: Lee's Gallant General*. Chapel Hill: University of North Carolina Press, 1985.

———. *Struggle for the Shenandoah: Essays on the 1864 Valley Campaign*. Kent, OH: Kent State University Press, 1991.

———. *The Shenandoah Valley Campaign of 1864*. Chapel Hill: University of North Carolina Press, 2006.

Gold, Thomas D. *History of Clarke County, Virginia and Its Connections with the War Between the States*. Berryville, VA: 1914.

Hale, Laura Virginia. *Four Valiant Years in the Lower Shenandoah Valley, 1861-1865*. Strasburg, VA: Shenandoah Publishing House, 1968.

Haselberger, Fritz. *Confederate Retaliation: McCausland's 1864 Raid*. Shippensburg, PA: Burd Street Press, 2000.

Hattaway, Herman, and Archer Jones. *How the North Won: A Military History of the Civil War*. Urbana: University of Illinois Press, 1983.

Hennessy, John. *The First Battle of Manassas*. Lynchburg, VA: H. E. Howard, 1989.

Ingersoll, L. D., *Iowa and the Rebellion*. Philadelphia: J. B. Lippincott & Co., 1867.

Jameson, Perry D., and Grady McWhiney. *Attack and Die: Civil War Military Tactics and the Southern Heritage*. Tallahassee: University of Alabama Press, 1982.

Johnson, R. U., and C. C. Buel, eds. *Battles and Leaders of the Civil War*. 4 vols. New York: Century, 1884-1887.

Kennon, L. W. V. "The Valley Campaign of 1864—A Military Study." In *The Shenandoah Campaigns of 1864-1865*. Boston: Military Historical Society of Massachusetts, 1907.

Krick, Robert K. *Lee's Colonels: A Biographical Register of the Field Officers of the Army of Northern Virginia*. 2nd ed., rev. Dayton, OH: Morningside Press, 1984.

———. *The Smoothbore Volley That Doomed the Confederacy*. Baton Rouge: Louisiana State University Press, 2002.

Knight, Charles R., *Valley Thunder: The Battle of New Market*. New York: Savas Beatie LLC, 2010.

Logan, Guy E., *Roster and Record of Iowa Soldiers in the War of the Rebellion Together with Historical Sketches of Volunteer Organizations, 1861-1866*. Des Moines: Emory H. English, State Brinter, 1910.

Lowry, Terry. *Last Sleep: The Battle of Droop Mountain, November 6, 1863*. Charleston, WV: Pictorial Histories Publishing, 1996.

Luvaas, Jay, and Harold W. Nelson, eds. *The U.S. Army War College Guide to the Battles of Chancellorsville and Fredericksburg*. New York: Perennial Library, 1988.

Mahon, Michael G., *The Shenandoah Valley 1861-1865: The Destruction of the Granary of the Confederacy*. Mechanicsburg, PA: Stackpole Books, 1999.

———. *Winchester Divided: The Civil War Diaries of Julia Chase and Laura Lee*. Mechanicsburg, PA: Stackpole Books, 2002.

Mahr, Theodore C. *Early's Valley Campaign: The Battle of Cedar Creek, Showdown in the Shenandoah, October 1-30, 1864*. Lynchburg, VA: H. E. Howard, 1992.

Maxwell, Hue, and H. L. Swisher. *History of Hampshire County, West Virginia from Its Earliest Settlement to the Present*. Morgantown, WV: A. Brown Boughner, Printer, 1897.

McDonald, Archie P., ed. *"Make Me a Map of the Valley": The Civil War Journal of Stonewall Jackson's Topographer*. Dallas: Southern Methodist University Press, 1973.

McManus, Howard Rollins. *The Battle of Cloyds Mountain: The Virginia and Tennessee Railroad Raid, April 29 May 19, 1864*. Lynchburg, VA: H. E. Howard, 1989.

Meaney, Peter J., O.S.B. *The Civil War Engagement at Cool Spring, July 18, 1864*. Berryville, VA: Peter J. Meaney, 1980.

Moore, Frank, ed., *The Rebellion Record*. 11 vols. New York: 1871.

Nash, Sister May Eleanor, S.S.J., Ph.B. *Colonel James A. Mulligan, Chicago's Hero of the Civil War*. St. Louis: Presented to the Faculty of the Graduate School of St. Louis University, 1929.

Noe, Kenneth W. *Perryville: This Grand Havoc of Battle*. Lexington: University Press of Kentucky, 2001.

Olcott, Charles S. *William McKinley*. Boston and New York: Houghton Mifflin, 1916.

Osborne, Charles O. *Jubal: The Life and Times of Jubal A. Early, CSA*. Chapel Hill, NC: Algonquin Books of Chapel Hill, 1992.

Patchan, Scott C. *The Forgotten Fury: The Battle of Piedmont, Virginia*. Fredericksburg: Sergeant Kirkland's Historical Society, 1996.

———. *Shenandoah Summer: The 1864 Valley Campaign*. Lincoln: The University Press of Nebraska, 2007.

Pond, George E. *The Shenandoah Valley in 1864*. New York: Charles Scribner's Sons, 1883.

Reid, Whitelaw. *Ohio in the War*. 2 vols. Cincinnati, OH: Moore, Wilstach and Baldwin, 1868.

Rhea, Gordon C. *The Battles of Spotsylvania Courthouse and the Road to Yellow Tavern, May 7-12, 1864*. Baton Rouge: Louisiana State University Press, 1997.

————. *Cold Harbor: Lee and Grant, May 26 - June 3, 1864*. Baton Rouge: Louisiana State University Press, 2002.

————. *To the North Anna River, Grant and Lee, May 13-25, 1864*. Baton Rouge: Louisiana State University Press, 2000.

Ruffner, Kevin Conley. "'More Trouble Than a Brigade': Harry Gilmor's 2d Maryland Cavalry in the Shenandoah Valley." *Maryland Historical Magazine*, 89:388-411.

Scribner, Theo. T., *Indiana's Roll of Honor*. Indianapolis: A. D. Streight, 1866.

Sears, Stephen. *To the Gates of Richmond: The Peninsula Campaign*. New York: Ticknor and Fields, 1992.

Sheppard, James C. "Brigadier General Alfred N. Duffié: Adopted Son of Staten Island." *Staten Island Historian*. July - September 1973.

Smith, Gerald J. *One of the Most Daring of Men: The Life Of Confederate General William Tatum Wofford*. Murfreesboro, TN: Southern Heritage Press, 1997.

Stackpole, Edward J. *Sheridan in the Shenandoah: Jubal Early's Nemesis*. Harrisburg, PA: Stackpole Company, 1961.

Starr, Stephen Z. *The Union Cavalry in the Civil War*. 3 vols. Baton Rouge: Louisiana State University Press, 1979-1985.

Stiles, Robert. *Four Years under Marse Robert*. New York and Washington, DC: Neale Publishing, 1903.

The Story of American Heroism. New York: Wilson, 1896.

Styple, William B., ed., *Generals in Bronze: Interviewing the Commanders of the Civil War*. Kearny, NJ, Belle Grove Publishing, 2005.

Tucker, Spencer C. *Brigadier General John D. Imboden: Confederate Commander in the Shenandoah*. Lexington: University Press of Kentucky, 2003.

Walker, Charles D. *Biographical Sketches of the Graduates and Eleves of the Virginia Military Institute Who Fell During the War Between the States*. Philadelphia: J. B. Lippincott and Co., 1875.

Warner, Ezra J. *Generals in Blue: Lives of the Union Commanders*. Baton Rouge: Louisiana State University Press, 1964.

————. *Generals in Gray: Lives of the Confederate Commanders*. Baton Rouge: Louisiana State University Press, 1970.

Wert, Jeffry. *From Winchester to Cedar Creek: The Shenandoah Campaign, 1864*. Carlisle, PA: South Mountain Press, 1987.

Williams, T. Harry. *Hayes of the Twenty-Third: The Civil War Volunteer Officer*. New York: Alfred A. Knopf, 1965.

Wittenberg, Eric J., *Glory Enough for All: Sheridan's Second Raid and the Battle of Trevilian Station*. Washington, D.C.: Brassey's, 2002.

————. *Little Phil: A Reasssessment of the Civil War Leadership of Gen. Philip H. Sheridan*. Washington, D.C.: Brassey's, 2002.

————. *The Union Cavalry Comes of Age: Hartwood Church to Brandy Station, 1863*. Washington, D.C.: Brassey's, 2003.

————, ed. *Under Custer's Command: The Civil War Journal of James Henry Avery*. Washington, D.C.: Brassey's, 2000.

Index

Scott C. Patchan

A lifelong student of military history in general, and the Civil War in particular, Scott Patchan is a graduate of James Madison University in the Shenandoah Valley. He is the author of many articles and books, including *The Forgotten Fury: The Battle of Piedmont* (1996), *Shenandoah Summer: The 1864 Valley Campaign* (2007), and *Second Manassas: Longstreet's Attack and the Struggle for Chinn Ridge* (2011).

Patchan serves as a director on the board of the Kernstown Battlefield Association in Winchester, Virginia, and is a member of the Shenandoah Valley Battlefield Foundation's Resource Protection Committee.